Delacroix

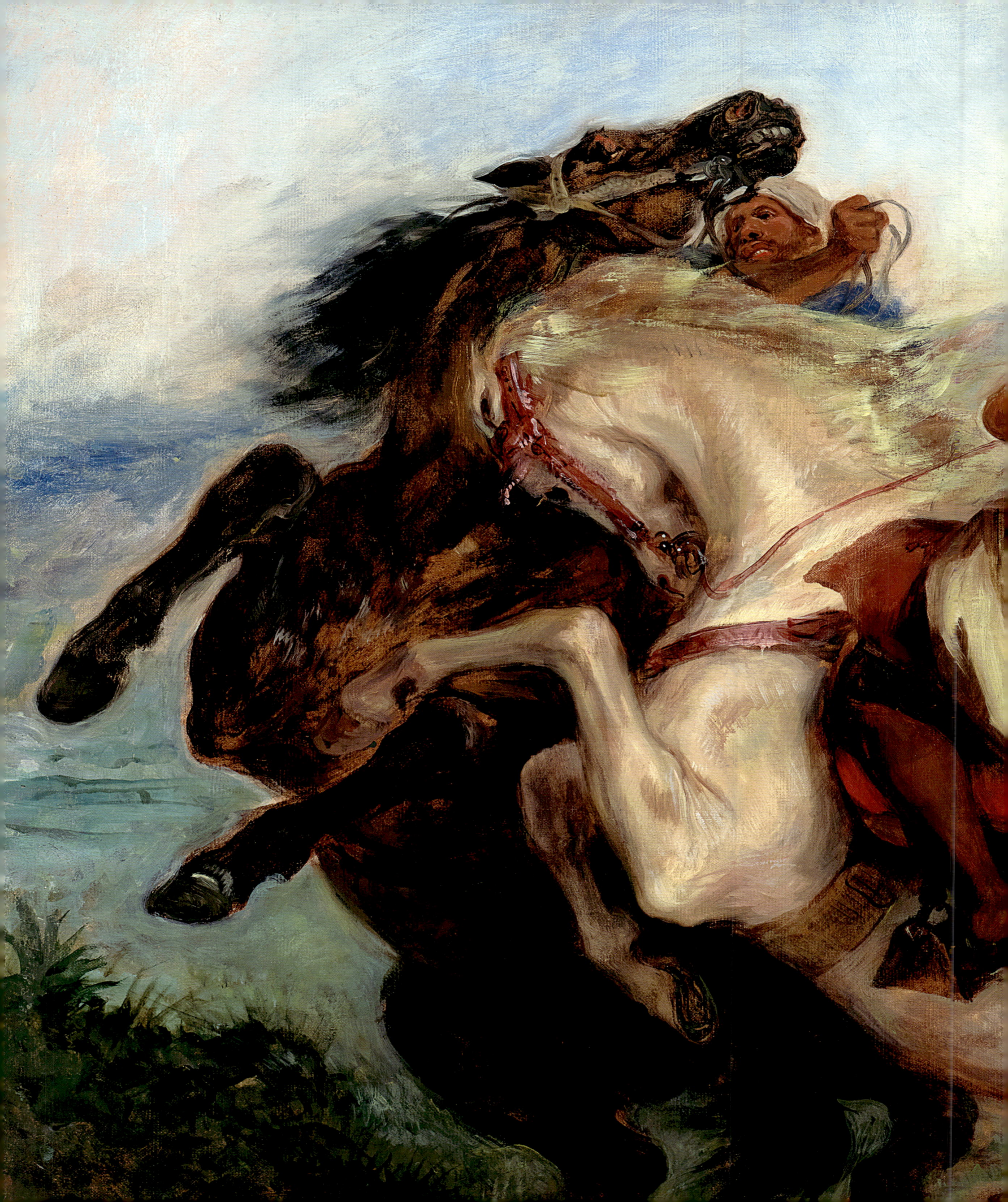

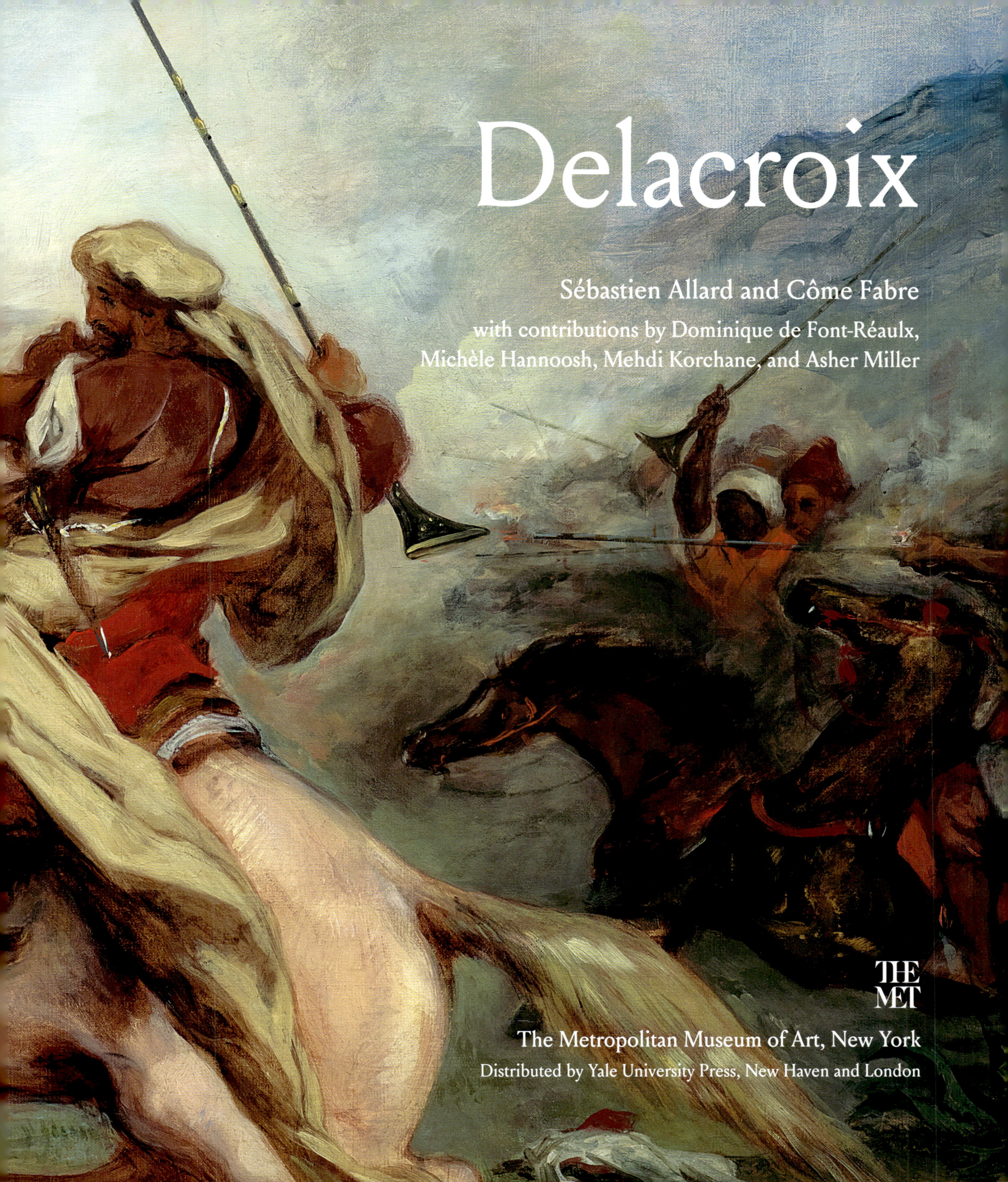

Delacroix

Sébastien Allard and Côme Fabre

with contributions by Dominique de Font-Réaulx,
Michèle Hannoosh, Mehdi Korchane, and Asher Miller

THE
MET

The Metropolitan Museum of Art, New York

Distributed by Yale University Press, New Haven and London

This catalogue is published in conjunction with "Delacroix," on view at the Musée du Louvre, Paris, from March 29 through July 23, 2018, and at The Metropolitan Museum of Art, New York, from September 17, 2018, through January 6, 2019.

The exhibition is made possible by the Eugene V. and Clare E. Thaw Charitable Trust.

Additional funds are provided by the Janice H. Levin Fund, the Sherman Fairchild Foundation, The Florence Gould Foundation, and the Gail and Parker Gilbert Fund.

It is supported by an Indemnity from the Federal Council on the Arts and the Humanities.

The exhibition is organized by The Metropolitan Museum of Art and the Musée du Louvre.

The catalogue is made possible by the Diane W. and James E. Burke Fund and the Janice H. Levin Fund.

Published by The Metropolitan Museum of Art, New York

Mark Polizzotti, Publisher and Editor in Chief
Gwen Roginsky, Associate Publisher and
    General Manager of Publications
Peter Antony, Chief Production Manager
Michael Sittenfeld, Senior Managing Editor

Edited by Elizabeth L. Block, with Sarah McFadden
Designed by Rita Jules, Miko McGinty Inc.
Production by Paul Booth
Bibliography and notes edited by Kirsten Painter
    and Jean Wagner
Image acquisitions and permissions by Jenn Sherman

Translations from the French of the essays by Sébastien Allard and Côme Fabre, Mehdi Korchane, and Dominique de Font-Réaulx are by Jane Marie Todd.

Photographs of works of art in the Metropolitan Museum's collection are by the Imaging Department, The Metropolitan Museum of Art, unless otherwise noted. Additional image credits are on p. 314.

Typeset by Tina Henderson in Louize and Proba
Printed on 150 gsm Condat Matt Perigord
Separations by Verona Libri, Verona, Italy
Printed and bound by Verona Libri, Verona, Italy

Jacket illustrations: front, detail, *Women of Algiers in Their Apartment*, 1834, cat. 83; back, detail, *Self-Portrait in a Green Vest*, ca. 1837, cat. 93
Title pages: pp. ii–iii, detail, *Collision of Arab Horsemen*, 1833/34, cat. 81
Frontispieces: p. vi, detail, *Young Tiger Playing with Its Mother (Study of Two Tigers)*, 1830, cat. 67; p. viii, detail, *Lion Hunt, sketch*, 1854, cat. 134; p. x, detail, *Christ in the Garden of Olives (The Agony in the Garden)*, 1824–26, cat. 17; p. xiv, detail, *Greece on the Ruins of Missolonghi*, 1826, cat. 26; p. 224, detail, *The Natchez*, 1823–24 and 1835, cat. 84; p. 234, detail, *The Triumph of Genius over Envy*, ca. 1849–51, cat. 117; p. 244, detail, *Orphan Girl in the Cemetery*, 1824, fig. 9; p. 254, detail, *Medea About to Kill Her Children (Medée furieuse)*, 1838, cat. 94; p. 266, detail, *The Sultan of Morocco and His Entourage*, 1856, cat. 138

The Metropolitan Museum of Art
1000 Fifth Avenue
New York, New York 10028
metmuseum.org

Distributed by
Yale University Press, New Haven and London
yalebooks.com/art
yalebooks.co.uk

Cataloging-in-Publication Data is available from the Library of Congress.

ISBN 978-1-58839-651-8

Contents

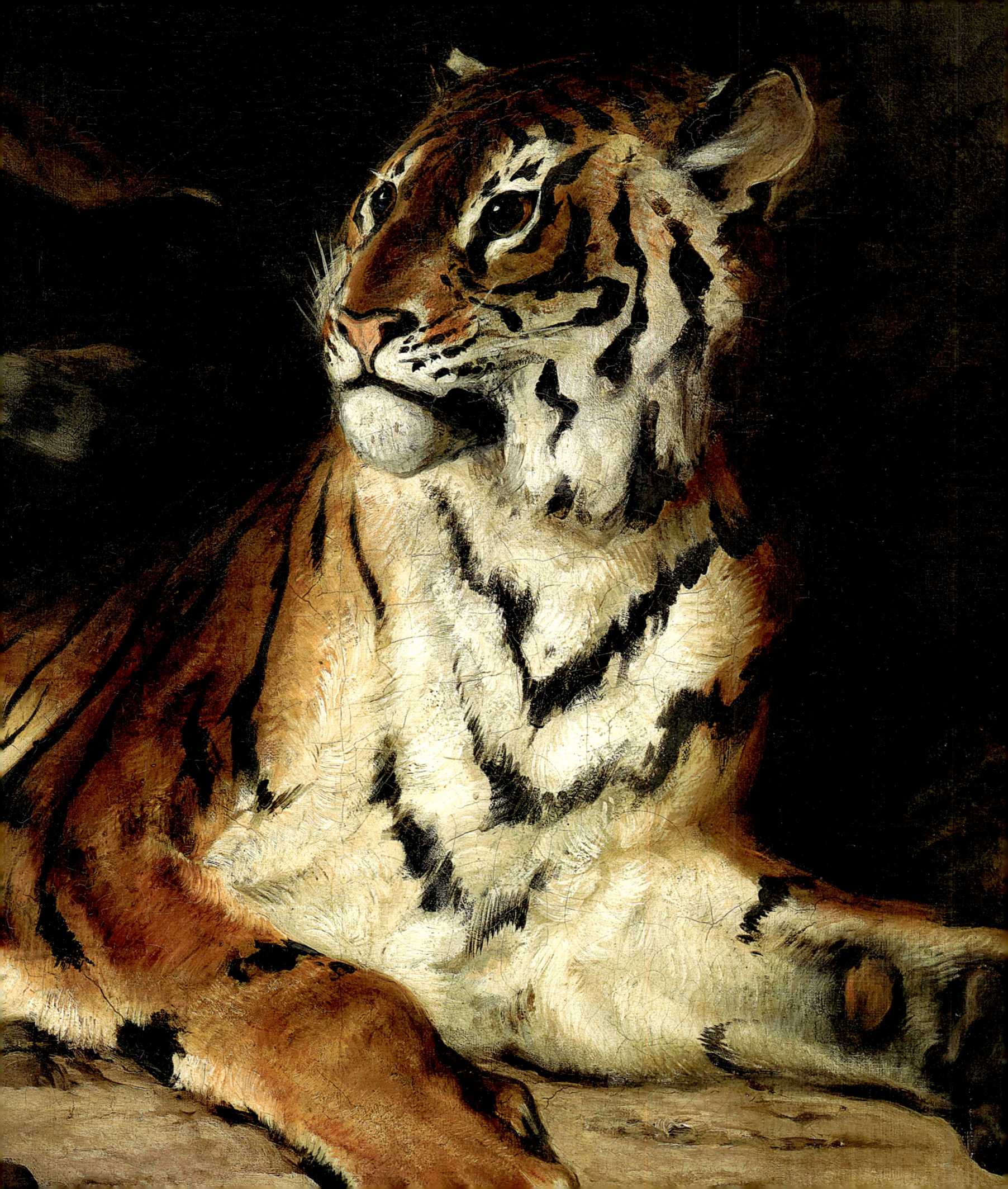

Foreword

Eugène Delacroix (1798–1863) was celebrated as a phenomenon in his lifetime and is a giant in the history of French art. No other figure of his time balanced his reverence for the past, including art, literature, and music, with his ambition and spirit of innovation. He was a key figure in the unfolding of what we think of today as modern, a defining feature of the nineteenth century, and as such he has been admired by a remarkably diverse company of writers, critics, and artists including Charles Baudelaire, Paul Cézanne, and Pablo Picasso. His career as a painter spanned more than forty years, from early showings at the Salons of the 1820s to the triumph of his retrospective display at the Exposition Universelle of 1855 and until the end of his life. In addition to his artistic achievement, Delacroix was a distinguished man of letters; he wrote eloquently, broadly, and reflectively.

To mark the centenary of Delacroix's death, a monumental exhibition curated by Maurice Sérullaz was organized by the Louvre. It was a fitting venue, given that this was the museum where Delacroix hoped his work would be preserved for posterity along with that of Raphael and Poussin, and for which he completed the ceiling of the Gallery of Apollo begun two centuries earlier by Charles Le Brun, the official painter of Louis XIV. Innumerable exhibitions have focused on one or another aspect of Delacroix's prolific production, but a complete retrospective has not been presented since 1963, and none has ever been mounted in North America. The present catalogue and its accompanying exhibition were conceived to reevaluate this complex and protean artist in light of the most recent research. At The Met, the exhibition has been organized by Asher Miller, associate curator in the Department of European Paintings.

The texts of this catalogue explore the continuities that lie behind the plenitude and variety of Delacroix's output. The challenge is a great one, because the scope of his production is exceptional, encompassing thousands of drawings, prints in every medium, hundreds of easel paintings including the immense canvases of the artist's youth, most of them preserved at the Louvre, as well as the decorative programs that adorn some of the most impressive civic and religious spaces in Paris.

We are enormously thankful to the Eugene V. and Clare E. Thaw Charitable Trust for its extraordinary support of this exhibition. We express our gratitude to the Janice H. Levin Fund for making both the exhibition and this catalogue possible, and to the Sherman Fairchild Foundation, The Florence Gould Foundation, and the Gail and Parker Gilbert Fund for their generosity to this presentation. We also extend our appreciation to the Diane W. and James E. Burke Fund for helping us bring this beautiful publication to realization.

We deeply appreciate the enthusiasm and generosity of the Louvre as well as some sixty other lenders, including many of the principal museums of the United States and Europe and numerous private collectors. We express our profound gratitude to them all. In addition to rarely lent masterpieces from the Louvre such as *Women of Algiers in Their Apartment*, there is the spectacular *Christ in the Garden of Olives*, taken down from its high perch in Saint-Paul-Saint-Louis and newly cleaned for the exhibition, *Greece on the Ruins of Missolonghi* from the Musée des Beaux-Arts, Bordeaux, the immersive *Battle of Nancy* lent by the Musée des Beaux-Arts in the city for which it was painted, and the fortuitous pairing of *Saint Sebastian Tended by the Holy Women* and *Medea About to Kill Her Children* from, respectively, the church of Saint-Michel, Nantua, and the Palais des Beaux-Arts, Lille.

A few days before his death, Delacroix wrote: "The chief merit of a painting is to be a feast for the eye. That is not to say that there is no need for it to have meaning; like beautiful poetry, if it offends the ear, then all the meaning in the world cannot redeem it." We wish this homage to the master to be a feast for the eye and also for the spirit.

Daniel H. Weiss
President and CEO, The Metropolitan Museum of Art, New York

Jean-Luc Martinez
President and director, Musée du Louvre, Paris

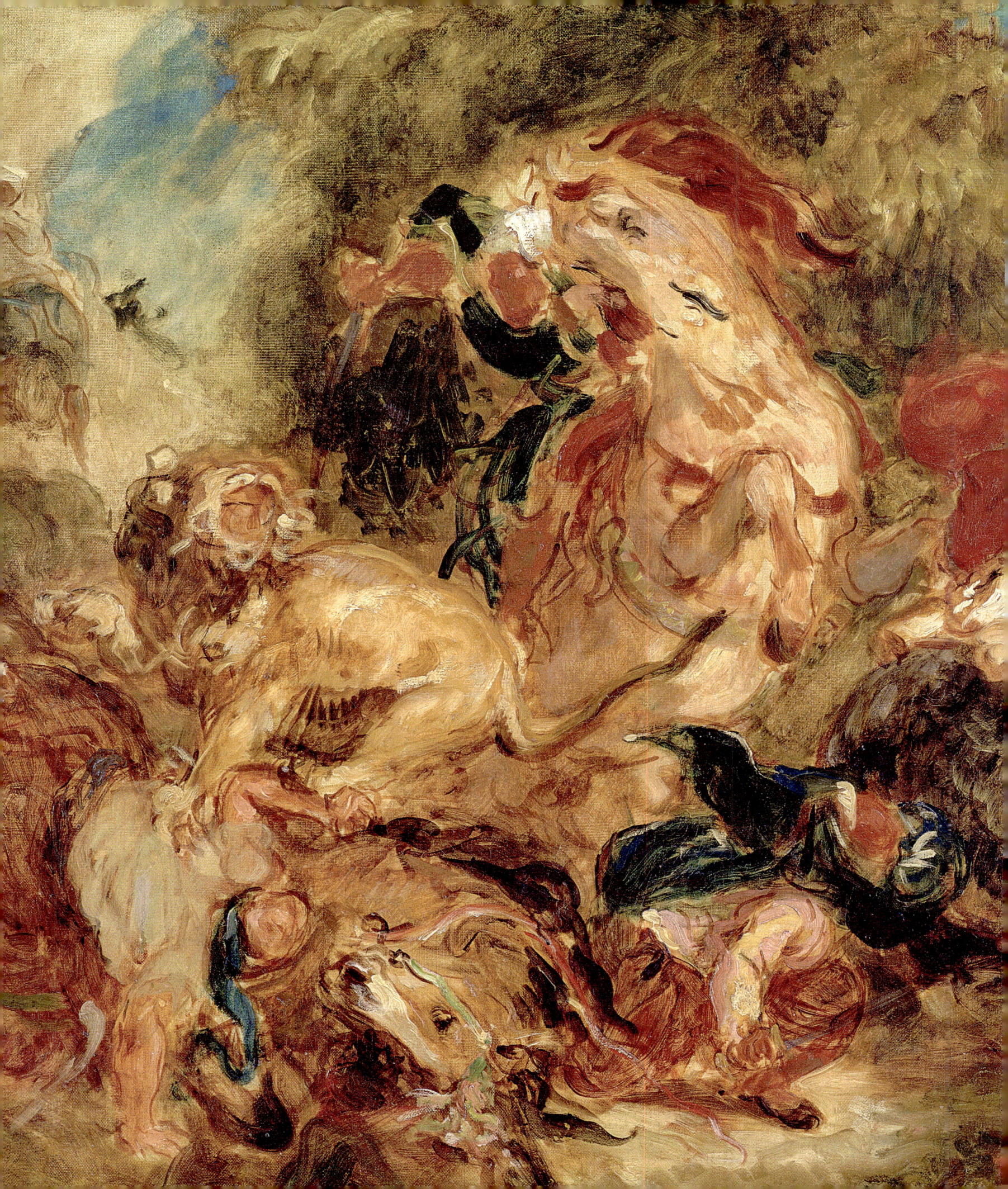

Lenders to the Exhibition

Belgium
Musées Royaux des Beaux-Arts de Belgique, Brussels

Canada
National Gallery of Canada, Ottawa

Czech Republic
Národní Galerie, Prague

France
Musée des Beaux-Arts, Arras
Musée des Beaux-Arts, Bordeaux
Palais des Beaux-Arts, Lille
Musée des Beaux-Arts, Lyon
Musée Fabre, Montpellier Méditerranée Métropole
Musée des Beaux-Arts, Nancy
Musée d'Arts de Nantes, Nantes Métropole
Fonds National d'Art Contemporain / Centre National des Arts Plastiques (Church of Saint-Michel, Nantua)
Musée des Beaux-Arts, Orléans
Les Arts Décoratifs, Musée des Arts Décoratifs, Paris
Conservation des Oeuvres d'Art Religieuses et Civiles de la Ville de Paris / Direction Régionale des Affaires Culturelles d'Ile-de-France (Church of Saint-Paul-Saint-Louis, Paris)
Institut National d'Histoire de l'Art, Paris

Musée du Louvre, Paris
Musée National Eugène-Delacroix, Paris
Musée d'Orsay, Paris
Petit Palais, Musée des Beaux-Arts de la Ville de Paris
Musée des Beaux-Arts, Tours
Musée des Beaux-Arts, Vannes

Germany
Staatliche Museen zu Berlin, Nationalgalerie
Kunsthalle Bremen—Der Kunstverein in Bremen
Städel Museum, Frankfurt am Main
Staatliche Kunsthalle Karlsruhe

Mexico
Pérez Simón Collection, Mexico

The Netherlands
Van Gogh Museum, Amsterdam
Museum Boijmans Van Beuningen, Rotterdam

Norway
The National Museum of Art, Architecture and Design, Oslo

Spain
Tubacex S.A.
Museo Thyssen-Bornemisza, Madrid

Sweden
Nationalmuseum, Stockholm

Switzerland
Kunstmuseum Basel – Öffentliche Kunstsammlung

United Kingdom
The National Gallery, London

United States
The Walters Art Museum, Baltimore
Museum of Fine Arts, Boston
Albright-Knox Art Gallery, Buffalo, New York
Harvard Art Museums/Fogg Museum, Cambridge, Mass.
Houghton Library, Harvard University, Cambridge, Mass.
Ackland Art Museum, University of North Carolina at Chapel Hill
Art Institute of Chicago
Kimbell Art Museum, Fort Worth
Museum of Fine Arts, Houston
The Morgan Library & Museum, New York
Philadelphia Museum of Art
Portland Art Museum, Oregon
Virginia Museum of Fine Arts, Richmond

Private Collections
Karen B. Cohen, New York
Roberta J. M. Olson and Alexander B. V. Johnson
Private collection, courtesy of Art Cuéllar-Nathan
Private collections, New York
Private collections

Contributors

Sébastien Allard
Chief curator and director, Department of Paintings, Musée du Louvre, Paris

Côme Fabre
Curator of nineteenth-century French paintings, Department of Paintings, Musée du Louvre, Paris

Dominique de Font-Réaulx
Director, Musée National Eugène-Delacroix, Paris

Michèle Hannoosh
Professor of French, University of Michigan, Ann Arbor

Mehdi Korchane
Independent scholar

Asher Miller
Associate curator, Department of European Paintings, The Metropolitan Museum of Art, New York

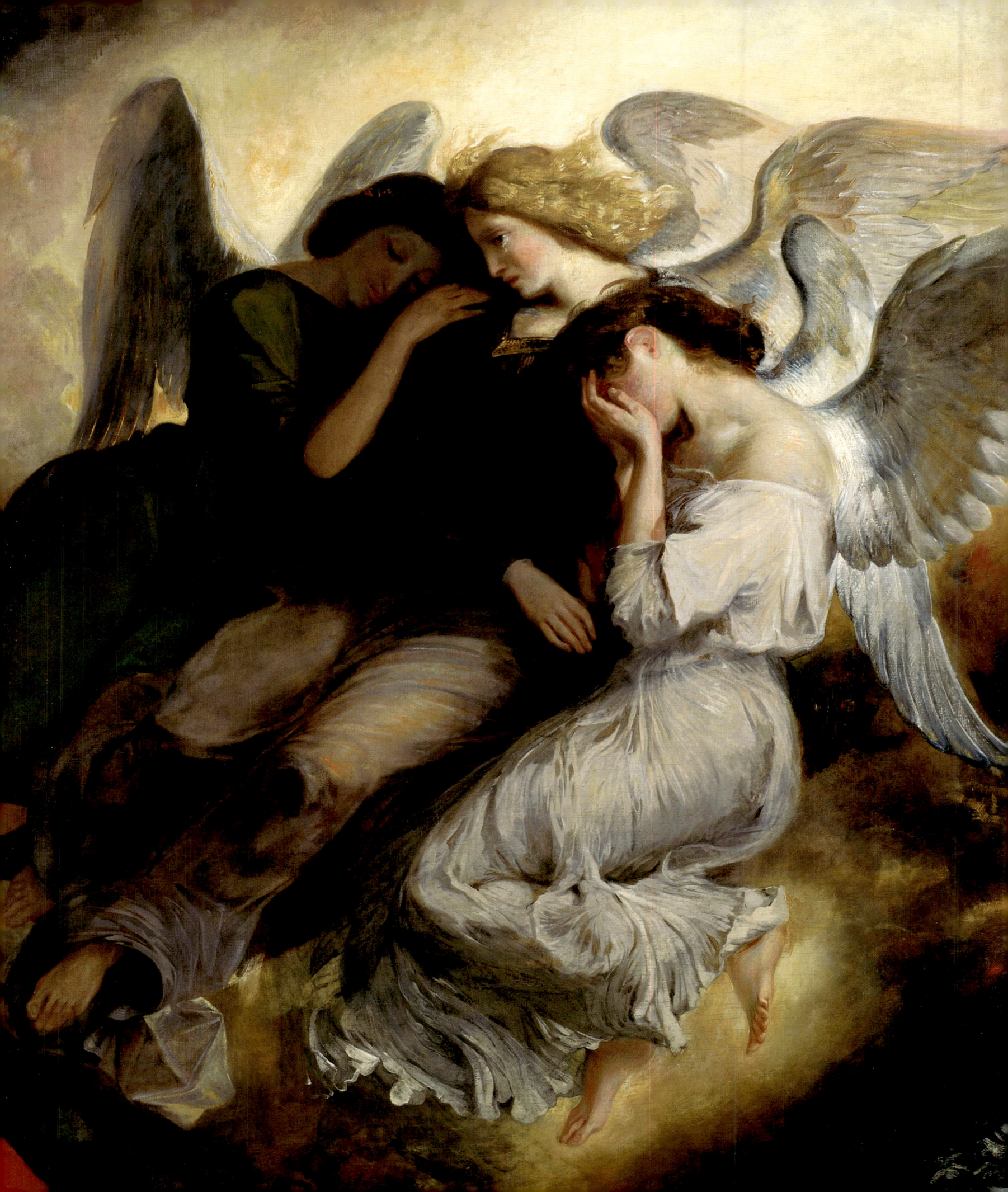

Preface and Acknowledgments

Whether encountering Eugène Delacroix for the first time or after long engagement with his life and work, readers of this volume will gain appreciation for one of the great creative imaginations of the nineteenth century. Museumgoers may be acquainted with Delacroix, but they can be forgiven for not feeling that they *know* him. His output is vast, diverse, and widely disseminated, and a definitive edition of his extensive writings has yet to appear in English. One place to begin is to look at the paintings—and drawings and prints—in person, as Van Gogh did when he wrote: "What I find so fine about Delacroix is precisely that he reveals the liveliness of things, and the expression and the movement, that he is utterly *beyond the paint*." The opportunity to discover Delacroix with fresh eyes is reason enough for the present exhibition.

Delacroix was unquestionably one of the most important figures in France, both within and outside the realm of the visual arts, to come of age in the wake of Napoleon. The inexhaustible richness of his production is here presented in all its complexity, with an emphasis on layers of association across the three main phases of his long career, the diverse genres he mastered, and the materials in which he worked. In the extensive texts that follow, the authors of this book build on and pay tribute to fundamental studies by such exemplary scholars as Adolphe Moreau, Alfred Robaut, Maurice Sérullaz, and Lee Johnson, breathing new life into the legacy of an artist whose art and writings reveal limitless capacity for self-reflection. This was the man about whom Théophile Silvestre wrote that his "character is violent and sulfurous, but his self-possession is total," and about whom Charles Baudelaire reflected, "Delacroix was passionately in love with passion, but coldly determined to express passion as clearly as possible."

Delacroix commenced formal training in the Paris atelier of the Neoclassical painter Pierre Narcisse Guérin, where he encountered the magnetic Théodore Gericault. But his artistic pedigree reached back even further—to Guérin's own master, Jacques Louis David, dean of the French school during the prior twenty-five years of Revolution and Empire. What distinguished Delacroix from the dozens of talented young artists who belonged to this storied circle was the strength of his ambition to conquer the public on his own terms: a deeply held conviction that his personal interests, creative impulses, and erudition were an appropriate foundation for art of enduring value. Hallmarks of his work, abundantly evident in the exhibition and catalogue, include novel subject matter, a theatrical sense of composition, a vibrant palette, and a vigorous painterly technique that prioritized the freshness of the initial sketch over traditional notions of finish.

A great deal of serious scholarship was inspired by now legendary monographic exhibitions held at the Louvre in 1930 and 1963. But it is also fair to say that Paul Jamot's assessment in the preface to the catalogue of the earlier show still applies, that Delacroix is an illustrious name and a great name, but *he* is not well understood. In other words, Delacroix is a major figure in the history of European painting who merits a close reappraisal. The present exhibition and catalogue provide a unique occasion to gain a deeper understanding of this defining figure of French painting. It is an opportunity to take the artist at his word, when he summed up the immediacy and urgency of his art: "Materially speaking, painting is nothing but a bridge set up between the mind of the artist and that of the beholder."

For enabling that most essential of Delacroix's credos to be brought to life, I am deeply grateful to the Eugene V. and Clare E. Thaw Charitable Trust. Its generous gift in memory of the late Eugene V. Thaw (1927–2018) makes it possible to enrich the legacy of a brilliant collector and visionary philanthropist by introducing visitors to The Met to one of the great artists of the Western canon. Delacroix held pride of place in Gene Thaw's pantheon, both as a collector and in his work as an art dealer. He appreciated that works which had passed through his hands would play an important role in this exhibition, and he looked forward to its fruition.

Projects of this size present unique financial challenges, and The Met is proud to acknowledge support from the Janice H. Levin Fund, the Sherman Fairchild Foundation, The Florence Gould Foundation, and the Gail and Parker

Gilbert Fund, the Diane W. and James E. Burke Fund, as well as the Federal Council on the Arts and the Humanities for its indemnification of *Delacroix*.

Delacroix is the glorious result of a group effort, of extraordinary people working together for more than four years on both sides of the Atlantic. I therefore express my gratitude to all who have steered the project since its inception: Daniel H. Weiss, president and chief executive officer of The Metropolitan Museum of Art, and Max Hollein, director, as well as his predecessor, Thomas P. Campbell; and in Paris, Jean-Luc Martinez, president and director of the Musée du Louvre. The idea for this catalogue and its accompanying exhibition originated with Henri Loyrette, former director of the Louvre, at the conclusion of the Delacroix exhibition presented in Madrid and Barcelona in 2011–12. It was nurtured by Marc Mayer, director of the National Gallery of Canada, and Paul Lang, formerly its deputy director and chief curator, and presently director of the Musées de Strasbourg; their participation in the early phases of the project was indispensable to laying a solid foundation on which to build, and has resonated at every stage since. The boundless energy, enthusiasm, and vision of Keith Christiansen, John Pope-Hennessy Chairman, Department of European Paintings at The Met, infused this collaboration with a level of collegiality and goodwill that dignifies the two august institutions, the highest aims of which this exhibition embodies. The erudition of Sébastien Allard, chief curator and director of the Department of Paintings at the Louvre, and Côme Fabre, curator of nineteenth-century French paintings, pervades every aspect of *Delacroix*, and we herald their commitment to excellence.

At The Met, I offer my warmest thanks to Quincy Houghton, deputy director for exhibitions, to her predecessor, Jennifer Russell, and to the entire exhibitions team: Gillian Fruh, manager for exhibitions; Martha Deese, senior administrator for exhibitions and international affairs; Linda Sylling, former manager for special exhibitions and gallery installations; Nina S. Maruca, senior associate registrar; Daniel Kershaw, exhibition design manager; Alexandre Viault, senior graphic designer; Jennifer Isakowitz, senior publicist; and Ann Meisinger, assistant educator. I recognize the efforts of Jason Herrick, chief philanthropy officer; Amy Lamberti, assistant general counsel; and Nicole Sussmane, legal assistant. The entire curatorial staff of the Department of European

Paintings is gratefully acknowledged for their support in ways large and small; the diligence of Jane R. Becker, Gretchen Wold, Rebecca Ben-Atar, Lisa Cain, Patrice Mattia, Andrew Caputo, Laura Corey, John McKanna, Rachel Robinson, and Garth Swanson is also deeply appreciated. The contributions of the following former interns were invaluable: Jack Shapiro, Alec Aldrich, Emily Cox, Emma Lasry, and Haley S. Pierce. For their expertise, I thank Michael Gallagher, Sherman Fairchild Chairman of Paintings Conservation, Charlotte Hale, and Cynthia Moyer in the Department of Paintings Conservation; Peter Van de Moortel, the Sherman Fairchild Fellow in 2014–16; and Marjorie Shelley, Sherman Fairchild Conservator in Charge, Department of Paper Conservation. Colleagues in the Department of Drawings and Prints who have been generous with their support and expertise are Nadine M. Orenstein, Drue Heinz Curator in Charge, Ashley Dunn, Perrin Stein, Mark McDonald, Elizabeth Zanis, David del Gaizo, and Ricky Luna. The work of photographer Juan Trujillo and digital imaging specialists Christopher Heins and Wilson Santiago was also instrumental to the project.

For the exhibition catalogue, I thank Mark Polizzotti, publisher and editor in chief, and his colleagues in the Publications and Editorial Department: Gwen Roginsky, Michael Sittenfeld, Peter Antony, Paul Booth, Anne Blood, and Jennifer Bantz, along with Sarah McFadden, Kirsten Painter, Jenn Sherman, and Jean Wagner. Elizabeth Block has overseen the publication of this volume, the splendid design of which was created by Miko McGinty Inc.

At the Louvre, I especially thank Pascal Périnel, Victorine Majani d'Inguimbert, Violaine Bouvet-Lanselle, and Camille Sourisse.

For their insightful texts in the present volume and advice on my own essay and other aspects of the exhibition, I am grateful to Dominique de Font-Réaulx, Michèle Hannoosh, and Mehdi Korchane.

In addition to the lenders, it is my distinct pleasure to acknowledge the following individuals for assistance and encouragement that took many forms in the realization of this project: Christopher Apostle, Helga Kessler Aurisch, Colin B. Bailey, Fred Bancroft, Sophie Barthélémy, Laura Bennett, Claire Bernardi, Molly Bernhard, Françoise Berretrot, Anders Bjørnsen, François Blanchetière, W. Mark Brady, Jo Briggs, Jean-Gabriel de Bueil and Stanislas Ract-Madoux, Caroline Campbell, the late Eric G. Carlson, Dawson W. Carr,

Laurence des Cars, Eric de Chassey, Karen B. Cohen, Deborah Coy, Maider Cuadra, Arturo and Corinne Cuéllar, Salomon Cuéllar, Philipp Demandt, Maite van Dijk, Michel Draguet, Flavie Durand-Ruel, Paul-Louis Durand-Ruel, Alexander Eiling, Ignatius J. Evans, Evelyne Ferlay, Olivier Gabet, Bruno Girveau, Eric Gordon, Gloria Groom, Charles Hack, Tracy Hamilton, Dorothee Hansen, Katie Hanson, John D. Herring, Paul L. Herring, Michel Hilaire, Eleanor Hoeger, Stine Hoel, Diana Howard, Holly E. Hughes, Thomas Hyry, Amy Indyke, Alexander B. V. Johnson and Roberta J. M. Olson, Ay-Whang Hsia, James C. Kelly, Edouard Kopp, Felix Krämer, Jon and Barbara Landau, Christophe Leribault, Sophie Lévy, Heather Lemonedes, Sylvaine Lestable, Victoria Sancho Lobis, Dominique Maréchal, Hope Mayo, Suzanne Folds McCullagh, James G. McGovern, Mitchell Merling, Kristina Mösl, Marie Monfort, Johannes Nathan and Antoinette Friedenthal, Richard Nathanson, Jill Newhouse, Peter Nisbet, Magnus Olausson, Carl-Johan Olsson, Stéphane Paccoud, Sylvie Ramond, Eva Reifert, Gaëlle Rio, Christopher Riopelle, Joseph Rishel, Mark and Rochelle Rosenberg, E. John Rosenwald, Christa M. Savino, Annie Scottez-De Wambrechies, George T. M. Shackelford, Guillermo Solana, Miriam Stewart, Susan Strauber, Elizabeth Taylor, Graciela Téllez Trevilla, Jennifer Thompson, Gary Tinterow, Jennifer Tonkovich, Isabelle Vazelle, Alvaro Videgain, Charles Villeneuve de Janti, George Wachter, Zoe Watnick, and Wheelock Whitney III. La Sauvergarde de l'Art Français, Paris, is acknowledged for making possible the conservation of *Christ in the Garden of Olives*. I extend special thanks to Katie Flanagan for her thoughtfulness and graciousness during critical stages of this exhibition as it unfolded. As ever, I am grateful to Heather Miller for her steadfast support and confidence.

Asher Miller
Associate curator, Department of European Paintings,
The Metropolitan Museum of Art

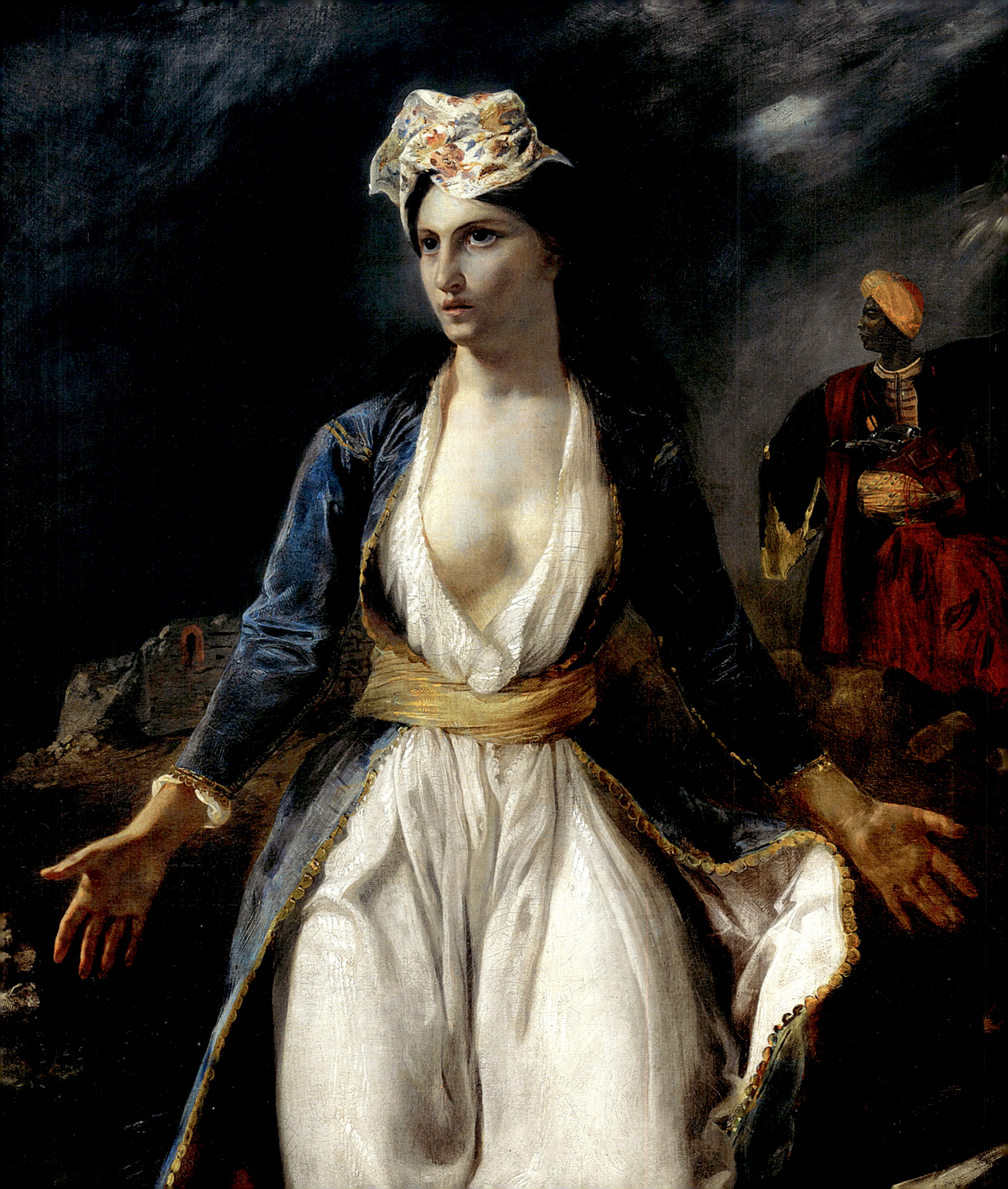

The Sphinx of Modern Painting

SÉBASTIEN ALLARD AND CÔME FABRE

"Fame Is Not an Empty Word": 1822–32

On September 3, 1822, while staying with his brother Charles Henry at Le Louroux, Eugène Delacroix (fig. 1) began keeping a journal.[1] This initiative marked the anniversary of the death of his "beloved mother" and also the occasion of his "present triumph," the exhibition of his first Salon painting, *Dante and Virgil in the Underworld*, or *The Barque of Dante*, as it is generally known, at the Musée du Luxembourg (fig. 2). The canvas had been the subject of heated debate at the Salon of 1822. A handful of contemporaries admired it: Adolphe Thiers, a young lawyer from Marseilles who had just arrived in Paris and was hoping to make a name for himself by writing reviews of the exhibition, praised it enthusiastically in *Le constitutionnel*, a liberal, opposition newspaper. But most critics did not understand the work, including the powerful critic Etienne Jean Delécluze, who would remain antagonistic toward Delacroix throughout his life. In *Le moniteur universel*, Delécluze called the painting a *tartouillade* (a daub).[2]

FIG. 1 Frédéric Villot (French, 1809–1875). *Portrait of Eugène Delacroix (after a Self-Portrait Drawing)*, 1847. Mezzotint and drypoint on paper, image 6⅜ x 4³⁄₁₆ in (16.2 x 10.7 cm); sheet 8¼ x 5⅛ in. (21 x 13 cm). Bibliothèque nationale de France, Paris (inv. N2)

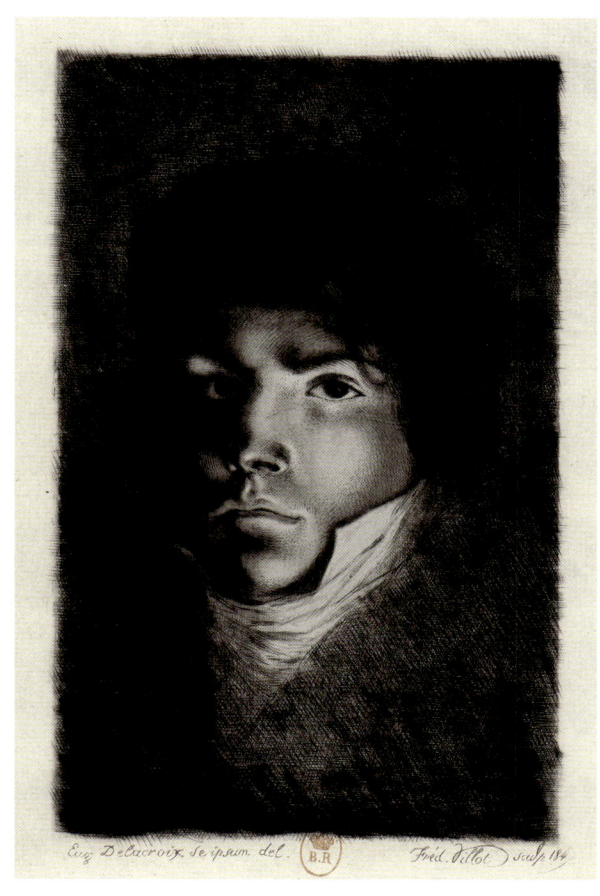

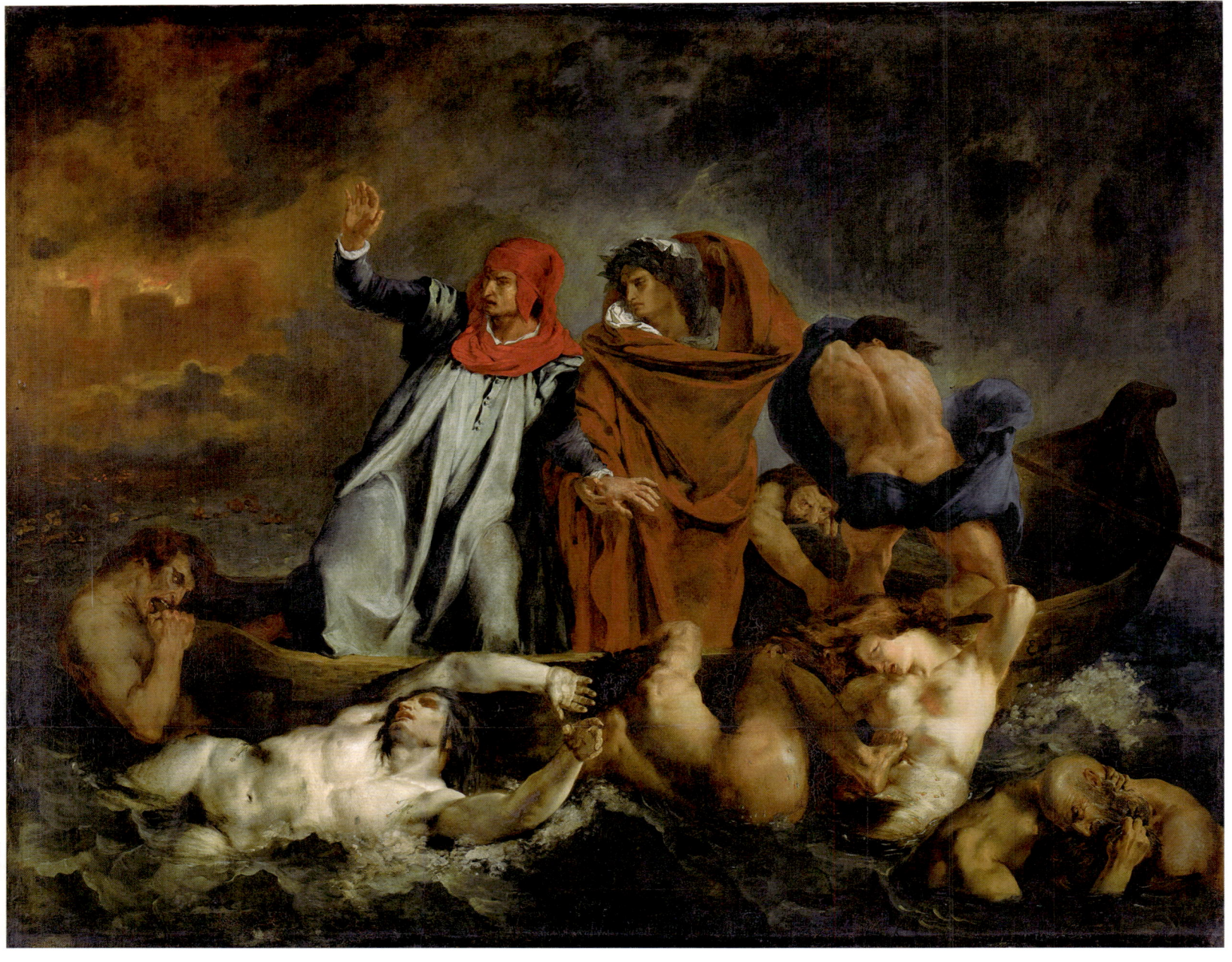

FIG. 2 *The Barque of Dante (Dante and Virgil in the Underworld)*, 1822. Oil on canvas, 74⁷⁄₁₆ x 96⁷⁄₈ in. (189 x 246 cm). Musée du Louvre, Paris (3820) (J 100)

The state's purchase of *The Barque of Dante*, arranged by comte Auguste de Forbin, director of museums, meant that the painting would enter the collection of the museum of living artists established in 1818 at the Palais du Luxembourg. Louis XVIII (r. 1814–24) intended the museum to fill the void left by the repatriation of works of art seized by French armies during the Napoleonic Wars. He wanted it to function as a symbol of both the glory of the French school and the munificence of royal patronage. This new museum—the Musée du Luxembourg—was conceived as "the antechamber to the Louvre"; every painting exhibited there would be transferred to the Louvre upon its maker's death. Delacroix, who was barely twenty-four when the *Barque* entered the collection in 1822, had just scored a major coup: although his career had hardly begun, he knew that after he died, is art would be displayed on the walls of the Louvre, like that of Raphael and Poussin. This prospect gratified him immensely. Not long after, he would write, "Fame is not an empty word for me. The sound of praise gives me real happiness."³

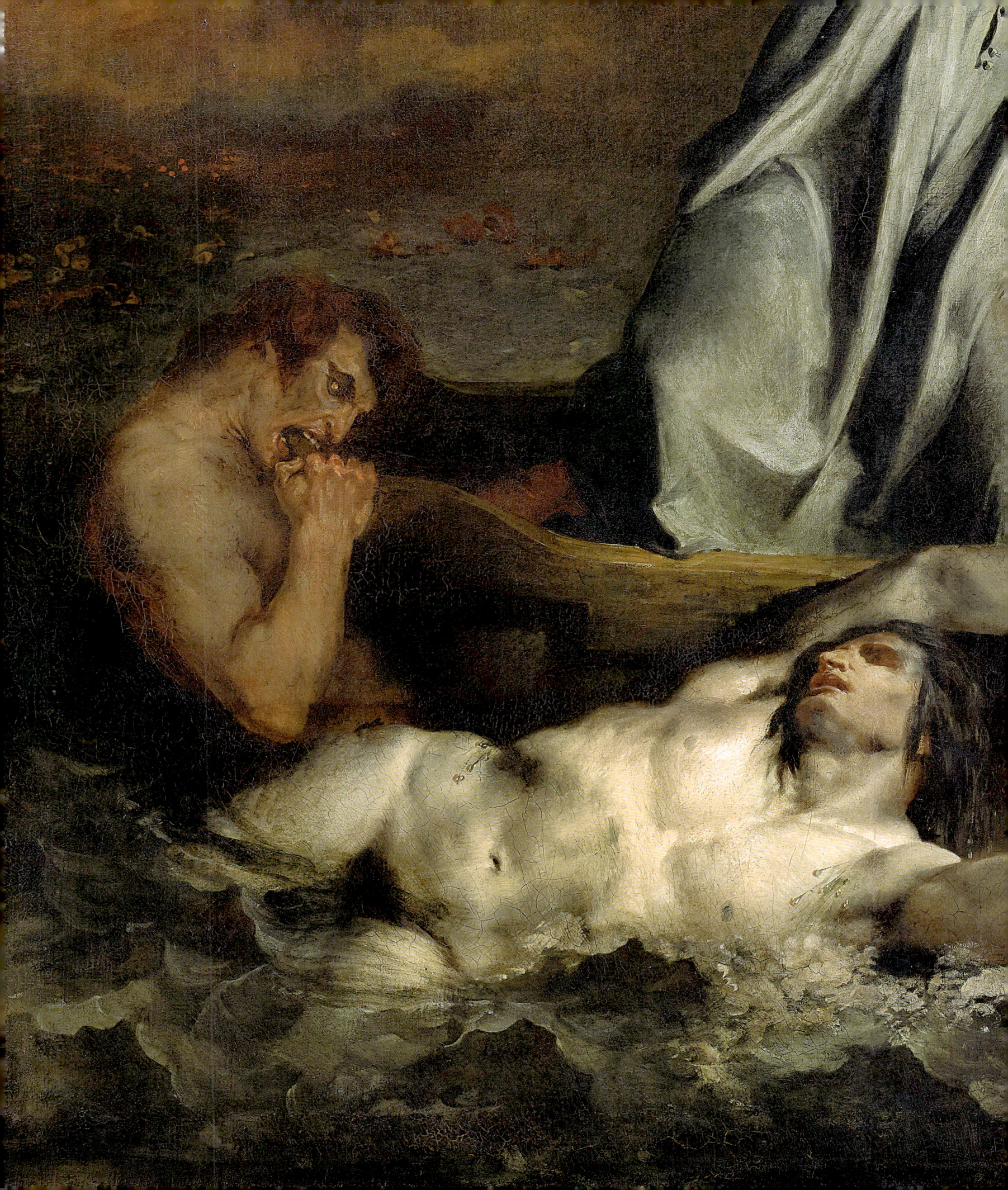

"Pray to Heaven That I May Be a Great Man"

Trained in the secondary schools of the French Empire, where fame was considered the cardinal virtue, Delacroix aspired to achieve it from his earliest years. He filled his student notebooks with variations on his signature that suggest something beyond mere experiments in penmanship. Written in roman and gothic styles, in color, and as rebuses, the inscriptions—"Delacroix," "de La Croix," "Della Croce"— were sometimes preceded by an emphatic "Monsieur." In November 1815, he wrote to his friend Achille Piron: "Pray to heaven that I may be a great man"—an entreaty that reveals his preoccupation with fame from a very young age.[4]

Delacroix's lineage was prestigious. His mother, born Victoire Oeben, was the daughter of the famous cabinetmaker Jean François Oeben; his uncle was the painter Henri François Riesener. Henri's wife, the former Félicité Longrois, was a favorite aunt, and their son Léon (also a painter), would become one of Delacroix's closest friends (see cats. 88, 89). Delacroix's father had been minister of foreign affairs under the Directory, and Delacroix often looked to him as a model.[5] His eldest brother, Charles Henry, a general and baron of the Empire, was made an honorary *maréchal de camp*, and his other brother, Henri, died courageously at the Battle of Friedland in 1807. Delacroix felt the need to distinguish himself, as indicated by a letter to his sister, Henriette de Verninac, after *The Barque of Dante* was purchased at the Salon of 1822 when, referring to a laudatory review by Adolphe Thiers, he suggested: "[My nephew] will be filled with pride for his uncle and will learn to respect one more great man."[6] However, his 1815 exhortation to Piron betrays a dual anxiety: that of failure and the passage of time. He exclaimed, "Oh, we are very old and have seen many things!" adding: "I have plans. I would like to do something, but nothing has come into focus just yet."[7]

Delacroix, born in 1798, belonged to the first generation to experience the acceleration of history captured by Alfred de Musset, who was twelve years the artist's junior, in *La confession d'un enfant du siècle*. Musset's book was published in 1836, twenty years after the events—the triumph of the Empire, its glory and fall—that left an entire generation of young people at loose ends, trapped between a reviled past and an uncertain future, yet in a world where everything seemed possible. On March 29, 1814, the eve of the allied forces' entry into Paris, Delacroix, as if disillusioned by Napoleon's imminent defeat, wrote in one of his school notebooks: "Wednesday, March 29: day of gunfire."[8] With the ensuing peace, his dreams of the military glory his brothers had known evaporated. What remained for him? His mother's death on September 3, 1814, left Delacroix and his sister utterly destitute. Indeed, Henriette had been forced to leave Paris. He observed with sadness the decline of his brother, also near bankruptcy; "surrounded by roughnecks and riff-raff," Charles was under pressure to conceal an extra-marital affair with the daughter of a tavern keeper.[9] The obligation to restore luster to the family name thus rested with Delacroix. It appears, then, that his desire for fame arose not solely from social ambition or classical virtue, but also from an acute historical consciousness.

His uncle Henri François Riesener had secured him a place in the studio of Pierre Narcisse Guérin, probably in 1813, and there he became friends with Théodore Gericault.[10] An artistic career was just one path among others that he considered following to fulfill his destiny, and for a long time he hesitated. The startling beginning to his *Journal*, which condensed in a few lines his first triumph and his mother's death, seems to have introduced unconsciously a causal relationship, as if her death had ultimately determined the direction he would take.

Whether or not this was so, Delacroix, intent on distinguishing himself, would take full advantage of the liberalization of art institutions under the aegis of the comte de Forbin at the beginning of the Bourbon Restoration. He would also make the most of the Salon, the premier exhibition of works by living artists, usually held biannually at the Louvre.[11] His generation would learn to capitalize on the goodwill of an administration eager to support new talents and intent on reinforcing the dynamism of the "French school." In 1816 Jacques Louis David, the father of that school, had fled to Brussels as a regicide,[12] and the remaining masters, especially David's students Antoine Jean Gros, François Gérard, Anne Louis Girodet—and also Guérin—were beginning to show signs of weakness.[13] In May 1821 Forbin wrote to his friend the painter François Marius Granet: "No one really knows what Gérard is doing. It's always very mysterious, but he is polite and has lovely manners. Gros takes little interest in others; he is as well-mannered as ever. I leave him alone in his sad corner. Girodet has retired to the countryside and no longer paints. Guérin is here, but he doesn't do much anymore either. The young people will try very hard, and the Salon will, I think, be very lively."[14]

In 1821, Delacroix, although only a beginner, understood that the Salon scheduled for the following year was an opportunity to be seized. Having just failed to win the Prix de Rome, he was troubled by a sense that time was slipping away. As he explained to his sister: "I would be very proud . . . to have the time to do something for the next Salon. These exhibitions are now so far apart that you can become old in the intervals between them . . . and it is good to win a bit of recognition, if possible."[15] The urgency with which he threw himself into the fray, although linked to his generation's awareness of an acceleration of historical time, was also rooted in his financial woes. To earn money, Delacroix designed machines with his friend Charles-Louis-Raymond Soulier and drew liberal-leaning political cartoons—a rare occurrence of overtly political views in his oeuvre—for the satirical newspaper *Le miroir*.[16] He also obtained work as a fine artist. In 1819, a patron commissioned him to paint a Virgin for the church of the village of Orcemont, near Paris, and in 1820 Gericault subcontracted to him a commission from the Ministère de l'Intérieur for a *Virgin of the Sacred Heart* (see fig. 110). Finally, in autumn 1821, Delacroix completed the decoration for the dining room in the newly built mansion of the great actor Talma. But his earnings from these projects fell short of his needs: his studies with Guérin and the Ecole des Beaux-Arts were costly, as were his materials, models, and the rental of scaffolding at the museum.[17] To improve his finances, he hoped to secure a commission or purchase by the state at the Salon.

1822: Trying His Luck

Under the auspices of the comte de Forbin, the Salon for the first time opened its doors to young artists who had not necessarily followed the well-established course of study culminating in the Prix de Rome competition. Even more than others, Delacroix immediately understood the Salon's importance: "I would really like to do a painting for the next Salon, especially if it could get people to know me somewhat," he wrote in 1821 to his friend Soulier, who was then in Naples.[18] Delacroix had advised Soulier a few weeks earlier: "Think about next year's Salon. You must plaster it with your watercolors and oil paintings. That's where you'll really make yourself known."[19] In 1821 Delacroix declined to try again for the Prix de Rome in order to join the fray at the Salon and

make a name for himself there. He may have been influenced by the example of friends and acquaintances. His master, Guérin, though a great defender of the traditional path, had had his first success as a painter at the Salon of 1799 with *The Return of Marcus Sextus*.[20] More recently, Théodore Gericault and Ary Scheffer, students of Guérin's and Delacroix's classmates, had won their spurs at the Salon of 1812 without having studied in Rome beforehand: Gericault with the *Portrait of Lieutenant M. D.,* later known as *Officer of the Chasseurs Commanding a Charge* (Louvre); and Scheffer with *Abel Singing a Hymn of Praise* (location unknown).[21] They were among the artists who were then adopting a new strategy of appealing directly to the public for approval before—or instead of—seeking official recognition, in the form of the Prix de Rome, from their colleagues.[22] This approach provoked a major upheaval within the tradition-bound fine arts system. The turmoil, bolstered by the unprecedented rise of the press in the early 1820s, was indeed felt at the Académie de France in Rome.

Although Delacroix would plan the specifics of his first Salon entry in an intelligent, pragmatic, and, above all, systematic manner, his reasons for submitting a painting to the exhibition were not based on principle, even though his future was at stake. In fact, it seems that he had not yet given up on the idea of eventually contending for the Prix de Rome. Aware of his technical deficiencies, he even entertained the possibility of training in the studio of Antoine Jean Gros, who at that time had the highest reputation for preparing students for the competitive exams.[23] Delacroix's decision to "try his luck," as he told Soulier, at the Salon was that of a young man in a hurry, hungry for recognition and driven by the need to secure a commission or a purchase.[24] The gambit paid off brilliantly, with the state's acquisition of *The Barque of Dante* and its exhibition in the Musée du Luxembourg at a time when not even Gericault or Gros had works displayed there. Delacroix's decision would determine the entire course of his career, not only his vocation as a painter but also his fondness for exhibiting his works to the public. Delacroix would be one of the few artists of his generation—Camille Corot was another—to put his reputation on the line by participating at the Salon until the very end of his career.

Delacroix skillfully prepared his submission to the Salon, probably guided by the successes and failures of Gericault at the previous exhibitions. The subject of the painting was clearly of paramount importance in attracting attention among

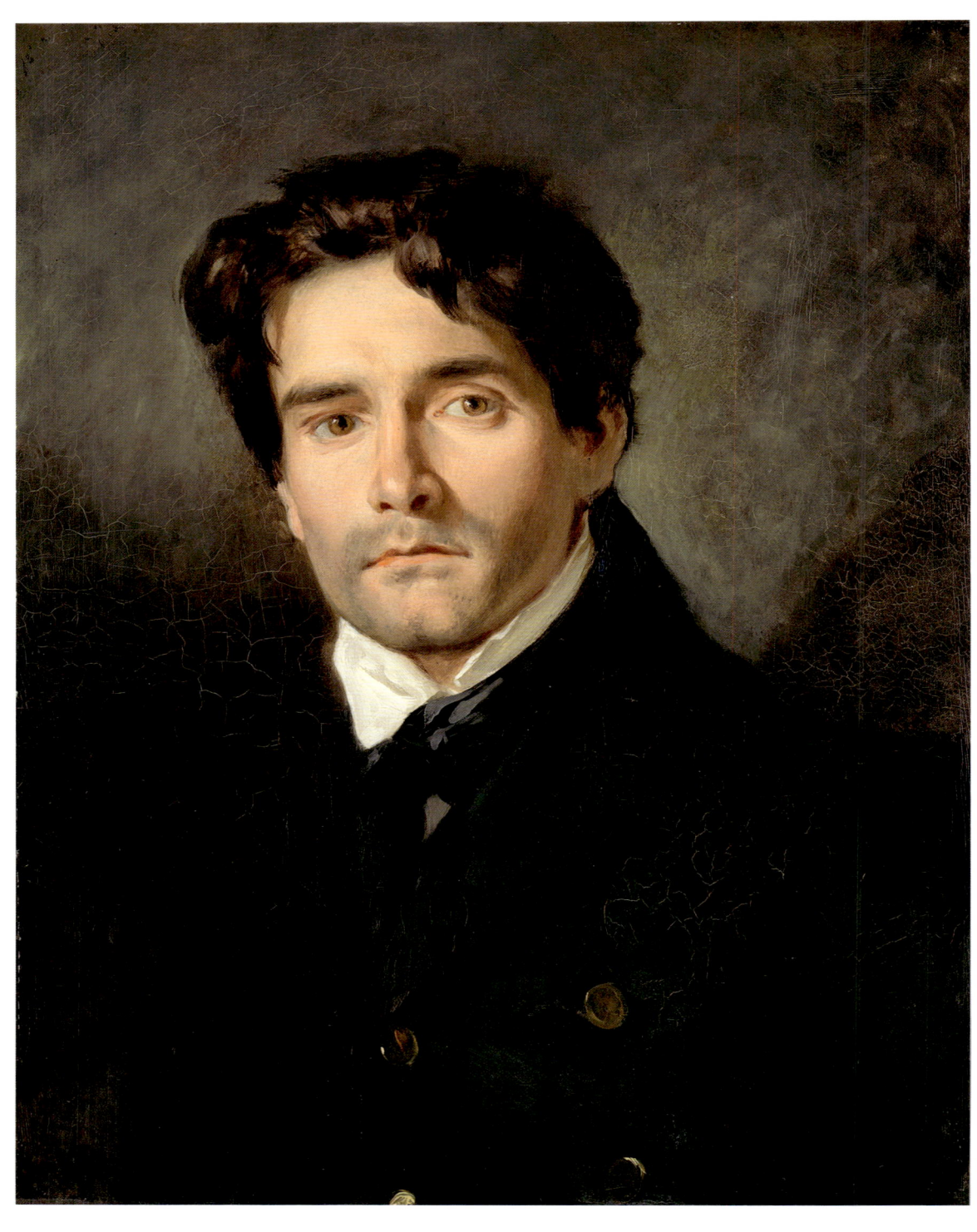

CAT. 88 *Léon Riesener (1808–1878), 1835*

CAT. 89 *Madame Henri François Riesener (Félicité Longrois, 1786–1847), 1835*

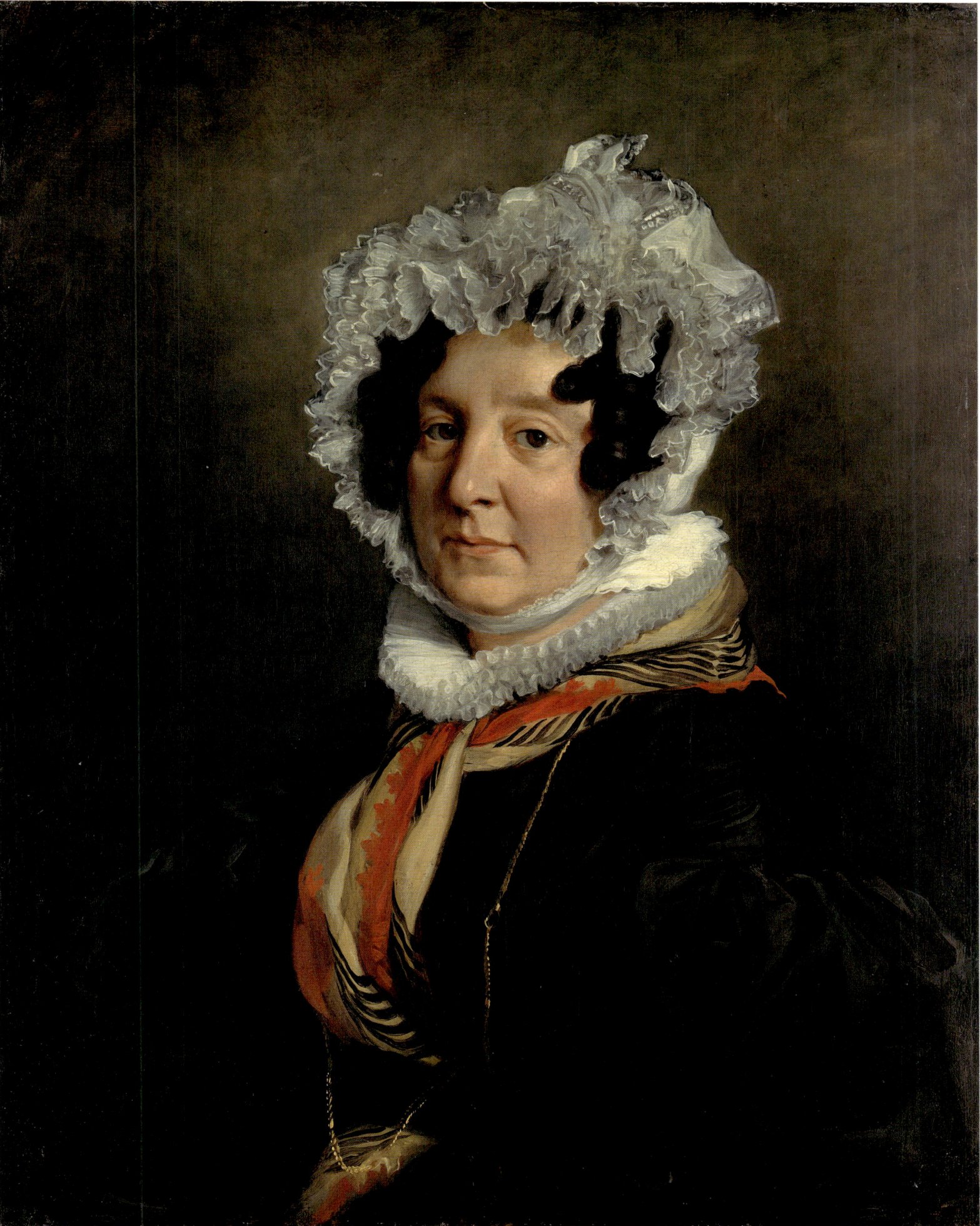

hundreds of works; an episode from Dante's *Divine Comedy,* the final choice, came after much deliberation. On September 15, 1821, Delacroix, still undecided about what he was going to paint, wrote to Soulier: "I am proposing to do a painting for the Salon, for which I will take as my subject the recent wars of the Turks and the Greeks. I believe that under the circumstances, if there is some merit in the execution, it would be a way to set myself apart."[25] In confiding this plan to his friend, Delacroix clearly expressed the hierarchical relationship between the subject and its execution. The standard by which interest in the work would be measured was, in fact, its subject. A Greek subject would have addressed a highly volatile and timely issue. In 1821, the Greek War of Independence against the Ottoman Empire had only just begun. The French government prudently maintained an official policy of strict neutrality in order to retain ties with all interested parties, including Russia. Moreover, because France's liberal faction openly sided with the Greeks, the Restoration government, which had just responded to the conspiracy of the Carbonari, was deeply anxious about the Greek independence movement. The risk, therefore, was that such a subject would be seen as a provocation.

In 1822 Delacroix, though of a liberal bent, wanted primarily to make a name for himself and secure a commission or a purchase. He knew the risks, having before him the example of Gericault's controversial *Raft of the Medusa,*[26] exhibited in 1819. He may also have listened to the advice of others, including Forbin, who scoured studios looking for young talent. Aside from the possibility of an immediate scandal, there was another risk. Given the uncertainty of the times, even if the work were purchased by the state, it might never hang in the Luxembourg owing to the vagaries of politics. Most of the great masters active under the Empire— Gros, above all—continued to pay a political price.[27]

Delacroix therefore abandoned his initial idea of a subject from contemporary history in favor of illustrating canto 8 of Dante's *Inferno.* That decision was made in late autumn 1821. Because the Salon was set to open on April 24, 1822, the artist, as would be his habit, worked relentlessly and with the utmost urgency, for as many as thirteen hours a day. In February, he wrote to his sister: "I am overwhelmed with work. If I manage to pull off what I am undertaking, I will have done a rather substantial painting in only two months, one that might contribute toward making me well known."[28] The painting was finished on April 15 (see fig. 2).[29]

"A Sublime Triviality That Thrills"

The choice of a subject inspired by Dante would prove tremendously effective. It is not known whether the idea was the artist's alone or if it was suggested to him by a devotee of Italian literature, such as the painter François Gérard. At the time, familiarity with *The Divine Comedy* was, for the most part, superficial in France. Painters were acquainted with the story of Ugolino and, consistent with the vogue for troubadour themes, the fateful love of Paolo and Francesca.[30] But Dante's epic poem had been part of Delacroix's cultural frame of reference since his years at the lycée. In 1814, he had copied passages from the poem into his school notebooks.[31] In 1819 or 1820, he made drawings in his notebooks inspired by the work and attempted to translate parts of it.[32] On September 28, 1819, he wrote to his friend Félix Guillemardet: "Sometimes when I am in the middle of the hunt, [but] my enthusiasm for the prey has waned, I remember Ugolino, whom I had the presence of mind to bring with me."[33] Delacroix wavered about which episode to illustrate before finally turning his attention to the moment in canto 8 when Dante, guided by Virgil in Phlegyas's boat, crosses the river to the Underworld.[34] He suddenly recognizes, amid the damned attempting to board the boat (cat. 6), the wrathful Filippo Argenti, condemned to devour himself. In the background, the infernal city of Dis is burning.

In choosing to illustrate a little-known passage from *The Divine Comedy,* Delacroix proposed a reformulation of certain principles of Neoclassical painting. With *The Return of Marcus Sextus,* his master Guérin had done the same, albeit inspired by classical tragedy filtered through the lens of Racine. In the 1820s, however, Delacroix's source, *The Divine Comedy,* was not only unconventional but also partly transgressive. Trying his hand at translating the story of Ugolino, Delacroix confided to Guillemardet: "[It] is extraordinarily difficult. In the original, there is a sublime triviality that thrills. The style drags as if to make you spend those six deadly days with Ugolino."[35]

The expression "sublime banality" aptly conveys what Delacroix was trying to achieve in his painting, seemingly anticipating by five years Victor Hugo's preface to *Cromwell.*[36] The Romantic generation to which Delacroix belonged, having grown up in a world both glorious and violent, could not fail to respond to the *terribilità* of *The Inferno.* The return of peace to Europe allowed for the dissemination and vogue for British gothic novels in France, and Delacroix read Dante in the light of these works. He devoured Matthew Gregory Lewis's

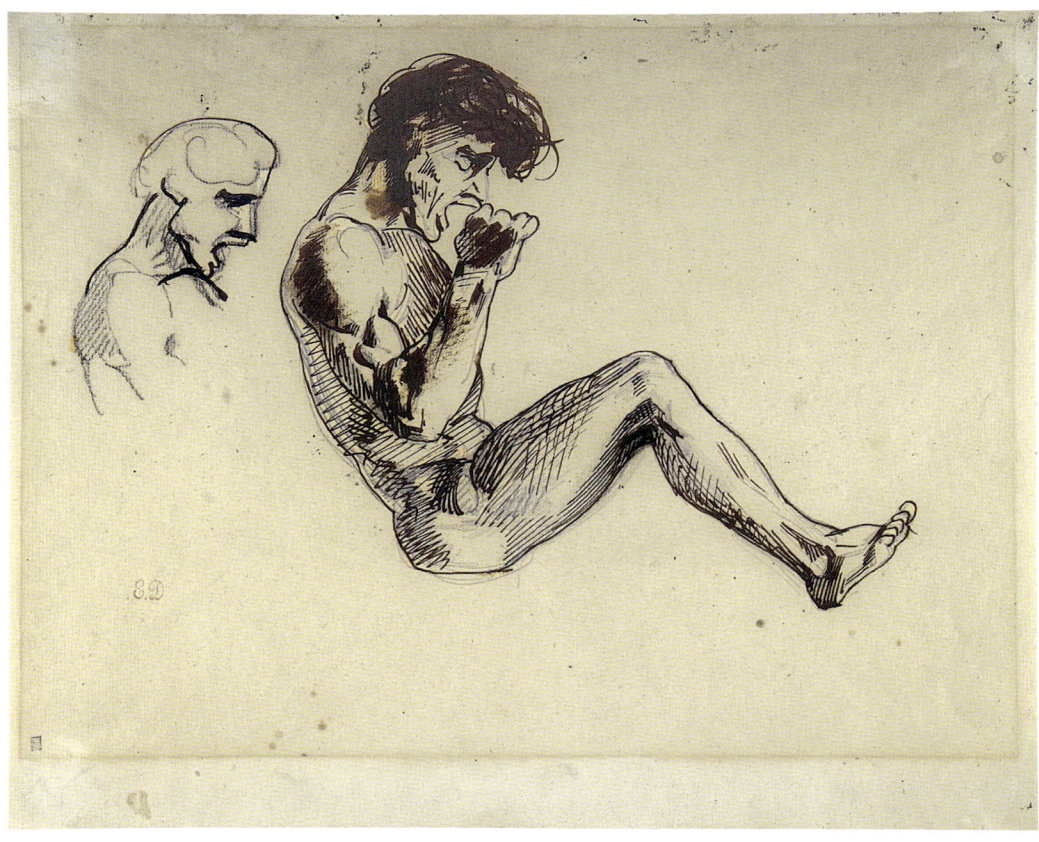

CAT. 6 *Studies of a Damned Man, for "The Barque of Dante,"* 1822

Monk, which combines eroticism, spellbinding supernatural-ism, and fiendish visions. He copied excerpts from the French translation of 1799 into his notebooks. The novel even inspired a poem he wrote in the early 1820s, at a time when he was rereading, translating, and illustrating Dante.[37]

The *Inferno*'s episode taking as its subject Filippo Argenti, which features a medieval hero, hellish clouds and dark waters, burning cities, and the damned devouring one another, moan-ing and screaming, was at odds with the ideal of balance pro-pounded by Neoclassical painting. It also introduced a new type of hero, one who is neither isolated nor triumphant. Delacroix captured Dante in a moment of doubt or hesitation, as he witnesses a scene, apparently terrifying, located outside the frame. That space beyond the frame, which the painter invoked regularly in his early paintings, stimulates the imagina-tion and elicits a new level of involvement on the part of the spectator.[38] This is the famous "bridge" Delacroix would later speak of between the minds of the painter and the beholder.

Dante, exiled from his own country and wandering in the Underworld, brings to mind the peregrinations of Oedipus, Belisarius, and Homer, who were often represented at the Salons during the Revolution. Like those heroes of antiquity, Dante is accompanied by a guide, Virgil. And yet Dante's status in the poem turns the notion of the hero on its head. The hierarchical relationship between classical charac-ters and their guides is abandoned: Dante and Virgil are treated as equals. The hero is thus split in two, a Romantic theme par excellence that recurs in Delacroix's early works, such as in the series of scenes from Goethe's *Faust* (see cats. 36–56). In the center of the canvas, Delacroix placed Virgil's hand grasp-ing Dante's, a kind of modern equivalent of the Neoclassical gesture of the oath. The oath, which conveys collective, unifying, and socially hierarchized values, as in David's *Oath of the Horatii* (1784; Musée du Louvre), is replaced in *The Barque of Dante* by the gesture of friendship, based on the free consent of individuals. In a climate of equality, friendship links concern for the self with concern for the other.

During these years, Delacroix's correspondence is filled with such ardent declarations addressed to Jean-Baptiste Pierret: "I am happy, really happy, only when I'm with a friend";[39] "Most holy friendship, divine friendship, dear heart! No, I am not worthy of you. You swathe me in your friendship.

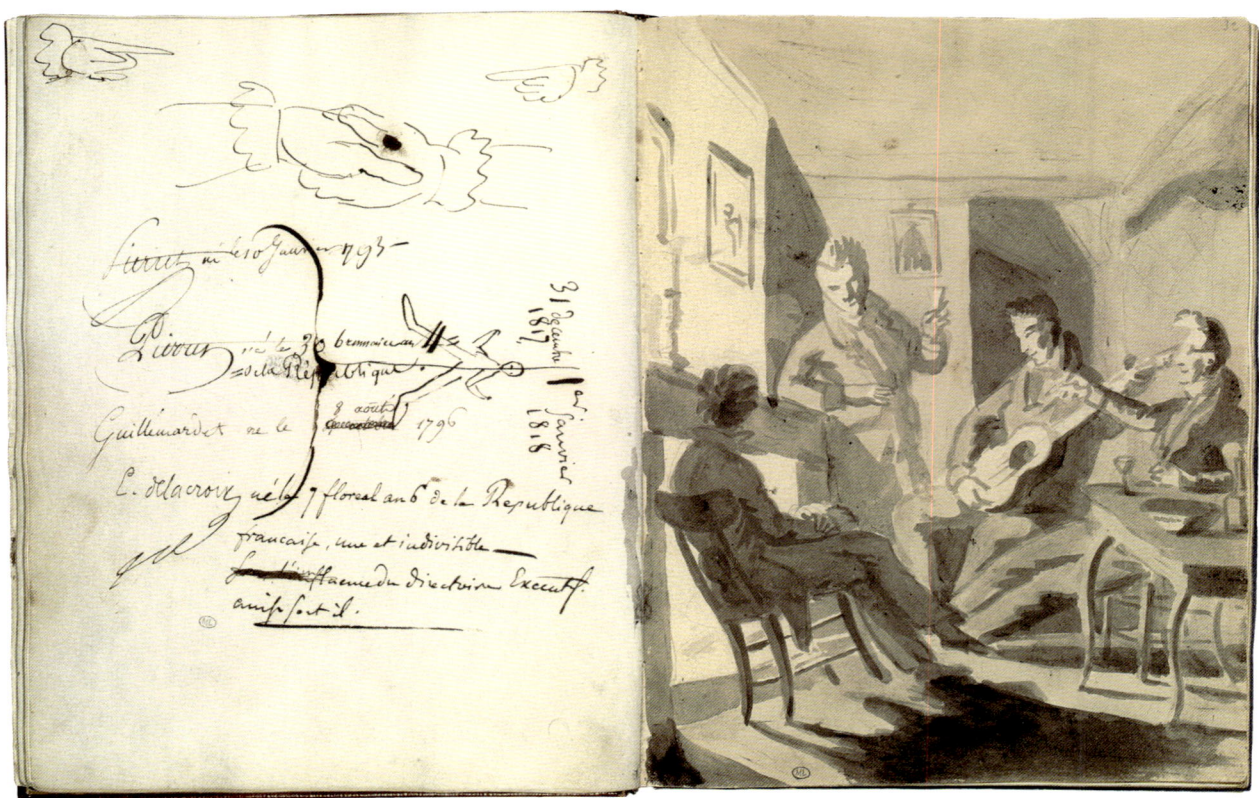

FIG. 3 *A Gathering of Friends on Saint Sylvester's Day (New Year's, 1817–18).* From the so-called *Saint Sylvester's Day Sketchbook*, folios 31 verso and 32 recto, 1817–18. Ink and wash on paper, overall 9¹³⁄₁₆ x 15¾ in. (25 x 40 cm). Musée du Louvre, Paris (RF 9140)

You are my conqueror, I am your captive. Good friend, truly you know how to love."⁴⁰ In the context of a new society that would highlight horizontal structures (generational, artistic), personal feelings were coupled with social practice, as indicated in a depiction of the traditional New Year's Eve celebration, *A Gathering of Friends on Saint Sylvester's Day (New Year's, 1817–18)* (fig. 3). In this drawing, Delacroix, Pierret, Guillemardet, and Piron are shown gathered by the fire, drinking, conversing, and enjoying music. On the left-hand page, each has signed his name and, three years after the fall of the Empire, given his date of birth according to the Revolutionary calendar. Delacroix, therefore, is shown to have been born on "the 9th of Floréal, Year 6 of the French Republic, one and indivisible"—as indivisible as their friendship, symbolized by the handshake that dominates the page. The same gesture unites Virgil and Dante in a shared fate and an initiation of sorts. The reference to the Revolutionary calendar in the midst of the Restoration, like Delacroix's use, in a letter to Piron written sometime after the Battle of Waterloo, of the "patriotic or revolutionary paper, however you want to interpret it," reveals the liberal, which is to say Bonapartist, ideas that united the four friends at the time.⁴¹

Monsieur Delacroix Shows "Promise of Real Talent"

Dante and Virgil, an entirely original subject, allowed the young painter to engage visitors to the Salon through a series of familiar associations. The boat and the cannibalism among the damned in the foreground evoked for his contemporaries Gericault's *Raft of the Medusa,* which had caused a scandal at the previous Salon. Some pointed this out, including Arnold Scheffer (brother of the painter Ary), who wrote several years later: "In that first work, imitating the manner of Gericault, M. Delacroix showed promise of real talent but not the originality that now marks his works."⁴² The painting's literary subject allowed the artist to avoid political risks, which Gericault himself had mitigated by giving his *Raft* the generic title "Shipwreck Scene" in the Salon catalogue, or *livret,* of 1819. The associations with Dante and Gericault called forth a third figure: Michelangelo. Evidence of that connection can be found in Delacroix's attempted translation of canto 3, devoted to the barque of Charon, recorded in one of his notebooks and illustrated on the right-hand page with a drawing inspired in almost every detail by Michelangelo's

Last Judgment in the Sistine Chapel.[43] Both the medieval poet and the Renaissance master gave expression to dark, dramatic inspiration. The moderns did so also, sometimes at the expense of form and with a certain immoderation. The critic Delécluze pointed this out in one of his first articles for *Le moniteur universel,* in which he attempted to define the essence of modern poetry—that is, poetry written since "that great rift in the arts brought about by Dante and Michelangelo." He contrasted the moderns, who, beginning with those two figures, had emphasized expressiveness, to the ancients, who, considering beauty the aim of art, had cultivated form. The critic, a former student of David's and a defender of the Grand Tradition, noted that "our painting was supposed to be expressive." At the same time, "in the interest of truth and art," he cautioned against "misusing that resource [expressiveness], which leads . . . imperceptibly to exaggeration and the neglect of indispensable studies in the arts of imitation."[44] With its dark subject, craggy faces, and the damned with their bloodshot eyes, *The Barque of Dante* obviously privileged expressiveness. Delécluze, though an expert on *The Divine Comedy,* therefore violently denounced Delacroix's painting, calling it a *tartouillade.*

A Real *Tartouillade*

In the idiom of the studio, a *tartouillade* was a weakly drawn painting in which everything was sacrificed to the brilliance of the colors. It is true that in his first Salon painting, Delacroix supplemented his allusion to Michelangelo's *terribilità* with, in Thiers's words, "the fecundity of Rubens."[45] The young painter belonged to the first generation of artists able to train with relative freedom at the museum—that is to say, the Louvre—directly in contact with the old masters, without the filter of academic teaching. In the early 1820s, Delacroix was fond of copying Peter Paul Rubens, especially the Nereids in *The Landing of Maria de Medici at Marseilles* (fig. 4), as seen in the great study at the Kunstmuseum Basel (see cat. 5). He knew only a few sculptures by Michelangelo firsthand, and they could have been of use to him only through the force of their invention. By contrast, the works of the Antwerp master were for Delacroix the essence of painting, and he sought to understand their mechanisms by observing and copying them. The tension between Michelangelo's influence, partly filtered through Gericault, and that of Rubens, apprehended in part

through Gros's example, expressed the new polarity in his mind between inventiveness in the classic sense of the term and craft, between inspiration and the materiality of paint. In 1824 Delacroix would express that polarity differently: "It would be a singular and very beautiful thing to bring together the styles of Michelangelo and Velázquez."[46]

The composition of *The Barque of Dante* was probably inspired not only by *The Landing of Maria de Medici at Marseilles* but also by Rubens's *Hero and Leander* (1604; Yale University Art Gallery), which Delacroix would have known through a large drawing by Lucas Vorsterman (ca. 1619; Musée du Louvre).[47] From his study of the Maria de Medici cycle, Delacroix learned the science of depicting flesh tones and reflections as well as the rational division of form into its colored components without the use of chiaroscuro. Contrary to what his assistant Pierre Andrieu would later claim, it is not possible to detect in the drops of water on the bodies of the damned the first hints of "optical mixture"; but Delacroix did express in the Salon painting his understanding of the importance of reflections for bringing color to life. "Delacroix had a very hard time rendering in all their natural truth the drops of water falling from the overturned nude figures," wrote the artist-manqué-turned-collector Alfred Bruyas. "These drops of water set him off on a search. The memory of Rubens's sirens in *The Landing of Maria de Medici at Marseilles* and the study of the gradations of the rainbow were his starting point."[48] But where Rubens displayed an economy of means by using the color of the sirens' flesh as local color, Delacroix, who was also trying to avoid black shadows, made use of a riot of colors: light is rendered by a brilliant white, gray tones by a green; reflections are conveyed with a yellowish dab, and the shadow by a red. Delacroix's extraordinary richness and chromatic inventiveness are already summed up in these few square inches of canvas, enlivened by the large red accent of Dante's hood, contrasted with its complementary color, the green of his mantle.

Wishing to attract attention by impressing the public, Delacroix balanced the boldness of a dark subject, the dramatic intensity of gesture and color, and the horrifying aspect of the figures trying to board the boat through a display of *beaux morceaux* (beautifully rendered passages) in what constituted the academic exercise par excellence: the nude. That is probably what led Gros to say that the painting was "Rubens refined."[49] Delacroix distributed these passages in the foreground, as a garland subtending the Dante-Virgil group. The rather ostentatious device allowed him to demonstrate his skill in combining references to antiquity—Phlegyas's back, for example, inspired by the Belvedere Torso—with a certain realism in the rendering of the flesh, with bodies folded up or splayed out in the extreme. Thiers was not mistaken in his enthusiasm for the artist who "throws down his figures, groups them, and bends them to his will with the boldness of Michelangelo and the fecundity of Rubens. I'm not sure which memory of the great artists takes hold of me as I look at that painting."[50] The frieze-like composition, which focuses attention on the foreground, probably allowed the artist to circumvent the difficulty he still had in defining space. The reason for this difficulty was his reliance on live models while building up his compositions. In the second part of his career, he would try to dispense with their physical presence, believing that having the model before his eyes during the execution of a painting obstructed the idealizing function of memory. In the 1820s, by contrast, the use of a model seemed a way of liberating himself from the constraints of academic teaching.

But let there be no mistake about the meaning of his painting of 1822, which is sometimes considered year 1 of the Romantic revolution. The young Delacroix was not wittingly engaged in undermining pedagogical fundamentals or Neoclassical principles. Did he not wish to study under Gros, the (overly) faithful student of David? And for his part, did not Gros, though an intransigent guardian of his master's teaching, try to attract the novice painter to his studio? Would not Delacroix's canvas, though judged imperfect (this was normal for a beginner), be almost unanimously admired as heralding a master? Unlike Ingres, whose talent was nurtured in David's studio and who, in 1806, said that "art needs to be reformed," Delacroix did not want to be "that particular revolutionary" who would carry out reform.[51] His primary objective was to make a name for himself. And yet, even while following in the footsteps of his more or less distant predecessors, remaining at heart a man of his time faithful to the principles of the *grand genre*, he systematically shifted and reformulated his positions, at least somewhat aware of the polarity between the ideal aspect of his art and its material composition.

In his early years, Delacroix was preoccupied with the apparent contradiction of the aspiration for immateriality existing within an art form produced by the materiality of paint deposited on canvas by an artist's hand, that "good, fat color" that he wanted to spread "thickly over a brown or red canvas."[52] This tension, which runs through a significant part of his early *Journal*, found its concrete expression in the relative

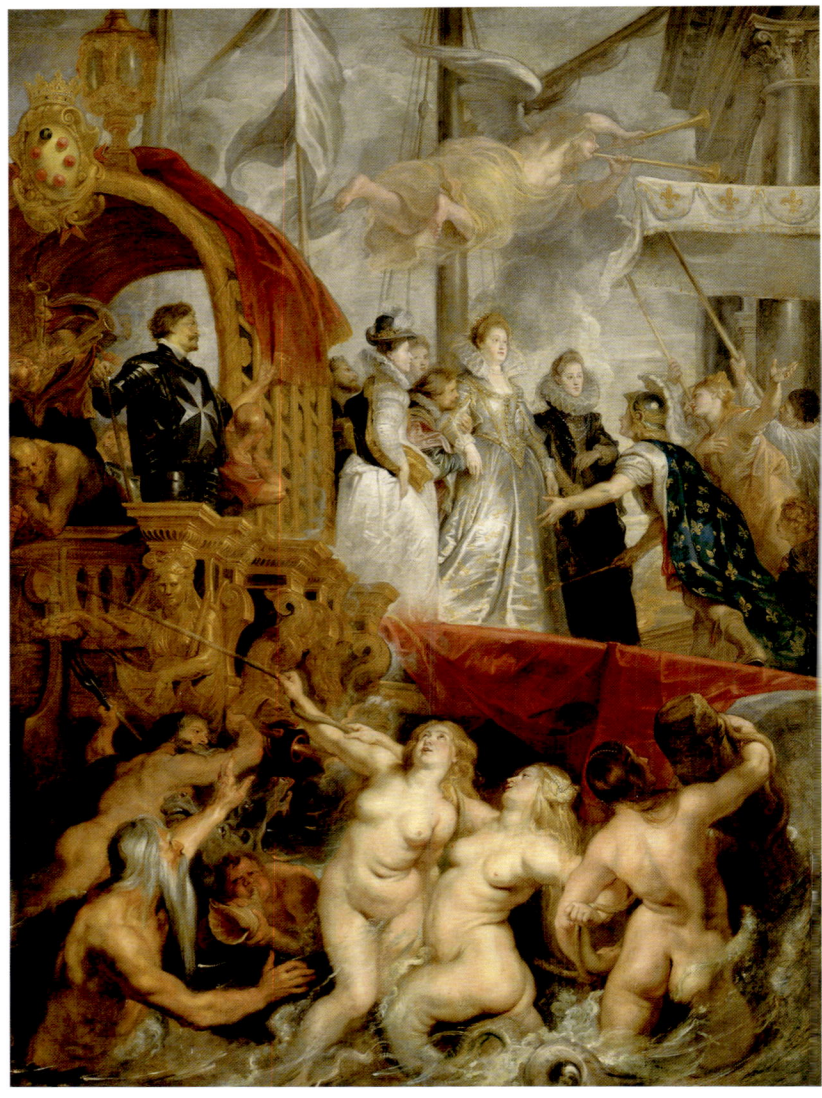

FIG. 4 Peter Paul Rubens (Flemish, 1577–1640). *The Landing of Maria de Medici at Marseilles on November 3, 1600*, ca. 1622–25. Oil on canvas, 12 ft. 11⅛ in. x 9 ft. 8⅛ in. (3.9 x 3 m). Musée du Louvre, Paris (1774)

importance he attributed to a painting's subject and its execution.[53] Delacroix's originality lay in reassessing and accepting the execution as "nobly" constitutive of the creative process; in that, he broke with almost three centuries of painting, defined as primarily *cosa mentale,* or *ut pictura poesis.* On May 11, 1824, he lamented, "How I would like to be a poet!" Then, correcting himself, he wrote, "But at least create in painting."[54] Two years earlier, in an important passage he would revisit several times in the *Journal* of his later years, he laid the foundations for what distinguishes the painter's art from that of the poet, namely, its relationship to materiality: "The art of

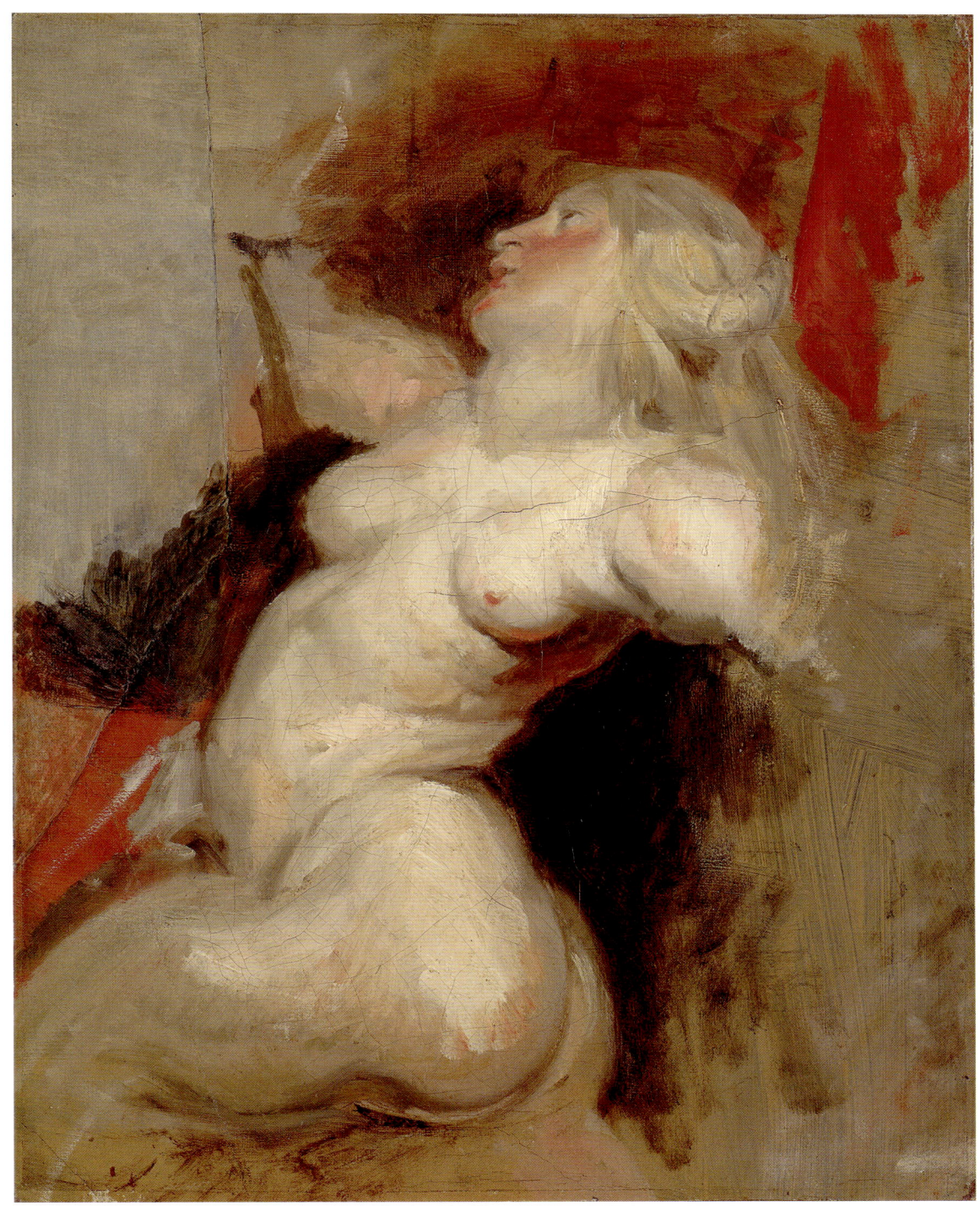

Nereid, after Rubens, detail from "The Landing of Maria de Medici at Marseilles," ca. 1822

the painter is all the nearer to man's heart because it seems to be more material."[55] The subtler critics, such as Delécluze, quickly understood the danger; the insulting *tartouillade* expressed exactly that: a formless form devoid of ideas. The violent attacks to which Delacroix would be subjected at the Salons of 1824 and, especially, 1827 would take aim at the artist's manner in particular. It was as if contemporaries found something repellent in an execution that was, in their view, too conspicuous, as if it prevented them from seeing the subject represented. Gros, who in 1822 had applauded Delacroix's good fortune, two years later looked upon the artist's *Scenes from the Massacres at Chios* (fig. 5) as the massacre of painting.

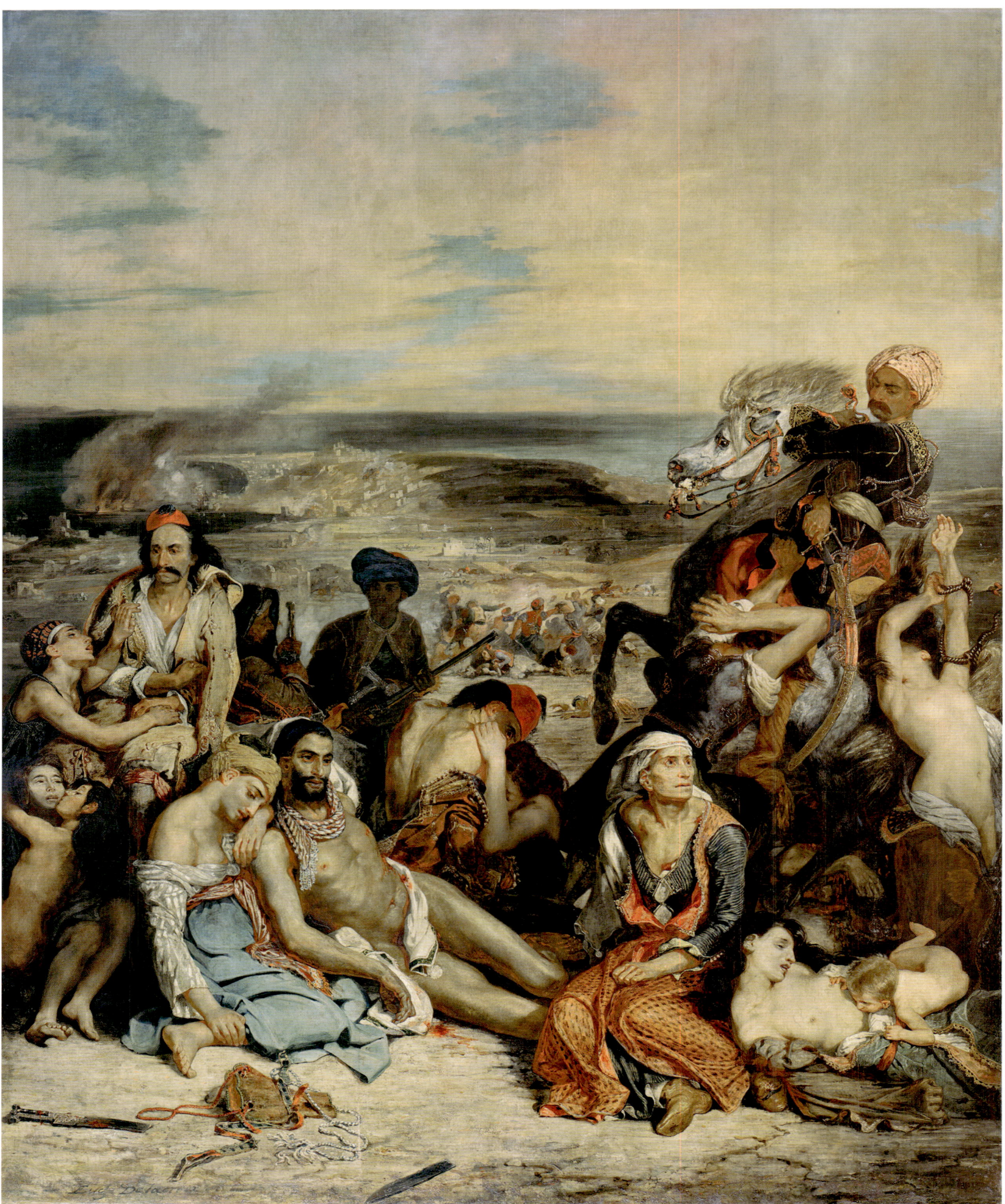

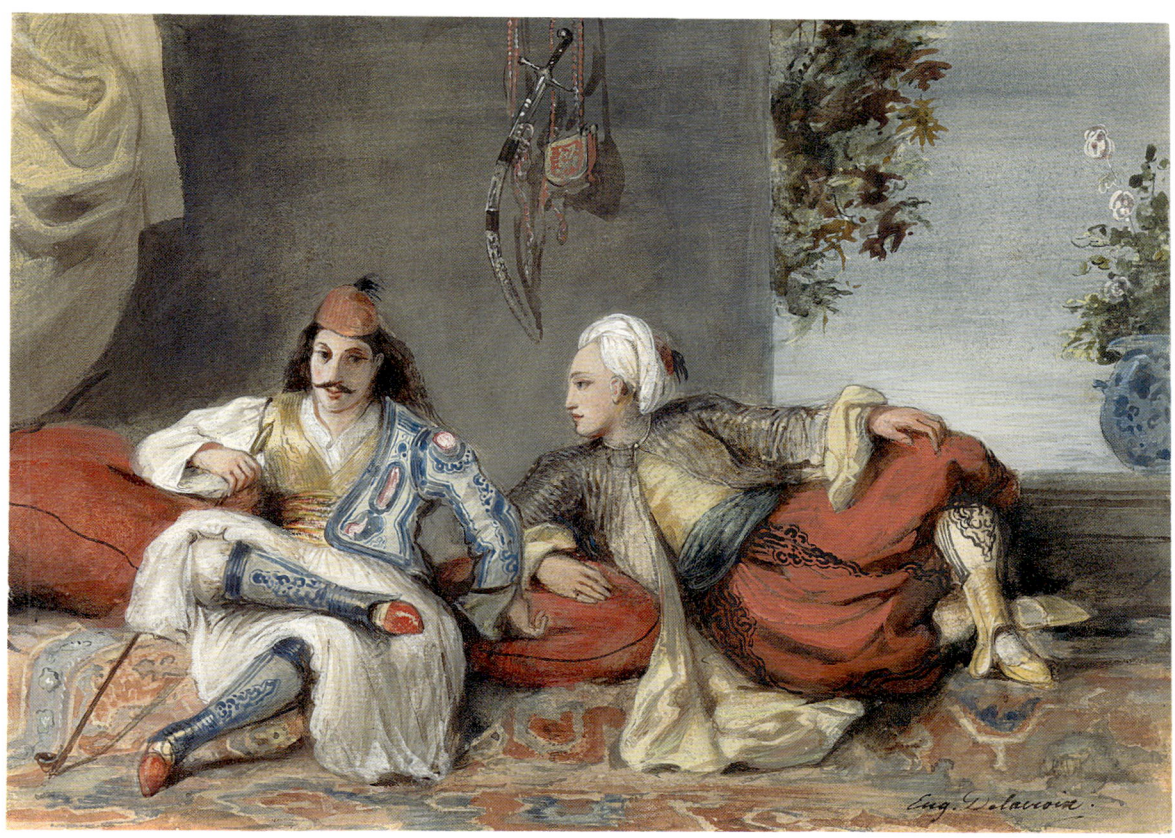

CAT. 35 *A Greek and a Turk in an Interior*, late 1820s

The Muse and the Market

Emboldened by his first success, Delacroix decided to exhibit at the following Salon, which was set to open in August 1824. On May 24 or 31, 1823, he recorded in his *Journal* the subject of the principal painting he would display: "I have decided to paint scenes from the massacres of Chios for the Salon."[56] The artist thus returned to an episode from the Greek War of Independence, a subject that he had abandoned in 1821. His earlier remark, "I believe that under the circumstances, if there is some merit in the execution, it would be a way to set myself apart," would prove to be prescient with regard to both the content and the role of the subject in attracting attention.[57] He chose one of the most terrible episodes in the war, one that had made a strong impact on Europeans owing to the profusion of dreadful details about it that had circulated in the press. In the spring of 1822, Ottoman troops massacred inhabitants of the island of Scio, now Chios, and sold several thousand men, women, and children into slavery in the principal cities of the empire. These killings and deportations caused a wave of outrage in the West. They were conveyed in numerous accounts, one by Olivier Voutier, a French colonel in the service of the Greeks and the discoverer of the Venus de Milo in 1820. Voutier's *Mémoires du Colonel Voutier sur la guerre actuelle des Grecs* was published in 1823. Delacroix moved in philhellenic circles, as did his nephew, Charles de Verninac, who introduced the artist to Voutier on January 12, 1824, the same day Delacroix noted that he was "really" beginning his painting. Its composition had been interrupted in November 1823, and its long and painstaking execution would keep him occupied throughout the spring.[58]

The artist's sincere interest in the Greeks who were trying to liberate themselves from the Ottomans is beyond

FIG. 5 *Scenes from the Massacres at Chios*, 1824. Oil on canvas, 13 ft. 8³⁄₁₆ in. x 11 ft. 7³⁄₈ in. (4.2 x 3.5 m). Musée du Louvre, Paris (3823) (J 105)

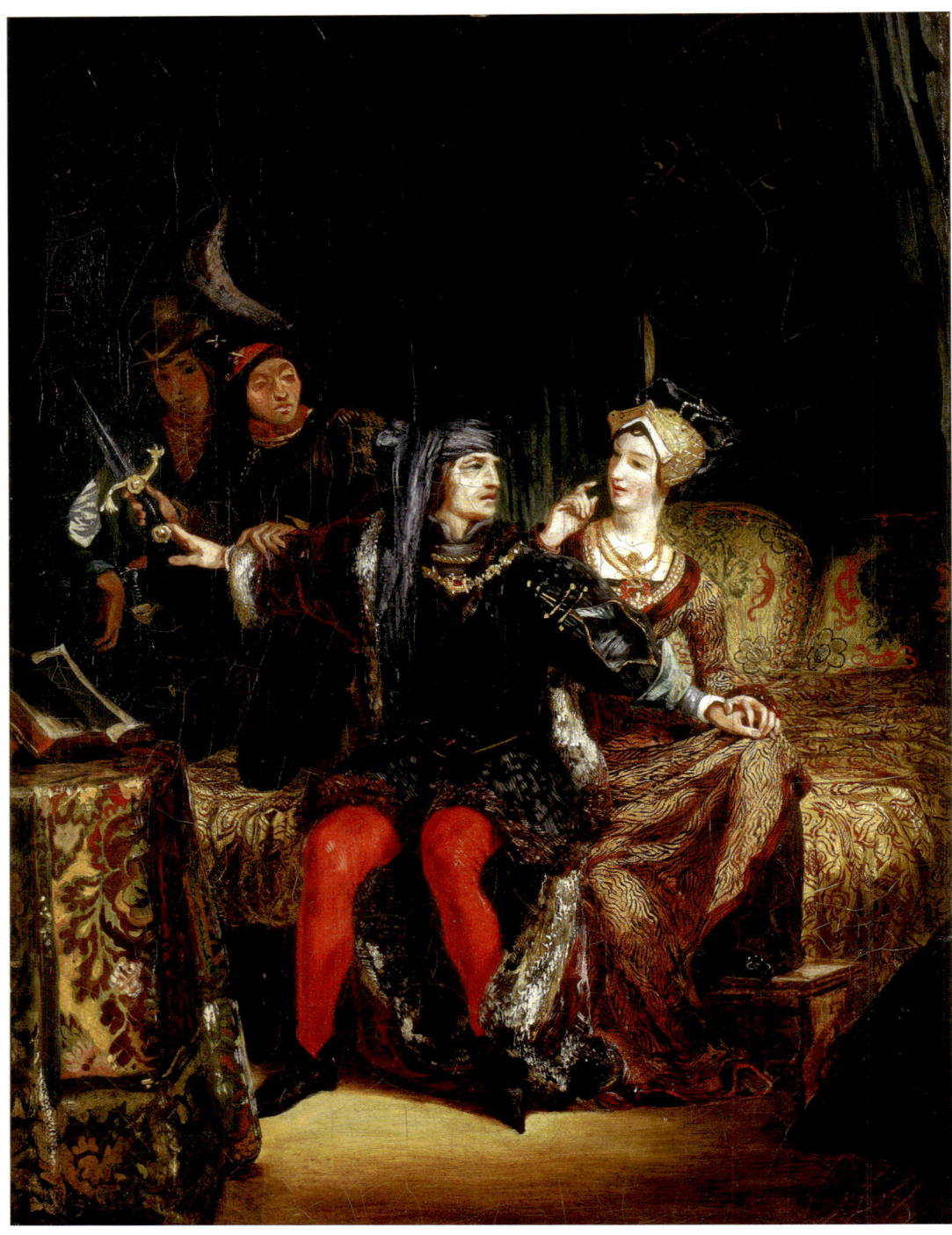

CAT. 23 *Charles VI and Odette de Champdivers, ca. 1825*

doubt: many traces are found in 1821 to 1823, and throughout the decade (see, for example, cat. 35). It is worth noting, however, that he acted with a great deal of discernment in postponing the execution of his idea for a subject taken from contemporary history. By 1824, though the official French position was still not decided, there was reason to hope that the country would side with the Greeks. The conflict, which had lasted three years, was on everyone's mind, and young people, following the example of the British poet-adventurer Lord Byron, were caught up in philhellenic enthusiasm. Delacroix had made a name for himself: his *Barque of Dante* had been purchased by the state and was on public display at the Musée du Luxembourg alongside works by widely acknowledged masters such as Joseph Marie Vien and David. Emboldened by this recognition, he could now brave the potentially polemical character of a topical subject.

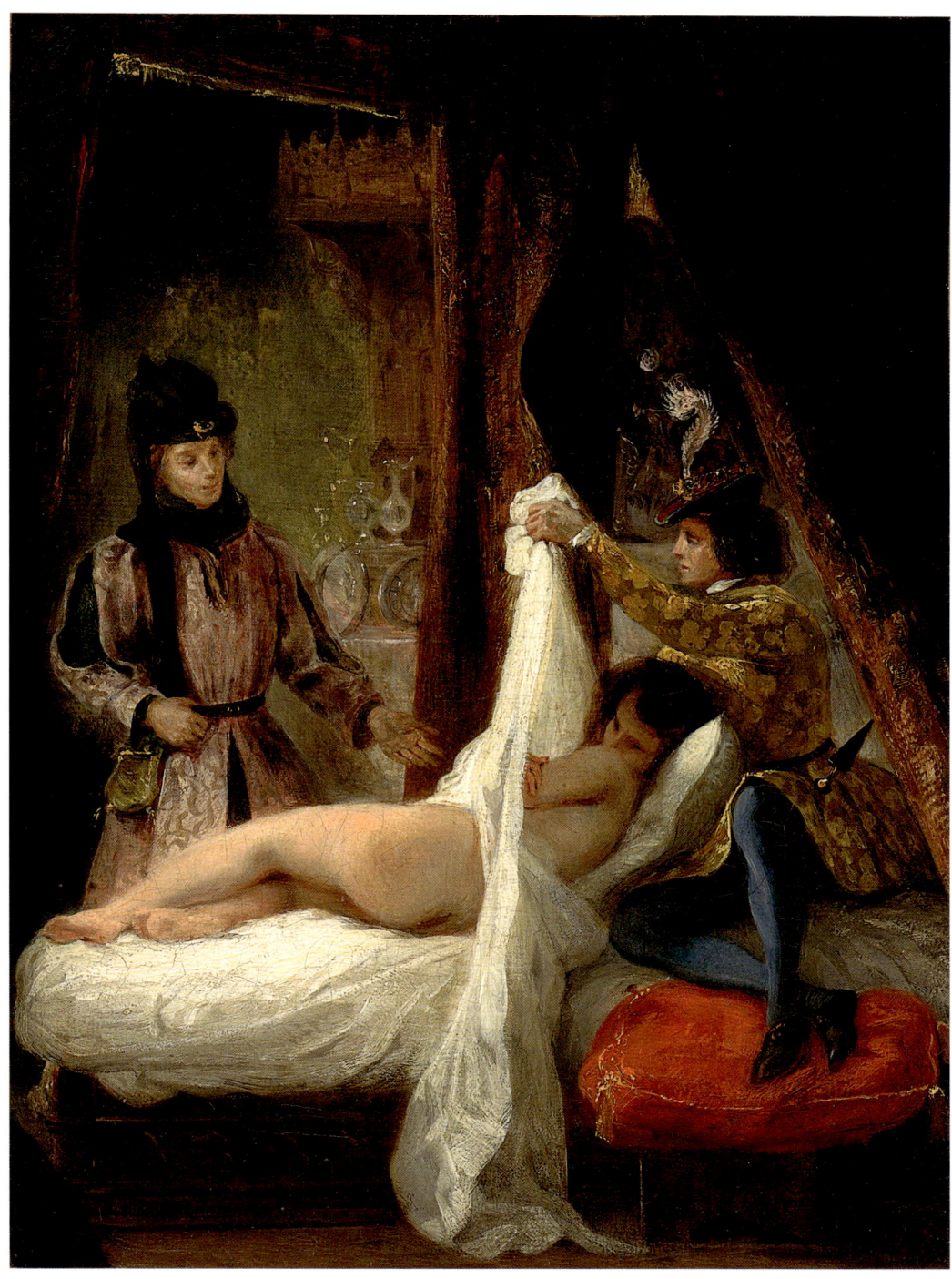

CAT. 24 *The Duke of Orléans Showing His Lover*, ca. 1825–26

Perhaps there was even a pointed interest in his doing so. With the liberalization of institutions, the art market had become considerably more complex; potentially, there were private buyers for his work. Delacroix, who had to make the most of his initial success, was keenly aware of this. Even as he was working on his large piece for the Salon, he made several dozen small paintings for private patrons, often for financial reasons. "[I] want to do small paintings, especially to buy something at the Gericault sale," he confided in his *Journal*.⁵⁹ Sometimes he just wanted to relax: "Instead of another fairly large painting, I should like to do several small paintings, but enjoy myself while painting them."⁶⁰ Then, aware of the time he considered having wasted on bread-and-butter jobs, he pulled himself together: "No more Don Quixotes and things unworthy of you. Concentrate deeply when you are painting and think only of Dante. In his works lie what I have always felt within myself."⁶¹

Delacroix was alluding here to *Don Quixote in His Library* (1824; Tokyo Fuji Art Museum). But the contrast between that painting and two of the most beautiful of his small canvases is striking. *Charles VI and Odette de Champdivers* (cat. 23) and *The Duke of Orléans Showing His Lover* (cat. 24) were painted somewhat later, about 1825, after his return from a trip to England. They are identical in format, and they function formally and iconographically as pendants. Both illustrate episodes from medieval history as recounted in literature, in particular, Pierre de Bourdeille Brantôme's *Les vies des dames galantes*. These brilliantly painted and intensely colored works, their material effects rendered in virtuoso fashion, appealed to admirers of minor historical subjects whose tastes had been shaped by the troubadour paintings of the Empire. Delacroix was inspired in this vein by his friend Richard Parkes Bonington, who was producing this very kind of painting at the time. For collectors, the licentiousness of *The Duke of Orléans Showing His Lover* would have enhanced its appeal: the duke, uncovering the lower half of his mistress's body while concealing the rest, exhibits her to her husband, who fails to recognize her. There may have been personal reminiscences behind the painting: in 1822–23, Delacroix shared a mistress, Madame Louise Rossignol de Pron, with his friend Soulier.

The evolving private art market, over which the state had little control, was not only for small paintings. In particular, as Elisabeth Fraser has shown, the duc d'Orléans (the future king Louis-Philippe), with his semipublic gallery at the Palais Royal, was making his mark as a collector of the most modern expressions of contemporary art.[62] Might Delacroix, who in 1828 would receive a commission from the duke for *Cardinal Richelieu Saying Mass in the Chapel of the Palais-Royal* (destroyed in 1848), have hoped for the duke's patronage if the state refused to purchase *Massacres at Chios*? One indication suggests that he did. Despite the scandal caused by the unveiling of *Massacres at Chios* at the Salon, the comte de Forbin, disregarding administrative procedure and without awaiting the king's signature, arranged to have the state purchase that painting and a few others not after the Salon ended, as custom required, but as it opened. Granted, King Louis XVIII was in a very bad way. It is therefore possible that Forbin, as the director of museums and an ardent supporter of youthful innovation, wished to speed up the works' acquisition in anticipation of Charles X's accession to the throne. Forbin responded somewhat impertinently to the vicomte Sosthènes de La

Rochefoucauld, the intractable director of fine arts, who was indignant about the breach of protocol: "I had the honor of proposing more promptly than usual that you acquire the paintings . . . to prevent these works, all of them remarkable, from being purchased by individuals who would establish themselves as patrons of the arts only to assail the government with a reproach as commonplace as it is unfair, namely, that it was not encouraging the arts."[63] Was the clever Forbin's quibble intended to legitimize the acquisition? And did Forbin mean to extricate himself from a difficult situation or from real danger?[64] Whatever the case, the episode aptly illustrates the competition between the state and the market.

Given that Delacroix created a work for the Salon with the idea that its purchase would remedy his financial situation and, above all, secure his standing, it is highly probable that he gave some thought to the private market. In view of Forbin's haste to acquire *Massacres at Chios* as soon as the Salon opened—probably before the controversy got out of hand—one may legitimately ask whether and to what extent the sympathetic official might have advised Delacroix. The fact remains that the strategy implemented by the artist was, once again, remarkably effective. The painting, exhibited at the Salon's opening and purchased shortly thereafter by the museum administration, was the object of everyone's attention and elicited particularly violent reactions.

Scenes from the Massacres at Chios

In elaborating a contemporary subject on a monumental scale, the painter reminded spectators of the scandal caused by Théodore Gericault's *Raft of the Medusa* at the Salon of 1819. Yet few Salon critics concerned themselves with the work's subject matter. Conversely, its execution was denounced so vehemently that *Massacres at Chios* soon came to be called a "massacre of painting." It is not incidental that this epithet may have originated with Gros, whom Delacroix would describe in 1846, in an article on the painter Pierre Paul Prud'hon, as "that son of Rubens who had the sad courage to hold out against all the magic toward which he was secretly inclined."[65] Delacroix, for his part, boldly confronted the expressive power of the paint, which he had discovered, at least in part, in Gros and in Rubens.

The massacre of Chios became the massacre of painting. The semantic slippage from the painting's subject to its form reduced the public's apprehension of the painting to its materiality, the dimension Delacroix had pondered constantly while painting it. As Marie Mély-Janin exclaimed in horror, "Everything here is harsh, coarse, rocky, rough, scruffy. Is it paint, or is it glue or putty? . . . Monsieur Delacroix rushes headlong without rules, without moderation; he piles on the color, he paints with a housepainter's brush."[66] The critic's vocabulary echoed the very words Delacroix had used when describing the painting in his *Journal* a few weeks earlier. The severity of the attack indicates the degree to which the painting appeared shocking and transgressive to the artist's contemporaries. In 1824 his position was too radical to be easily understood. The critics, taken aback by the display of form, the large brushstrokes, the surface effects, the extraordinary richness of color, and the abundant impasto in the foreground, did not make the connection—the famous "bridge"—between the harshness of the technique and the horror of the subject. Nonetheless, Delacroix invited them to do so in the entry he wrote for the Salon catalogue: "Scenes of the massacres of Chios. Greek families awaiting death or slavery (see the various accounts and newspapers of the time)." Going against the conventions of Neoclassical history painting, he rejected the use of dramatic argument, painting what in the language of the theater is called a tableau, rather than a scene.[67] Viewers must allow themselves to be won over by sensations engendered by an intentionally chaotic technique. The critic Auguste Chauvin felt this in spite of himself. Like Mély-Janin, he launched a diatribe against the canvas, condemning the "barbaric painter whose out-of-control imagination gives birth only to hideous wounds, contortions, agony, and who is always afraid he won't spill enough blood or cause enough agony."[68] Blinded by his disgust for the work, did Chauvin really look at the composition? In fact, the artist showed almost nothing of the horror of the battles, which take place in the distance, in a radiant landscape. What horror is shown is conveyed entirely by the materiality of the painting; it lies in the viewer's imagination, sparked by the absence of narration. No analysis of the work can separate the subject from the execution, as was done in Neoclassical criticism: the subject resides largely in the execution.[69]

Many did not understand *Massacres at Chios* and, like Stendhal and Thiers, likened it to a plague scene. "This work always seems to me a painting intended to represent a plague," Stendhal wrote.[70] Thiers noted that "everyone without exception has taken this massacre for a plague."[71] This association

recalled memories of Gros's *Napoleon Visiting the Plague Victims of Jaffa* (1804; Musée du Louvre), a painting withdrawn from public view during the Bourbon Restoration because it depicted Bonaparte, but which Delacroix had probably seen on a visit to Gros's studio at the close of the Salon of 1822.[72] The vagueness of the perceived plague theme may have diminished the political value of Delacroix's canvas. Thiers explained that the confusion regarding the painting's subject stemmed from the artist's failure to depict the right moment, that of the massacre itself. In rejecting unity of action, he did not "compose a principal scene." "M. Delacroix attempted to rival the randomness of nature. He therefore threw down his characters here and there, and no one knows how they could be in the place where they are."[73] Although the work's construction may have seemed faulty at the time, Thiers put his finger on one of the strong points of the painting as it is now perceived: the viewer's brutal confrontation with the spread-out bodies, which form a kind of wall across the bottom third of the canvas. Their pain and the manner in which they are painted stand in contradiction to the vast landscape that fills the remaining two-thirds of the composition.

The critic Charles Paul Landon expressed this view with utter clarity: "Instead of a carefully organized composition conforming to [accepted] artistic principles, one finds only a confused assemblage of figures, or rather half-figures, since none is developed completely. And the scene is so thoroughly obstructed that one does not glimpse the possibility of penetrating beyond the foreground."[74] That effect, already perceptible in *The Barque of Dante*, stems in part from the way the artist conceived his painting on the basis of models rather than adhering to a strictly defined composition. In fact, the rigid figures seem to be juxtaposed: highly differentiated in typology, age, and even skin color, they correspond to iconographic topoi (mother and child, lovers, two children, an old woman). It is as if the bodies' presence should suffice to tell the story: an individual hero, such as the one Delacroix had considered painting in 1821, is no longer needed. At the same time, the relationship between individual and collective histories is played out in the tension between the topos, which gives rise to discrete, personal stories, and the stereotypical character of the figures. Yet, this tension, which results in part from Delacroix's method of developing the composition directly from the model, obstructs the narrative, as Thiers observed.

Following pages: FIG. 5 *Scenes from the Massacres at Chios*, 1824, detail

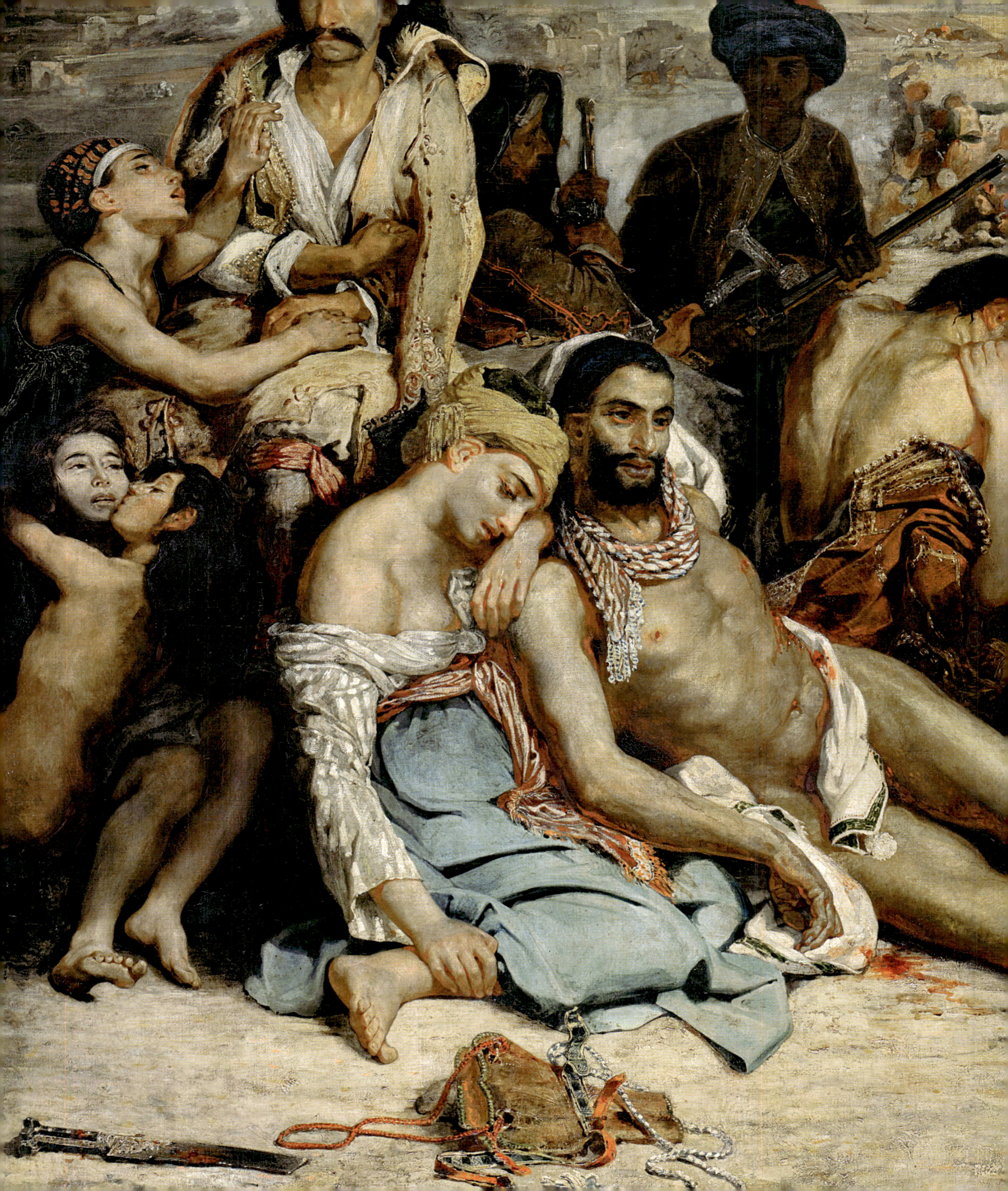

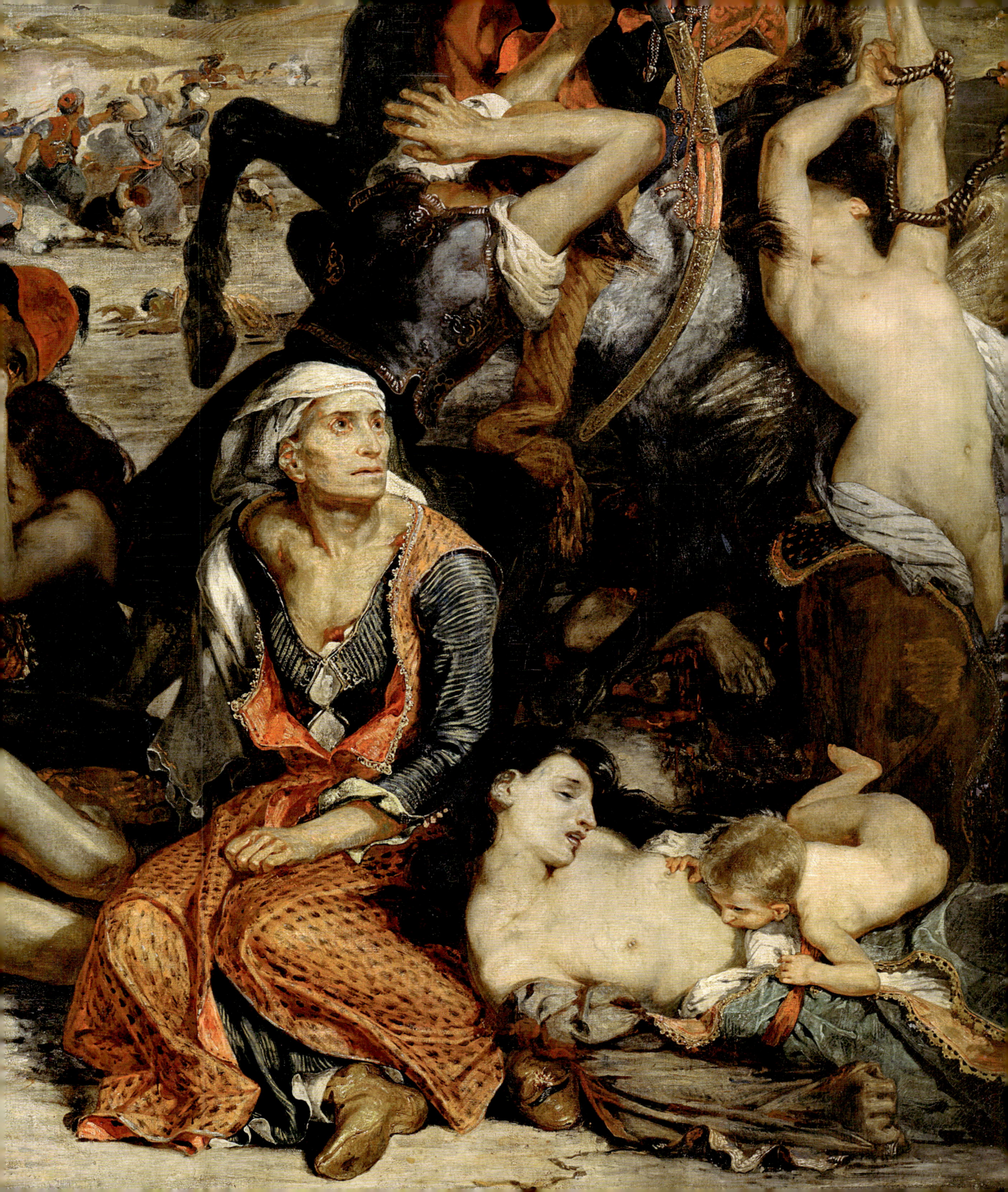

"Dolce Chiavatura"

If we follow the genesis of *Massacres at Chios* as it is recorded in Delacroix's *Journal*, we find that models were, in fact, its inspiration and, as with *The Barque of Dante*, that the work was elaborated from them. Although the artist executed a watercolor study setting out the main lines of the composition (fig. 6), he proceeded to paint it figure by juxtaposed figure, with the model before his eyes each time. Delacroix began the painting in earnest on Monday, January 12, 1824. On January 18, he noted, "Yesterday, Saturday, and the day before yesterday, Friday, did part of the woman front and center or the preliminaries for her. . . . I had a certain Provost, a model, on Tuesday the 13th, and began with the head of the dying man front and center."[75] On Sunday, February 29, he wrote: "did the other young man in the corner, based on little Nassau, and gave him three francs." On April 27, he painted the dead woman and her child based on "Mme Clément and her child." And so on. The entry of January 24 is particularly interesting because it shows that the model did not play the

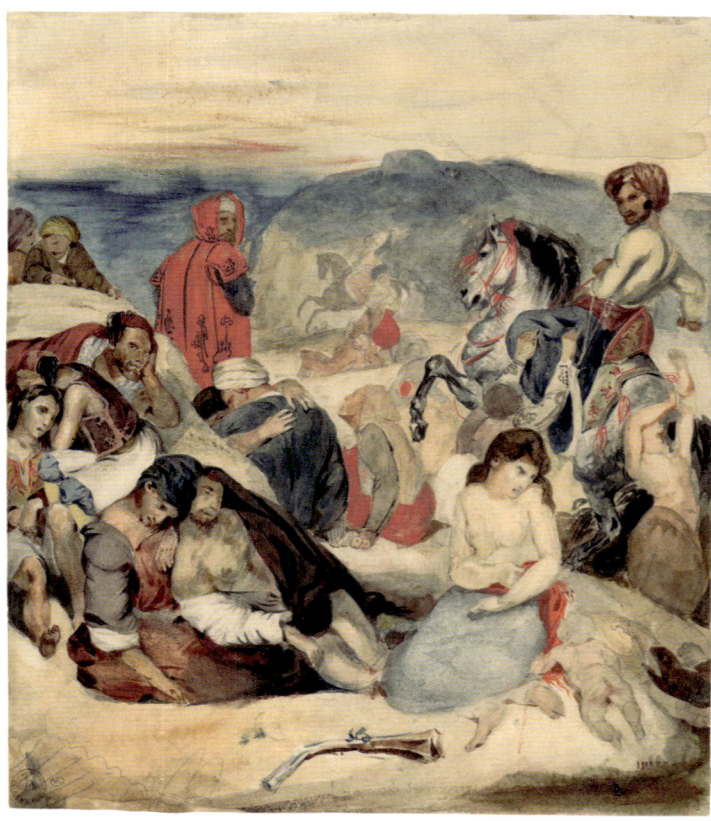

FIG. 6 *Study for Scenes from the Massacres at Chios*, 1823/24. Graphite, watercolor, and gouache on paper, 13⅜ x 11¹³⁄₁₆ in. (34 x 30 cm). Musée du Louvre, Paris (RF 3717 recto)

role merely of a fragment of reality to be transfigured on the canvas. "Today I drew and painted in the head and breast, etc. of the dead woman in the foreground." He added: "I again had *la mia chiavatura dinanzi colla mia carina Emilia*. It in no way dampened my enthusiasm. You have to be young for this kind of life. Everything is now painted in except for the hand and the hair."[76] Delacroix used the term *chiavatura* to refer to sexual intercourse. Although artists often had such relations with models, for Delacroix, while he was working on *Massacres at Chios*, there was a close connection between erotic relationships and artistic creation. Their inextricability is conveyed even in the way he relates the episode, which is far from an isolated event. The reference to sex appears without transition in the middle of the description of his work, as if painting the hair and the hands, among the most sensual of anatomical details, were the direct consequence of the sexual act. Delacroix needed to possess his models in order to paint them.

On January 26, he saw Emilie again: "For three studio sessions I gave Emilie Robert twelve francs . . . I had a nice *chiavata*."[77] And on March 3, he wrote: "Emilie dropped in for a moment and I took full advantage; this made me feel a little better. Work hard at your picture. Think about Dante. Reread him. Shake a leg, keep at it to keep your mind on great ideas. How will I profit from my near-solitude if I have only commonplace ideas?"[78] And five days later: "did the head and torso of the young girl attached to the horse.—*Dolce chiavatura*."[79] On April 18, he mentioned a woman named Laure and once again associated his ardor for his work with the expression of sexual desire, which vanished at the end of the session: "At the studio by nine. Laure came. Made progress on the portrait. It is strange that, having desired her all during the session, as she was leaving, in quite a hurry actually, it wasn't quite the same. I suppose I needed time to collect myself."[80] On April 20, he mentioned a certain Hélène: "The girl came this morning to pose. Hélène slept or pretended to. I don't know why I stupidly thought I had to act like an admirer. But no attraction there. I used the excuse of a headache. . . . As she was leaving and it was too late, the wind had changed."[81] This description brings to mind a study of a reclining nude (cat. 18): first identified—but without evidence—by Alfred Robaut as Mlle Rose, she could be the sleeping Hélène. Again on May 28, Delacroix wrote: "In the last few days I have resumed my painting wholeheartedly. I worked on adjusting the dead woman. To a woman who came with a child—one franc. In the morning Laure came; she and the

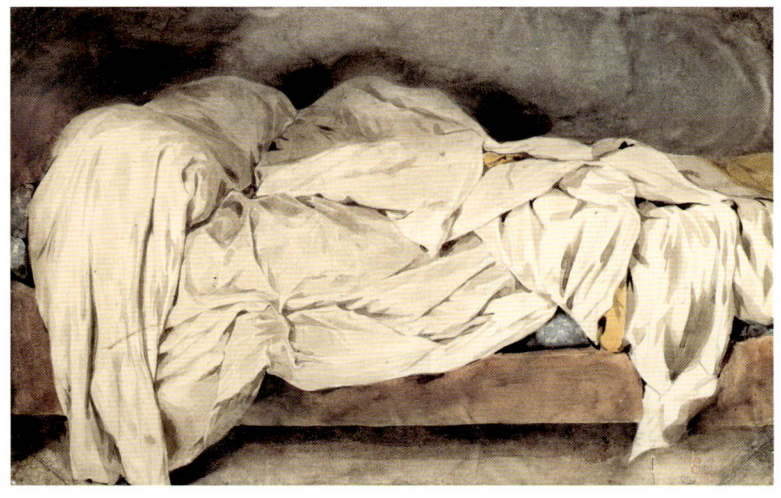

chiavatura—five fr.—Also yesterday, another with *la nera*."[82] The magnificent watercolor depicting an unmade bed (fig. 7), which refers both to the pose and to the sexual encounter, is the symbol of that dual relationship with the model. She is a source of inspiration and also an object of desire, or a source of inspiration inasmuch as she is an object of desire.

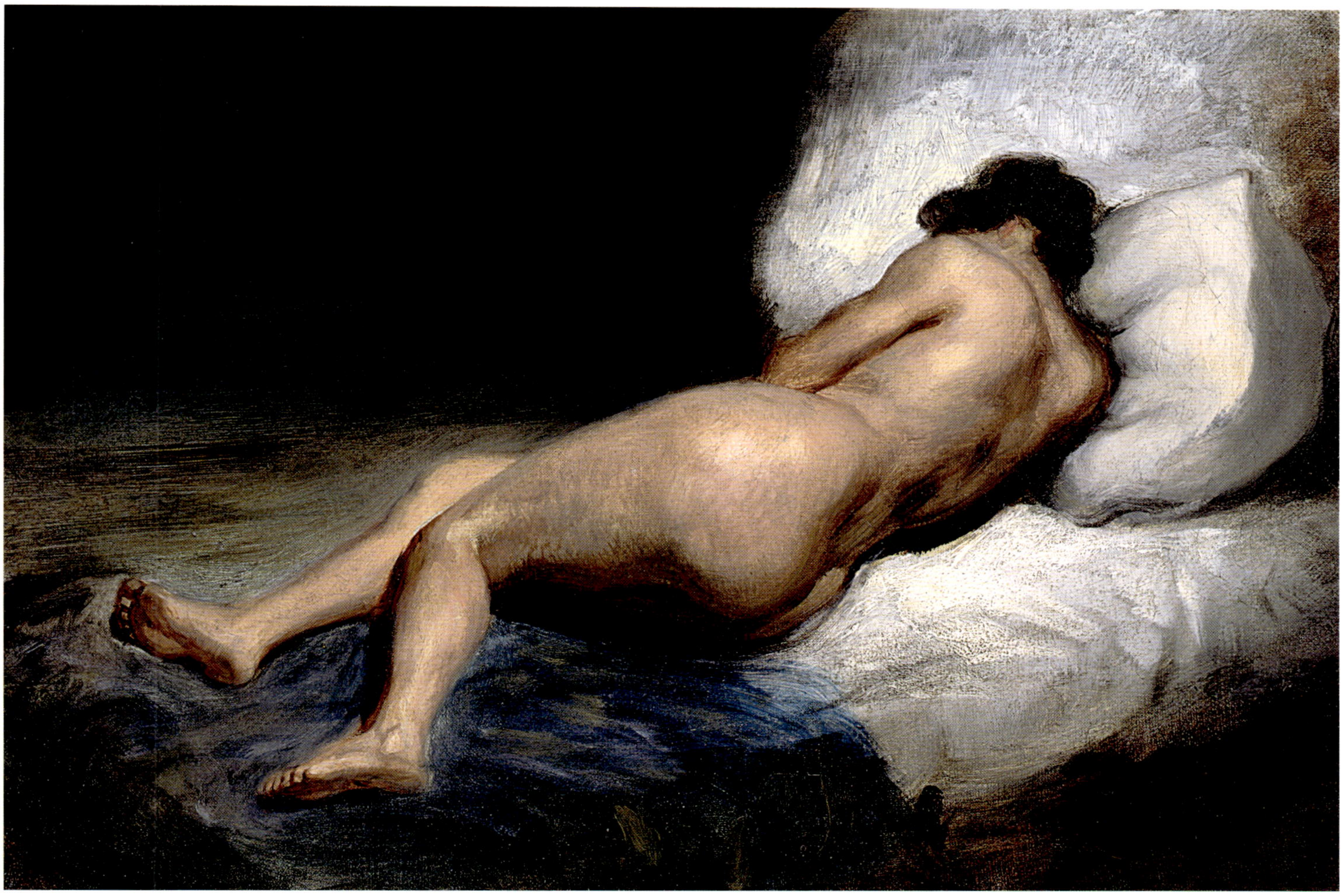

An evolution had occurred in Delacroix's conception of the nude from the time of his formative years to his recent, more personal works. The earliest studies, some of which were probably executed in Guérin's studio, respect the protocol of the academy figure frozen in a conventional, at times rhetorical pose (cat. 1).[83] Mademoiselle Rose (see cat. 2), viewed frontally, is seated with her ankles crossed; she rests her upper body on her left arm; her other arm is raised. The model's right arm was undoubtedly supported by a rope to

FIG. 7 *Unmade Bed*, ca. 1825–28. Graphite, watercolor, and brown wash on paper, 7¼ x 11¾ in. (18.5 x 29.9 cm). Musée du Louvre, Paris (RF 31720)

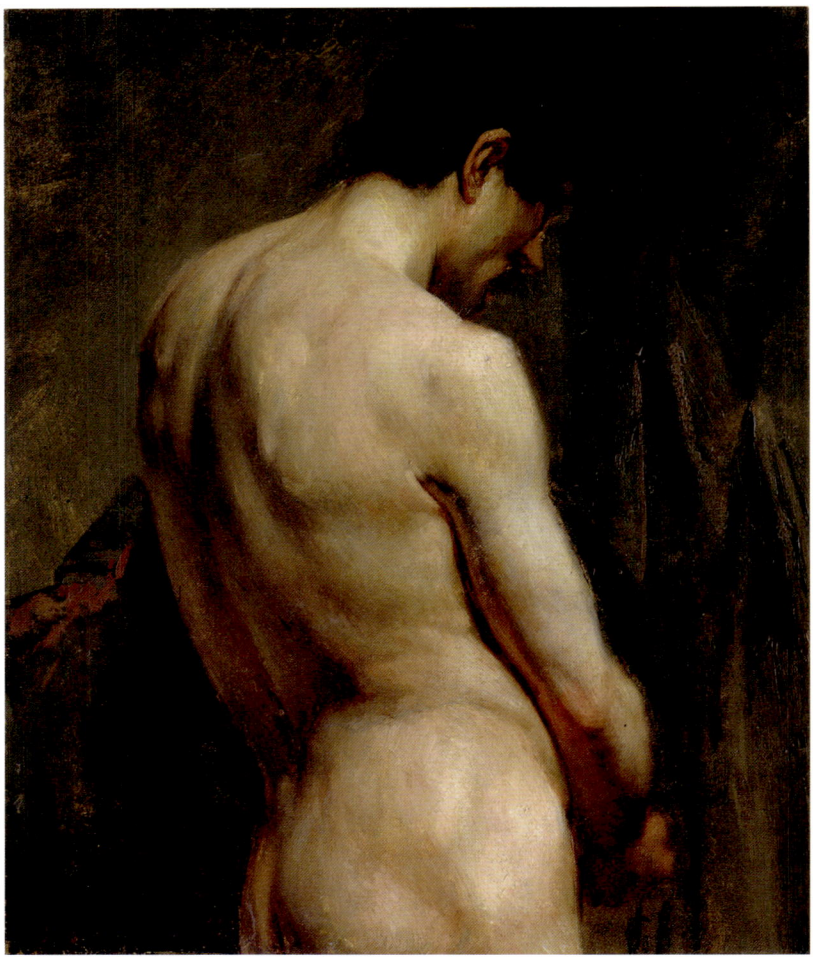

CAT. 1 *Male Academy Figure: Half-Length, Side View*, ca. 1818–20

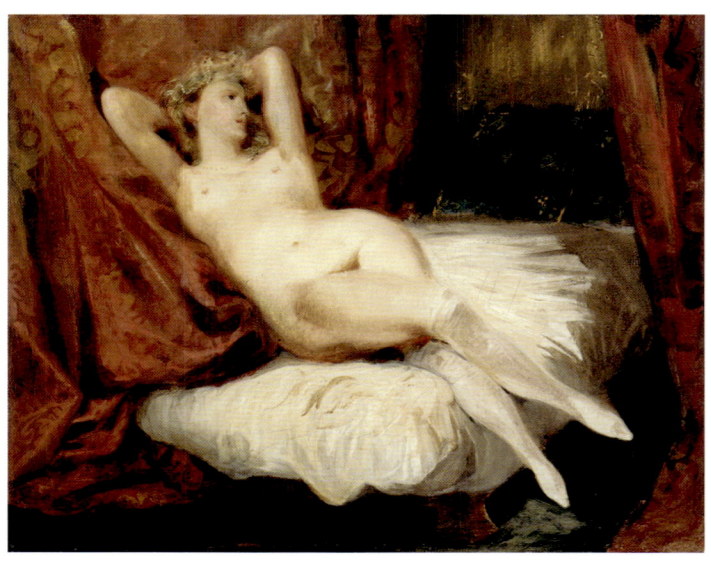

FIG. 8 *Female Nude Reclining on a Divan*, or *Woman with White Stockings*, ca. 1825–26. Oil on canvas, 10¼ x 13 in. (26 x 33 cm). Musée du Louvre, Paris (RF 1657) (J 7)

enable her to hold the pose. The figure's face is shown in profile, her eyes modestly lowered. By contrast, in the studies Delacroix did in his own studio, he depicted the desire and sexual availability of half-dressed women, often with their breasts exposed, facing the painter (fig. 8).

The distinctive presence of the model in Delacroix's early works, though it may sometimes undermine the painting's unity, as Landon remarked, is much more significant than it appears at first glance. During those years, the model was the fulcrum around which the artist was able to revitalize history painting by challenging Neoclassical composition. Within the Neoclassical system, the *idea* had primacy. Once the idea for a painting had been established, the artist would copy works of antiquity and works by the masters before bringing his composition to life by means of a live model. Conversely, Delacroix began with the model, then saw how he would compose the work. This was the method he used for *The Barque of Dante* (fig. 2).

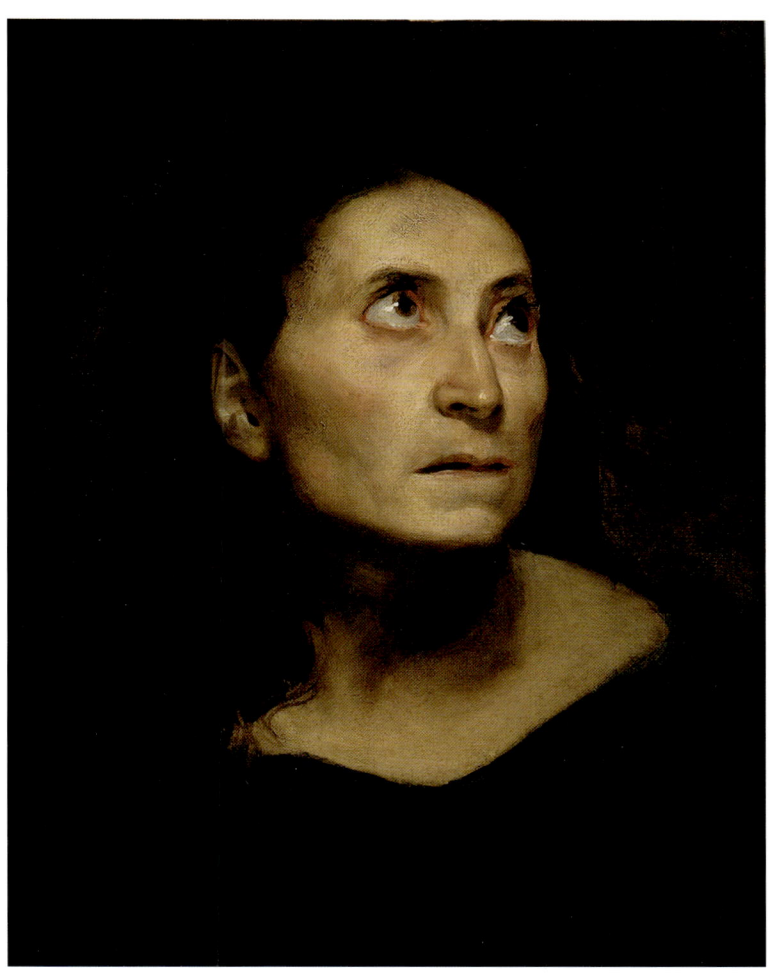

CAT. 7 *Head of an Old Greek Woman*, 1824

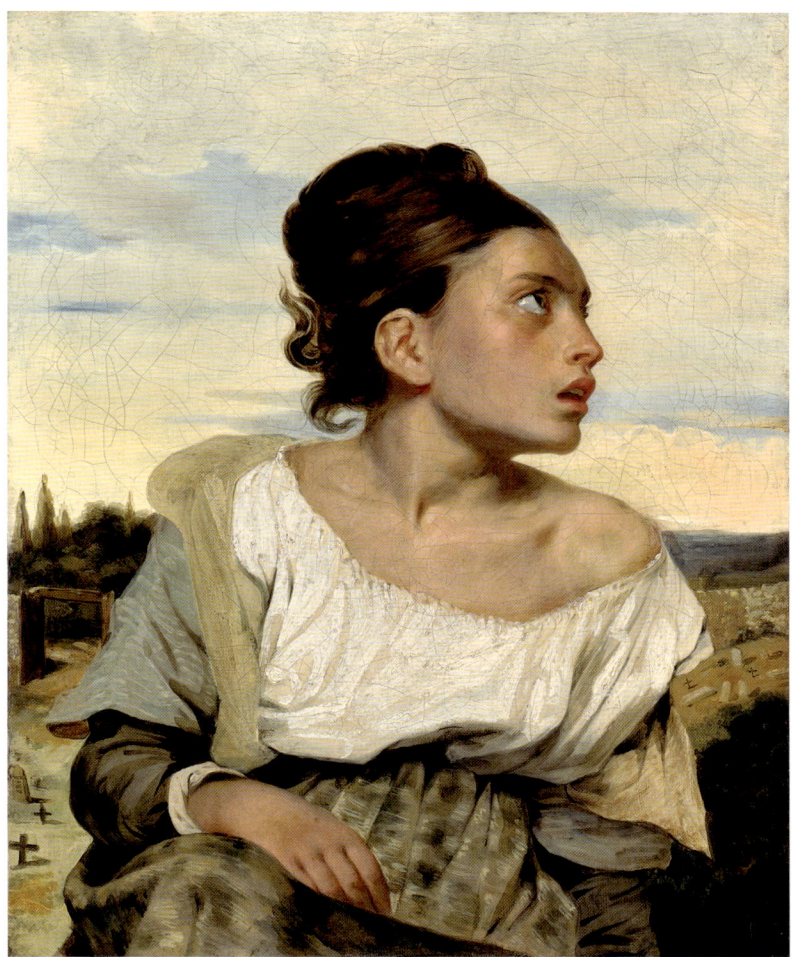

FIG. 9 *Orphan Girl in the Cemetery*, 1824. Oil on canvas, 25¹³⁄₁₆ x 21⁷⁄₁₆ in. (65.5 x 54.5 cm). Musée du Louvre, Paris (RF 1652) (J 78)

Working from life drawings (the models for the damned maintained their poses with the help of ropes), he transferred the figures to the canvas and then, recognizing an imbalance in the composition, changed their positions.[84] In a sense, the choice of works he exhibited at the Salon of 1824 was emblematic of that method. Alongside the *Massacres at Chios*, Delacroix displayed two studies that were listed under the same number in the Salon catalogue, but without descriptions. In all likelihood, these were *Head of an Old Greek Woman* (cat. 7) and *Orphan Girl in the Cemetery* (fig. 9), both preliminary oil studies for the large painting. *Orphan Girl* (not its original title) portrays a beggar girl to whom Delacroix alluded in his *Journal* on February 17, 1824, when he indicated that she was the model for the figure of the young Greek boy at the far left of the composition. That figure seems to have been the element upon which the entire painting was elaborated. At the same time, it manages to support the painting all on its own, displaying the dramatic

and expressive autonomy of a real model. The Greek youth is not only a study of the expression of an emotion but also an actual embodiment of a story, a destiny.

Flesh and the Nude

By beginning with a man or woman who posed for him rather than a model from antiquity, Delacroix adopted a fundamentally new relationship to the model, one in which the ideal had to yield to the expression of a form of realism. The artist was now in search not of perfection but of life, as he plainly stated:

> Never seek an empty perfection. Some faults, some things which the vulgar call faults, often give vitality to a work. My picture is beginning to develop a rhythm, a powerful spiral momentum. I must make the most of it.

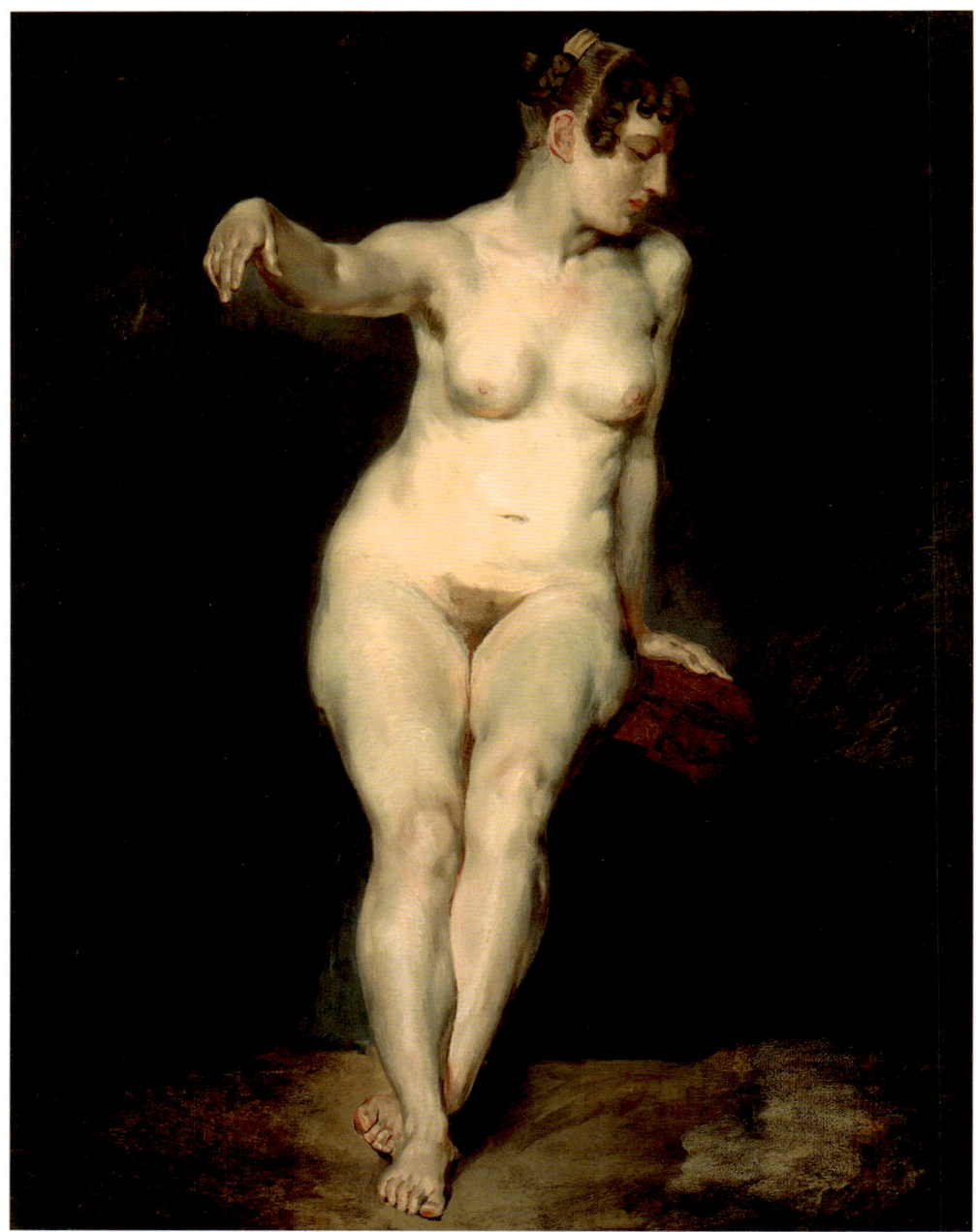

CAT. 2 *Female Academy Figure: Seated, Front View (Mademoiselle Rose)*, ca. 1820–23

I must keep that good black color, that happy, rather dirty quality, and those limbs which I know how to paint and few others even attempt. The mulatto will do very well. I must get fullness. Even though it loses its naturalness, it will gain in richness and beauty.[85]

In his studies, the artist attended less to the form and structure of objects and bodies than to their surface and color. The young Delacroix achieved mastery of the color of human bodies through observation and his original conception of the most academic of exercises: the nude. In the *Female Academy*

Figure: Seated, Front View (Mademoiselle Rose) (cat. 2), which portrays a model who was probably nicknamed Rose, the artist was less intent on scrupulously representing anatomy (the foreshortening of the right arm is slightly exaggerated) than on rendering the iridescence of feminine flesh tones, which range from pink to green and then from green to brown. Here Delacroix captured in a new way the secret of life palpitating beneath the skin and, more particularly, the role of reflections, which he had learned from Rubens. Especially on the thighs, the skin's material substance is conveyed with hatchings of various colors applied with a brush. On an empirical level, this

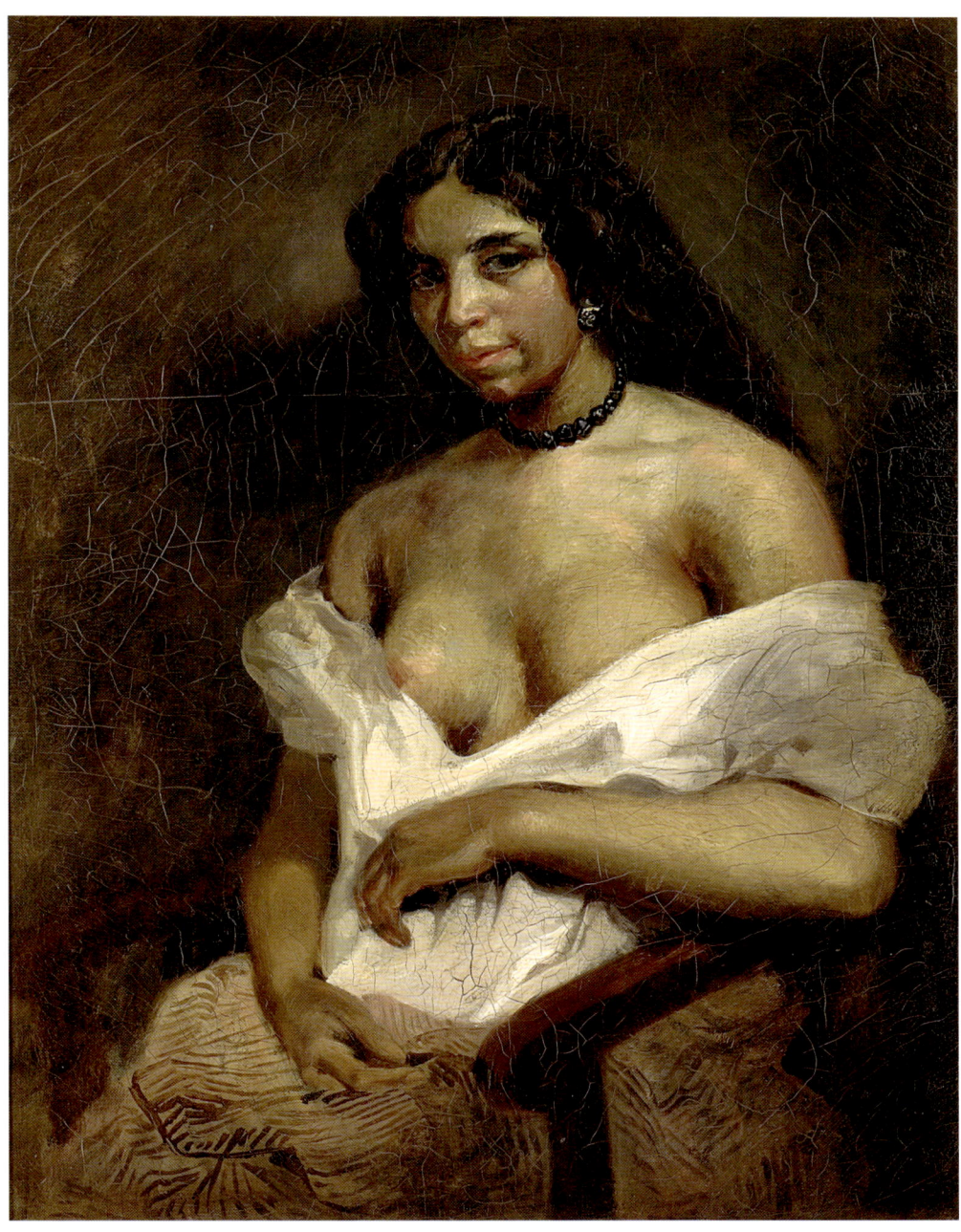

CAT. 10 *Portrait of Aspasie*, ca. 1824

technique anticipates optical mixture, which Delacroix would practice more systematically beginning in the early 1830s. The effect was enhanced by the choice of a dark ground, which projects the body forward and accentuates its luminosity.

An added layer of virtuosity is found in *Portrait of Aspasie,* painted about 1824, now in the Musée Fabre, Montpellier (cat. 10). Delacroix kept the portrait in his studio until late in his career and seems to have accorded it a certain importance: the model's first name appears on a list of works the artist entered in his *Journal* on October 4, 1857.[86] Preceded by two small, highly refined canvases (fig. 10 and private collection),

the painting is midway between a study and a portrait. The size of the canvas and the pose of the sitter—a woman seated in a chair, her gestures subtle, her gaze directed toward the viewer—are consistent with the canons of portraiture. By contrast, the bare throat and breast were possible within the context of this genre only because Delacroix used a studio model, one who was, moreover, a woman of mixed race. The composition therefore plays on an ambiguity: on the one hand, the model is idealized, ennobled by the pose; on the other, her state of undress underscores her inferior status, her subordination to the painter's artistic and perhaps sexual desire.[87]

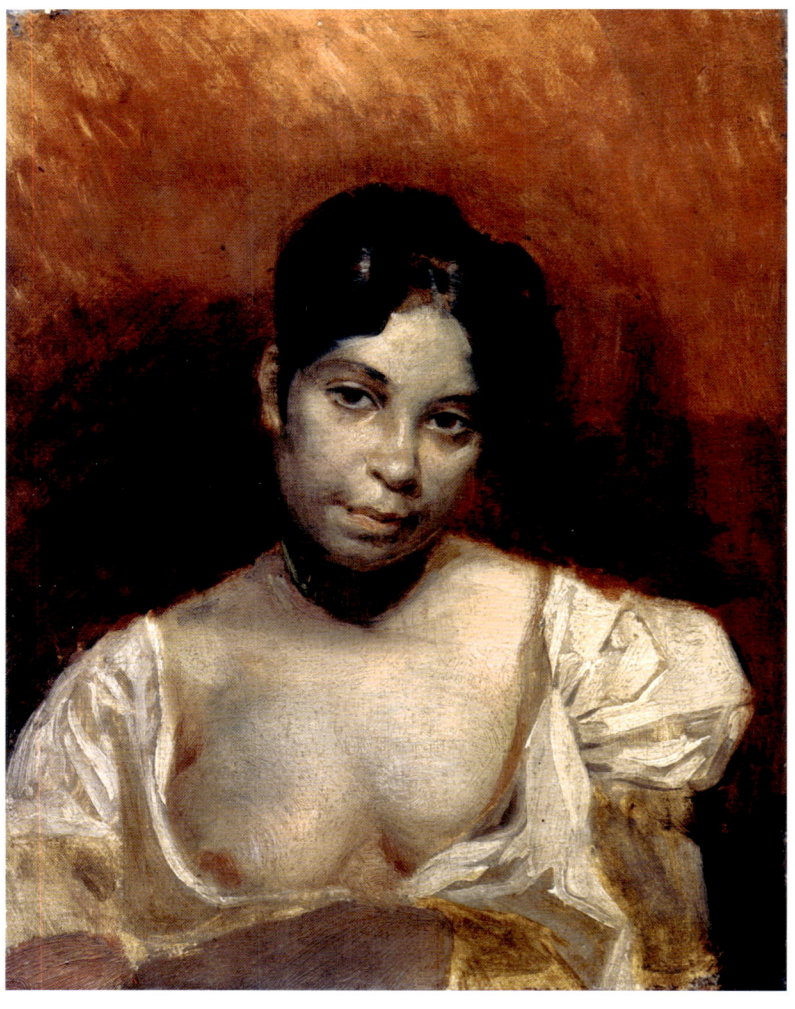

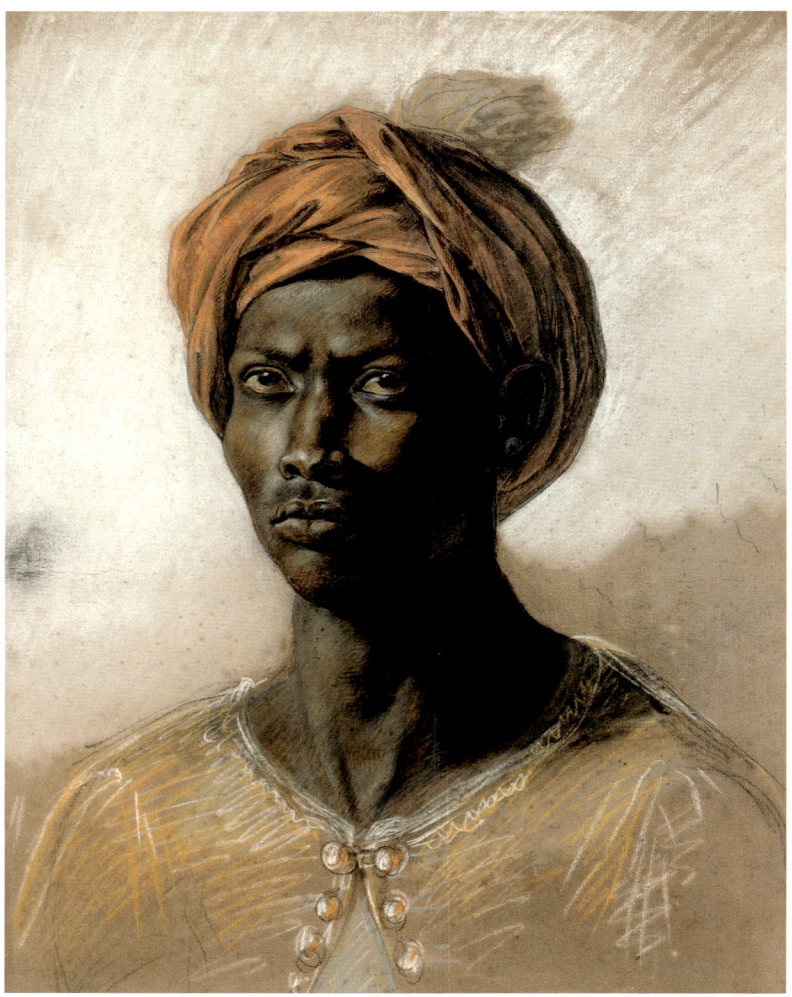

FIG. 10 *Aspasie (Red Background)*, ca. 1824. Oil on canvas, 10⅝ x 8⁷⁄₁₆ in. (27 x 21.5 cm). Private collection (J 80)

FIG. 11 *Model Wearing a Turban*, ca. 1824–26. Pastel on buff paper, 18½ x 14¹⁵⁄₁₆ in. (47 x 38 cm). Musée du Louvre, Paris (RF 32268) (Johnson 1995, no. 14)

There has been speculation about whether the woman in the two small studies was the Aspasie depicted in the painting in Montpellier. But there is no question that the same woman modeled for all three works. In the study of Aspasie against a red background (fig. 10) the model also shows a bare breast, with the nipple visible, as in the larger painting; and the other study (private collection) shows a similar expression in the eyes and the hint of a smile. In addition, there is a preliminary drawing for the painting in which the face is identical to the one in *Aspasie (Red Background)*. The canvas from the Musée Fabre is thus the idealized version of a model elaborated on the basis of these two studies.

The work's originality lies in its treatment of the woman's skin color. In the parlance of the time, she was considered neither altogether black nor white and regarded as *sang mêlé*, that is, of mixed blood.[88] Delacroix may thus be seen as

extending the investigation of nonwhite figures previously undertaken by his friend Gericault; another example is a pastel study of a dark-skinned man in a turban (fig. 11). In his depictions of Aspasie, Delacroix explored a relatively wide range of pictorial possibilities. The matter at hand was evidently to capture the ways in which dark skin reflects light and to render its texture. He therefore underscored with a darker brown parts of the anatomy, such as the armpits and the back of the hand—here given a velvety quality—that are mostly ignored in strictly academic nudes. He also played on the contrast between the brown complexion and the intense red of the lips. A comparison of the three Aspasies shows that he was studying how the face and body interact with a colored ground, which goes from red to green in the painting in Montpellier. The three versions thus constitute a true study of color conducted at the same time as *Massacres at Chios*.

This manner of treating the nude in terms of its color rather than its structure struck some visitors to the Salon when they saw *Massacres at Chios*. The reviewer for *Le globe* noted: "[Delacroix] has almost, and for no reason, made some bodies green, others yellow, others reddish-brown; he has brought together the most different colorings."[89] The critic thus pointed out the novelty, in that day, of the rendering of diverse flesh tones. Delacroix's unfortunate Greeks, men and women of flesh and blood, some pale, others tanned, present a striking contrast to the Neoclassical heroes painted by David's imitators, with their uniforms and marmoreal whiteness directly influenced by Greco-Roman statuary. The painting served as a pictorial manifesto, and it also carried a reflection on history, if not on politics. Delacroix, a "child of the century" who witnessed the fall of the Empire at an early age, meditated throughout his life on the greatness, decline, and perpetuation of civilizations. For him, was not the idea of "mixed blood" a condition for the survival of civilizations? The diverse skin colors of the Greeks he painted in *Massacres at Chios* have nothing in common with the abstract ideal of Hellenic purity so vaunted by the Neoclassical writers and painters.

"Greek Families Awaiting Death or Slavery"

With his subject taken from contemporary history, Delacroix painted not heroes of antiquity but the men, women, and children of his own time, as the text in the Salon catalogue indicates: "See the various accounts and newspapers of the time." This was not the ideal Greece of Pericles or Leonidas but the very real Greece, gateway to the Orient, of a people fighting for their freedom. That historical and (in the strict sense) embodied vision must have been transgressive at the time. We have trouble perceiving that quality in the painting today, but it accounts for audiences' general blindness to his subject, which most interpreted as a plague or derided as "filth." The philhellenism of Delacroix and some of his contemporaries combined political and artistic demands. Auguste Jal, in his review of the Salon of 1824, became their spokesman: "I have had enough of the old Greeks; it's the modern Greeks who interest me. . . . Farewell, ancient Greece, which saw so much bloodshed. . . . Hail to you, Hellenia, young and proud, who are stepping out of your cradle in ruins, to the cries of fatherland and freedom!"[90]

One may well wonder to what extent young artists of Delacroix's generation were driven by the unconscious need to approach, by means of a necessary displacement in time and space, the unthinkable in the national past—namely, massacres. Such a question need not impugn the sincerity of that generation's engagement with contemporary phenomena such as the philhellenic movement. But it was a burning question for Delacroix, who was among the direct descendants of the generation that had actively participated in the events of the Revolution, including the tragic hours of the Reign of Terror. He always proclaimed pride in his father, a deputy and diplomatic emissary at the Convention, whose aura was preserved by his early death. It is significant that the anecdote Delacroix recalled most fondly concerned his father's resistance to agitators backed by the most extremist elements of the Revolution. He thereby found reassurance in his father's supposed moderation. Two other massacres were on view at the Salon of 1824: Léon Cogniet's *Scene from the Massacre of the Innocents* (Musée des Beaux-Arts, Rennes) and Charles-Emile Callande de Champmartin's *Massacre of the Innocents* (Louvre). These were followed in 1827 by Ary Scheffer's *Souliot Women* (Louvre). Other scenes of mass execution appearing at the Salons of the period are worth noting: Horace Vernet's *Massacre of the Mamelukes in Cairo in 1811* in 1819; and Champmartin's *Massacre of the Janissaries* in

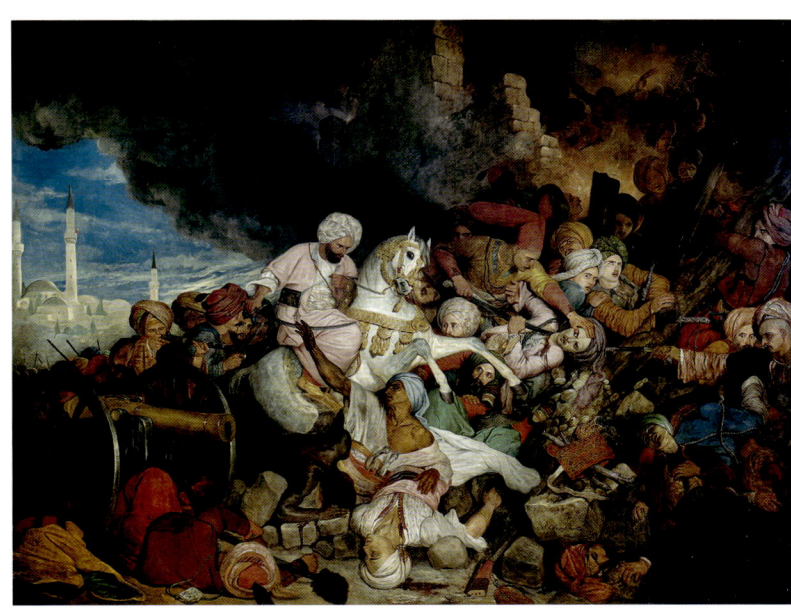

FIG. 12 Charles-Emile Callande de Champmartin (French, 1797–1883), *Massacre of the Janissaries*, 1826. Oil on canvas, 18⅝ x 24¾ in. (47.2 x 62.8 cm). Musée d'Art et d'Histoire, Rochefort (inv. 2007.8.15)

1827 (fig. 12). Although Vernet's and Champmartin's paintings do not portray innocent civilian populations and therefore did not have the cathartic quality of Delacroix's painting, they did swell the ranks of slaughter that assaulted the eyes of visitors to the Salon. These spectacular stagings of massacres in paint possibly satisfied a need for expression and a need to appeal to the collective memory of the French. The Revolution had revived in modern France the ancient practice of massacres that had bloodied the country during the religious and political conflicts of the sixteenth century. But in the 1820s, painters took their subjects from the Bible or from current events in foreign countries, thus maintaining a certain distance through art and exoticism.

The Empire had permitted the representation of war only in its disciplined and reputedly civilized forms—confrontations between professional armies, preparations for those encounters (the readying and deployment of forces), and their aftermaths (battlefield visits, care of the wounded, acts of clemency toward prisoners, the signing of peace treaties)—within the highly controlled context of propaganda. The liberalization of the art scene in the first years of the Restoration allowed for freer artistic expression, opening

the door to paintings of fratricidal battles and the mass extermination of ethnic groups, with all the disorder, injustice, terror, and ambiguity they suggested. These scenes, with their depictions of civilian populations, including women and children, exerted a much stronger appeal to emotion. Delacroix's monumental work, or *grande machine*, as it was called, brought viewers face to face with the tragedy of the Greeks, who formed a kind of fixed wall before them. It also forced beholders to acknowledge their own responsibility, insofar as the victims seem to have no hope of rescue. Prostrate, they await death or slavery, as the Salon catalogue explains. The sparsity of movement and the action, frozen or relegated to the margins, compel spectators to focus on the bodies and the suffering souls, tormented by shame and despair. It is a vision of horror to lead the audience itself to revolt.

The contrast between the pathos of the scene and the luminosity of the landscape, between the coarseness of the brushwork in the lower part of the canvas and the delicate treatment of the sky, conveys a kind of dereliction that is expressed in the eyes of the old woman, inspired by *Orphan Girl in the Cemetery* (see fig. 9). Delacroix disconcerted the Salon audience not only by accumulating a large number of

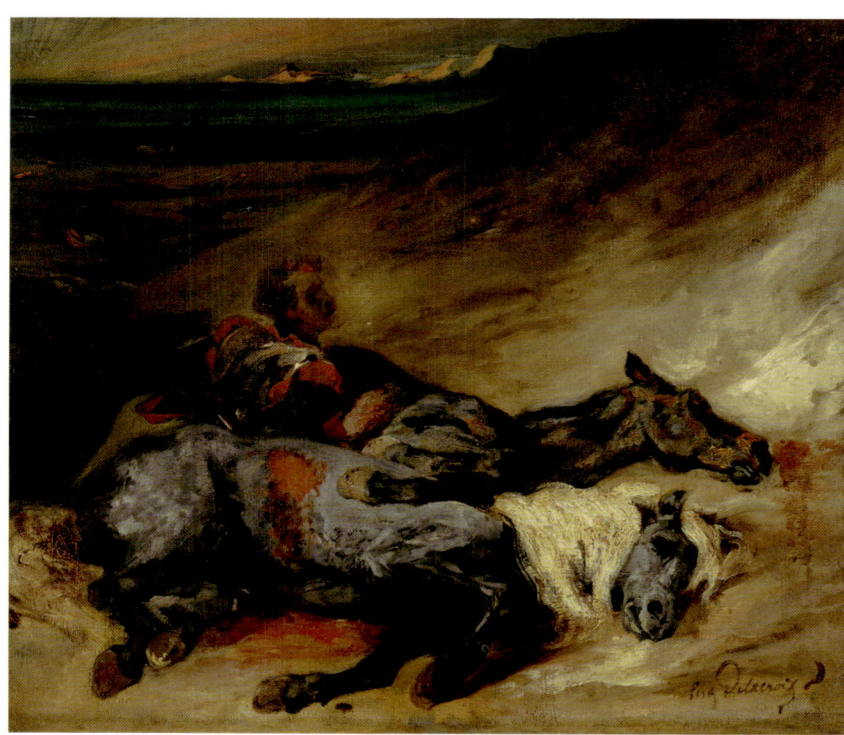

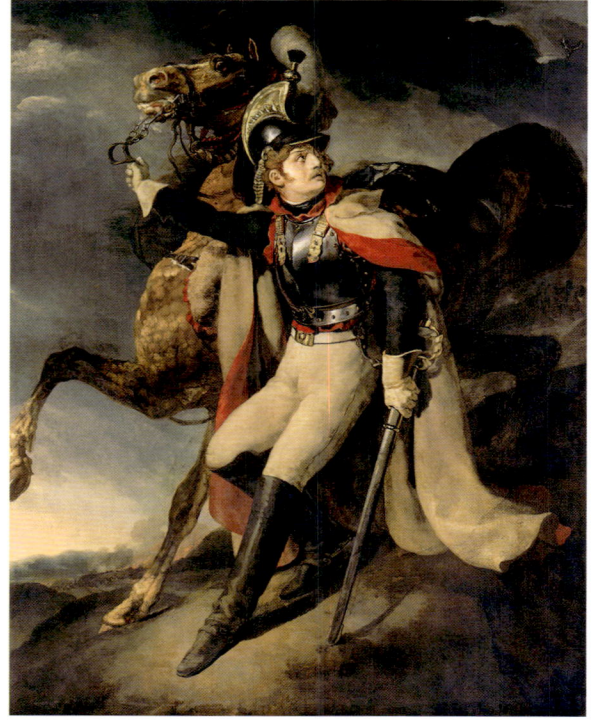

FIG. 13 *A Battlefield, Evening*, 1824. Oil on canvas, 18⅞ x 22¼ in. (48 x 56.6 cm). The Mesdag Collection, The Hague (inv. hwm 0112) (J 104)

FIG. 14 Théodore Gericault (French, 1791–1824). *Wounded Cuirassier*, 1814. Oil on canvas, 11 ft. 18¹⁵⁄₁₆ in. x 9 ft. 7¾ in. (3.6 x 3 m). Musée du Louvre, Paris (4886)

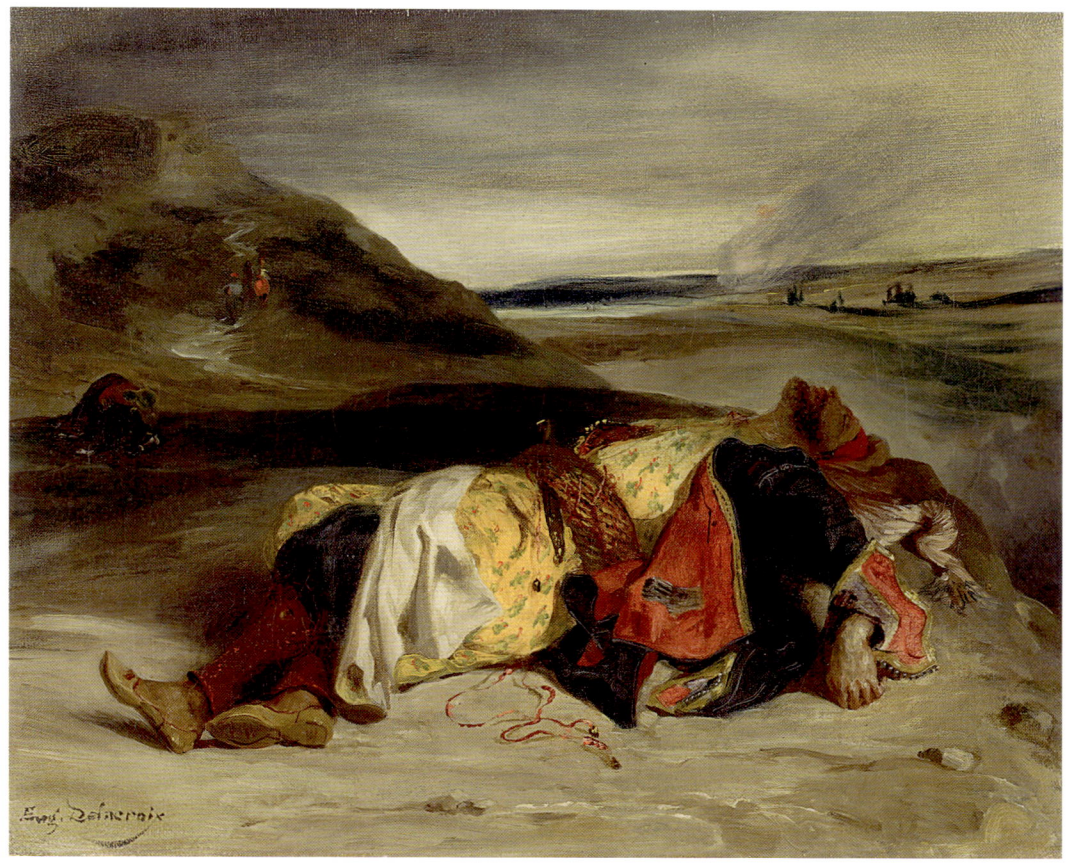

FIG. 15 *Turkish Officer Killed in the Mountains*, or *The Death of Hassan*, 1826. Oil on canvas, 13 x 16⅛ in. (33 x 41 cm). Private collection (J 113)

wretched human figures and emptying out the central zone, normally the place of the hero. He caused astonishment also by extending the background to a far-distant horizon, thus tapping into a different pictorial subgenre: the topographical battle painting, of the type exemplified by Louis François Lejeune during the Empire. The artful spatial arrangement provided Delacroix a high vantage point overlooking one end of the island. The landscape unfolds across fields and farms punctuated by palm trees before ending at a city on a bay, with a port at its edge. Fires on land and at sea attest to the ubiquity of fighting and destruction. Sea and sky, undisturbed by vertical intrusions (trees, rocks, masts), occupy a third of the painted surface. The sky is astonishingly empty and flat, traversed only by long trails of cloud: it is two-dimensional, motionless, and uninvolved with the action on the ground. The merciless indifference of nature signals the immanence of human despair. The artist took the opposite course from that of his model, Gros's *Napoleon Visiting the Plague Victims of Jaffa*, in which Bonaparte seems to rise up like a magician from the tragedy under way. The allusion by some critics to a plague, though it obviously brings to mind Gros's masterpiece, is also,

perhaps, an apt expression of dismay in the face of such powerlessness. The absence of a divine miracle or any other transcendence makes more urgent the call to others—namely, viewers at the Salon—for help. The painting plays on the cathartic effect of a contemporary tragedy.

War as seen by Delacroix is at odds with the heroic vision still present in Gericault; in *Massacres at Chios*, war has no panache. Delacroix's *A Battlefield, Evening* (fig. 13), realized during the same period, was inspired by Gericault's *Wounded Cuirassier* (fig. 14), exhibited at the Salon of 1814. But where Gericault transfigured the despair of defeat and the soldier's isolation into heroism, Delacroix presented the spectacle of disillusionment: all is desolation. In Gericault's painting, the cuirassier is the unfortunate double of the groom attempting to restrain one of the two *Horses of Marly* (1745; Musée du Louvre), but he is still in control of his mount.[91] In *A Battlefield, Evening,* by contrast, the soldier crawls, pitiable and alone, amid the cadavers of horses, in mud and blood. Blood is also found in the foreground of *Massacres at Chios*, especially on the Christlike figure in the center of the composition. Two years later, for an exhibition at Galerie Lebrun held as a

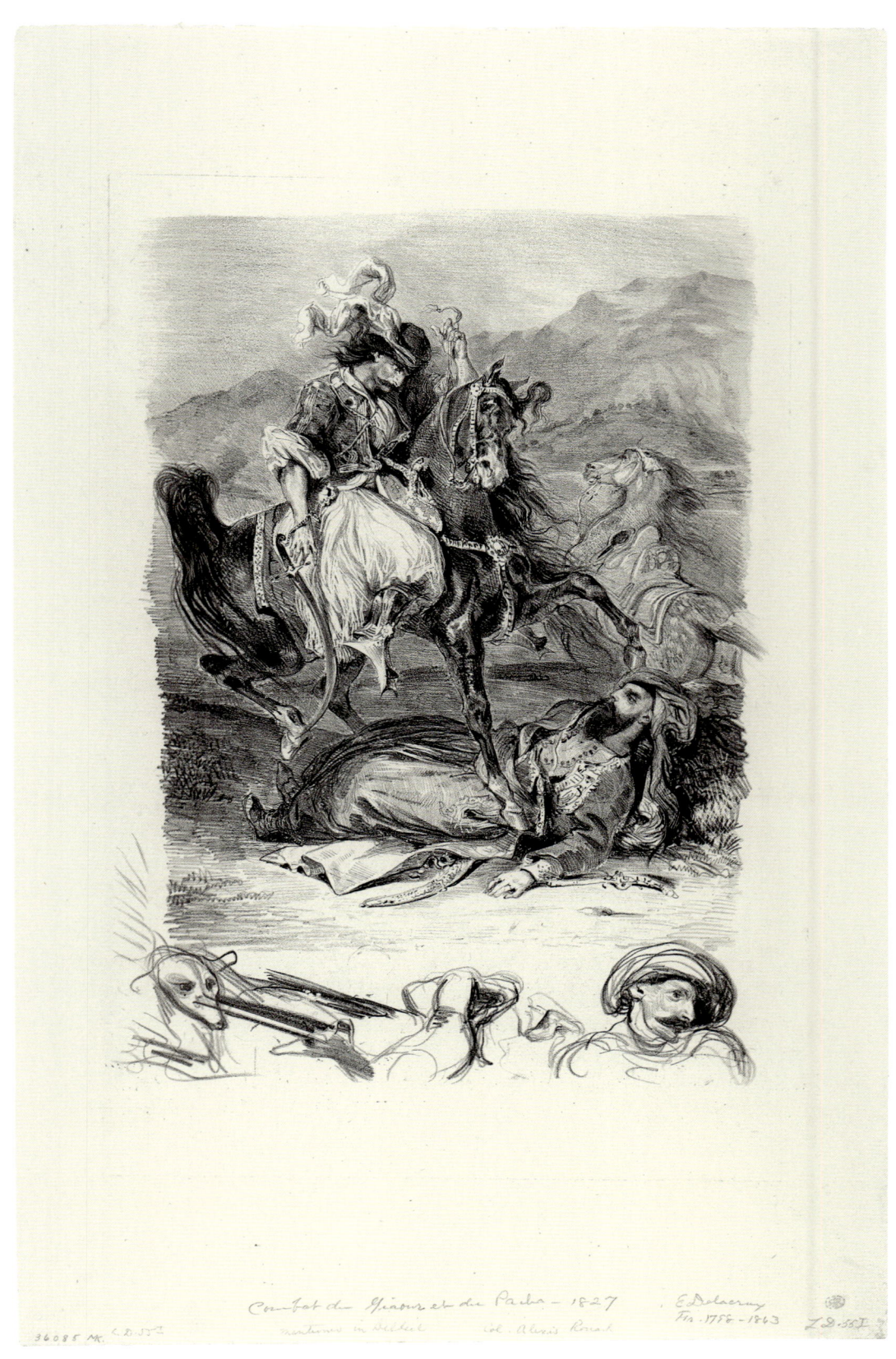

FIG. 16 *Combat of the Giaour and the Pasha,* 1827. Lithograph, first state of two, with remarques, sheet 16 x 11 in. (40.6 x 27.9 cm). The Metropolitan Museum of Art, New York, John J. McKendry Fund, 1996 (1996.424) (D-S 55)

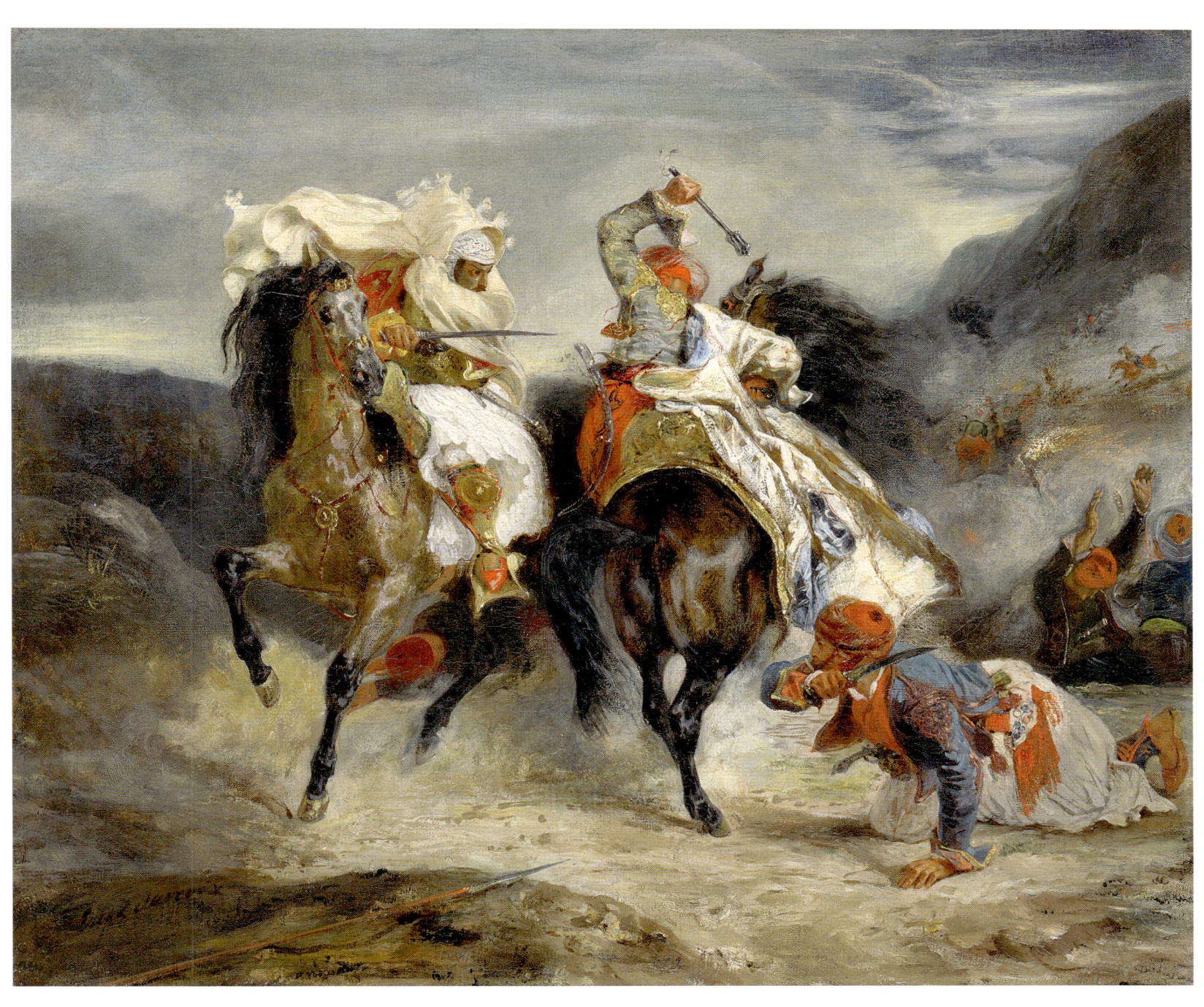

CAT. 27 *Combat of the Giaour and Hassan*, 1826

benefit for the Greeks, Delacroix displayed *Turkish Officer Killed in the Mountains,* or *The Death of Hassan* (fig. 15). The corpse, dressed in a magnificent uniform, lies abandoned while a village burns in the background, as in *Massacres at Chios*. The unusual nature of this representation, centered on a corpse, was pointed out in Ludovic Vitet's contemporaneous critique, which classified the painting as a study.[92]

For a second time, Delacroix had gambled and won. His stature was reinforced by the royal museums' acquisition of *Massacres at Chios*, but the critics were harsh, and for the most part they did not understand the painting. The painter François Joseph Navez, a student of David's in Brussels, summed up the situation in a letter to his fellow artist Louis Léopold Robert: "*The Massacre at Chios* is only an intention, it is neither drawn nor painted, but it is impossible to give a more accurate idea of misfortune. . . . All of that is characterized so well that it penetrates; there is originality in the color. He will go far if he studies, but he will lose his way if he continues on this path."[93] When Navez indicated that the painting was only an intention, he was likely referring to the absence of unity, which was caused partly by the young artist's method of composing his paintings on the basis of the model. It appears that Delacroix was highly sensitive to that frequently made criticism of his work. Had he himself not recognized this flaw? His *Journal* entries on the genesis of *Massacres at Chios* document his distress over the fragmentation of the scene and the difficulty he had in putting together the various pieces, painted brilliantly but in isolation. He began to execute the figures in early 1824, and toward the end of March he worried about the "disjointedness" of the work under way. On May 9, 1824, he noted: "My painting is beginning to take on a different appearance; disjointedness is giving place to sombreness. . . . I am changing the plan."[94] Following his own advice, he resumed reading Dante.

A few weeks later, while visiting the Paris art dealer John Arrowsmith, Delacroix saw five canvases by the English painter John Constable, including his famous *Hay Wain* (1821; National Gallery, London).[95] According to Théophile Silvestre, Delacroix was so struck by these paintings that he retouched his own composition.[96] Frédéric Villot wrote in 1856 that, at the time, "he made the light denser, introduced rich gray tones, gave transparency to the shadows through the use of glazes, made the blood circulate and the flesh quiver."[97] Whatever the exact influence of the British painter and the precise time when this retouching took place, a virtuoso

Delacroix added vibrant touches of red, black, and yellow to his *Massacres at Chios*, which he probably considered too monochrome and lacking in homogeneity. He thereby gave it more brilliance.

Delacroix, in his ardor to take up brushes and paint, neglected the tedious academic work of preparing the composition. Such preparation typically required, after the overall composition had been defined in a sketch, a careful, separate study (drawn, or sometimes painted) for each of the important elements (heads, limbs, principal accessories), which were then transposed by means of a grid and assembled on the canvas, to be executed in oil. Once his painting was completed, Delacroix became aware of the dangers of his own virtuosity, the risks inherent in his way of composing on the basis of "beautiful pieces" painted directly on the canvas. In reevaluating the execution phase of his creative process, he wrote, "I must make many sketches and take my time. That above all is where I need to make progress. . . . The main thing is to avoid that infernal facility of the brush. Instead, make the medium difficult to work with, like marble—that would be completely new. Make the medium resistant, so as to conquer it patiently" (see fig. 104).[98]

Lessons from England: The Merging of Genres

The conquering strategy that Delacroix had employed successfully since 1822 would attain its highest achievement at the Salon of 1827–28. His career up until that moment was summarized by Charles Paul Landon as follows:

> M. Delacroix made his debut in the fine arts at the moment most favorable to him. Twenty years earlier, his works would have caused only unwelcome astonishment; they might have been spurned by the public. . . . Perhaps the jury would not even have accepted them for the Salon. Today, by contrast, M. Delacroix has champions and proselytes, admirers, copiers. The judges awarded him a medal of encouragement at the Salon of 1824. He has gained a following; he is praised, supported. He is entrusted with major projects.[99]

Delacroix, now recognized, was determined to show the range of his talent. He presented the jury with seventeen paintings. Four were rejected, including his portrait of a

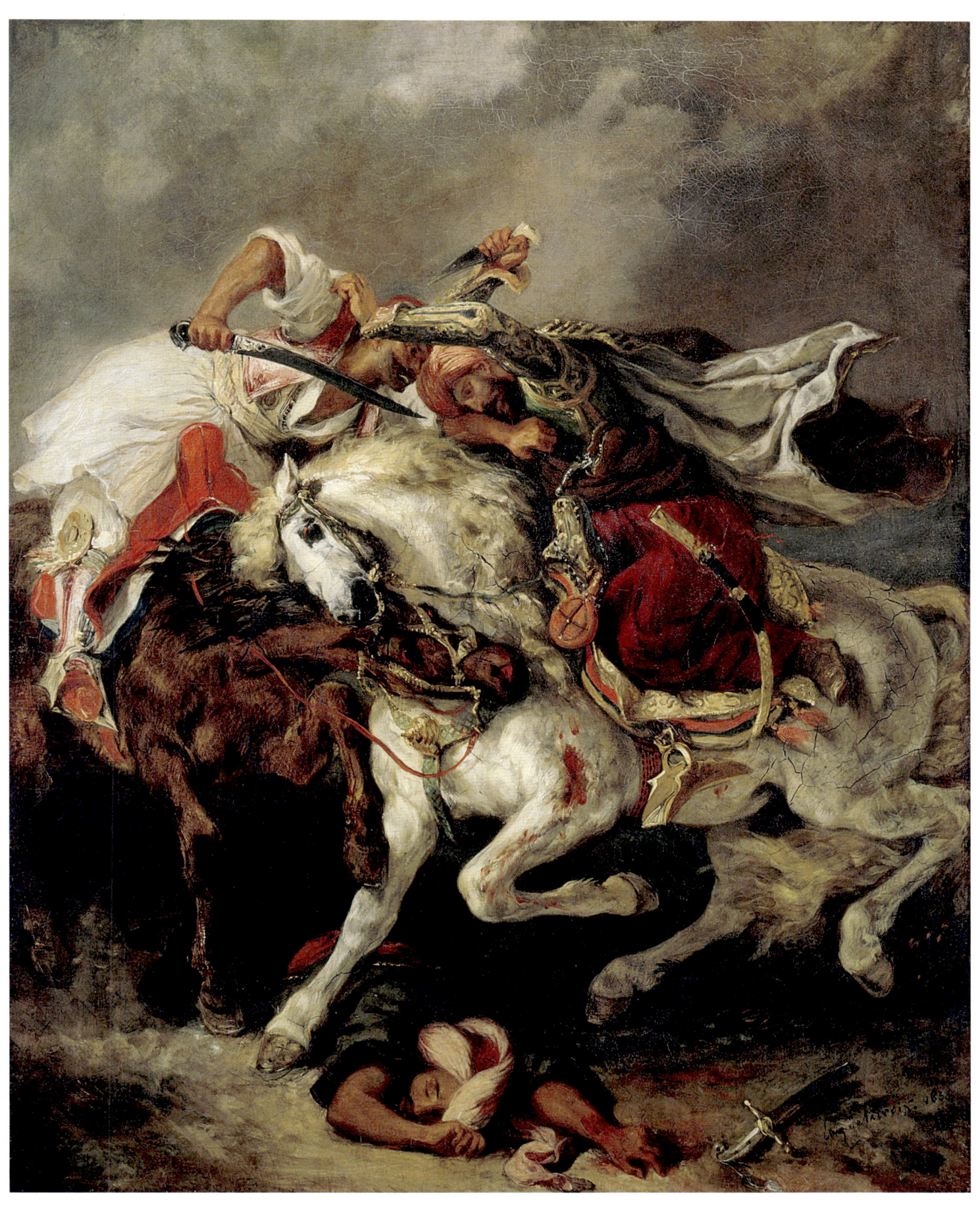

CAT. 87 *Combat of the Giaour and Hassan*, 1835

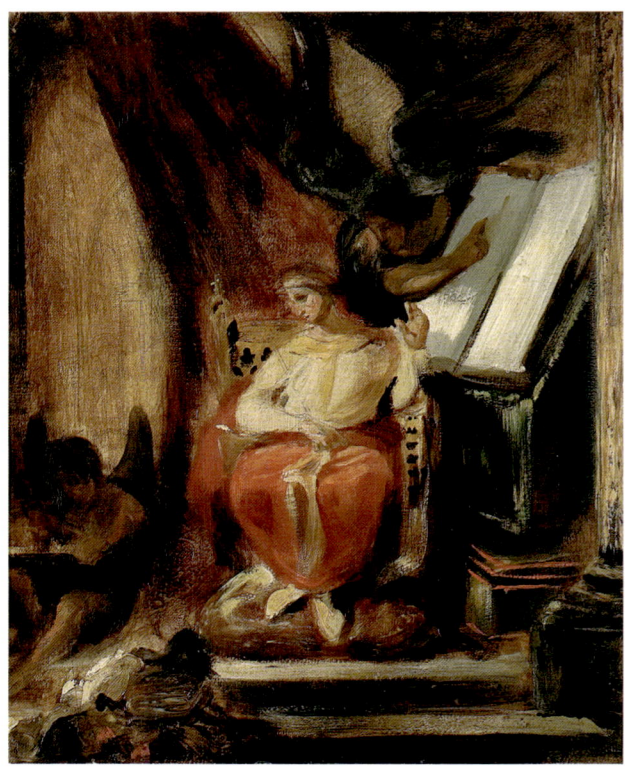

CAT. 28 *Justinian Drafting His Laws, sketch*, 1826

friend, *Louis-Auguste Schwiter* (see cat. 30), and *Combat of the Giaour and Hassan* (cat. 27), inspired by Lord Byron, which he treated in a contemporary lithograph (fig. 16) and whose subject he returned to in a painting nine years later (cat. 87). The following were accepted: a portrait, *Count Demetrius de Palatiano (1794–1849) in Suliot Costume* (see cat. 25); two public commissions, *Christ in the Garden of Olives (The Agony in the Garden)* (see cat. 17), awarded by the prefecture of the Seine for the church of Saint-Paul-Saint-Louis, and *Emperor Justinian*, for the halls of the Conseil d'Etat at the Louvre (destroyed in 1871; see cat. 28); a contemporary subject, *Scene from the War between the Turks and the Greeks*; literary subjects, *The Execution of Doge Marino Faliero* (exhibited the previous year at Galerie Lebrun) (fig. 25), *Faust in His Study*, and *Milton Dictating "Paradise Lost" to His Daughters*; Oriental subjects, *Head Study of an Indian Woman*[100] and *Young Turk Stroking His Horse*;[101] an animal subject, *Two English Farm Horses*;[102] and genre subjects, *Mortally Wounded Brigand Quenches His Thirst* (cat. 22), painted for Alexandre Du Sommerard, and *Still Life with Lobsters* (fig. 17).

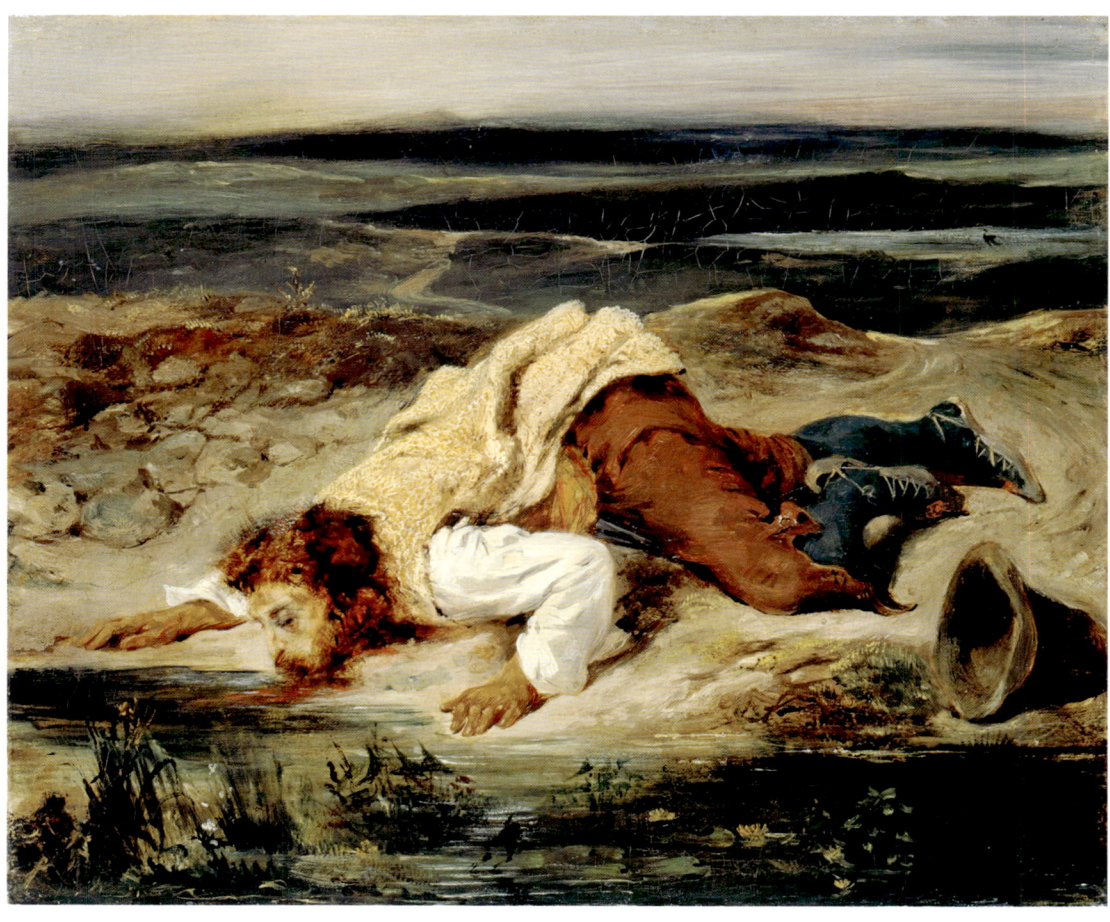

CAT. 22 *Mortally Wounded Brigand Quenches His Thirst*, ca. 1825

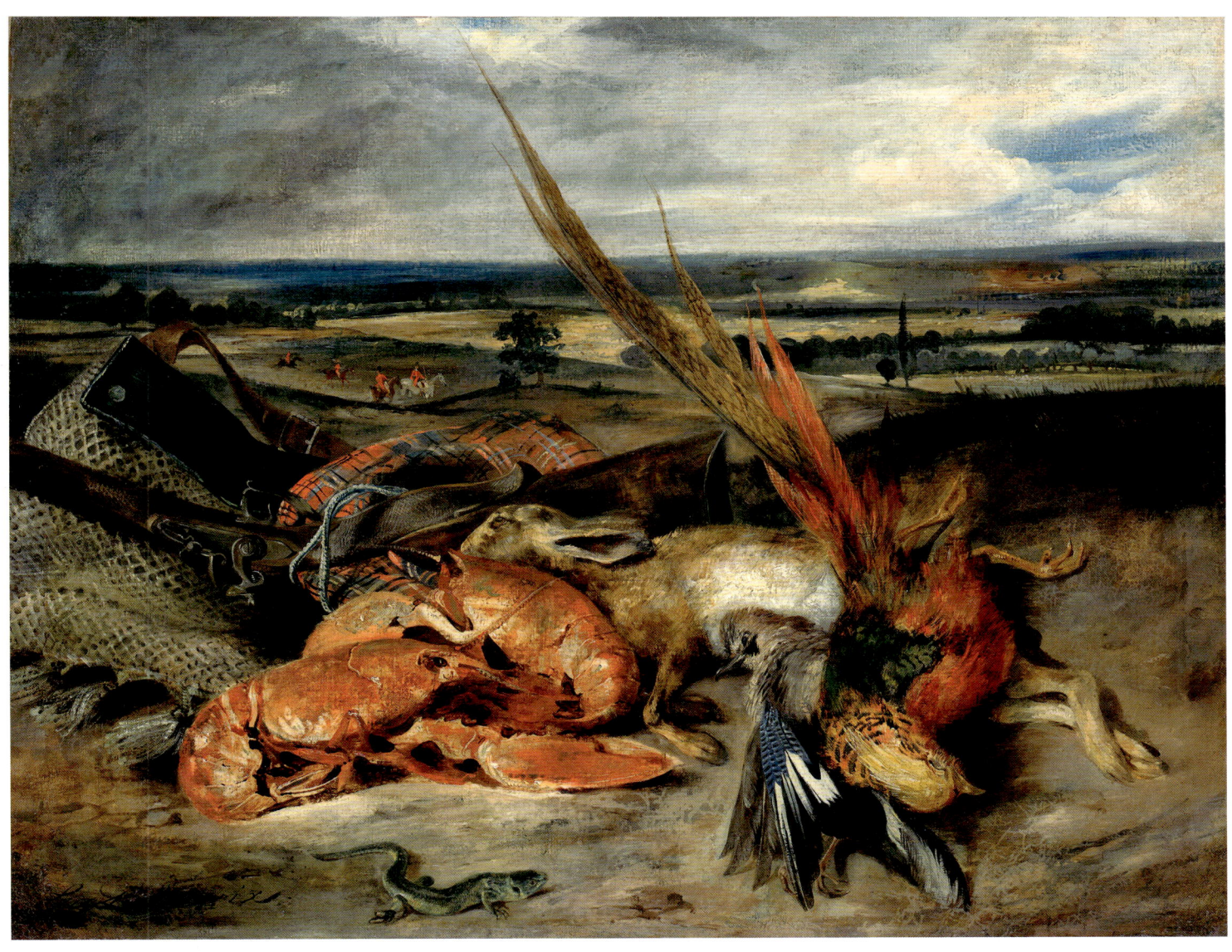

FIG. 17 *Still Life with Lobsters*, 1826–27. Oil on canvas, 31½ x 41¾ in. (80 x 106 cm). Musée du Louvre, Paris (RF 1661) (J 161)

With the rejected portrait of Schwiter, the accepted portrait of the count de Palatiano, and *Still Life with Lobsters,* the artist's repertoire had broadened. He was making incursions into the minor genres, a process that would continue at the Salon of 1831 with *Young Tiger Playing with Its Mother (Study of Two Tigers)* (see cat. 67). Delacroix had come under the influence of British art after seeing the paintings of Constable and Sir Thomas Lawrence exhibited at the Salon of 1824 and in England, which he visited in 1825 on the advice of his friend Thales Fielding (cat. 13). Assimilating that influence in an original way, he began painting works in which different genres were combined. *Still Life with Lobsters* (fig. 17), commissioned for the dining room of General Charles Yves

César Cyr du Coëtlosquet, is somewhere between a still life and a landscape painting, with a hunting scene added in the background. An homage to both the seventeenth-century Flemish and Dutch masters and the most modern landscape artists, with sky effects visibly inspired by Constable, the painting flaunts its incongruity. Fresh game from a hunt lies on the ground next to cooked lobsters, traditionally shown on kitchen tables, and a salamander scuttles out of the still life. Delacroix, wishing primarily to display his virtuosity in rendering matter with color, was playing with clichés: perhaps he was alluding to the four elements. He treated these tropes with a certain ironic offhandedness, as he himself remarked to his friend Soulier: "I completed the general's animal painting

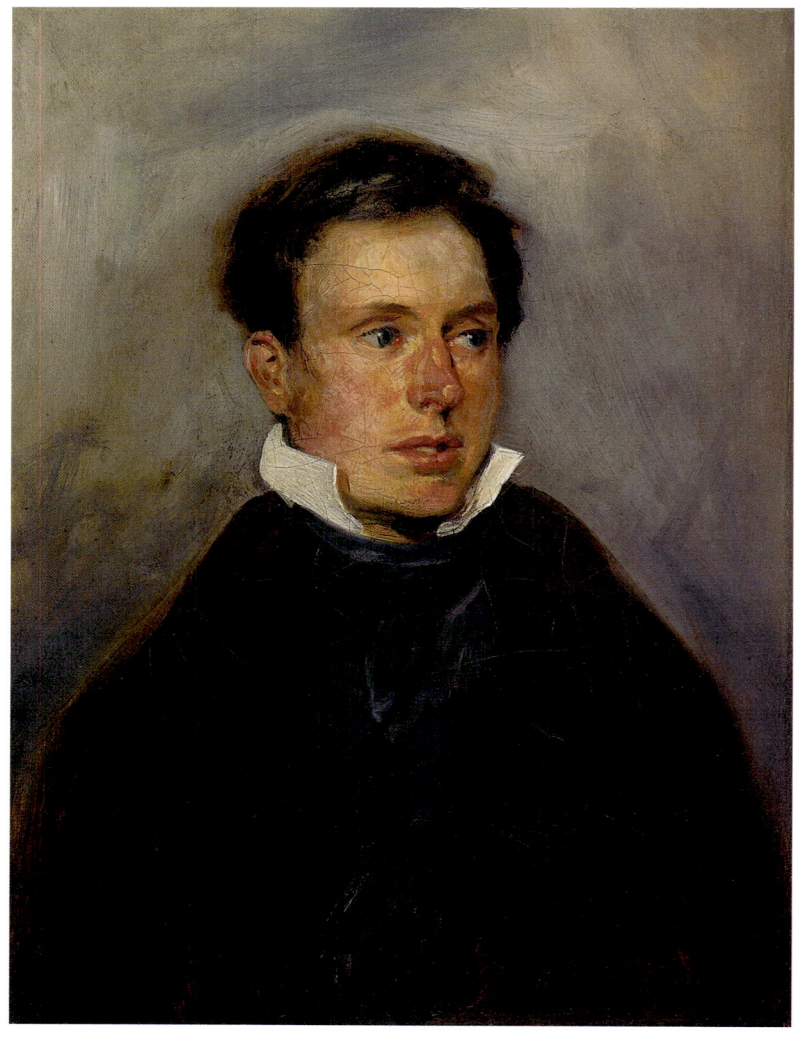

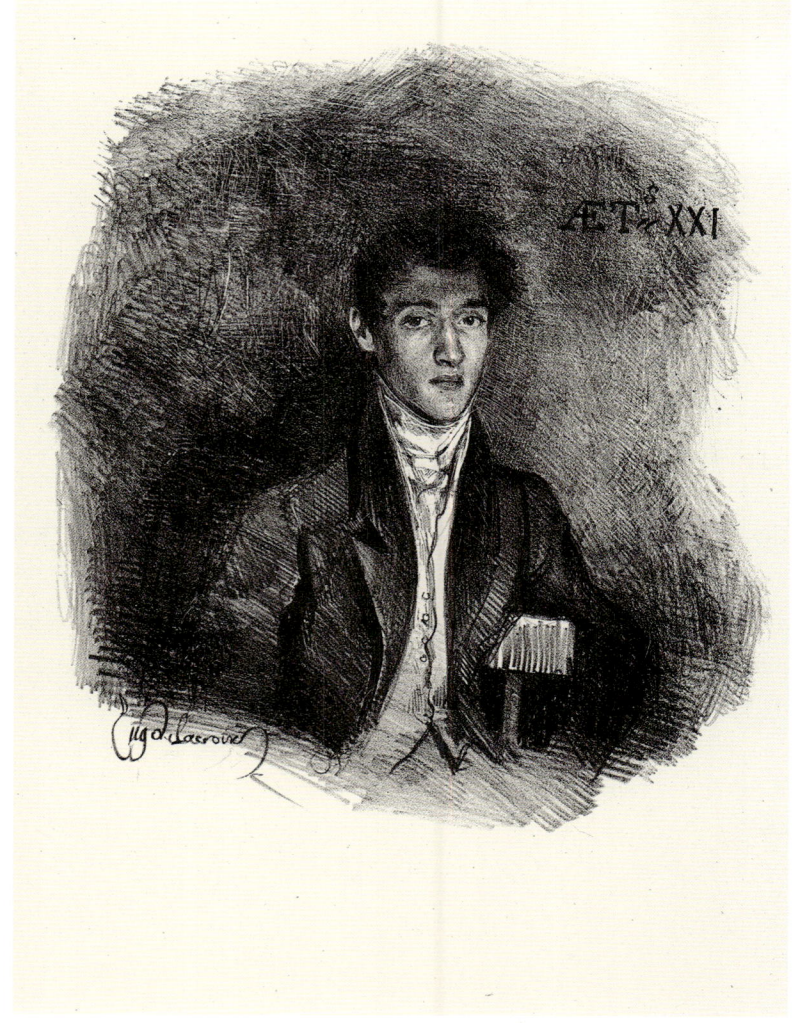

CAT. 13 *Thales Fielding (1793–1837), ca. 1824–25*

CAT. 29 *Baron Schwiter (Louis Auguste Schwiter, 1805–1889), 1826*

and dug up a rococo frame for it, which I am having regilded. It will do the trick. It has already made quite a splash with a load of art lovers, and I think it will be amusing at the Salon."[103]

With the portrait of his friend Louis Auguste Schwiter, son of a marshal of the Empire who became a baron in 1808, Delacroix attempted to combine a portrait with landscape painting (cats. 29, 30). The canvas, probably begun in 1826, a few weeks after he returned from London, conveys the personal, French manner in which Delacroix reinterpreted British portraiture. Schwiter exhibited the Anglomania of a dandy and lived in luxury in Paris. The choice of an "English-style" representation of Schwiter standing in a garden setting therefore seemed a fitting way to express his character. Leaving aside

the ostensibly relaxed poses of Thomas Lawrence's sitters, Delacroix preferred a formality that dates back to the origins of the aristocratic portrait. The model's strict frontality is affected; his attitude is slightly ill at ease, a combination of naturalness and artifice. In an effort to represent not so much his friend's psychology as the idea of refined elegance, the artist played on the expressive distortions of a very slender body with overly long arms. The impact of the clothing and pose competes with and even masks Schwiter's personality and sexual proclivities.

The model's attire is studiously stylish: in his black suit with its pinched waist, his long trousers (an invention of the famous Beau Brummel), his leather gloves and patent leather pumps, he seems dressed for a ball rather than a walk in the

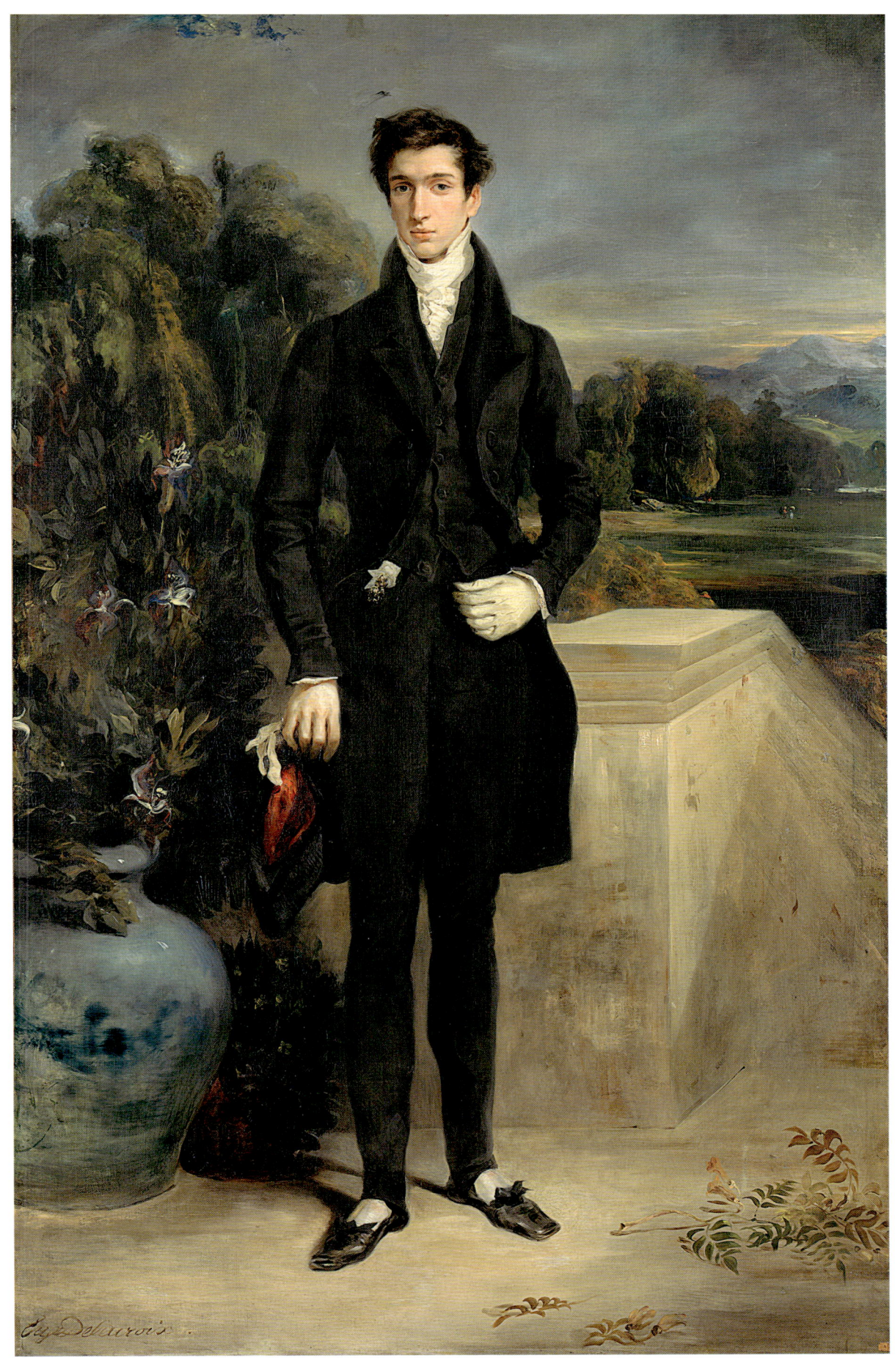

CAT. 30 *Louis Auguste Schwiter (1805–1889), 1826–27*

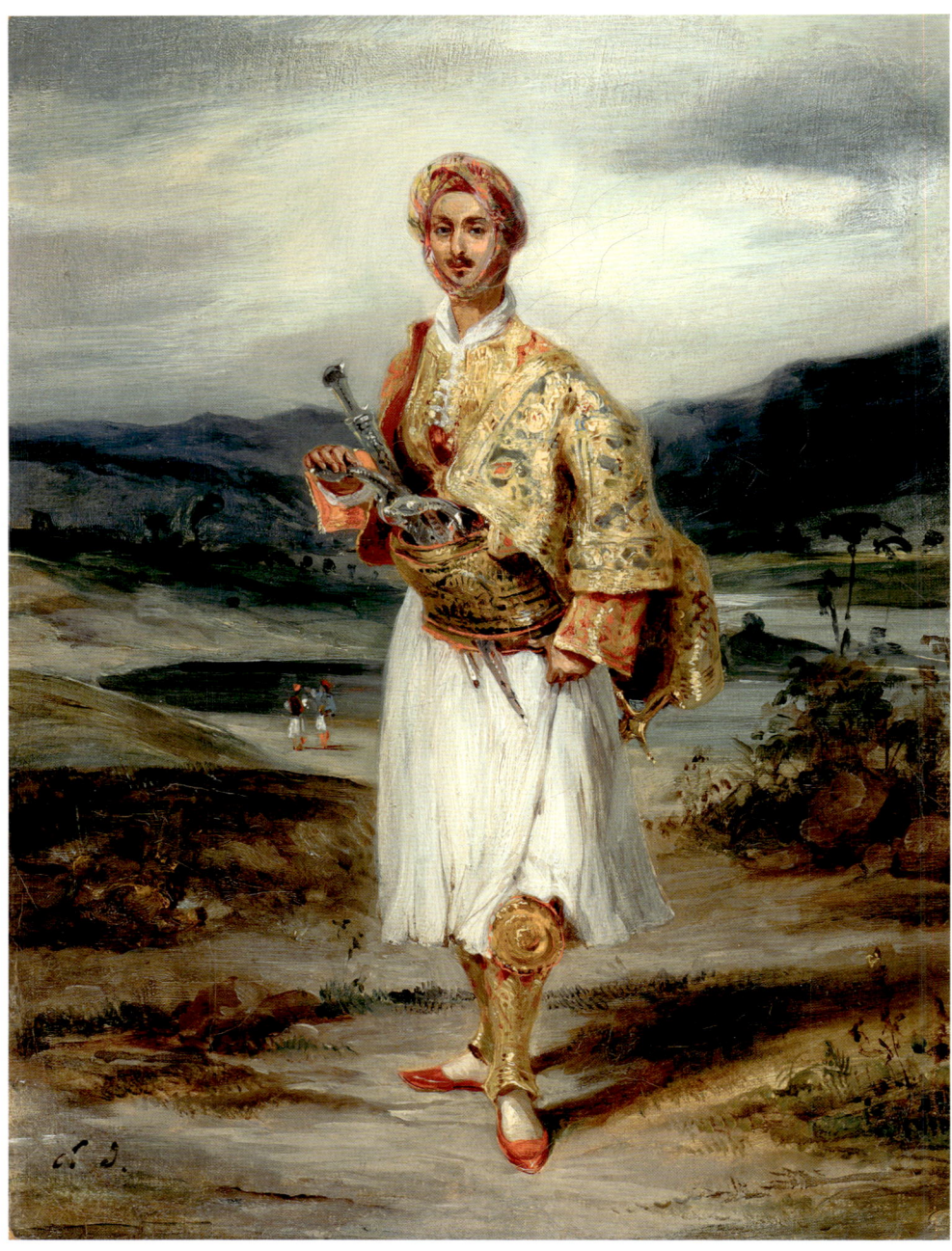

CAT. 25 *Count Demetrius de Palatiano (1794–1849)*
in Suliot Costume, ca. 1825–26

park. Delacroix pushed the conventions of the English-style portrait to their limits in this work—especially the relationship between figure and ground—to express the artificiality of the dandy's attitude. The same is true for the portrait of Demetrius de Palatiano (cat. 25), in which the exoticism of the outfit is reinforced by the surroundings of an English landscape garden, with its minuscule promenading figures, and by the count's conventional pose, proudly struck, one foot in front of the other. The question is whether the surroundings are at odds with the figure, serving merely as a theatrical set, or whether the figure is inserted bizarrely into his environment. We know that Demetrius de Palatiano, an aristocrat from Corfu, enjoyed parading in the center of Paris wearing the sumptuous attire of his homeland, deliberately flouting Western fashions. In the context of the philhellenic movement of the time, which was stimulated by the writings of Byron and embraced by Delacroix, the extravagant count was met with astonishment and admiration—and he made the most of it. Schwiter, with his extreme elegance, did the same. The vaunting of fancy dress at the expense of "natural"

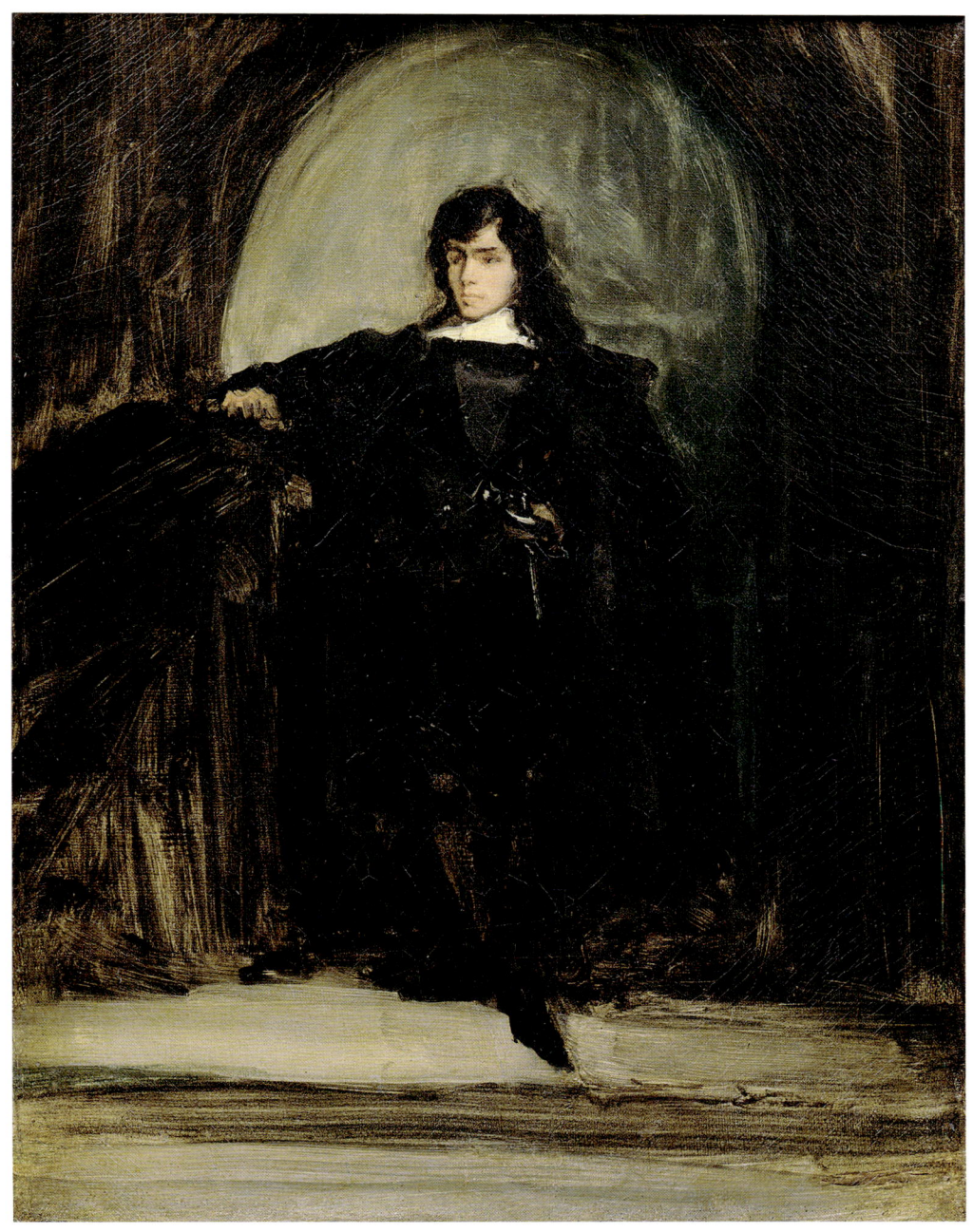

CAT. 4 *Self-Portrait as Ravenswood*, ca. 1821–24

expressiveness derives partly from masquerade, the vogue for disguises, which is present also in Delacroix's *Self-Portrait as Ravenswood* (cat. 4), and in his appearances at masked balls, which, according to Alexandre Dumas, he attended dressed as Dante. With the exception of Palatiano, who intentionally played up his natural "strangeness," these masquerades involved borrowed identities, designed to highlight one aspect of the model's personality, but not more.

Self-Portrait as Ravenswood is both a portrait of a literary hero and an allusion to the financial difficulties of the artist,

whose response to his early reversal of fortune may be read in the nobility of his pose. Edgar Ravenswood is the protagonist of *The Bride of Lammermoor,* a novel by Sir Walter Scott, published in 1819 and very much in vogue at the time. The young nobleman loses fortune and property when his father dies, as Delacroix did in the early 1820s with the catastrophic settlement of his mother's estate.[104] Delacroix had read *The Bride of Lammermoor* and identified with the story. Might not the portrait of Schwiter, dignified and majestic in its way, and with its imposing format, express a certain convivial irony toward the

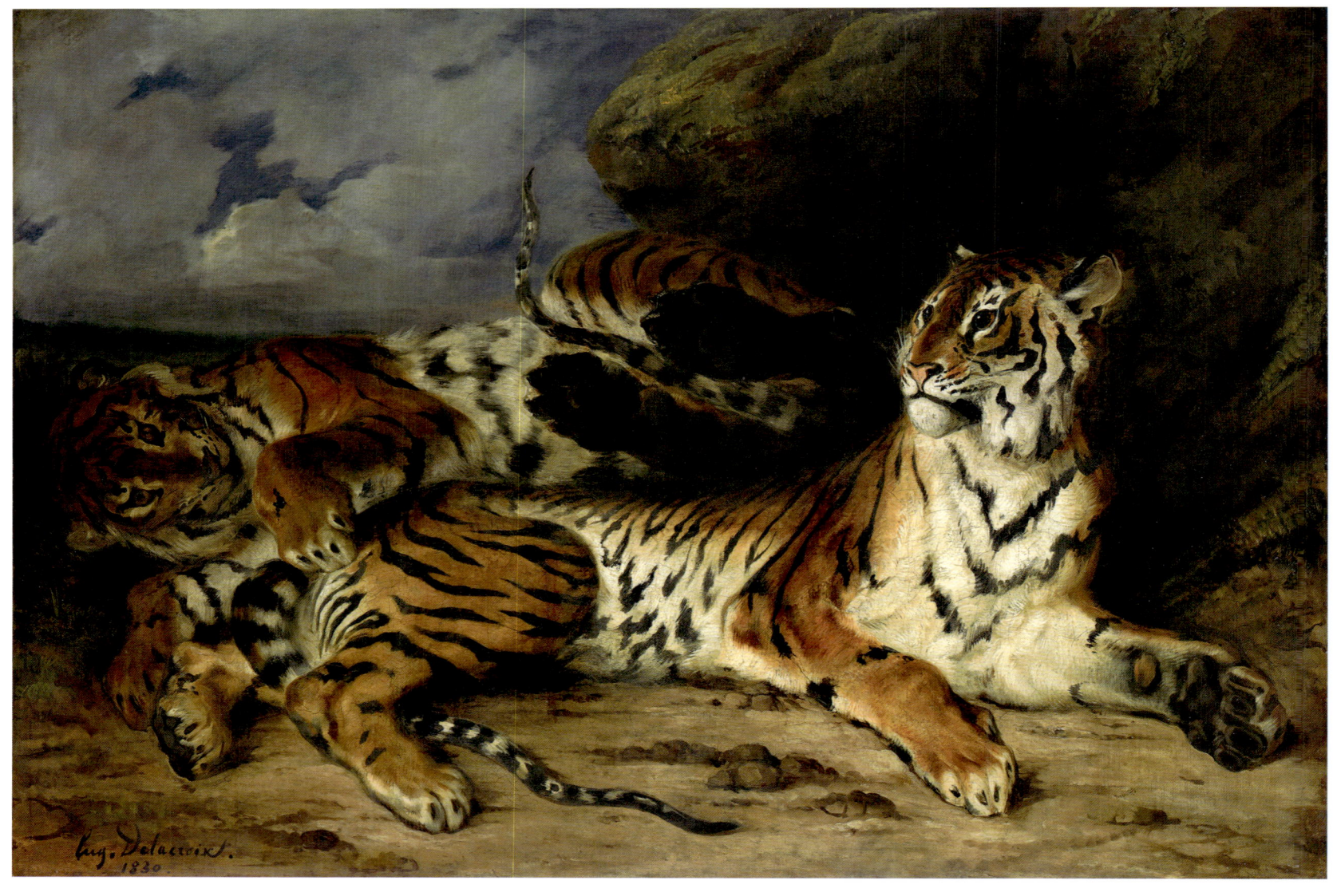

CAT. 67 *Young Tiger Playing with Its Mother (Study of Two Tigers)*, 1830

artist's friend, a Frenchman who posed in English-style finery? Revealing the subject's dandyism as an assumed identity, the work discloses the artificiality of the young man's pretentions.

The dignity found in the Schwiter portrait was also present in a painting shown at the Salon of 1831, the imposing *Young Tiger Playing with Its Mother* (cat. 67). As indicated by Delacroix's many renderings in graphic media of domestic cats, tigers, and lions (cats. 60, 62, 63, 65, 66), the artist had a particular predilection for felines. This enormous work is one of a kind in his oeuvre partly because of its monumental format, which is close to that of a history painting, and partly because of the calmness of the image. Contemporaries were disturbed by the unexpected scale of this animal painting. A change in its title points to the difficulty they had in

understanding the status of the work within the traditional hierarchy of genres. Although presented to the Salon jury under the title "Young Tiger Playing with Its Mother," which was probably proposed by the artist, it appears in the catalogue as "Study of Two Tigers." The second formulation is clearly inadequate. The confusion stemmed from the fact that in heroizing the animal, Delacroix dispensed with narrative and dramatic action: there is no hunt, no tiger attacking a wild horse (cats. 57, 58), no horse frightened by a storm, as in the watercolor at the Szépművészeti Múzeum in Budapest (fig. 18; see also cat. 59). The subject is made heroic by a composition that, rather than seeking to capture the savage energy of nature, proffers analogies between the animal kingdom and humanity. *Young Tiger Playing with Its Mother* is, in

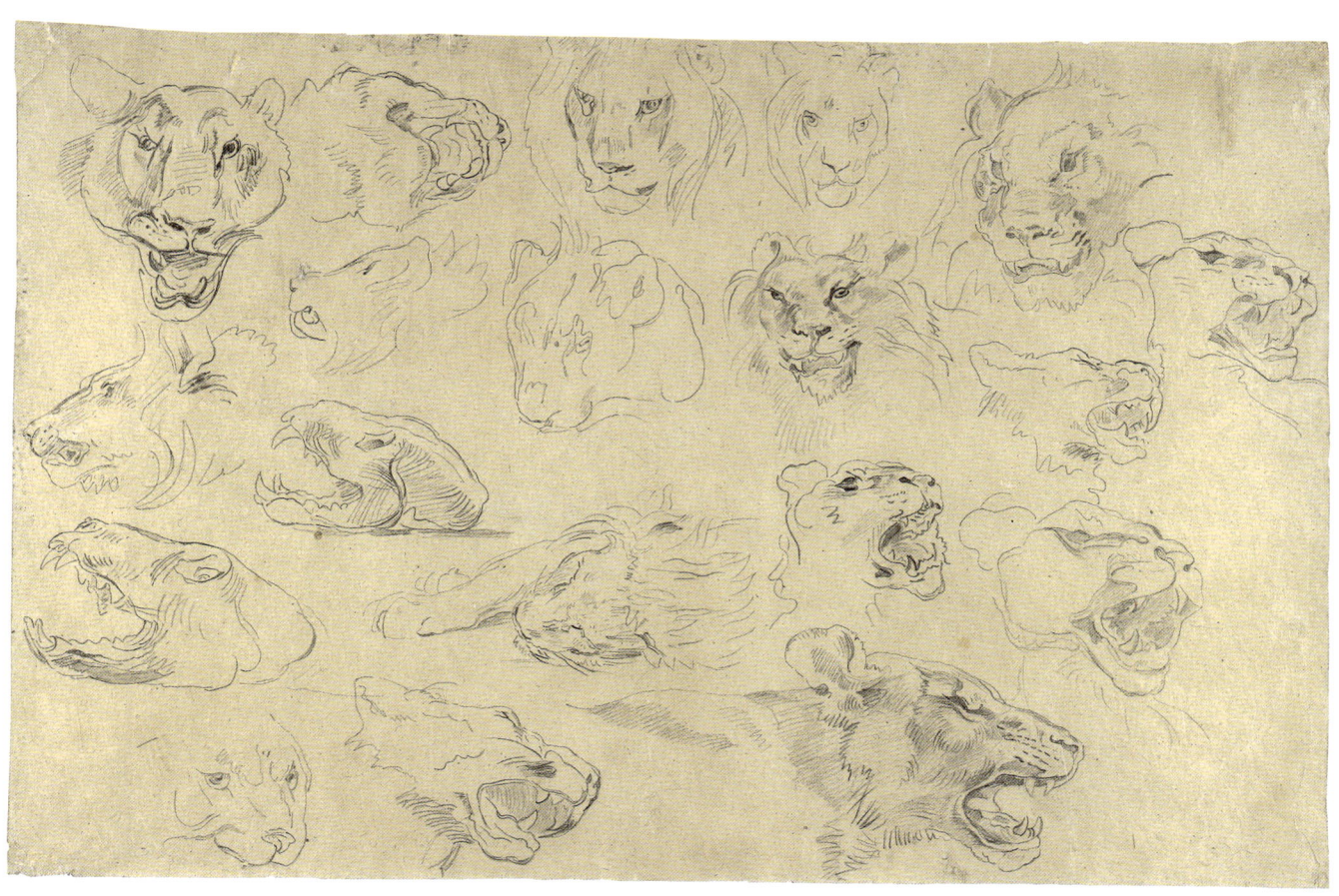

CAT. 62 *Nineteen Studies of Heads and Skulls of Lions*, ca. 1828–30

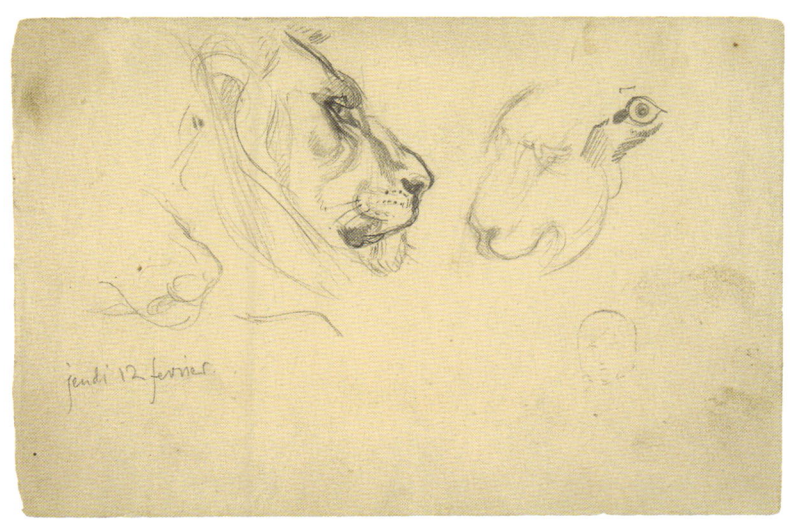

CAT. 60 *Studies of a Lion, from* Sketchbook with Views of Tours, France and Its Environs, *1828–29*

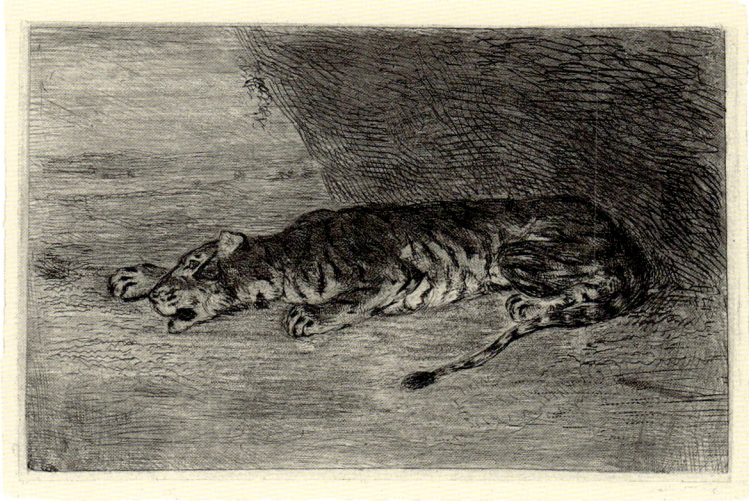

CAT. 63 *Tiger Lying at the Entrance of Its Lair*, ca. 1828–30

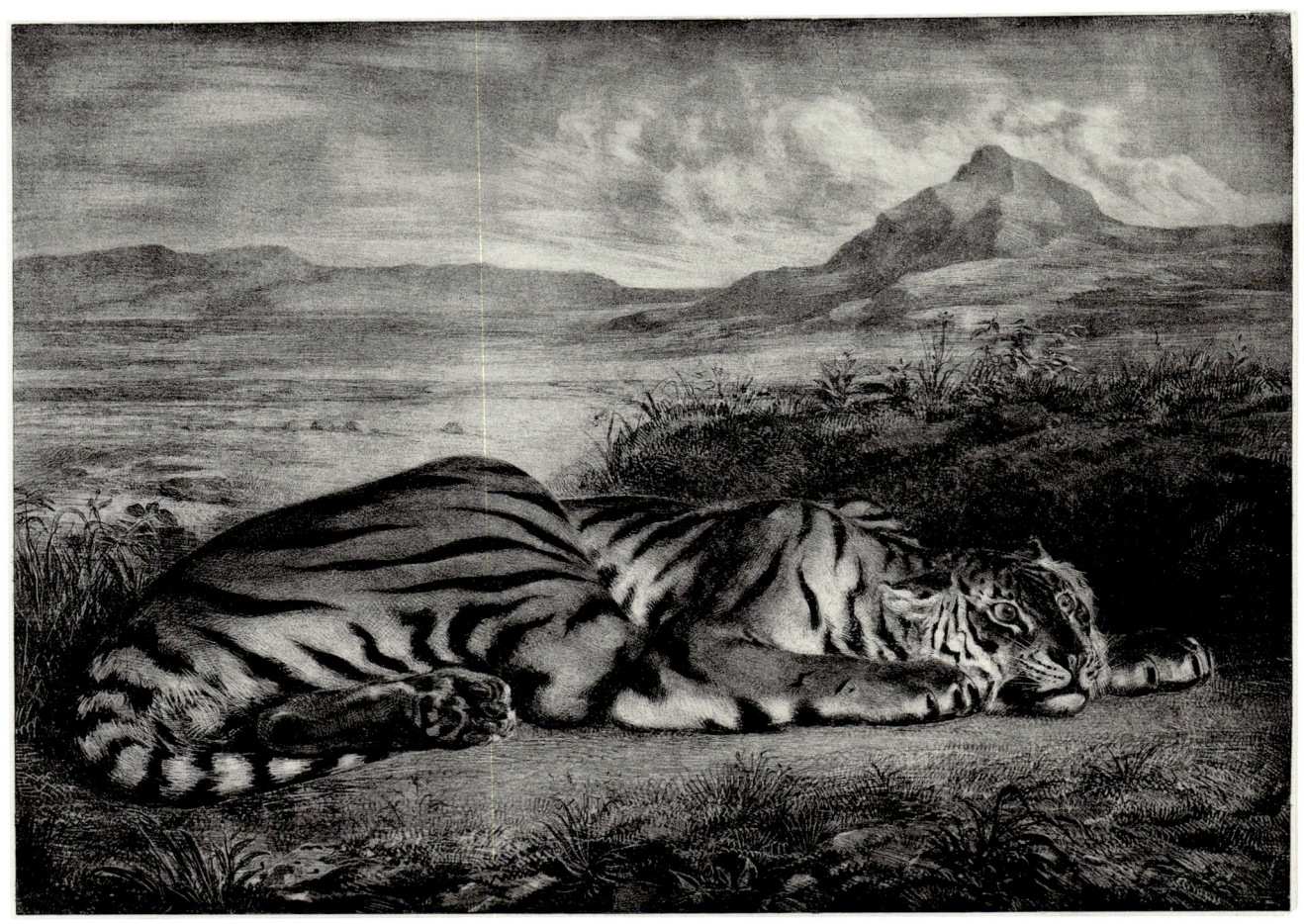

CAT. 65 *Royal Tiger*, 1829

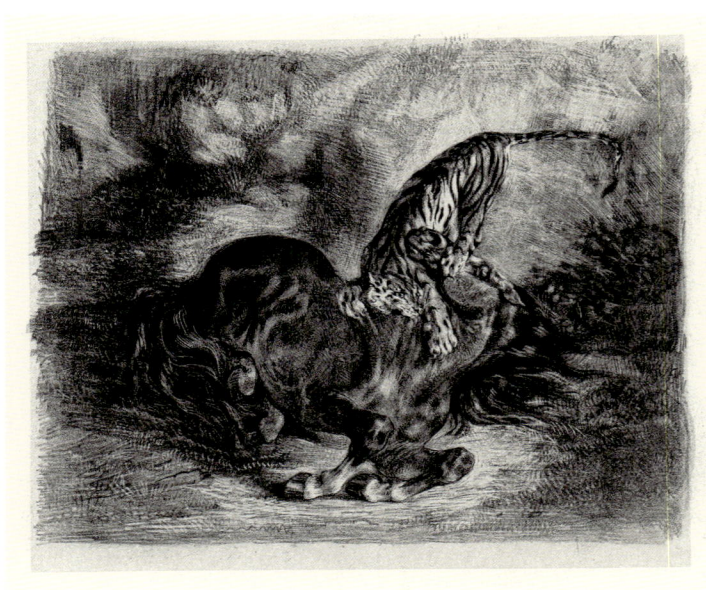

CAT. 57 *Wild Horse Felled by a Tiger*, 1828

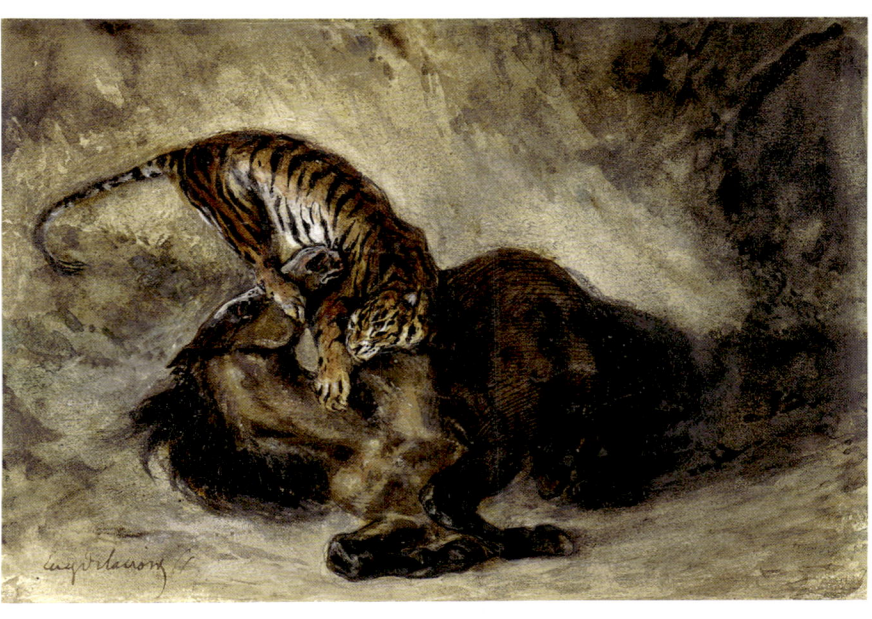

CAT. 58 *Wild Horse Felled by a Tiger*, 1828

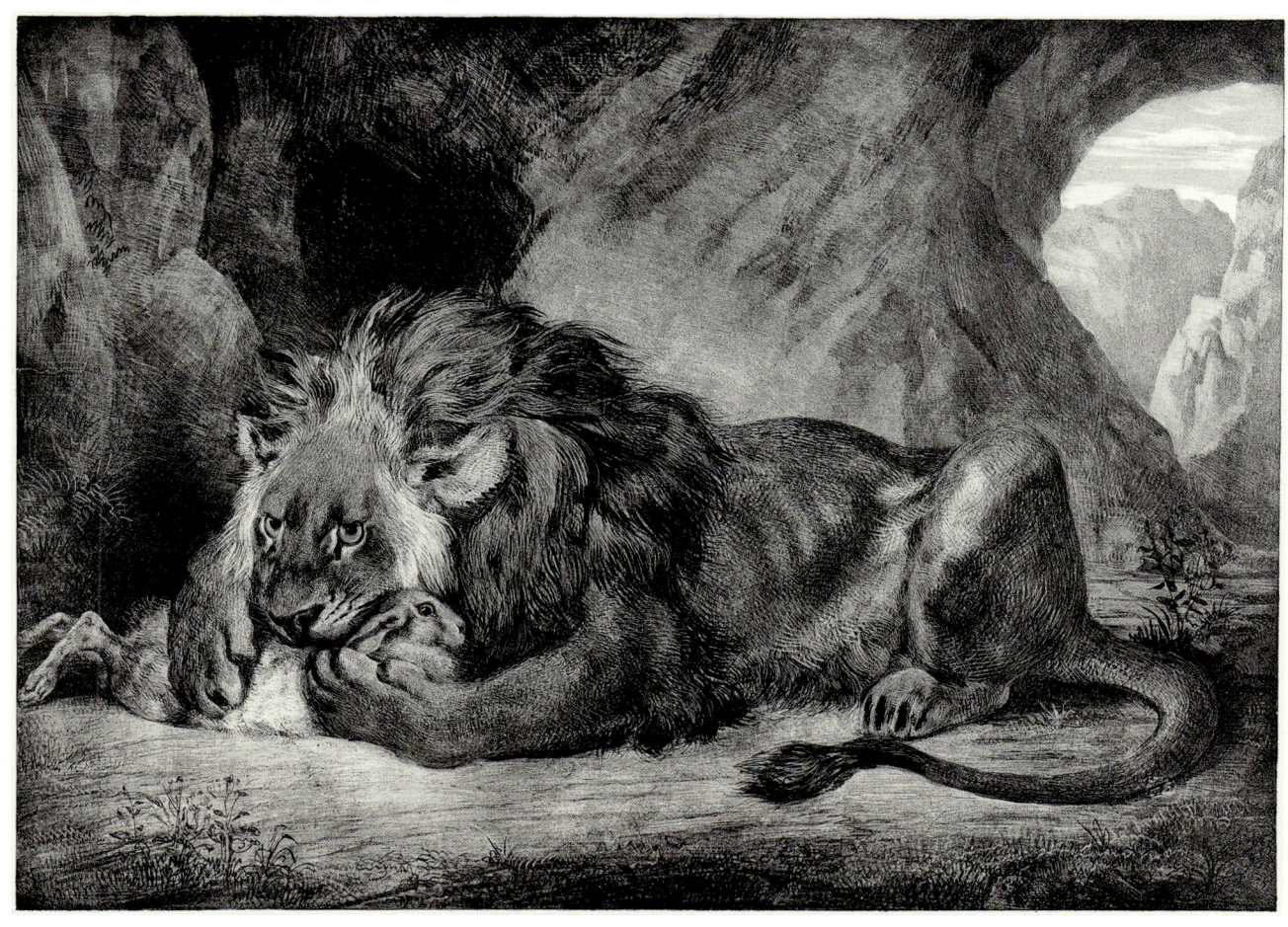

CAT. 66 *Lion of the Atlas Mountains*, 1829–30

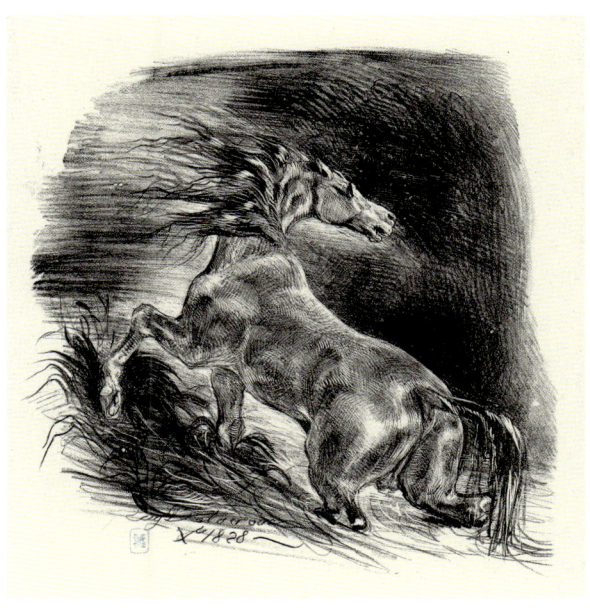

CAT. 59 *Wild Horse*, 1828

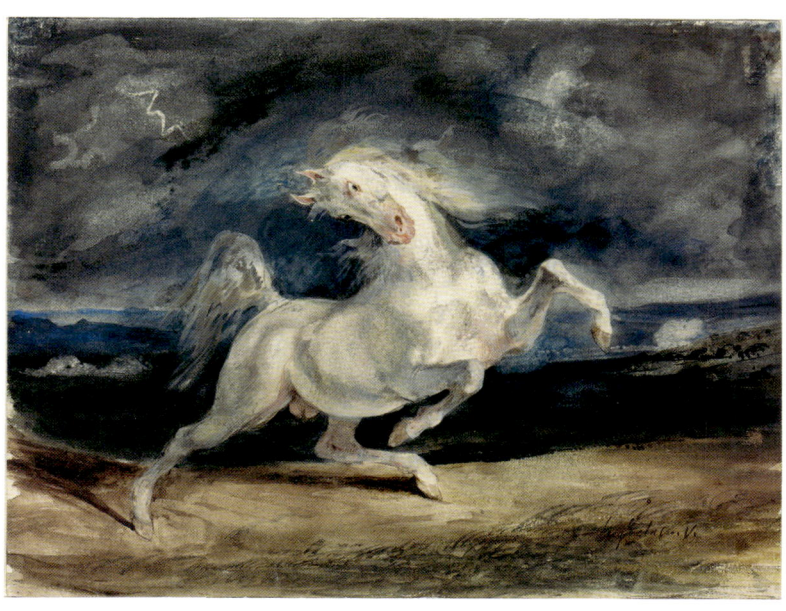

FIG. 18 *Horse Frightened by a Storm*, ca. 1825–29. Watercolor on paper, 9¼ x 12⅝ in. (23.5 x 32 cm). Szépművészeti Múzeum, Budapest (inv. 1935-2698)

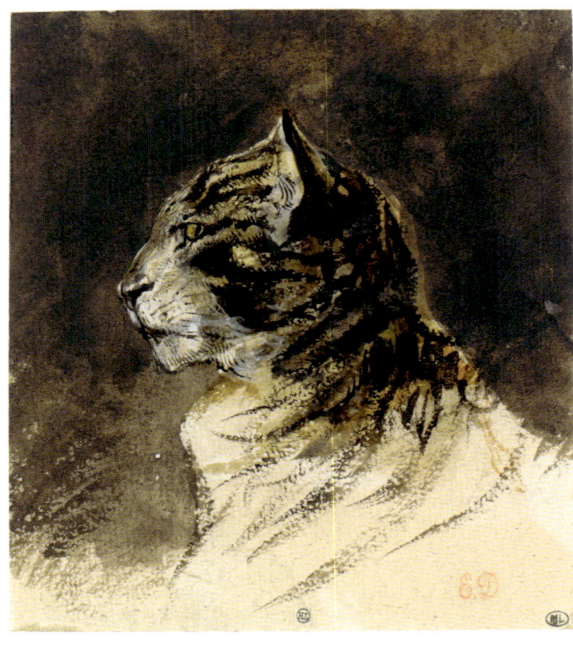

FIG. 19 *Head of a Cat*, ca. 1824–29.
Watercolor with gum arabic on paper,
6⁵⁄₁₆ x 5⁹⁄₁₆ in. (16 x 14.2 cm). Musée du
Louvre, Paris (RF 794)

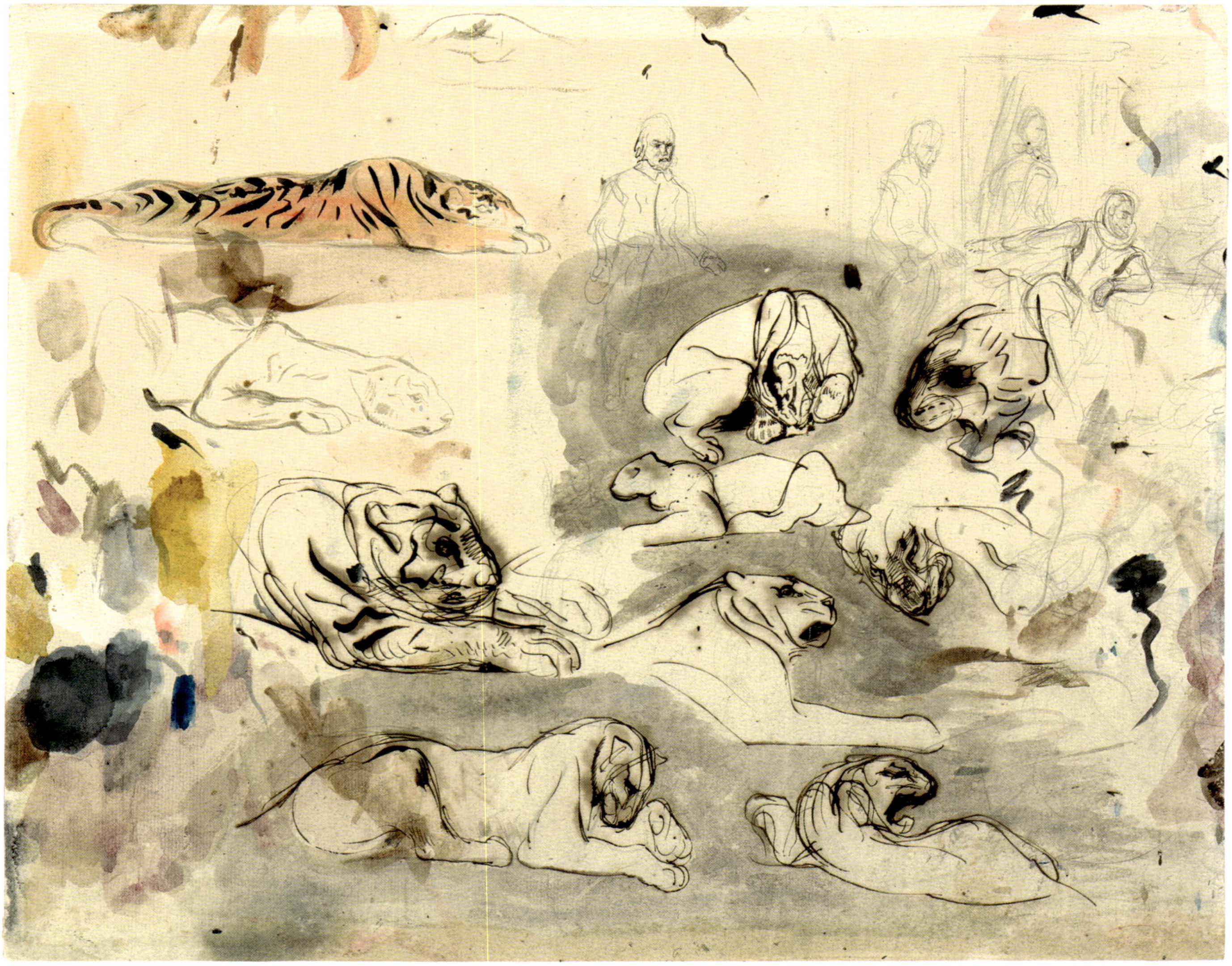

CAT. 61 *Sketches of Tigers and Men in Sixteenth-Century Costume, ca. 1828–29*

fact, a portrait. The nobility of the mother tiger's pose is akin to Schwiter's rather remote haughtiness (see cat. 30); the dandy resembles the feline. Some critics would, in fact, find fault with Delacroix for rendering the animals' expressions more accurately than those of men: "That unusual artist has never painted a man who looks like a man in the way his tiger looks like a tiger," wrote the editor of the *Journal des artistes*.[105] There is a similar anthropomorphism in the Louvre's *Head of a Cat* (fig. 19). The profile pose, recalling the portraits of great men found on ancient coins and medallions (see cat. 21), is here adapted to a feline. In these works, Delacroix seems to reverse theories of physiognomy: rather than likening man to an animal, he highlights an animal's resemblance to man.

The large painting owes its originality to the artist's close observation of animals and a notion of the animal kingdom marked by the quarrel between the naturalists Georges Cuvier and Geoffroy Sainte-Hilaire. Just as the Louvre was a place where the young Delacroix could freely study the old masters and thereby emancipate himself from academic precepts, the Muséum d'Histoire Naturelle, located in the Jardin des Plantes in Paris, offered him the opportunity to examine and draw live animals, particularly wild creatures difficult to see elsewhere (see cat. 60). On his regular visits there, he was also able to study the skinned corpses of animals, including that of Admiral Rigny's famous lion. In 1829, Delacroix and the sculptor Antoine Louis Barye studied that specimen by lamplight in an effort to understand the function of every muscle. The painter's work on skinned animals and feline remains can be discerned in works from 1829 and 1830. *Young Tiger Playing with Its Mother* was preceded by several water-colors and ink wash drawings of tigers at rest (for example, cat. 61), their heads lowered to the ground between their front paws. That position, found also in the lithograph *Royal Tiger* (cat. 65), is reminiscent of a skinned tiger drawn in one of the artist's notebooks now in the Louvre. In the painting, Delacroix righted his model's upper body in such a way that it holds its head erect—with anthropomorphic nobility.

According to the nineteenth-century critic and historian Hippolyte Taine, Delacroix was especially struck by the fact that the "lion's front leg was the huge arm of a man, but twisted and turned backward," and that "there were in all human forms more or less vague animal forms that had to be teased out." The artist is said to have gone even further, claiming that, on the basis of these forms, "you manage to discover in [man] the more or less vague instincts that link his nature to one animal or another."[106]

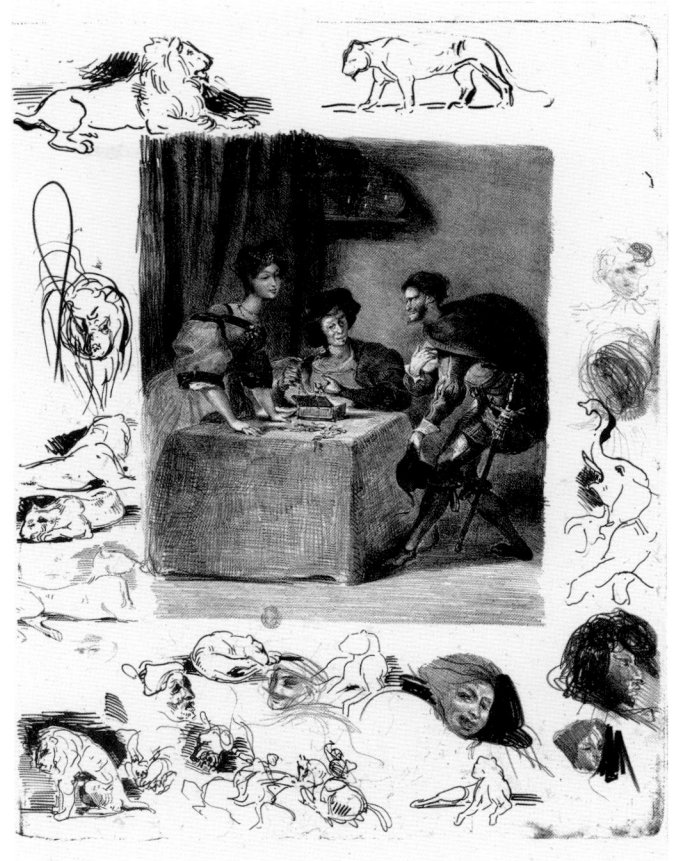

CAT. 48 *Faust, plate 9: Mephistopheles Introduces Himself at Martha's House*, 1827

We may wonder whether a self-portrait of the painter might have slipped into the improbable cat's head. (Only a few years later, Charles Baudelaire would compare Delacroix to a tiger.) The similarities between man and animal in the painter's understanding of the species are easily identifiable in the marginalia of some of the *Faust* engravings. In *Mephistopheles Introduces Himself at Martha's House* (cat. 48), the attitude of Mephistopheles, his back rounded, echoes that of the seated lion in the lower left corner of the sheet. From an expressive standpoint, it appears that the association between the tempter and the lion signals a natural savagery behind Mephistopheles's obsequious attitude. The presence of felines all around the image, either watchful or at rest, was a technical experiment, but it introduced a disturbing atmosphere very much in keeping with the subject. A similar expressive association can be found in a superb preliminary sheet for *The Death of Sardanapalus*: a dog's terrifying maw in the midst of nude women awaiting death embodies the sadistic pleasure the Assyrian king feels as he contemplates the atrocity he has ordered.[107]

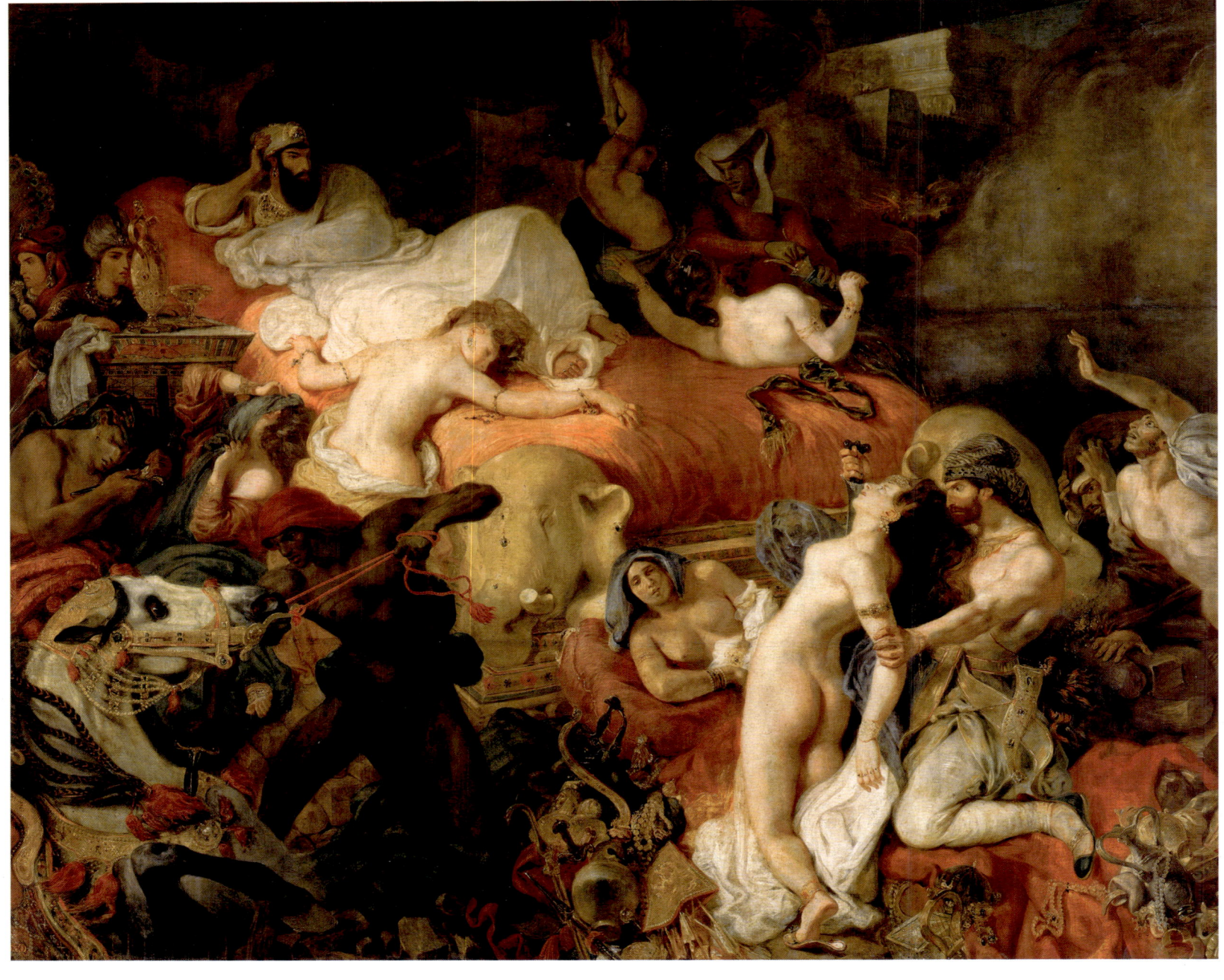

FIG. 20 *The Death of Sardanapalus,* 1826–27. Oil on canvas, 12 ft. 11½ in. x 16 ft. 2⅞ in. (3.9 x 4.9 m). Musée du Louvre, Paris (RF 2346) (J 125)

He Painted with a "Drunken Broom"

The Death of Sardanapalus (fig. 20) was meant to be Delacroix's major exhibit at the Salon of 1827, but the painting was not ready in time for the opening on November 4. When it finally arrived in January 1828, it provoked anger and indignation. Charles Paul Landon fumed: "Are we to give the title of composition to this incomprehensible hodgepodge of men, women, dogs, horses, logs, vases, instruments of every kind,

enormous columns, oversize bed, all thrown down pell-mell, without stylistic effects or perspective, and hanging in mid-air!"[108] It was such a disaster that Delacroix called the work "Massacre No. 2" and the museum administration refused to purchase it. Inspired by Byron's drama of the same name, Delacroix, perhaps channeling Diodorus Siculus, Byron's ancient Roman source, accentuated the dark side. The canvas was almost unanimously reviled and caused an unprecedented scandal. A deadly orgy depicting the suicide of a king avid for

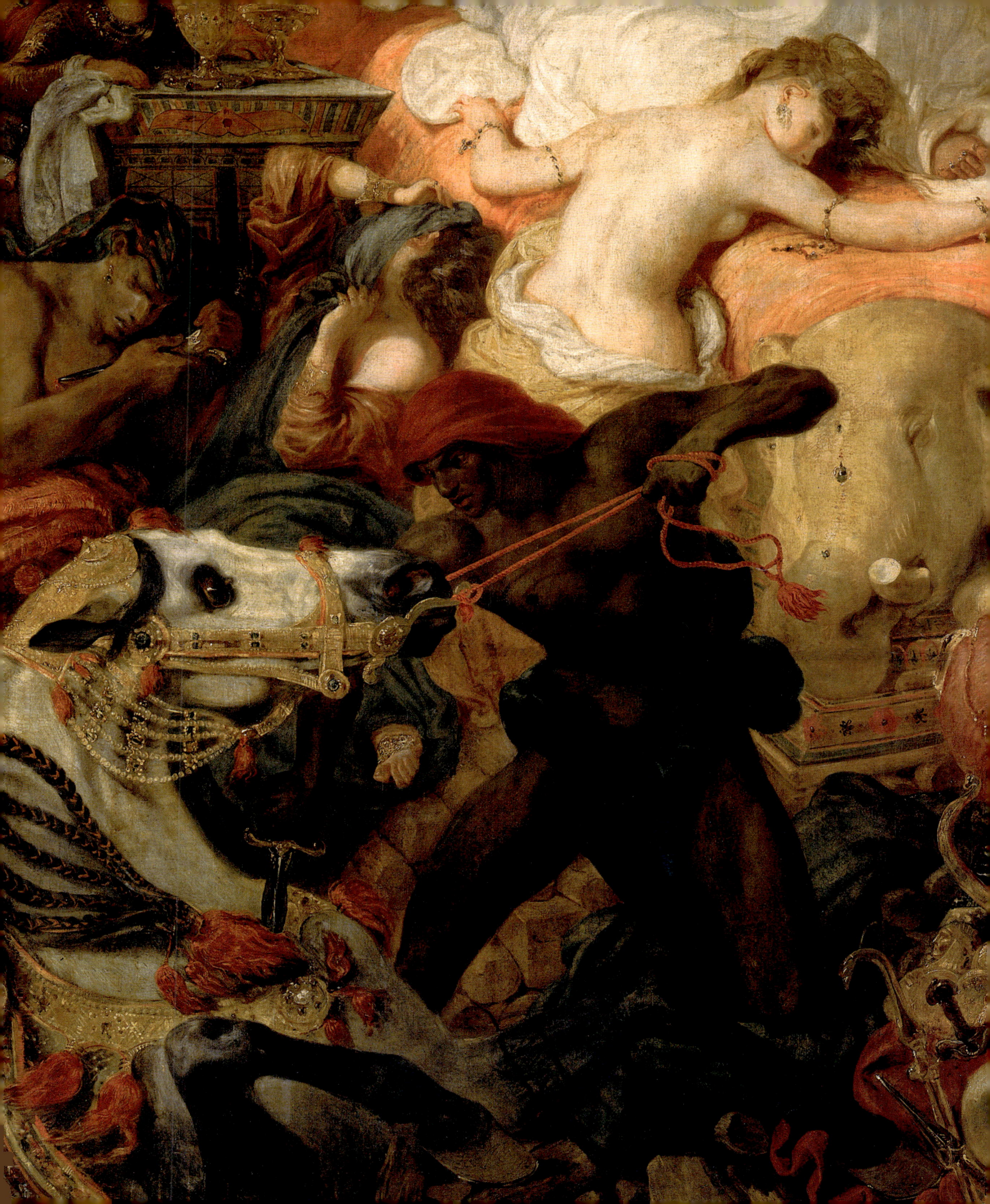

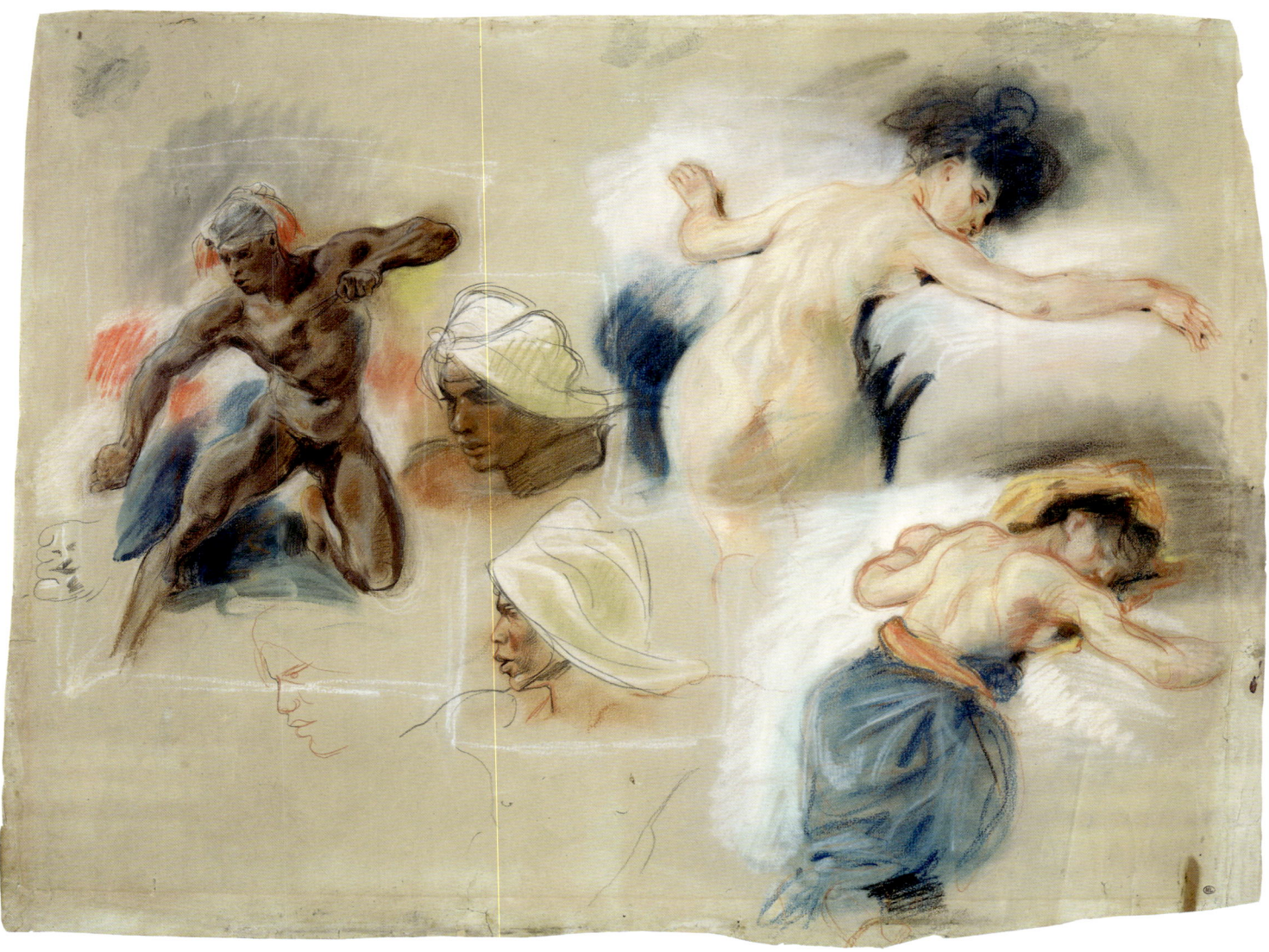

FIG. 21 Sheet of studies for *The Death of Sardanapalus,* 1827. Chalk and pastel on paper, 17³⁄₁₆ x 22¹³⁄₁₆ in. (43.7 x 58 cm). Musée du Louvre, Paris (RF 29665) (Johnson 1995, no. 1)

sex and luxury had inspired a wildly bold brush, which a few years later Théophile Gautier would call a "drunken broom." The artist flouted the principles of art, decency, and modesty. On a giant canvas, the color explodes in a welter of reds and golds both sensual and apparently disordered. Here, Delacroix, in his quest for a modern mode of expressiveness, followed the path of chromatic overexuberance rather than the exaggeration of Michelangelesque form, as he had in his *Barque of Dante.* This homage to Rubens was accompanied by contempt for the elementary rules of drawing and composition: the bodies are entangled, distorted, and stretched; a tremendous horse rears up; and the king's bed, on a diagonal seemingly reminiscent of *The Raft of the Medusa,* appears to be tipping over onto the

viewer. All the figures, as Jean-Pierre Thénot noted in a manual on perspective, "are drawn from the same place and at the same height, without concern for the horizon in the painting or in nature."[109] The space overflows with bodies, animals, objects, and jewelry. The unity of the composition is compromised by that accumulation and further undermined by the apparently arbitrary framing. As Ludovic Vitet remarked: "On every side, the meaning is interrupted by the border."[110] The viewer's gaze, disturbed by the distortions in perspective, runs up against the frame, which imprisons the eye inside the composition.

Although the work was preceded by many preliminary studies (fig. 21) and an imposing sketch (cat. 31), Delacroix again let himself be carried away by the extraordinary

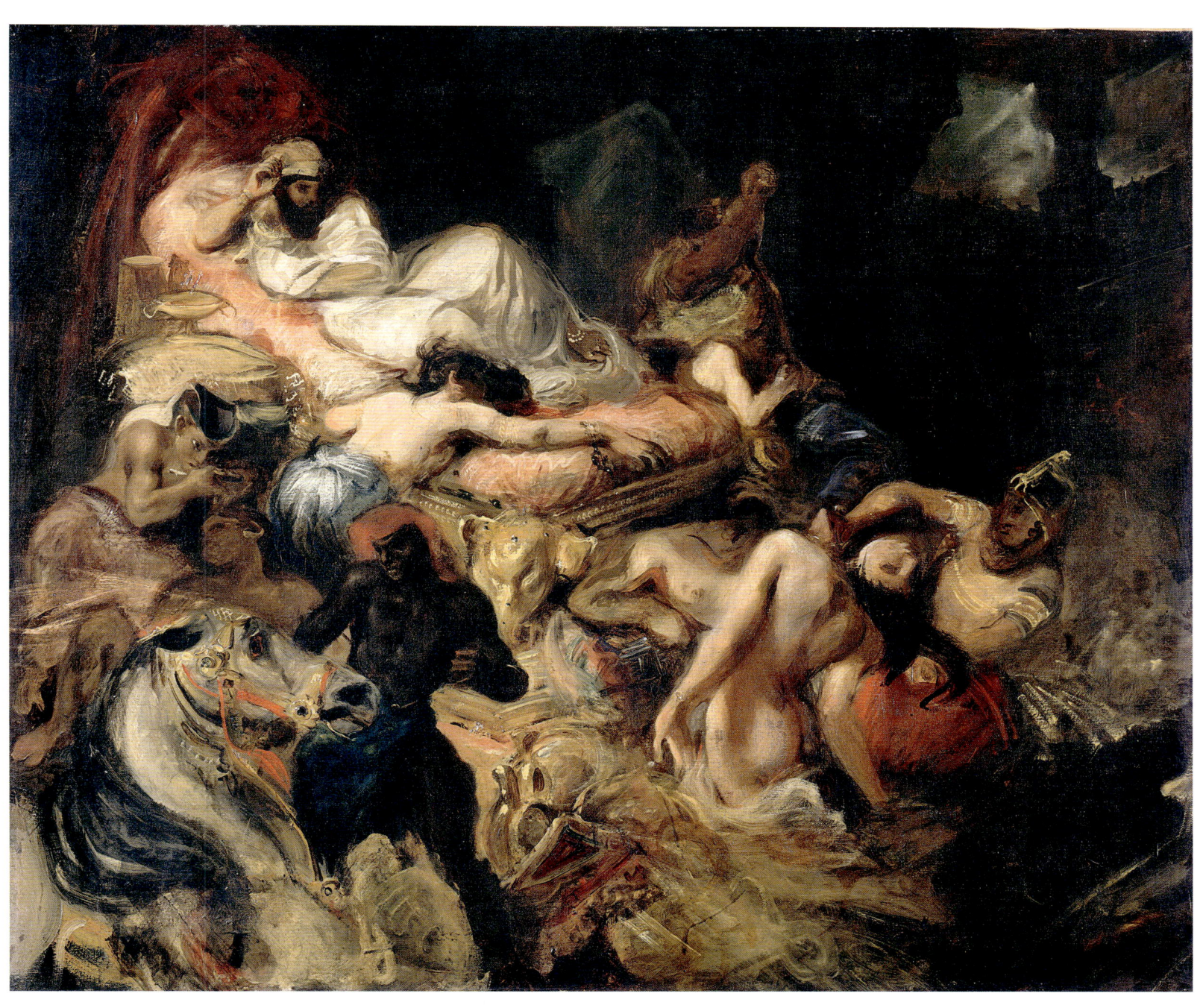

CAT. 31 *Death of Sardanapalus, sketch, 1826–27*

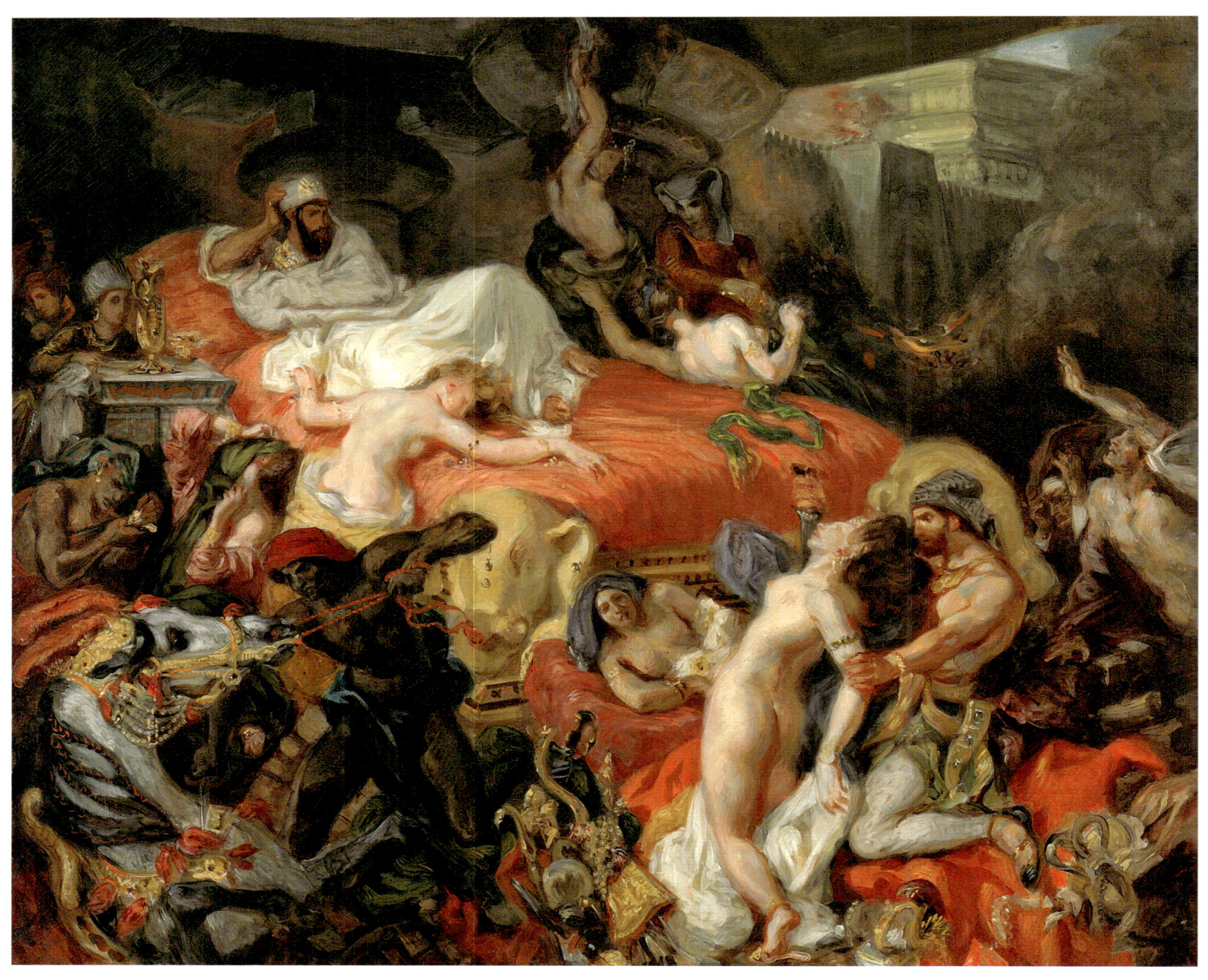

CAT. 104 *The Death of Sardanapalus, 1845–46*

impetuousness and virtuosity of his brush and by his attention to detail and the model, developing the composition during the execution phase as he added in the figures. In February 1849, on a visit to Charles Rivet, a childhood friend to whom Delacroix would give the sketch for *Sardanapalus*, the artist explained how the idea for the work had come to him. (By then, Delacroix had sold the Salon picture, which prompted him to paint a replica for himself; see cat. 104). According to Rivet, the artist had been struck by the ferocious denouement of Bryon's tragedy: the despot, ruler of Nineveh, immolates himself along with everything he has loved in order not to be taken by his enemies. "The scene as he first imagined it was filled with grief and horror." Rivet's account conveys the almost hallucinatory quality of literary inspiration, which gives birth to a world seemingly composed of phantoms. Indeed, Delacroix had declared in 1824, "What is real for me are the illusions I create through painting."[111]

After the moment of inspiration, Delacroix made a wild, dark sketch. When he moved on to the execution, he set out to paint one of the half-nude slave girls from a live model. He was then swept up in the seductiveness of imitation and "made the opal and gold on the torso palpitate with brilliant reflections." The magnificent pastels (including fig. 21) the artist realized in the presence of live models confirm Rivet's concluding statement: "He lost the general tone of the painting in order to preserve what he had done with such verve and felicity. Therefore, he gradually modified all the accessories, and the entire scene took on a completely different effect from what it was supposed to express at first."[112] This text shows the active role that the execution played in Delacroix's apprehension of the subject. The sensuality of the composition resulted from his handling of material substance, a process that modified his initial understanding. His imagination was sparked during the execution phase: execution is also creation. In 1849, twenty-one years after exhibiting the work, Delacroix, now better in control of his craft, criticized the seductiveness of color, as if he had once again yielded to the facility of the brush, a temptation he had denounced in 1824. "My palette is no longer what it was. It may be less brilliant, but it no longer loses its way. It is an instrument that plays only what I want it to play." Delacroix also observed in 1849 that in 1827 or 1828, the overall spirit of the composition had been altered by the execution of a single element—the body of one of the figures.

In a sense, Sardanapalus, both greedy for and detached from the surging wave of objects and bodies, is the artist's

double. Delacroix was the organizer of the sadistic conflagration, the compulsive collector of his own most beautifully painted elements, which he liked to pile up and spread out in precarious equilibrium, at the risk of seeing them collapse and overflow their boundaries. Delacroix filled the composition with everything he knew how to paint, everything he had ardently elaborated in virtuoso studies during his early years: clothing, jewelry, fabrics, babouches, weapons and gold, male and female nudes, horses, multiple shades of skin (see cats. 9, 11, 12, 14–16, 34; fig. 22). The welter accounts for the impression of confusion decried by Delécluze, who failed to understand that this apparent flaw was meant to render the chaos of imminent destruction: "The spectator was unable to penetrate a subject whose every element is isolated, where the eye cannot disentangle the confusion of lines and colors."[113]

Although he focused his attention on the details, Delacroix gave some of the figures a new inflection. While the woman in the foreground brilliantly displays the artist's fidelity to the model, and the man with raised arms at the far right along with his desperate companion recall Gros's naturalistic prototypes in *Napoleon Visiting the Plague Victims of Jaffa* and *Embarkation of Marie-Thérèse, Duchess of Angoulême, at Pauillac* (1818; Musée des Beaux-Arts, Bordeaux), the faces of Sardanapalus and the women in the background have simplified features.[114] About 1827, Delacroix, inspired by Moghul manuscripts, medieval engravings, Indian paintings, and ancient coins (see cats. 20, 21), sought to stylize his brushstroke. He now insisted on profiles drawn with sharp edges: modeling was replaced by linear contours, and the forms became more geometric. In that move toward primitivism, he was trying not only to imprint an Oriental character on his composition but also, through a more synthetic approach, to free himself from the tyranny of the model and restore a certain ideality.

Delacroix and the Question of the Hero

The image of the ruler of Nineveh, motionless in the midst of futile turmoil, would be compared to David's *Leonidas at Thermopylae* (1812; Musée du Louvre).[115] Sardanapalus seems to be the negative counterpart of Leonidas. David's masterpiece was formidable at the time, one of his few large paintings then on view. Another was *The Intervention of the Sabine Women* (1799; Musée du Louvre).[116] Both were hanging in the Louvre in March 1826, when Delacroix conceived the idea for *The Death*

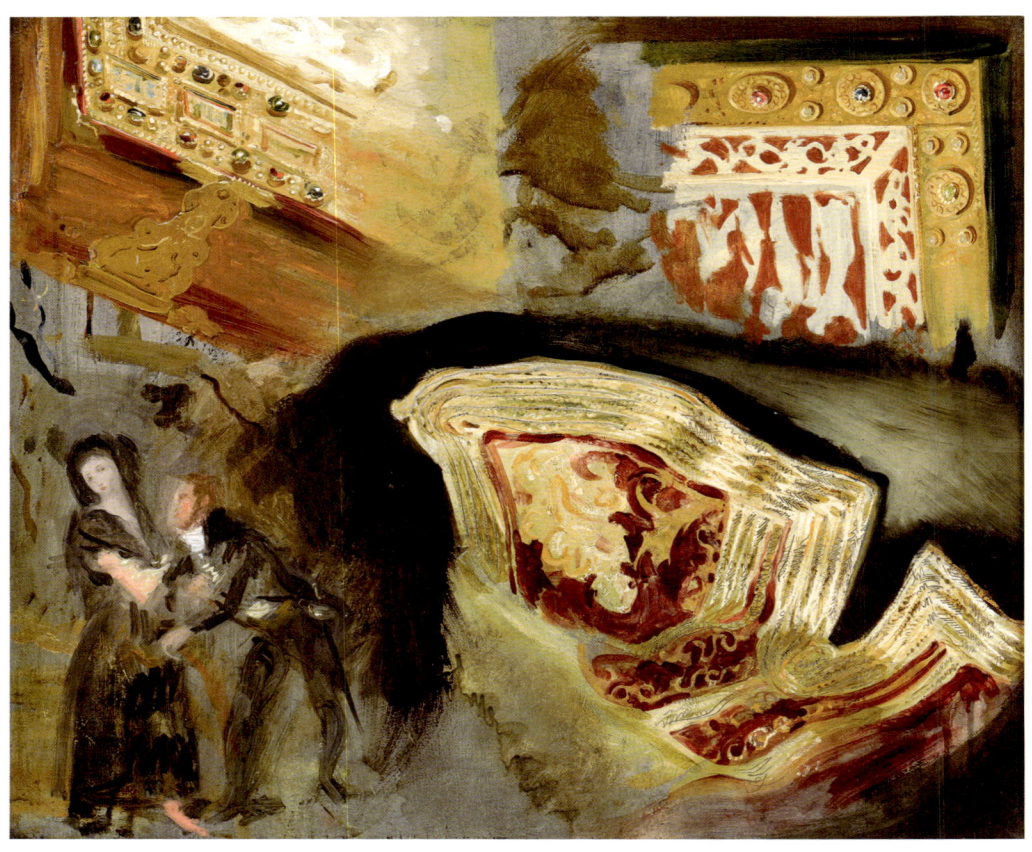

CAT. 14 *Studies of Bindings, an Oriental Jacket, and Figures after Goya,* ca. 1822–26

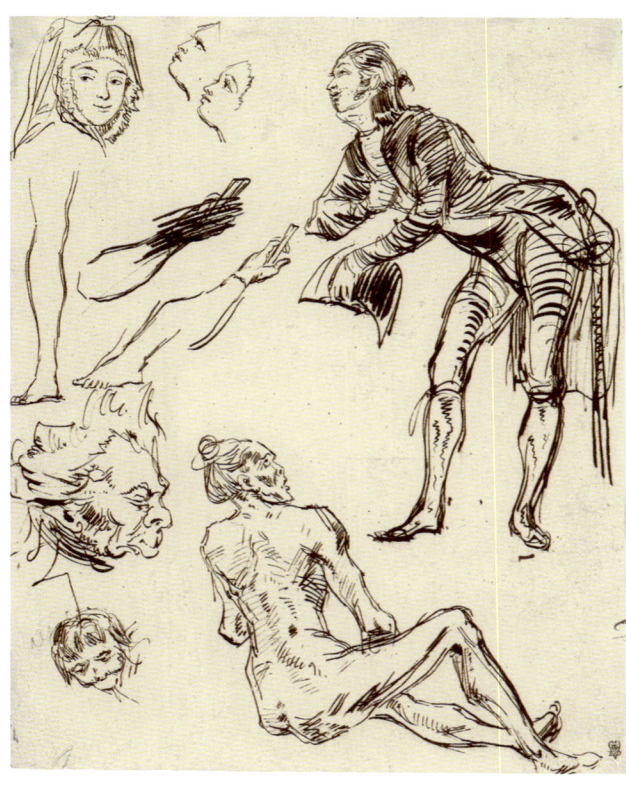

CAT. 11 *Sketch after Goya's "Caprichos,"* ca. 1822–24

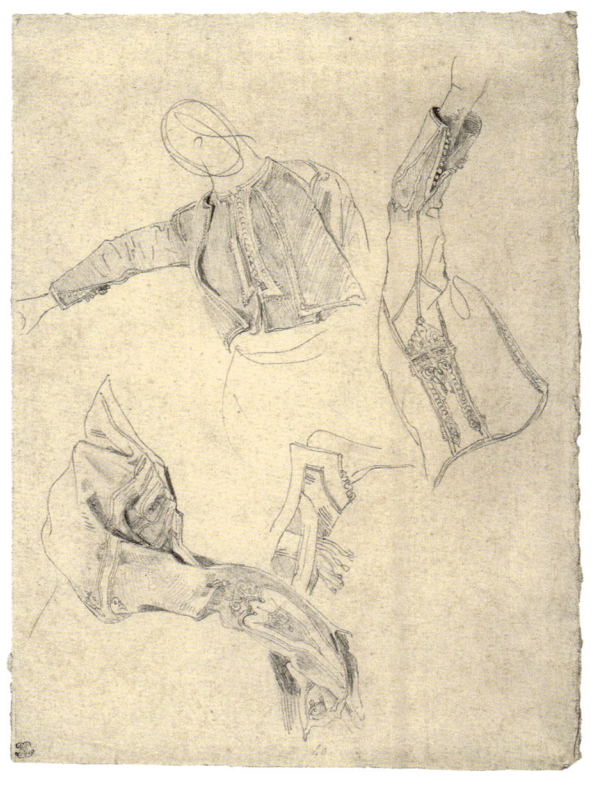

CAT. 16 *Study of Greek Costumes,* ca. 1823–26

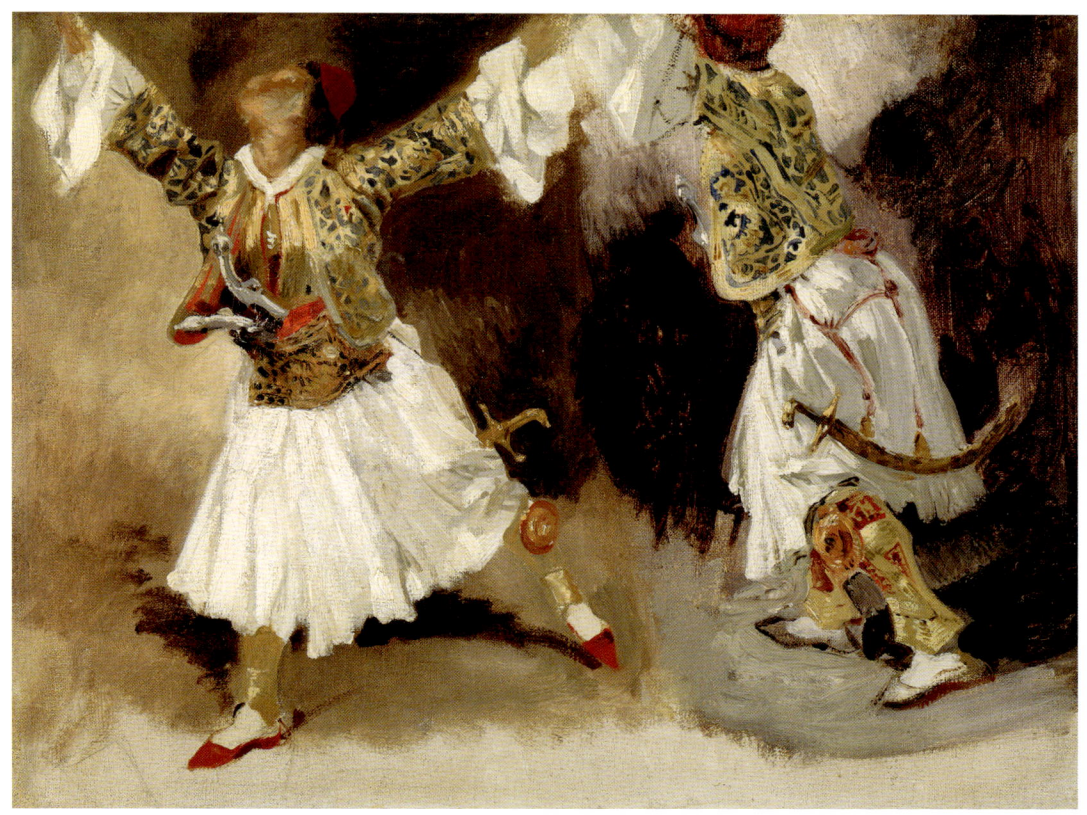

FIG. 22 *Two Studies of a Figure in Greek Costume (Front and Side Views)*, ca. 1823–26. Oil on canvas, 13¾ x 18⅛ in. (35 x 46 cm). Musée du Louvre, Paris (MNR 143) (J 30)

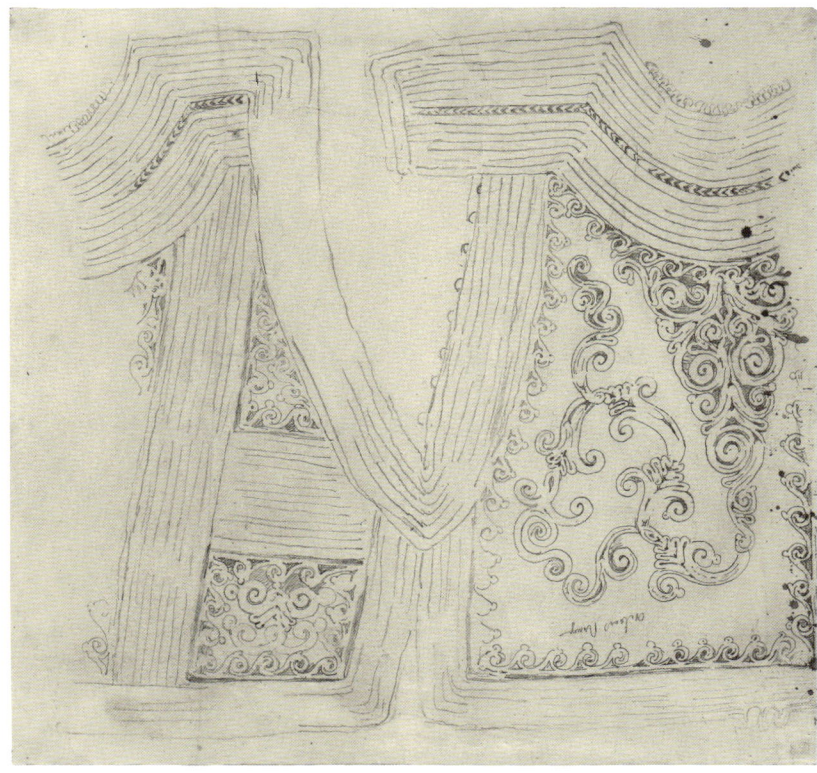

CAT. 15 *Study of an Oriental Vest*, ca. 1822–26

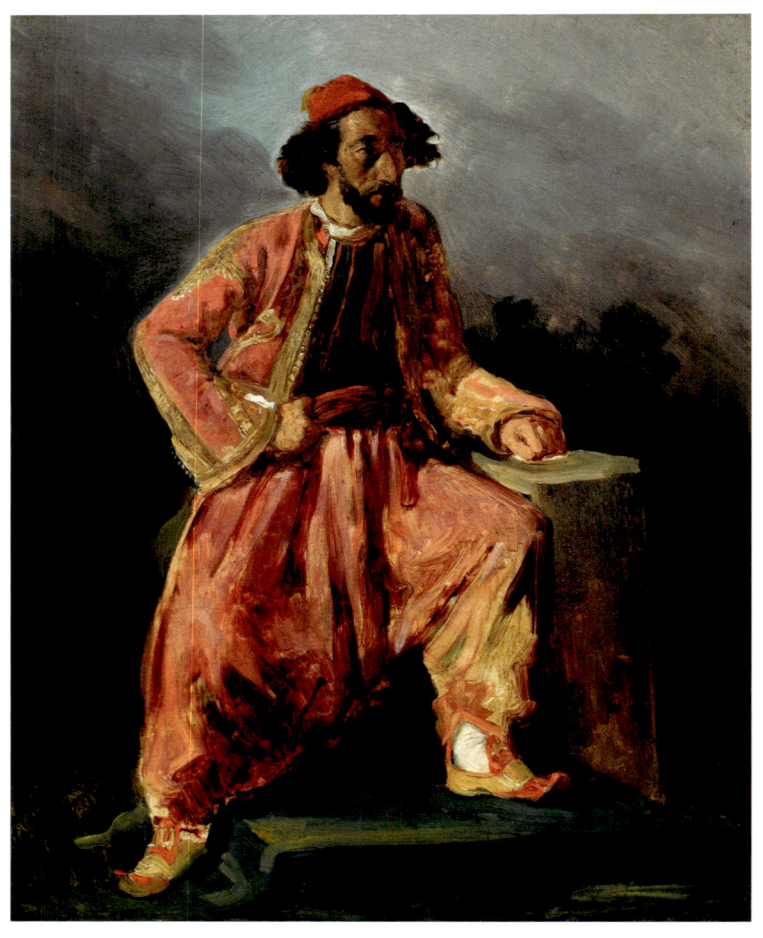

CAT. 34 *Seated Turk (possibly Paul Barroilhet, 1805–1871),*
ca. 1827–30

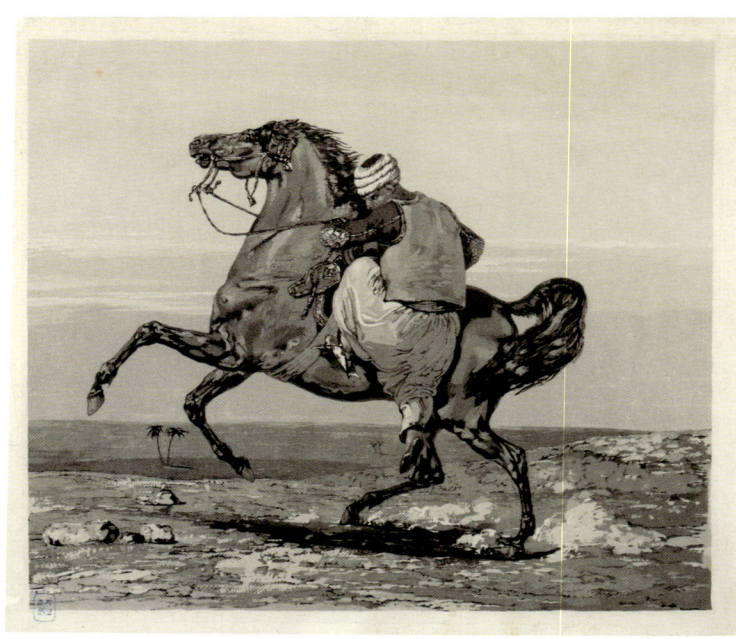

CAT. 9 *Turk Mounting His Horse,* 1824

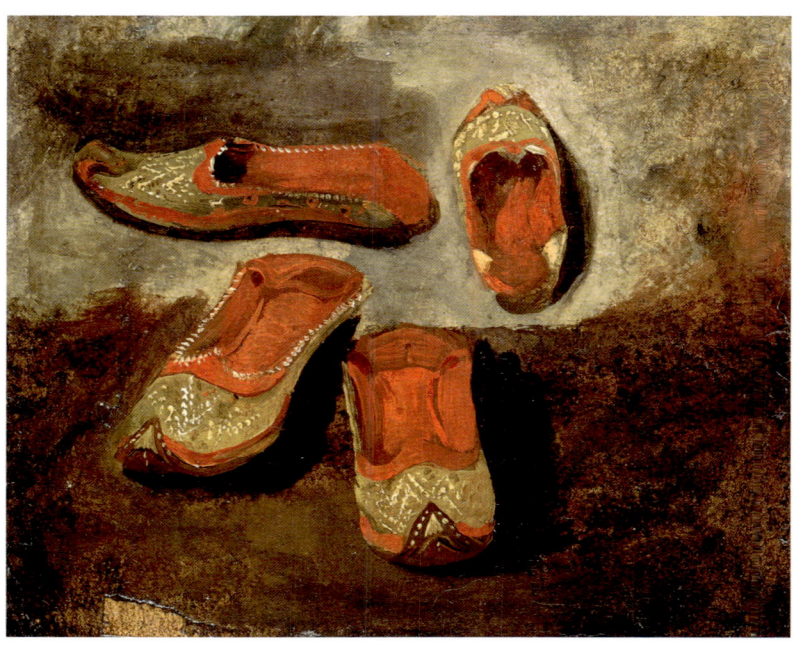

CAT. 12 *Study of Babouches,* ca. 1823–24

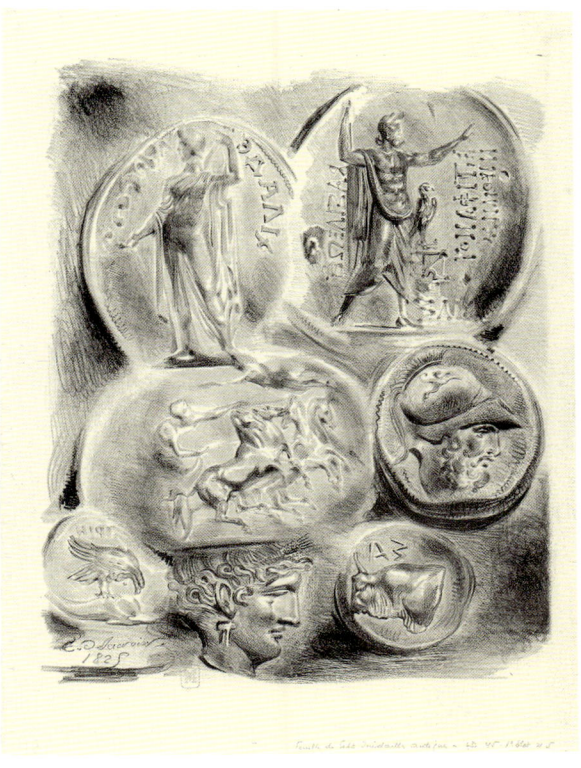

CAT. 20 *Studies of Seven Greek Coins*, 1825

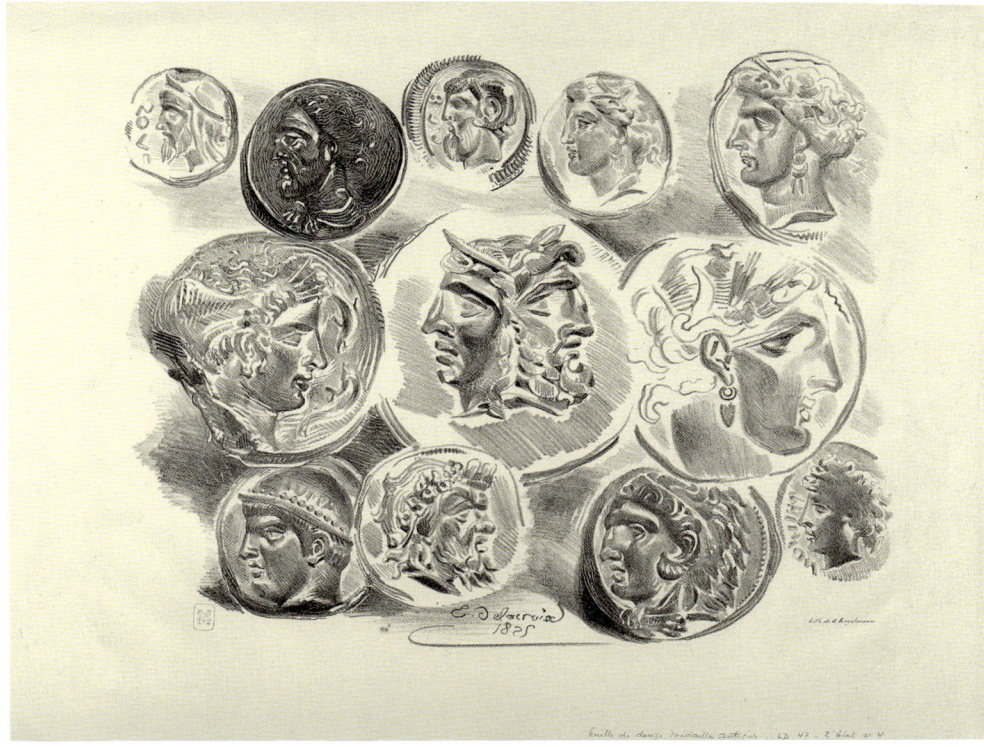

CAT. 21 *Studies of Twelve Greek and Roman Coins*, 1825

of Sardanapalus. In formal terms, the Salon painting, in the way it violated the rules by making the execution phase visible, struck a blow against the Davidian ideal of composition. Furthermore, even with his first works, Delacroix had challenged the heroism traditionally associated with history painting in general and with the *exemplum virtutis* in particular. Delacroix's Sardanapalus, deliberately darker than the figure in Byron's tragedy, is stylized as an egotistical monster, a distant and inaccessible despot in a pose wavering between indolence and melancholy. Unlike Leonidas, he is impervious to the unhappiness around him, which he himself has caused. He is an allegory of immoderation and greed, dwarfed by the mad accumulation of living beings assembled under his final order and for his own pleasure. He appears enigmatic and paradoxical, at once creator, beholder, and destroyer of his own collections.

Delacroix, a child of the Revolution, witness to the glory of empire and the fall of the hero, was a man of his generation. As such, he could no longer accept unquestioningly the heroism inherent in history painting. His painting therefore challenged the hero's unique, positive, unifying, and exemplary status. *Massacres at Chios* (fig. 5) even sanctioned the hero's disappearance in favor of a collective of anonymous

men, women, and children whose bruised bodies display the pathos of a vanquished resistance. Very often, Delacroix pushed the hero to the margins of the composition; decentered, he is under threat of losing his preeminent place. Such is the case in *The Battle of Nancy* (cat. 69), commissioned by the Ministère de l'Intérieur in 1828 for the city of Nancy, where the work was to be sent in anticipation of a visit by King Charles X. The subject, the death of Charles the Bold, was assigned to the artist after consultation with the city's Société Royale des Sciences, Lettres et Arts.[117] Just as *Massacres at Chios* paid tribute to Gros's *Napoleon Visiting the Plague Victims of Jaffa*, this composition is a reinterpretation of Gros's *Napoleon on the Battlefield of Eylau* (fig. 23), which had impressed visitors to the Salon of 1808 with its display of frozen corpses in the foreground. The Battle of Nancy took place on January 5, 1477, and it inspired in Delacroix the original idea for a field of ice and snow. In the magnificent sketch (fig. 24), he even replicated the topography of the battlefield of Eylau, a feature that Dominique Vivant Denon, the director general of museums, had required for the competition Gros won in 1808. Conceived as a vast landscape in which the warm effects of a sky at dusk enter into dialogue

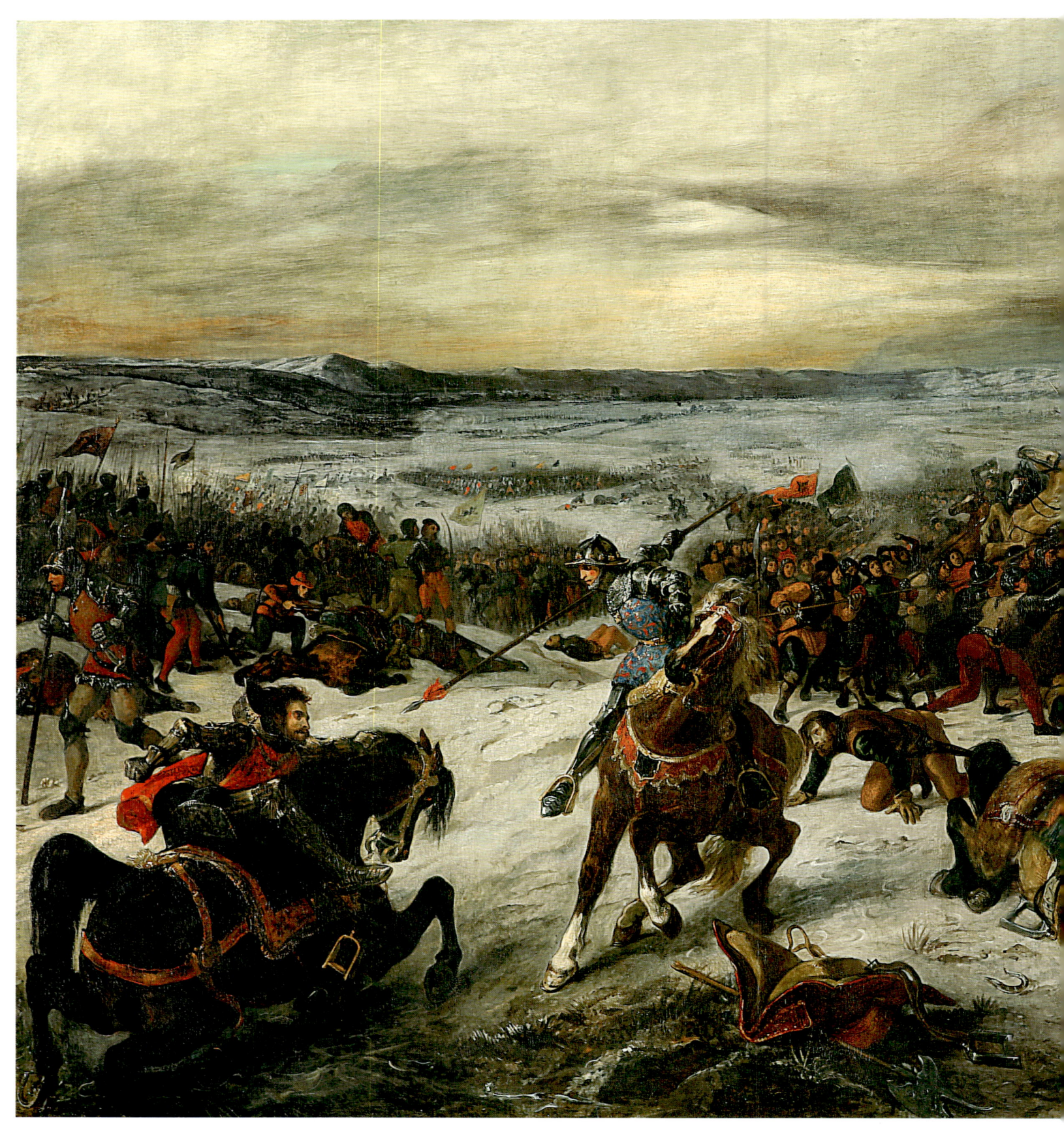

CAT. 69 *The Battle of Nancy and the Death of Charles the Bold, Duke of Burgundy, January 5, 1477, 1831*

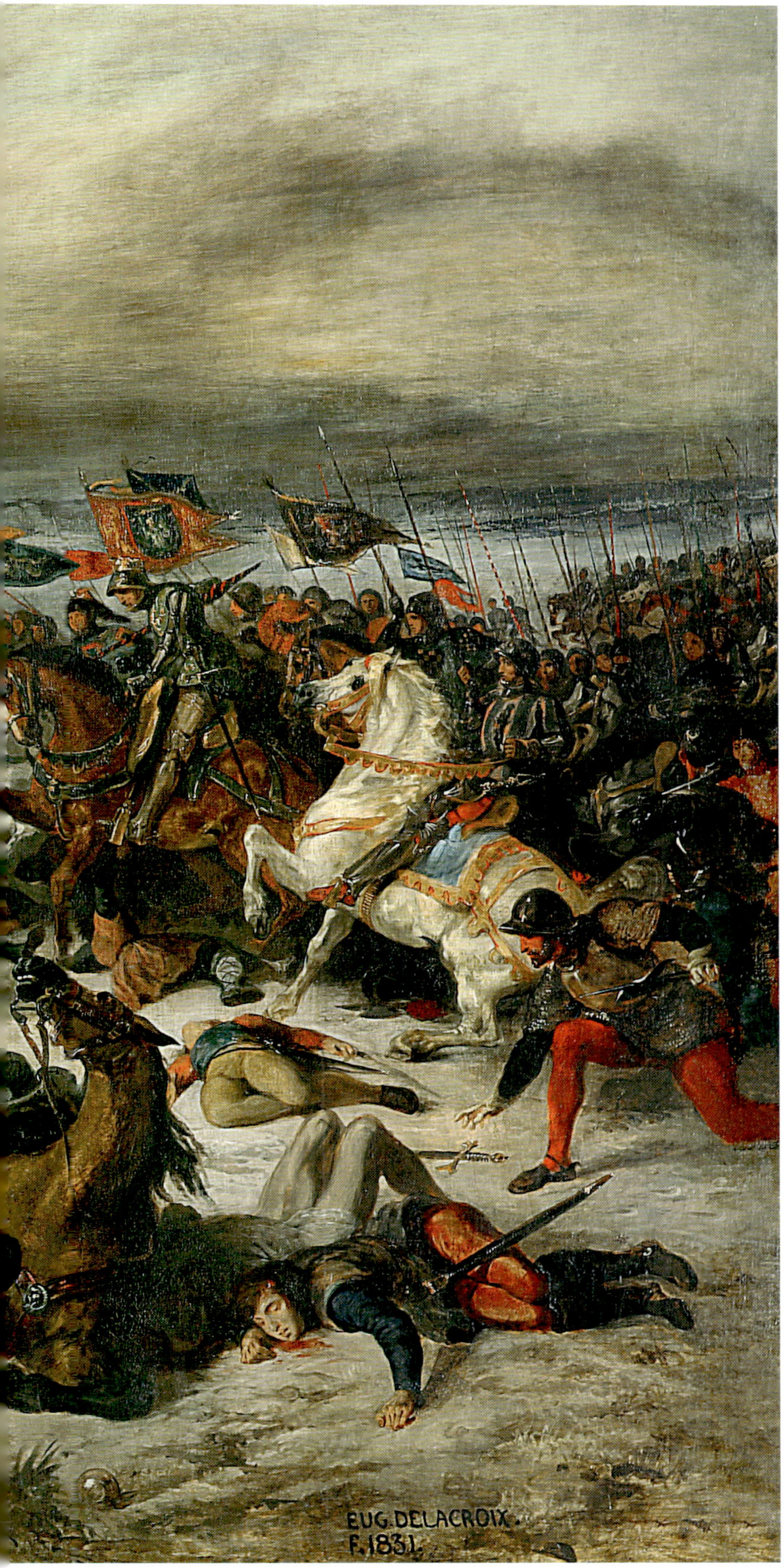

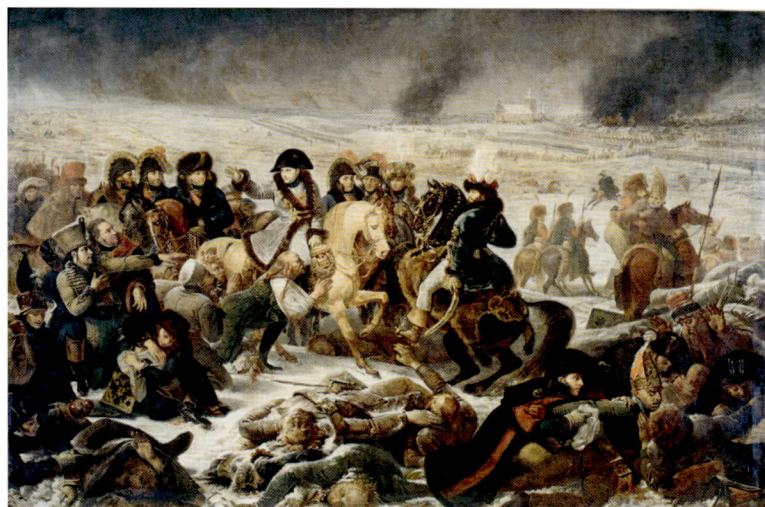

FIG. 23 Antoine Jean Gros (French, 1771–1835). *Napoleon on the Battlefield of Eylau, February 9, 1807*, 1808. Oil on canvas, 17 ft. 1½ in. x 25 ft. 8¹¹⁄₁₆ in. (5.2 x 7.8 m). Musée du Louvre, Paris (5067)

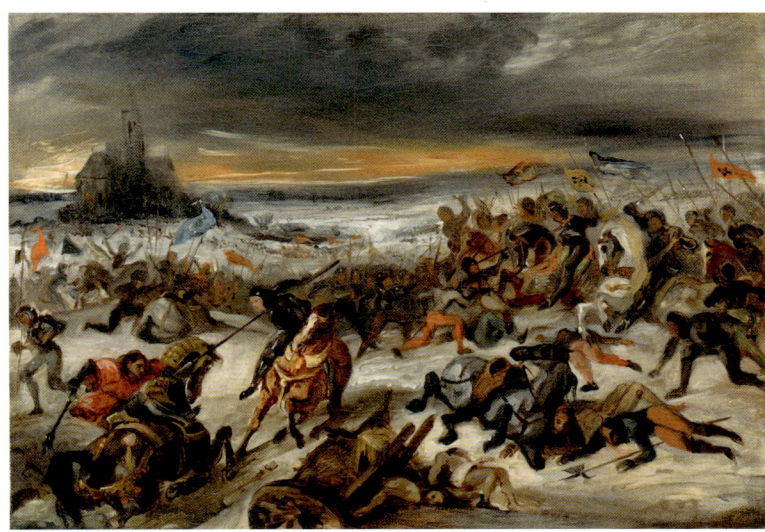

FIG. 24 *The Battle of Nancy*, sketch, 1828/29. Oil on canvas, 18½ x 26¾ in. (47 x 68 cm). Ny Carlsberg Glyptotek, Copenhagen (inv. MIN 1905) (J 142)

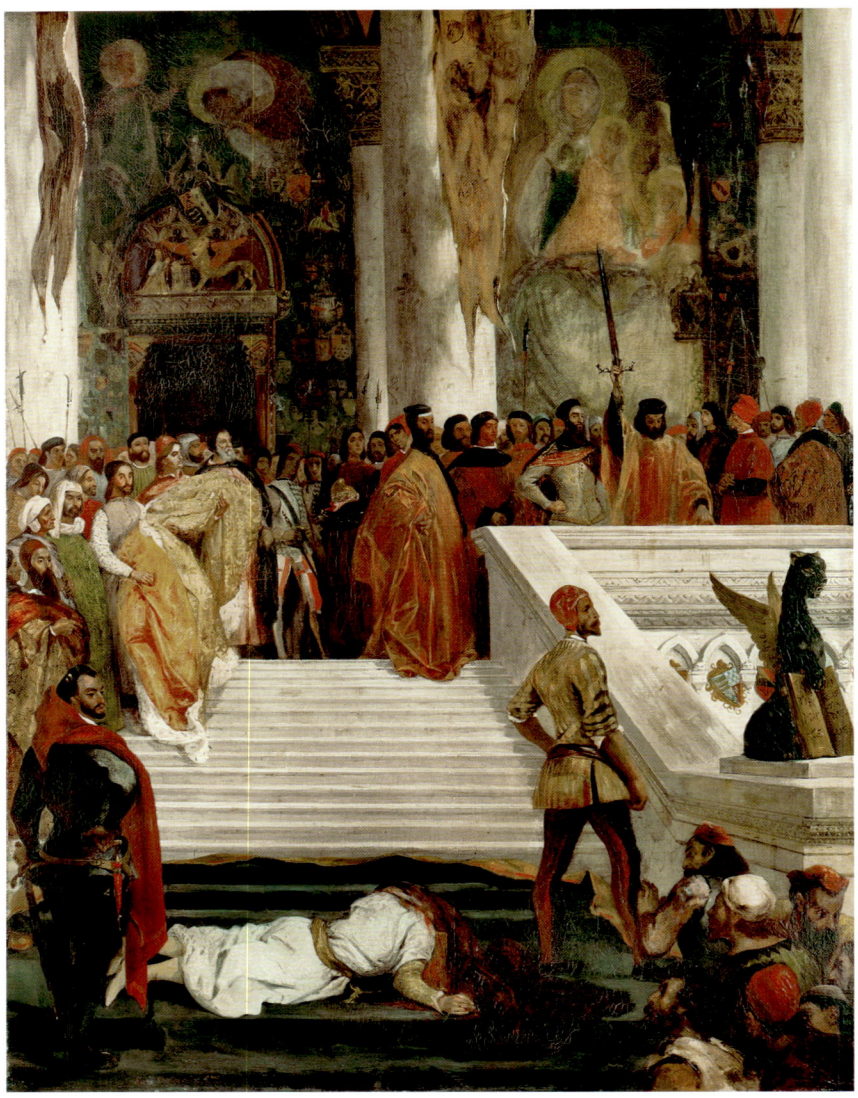

FIG. 25 *The Execution of Doge Marino Faliero*, 1825–26. Oil on canvas, 57⁵⁄₁₆ x 44¹³⁄₁₆ in. (145.6 x 113.8 cm). The Wallace Collection, London (inv. P282) (J 112)

with the coldness of the frozen, uneven ground, the painting is, effectively, in search of a hero: Charles the Bold is being pushed outside the frame, and therefore out of history, by the long spear of an anonymous knight. Once again, Delacroix reversed the conceit of his model, in which the emperor arrives as a hero to reestablish order through clemency.

The Execution of Doge Marino Faliero (fig. 25) was inspired by Byron's tragic drama *Marino Faliero, Doge of Venice* and was displayed for the first time in the 1826 exhibition held as a benefit for the Greeks. In Delacroix's painting, the doge's decapitated corpse lies at the foot of the stairs, his neck still on the block, and his head, which has fallen to the ground, hidden under a cloth. The executioner turns away from the corpse, while on the balcony above him, a member of the

Council of Ten exhibits the blade—the instrument of justice— to the people, who are gathered outside the spectator's view. The composition is devoid of psychology and violent action. To borrow Auguste Jal's formulation, the artist "presented the cold denouement of a tragedy whose movements are hidden from us."¹¹⁸ The center of the painting is an empty white staircase, an expression of deposed power symbolized by the lifeless body that has fallen to the level of the plebs ready to invade the court of the Doge's Palace. The staircase separates two intensely colored spaces, warmer at the top, cooler at the bottom. The force of history lies not in the body of the hero executed for high treason but in the accessories, the *corno ducale* (ducal hat) and the enormous gold mantle, that have been carried to the top of the steps.

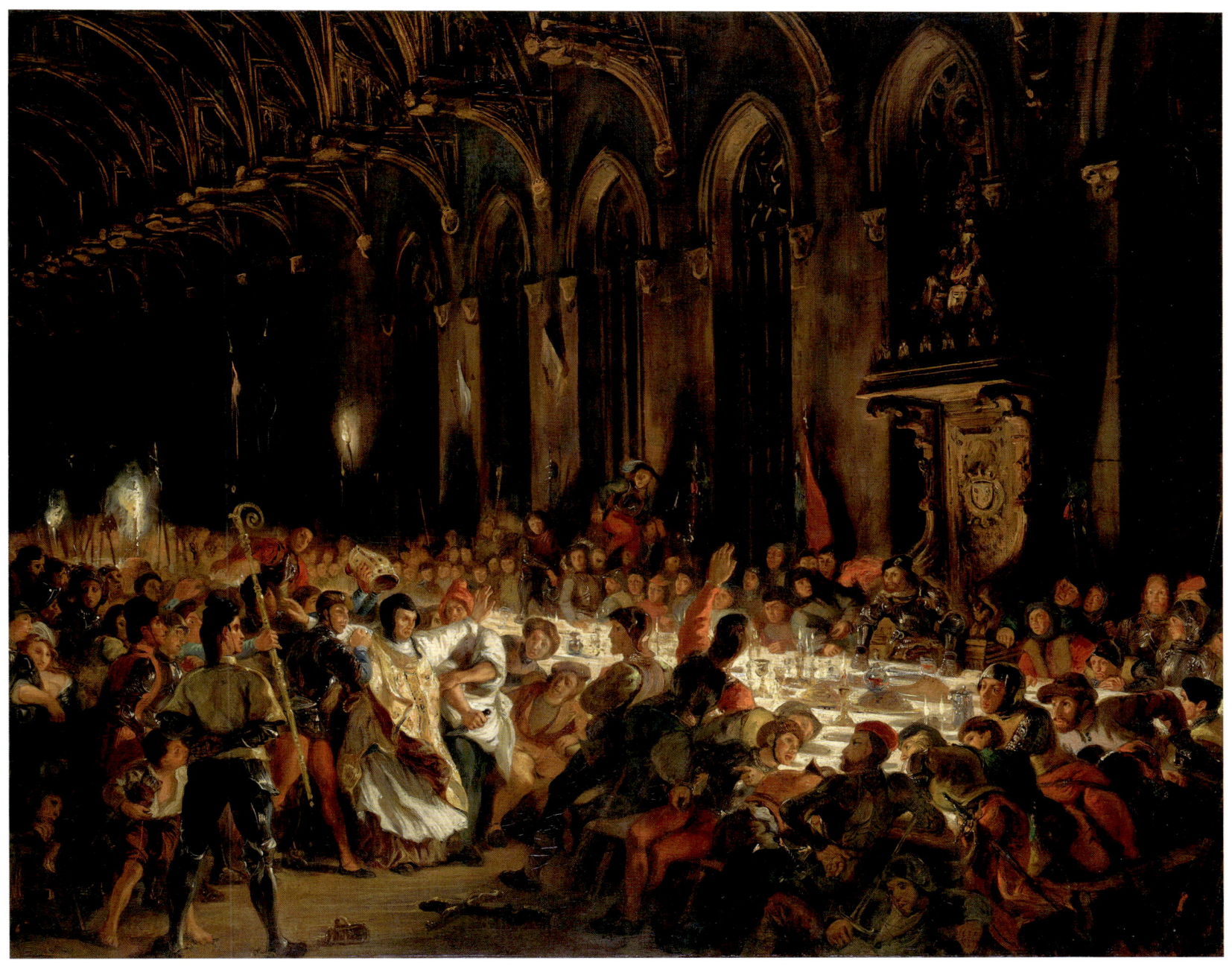

CAT. 64 *The Murder of the Bishop of Liège*, 1829

The high stakes of power and death are conveyed by the rhetoric of gesture, which is relegated to the middle ground, and also by the deployment of textiles—by color. The yellow underside of the blue carpet on which the doge's corpse lies mirrors the gold of the ducal robe. The violence of the scene is expressed by dabs of red scattered through the composition (the executioner's cloak, the patricians' clothing, the men's caps), conjuring blood. As in *Massacres at Chios* and *Greece on the Ruins of Missolonghi* (see cat. 26), blood is depicted in the foreground, where it streams onto the block and soaks into the carpet. The splendor of the fabrics displayed in the upper

register is sullied by the doge's execution below. The result is an ambiguous composition in which, to borrow Ludovic Vitet's expression, "jokers will surely say that the main character is the staircase."[119] The work undermines the classical rules of history painting, which require a clearly expressed moral lesson. Here, a state ceremonial is deprived of a hero.

The Murder of the Bishop of Liège (cat. 64) is as animated as *Marino Faliero* is static. In this work, inspired by Sir Walter Scott's historical novel *Quentin Durward,* published in 1823, Delacroix was less interested in the tragic hero than in the violent encounter between the bishop, who is being stripped

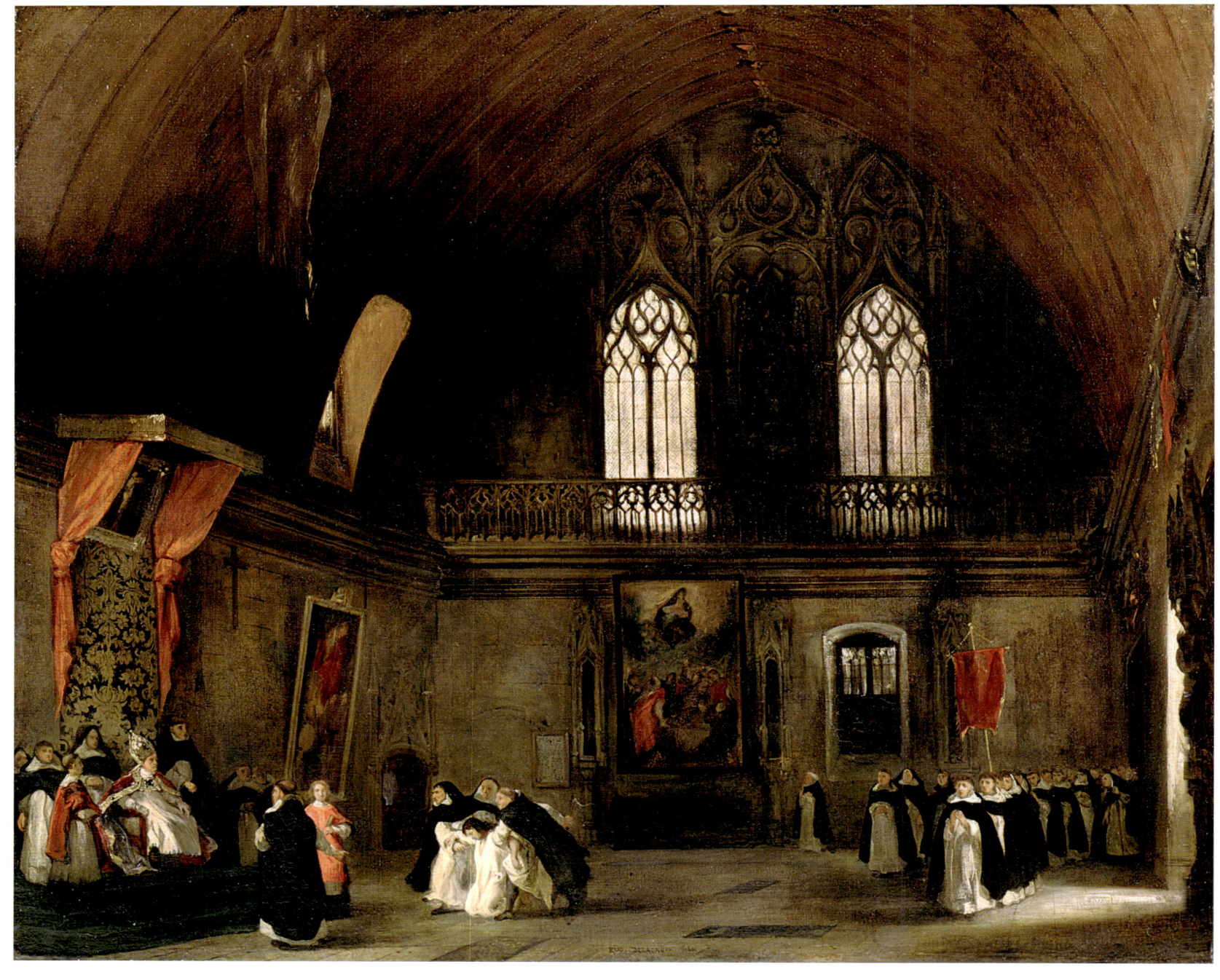

CAT. 71 *Interior of a Dominican Convent in Madrid (L'Amende Honorable)*, 1831

of his liturgical props, and the ferocious William de la Marck, "the wild boar of the Ardennes." Architecture is a full-fledged actor in this and other of the artist's works from the 1820s in which dramas play out before spectators. *Marino Faliero's* large staircase shows the influence of theater on Delacroix, and *The Murder of the Bishop of Liège* and *Interior of a Dominican Convent in Madrid (L'Amende Honorable)* (cat. 71) attest to the impressions he formed during visits to historical monuments, including the Gothic halls of the Palais de Justice in Rouen and of Westminster Abbey in London.

The assassination scene takes place during a banquet: the exaggerated perspective, accentuated by the brilliance of the white tablecloth, structures the composition; like the marble staircase in *Marino Faliero*, the banquet table separates the protagonists. The physiognomy and attitude of the executioner are similar to those in *A Blacksmith* (cat. 80), etched at nearly the same time. Armed with a crude knife, he is shown rolling up his sleeves to do his dirty work. The impression of a stifling atmosphere, rendered by the warm colors, chiaroscuro, gleaming glasses, light of the torches, vast crowd,

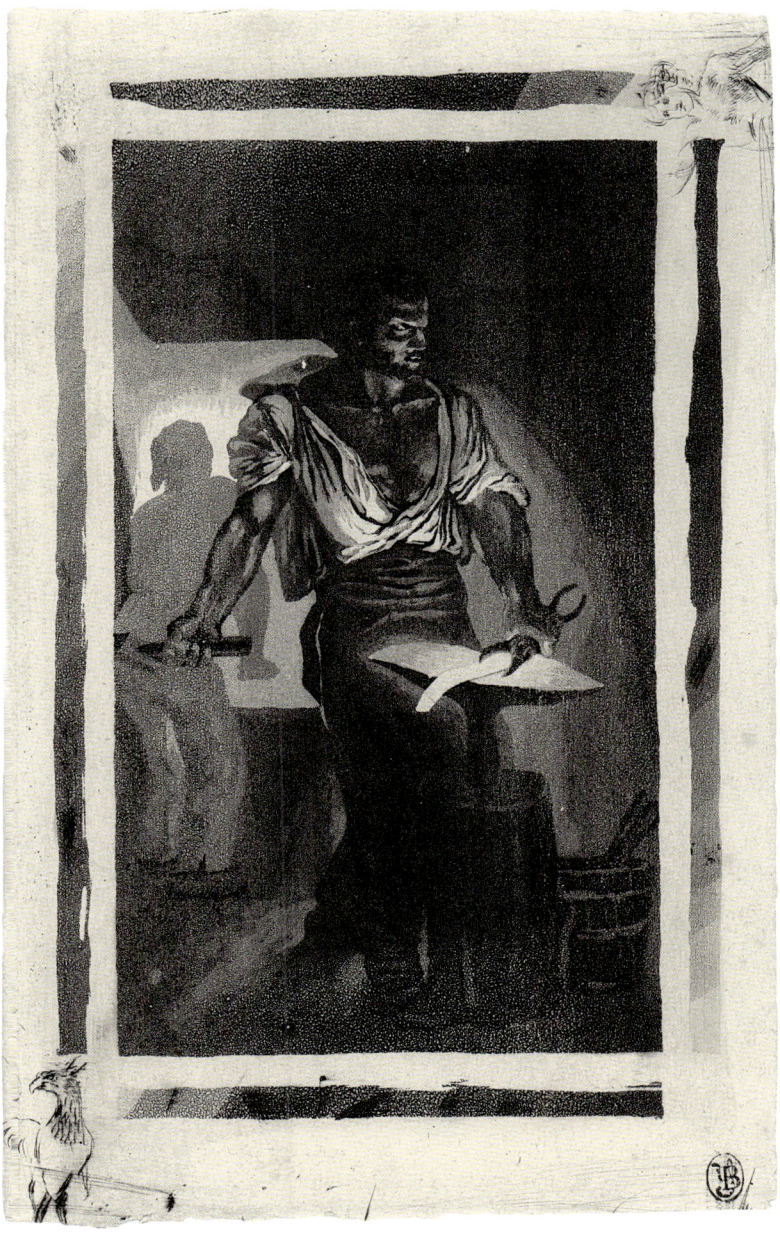

guests' brutal, frenetic body language, and accumulation of ruddy faces resembling grimacing masks would spark memories of the massacres perpetrated during the Revolution and, for those viewing the painting a few years later, the sack of the archbishop's palace in Paris, which took place in February 1831. What is depicted is less an individual story than a violent spectacle in which, as Alain Corbin argues, a mob creates a bloody representation of itself.[120] Gautier described the painting well: "This little canvas screams, vociferates, blasphemes . . . you hear the obscene songs of that drunken rabble of soldiers.

What brigands they make! What jovial and bloodthirsty brutality! How they swarm and yelp, how they blaze and reek!"[121]

When the hero does not melt into the anonymity of a collective, when he is not pushed to the margins of the composition, he is very often split in two to convey the complementary and dialectical facets of a divided humanity: animal instincts and divine aspirations, good and evil, emotion and reason. Introduced in 1822 with *The Barque of Dante*, the theme of the double was developed in Delacroix's prints, particularly the series of lithographs inspired by *Faust,* which the publisher Motte commissioned to accompany Albert Stapfer's 1823 French translation of Goethe's tragedy (see cats. 36–56). The print series was published in 1828, but Delacroix seems to have taken an interest in the subject considerably earlier. In 1824, he wrote in his *Journal* of his interest in engravings after Faust that he had seen. They were probably either the prints done by the German painter Peter Cornelius beginning in 1811 and published in 1816, or those by Moritz Retzsch, published the same year. His interest was aroused again by the spectacular theatrical performance of George Soane and Daniel Terry's *Devil and Dr. Faustus,* loosely based on Goethe's play, that he attended in London in 1825. The painter presented an original interpretation that would captivate Goethe himself. Taking advantage of the narrative possibilities created by the series format, he focused primarily on the reciprocal evolution of the hero and his evil genius—Marguerite having been destroyed by their relationship from the start. In the earliest prints, such as *Faust Trying to Seduce Marguerite* (see cat. 47), Delacroix represented the two men as monstrously alike. Later on, he tended to give a more human physiognomy to Faust and animalistic features to Mephistopheles (see cat. 53), emphasizing the diabolical and almost schizophrenic character of the partnership prior to its dissolution.

Shortly before, with *Macbeth Consulting the Witches* (see cat. 19), Delacroix had proposed a more ambiguous representation of a hero split in two, threatened by the danger of schizophrenia. This plate epitomizes Romantic lithography. Delacroix reversed the normal practice for the medium: instead of drawing with a lithographic pencil, he covered the stone completely with violent black hatching; then, with a stylus, he drew the shapes and physiognomies, making them emerge literally from the darkness. With the same tool, he released and modulated a flood of light. The virtuosity of the

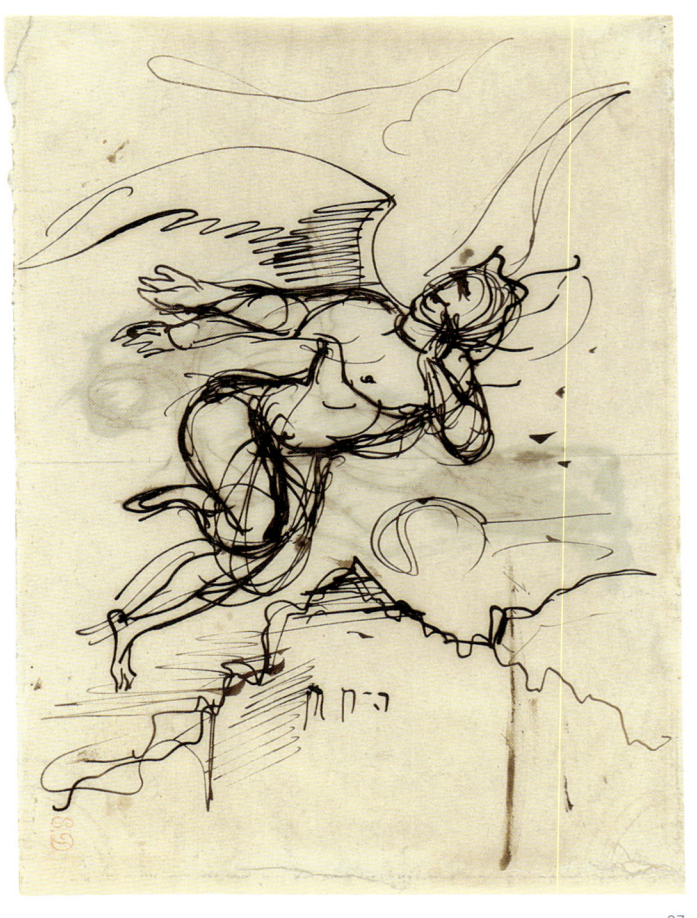

37

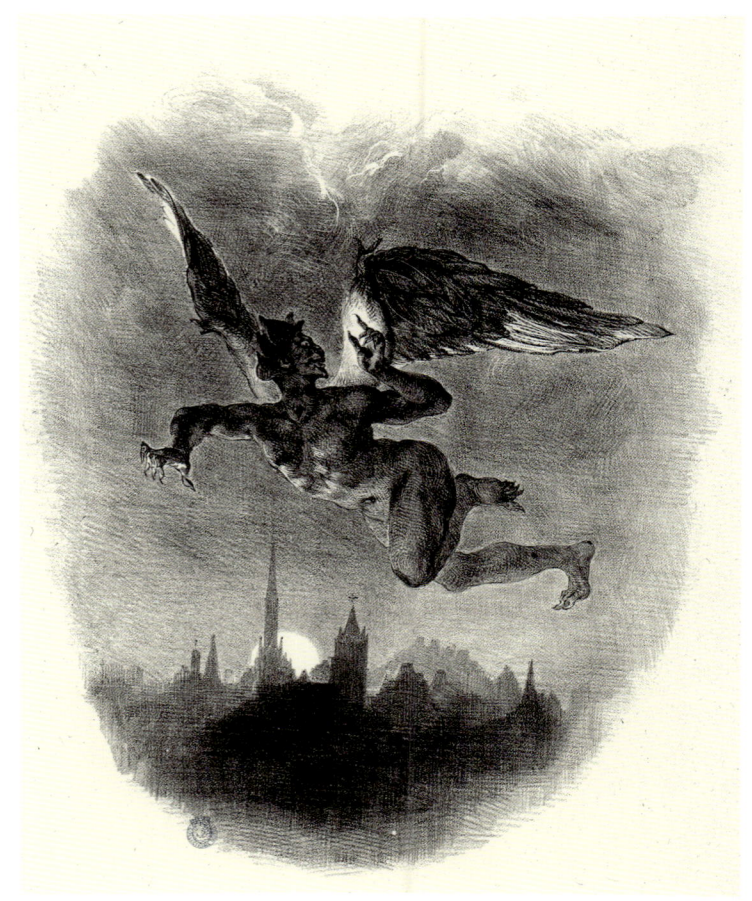

38

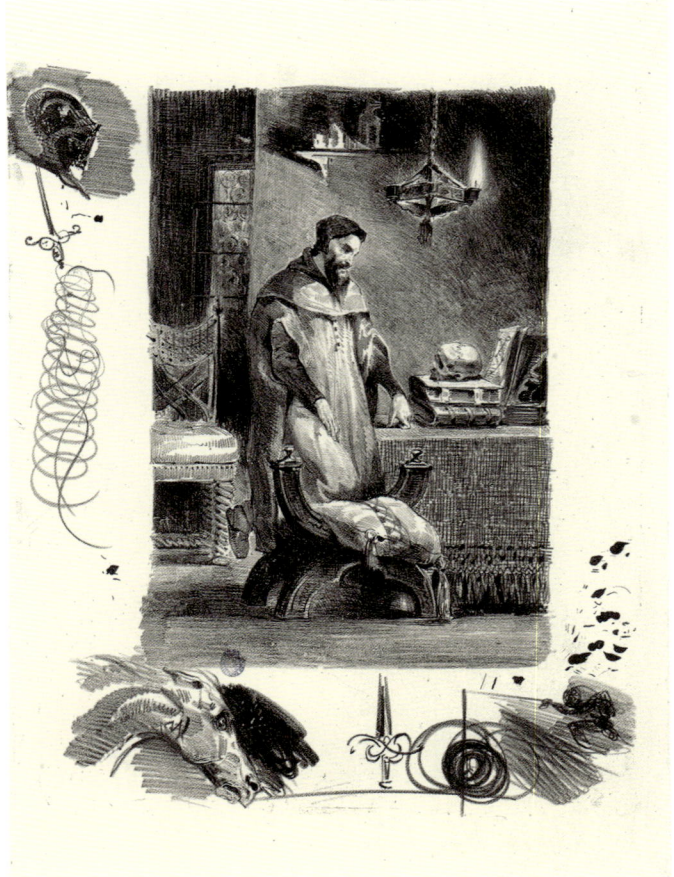

39

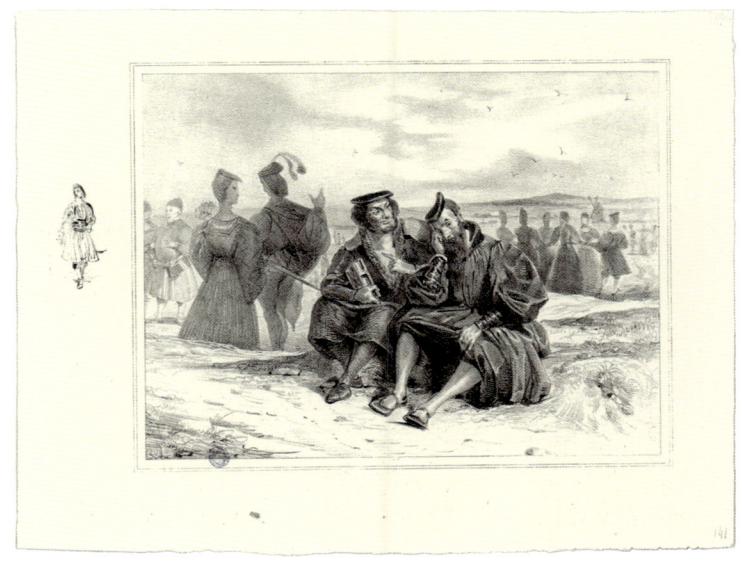

40

CAT. 37 *Mephistopheles Flying over the City
(Study for "Faust," plate 1), ca. 1825–27*

CAT. 38 *Faust, plate 1: Mephistopheles Aloft, 1826/27*

CAT. 39 *Faust, plate 2: Faust in His Study, 1826/27*

CAT. 40 *Faust, plate 3: Faust and Wagner, 1826/27*

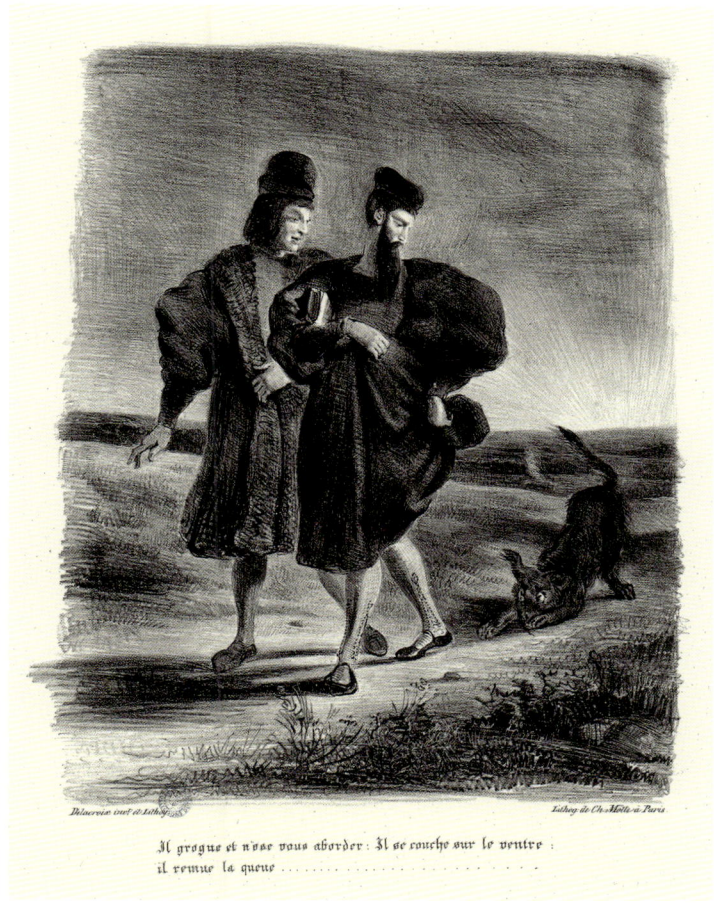

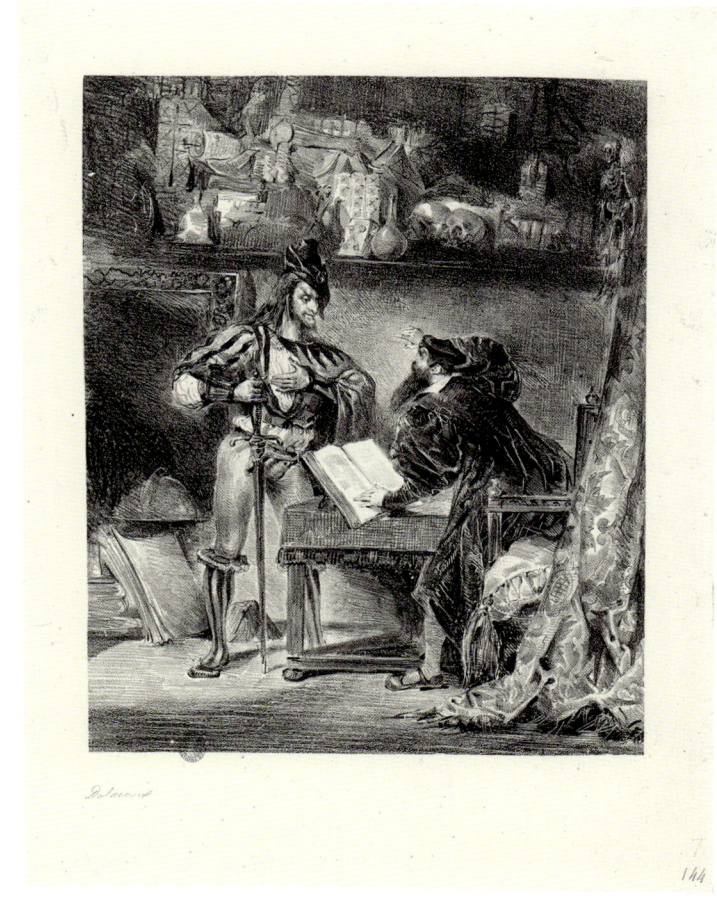

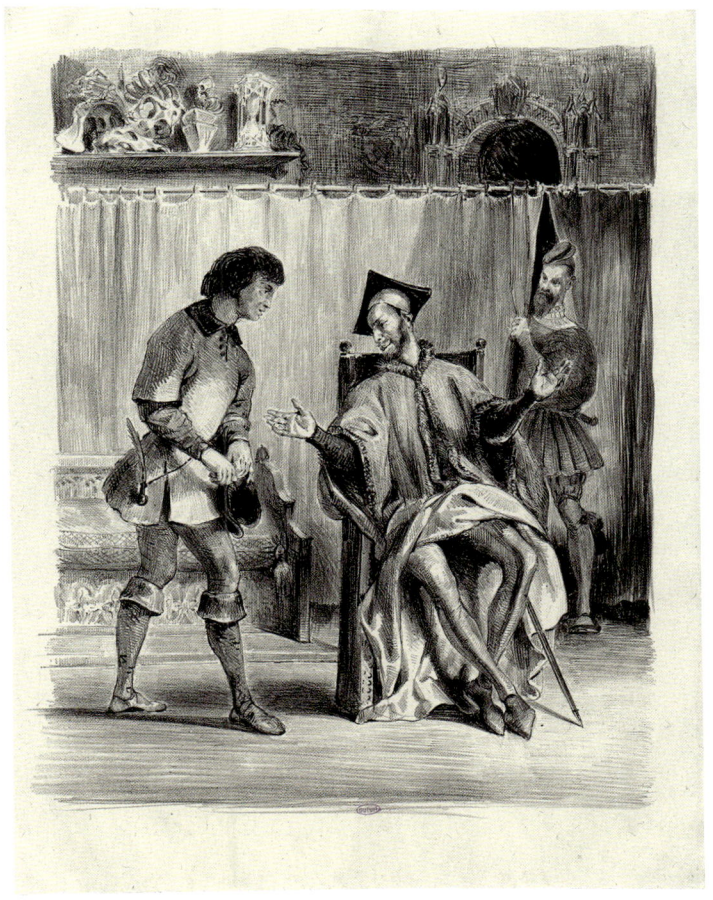

CAT. 41 *Faust, plate 4: Faust, Wagner, and the Poodle, 1826/27*

CAT. 42 *Faust, plate 5: Mephistopheles Appearing to Faust, 1826/27*

CAT. 43 *Faust, plate 6: Mephistopheles Receiving the Student, 1826/27*

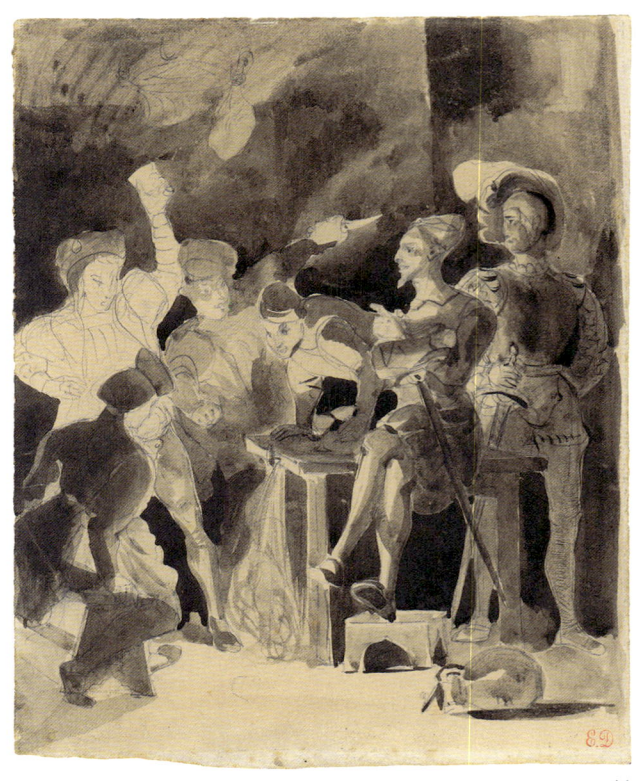

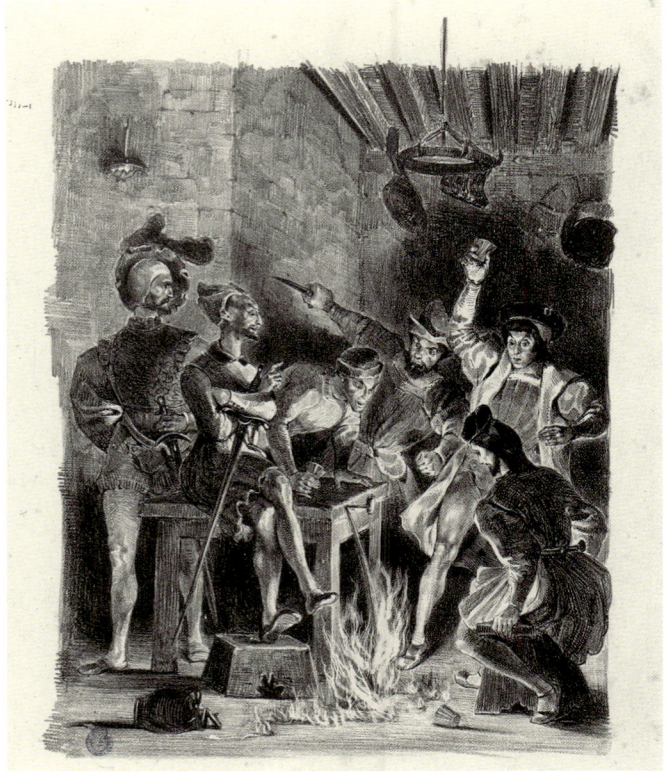

44

45

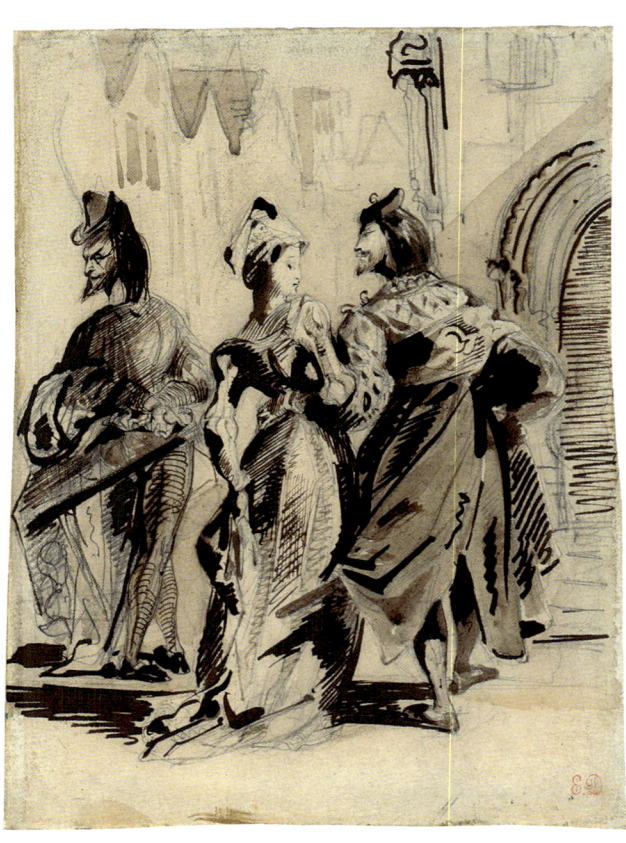

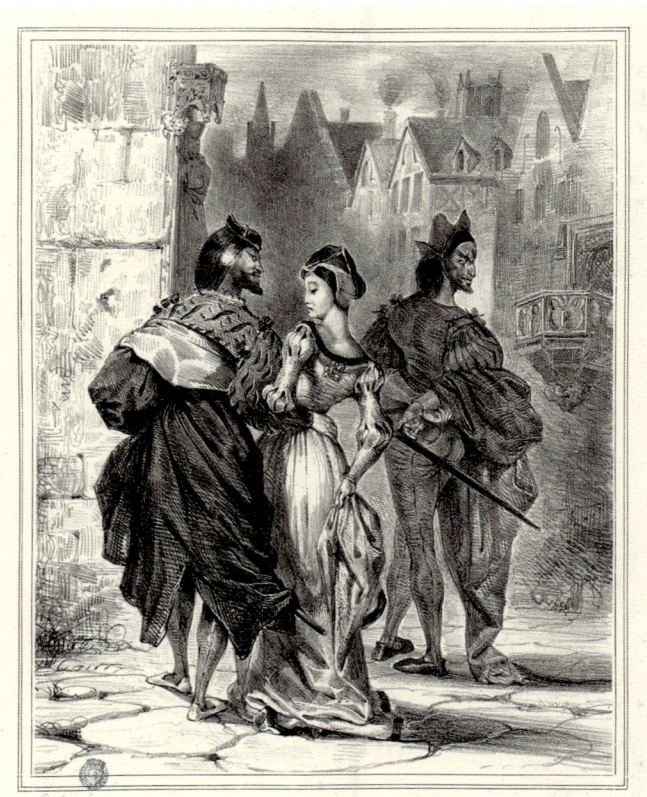

46

47

CAT. 44 *Faust and Mephistopheles in the Tavern (Study for "Faust," plate 7)*, 1825/26

CAT. 45 *Faust, plate 7: Mephistopheles in Auerbach's Tavern*, 1826

CAT. 46 *Faust, Marguerite, and Mephistopheles in the Street (Study for "Faust," plate 8)*, ca. 1825–27

CAT. 47 *Faust, plate 8: Faust Trying to Seduce Marguerite*, 1826/27. For plate 9, see cat. 48

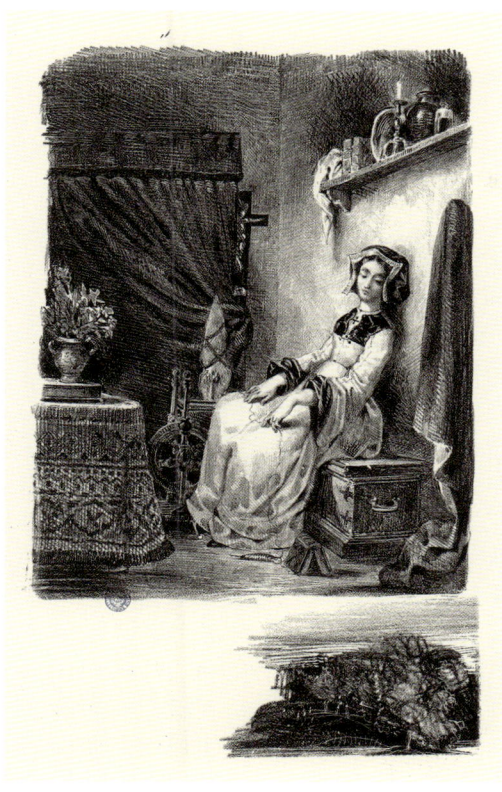

49

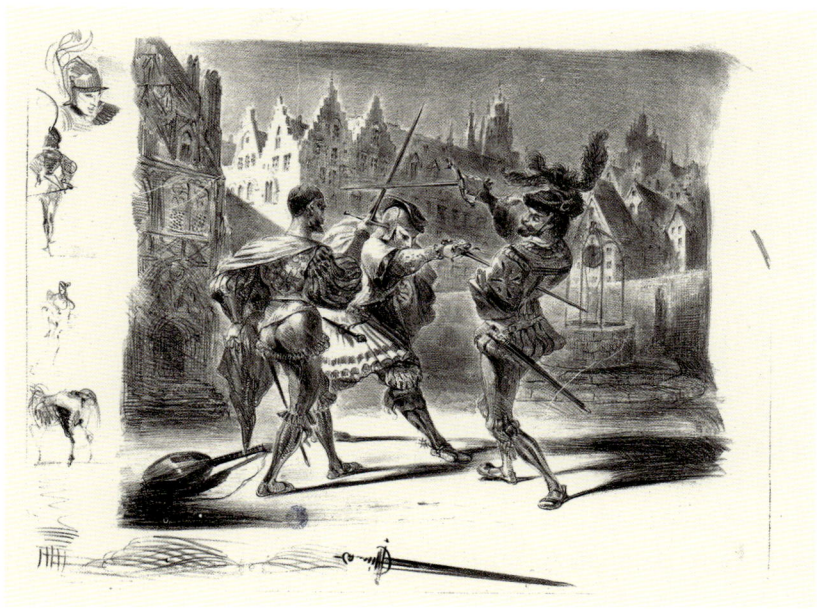

50

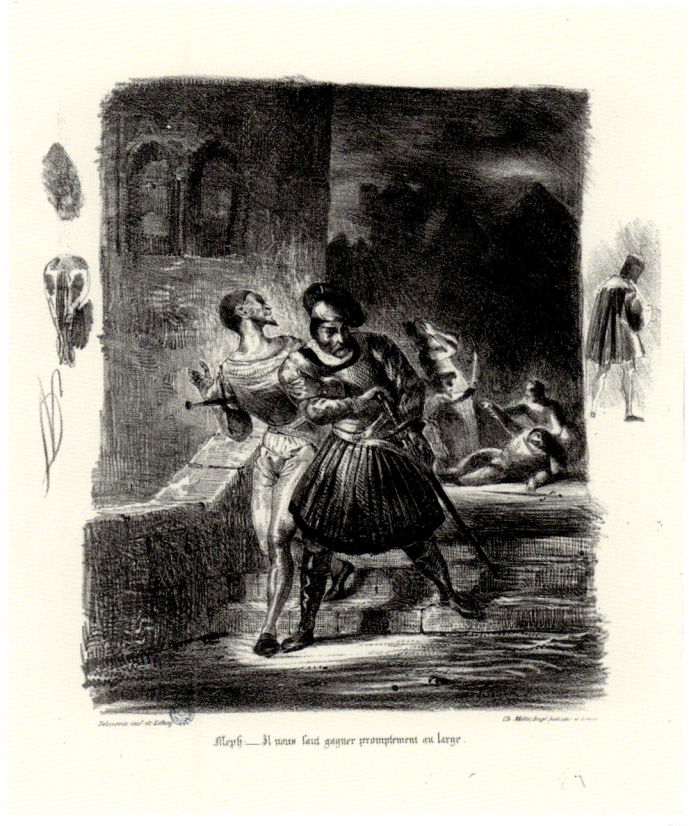

51

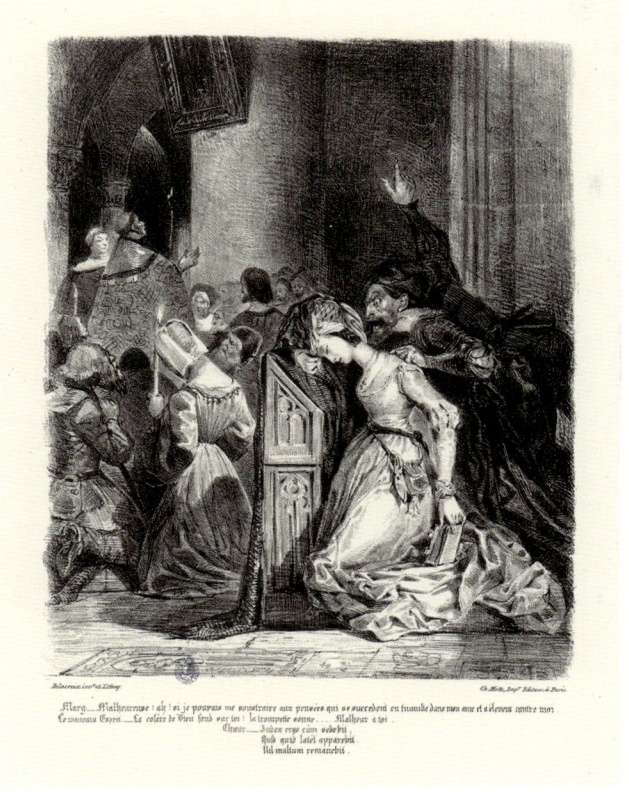

52

CAT. 49 *Faust, plate 10: Marguerite at the Spinning Wheel, 1826/27*

CAT. 50 *Faust, plate 11: Duel between Faust and Valentin, 1826/27*

CAT. 51 *Faust, plate 12: Mephistopheles and Faust Fleeing after the Duel, 1826/27*

CAT. 52 *Faust, plate 13: Marguerite in Church, 1826/27*

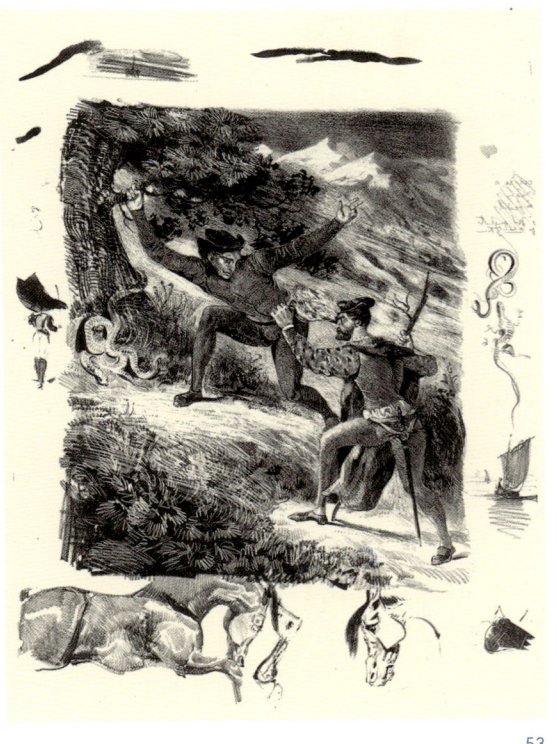

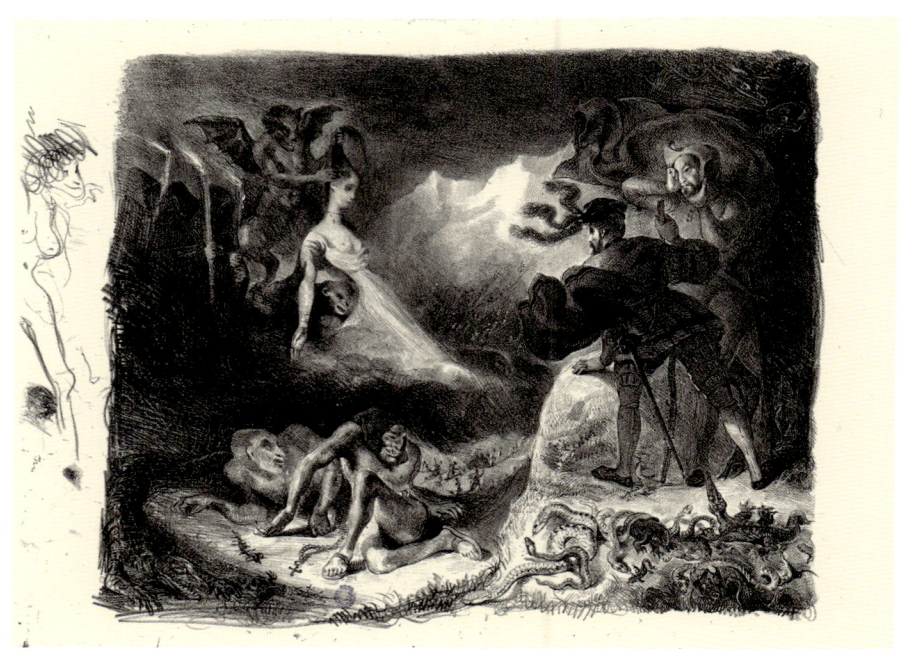

53

54

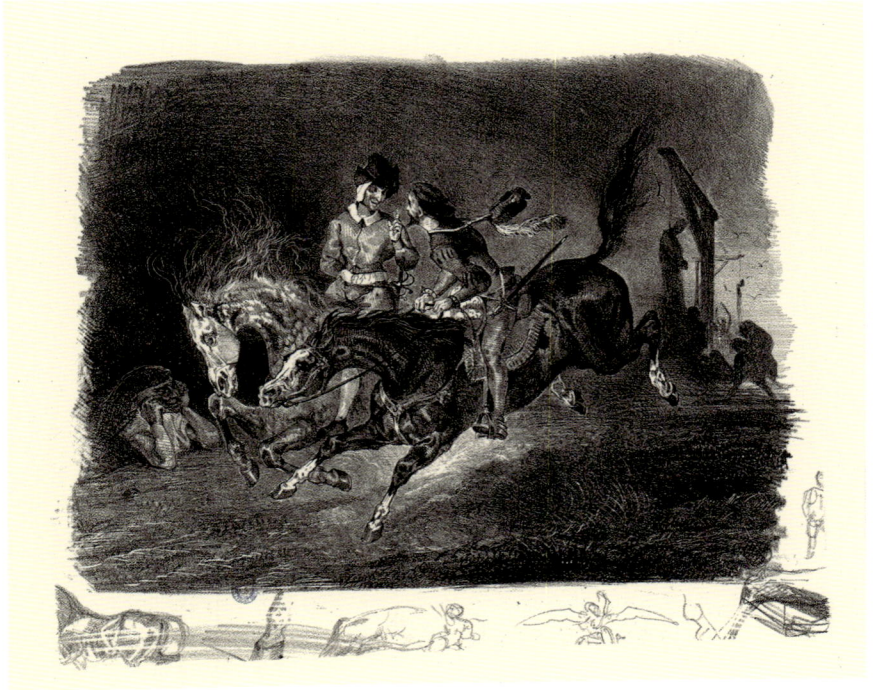

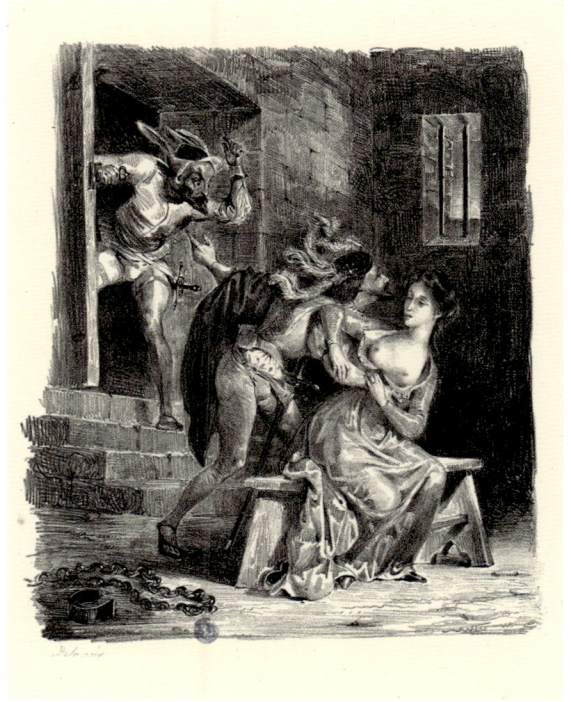

55

56

CAT. 53 *Faust, plate 14: Faust and Mephistopheles in the Harz Mountains, 1826/27*

CAT. 54 *Faust, plate 15: Marguerite's Ghost Appearing to Faust, 1826/27*

CAT. 55 *Faust, plate 16: Faust and Mephistopheles Galloping on Walpurgis Night, 1826*

CAT. 56 *Faust, plate 17: Faust with Marguerite in Prison, 1826/27*

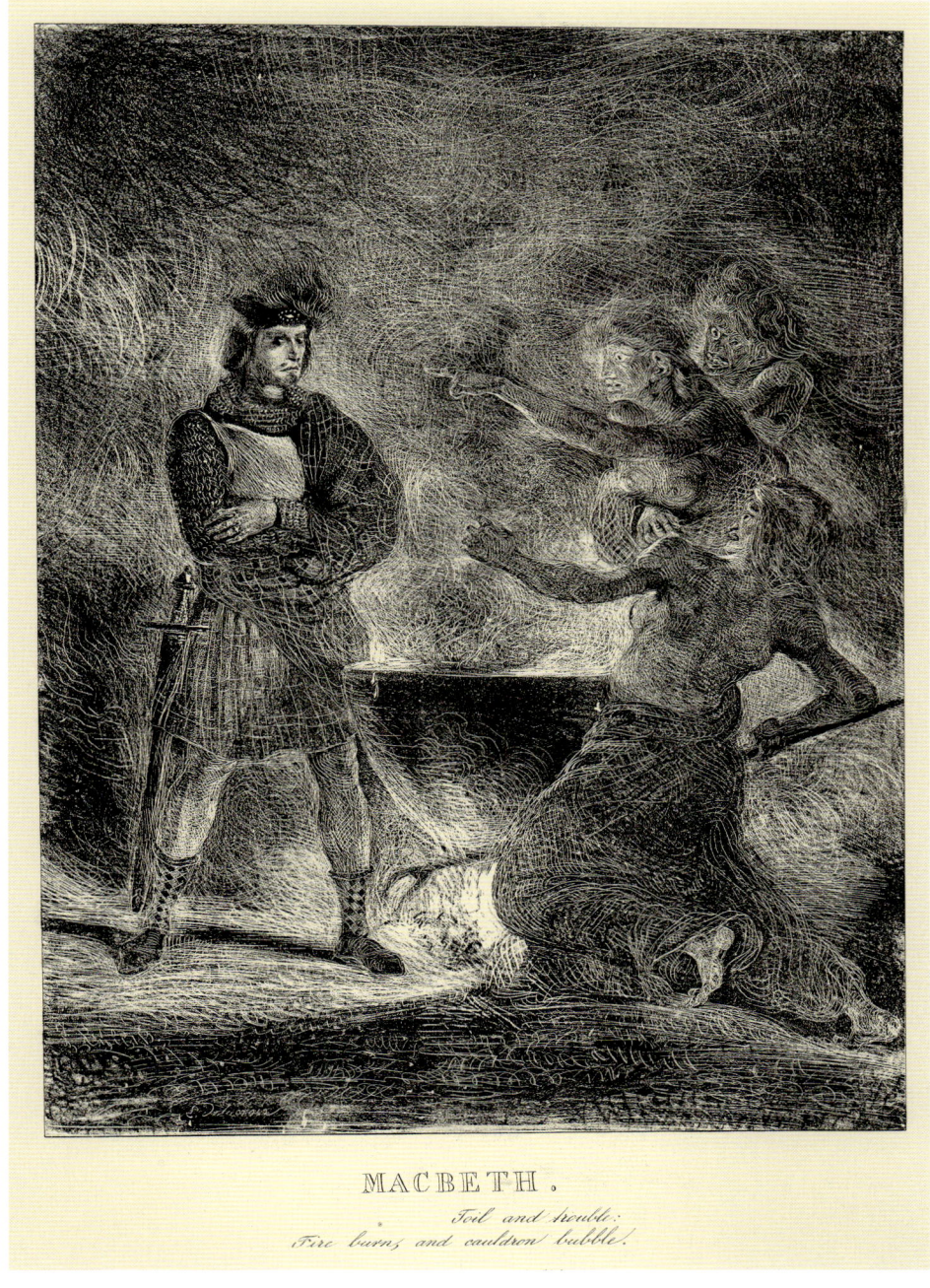

MACBETH.

Toil and trouble;
Fire burns and cauldron bubble.

CAT. 19 *Macbeth Consulting the Witches,* 1825

line obtained by scraping—sinewy for the witches, more undulating for the diabolical vapors, very strong and insistent for the fire, subtle for the drops overflowing the kettle—produced an impression of instability that raises doubts about the reality of the scene. Does Macbeth really see the witches, or are they the figments of his guilty conscience, now fully in the grip of evil? The dazed expression in his eyes might suggest they are mere imaginings. Delacroix, who knew only the written text of *Macbeth* at the time, did not choose the first encounter between the witches and the hero on the brink of becoming an assassin. He opted for the much more ambiguous first scene of act 4. Macbeth is portrayed at the moment of his fall, when murder becomes an end in itself and no longer necessarily serves his political plans. The witches then conjure up scenes of prophecy, as frightening as they are incomprehensible.

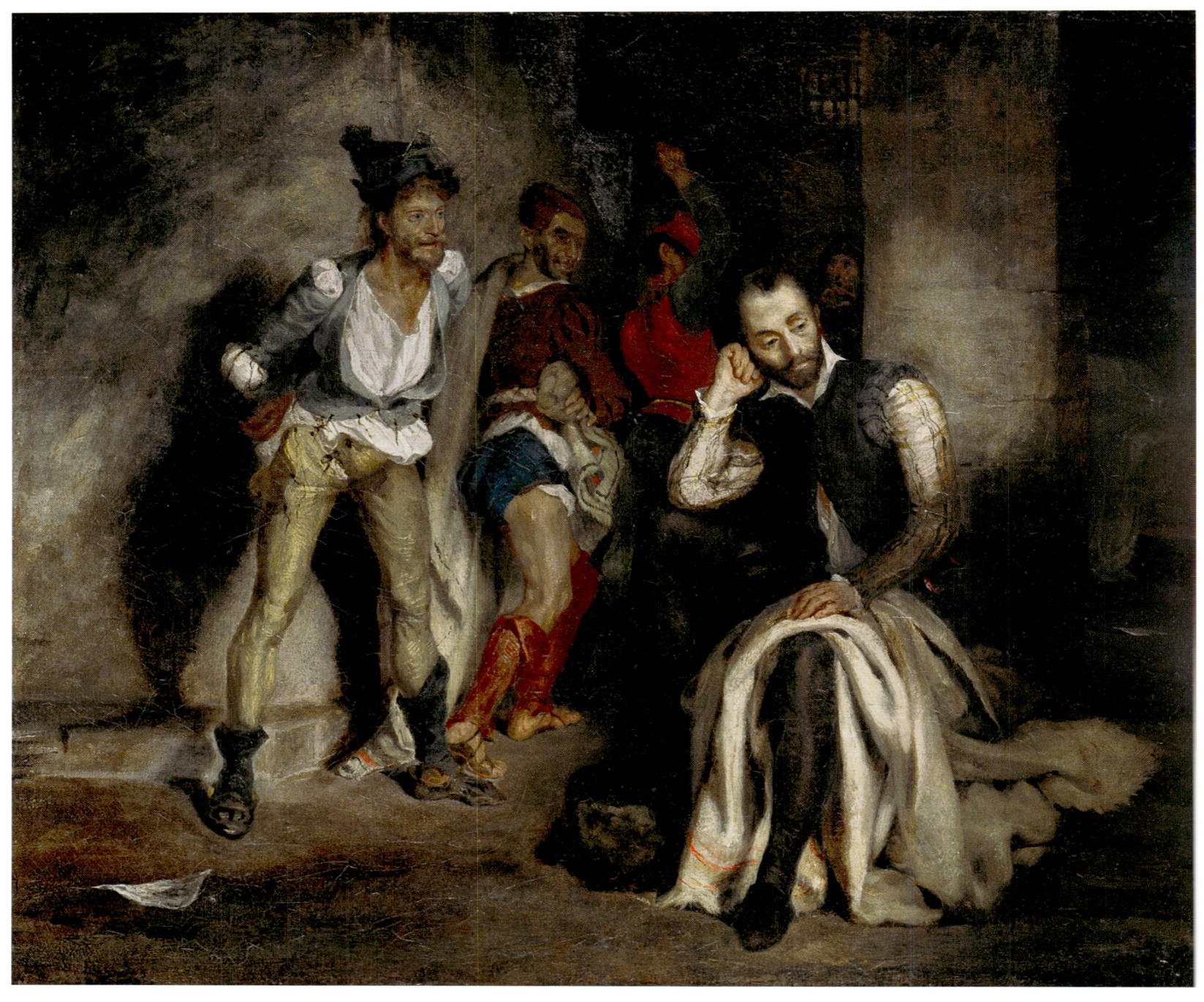

CAT. 8 *Tasso in the Hospital of St. Anna, Ferrara,* 1824

The expression of the madness that threatens heroes also appears in the first version of *Tasso in the Hospital of St. Anna, Ferrara* (cat. 8). The poet, depicted in the pose of a melancholic, is confined in the madhouse of St. Anna in Ferrara, where he is taunted by other inmates. In this original rendering of the confrontation between the poet and a madman, Delacroix gave the hero and his tormentor similar facial features. The madman stands before a wall onto which his

menacing shadow is cast. He, like the author of *Gerusalemme Liberata,* appears in a halo of light; he is the inverted image of the poet assailed by his inner demons. Rather than focusing on the picturesque aspect of a subject so beloved of the Romantics, Delacroix expressed its violence: Tasso's illuminated face stands out against a dark scene showing a guard violently whipping a wretched creature whose head barely emerges from the obscurity of the background, a possible allusion to the torments of Tasso's soul at the time. Whereas Tasso's melancholy conveys the image of the accursed poet, alone and misunderstood, Sardanapalus's reveals the sadistic egotism of the despot. In the 1820s, it is clear that Delacroix took care to deliberately undermine the triumphant heroism traditionally associated with history painting.

In its immoderation and profusion, *The Death of Sardanapalus* was an experiment pushed to the extreme. The artist abandoned himself fully to his own virtuosity and yielded willingly to the seductiveness of his materials. His brush is jubilant; the color explodes. He pursued the most diverse, even contradictory of paths while continuing to apply what he had learned from his previous works. His unbridled imagination was fueled by the observation of live models transformed into beautifully painted pictorial elements that accumulate even at the risk of jeopardizing the composition's balance. Delacroix was spurred on by the Oriental subject, but the work's monumental failure, the violent reactions of visitors to the Salon, seems to have convinced him of the hazards of this type of painting, in which the material threatened to smother the idea. In a sense, *Sardanapalus* was by its very nature a dead end, and he now had to find a way out—to employ greater rationality. At the following Salon, Delacroix's awareness of the situation and acumen about his art led him to reverse course. In *July 28, 1830: Liberty Leading the People* (fig. 26), he presented a painting in which everything is perfectly in its place, composed and balanced.

Toward Real Allegory: *Greece on the Ruins of Missolonghi*

Delacroix had begun to explore that "more reasonable" path in *Greece on the Ruins of Missolonghi* (cat. 26) a year prior to the scandal at the Salon of 1827–28. It is as if, in the 1820s, the young artist was moving in various directions simultaneously; he would abandon works and then return to them, correcting the flaws he had identified or trying his hand at new genres. In 1826, when a philhellenic committee organized an exhibition at the Galerie Lebrun as a benefit for the Greeks, the artist, who two years earlier had painted *Massacres at Chios*, made the bold choice of presenting an allegory, a genre considered outmoded, even anachronistic at the time. *Greece on the Ruins of Missolonghi* was an evocation of the nearly year-long resistance proudly mounted in 1825 by the residents of

the city of Missolonghi against Ottoman troops that were partly composed of Egyptian divisions. The triumphant, dark-skinned soldier who appears in the middle ground is probably an Egyptian. The Greek resisters, worn down by starvation and disease, were ultimately forced to yield, but they blew themselves up rather than surrender. The survivors were massacred. For philhellenes, and for Delacroix in particular, the reference to Missolonghi held added significance. Byron had succumbed to a fever in that city in 1824, on his way to bring funds and assistance to the insurgents. The younger generation of France, eager for glory and battle, had been roused to the Greeks' cause through Byron's writings. The canvas of 1826 can therefore be read as a memorial to the recently deceased poet, who so often inspired Delacroix, especially in the artist's many versions of the *Combat of the Giaour and the Pasha* (see fig. 16; cats. 27, 87).

But the allegory *Greece on the Ruins of Missolonghi* transcends the specificity of current events and offers a reflection on the meaning of history. Horror and signs of violence appear in the middle ground, where severed heads are placed on a wall, and in the foreground, where a hand emerges from the blood-streaked rubble. These virtuoso details, chilling in their realism, are vivid reminders of the reality of the massacre, as are the details in *Massacres at Chios* (see fig. 5). Conversely, the Egyptian victor's mien does not horrify; it is as if Delacroix withholds judgment. Early commentators' remarks about the agitated state of the allegorical figure of Greece are unfounded; her gesture is not one of denunciation, imprecation, and terror. She seems to accept as ineluctable the sacrifice imposed on her as she exhibits her wounds to the viewer. The painting marks the beginning of the artist's reflections on the greatness and decline of civilizations, a subject that would haunt his imagination throughout his life.

In 1826, with his bold choice of allegory, Delacroix again revitalized a genre, anticipating by nearly thirty years the "real allegory" of Gustave Courbet (see fig. 119). In fact, the painting manages to escape the didacticism intrinsic to allegory and its abstract vocabulary. An isolated woman, like the model for *Orphan Girl in the Cemetery* in 1824 (see fig. 9), is sufficient to represent all the misfortunes of Greece. But the figure of Greece is so laden with artistic references that viewers cannot fail to decipher its symbolic meaning. The attitude of the woman alludes to traditional Pietàs, and particularly to an engraving by Marcantonio Raimondi after Raphael, *The Virgin*

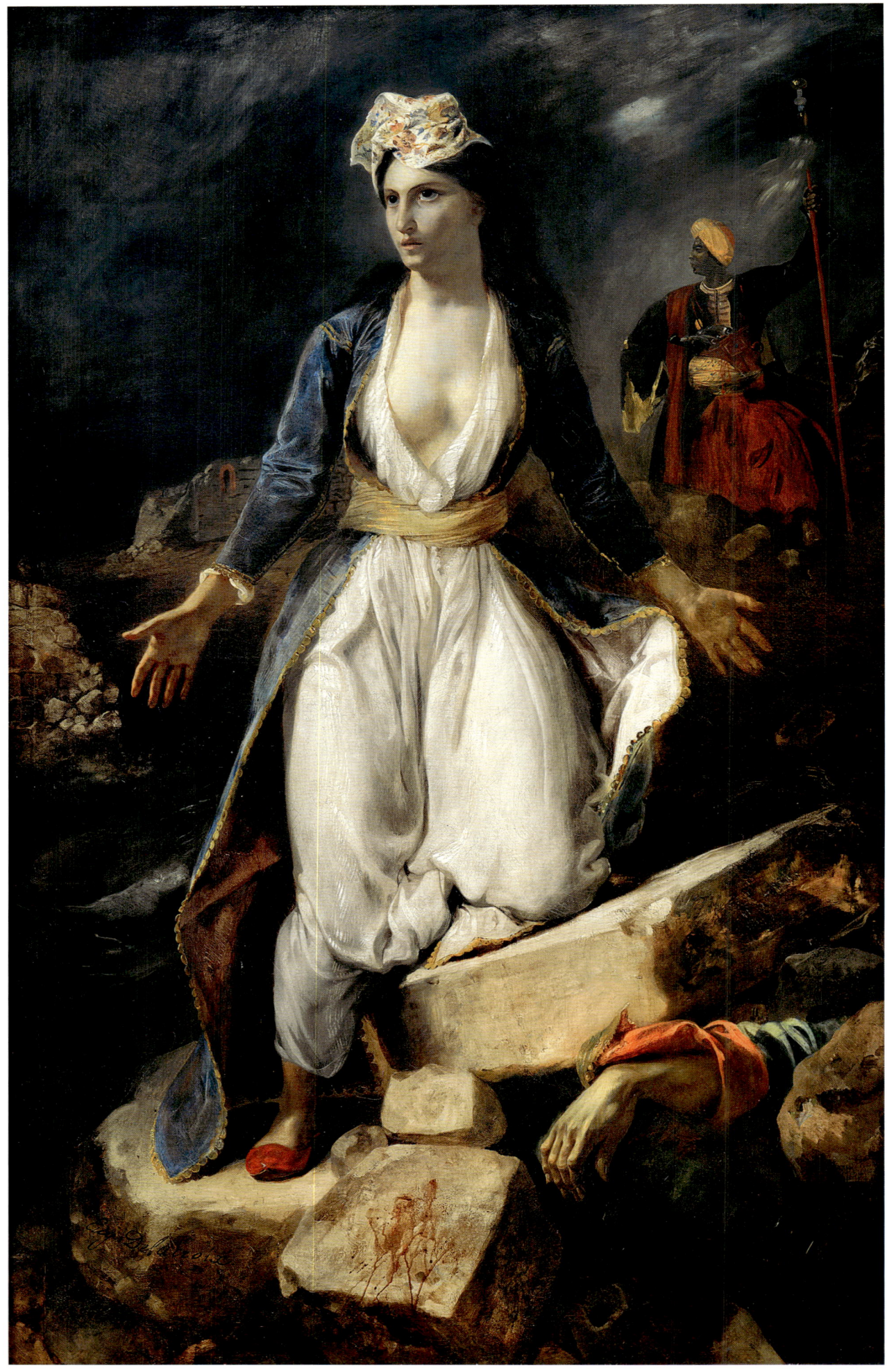

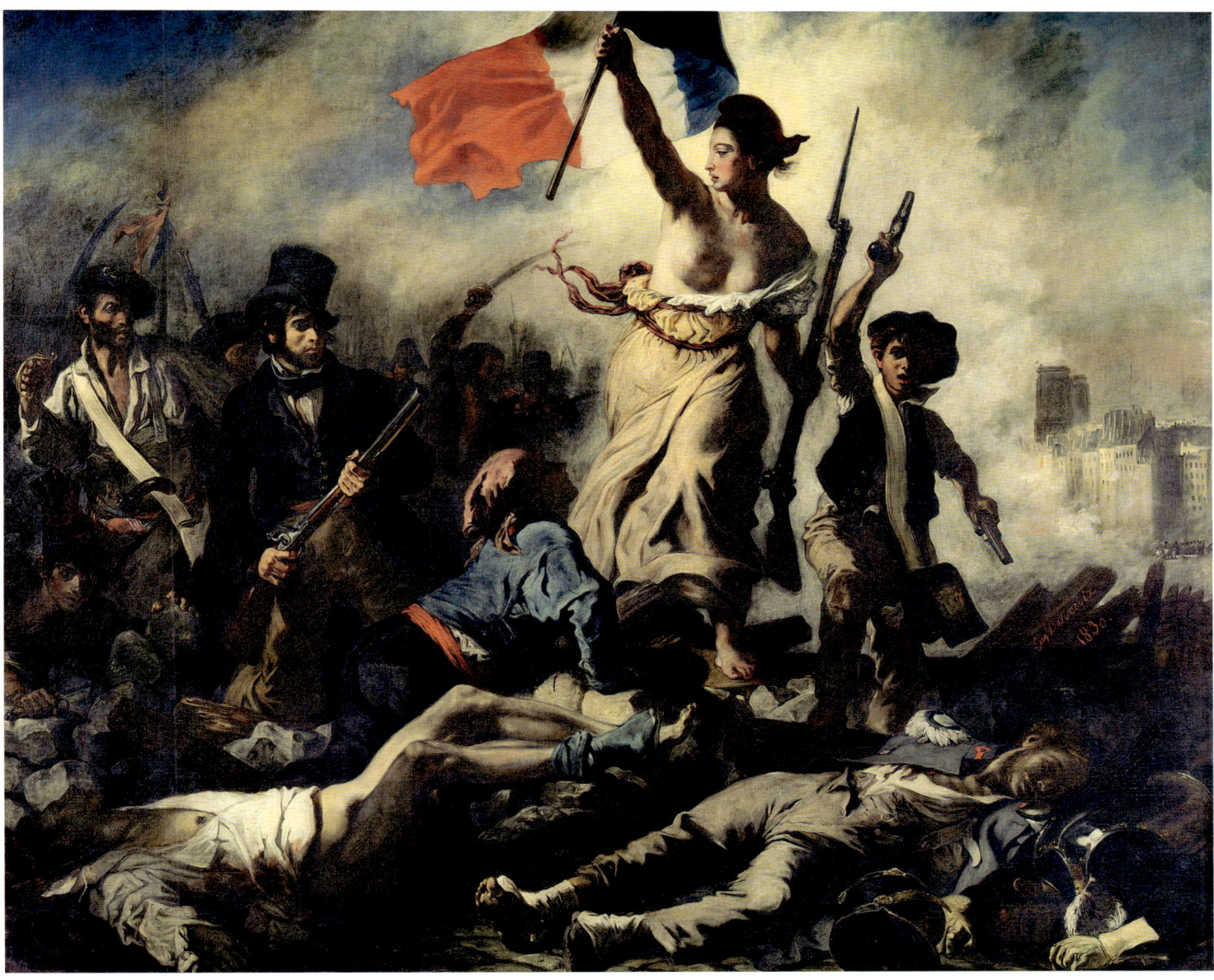

FIG. 26 *July 28, 1830: Liberty Leading the People*, 1830. Oil on canvas, 8 ft. 6⅜ in. x 10 ft. 7¹⁵⁄₁₆ in. (2.6 x 3.2 m). Musée du Louvre, Paris (RF 129)

*Weeping over the Body of the Dead Christ.*¹²² In an early idea for the composition sketched on several sheets of a notebook in the Louvre, Delacroix considered representing the desperate figure standing over the corpses of her children. He was inspired by the figure of the kneeling woman in the center of David's *The Intervention of the Sabine Women*. Delacroix's model is said to have been a certain Laure, who posed for *Woman with a Parrot* (see cat. 33), but the artist ended up painting a more geometric face, which would be further idealized when he rendered it in profile in *Liberty Leading the People*.

A Barricade

Delacroix used the idea of allegory again in *Liberty*, one of his most famous paintings (fig. 26). Exhibited at the Salon of 1831, the work was painted to celebrate the Revolution of 1830, which brought down the Bourbon king Charles X and put Louis-Philippe d'Orléans (r. 1830–48) on the throne. On a barricade in the heart of Paris, a bare-breasted woman advances, accompanied by the people she leads. She brandishes the blue, white, and red flag inherited from the

CAT. 26 *Greece on the Ruins of Missolonghi*, 1826

Revolution of 1789 and adopted by the new king. In contrast to the static figure of a defeated and aggrieved Greece, the ill-fated heir of a brilliant ancient civilization, the energetic Liberty is on the march; she is the surging hope of a brighter future. If in the 1820s the violence of civil war and urban slaughters could have legitimately appeared to Delacroix as events that had occurred in other times and places, that was no longer the case after the revolution of July 1830. As he wrote to his nephew, Charles de Verninac: "Three days in the midst of shellfire and gunshots, people fighting everywhere. Someone like me, simply out for a walk, had as great a chance of being hit by a bullet as the heroes of the moment who marched on the enemy with pieces of iron inserted into broomsticks."[123] Delacroix witnessed insurrection and the phenomenon of the barricades, which had reappeared in Paris in 1827. These modern forms of massacre invaded his own urban and social environment—the streets of Paris—and involved his compatriots, members of his own generation. For the first time, Delacroix was confronted with the difficulty of rendering a historical event to which he was a direct witness and in which he played a part. How to synthesize multiple and successive incidents in a single image? How to convey the complexity and ambiguity of the event, the tangle of facts and interpretations, reality and imagination?

Liberty Leading the People, which Delacroix nicknamed "Barricade," seems to concentrate the imaginary characteristics of the barricade identified by Alain Corbin, beginning with its ephemerality and deadliness: "The barricade, haunted by promises of the future, is a temporary structure; it is quickly transformed into a tomb, a space outside time, where a funeral ceremony seems to play out."[124] Delacroix's painting memorializes a fragile construction, spontaneous and transitory; it conveys what the barricades were like in July 1830 and simultaneously evokes the tomb, the sacrificial altar, that these sites became for the victims of the street battles, whatever their political camp. There is a disturbing resonance between the primitive, popular architecture of the barricade and the deadly mound of humanity that both shapes and fuels the pyre in *Sardanapalus*. Employing the same pyramidal composition, Delacroix expressed in both paintings the idea of bodily sacrifice for the sake of freedom. But the works illustrate opposite political extremes: on one hand, the civil liberty of a people united against the arbitrariness of government; on the other, a monstrous tyrant's ultimate caprice, the freedom to destroy himself. The pyre of *Sardanapalus* is merely the stuff of dreams

or legend; the commander of the impending conflagration is a strange figment, a cross between a Byronian theatrical character and an obscure figure from millennia past. As in *Massacres at Chios*, in which Delacroix transmuted contemporary newspaper reports into bodies and spaces, the artist, stimulated by his readings, relied on the power of his imagination to construct the enormous scene. He gradually gave it weight and substance, as he added the realistic effects provided by his many models and the accessories he gathered in the studio.

The construction of *Liberty Leading the People*, painted in the wake of the revolution of 1830, took the opposite course. The artist assembled his image from things he had seen, heard, and felt, things with a strong but only temporary presence: piles of paving stones, beams, and barrels that had been cleared away by the early days of August; corpses rapidly carried off, washed, and buried; the noise of alarm bells and gunfire, which quickly fell silent. He then proceeded to derealize and abstract these elements through smoke effects similar to those that precede the descent of a deus ex machina onstage. In the painting, the theatrical fog served to attenuate the presence of the urban environment and cast into relief the human figures in the foreground. The very title, *July 28, 1830: Liberty Leading the People*, affirms the deliberate ambiguity of the work, the universal message of which is conveyed through the commemoration of a specific historical event. Liberty, her feet and breasts bare, carries the Revolutionary tricolor— the blue, white, and red—rehabilitated by the new regime and serving as the composition's chromatic fulcrum. Like the barricade, with its contradictory symbolic associations—it is both a space of liberation and a tomb—Liberty is ambiguous: half-goddess and half-woman of the people. "A fishwife," some critics would howl, perhaps remembering the actions of women during the earlier Revolution and disturbed by their active roles on the most recent barricades.[125]

While Delacroix assigned a traditional female role—that of *mater dolorosa*—to the allegorical figure in *Greece on the Ruins of Missolonghi* (cat. 26), five years later he had other plans for Liberty. That figure, an homage to Gros's *Bonaparte on the Bridge at Arcole* (1796; Musée National du Château, Versailles), is leading the people. To be sure, all of her followers are male and correspond to types, even stereotypes: a Paris urchin carrying a shoulder bag probably taken off a corpse; a student from the Ecole Polytechnique, with his beret; an

FIG. 26 *July 28, 1830: Liberty Leading the People*, 1830, detail

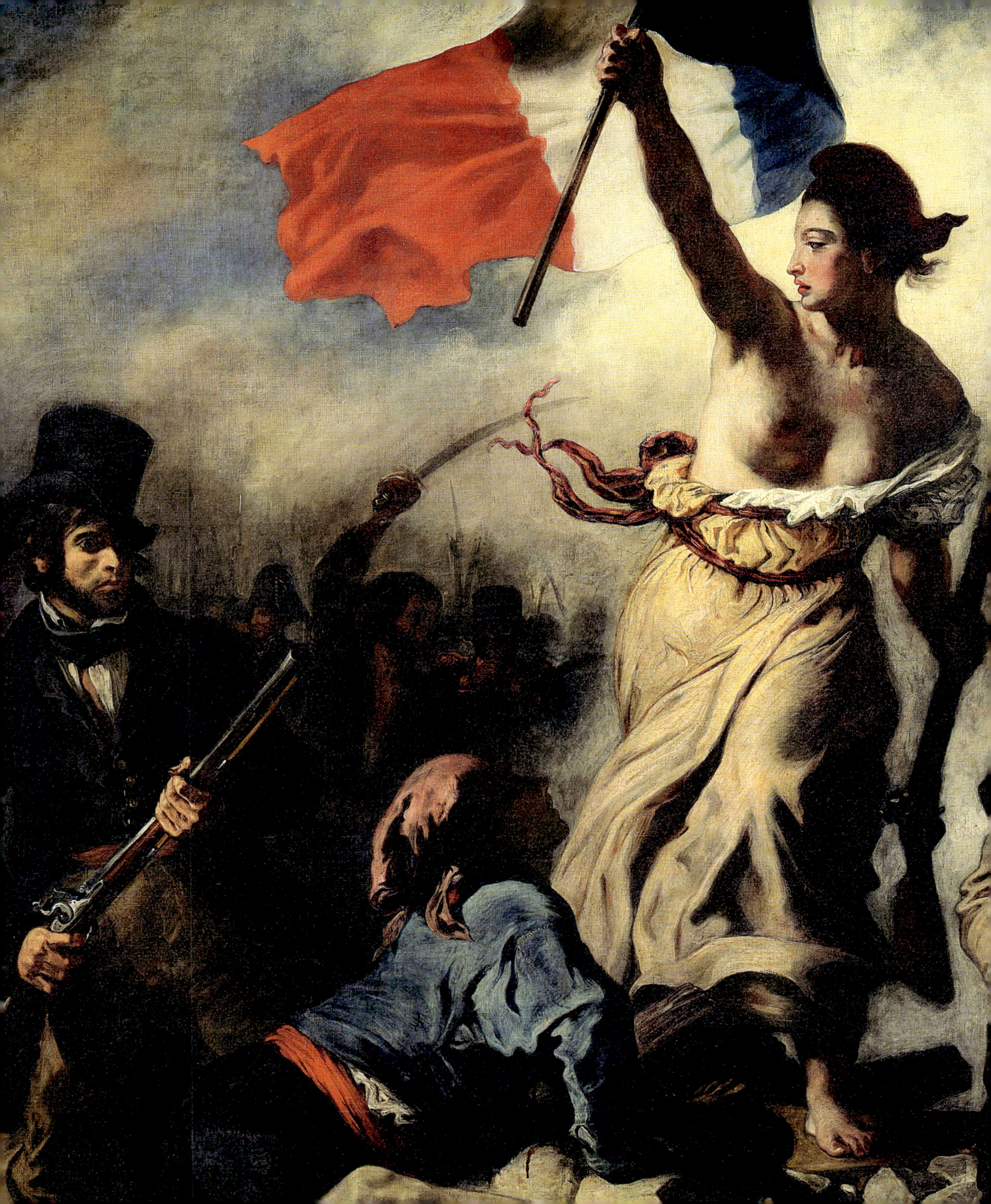

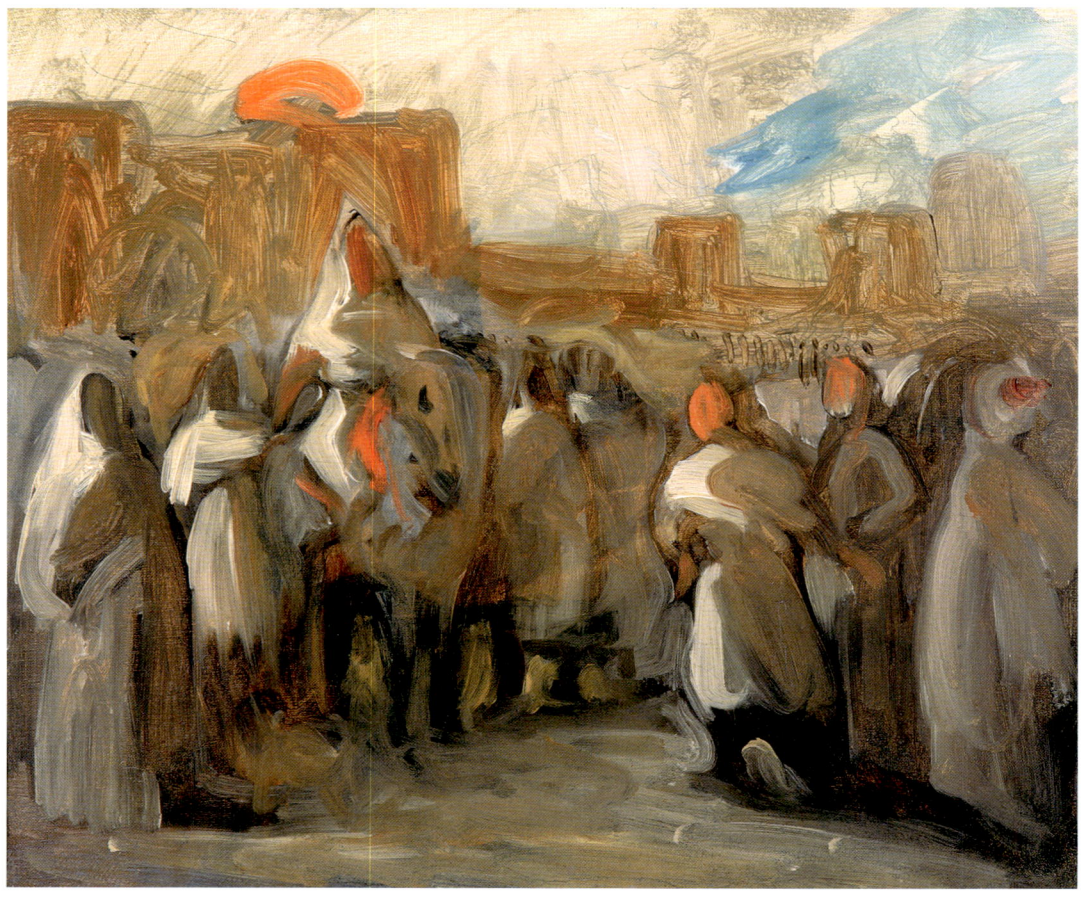

FIG. 27 *The Sultan of Morocco*, sketch, ca. 1832–33. Oil on canvas, 12³⁄₁₆ x 15¾ in. (31 x 40 cm). Musée des Beaux-Arts, Dijon (inv. DG 86) (J 369)

industrial worker; a craftsman wearing a top hat; a peasant dressed in overalls and red flannel belt.[126] Unlike the unfortunate Greeks in *Massacres at Chios*, the common people of Paris are not depicted in a state of paralysis, passively awaiting their cruel fate: they are the authors of their own history. The force of Delacroix's composition stems from the artist's capacity to depict the revolution as a perpetually ongoing process.

In his early paintings, Delacroix made significant use of both the fictive space of the image and the real space of the gallery in which the painting would be seen.[127] In *Liberty Leading the People*, he used that technique with formidable originality and effectiveness. Although the composition is strictly and classically pyramidal, the flag, because it is cropped at the top, introduces an unexpected dynamic. Even more striking is the forward movement of the figures—most notably, Liberty—who stride toward the spectator with extraordinary violence; the viewer is, in some sense, set upon. The people, on the march toward their liberation, advance on their audience, whose only options are to join in or be

crushed. The motionless frontality of *Massacres at Chios* and *Greece on the Ruins of Missolonghi* was intended to shock visitors to the Salon and appeal to their responsibility as citizens and human beings. The brutal intrusion of Liberty into the viewer's space, followed by her cohort of armed men and children, leaves no room for hesitation: the time for reflection has given way to the moment for action.

Although the state purchased the painting, the subversive power of the image was so great that, by 1832, it was judged dangerous to the July Monarchy (the government of Louis-Philippe). The canvas was therefore removed from the walls of the Musée du Luxembourg. It then suffered the same fate as masterpieces by David, Gros, and Girodet upon the fall of the Empire: at the request of Hippolyte Royer-Collard, director of fine arts, the painting was placed in storage. In 1839 the regime, which was trying to suppress memories of how it had come into power, even agreed to return it to the artist. Owing to the revolution of 1848, the work resurfaced at the Musée du Luxembourg; yet it was barely back on view

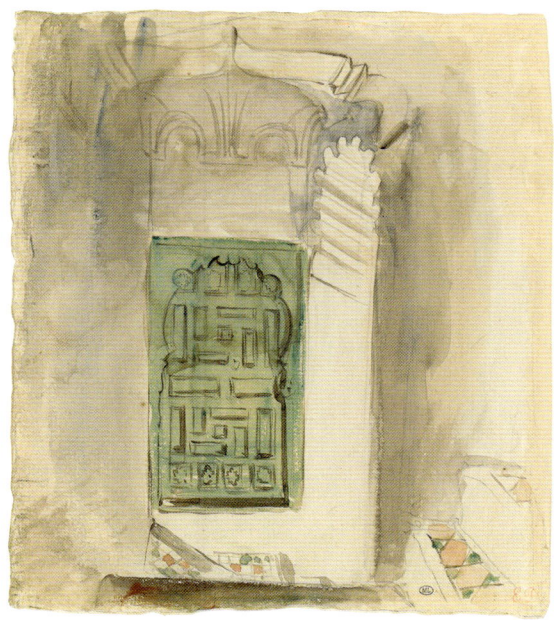

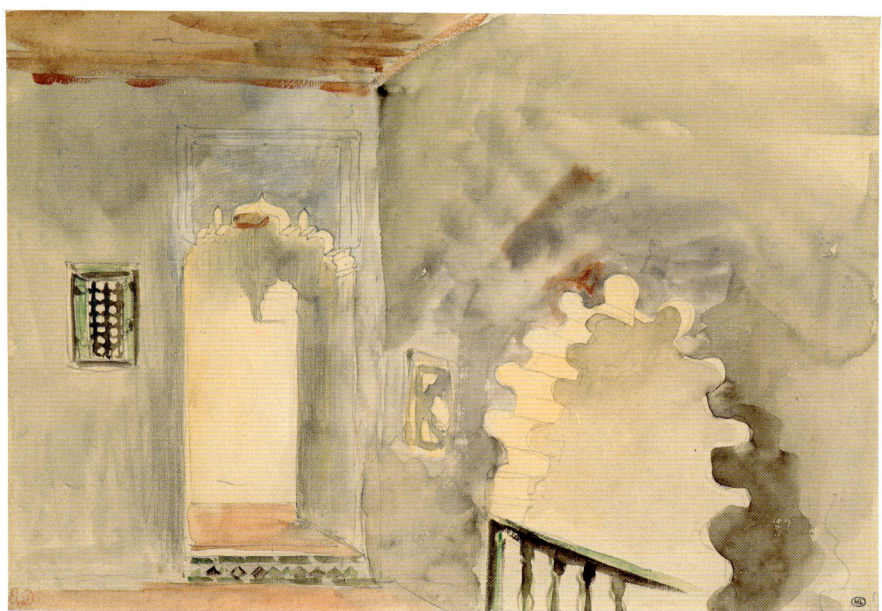

FIG. 28 *Moroccan Interior: The Green Door,* 1832. Watercolor over graphite on paper, 9⅝ x 7¹⁵⁄₁₆ in. (24.4 x 20.2 cm). Musée du Louvre, Paris (RF 4528)

FIG. 29 *Interior with Moorish Archways,* 1832. Watercolor over graphite on paper, 9⁷⁄₁₆ x 13⁷⁄₁₆ in. (23.9 x 34.2 cm). Musée du Louvre, Paris (RF 9266)

when it disappeared again into the storerooms, for fear that it could be interpreted as an incitement to riot. Not until the Exposition Universelle of 1855, and with special dispensation from Emperor Napoleon III, was the painting once again displayed to the public.

After the Salon of 1831, Delacroix faced the question of how to continue, how to find new inspiration. In under ten years he had explored and revitalized nearly every genre: history painting, modern subjects, animal painting, portraiture, still life, literary subjects, the nude. He had also experimented in many ways, setting off in new directions, then leaving them only to return to them later. *Liberty Leading the People* was both his most balanced and most subversive composition, and the first one in which he had managed to evade the "facility of the brush." His thirst for fame had been more than satisfied at the Salon. Despite the repeated scandals and the bitter failure of *The Death of Sardanapalus,* many of his works had been acquired by the state and hung in the Musée du Luxembourg in anticipation of their eventual transfer to the Louvre. In the eyes of the public, who were influenced by unprecedented developments in the press, he appeared— very much in spite of himself—to be the leader of the "young innovators," the "apostles of the ugly" whom the Neoclassical critics violently denounced. His networks had become more extensive, and he was beginning to benefit from very promising

support, like that of Adolphe Thiers, one of the first to sing his praises in 1822 and now an influential administrator.

At the end of 1831 comte Charles de Mornay made Delacroix a proposal that would come as a godsend. Mornay asked Delacroix to accompany him on a diplomatic mission to Morocco, where they were to meet with Sultan Moulay Abder-Rahman in an effort to establish good relations with his country, an encounter that the artist would depict multiple times (see, for example, figs. 27, 37, and cat. 138). The journey, which unfolded between January and July 1832, took the artist to Meknes, with stops in Spain and, on the return trip, Algeria, where he visited Oran and, from June 25 to 28, Algiers. The trip offered him the opportunity to step back and find new sources of inspiration through contact with the living antiquity he went in search of: "I use part of my time for work, another considerable part to let myself live. But it never occurs to me to think about my reputation or the Salon I had to miss, as they said."[128]

"Living Antiquity"

The preeminence of the subject and the tension between the subject and execution of a work gave rise to another question, namely, a painting's purpose. Should a painting contain a lesson, as Neoclassical doctrine proclaimed, or should it be

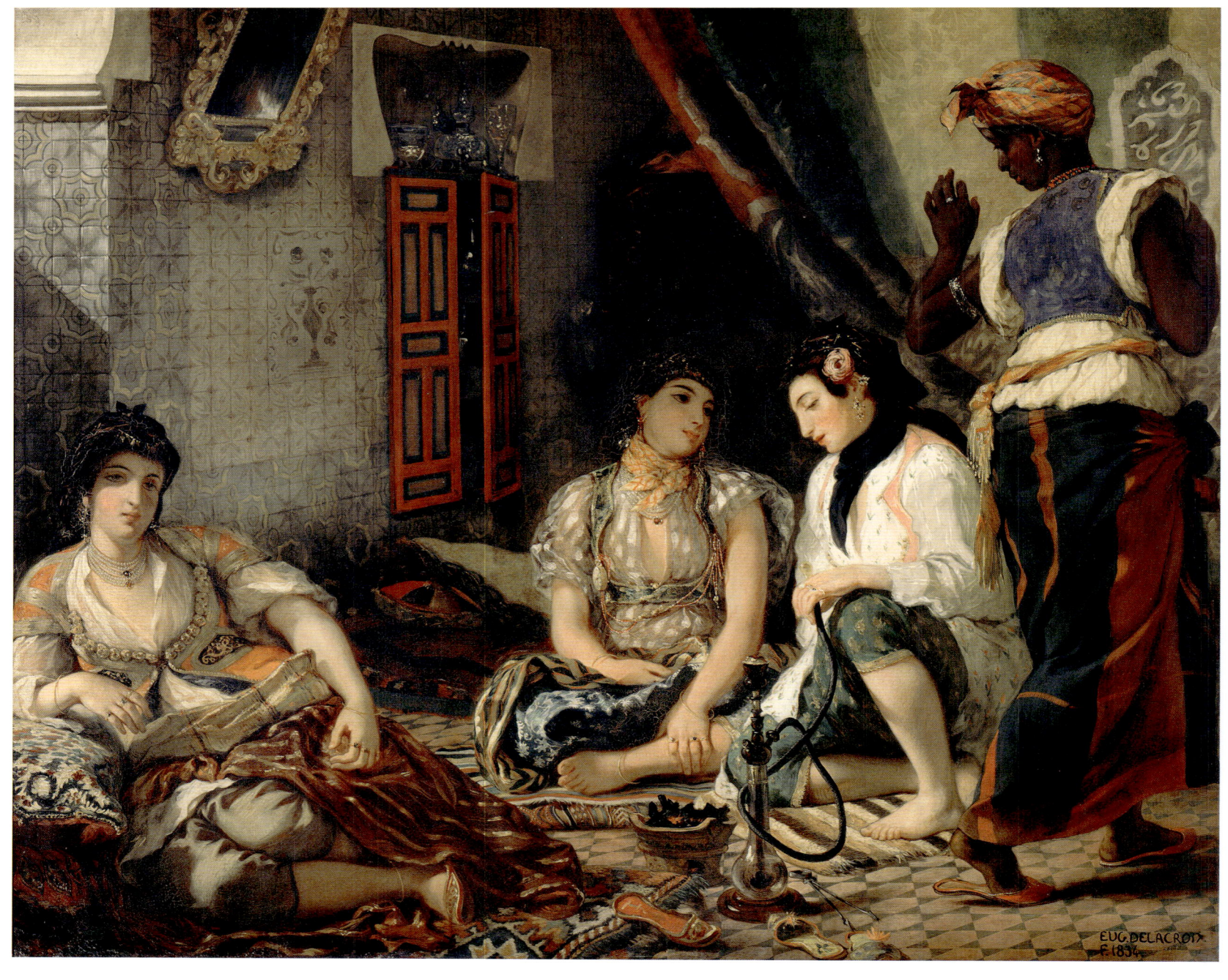

Women of Algiers in Their Apartment, 1834

a feast for the eye above all else? Delacroix could not decide, though he concluded his *Journal* with this remark: "This does not mean that there need be no sense in it [painting]." He hastened to add, however, "It is like beautiful verses."[129] Such an idea, formulated in 1863, may of course have had Realism as its target, at least in part. The artist, though he admired the direction of Courbet's painting, rejected the supposedly

prosaic subjects of Realism and what it put on display. In the same way, the subtle correction Delacroix made in his *Journal* demonstrated his lack of sympathy for the doctrine of art for art's sake. Nevertheless, his remark, in its very simplicity, undermined the theoretical edifice on which the classical system of painting had been built. That assault was at least as important as the blows he struck against Realism. In fact, his reassessment of *delectare* versus *docere,* giving pleasure versus teaching a lesson, in other words (at least in part), form versus content, signifier versus signified, finally amounted to a disruption of the traditional ideology of *ut pictura poesis.* Delacroix, who belonged to a generation inculcated with that ideology, could not go quite so far and, in his constant vacillations, his corrections of his ideas by means of nuance, he attempted to stay on track. The classical system, based on the association of the painter and the poet, obscured the fact that the poet, at least before the advent of modern poetry, had to make himself understood before seeking to please, whereas the painter sometimes followed the reverse course.

Women of Algiers in Their Apartment (cat. 83), a painting inspired by Delacroix's trip to the Maghreb in 1832 and exhibited at the Salon of 1834, played a decisive role in that problem. Its imposing format is suggestive of a history painting enlivened by an action, but its title (and hence its subject) is that of a genre scene. Nevertheless, this particular Oriental scene shuns all picturesqueness. In the entry for the Salon program, Delacroix took care to substitute the Western word "apartment" for "harem," as if he were rejecting the exoticism implied by his subject, as if he were seeking to minimize the cultural distance, if not to create a form of empathy despite that distance. That is one indication of the gap between the seriousness of the representation of *Women of Algiers* and the poetry of the bazaar that lay behind many Orientalist canvases of the time. The work's status is therefore indeterminate. Although we are now accustomed to such fluidity, it disturbed contemporaries, as Amédée Cantaloube noted: "Although his *Algerian Women* seems at first sight to be only a genre study, generalizing strains can be found in it."[130] The opposition between "genre study" and "generalizing strains" conveys the tension between genre scenes and history painting. Delacroix was aware of it; in fact, his experience of the Orient seems to have been dominated by that tension.

In a letter of 1832 to his friend Pierret, he wrote: "Imagine, my friend, what it is like to see figures like consuls—Catos, Brutuses—lying in the sun, walking in the streets, mending old shoes." The painter thus arrived in the Maghreb with his eyes filled with Western culture, believing he had found in Algeria and Morocco the "living antiquity" he had come looking for. Everywhere he saw Catos, Brutuses, Ciceros.[131] But he found them idling in the sun or cobbling shoes, at a great remove from the heroization that time had bestowed on the Greeks and Romans. "Imagine, my friend, what it is . . ."

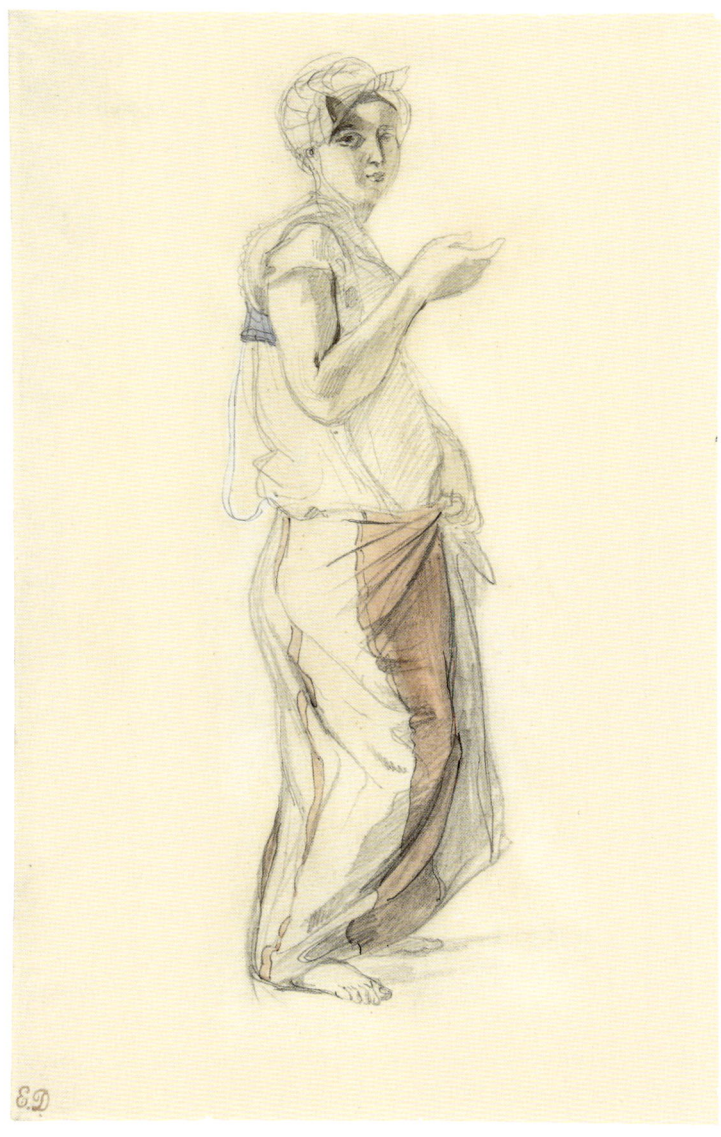

CAT. 82 *Figure Study for "Women of Algiers,"* 1833/34

conveys his astonishment and a kind of admiration. Delacroix continued: "If the school of painting persists in proposing to the nurslings of the Muses the family of Priam and Atreus as their subjects, I am convinced—and you will be of the same opinion—that it would be infinitely better for them to be sent as ship's mates on the first vessel to the Barbary Coast than to wear down the classical territory of Rome any longer."

In the canvases inspired by the Orient, Delacroix desired to escape the picturesque, the superficiality of alluring descriptiveness, in order to restore the ideal that makes for true painting. When he evoked Catos lying in the sun, the expression must be taken seriously. The greatness of a work is not measured

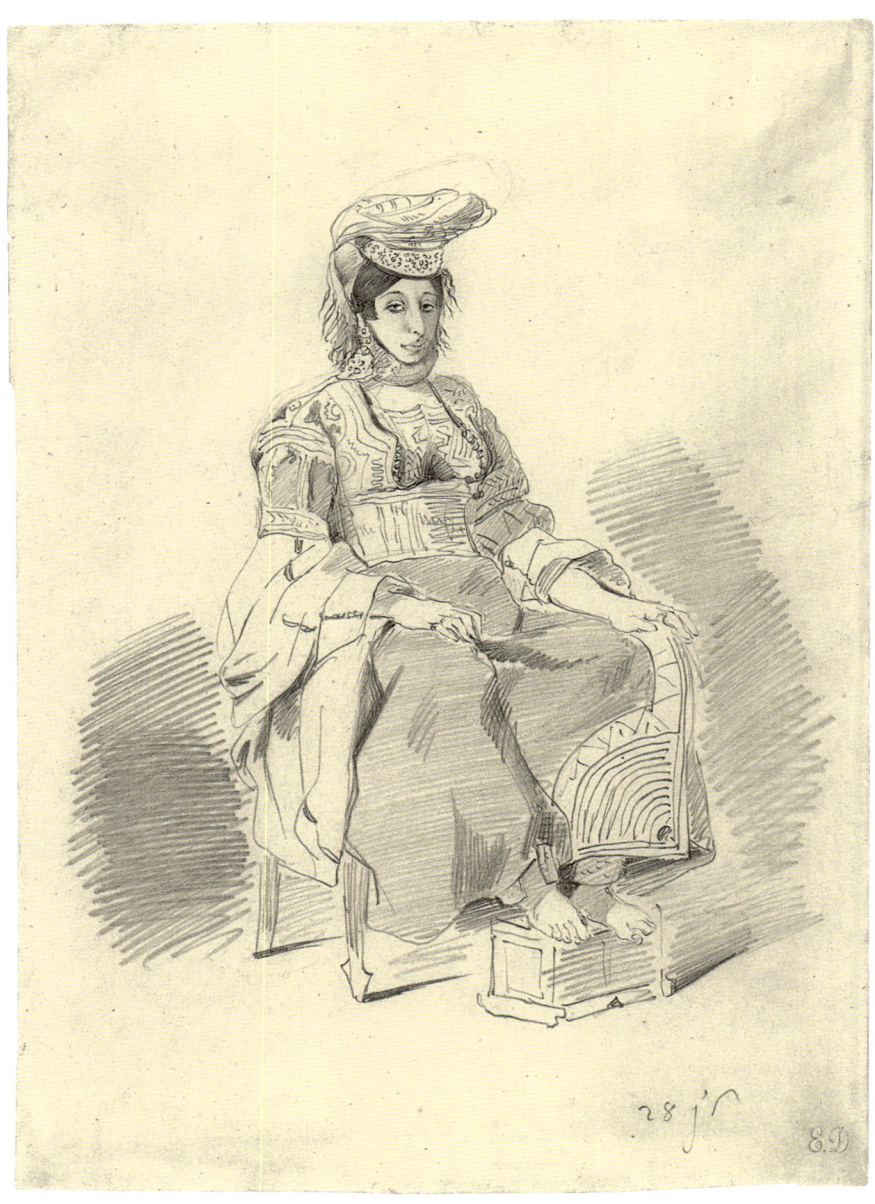

CAT. 72 *Jewish Woman of Tangier*, 1832

solely by the nobility of its subject but by the nobility with which it is rendered. Delacroix added geographical distance to chronological distance, which is the essence of the historical subject. For him, "the thing seen" did not culminate in a form of realistic representation, as it did for many of his fellow artists, but in a poetic recomposition founded on the idealizing work of memory. Therein lay its novelty. The subject was less in the rendering than in its perception by the artist. That idea runs through Delacroix's entire career, from the remark in his *Journal* in 1824, in which he declared that nothing was true for him but the illusions he created, to a letter of June 8, 1855, to his friend Marie-Elisabeth Cavé, wife of a director of

the fine arts and inventor of a method of drawing: "Truth in the arts is relative to the person who is writing, composing, etc."[132] Delacroix managed to avoid the repetitive and superficial picturesqueness of many painters who traveled to North Africa, the Middle East, and the Ottoman Empire. The Moroccan expedition was a liberation. Wherever he stopped, Delacroix, always with notebook in hand, made a sketch: costume details, heads, expressions, settings, landscapes, horses, objects, trees, plants, relics of antiquity, languid women (cats. 72–76, 78, 79, 81; fig. 30). He showed a particular fondness for doors and thresholds (see figs. 28, 29), which seem to symbolize, as in *Street in Meknes* (see cat. 77), more

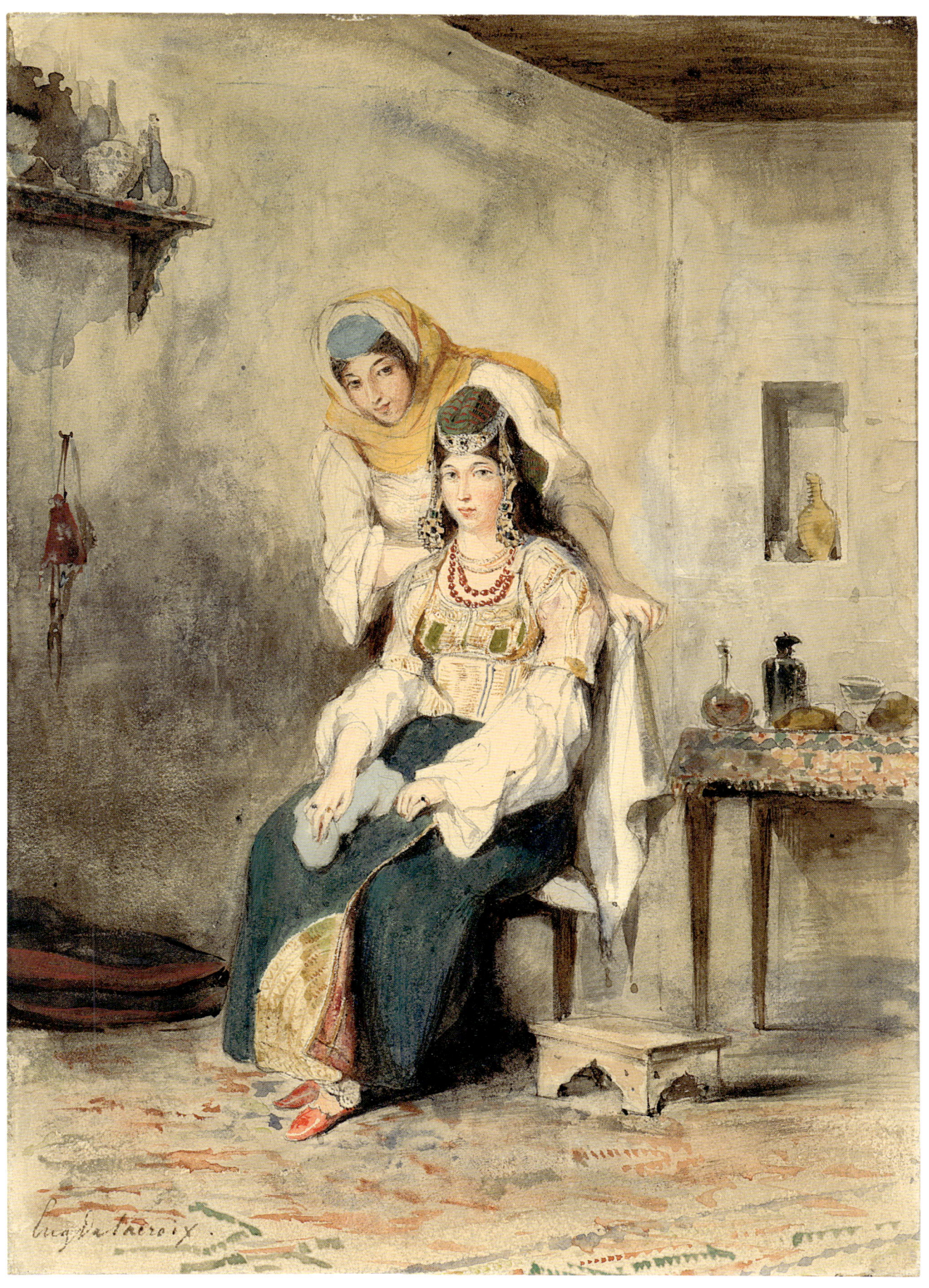

CAT. 76 *Saada, the Wife of Abraham Ben-Chimol, and Préciada, One of Their Daughters, 1832*

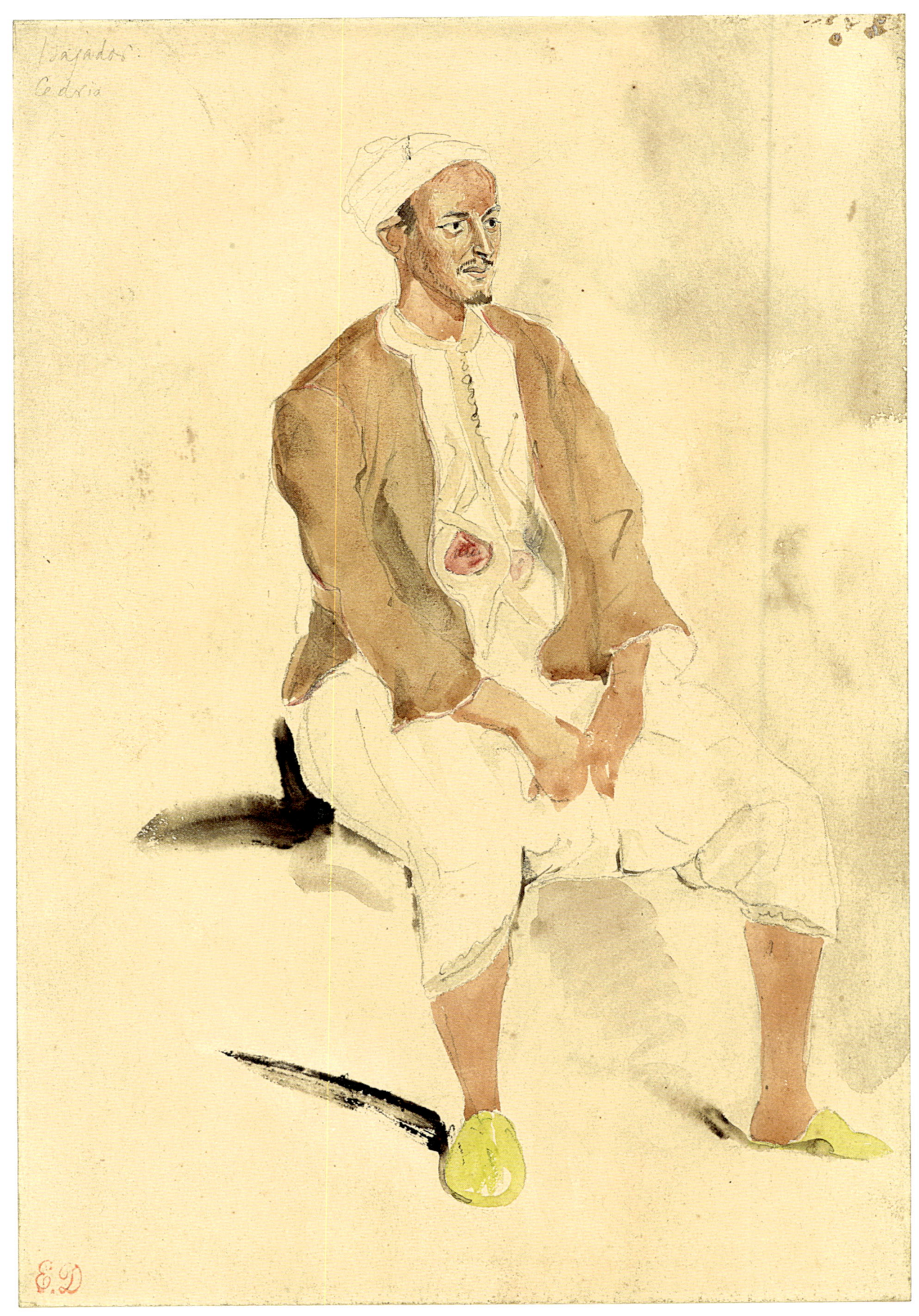

CAT. 75 *A Man of Tangier*, 1832

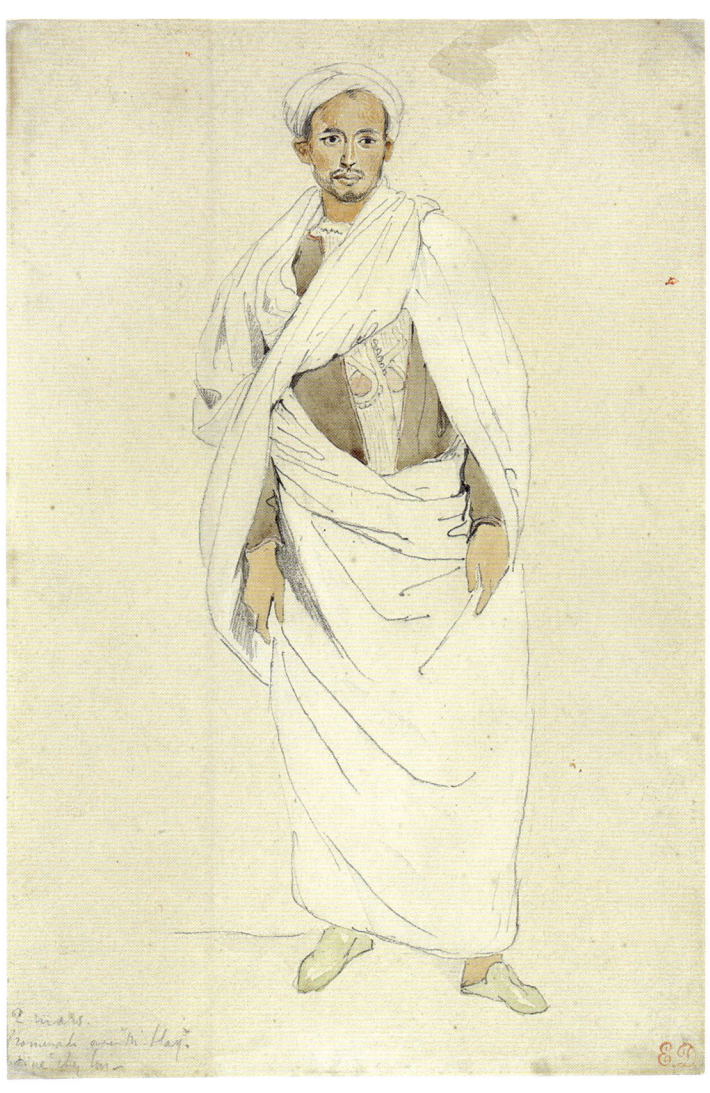

CAT. 74 *Standing Moroccan,* 1832

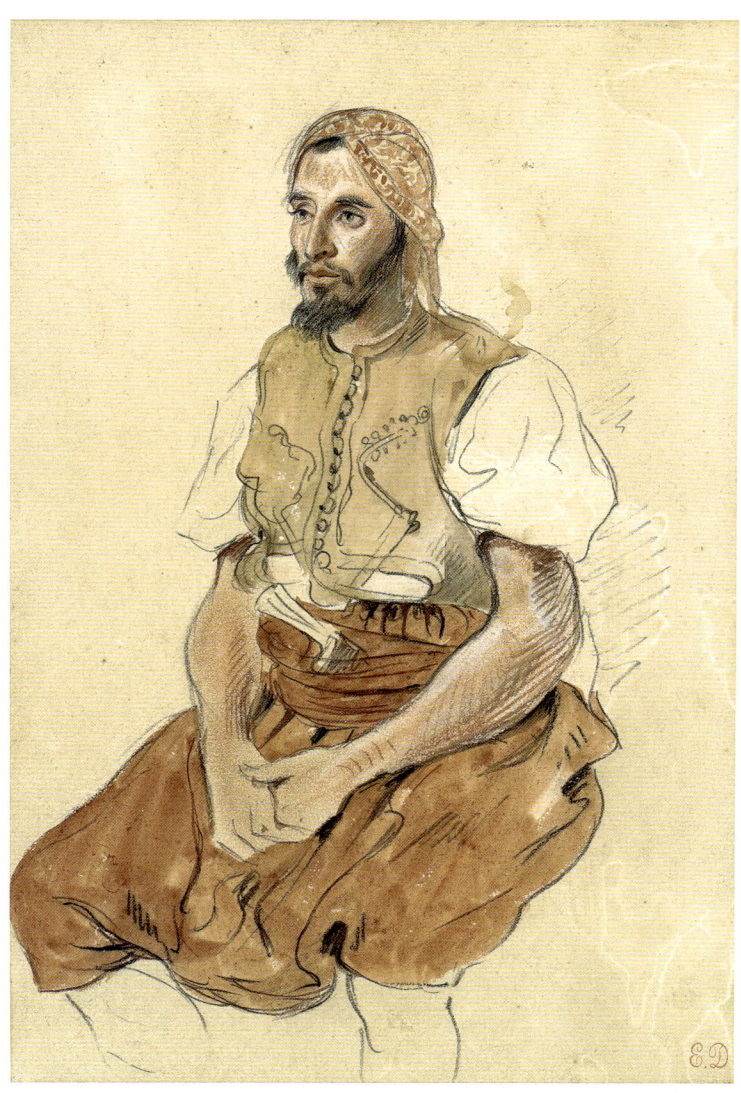

CAT. 73 *Portrait of Schmareck, Tanner at Tangier,* 1832

FIG. 30 *Notes and Sketches Made at Tangier,* "North African Sketchbook," folios 12 verso and 13 recto, January–April 1832. Pen and brown ink with watercolor, overall 6½ x 7⅞ in. (16.5 x 20 cm). Musée du Louvre, Paris (RF 39050)

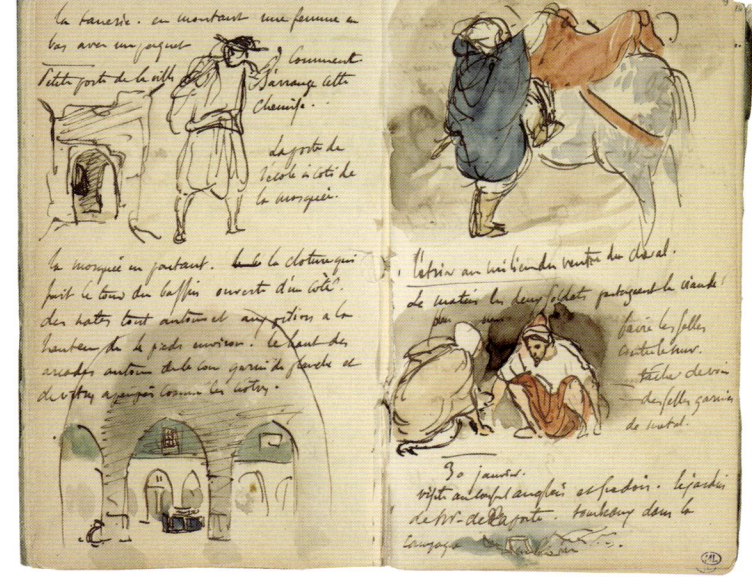

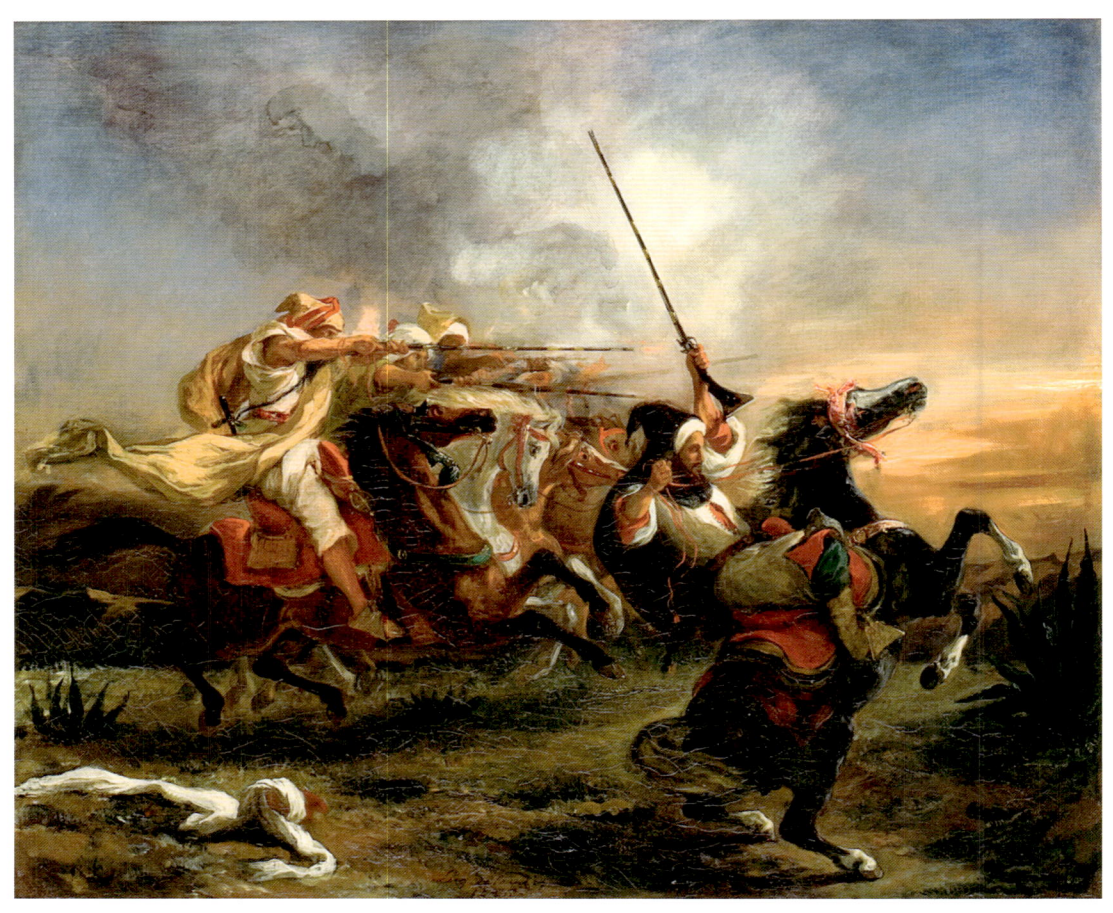

CAT. 78 *Moroccan Military Exercises*, 1832

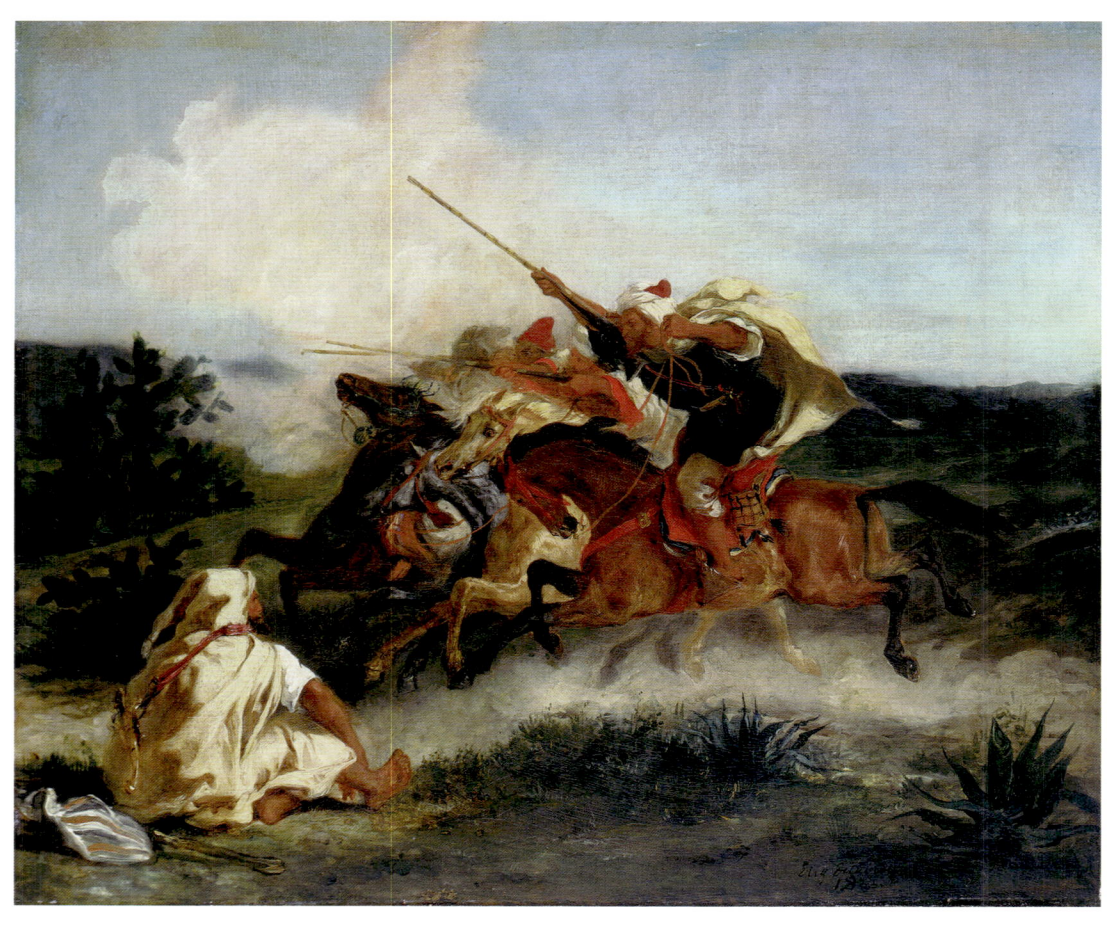

CAT. 79 *Arab Cavalry Practicing a Charge (Fantaisie Arabe)*, 1833

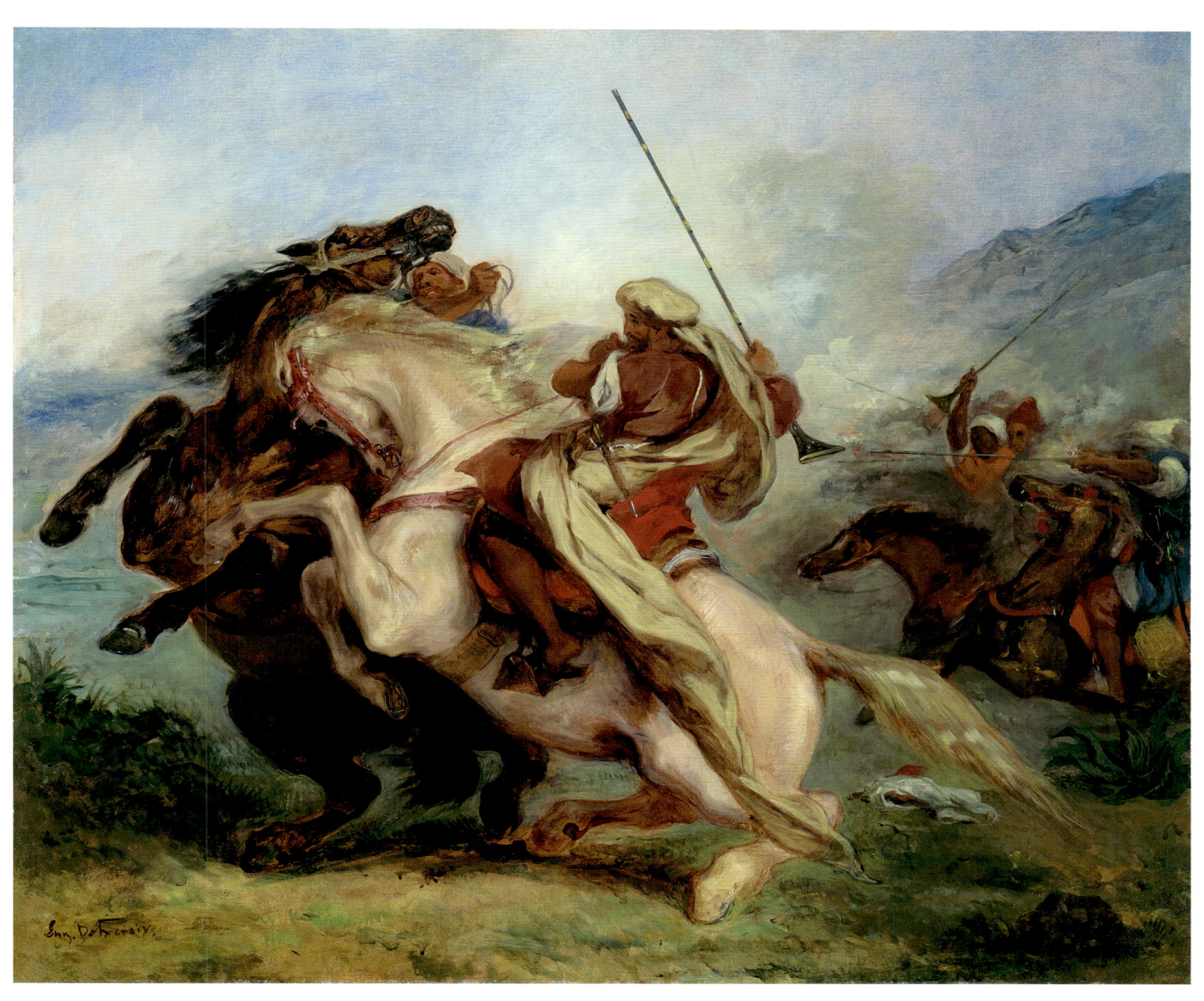

CAT. 81 *Collision of Arab Horsemen*, 1833/34

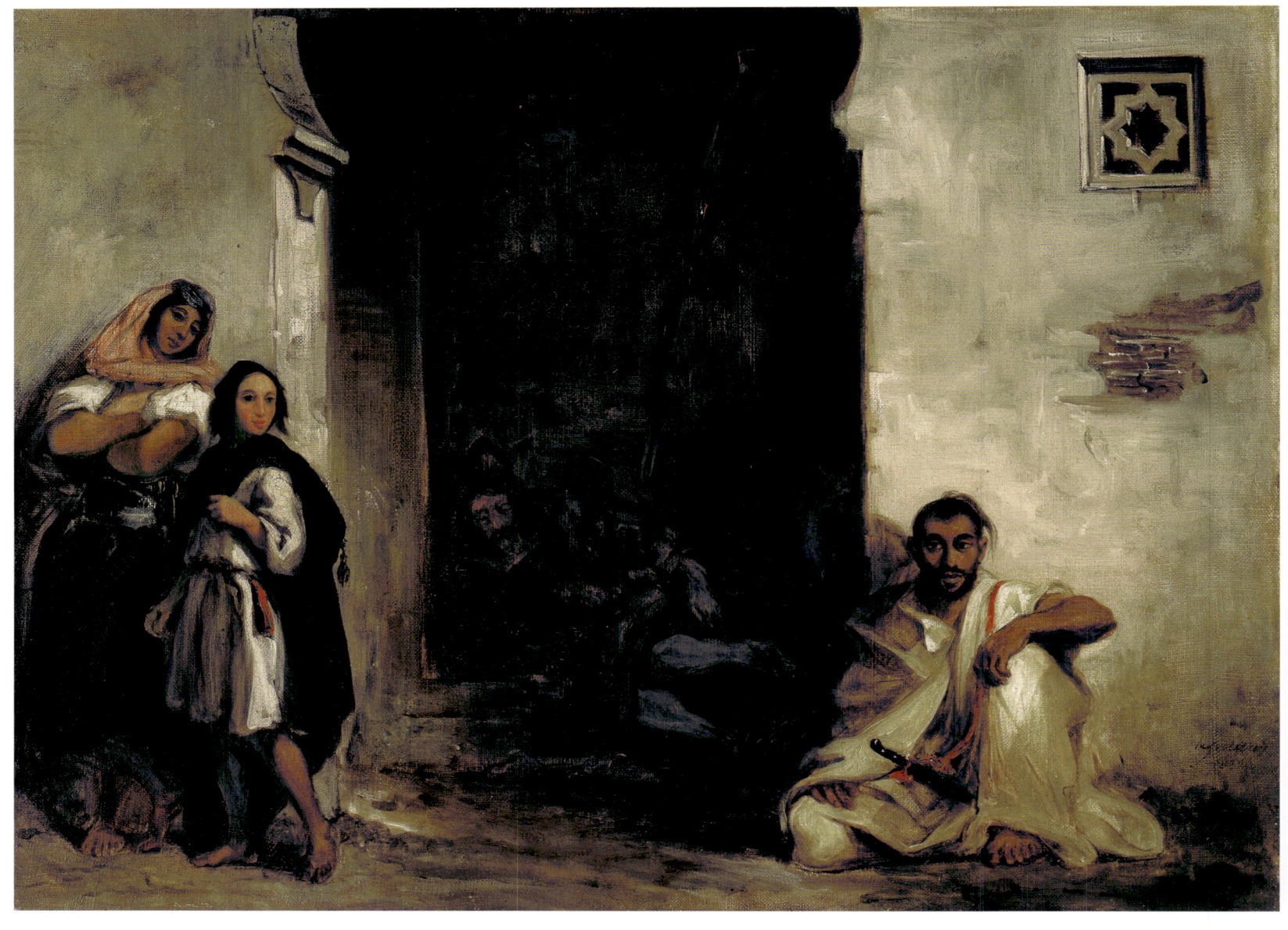

CAT. 77 *Street in Meknes*, 1832

than a form of mystery; rather, they suggest the discovery of and encounter with the Other.

Delacroix thus accomplished an enormous amount of work from life and outdoors, often in watercolor, a medium with unpredictable effects that certainly sharpened his perception. This intense activity played a fundamental role in his future reflections on the effects of observing the world—trees, flowers, tiger's stripes, rocks, waves, sand, and so on—and on his inspiration and growing attention to the landscape, as indicated somewhat later by such works as *Startled Arabian*

Horse in a Landscape (cat. 97) and *Arab Players* (cat. 107). Visits to museums and copying the masters, the foundations of the history painter's art, were no longer the only sources of technical inspiration: sometimes he had only to go out into the street. In 1821–22 Delacroix had discovered the secret of depicting glistening drops of water by studying those that Rubens had painted on the bodies of the Nereids in *The Landing of Maria de Medici at Marseilles* (see fig. 4);[133] in the 1830s, if Charles Blanc is to be believed, it was upon observing a yellow taxi that the artist became aware of the role complementary colors play in shadows.[134] In the interval, he had the experience of travel. He thus freed himself from the overly literary—and therefore exceedingly narrative—aspects of his previous sources of inspiration in order to devote more space to sensation, highlighting the tension between the subject and the motif.

Above all, extensive note-taking allowed Delacroix to liberate himself not only from studio formulas but also from the studio itself and, consequently, from an imitative conception of the model. During his journey, he made no oil paintings, but he assembled a collection of motifs, a dictionary of forms and subjects, that he would use for the rest of his career. His manner of filling certain travel notebooks with long lists of succinctly written images reveals his urgent need to record sensations in order to invoke them subsequently in all their richness:

> The nights on the terraces
> The cranes on the houses of Alcassar
> The nervousness that makes us go through the city
>   without stopping
> The fury of the consul's horse
> The man it had half eaten, etc.[135]

Extensive written descriptions would have run the risk of fixing the scene in place and reducing its capacity to inspire in the future.

He would soon write lists of biblical and historical subjects in his *Journal*. Henceforth, not only books and engravings but also his own notebooks, which contained his memories—whether recorded as drawings, watercolors, or in written form—would trigger his imagination and awaken inspiration. This process is illustrated in two late works, *Guard-Room at Meknes* (see fig. 94) and *Arab Horses Fighting in a Stable* (see cat. 144).

"Drowsy Reverie"

These paintings raise anew the question of the model and its function. When Delacroix turned to his travel notebooks after his return to Paris, he no longer had the model before his eyes; he had only the memory of it. Just as while he was reading, Delacroix inserted himself into the empty spaces, the blanks in the text, in order to reinvent the narrative through painting, so, too, he would summon from the depths of his memory, using the precious material compiled during his trip,

a sensation partly liberated from the grip of the thing seen. Imagination thus played a major role in his art; his paintings would achieve the ideal that constitutes the greatness of history painting. Unfortunately, because Delacroix did not keep a journal while working on his large Oriental scenes, we cannot follow precisely the idealizing process of memory that was involved in their making. A slightly later text sheds light on the subject, however. On October 8, 1847, Delacroix compared a work by Claudius Jacquand to a painting by Narcisse-Virgile Diaz de la Peña. Jacquand's painting, despite its realistic rendering, seemed false to him; the meticulous imitation of the most insignificant objects led only to dullness and clumsiness. In Diaz's work, by contrast, "everything came out of the painter's imagination, but the memories are faithful to life." Regarding Jacquand, Delacroix concluded: "It is as if this painting were done by a man incapable of even the slightest recollection of objects, for whom the detail he has before his eyes is the only striking one."[136] The passage of time, in bringing loss, opens up empty spaces into which many possibilities, multiple interpretations, insinuate themselves.

Women of Algiers (see cat. 83), *Convulsionists of Tangier* (see fig. 34), *Moroccan Chieftain Receiving Tribute* (cat. 92), and *Jewish Wedding in Morocco* (see fig. 31), though inspired by events that Delacroix had witnessed, avoid the descriptive exoticism that marked the heyday of Orientalism; instead, they offer reminiscences. Memory allowed him to reproduce the model while idealizing it in order to produce art from nature rather than, like Jacquand, a prosaic copy. The work's originality would be determined by the artist's capacity to be himself. The distance Delacroix introduced into *Jewish Wedding in Morocco*, by viewing the principal figures from afar and by representing in the foreground men viewed from the back and partly immersed in shadow, leads viewers—as if they were Western visitors—to the threshold of a house not completely open to them. Despite the abundance of costumes, jewelry, musical instruments, and exotic details, the scene retains its mystery and avoids cumbersome pseudo-realistic description. Several critics used the term "reverie" to capture the idealizing role of memory. Amédée Cantaloube, for example, saw in *Women of Algiers* "an entirely foreign culture of charming beings, listless in drowsy reverie."[137] He had previously noted that "Delacroix, when dealing with the Orient, did not specialize in searching for local color or reproducing this or that picturesque corner in the interest of slavish exactitude."[138] The real is not the true.

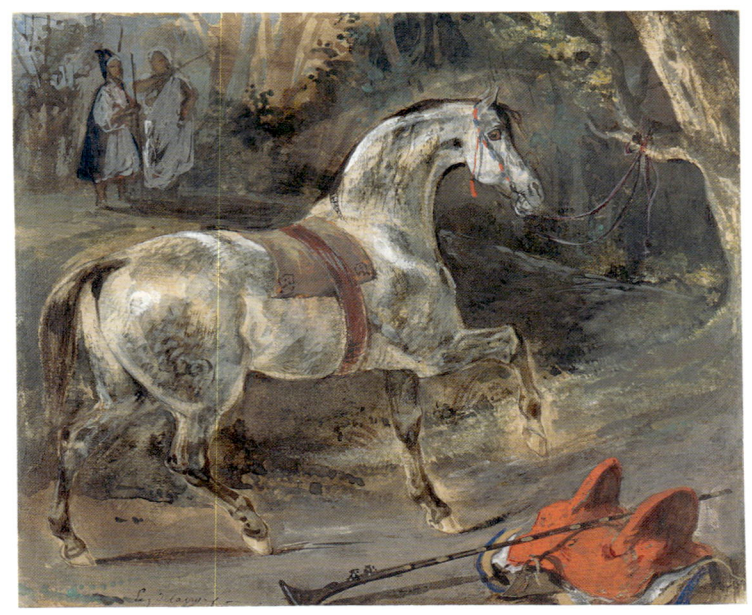

CAT. 97 *Startled Arabian Horse in a Landscape*, ca. 1835–40

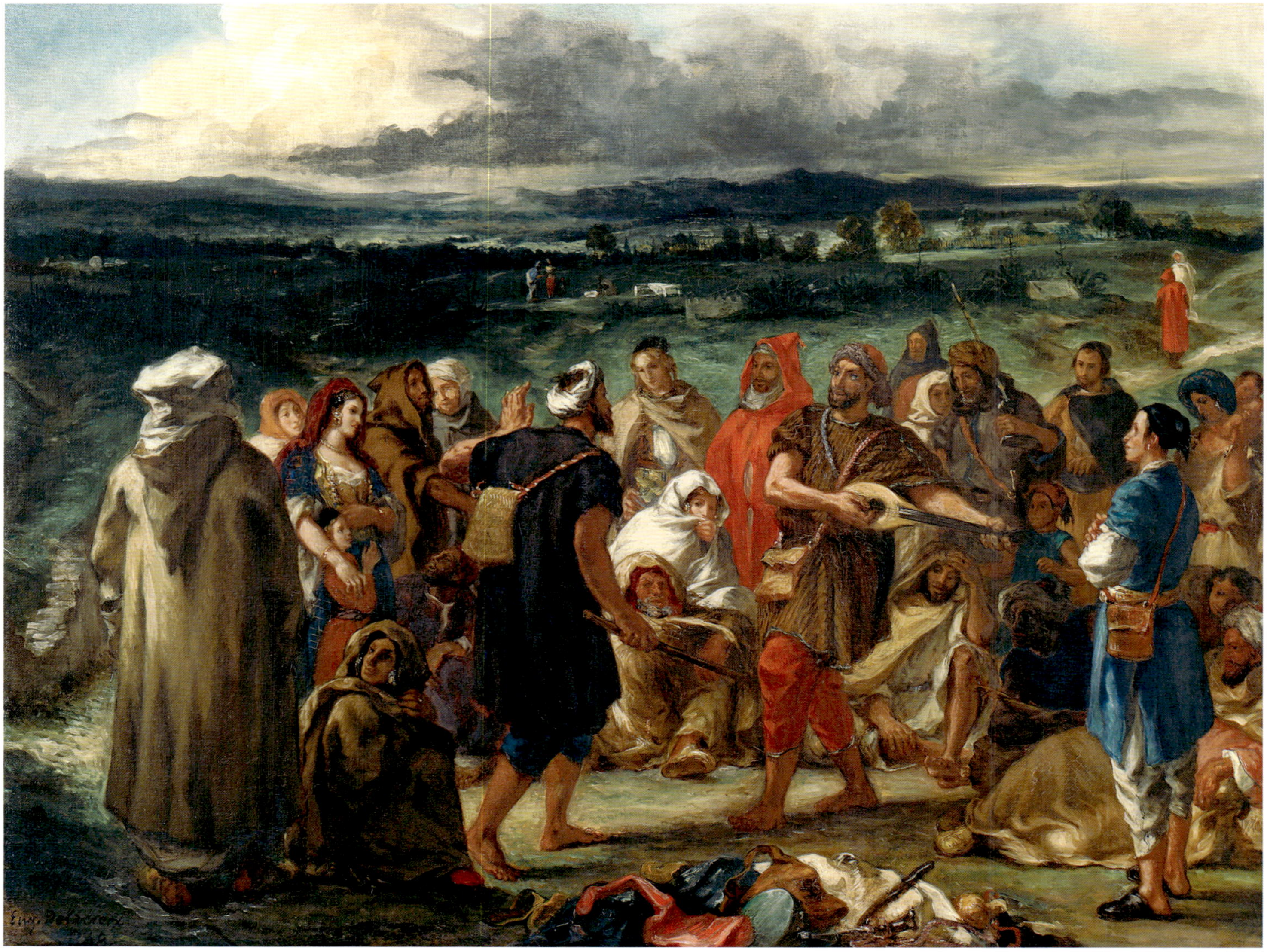

CAT. 107 *Arab Players*, 1848

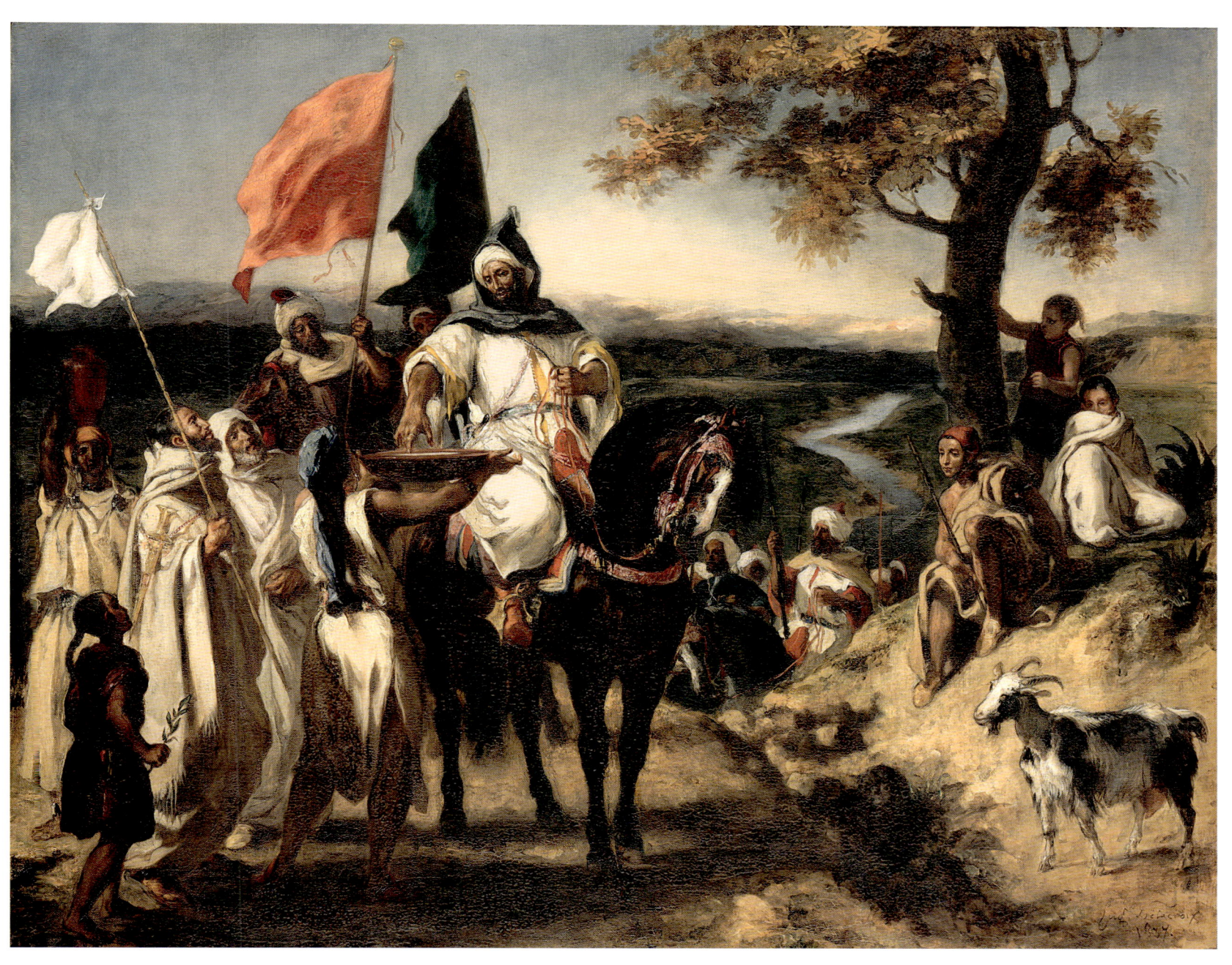

CAT. 92 *Moroccan Chieftain Receiving Tribute*, 1837

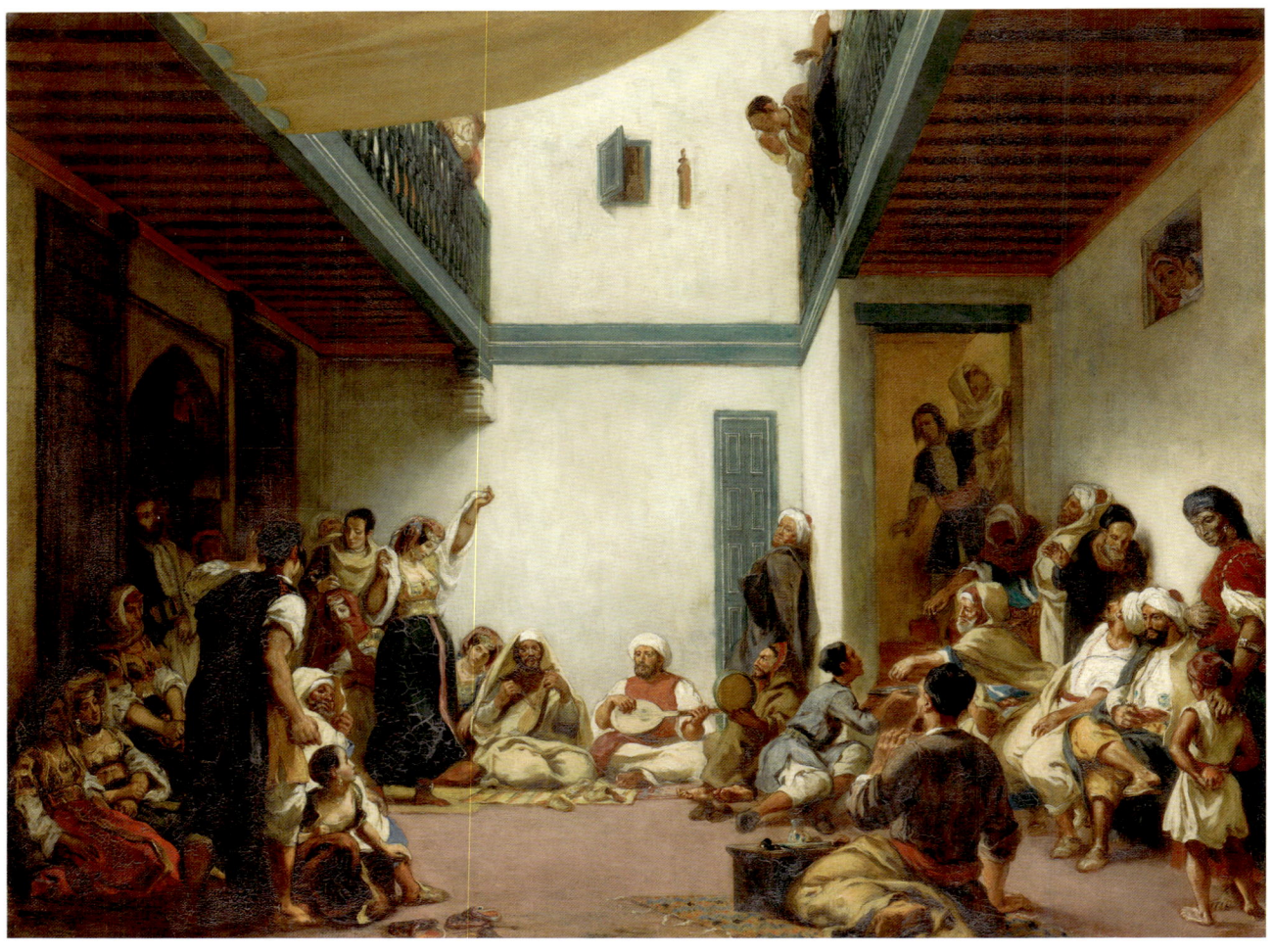

FIG. 31 *Jewish Wedding in Morocco*, 1841. Oil on canvas, 41⁵⁄₁₆ x 55⁵⁄₁₆ in. (105 x 140.5 cm). Musée du Louvre, Paris (3825) (J 366)

The second version of *Women of Algiers* (fig. 32) provides the most striking example of this phenomenon. Unlike the painting of 1834, the version of 1849 appears to have been conceived primarily as a reminiscence. In light of its Rembrandtesque chiaroscuro, the painting could be called "Souvenir of Morocco" (with a nod to Camille Corot, who employed this formulation in several of his titles). The women, observed from a greater distance than in the 1834 version, look like apparitions. They are presented theatrically through the gesture of the black servant, who lifts the curtain concealing them. This figure was the artist's invention, even in the first version of the painting, for which Delacroix posed a Caucasian model in his studio (see cat. 82). Delacroix painted a mystery to be unveiled, as it were. The instrument of that unveiling is the slave, placed in the intermediate space between the spectator and the Algerian women, who strike poses as in a tableau vivant. Delacroix thus introduced a narrative element that paradoxically evokes Charles

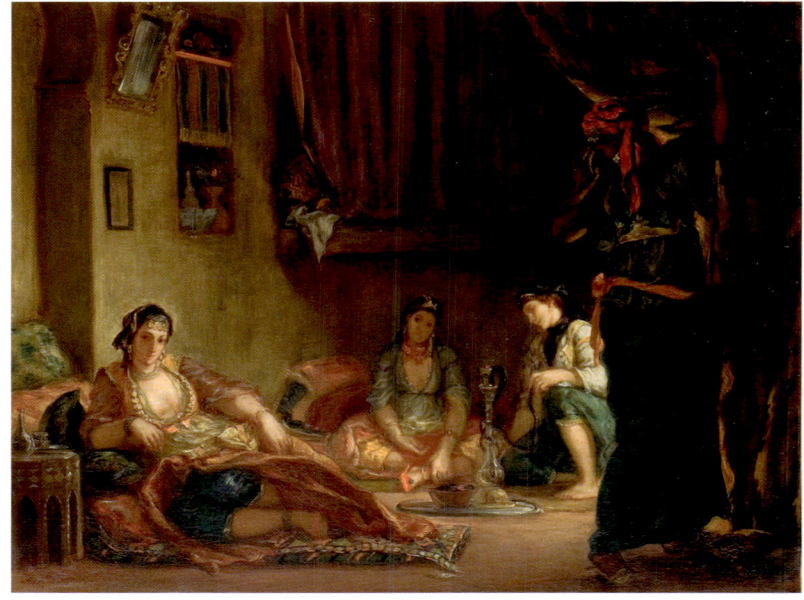

FIG. 32 *Women of Algiers in Their Apartment*, 1849. Oil on canvas, 33⁷⁄₁₆ x 44¹⁄₁₆ in. (85 x 112 cm). Musée Fabre, Montpellier (inv. 868.1.38) (J 382)

Cournault's description of a visit to a harem in 1832: "After crossing a dark hallway, when you enter into the part of the house reserved for them, the eye is truly dazzled by the bright light, by the fresh faces of women and children, who appear all of a sudden in the midst of that heap of silk and gold."[139] In this later version of the work, though the women are no more active than in the canvas of 1834, the dramatic effect, obtained by the contrasts of light, introduces a form of narration that seizes the beholder and distills the sense of time and action. The painting functions as a kind of revelation, because its true subject resides in the experience of a visitor entering a harem.

"It Is Paint and Nothing More"

The first painting on this subject, which the artist exhibited at the Salon of 1834, was done in a completely different spirit. *Women of Algiers* can be seen as a manifesto. Executed shortly after Delacroix's return to France, it tests the limits of the relationship between idea and execution, subject and material object. Unlike *Jewish Wedding in Morocco* (fig. 31), inspired by a ceremony in Tangier that Delacroix attended on February 21, 1832, and unlike *Convulsionists of Tangier* (fig. 34) or even *Portrait of Aspasie* (see cat. 10), this work has a problematic subject.[140] What did the artist's contemporaries see in it? Nothing. Nothing but paint. After a visit to the Louvre in 1877, the Symbolist painter Fernand Khnopff exclaimed: "Of all the Delacroix paintings there, the one I like least is *Women of Algiers.* The color is beautiful, but there is nothing but that, and that is not enough: I need an action, a subject, something that moves me."[141] In other words, he needed a narrative subject. In the same years, Charles Blanc, in an obvious allusion to Delacroix, expressed a similar judgment: "In passionately pursuing the triumph of color, the painter risks sacrificing action to spectacle. So what do our colorists do? They go to the Orient, to Egypt, to Morocco, to Spain."[142] The spectacle to which Blanc referred was clearly that of color. In 1834, such a spectacle was already quite something; it was new, as Blanc himself indicated, referring to *Women of Algiers.* "This essential piece is of interest only because of the paint. . . . It is paint and nothing more; fresh, vigorous, energetically displayed."[143] Delacroix had thus partly realized his dream of spreading matter across the canvas as the ideal of art, of dispensing with any bothersome mediation of a subject. At least that is how the painting was perceived.

Granted, the women painted by Delacroix are inactive. "It's as if you were seeing flowers vegetate," exclaimed Paul de Saint-Victor, adding: "No shadow of a thought ever crossed their faded cheeks; no passion ever hastened the rise and fall of their heavy bosoms."[144]

But might not these women be interesting in themselves? The title of the painting, in its combination of East and West, introduced an ambiguity. The fusion between the promise of a dreamlike, feminine, and Algerian distance and the prosaic notion of an "apartment" immerses these seemingly vacant women in a profuse luxury of place and finery. Although they might seem foreign to us, they are less foreign than they appear at first glance. The pose of the reclining figure on the left brings to mind the ancient *Sleeping Ariadne* (Vatican Museums); the Algerian woman embodies the living antiquity that dazzled the artist. These women resemble us; they are modern. The presence of a timepiece, so rarely remarked upon yet located almost in the middle of the painting, hanging from the bodice of the woman in the center, expresses the idea both symbolically and materially. The precious object does not date back to the dawn of time; it belongs to the nineteenth century. It is therefore the surroundings that introduce an element of strangeness. The harem has been renamed an apartment, but there is nothing bourgeois about it: it has a luxury, a decorative profusion, that combines Arab faience, Oriental carpets, and Venetian mirrors, the art of the Maghreb and Western imports juxtaposed.

It is as if the spectator (most often male) were struggling to accept the face-to-face encounter with these listless beings, who belie the image he might have had of a harem. Except for their apparent indolence, the women have none of the sexual allure of the odalisque, a Western male fantasy projected onto an Orient under invasion, and a subject Delacroix painted several times. With the trip to the Maghreb, he liberated himself from the literary clichés he had fallen for so brilliantly in his early works. The women of Algiers are neither nude nor, worse, undressed, to satisfy the lustful, dominating gaze of the European male. Like Ingres's *Grande Odalisque* (fig. 33), which inspired Delacroix's *Woman with a Parrot* (cat. 33), they neither offer their favors nor pretend to decline them. Delacroix's voyeurism, if it is voyeurism, is more apparent in the 1849 canvas—through the servant's unveiling of the tableau—than in the scene of 1834. We may therefore wonder whether Baudelaire's famous dictum "This little domestic poem . . . gives off a strong whiff of a place of ill repute"

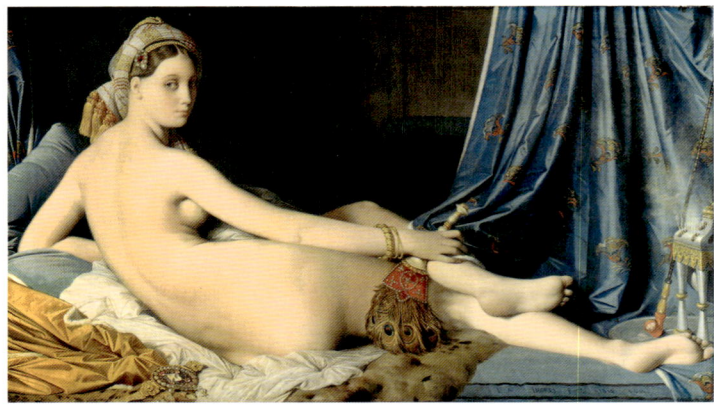

FIG. 33 Jean Auguste Dominique Ingres (French, 1780–1867). *Grande Odalisque*, 1814. Oil on canvas, 35¹³⁄₁₆ x 63¾ in. (91 x 162 cm). Musée du Louvre, Paris (RF 1158)

might not apply better to the painting in Montpellier, which the poet may have seen as it was being completed.[145] However, in his allusion to a place of ill repute, Baudelaire may have been attempting to introduce the role of sexuality traditionally associated with the harem, an aspect Delacroix engulfed in a more general sensuality.

The more disturbing the power of woman, the less she is seen. There is a certain paradox in considering this type of blindness in the context of Delacroix's opening up of the harem to Western eyes—his conferral of the status of subject on women who had been denied by male authority and by colonialism, which had violated their private realm. But perhaps, as Patrick Vauday has aptly remarked, he did these things in an ambiguous manner.[146] The emptiness of the women's

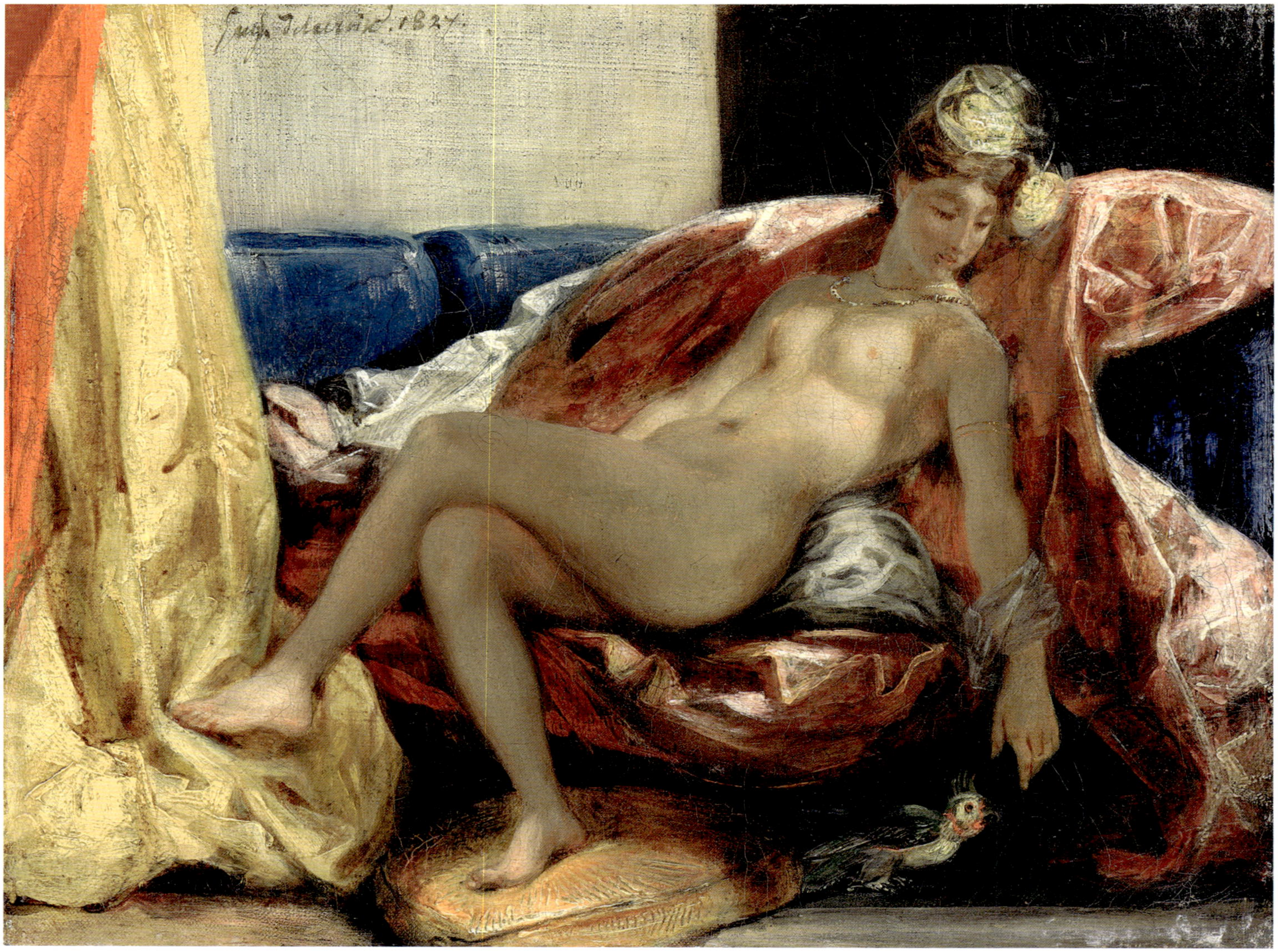

CAT. 33 *Woman with a Parrot*, 1827

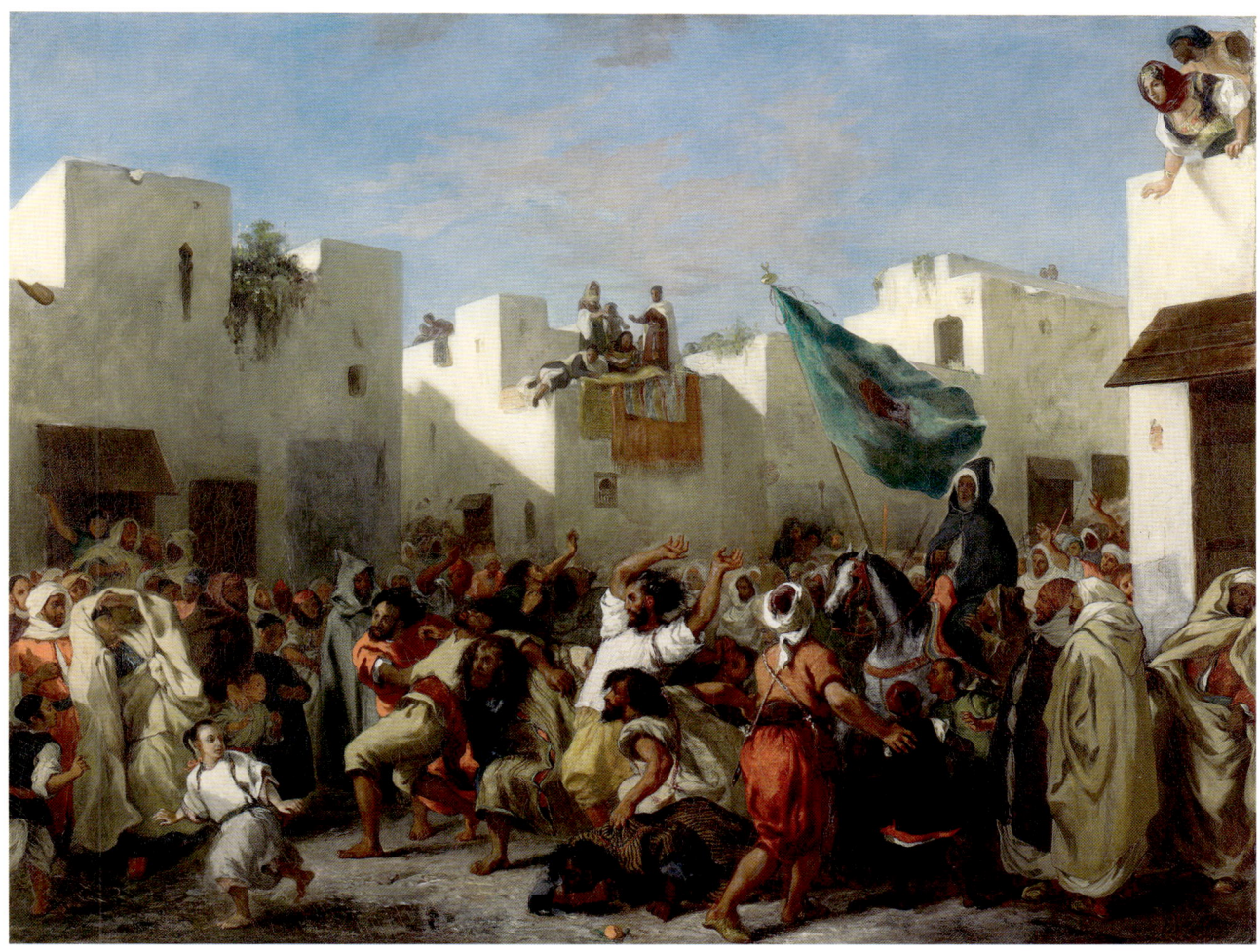

FIG. 34 *Convulsionists of Tangier*, 1837–38. Oil on canvas, 37⅝ x 50⅝ in. (95.6 x 128.6 cm). Minneapolis Institute of Art, Bequest of J. Jerome Hill (73.42.3) (J 360)

gaze reveals their effort to withdraw from the presence of the intruder, whether the visitor to the harem—the colonizer—or the male visitor to the Salon. The result is an absent presence, as if these women were blending into the decorative overexuberance of the canvas, obliging viewers to shift their attention to the material substance of the paint itself.

That is what the artist wanted. Paul Signac pointed out this inversion of the relationship between the women represented and the frame, describing how their flesh dissolves into the decorative continuum: "If the setting shines more brilliantly than the jewels, it is because Delacroix made the most insignificant surfaces—fabrics, door hangings, carpets, faience—shimmer by introducing a number of small details and ornaments whose various colors come to quiet or excite those parts of the painting, even as he painted almost monochrome flesh, because in real life, that is what it looks like."[147] This intentional weakening of the representation prevents the painting from telling a story. That is the reason, according to Alexandre-Gabriel Decamps, that the public saw it "only as a scene without emotion, a painting without an entry."[148] The allusion to an "entry," an explanatory text published in the Salon catalogue, is obviously metaphorical. Nonetheless, the subjects of other Moroccan works by Delacroix—*Jewish Wedding in Morocco* (fig. 31), *Moroccan Chieftain Receiving Tribute* (cat. 92), *Convulsionists of Tangier* (fig. 34)—were precisely explained in such entries, whereas, for the painting of 1834, the artist dispensed with all commentary that might have helped viewers interpret the image. Furthermore, he clouded its meaning by using the term "apartment" rather than "harem" in the title, thus merging Western and Eastern realities. In this fashion, he accentuated the "display of paint," the essence of his art. When compared with *Sardanapalus*, however, *Women of Algiers* shows a shift in Delacroix's interest from the material substance of paint to color.

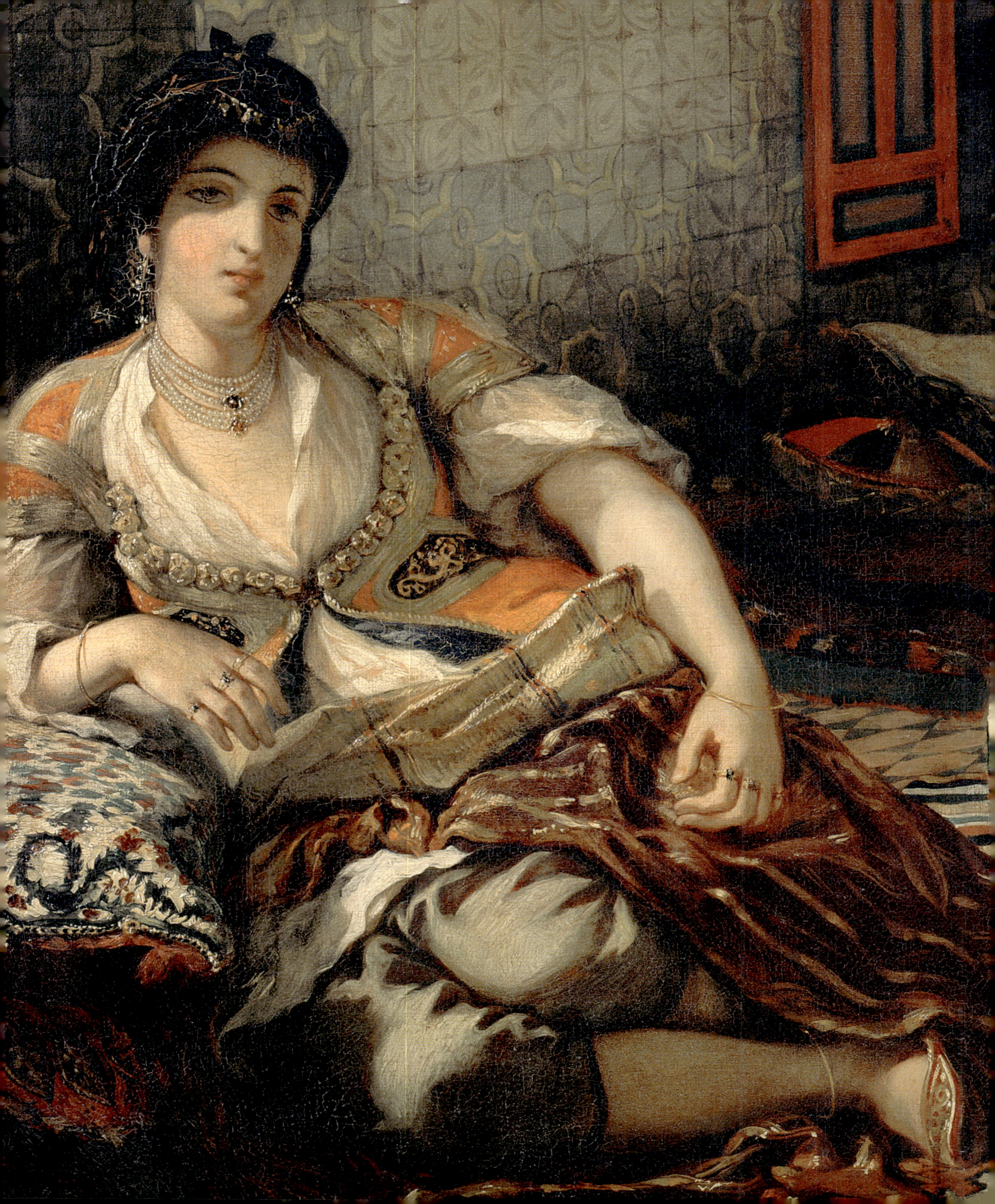

"The Shades Interpenetrate Like Silks"

In the painting of 1834, Delacroix succeeded in "attracting interest by means of paint alone, unaided by a subject, which can be interpreted in a thousand different ways and too often distracts the eye of casual viewers."[149] As in *The Death of Sardanapalus*, but by opposite means, he managed to assert the power of the execution in the completed work and to remind viewers that every painting consists of the substance of paint itself. In *The Death of Sardanapalus*, that assertion came about through struggle, in the competition between a violent, dark, and sensual subject and an overwrought execution that flaunted itself in order to rise to the level of the representation. In *Women of Algiers*, by contrast, the weakening of the narrative allowed the execution to predominate almost naturally, in a process that culminated in a form of abstraction—the abstraction of color. Delacroix no longer sought to emphasize the concrete materiality of his medium. In 1824 he had described his oil paints in terms of their physical characteristics—as "fat" and "thick"; beginning with *Women of Algiers*, however, he would reduce the visibility of the brushwork and play instead on the vibrations and the level of intensity of the color. His visit to Morocco, and probably, as Charles Blanc reported, his observation of moiré fabrics, led him to an awareness of the interweaving of colors and the intensity that colors acquire when they interact with one another. The weaving metaphor is particularly apt. As Maxime du Camp recounted in his *Souvenirs littéraires*: "I saw him one evening near a table where there was a basket full of wool skeins. He picked up the skeins, grouped them, rearranged them up, divided them by shade, and thereby produced extraordinary color effects. I heard him say: 'The most beautiful paintings I have seen are certain Persian carpets.'"[150] If the anecdote is true, the association of carpets and paintings once again raises the question of the place of the subject.

In *Women of Algiers*, Delacroix experimented intuitively and for the first time with the law of simultaneous contrast and the optical mixture of complementary colors, which would be theorized by the chemist Michel Eugène Chevreul five years later, in 1839. This manner of paint application confers on the viewer an active role, since the mixing of colors occurs in the eye and brain rather than on the palette. A more intense green

is achieved, for instance, when a painter, instead of mixing a yellow with a blue on his palette, juxtaposes a dab of blue and a dab of yellow directly on the canvas, following a method Delacroix would call *flochetage*. Some critics would denounce the technique for creating "the fuzzy effect of a tapestry viewed from the wrong side."[151] In *Women of Algiers* a good example can be found in the cushion on which the reclining figure at the left is resting. The extraordinary vibration of the painting originates in the *flochetage*. Passages of pure color structure the composition: blue (the servant's vest and the stripes of her dress, the silk garment worn by the figure in the center, the patterned floor tiles); red (the servant's dress and slippers, the doors and hangings, the patterns in the carpets), and yellow (the gold objects and textiles). The black skin and turning motion of the servant, who is standing, provide a counterpoint to the milky flesh tones and immobility of the other women. Between these areas, the artist deployed a dizzying array of virtuoso contrasts between primary, secondary, and complementary colors, enriching one another even in the smallest details of the scarves and fabrics. The orange of the reclining woman's bolero interacts with the complementary blue of the garment's lining, which mirrors the servant's vest on the other side of the composition. In the foreground, the red babouche edged with gold seems to have been cast casually onto the green fringe of the carpet—that is, on its complementary color.

Referring to *Women of Algiers*, Paul Cézanne declared that "the shades interpenetrate like silks" to such an extent that the materiality of the objects dissolves in the symphony of colors.[152] The projected space of the painting, built on the intricacy of these colored dabs, resembles the Persian carpets the painter considered the most beautiful of paintings, like the fabrics he accumulated in his masterpiece. Charles Blanc chose the comparison of a shawl: "When we look at a cashmere shawl from a few steps away, we usually perceive shades that are not in the fabric but are themselves composed inside our eye by the effect of reciprocal reactions of one shade with another."[153] The result is an infinite variety of color impressions that language cannot describe: "In *The Women of Algiers*, a blouse dotted with little flowers gives rise to a third, undefinable tone that the eye perceives but that language cannot name precisely. A copyist will never obtain it if he tries to compose it beforehand and deposit it on the canvas with the tip of his brush."[154] The painter's art long preceded the art of discourse; a painting doesn't require a catalogue entry.

Delacroix was right: when he made a beautiful painting, he was not writing down an idea.

Above all, *flochetage* entailed a departure from the classical notion of local color, which is predicated on the essence of a thing. The principle assumes that every object possesses a natural color that can be isolated by precisely drawing the model. Black is then added to that color to produce shadows, in a subtle chiaroscuro.[155] Delacroix realized that the addition of black only muddied the color because the shadows themselves are colored, resulting, as they do, from reflections. He seems to have made the discovery in Morocco, where in one of his albums he wrote: "Adding black is not the same as adding gray tones: it muddies the color, whose true gray tone is to be found in the opposite color; therefore, green shadow in the red."[156] Well-defined contours do not exist in nature, and the color of an object contaminates that of its neighbors. If local color is rooted in the search for an essence or in the objective consistency of things, *flochetage* highlights the vibration, even the instability, of the sensation. An object can be valorized by its identity, but that identity is not realized in isolation. It comes into being in the porousness between the object and its environment, like the red babouche on the carpet's bold green fringe.

The glorification of luminous color and matter was Delacroix's great discovery in *Women of Algiers*. The work has the value of a manifesto insofar as its subject is dissolved in the effects of color; the tension between the subject and its realization is here at its height. However, a classically trained artist such as Delacroix knew that this boldness, this exhibition of color as matter, ran the risk of lowering the painting to the ranks of the merely decorative, or to art for art's sake. The many allusions by his contemporaries to tapestries, carpets, and cashmere, though often laudatory, are proof of the risk. In 1841 Gautier noted that *Entry of the Crusaders into Constantinople* (see fig. 36) had been maliciously compared to a Gobelins tapestry:

> *Baldwin* elicits the strongest criticism, and its success is the most contested: it is criticized primarily for a

certain Gobelins tapestry look. The reproach is well founded, but there is nothing very alarming about it. Gobelins tapestries are very beautiful, and the color is proof of the painter's delicacy of feeling. In executing a ceremonial piece, he gave it something of the ornamental aspect of a wall hanging, which is altogether appropriate, since, after all, the painting will decorate a gallery.[157]

The painting reduced to an objet d'art: that was the danger Delacroix would try to ward off.

After experimenting with the "facility of the brush" in *The Death of Sardanapalus*, and then moving away from that virtuosity, Delacroix became absorbed in the seductiveness of color only to master it more completely. The artist's career, as detailed in his writing, was composed of these experiments, advances, formulations, followed by rectifications, which, like *flochetage*, constantly made the meaning in his paintings more precise without ever providing a definitive interpretation. Therein lay Delacroix's difficulty. After the brilliant feat of *Women of Algiers*, for example, he returned even in the canvases inspired by his travels to privileging subject over execution (*Convulsionists of Tangier*, *Jewish Wedding in Morocco*) and, in the later version of *Women of Algiers*, to using chiaroscuro effects as a means of dramatization.

The simultaneous exhibition of *Medea About to Kill Her Children* (see cat. 94) and *Convulsionists of Tangier* (see fig. 34) at the Salon of 1838 seemed an attempt to resolve the dialectic between color and subject. The confrontation between an ancient act of rage and a contemporary form of trance was probably not coincidental. The images seem to represent two aspects of a single passion expressed in two different "genres" at two historical moments. That is what Théophile Gautier appeared to sense, without saying so explicitly, in his review of the Salon: "It [the *Medea*] is an ancient subject treated with modern intelligence using forms more human than ideal. That contrast has a piquancy to it, and the most worn-out subjects in the world would take on a youthful vitality and novelty if understood in that way. There is a complete revolution in that idea."[158]

Delacroix's first decade as an artist can be understood reasonably well through his participation in the Salon, the question of originality, the stakes of fame, and his desire to master and combine multiple pictorial genres. By contrast, the strategies that guided his prolific artistic output after 1832 are more difficult to decipher. In the second decade, Delacroix continued to work simultaneously in all the genres he had mastered in the 1820s: political and biblical history, battle scenes, poetry and theater, animal pictures, Moroccan genre scenes, portraits, and still lifes. He further expanded his repertoire while executing the large decorative projects that absorbed him beginning in 1833. From that point forward he proved himself in the loftiest categories of academic painting—allegory, myth, and ancient history—as well as their counterpoint, ornamental painting (floral compositions and large-scale murals). Thus it was that Delacroix distinguished himself as an all-around genius in the second half of the 1830s (cat. 93). He was forty and his career spanned just fifteen years when Théophile Gautier lauded him in his review of the Salon of 1838:

> M. Eugène Delacroix is one of the most adventurous talents of the time; he has a certain restlessness, a certain feverish genius, that impels him to experiment in all sorts of ways; no one has looked more deeply into himself. . . . M. Eugène Delacroix, in his desire to achieve perfection, has attempted every form, every style, and every color; there is no genre he has touched without leaving some noble and luminous trace. Few painters have covered as vast a field as M. Delacroix; his oeuvre is already nearly as impressive as that of a golden-age Venetian. He has done frescoes, monumental works, history paintings, genre paintings, battle scenes, interiors, horses as skillfully as Gericault, lions and tigers as fine as those of Barye or Desportes.[1]

Gautier's enthusiastic description masks, however, the change in the relative importance of the different categories within Delacroix's iconographic repertoire. In fact, the artist's search for original painting subjects, which up until then he had drawn largely from recent literature or political history,

had slowed. After the first years of the reign of King Louis-Philippe, Delacroix lost interest in painting the disasters of war of his time and the spirit of the revolutions that were unsettling Europe's political order; the Revolutions of 1848–49 were not reflected in his paintings. While still engaging his favorite literary references—Byron, Dante, Shakespeare, Scott, Tasso—he focused the greater part of his research on iconography associated with the sixteenth- and seventeenth-century pictorial traditions of France, Italy, and the Low Countries. These included martyrdoms and miracles taken from the Gospels and lives of the saints, which featured in more than seventy paintings between 1832 and 1863; attributes of virtue drawn from biographies of illustrious men of antiquity; fables of Greek mythology (Hesiod, Ovid); and episodes from chivalric romances of the Renaissance (Ariosto, Tasso). All these subjects occupied a much larger place in Delacroix's oeuvre in the years after 1832 than they had during his first decade as an artist.

The traditional character of his subjects was combined with a growing eclecticism in his compositions. Delacroix devoted new attention to studying the great geniuses of the past, seemingly at the expense of his rivalries with contemporaries. From then on, he emulated revered painters as diverse as Rubens, Titian, Veronese, Rembrandt, Poussin, and Raphael, whose work would inform his large decorative projects and his reflections on art. His increasingly transparent quotation of painterly references began to be remarked upon in the mid-1830s. Gustave Planche, for example, on seeing *Saint Sebastian Tended by the Holy Women* (see cat. 90) at the Salon of 1836, rightly raised questions about his disparate choices, though he was sympathetic to them:

> This year's color obviously recalls Titian; last year, *Christ on the Cross* brought to mind Rubens; in 1834, *Women of Algiers* was reminiscent of Veronese. How does M. Delacroix pursue with such tireless perseverance both imitation and originality? How, even while retaining the individuality and indelible characteristics of his own thought, does he reproduce by turns the Flemish style and the Venetian style? Why does he sometimes select Veronese and sometimes Titian from

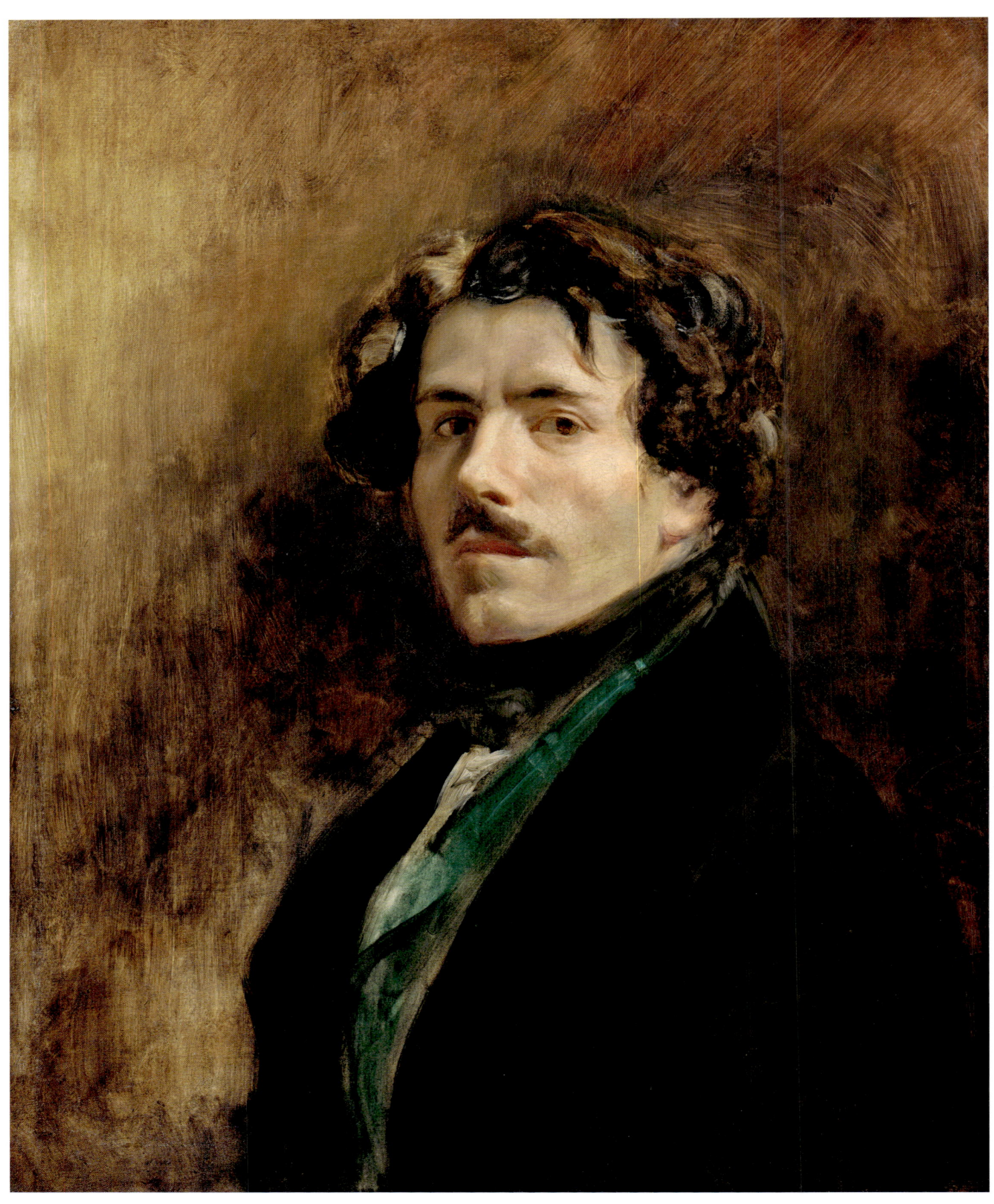

CAT. 93 *Self-Portrait in a Green Vest*, ca. 1837

among the Venetian masters? Is it not because of his immoderate desire to do things well? Must we not believe that M. Delacroix, sincere in each of his works, in every ambition he realizes, is never satisfied with himself and is perpetually seeking a new manner, as if he had not yet found one? Is that not the conclusion that arises naturally in the presence of the artist's works, so numerous and so varied?[2]

What is interesting about Planche's questioning is that it conveys the impression that, beginning in 1834, Delacroix's submissions to the Salons did not reflect as consistent a plan as did the works he had exhibited at the Salons of the 1820s. (The exception was the *Battle of Nancy*, see cat. 69, commissioned in 1828 and a product of its time.) The later works display a bewildering diversity of textual and stylistic references, as can be seen by examining Delacroix's participation at the Salons held between 1833 and 1849.

After his trip to Morocco in the first half of 1832, the artist had barely enough time to submit a few watercolors and portraits to the Salon of 1833. His return to history painting was evident in 1834, with *Women of Algiers in Their Apartment,* a large-format Moroccan genre scene done in the manner of Veronese (see cat. 83), and in 1835, with *Christ on the Cross,* his first Christian martyrdom, which was greatly influenced by Rubens (see cat. 85). The following year, Delacroix exhibited a second Christian martyrdom, *Saint Sebastian,* in which certain motifs were indebted to Michelangelo and Rubens but the overall composition of which is usually associated with Venetian influence (see cat. 90). He showed only one work at the Salon of 1837, *Battle of Taillebourg,* a large picture commissioned for the Musée de l'Histoire de France at Versailles, clearly inspired by Rubens's *Battle of the Amazons* (1615; Alte Pinakothek, Munich). This was followed in 1838 by a scene from Greek mythology, *Medea About to Kill Her Children* (see cat. 94), in which critics noted a curious mix of Correggio, Michelangelo, and Rembrandt. It was accompanied by a sort of genre painting, *Convulsionists of Tangier,* a large outdoor Moroccan scene (see fig. 34).

The following year, at the Salon of 1839, both of Delacroix's submissions drew on Shakespearean sources, but to very different effect. The open, well-balanced *Hamlet and Horatio in the Graveyard,* his second painted version of the subject (cat. 96), was set against the monumentality of the Caravaggesque *Cleopatra and the Peasant* (see cat. 95). In 1840

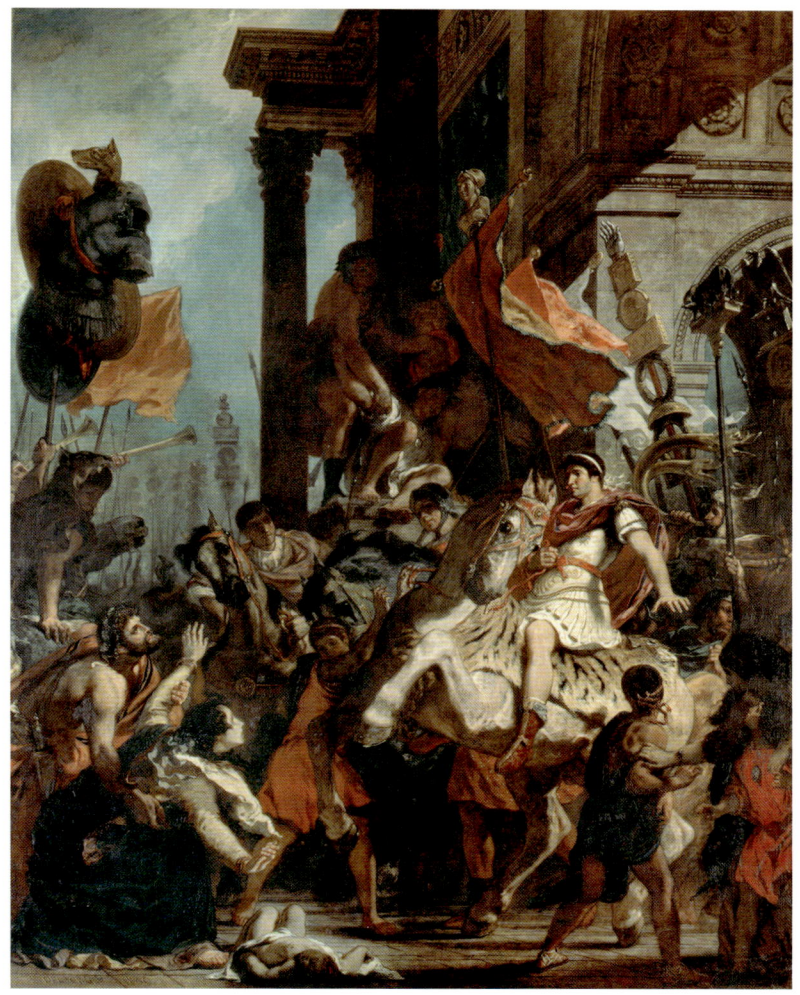

FIG. 35 *The Justice of Trajan,* 1840. Oil on canvas, 16 ft. 15/16 in. x 12 ft. 9 9/16 in. (4.9 x 3.9 m). Musée des Beaux-Arts, Rouen (inv. D 1844.1) (J 271)

and 1841, the splendor of Delacroix's palette burst forth, and the critics were enchanted by his remarkably rich, luminous *grandes machines.* The Salon of 1840 was dominated by the spectacular *Justice of Trajan* (fig. 35), an ancient subject that Delacroix had discovered in Byron and treated with the eloquence of Veronese and Rubens. This was followed in 1841 by three submissions: *Entry of the Crusaders into Constantinople* (fig. 36), his second medieval history painting commissioned for Versailles; a Byronian *Shipwreck* (see cat. 98) that evoked Gericault and embodied the results of Delacroix's own first seascape studies; and a genre scene, *Jewish Wedding in Morocco,* in which architecture plays a leading role (see fig. 31).

Troubled by ill health and absorbed in major decorative works, Delacroix abstained from exhibiting for three years in a row, returning in 1845 with large compositions that seemed

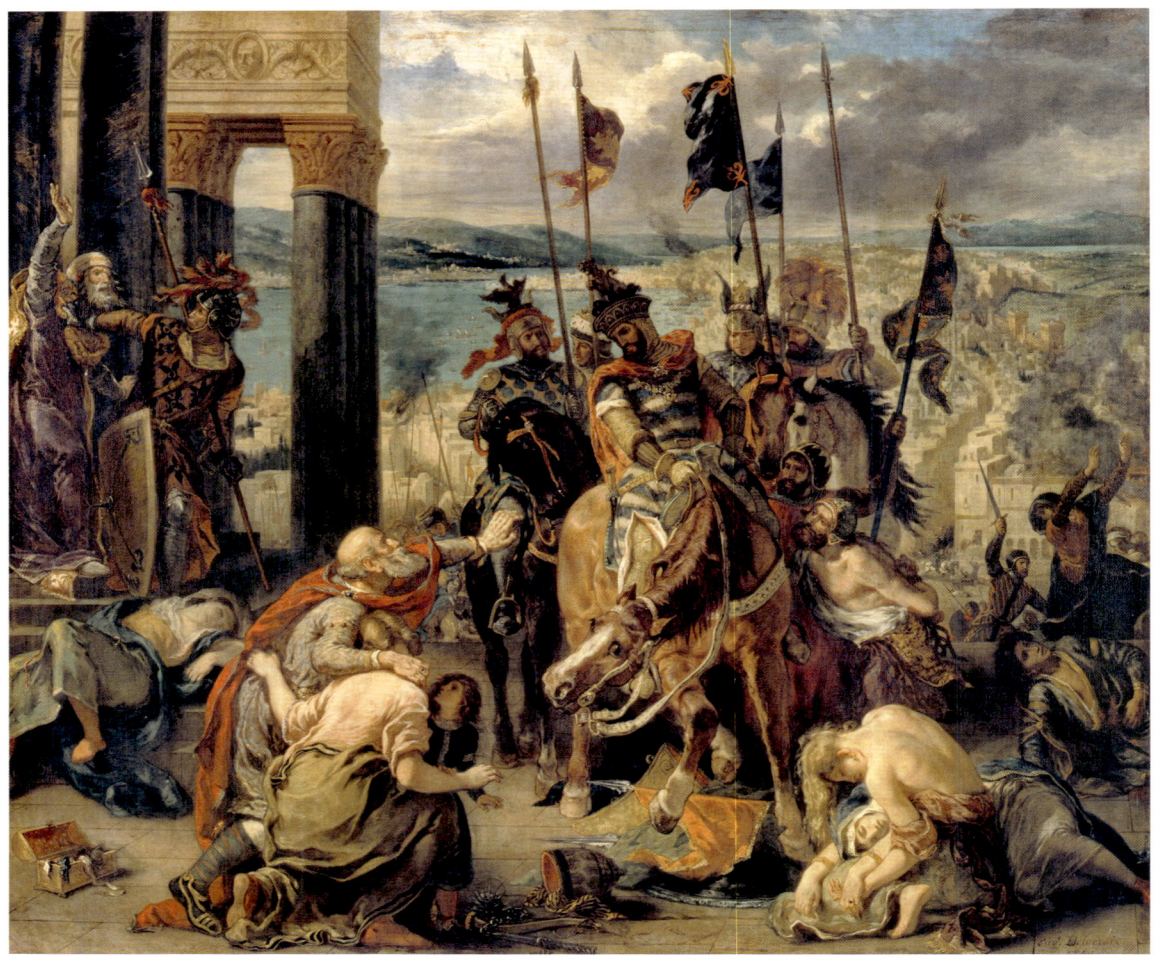

FIG. 36 *Entry of the Crusaders into Constantinople*, 1840. Oil on canvas, 13 ft. 5⁷⁄₁₆ in. x 16 ft. 4¹⁄₁₆ in. (4.1 x 5 m). Musée du Louvre, Paris (3821) (J 274)

solemn and somber compared with those he had shown the Salons of 1840 and 1841: *Last Words of Marcus Aurelius* (1844; Musée des Beaux-Arts, Lyon), a tribute to the great Roman emperor and Stoic in which Delacroix measured himself against Poussin's *Death of Germanicus* (1627; Minneapolis Institute of Art) and David's *Death of Socrates* (1787; Metropolitan Museum); *The Sultan of Morocco and His Entourage* (fig. 37; see also cat. 138), with a static character, majesty, and silence that are diametrically opposed to the turmoil in *The Justice of Trajan;* and finally, a *Cumaean Sibyl* inspired by Dante and a *Mary Magdalene in the Wilderness,* each massive, sculptural, and enigmatic in its way (see fig. 122). A change of course was discernible in the Salons of 1846 and 1847: Delacroix displayed only small paintings invoking his memories of Morocco and the Romantic literary references of his youth—Shakespeare, Scott, Byron, Goethe—sometimes reinterpreted after old lithographs. The Salon of 1848 offered additional surprises, with the exhibition of *The Lamentation (Christ at the Tomb),*

a large, austere, neo-Caravaggesque meditation (see cat. 106); and, even more remarkable in the highly charged political context of the Salon of 1849, the darkest, most Rembrandtesque version of the *Women of Algiers in Their Apartment* (see fig. 32), accompanied by an *Othello and Desdemona* imbued with the same atmosphere of mystery (see fig. 116). These two submissions contrasted sharply with a pair of neo-Baroque floral compositions, opulent and densely filled (see cats. 109, 110). A series comprising paintings as heterogeneous as these came across as incomprehensible, impossible to relate to a unified, well-thought-out strategy: the submissions to the Salon were obviously inconsistent from one year to the next. However, the best-informed critics understood that Delacroix was employing at least three different strategies at once: the transposition and elaboration of experiments carried out in the large decorative programs; ceaseless dialogue with Rubens; and further development of his own repertoire of favorite motifs.

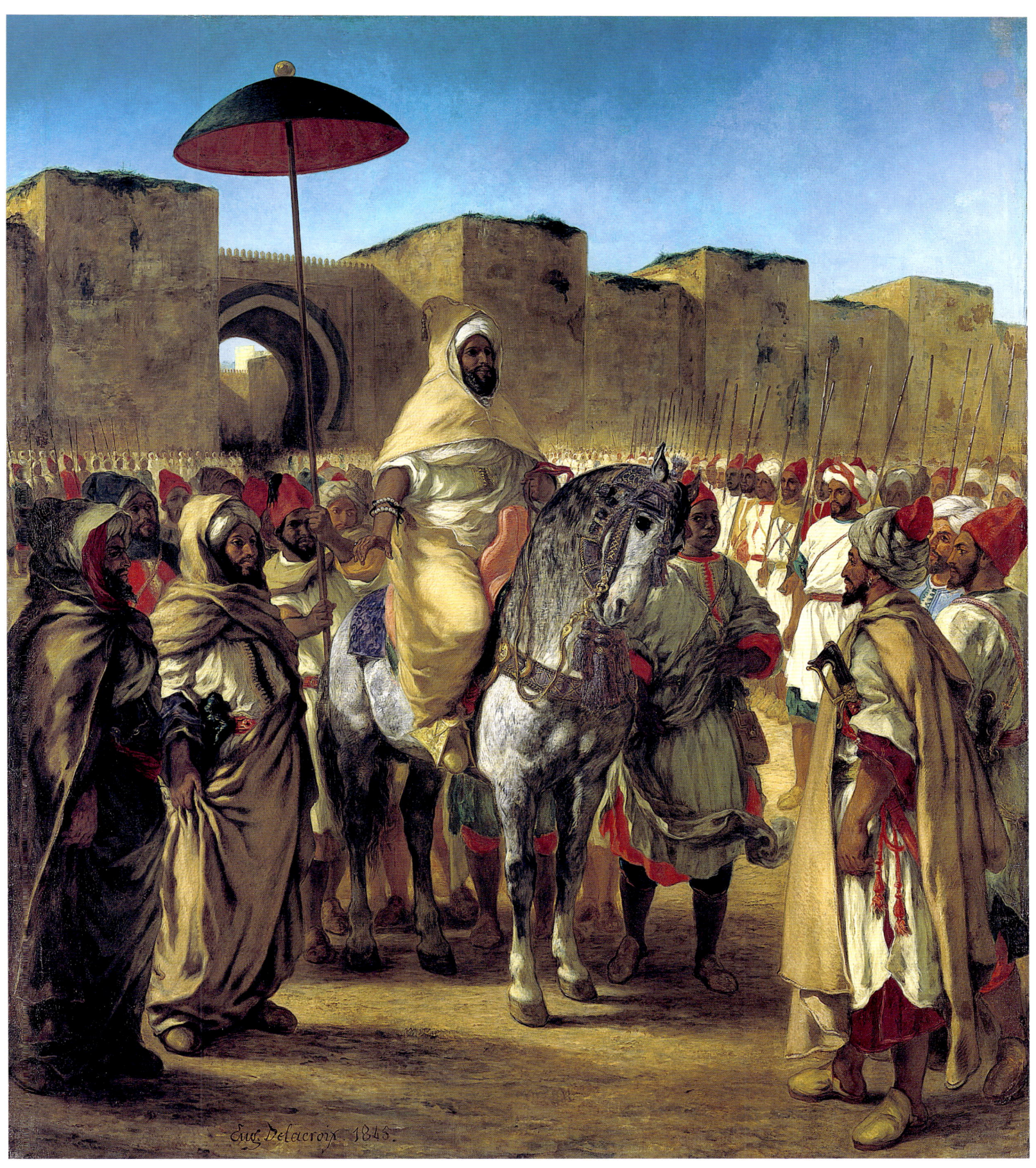

FIG. 37 *The Sultan of Morocco and His Entourage (Moulay Abd-er-Rahman, Sultan of Morocco, Emerging from His Palace in Meknes, Accompanied by His Guard and Principal Officers)*, 1845. Oil on canvas, 12 ft. 7³⁄₁₆ in. x 11 ft. 3¹⁄₁₆ in. (3.8 x 3.4 m). Musée des Augustins, Toulouse (inv. 2004 I 99) (J 370)

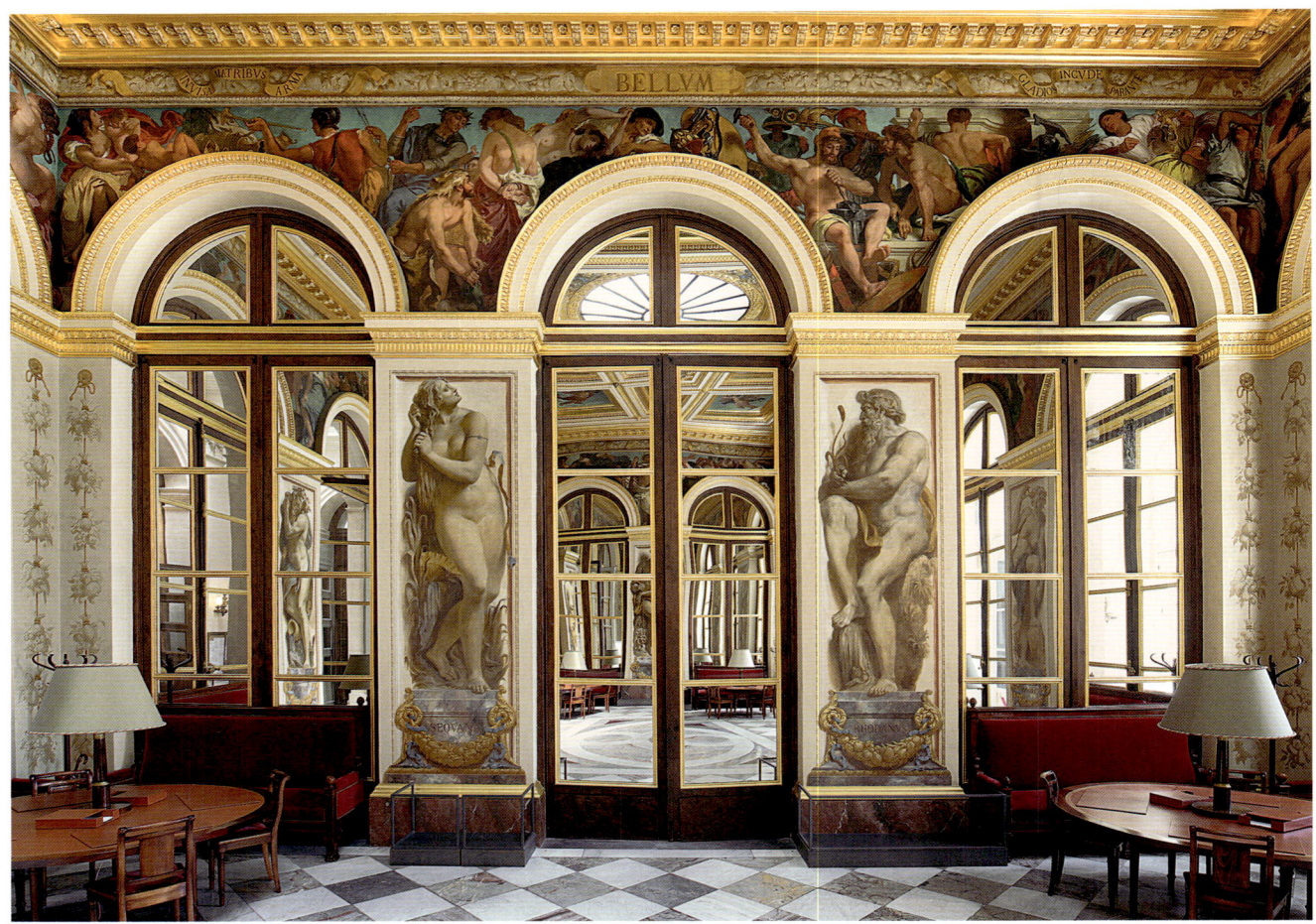

FIG. 38 Eastern wall of the Salon du Roi, Assemblée Nationale (Palais Bourbon), Paris, featuring the frieze painting *War (Bellum)* and the pier paintings *The Seine (Sequana)* and *The Rhone (Rhodanus)*, 1833–37. Oil and wax on plaster

A number of the historical compositions that Delacroix presented at the Salon can be understood as the visible portion of a creative output with a center of gravity that lay elsewhere—in the monumental decorative works. Enormous but largely inaccessible, these projects were an essential source of renewal in his painting. Gautier, Planche, and an anonymous critic at *L'artiste*, likely tipped off by the painter, seem to have been the first to realize this.

The second thread Delacroix pursued was a dialogue with the masters, particularly Rubens, who was for him the absolute and infinitely prolific master. Delacroix was stimulated by every new encounter with Rubens's masterpieces during his visits to French museums in Nancy, Bordeaux, and Rouen and in Belgian churches, but also through engravings. He entered into competition with the Flemish master and regularly sought to cross swords with him by reinterpreting his seminal works, both religious—*Christ on the Cross, Christ at the Column (The Flagellation)*, *Christ Calming the Sea*

(see fig. 79), *The Entombment of Christ*—and profane—*The Lion Hunt, Hippopotamus and Crocodile Hunt* (see fig. 59), *Abduction of the Daughters of Leucippus* (see fig. 101), *The Battle of the Amazons*.

A third driving force of his art was superimposed on the first two. The recurrence of the same subjects in successive submissions to the Salon reveals that an increasing share of Delacroix's output followed the principle of repetition with variations. That is, the artist reprised his own earlier subjects and motifs, most of which originated in the late 1820s and early 1830s. *Saint Sebastian,* for example, exists in no fewer than six versions. Such extensive self-referentiality adds to the complication of interpreting Delacroix's work. The "reprises," usually in small formats, were no doubt a form of relaxation for the painter, who enjoyed retracing his own steps, free of competition, to develop an early idea along new lines. They also satisfied the demand of the burgeoning art market and thus served a commercial purpose. On a deeper level, however, it seems that they were prompted by a reflexive proclivity characteristic of the now-mature artist, who was alert to the passage of time and its effect on his oeuvre.

The Canvas and the Wall

Delacroix's interest in large mural decoration, now well known, arose in the 1830s. As early as 1830–31, he competed for the opportunity to decorate the wall behind the rostrum of the Chamber of Deputies in the Palais Bourbon, seat of the Assemblée Nationale, though the sketch he submitted was rejected (see cat. 70). In 1838 the decoration for the Salon du Roi (fig. 38), entrusted to the artist five years earlier, had only just been completed when he was awarded a commission for the decoration of the library in the Chamber of Deputies (fig. 39). The assignment resulted from his efforts to secure a project "that would satisfy my need to work big, [a need] which becomes insistent once you've had a taste of it,"[3] and it occupied him for a decade. Its execution was slowed by his acceptance in 1840 of two additional mural projects: the cupola and hemicycle of the Peers' Library at the Palais du Luxembourg (fig. 40) and the Chapel of the Virgin at the church of Saint-Denys-du-Saint-Sacrement (see fig. 48), commissioned by the prefecture of the Seine. The same year, Delacroix accepted a commission to create cartoons for stained-glass windows for the Manufacture Nationale de Sèvres. During the advent of the Second Republic, between 1848 and 1851, he even tried having himself named director of the manufacture des Gobelins.[4] Under the republican government led by Napoleon Bonaparte, he received commissions for two Parisian projects: a section of the ceiling in the Louvre's Gallery of Apollo (1849–51; see fig. 53) and a chapel in the church of Saint-Sulpice (1849–61; see figs. 69, 70). In addition, the City of Paris asked him to decorate a salon in the Hôtel de Ville (1851–54).

Plagued by frequent illness from 1842 onward, Delacroix was obliged to delegate to assistants parts of the considerable labor required to execute these projects. It was the first time he had taken such a step. Inevitably, there were disagreements with the architects, patrons, and his own assistants, and the work took a toll on his fragile constitution. Despite all that, and despite the decidedly poor financial compensation he received when compared to what he earned for his highly prized small paintings, Delacroix left none of these undertakings unfinished.

The passion that enabled him to surmount so many obstacles cannot be explained solely by the prestigious nature of the commissions. Mural painting resonated deeply with his new ambitions, which were those of a mature artist aware that the strategy of his early years, which focused almost exclusively on the Salon, no longer sufficed.

The failure of *The Death of Sardanapalus* (see fig. 20) at the Salon of 1827–28 is usually seen as having broken the momentum of Delacroix's career, provoking a phase of discouragement that lasted several years. Then came the Revolution of July 1830, which rid him of the enmity of the vicomte Sosthènes de La Rochefoucauld, director of fine arts, followed by the trip to Morocco in 1832, which opened up new perspectives. These events have long been understood as the positive, liberating factors that enabled the artist to strike

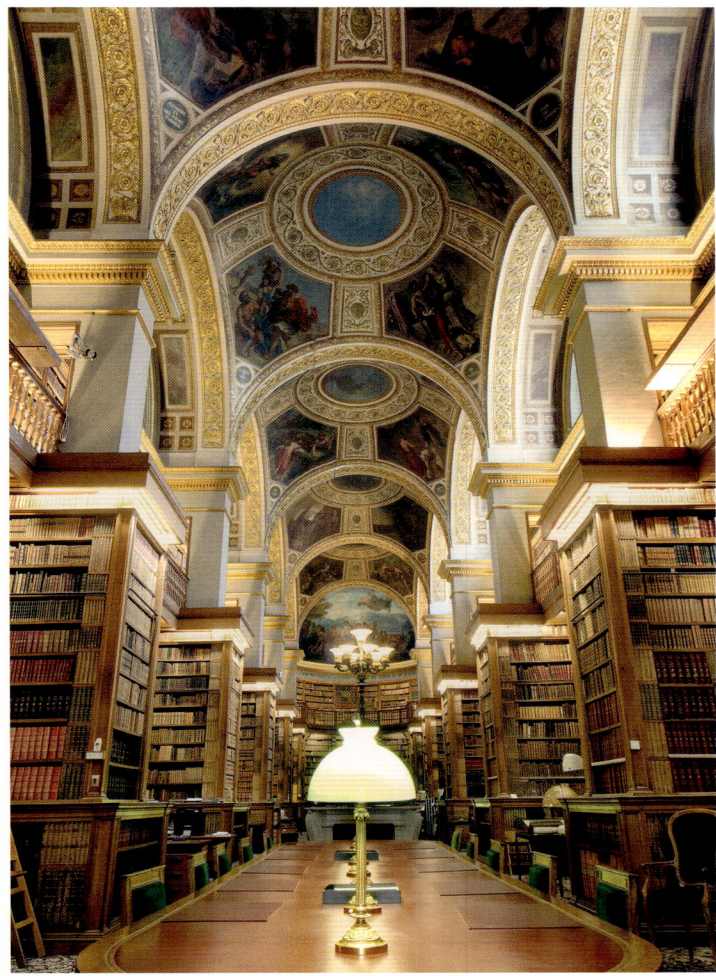

FIG. 39 Interior view of the Deputies' Library, Assemblée Nationale (Palais Bourbon), Paris, featuring ceiling paintings by Delacroix, 1841–47. Oil and wax on plaster

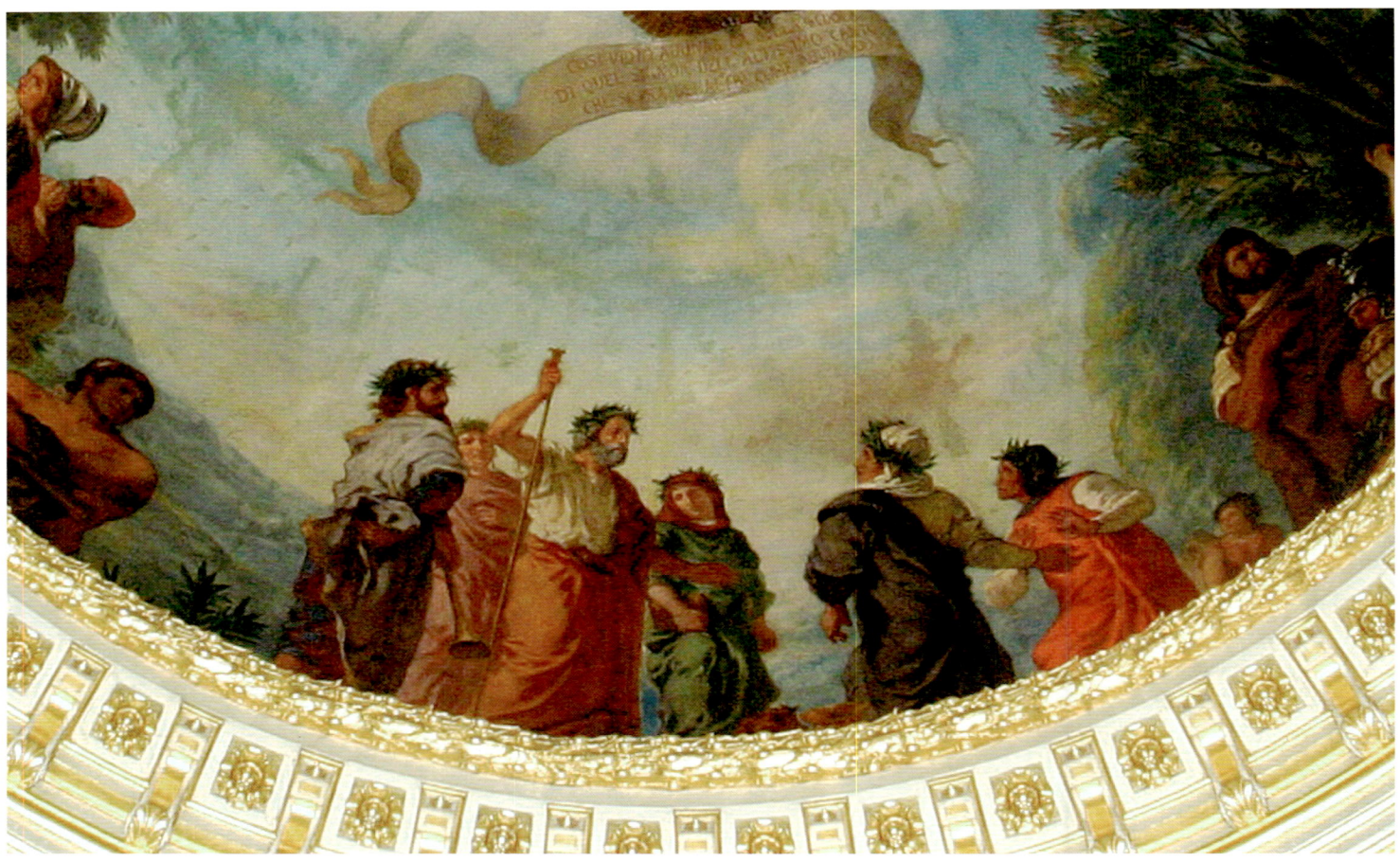

FIG. 40 *Dante and the Spirits of the Great*, 1841–45. Diam. 22 ft. 4 in. (6.8 m). Detail of cupola of the Peers' Library, Palais du Luxembourg, Paris

out in new directions. However, careful examination of Delacroix's early relations with the administration leads to a different hypothesis, one that attributes the leveling off in the artist's career trajectory not to supposed hostility from the department of museums under Charles X but to something rather different.

In fact, the painter had achieved his professional objectives at a very young age and as a result quickly found himself at an impasse. It was the young Delacroix's ambition to achieve glory by having his works exhibited in museums while preserving his originality through his participation at the Salons. He had the extraordinary privilege of having one of his paintings admitted to the Musée Royal des Artistes Vivantes the first time he participated at the Salon, in 1822. At the age of twenty-four, ahead of some of his most promising fellow artists from Guérin's studio (Théodore Gericault, Léon Cogniet), Delacroix secured a place alongside David, Prud'hon, and Girodet at the Musée du Luxembourg. The museum acquired a second work by Delacroix in 1824. This

streak of good fortune ended in 1828, when the department of museums refused to purchase *The Death of Sardanapalus* or any of his other submissions to the Salon of 1827–28. The painter had surely gone too far in asserting his artistic singularity, but the refusal was based above all else on the administration's belief that Delacroix was sufficiently well represented at the Musée du Luxembourg and found it more judicious to continue its support in the form of commissions. It did so generously; however, commissions imposed significant constraints and resulted in the dispersal of his works. Each commission was for a specific site and came with a preselected subject, format, and deadline for completion. Delacroix was loath to see his major history paintings sent off to museums far from Paris (see cat. 69) or to locations in the capital that were relatively inaccessible. For example, the third room of the Conseil d'Etat at the Louvre, where *Emperor Justinian*, commissioned in 1826 (see cat. 28), was displayed, was open to the public for only a few days during the Salon of 1827–28, and *Christ in the Garden of Olives* (see cat. 17) was hung high in the

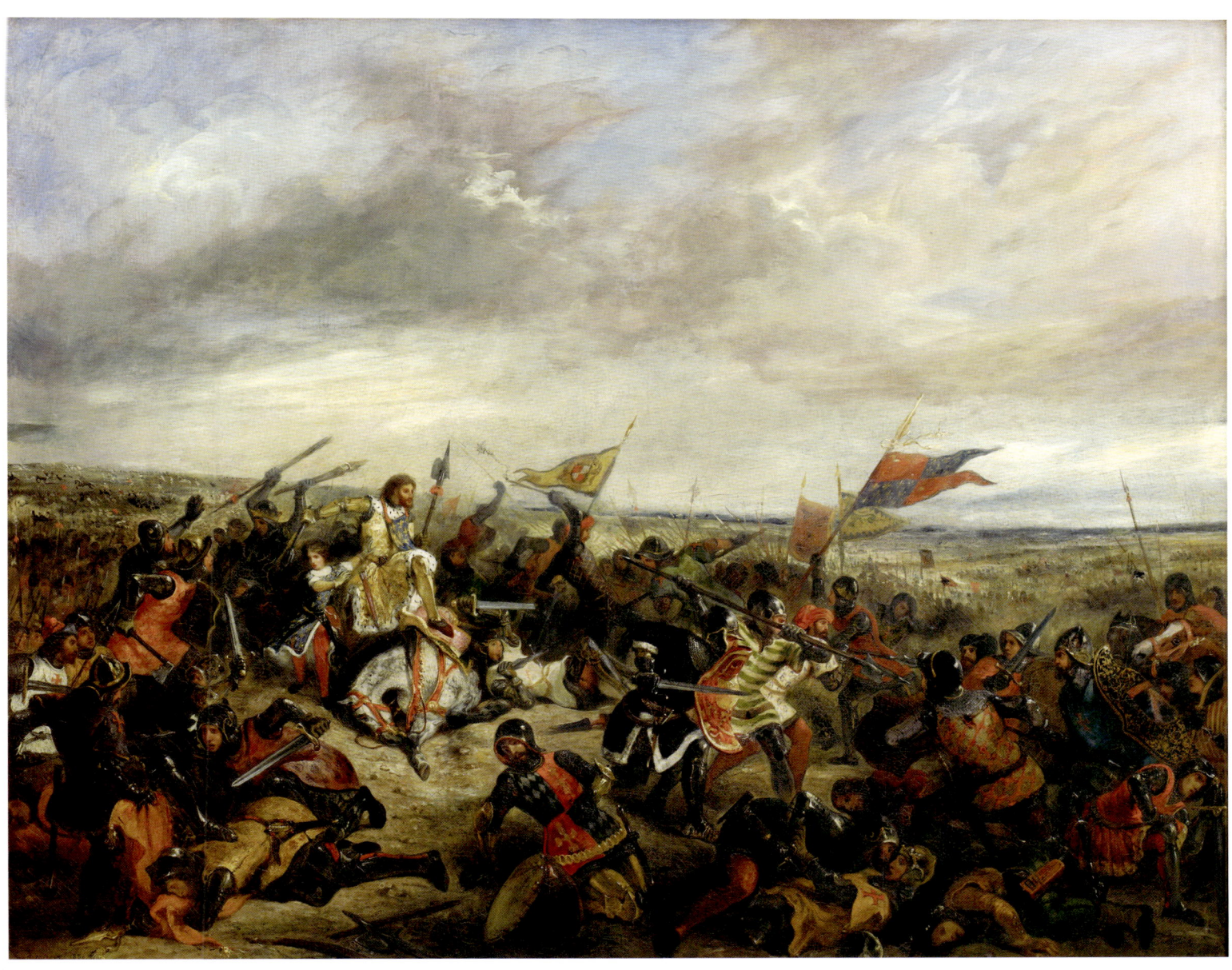

CAT. 68 *The Battle of Poitiers*, 1830

transept of the church of Saint-Paul-Saint-Louis.[5] In the case of one private commission, *The Battle of Poitiers* (cat. 68), the artist was obliged to take legal means to obtain the return of the painting after his patron, the duchesse de Berry, was forced into exile.

Although the change of regime in 1830 and the trip to Morocco in 1832 provided him with breathing room, they were not sufficient to revitalize his art over the long term. In the early days of the July Monarchy Delacroix hoped once again that he would see more of his history paintings enter the Musée du Luxembourg. He was not disappointed; the department of museums made purchases at the conclusion of the

Salons of 1831 (*Liberty Leading the People*) and 1834 (*Women of Algiers in Their Apartment*) (cat. 83). The bright spell was short, however. *Liberty Leading the People* was quickly relegated to storage for political reasons, and Delacroix failed to win the competition of 1830–31 for two historical compositions destined for the Chamber of Deputies (cat. 70). In the end, the works by Delacroix that the state acquired after 1834 were most often bought by the Ministère de l'Intérieur and not by the intendance de la Liste civile, which oversaw acquisitions selected by the king for the department of the Musée du Louvre and the Musée du Luxembourg. Because the Ministère de l'Intérieur was responsible for procuring works of art for

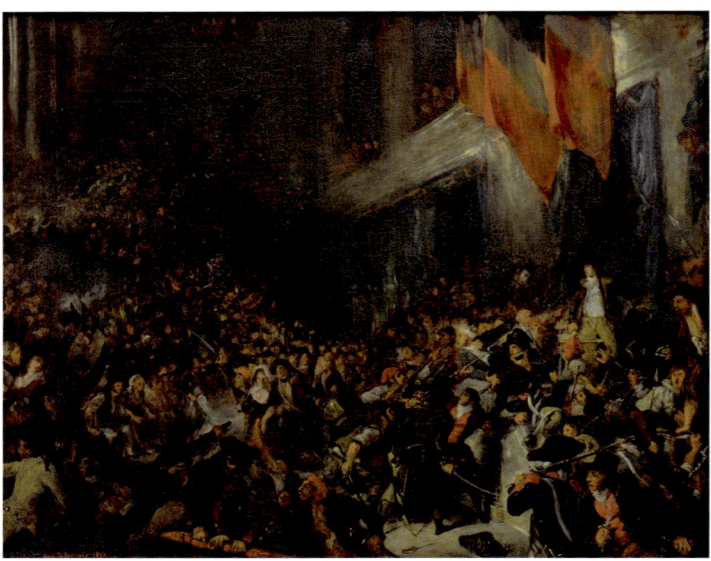

CAT. 70 *Boissy d'Anglas at the Convention, sketch,* 1831

provincial churches and museums, the large compositions by Delacroix that the administration purchased were systematically sent away from Paris. *Christ on the Cross* (see cat. 85) was dispatched to the church of Saint-Paterne in Vannes, and *Saint Sebastian* (see cat. 90) was acquired for the church of Saint-Michel in Nantua at the request of a deputy from the department of Ain. Delacroix was sorry to see these scenes of martyrdom transported to churches. He had not intended them for religious institutions but rather to be placed in museums, next to masterpieces of religious art. Furthermore, he worried about the damage his works would suffer at the hands of uncomprehending clergy and in the poor atmospheric conditions of churches.

These fears were confirmed some twenty-five years later, as documented in an alarmist letter Delacroix sent to the state finance minister, Achille Fould:

I have learned that this work [*Christ on the Cross,* cat. 85], long placed in a dark, damp chapel of the church [Saint-Paterne, Vannes], is threatened with complete destruction if the situation continues. I take the liberty of appealing to Your Excellency, to ask if it might be possible to have the city return the threatened painting to Paris. . . . In addition, it was suggested to me that the unfavorable place allotted to my painting might be explained by a Mary Magdalene figure that the clergy did not find sufficiently draped.[6]

Delacroix spoke from experience: he had already observed the deterioration of *Christ in the Garden of Olives* (cat. 17), which had hung in the transept of the church of Saint-Paul-Saint-Louis since its completion. In 1837 Théophile Thoré reported that "the moisture [was] beginning to dull the colors."[7] In 1855, when it had become "barely visible under the layers of mold and varnish," Delacroix restored it in order to display it at the Exposition Universelle. He was afraid that, by returning it to the church, "given the height at which it [was] placed and the difficulty of maintaining it, it [would] perish within a few years."[8]

Does that explain why for ten years, between 1837 and 1846, Delacroix chose not to display large religious compositions at the Salon? His strategy at least ensured that paintings acquired by the Ministère de l'Intérieur would be sent to museums and not churches. In 1838, the year after he exhibited the *Battle of Taillebourg,* commissioned for the museum at Versailles, Delacroix submitted *Medea About to Kill Her Children* (see cat. 94), which the ministry bought and sent to the Palais des Beaux-Arts, Lille. At first, the artist protested vehemently, insisting that the work be purchased by the intendance de la Liste civile for the Musée du Luxembourg. The Ministère de l'Intérieur, no longer run by Adolphe Thiers but by the comte Duchâtel, refused to give in. It merely agreed to have the painting lent to the Paris museum for a year before being sent permanently to Lille.

Delacroix expressed his resentment to his friend Edmond Cavé, head of the division des Belles-Lettres et des Arts à l'Intérieur at the Ministère de l'Intérieur: "I accept the proposal you were kind enough to make on the minister's behalf, though the temporary exhibition at the Musée du Luxembourg far from fulfills my objective, which was to ensure that the painting would not leave Paris."[9] The next acquisition by the Ministère de l'Intérieur was the occasion for further wrangling: *The Justice of Trajan* (see fig. 35), exhibited at the Salon of 1840, was acquired two years later for the Musée des Beaux-Arts, Bordeaux. Delacroix was fond of the city, where his father had been prefect and where his elder brother lived, but he lacked confidence in the upkeep of the museum's facilities and believed the site was too far from Paris. He seized the initiative, convincing the mayor of Bordeaux to trade the painting for another, and once more appealed to Cavé: "I saw the mayor of Bordeaux, who would be open to an exchange for the *Trajan.* You know how much I desire that, in the first place, it go to Rouen, and, in the second, that it not go to

Bordeaux. I'm convinced they do not even have a place high enough for it. The painting would be left in a corner, rolled up for who knows how long, as others have been that deserved better."[10] He won his case and had *The Justice of Trajan* assigned to the Musée des Beaux-Arts, Rouen.

Likewise, in 1845, when the Ministère de l'Intérieur announced its intention to acquire *Last Words of Marcus Aurelius* for the Musée des Beaux-Arts, Toulouse, Delacroix, not satisfied with that painting, arranged with Cavé to substitute the *Sultan of Morocco* (see fig. 37), which had just been exhibited at the Salon of 1845.[11] After 1834, when the state purchased its last Delacroix painting for the Musée du Luxembourg, the artist was able to see only one more of his works enter that museum: *Jewish Wedding in Morocco* (see fig. 31). The painting was donated by the crown prince, the duc d'Orléans, a major patron of the arts and the owner of Delacroix's *The Murder of the Bishop of Liège* (cat. 64), among other works by the artist, immediately after he purchased it.

As he gained experience, Delacroix was increasingly concerned about the destination of his works and their preservation. He had learned about the fragility of oils painted on canvas, their sensitivity to variations in atmospheric conditions and their vulnerability to damage through mishandling. He was therefore deeply affected by the degraded state of *The Death of Sardanapalus* (see fig. 20), which he saw at the Château des Prés d'Ecoublay in September 1849 following the death of its owner, Daniel Wilson. He worried about his "poor painting, which will meet who knows what fate and whose condition at the moment is deplorable: the canvas is loose; the bottom seam is split along its entire length and held together here and there by stitches."[12] At the end of his life, he realized that even museums were no guarantee against risk, and that botched restorations were something to fear. He concurred with the disapproval expressed by some members of the press when Frédéric Villot, curator of paintings at the Louvre—and, as it happened, a friend of Delacroix's—undertook a contested restoration of Veronese's *Wedding at Cana* in 1853.[13] A year later, Delacroix learned that his own masterpiece had been stripped of its varnish: "[Louis d'] Arnoux came by during the day. . . . He says that the *Massacre [of Chios]* was not improved by having its varnish removed; without having seen it, I am almost of the same opinion. Like the Veronese, the painting will have lost the transparency of its shadows, as is almost bound to happen. Haro . . . spoiled the portraits by Uncle Riesener of my two brothers as

children."[14] Thus, whenever he could, he reserved the right to do the necessary retouching of his works himself. In 1860 he treated *The Barque of Dante,* the cracks of which, caused by differences in drying times of the layers of paint, had become obtrusive.[15]

Baudelaire provided a revealing account of Delacroix's concerns:

> One of the painter's major preoccupations in his final years was the judgment of posterity and the uncertain material durability of his works. Sometimes his sensitive imagination was inflamed by the idea of immortal glory, sometimes he spoke bitterly of the fragility of canvases and paint. On other occasions he mentioned with envy the old masters—nearly all of them—who had the good fortune of having their paintings reproduced by skillful engravers . . . and he ardently regretted not having found such a translator of his own works. The brittleness of paintings, when compared to the solidity of prints, was one of the habitual themes of his conversation.[16]

Baudelaire had heard Delacroix speak on these matters; he had also read an article Delacroix had published on Prud'hon, whose paintings had deteriorated considerably over time: "All the genius in the world cannot prevent a varnish from yellowing, a thin coat of paint from disappearing. . . . All the elements are the enemies of painting: air and sun, dryness and dampness. And these are not even the cruelest. An ignorant retoucher often finishes in a single stroke the work of destruction that the centuries have not completed."[17]

Confronted with the fateful fragility of his paintings on canvas and frustrated by their systematic and uncontrollable dispersal, Delacroix suffered another spell of inertia. In his view, the limits of easel painting lay paradoxically in the absolute freedom the practice afforded: the artist, alone in his studio, nose to the canvas, has only self-discipline to prevent him from spoiling the work at hand. He can return to it indefinitely, refining or complicating the composition, superimposing layers of oil and glaze, but he risks losing his way. Over the years, Delacroix became persuaded that an artist's first impulse was the right one and that the pleasure of execution was a trap that threatened a painting's unity and originating idea. He was stimulated by the constraints of the large decorative works, which required clean, rapid execution and a distanced view. A passage from his *Journal* written in 1847, as he was completing the decoration for the library of the Palais Bourbon, attests to this:

> I painted the small figure of the man fallen forward, pierced by an arrow, in a few instants. That is the way one ought to do painted sketches that would then have the freedom and freshness of a jotting (*croquis*). Small paintings annoy me, bore me. Easel paintings do too, even large ones done in the studio. You wear yourself out ruining them. One should put into large canvases all the fire that usually goes only onto walls. Cournault told me that is what Rubens did in his *Battle of Ivry* in Florence.[18]

It is therefore clear why Delacroix's first large decorative project, entrusted to him in 1833, was his road to Damascus: it revitalized him in the profound and lasting way that he needed.

Mural painting satisfied Delacroix's desire to move about in his paintings, his "need to work big," while guaranteeing him stability and continuity.[19] He was assured that his paintings would remain in place and long outlast him, provided that the building that sheltered them was sound, located in the historic heart of Paris, and linked to a prestigious institution, whether the state (Palais Bourbon, Palais du Luxembourg, Palais du Louvre), the church (Saint-Denys-du-Saint-Sacrement, Saint-Sulpice), or the city itself (Hôtel de Ville). It must have seemed to him that by integrating his paintings morally and materially into a great monument of Paris, he would achieve an immortality comparable to that offered by a museum.

The large decorative projects compelled him to innovate on a regular basis, and for this reason, too, they were stimulating. Every site, by virtue of its architectural configuration (caissons, cupola, apse, hemicycle), function (library, gallery, chapel, vestibule, reception hall), and preexisting artistic features, required him to devise a tailor-made solution and explore new iconographic territory. He also had to evaluate carefully how the works would be received. The paintings for the Salon and the museum, seen frontally and fairly close up, dramatically engaged a diverse, inquisitive audience made up of art critics and the urban public. Paintings in palaces and churches, seen from a greater distance, tower over and envelop viewers. Delacroix's works at the Palais Bourbon and the Palais du Luxembourg were viewed mainly by representatives of the nation who went to the library to read, learn, and meditate on the meaning of history, taking the great men of the past as their models and finding inspiration in them when fashioning their laws. In these locations, painting became the vehicle of a moral and historical discourse that called for the greatest intelligibility even as it assured the serenity of the surroundings. By contrast, in the Chapel of the Virgin at Saint-Denys-du-Saint-Sacrement, practicing Christians, imploring divine assistance, gave free rein to their emotions and devotional fervor. There, the register of Delacroix's painting was one of somber pathos and high contrast. Finally, public spaces of palaces, designed to welcome the eminent guests of a city or parliament, had to convey the solemnity, pride, and joy resulting from good government.

Delacroix's taste for large decorative projects was heightened by the notion that he was intervening physically in a monumental ensemble to which illustrious masters of the past had contributed, and where his own painting could freely engage in dialogue with theirs. That relationship was even stronger and more immediate than in a museum. In the French royal collections, works by living artists were strictly separated from those of artists who had died; their productions were housed in institutions on opposite sides of the Seine. While working in the Palais du Luxembourg, Delacroix was conscious of the fact that he was the successor of Philippe de Champaigne and, even more, of his idol, Rubens. But his most immediate link to tradition occurred when he painted, starting in 1850, the central compartment of the ceiling of the Gallery of Apollo at the Louvre: the work was at the heart of a painted, sculpted, and ornamental program overseen two centuries earlier by Charles Le Brun, the *premier peintre* of Louis XIV.

Delacroix's activity as a decorative painter, as demanding as it was, did not put an end to his work as an easel painter. He pursued the two practices simultaneously, believing they were complementary. In fact, the large decorative murals— except for those in churches, which were sometimes poorly lit—were not easily accessible. The decorations done for the Palais Bourbon or the Palais du Luxembourg, apart from the few days after their unveiling when they were discussed by a small group of journalists, were visible only as a special favor

CAT. 138 *The Sultan of Morocco and His Entourage*, 1856

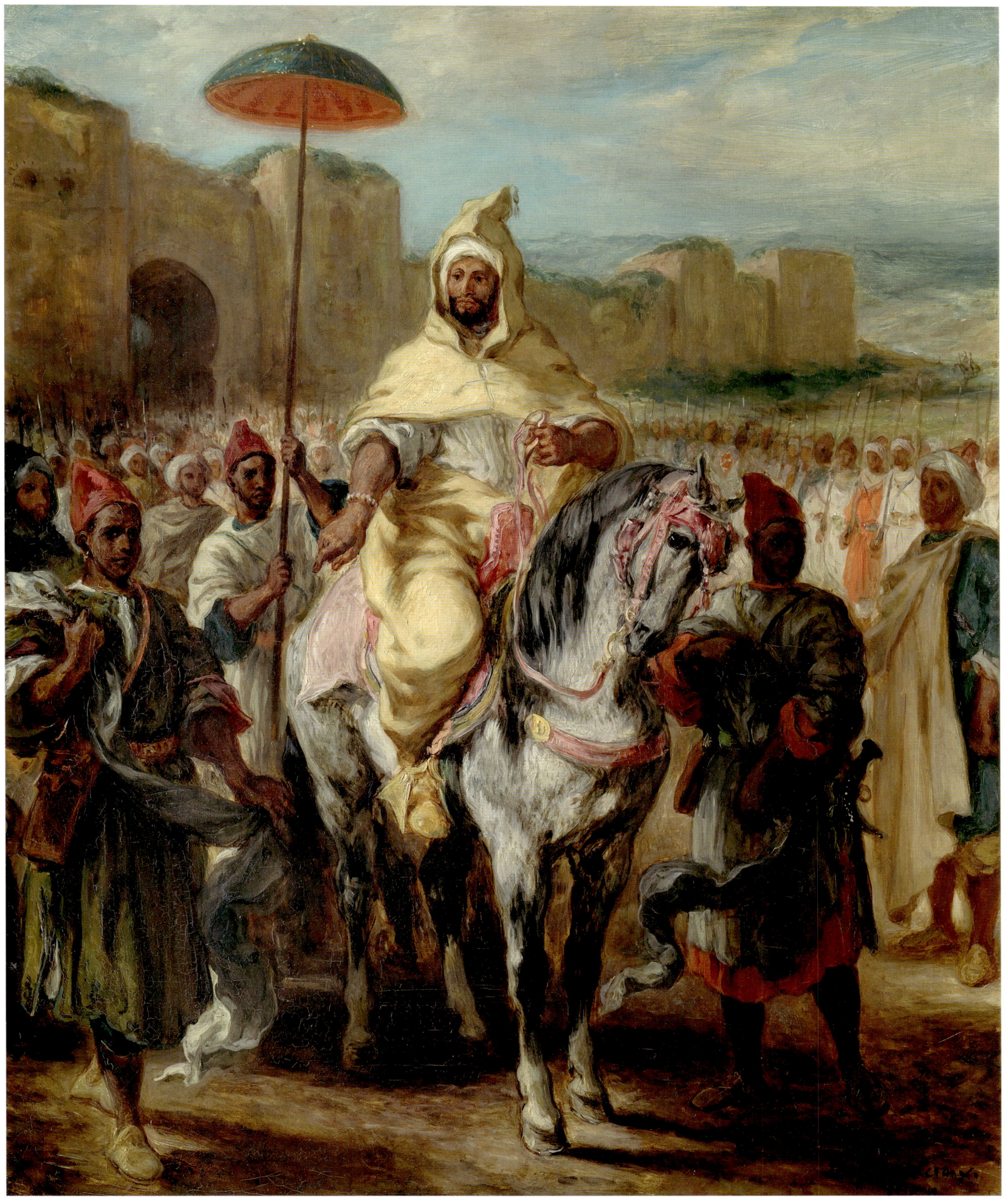

or by invitation, and were not reproduced and disseminated as engravings. The regular frequency and public nature of the Salon therefore remained invaluable to Delacroix. That venue allowed him to give the public and the critics a sense of the renewal that his painting was undergoing elsewhere, in the context of architecture and the great tradition.

It is therefore fruitful to ask to what extent the challenges raised by his large works conditioned and shaped his easel paintings (see fig. 37 and cat. 138). What role did Delacroix assign to these paintings? Were they primarily a sort of an echo chamber, a medium in which to further elaborate the mural experiments? Or could they also serve as a testing ground, a laboratory? Between 1833 and 1855, Delacroix appears to have applied three successive and overlapping artistic approaches in these works.

The First Large Decorative Experiment: The Grammar of Bodies

Delacroix's first public commission for a large decorative work, the Salon du Roi in the Palais Bourbon (see fig. 38), was confirmed by decree on August 31, 1833, by Adolphe Thiers, then minister of trade and public works. The architectural framework, a rigid Neoclassical setting— symmetrical, highly compartmentalized, lit only indirectly—was unforgiving. Within this space, Delacroix had to elaborate a fully allegorical program extolling national prosperity. The square plan of the salon determined the selection and placement of four female allegories, each presiding over one side of the room, representing Agriculture and Industry, sources of French abundance, and Justice and War (*Bellum*), forces inspiring respect for the monarchy both inside the country and abroad. These four figures, represented in reclining poses in the narrow, horizontal ceiling compartments, identify the theme developed vertically in the friezes. There, a throng of about sixty figures of men, women, children, and elderly people nearly covers the turquoise ground. Having received permission to remove the carved band beneath the cornice, Delacroix had just barely sufficient room to establish a connection between the spandrels, defined by the arched shape of the bay windows. Making the most of the complex surface thus obtained, he emphasized it as he pleased, filling each section to the maximum with piled-up, huddled bodies that crawled and slid over the arches. Delacroix made abundant use

of the child figures, whether putti, winged spirits, or urchins, to fill in the smallest vacant space. Critics were somewhat disconcerted by the joyful crush of bodies: "My primary criticism of M. Delacroix is that his figures are all crammed together, and his planes are not sufficiently layered."[20]

Farther down, the overcrowding verges on the comical. On the piers, deities of the rivers and seas of France are represented as stone sculptures painted in trompe l'oeil grisaille heightened with blue and gold. The bodies of the voluptuous *Sequana* (The Seine) and the solidly built *Rhodamus* (The Rhone) seem to contort inside undersize niches. The illusory space carved out around the voluminous figures, which are rendered more in the round than in bas-relief, is inadequate to contain them. They seem to burst open the frame and leap out from the wall.

Playing mischievously with the architectural setting and casually rivaling sculpture, Delacroix suffused the work with an abundance that created an impression of clutter—to the point of disorder and overload. He developed a particularly carnal grammar of bodies: the figures are monumental, heavy, and extensively modeled; their flesh is pink or bronze. When not half-naked, most are draped in colored wool trimmed with silk accessories. They conjure an unspecified traditional Mediterranean society between ancient Rome and the Morocco Delacroix had recently discovered. And they seem to give off heat, to possess a vitality bursting with energy. The atmosphere they create is a far cry from the chilly abstraction so often associated with allegorical painting.

While feigning difficulty in containing the lively crowd, the artist maintained close control over the figures' symbolic role. He guaranteed their aesthetic unity and avoided any cumbersome realism, thus averting the inexorable obsolescence of modern dress and naive adherence to the ideology of progress or any other social discourse. In contrast to their counterparts in *Massacres at Chios* (see fig. 5), painted ten years earlier, the figures here possess none of the individual traits of the professional models who posed for them. The faces are hardly distinguishable from one another or are simply obscured by shadow or an overlapping arm. All the figures, whether young or old, bear the same trademark, recognizable in their bodily proportions and the standardization of their faces.[21] They are not individuals but painted figures invented by the same hand and animated by the same creative principle. They are differentiated only by the roles they play in the present, not by personal histories or destinies that would have granted them the autonomy to escape the total control of their demiurge.

Such saturation of the space—tumultuous but never exorbitant—was certainly influenced by the festive spirit of Mannerist court art, masterfully represented in France by the painted and sculpted decorations of Rosso Fiorentino, then of Niccolò dell'Abate, for the Château de Fontainebleau, decorative works considered the first expression of a French national style. In the early 1830s, they were the object of an unprecedented surge in interest led by the ornamentalist painter Claude Aimé Chenavard and befitting the taste of the time. Delacroix is known to have visited the Château de Fontainebleau in early January 1832; it was his first stop en route to Morocco.[22] Other references to the French Renaissance were on his mind when he laid the groundwork for the decoration at the Salon du Roi. In the margins of a drawing study for the fictive niches on the pilasters, Delacroix noted, for the base, "see the pedestal for Germain Pilon's graces," a reference to the *Monument to the Heart of Henri II* (1561; Musée du Louvre).[23]

Without imitating the elongated bodies of the School of Fontainebleau, Delacroix adopted the playful refinement and theatricality of its art, qualities that allow the figures to play their role in a painted narrative while creating the illusion of complicity with the viewer by means of an outward gaze. Théophile Gautier rightly recognized this influence in the Salon du Roi:

> Were it not for the gloomy style of the architecture, which dispels the illusion, you might believe, upon seeing these cheerful and luminous paintings, that you were in a Renaissance hall decorated by some artist summoned from Florence—Primaticcio or Il Rosso. The style is that elegant and supple, and these beautiful allegorical women, nude or caressed by light draperies, have about them just such an air of royalty and familiarity with magnificence.[24]

Alexandre-Gabriel Decamps, though he missed the reference to Fontainebleau, sensed that Italian roots had been tapped:

> It is indisputable that modern art has never given us works better able to invoke the style and execution of beautiful Italian paintings. Remarkably, M. Delacroix has never traveled to Italy; he has not seen the frescoes of Venice or Florence or Rome. But it so happens that

he has intuited them without copying them and that he belongs to the great family of true painters. . . . There is something of Veronese in the fresco on which he painted Justice; there are memories of Roman art in the fresco that represents Agriculture; there is something of Michelangelo in the admirable figure of the blacksmith in the foreground of the frieze where the emblems of War are depicted. But overall, despite the allegorical style, the ensemble has a character so modern, so new, that it is clear the artist has studied the admirable qualities of the great masters, but without becoming such a slave to any of them that he imitates their flaws.[25]

In addition to elaborating a grammar of bodies for the large decorative works, Delacroix was obliged to modify his palette in order to create light in a place where the architecture afforded very little. Tasked with producing the illusion that the walls had been breached and the space opened up to radiant skies to ensure his work's legibility, he had to reject the easy solution of using dark grounds to highlight the figures; he also had to convert contrasting values into contrasting colors. Delacroix brightened his palette, warmed his shadows, and chose sky-blue grounds to create an impression of luminosity and air. Those measures, first applied in the Salon du Roi, were fully mastered in the cupola of the Peers' Library nearly ten years later (see fig. 40). The critics hailed him:

> In the cupola of the Luxembourg, the victory won by M. Delacroix over the miserliness of M. de Gisors [the architect] can be considered a real tour de force. The painter was in some sense obliged to create the light he needed to illuminate his figures. He had to seek in the tone of the draperies, the hue of the sky, the rays that the architecture refused him. It was an arduous struggle, but the painter emerged the victor in that fierce battle: he metamorphosed shadow into light.[26]

This paean from Gustave Planche was echoed by Gautier: "By the magic of his palette, this painting illuminates itself; the colors do not receive daylight, they provide it."[27]

The first painterly adjustments that Delacroix made when he undertook the large decorative paintings found their way into several history paintings done during the course of the Salon du Roi project or immediately after its completion. It is possible that they appeared as early as 1834, in the

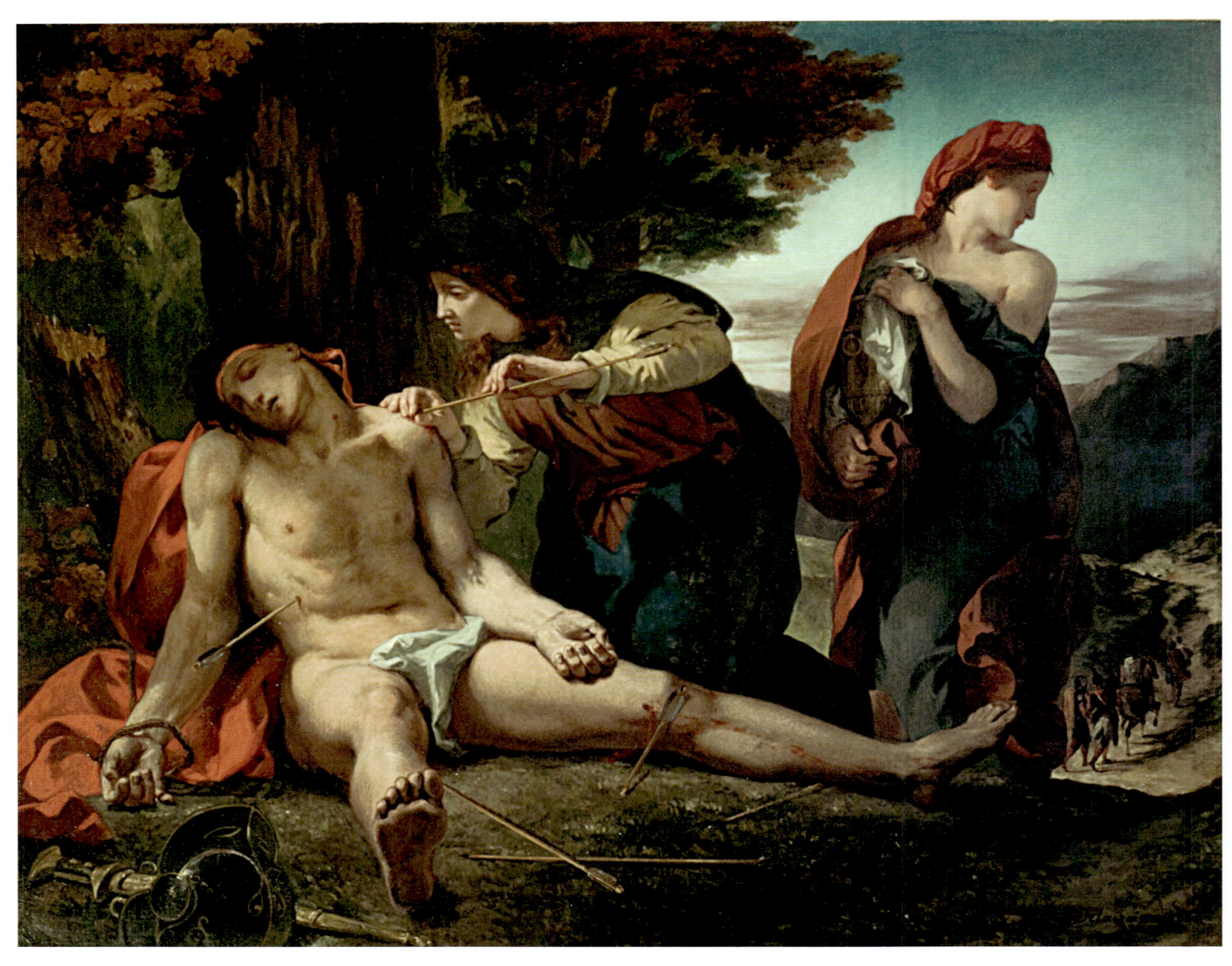

CAT. 90 *Saint Sebastian Tended by the Holy Women*, 1836

ornamental abundance and monumental placidity of *Women of Algiers in Their Apartment* (see cat. 83). His mural practice made its full migration to the studio two years later, with *Saint Sebastian* (cat. 90), exhibited at the Salon of 1836. Although Delacroix very clearly borrowed the overall composition and the saint's pose—head tilted to one side, collapsed torso, and stiff, spread legs—from Rubens's *Lamentation* (ca. 1612; Liechtenstein Museum, Vienna), he radically distinguished himself in the general tone, which is much less cold, gray, and macabre than the one chosen by the Flemish master. In fact, in the *Saint Sebastian*, sorrow is transcended by the solid volumes, simplified forms, and radiating force of a warm and slightly acid palette. Also taken from the Salon du Roi are the turquoise blue ground, which sets off the rosy flesh tones and red drapery, and the shallow, elliptical background, with its surprisingly flat trees and grassy embankment. The faces are schematic, generic, and obscured by shadows. Consequently, the main narrative function rests with the bodies themselves, whose proportions relative to the frame are colossal, unprecedented in Delacroix's history painting. The saint's massive body is worthy of Michelangelo's Slaves. His powerful musculature is accentuated by the raking light; his undersize head dissolves in the shadows, while his dramatically foreshortened hands and feet project forcefully outward, toward the viewer.

Gustave Planche aptly described the changes he saw: "M. Eugène Delacroix's *Saint Sebastian* will confound the expectations of many. Those who have attentively followed the projects the artist has undertaken and completed in the last fourteen years will be astonished by this new transformation of an adventurous and innovative genius."[28] Planche explained that he had not yet been able to see the room Delacroix had painted at the Chamber of Deputies, but another, evidently better-informed critic, who wrote for *L'artiste,* promptly made the connection. He too began by emphasizing the impression produced by *Saint Sebastian,* which was so unlike the clamor of Delacroix's *grandes machines* at the Salons of the 1820s. Then he added: "If, therefore, you look with attention . . . you will notice in the figure of the saint, especially in the torso, a grand and simple style, an expansive and vigorous execution. No doubt the decorative projects executed by the artist at the Chamber of Deputies contributed to the development of these qualities."[29]

Parallel to the last phase of decoration of the Salon du Roi, which ended with the large trompe l'oeil grisailles on the piers, Delacroix worked on *Medea About to Kill Her Children*

(cats. 91, 94). In a less exaggerated manner but following a process identical to that used for the river and sea deities, Delacroix inscribed the larger-than-life figure of Medea in an intentionally shallow setting, a cave where, abandoned by the unfaithful Jason, the queen would commit infanticide. The sculptural quality of that scheme was fundamental to the work, already present at the earliest stage of its development. Several preliminary drawings indicate that *Medea* and *Saint Sebastian* were conceived at the same time (fig. 41). The charitable saint and murderous queen, unlikely pendants brought together on a single sheet, seem to have occurred to the painter primarily as complementary figures; the drawing studies provide no information about the overall compositions or how the figures would be framed. Like trompe l'oeil statues in grisaille, the figures are modeled in a pen-and-ink wash on an undifferentiated ground.

Planche, well informed about the decoration of the Salon du Roi by the time it was unveiled in October and November 1837, linked the work to *Medea About to Kill Her Children* in his review of the Salon of 1838: "[*Medea*] is, to be sure, a painting of rare merit, perhaps the most beautiful that M. Delacroix has ever produced, since in it you find all the qualities he has developed one after another in the decoration for the Salon du Roi at the Chamber of Deputies."[30] Théophile Gautier confirmed the soundness of Planche's assertion:

> The Chamber of Deputies, which is not yet known to the public . . . is worthy of the best *stanze* of Rome and the most vaunted *scuole* of Venice. These allegorical, mythological paintings, altogether unusual for M. Delacroix, are additional proof of the marvelous suppleness of his talent. Over the course of this major project, these paintings will no doubt influence the painter's future. He has adopted a more expansive, grander manner; he has inserted sobriety in his color, decorum in his style. He has made his spirit bow to all the architectural requirements, has confined himself within bizarre compartments and unforgiving shapes. It is an excellent study and will affect the paintings he will do subsequently. . . . *Medea About to Kill Her Children* is linked to the same order of ideas that produced the frescoes in the throne room [the Salon du Roi]. It is an ancient subject worked out with modern intelligence and in forms more human than ideal.[31]

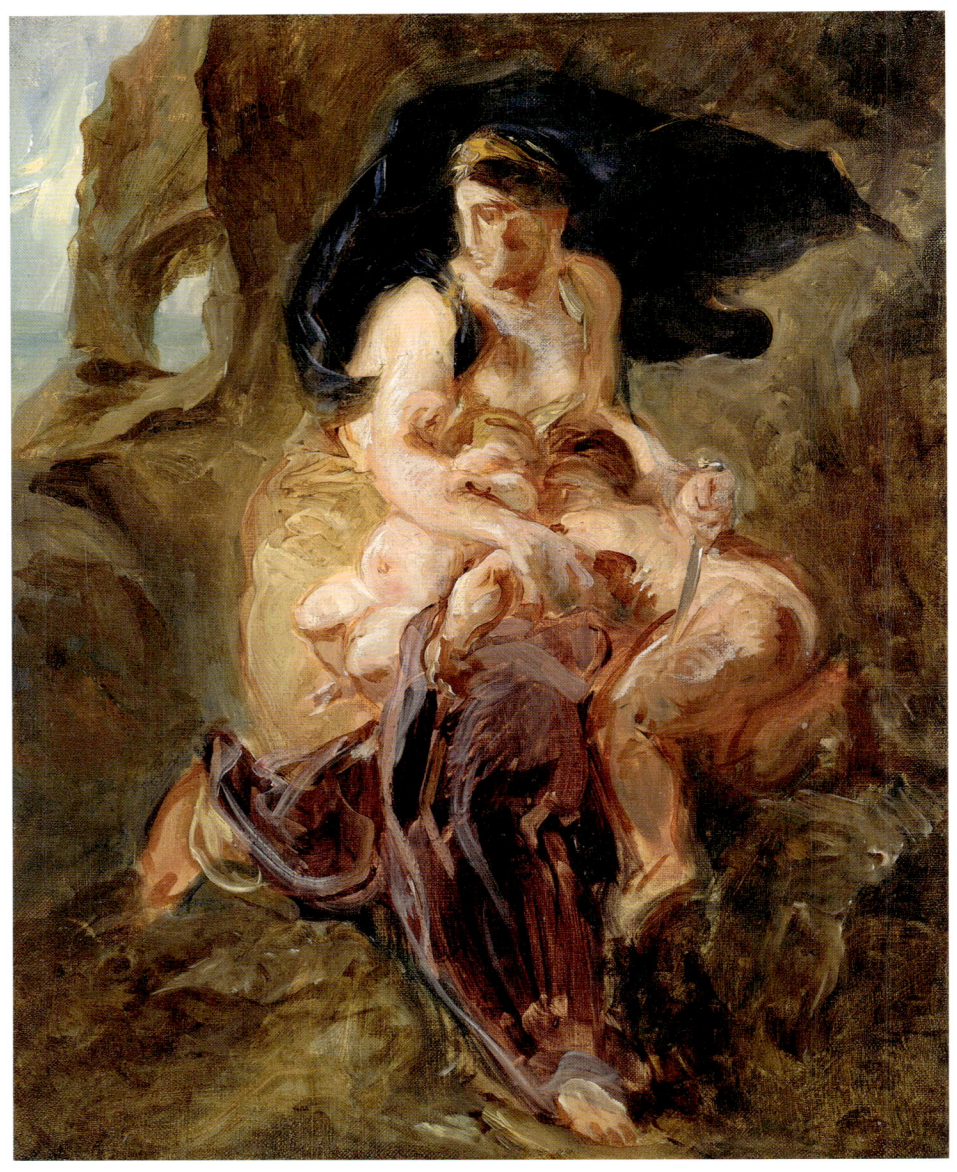

CAT. 91 *Medea About to Kill Her Children, sketch,* ca. 1836

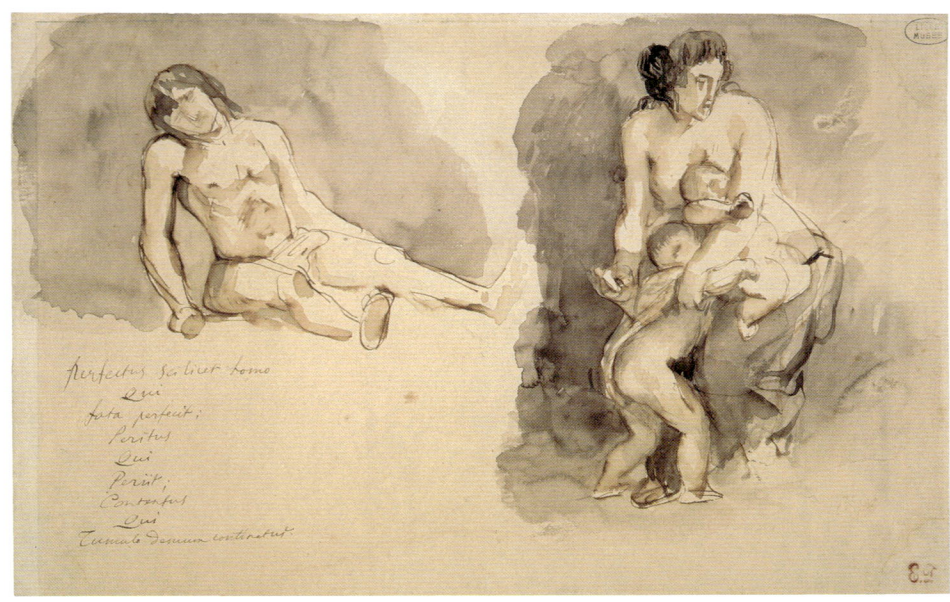

FIG. 41 Studies for *Saint Sebastian* and *Medea*, ca. 1835. Pen and brown wash, 7½ x 12⅜ in. (19.1 x 31.5 cm). Palais des Beaux-Arts, Lille (inv. Pl. 1279)

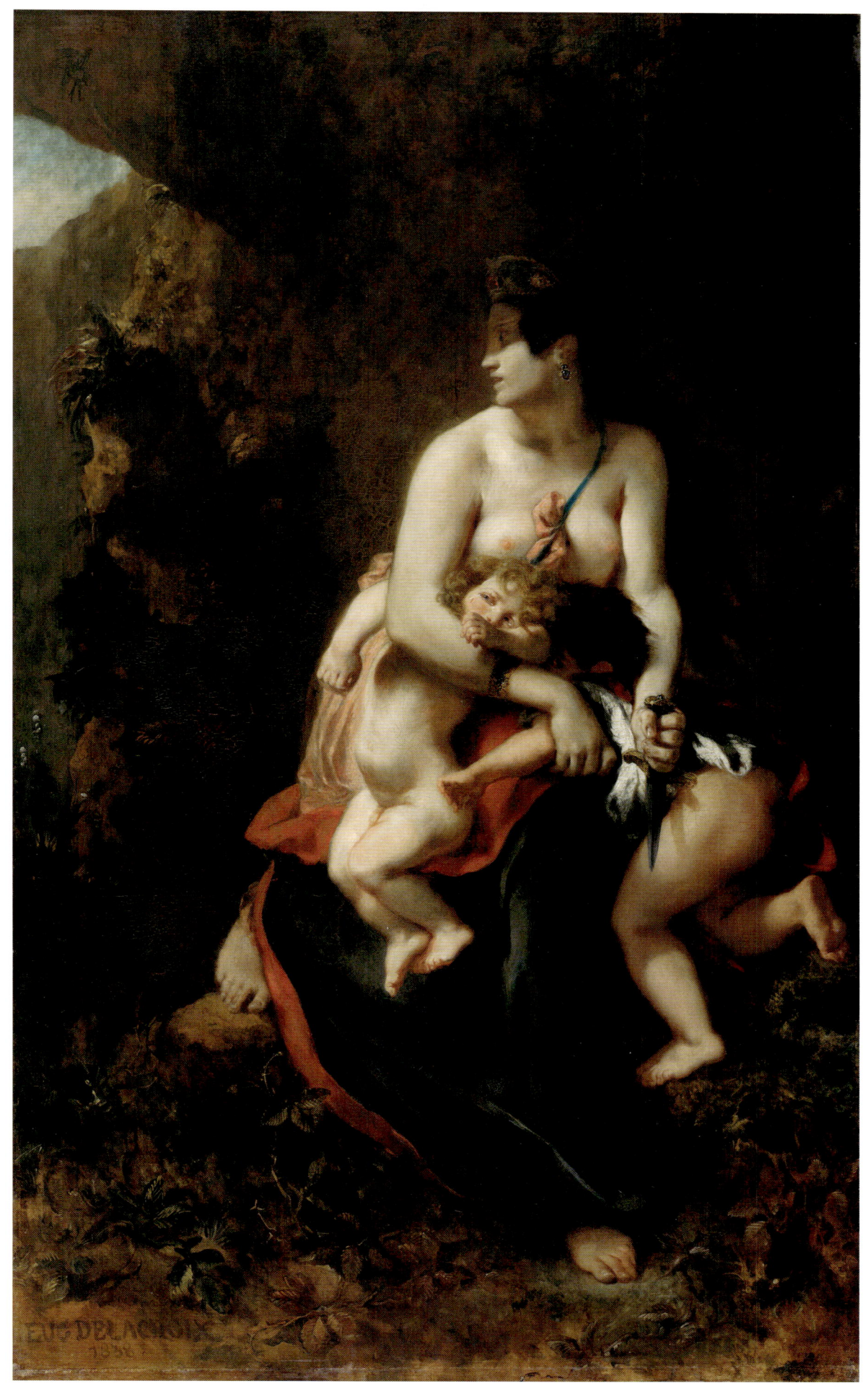

CAT. 94 *Medea About to Kill Her Children (Medée furieuse)*, 1838

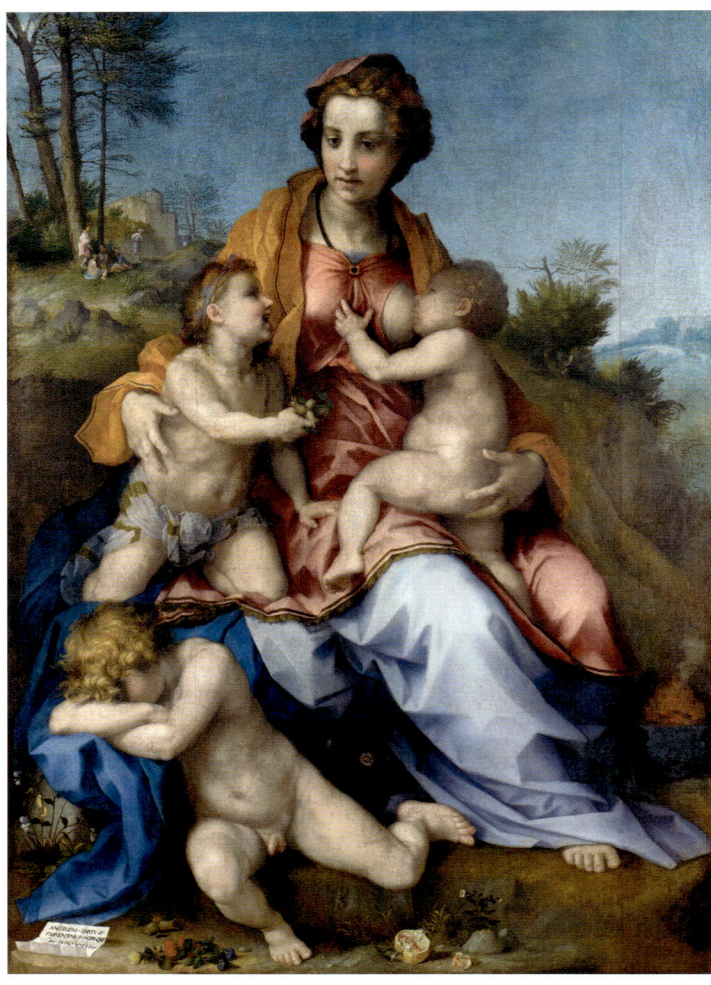

FIG. 42 Andrea del Sarto (Andrea d'Agnolo) (Italian, 1486–1530). *Charity*, 1518–19. Oil on wood transferred to canvas, 72¹³⁄₁₆ x 53¹⁵⁄₁₆ in. (185 x 137 cm). Musée du Louvre, Paris (712)

Medea About to Kill Her Children was Delacroix's first large painting on a mythological theme and marked a decisive point of transition in his career. Yet the subject had preoccupied him for a long time, as attested in a notebook entry from the early 1820s and by the famous comment he wrote in his *Journal* after returning from a performance of Gioachino Rossini's *Moses in Egypt* at the Théâtre-Italien in March 1824: "I am preoccupied by *Medea*."[32] He had probably been reminded of Simon Mayr's opera *Medea in Corinth,* performed in Paris in 1823 with Giuditta Pasta in the title role. It is worth considering whether, fifteen years later, the memory of Pasta's performance contributed to the artist's own interpretation of Medea, in oil. He rendered her in perfect left profile, her upper face masked in shadow, crowned with a gold diadem set with precious stones and pearls. It appears that she was

modeled on John Hayter's 1827 portrait of Pasta in the role and costume of Medea.[33] Virginie Bernast has suggested, "if Delacroix heard Madame Pasta in the role of Medea, the memory of that performance was likely revived by Giulia Grisi's Norma at the Théâtre-Italien in Paris between 1835 and 1847. . . . Like Medea, the Druid priestess Norma is tempted to commit infanticide after Pollione, a Roman proconsul, abandons her for . . . Adalgisa."[34]

It is possible that this play of references was also at work in Delacroix's oeuvre: with *Medea,* he made an astonishing return to the twin theme of Greece and tragedy—the two were forever linked in his mind—by painting a peculiar kind of pendant to *Greece on the Ruins of Missolonghi* (see cat. 26), although this was certainly not his intention. That work features an allegorical figure of modern Greece, successor to the golden age of antiquity, weeping over her enslavement and the murder of her children by the Ottoman Turks. A decade later Delacroix proposed, with *Medea,* a mirror image—the representation of a Greece prior to civilization. Savage, intuitive, animalistic, Greece herself is the one who kills her offspring. The formal self-reference is obvious: as in *Missolonghi,* the main action is kept offstage; echoes of *Liberty Leading the People* are evident in the protagonist's face turned in profile, her bare breasts, and the position of her legs.[35] In addition to the self-reference, Delacroix alluded to the great masters of the past to an unparalleled degree in *Medea.* The pyramidal composition is a reference—particularly jarring, even parodic in this context— of Andrea del Sarto's *Charity* (fig. 42), while the sculptural force of the queen is inspired by Michelangelo's three-dimensional works. Delécluze posited a connection between Correggio's *Venus and Cupid with a Satyr* (formerly known as *Sleep of Antiope*) and the velvety softness of Medea's skin. By contrast, the rosy, glistening flesh tones of the children seem unquestionably Rubensian, while their whimpering expressions and wriggling postures seem to be borrowed directly from Rembrandt's *The Rape of Ganymede* (fig. 43). Far from eliciting a smile, these commonplace signs of terror render the horrifying truth of the situation, that of children who sense that they are about to die at the hands of the person in whom they have naturally put their complete trust.[36] Delacroix made ingenious use of the narrative power of the lighting: as the shadow cast by the dagger onto the child's thigh symbolically cuts into its flesh, the mother's blinding hatred is evoked by the penumbra that swallows up her gaze. At the same time, her brightly lit breasts and hands accentuate her monstrous animality.

The painting was a total success with the critics, converting even the most traditional among them. They praised Delacroix for applying his unique talent (that of using color to express the intensity of life's most savage aspects) to a tragic subject enshrined in ancient and humanistic literature but lacking an iconic counterpart in the art of Greco-Roman sculptors and modern masters. In *Medea*, Delacroix summed up the complexity of narrative and character in a compact, autonomous group, borrowing from sculpture this means for conveying content without providing context. He thereby succeeded in inventing an iconography, the canonical force of which was equal to that of the *Laocoön*.

Delacroix's subsequent emulation of sculpture was less pronounced and more fragmentary: he opted for half-length representations (*The Cumaean Sibyl,* undertaken the same year as *Medea* but exhibited at the Salon of 1845) and even tighter framing. For example, the enigmatic head of *Mary Magdalene in the Wilderness* (rejected by the Salon of 1845; see fig. 122) seems to have been torn off a statue or a tomb effigy. His last real success involving sculptural borrowings was *Cleopatra and the Peasant* (cat. 95), exhibited at the Salon of 1839. The subject may have been inspired by act 5, scene 2, of Shakespeare's tragedy *Antony and Cleopatra*. The defeated queen, preferring suicide to the humiliation of the Roman victory, stoically ponders her own death, which takes the form of an asp that a peasant has secretly delivered to her in a basket of figs. This Shakespearean meditation on the vanity of power and the world posits *Cleopatra and the Peasant* as the female pendant to *Hamlet and Horatio in the Graveyard* (see cat. 96), also exhibited at the Salon of 1839. Delacroix avoided the Baroque convention of representing the queen in her death throes, preferring to depict the moment just before she was bitten by the serpent. References to ancient art are still present. Cleopatra assumes the melancholic pose of the Roman goddess Pudicitia, while the peasant's coarse features are borrowed from those of sculpted satyrs or Greek comic masks. Delacroix revitalized these appropriations from the antique, giving the peasant's thick hands vibrant reddish highlights, darkening the figures' hair, and accentuating the sparkle of the jewels and the sheen of the fur.

This type of composition—with its monumental, three-quarter-length figures standing out against a dark ground—can probably be related to the library project at the Palais Bourbon (see fig. 39). The latter, commissioned in the summer of 1838 and completed at the end of 1847, occupied

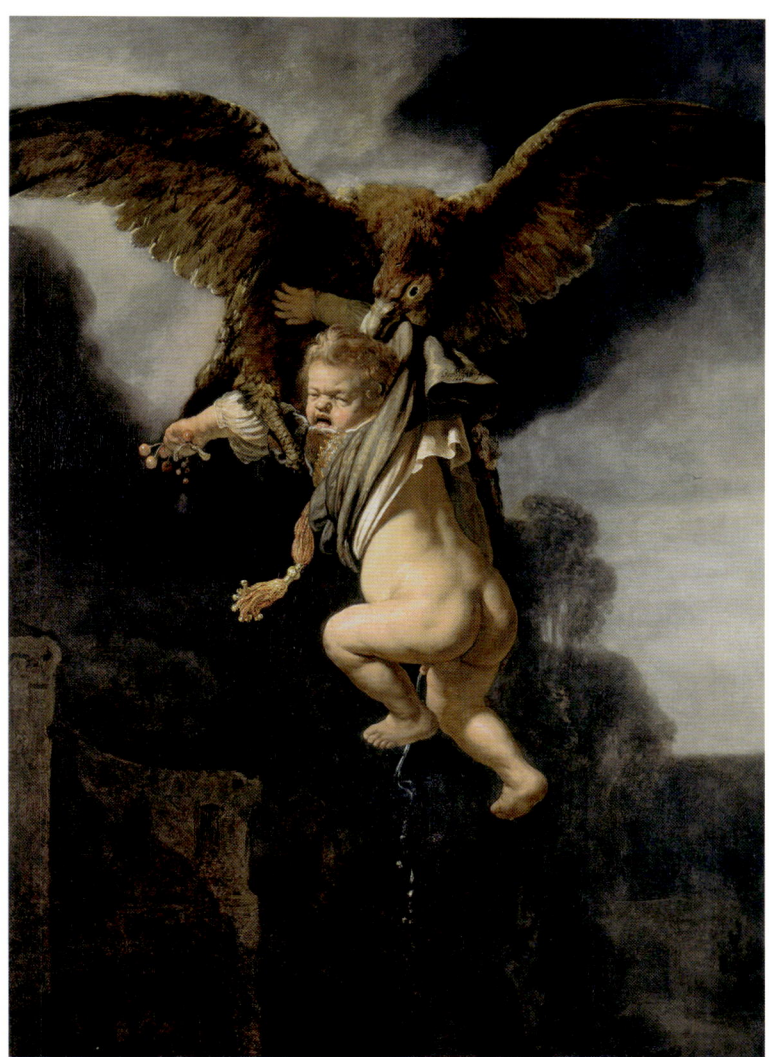

FIG. 43 Rembrandt (Rembrandt van Rijn) (Dutch, 1606–1669). *The Rape of Ganymede*, 1635. Oil on canvas, 69¹¹⁄₁₆ x 50¹³⁄₁₆ in. (177 x 129 cm). Staatliche Kunstsammlungen, Gemäldegalerie Alte Meister, Dresden (inv. 1558)

Delacroix intensively in the early 1840s. He was obliged by the studious atmosphere to employ his formidable powers of invention in a more serious and serene register than he had in the Salon du Roi. In addition to the two hemicycles, one at each end of the library, there were five cupolas to decorate. Each cupola was dedicated to a specific theme—Law, Philosophy, Theology, Poetry, the Sciences—and each was supported by four hexagonal pendentives. The challenge was threefold: to make erudite and little-known subjects comprehensible; to bring them to life even though they pertained less to actions than to ideas; and to counter the effect of monotony that the large number of pendentives—twenty in all—would likely produce.

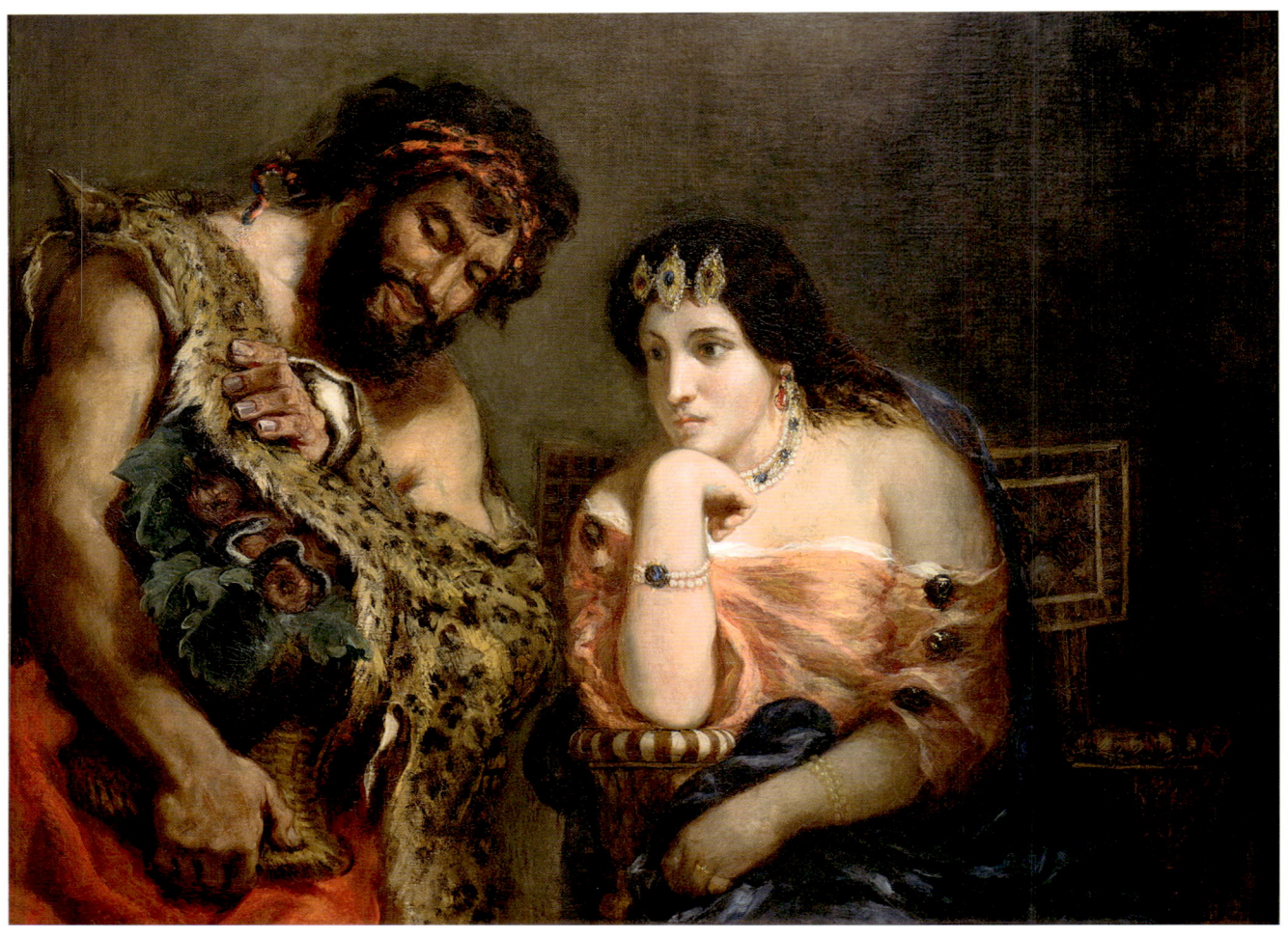

CAT. 95 *Cleopatra and the Peasant*, 1838

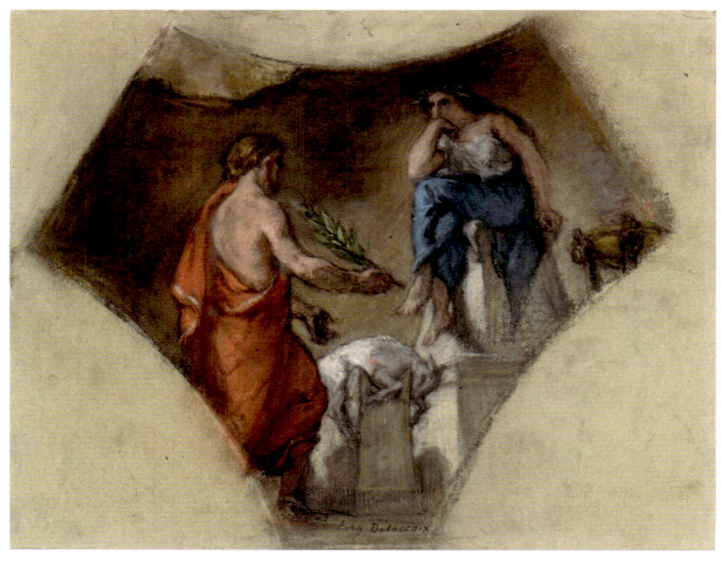

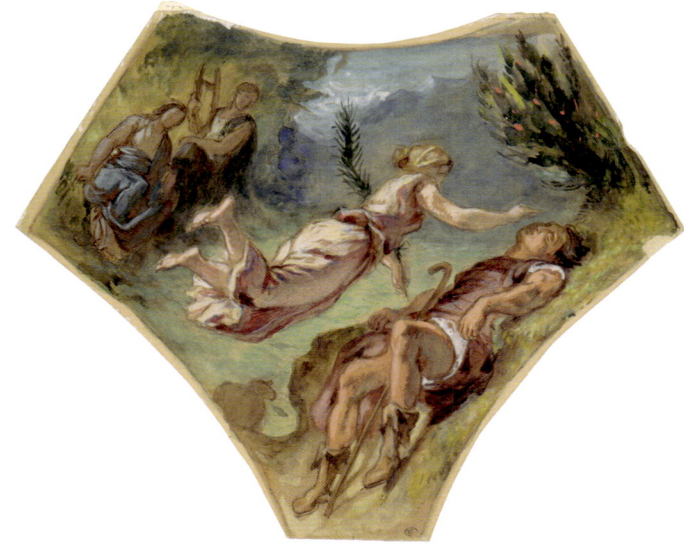

FIG. 44 *Lycurgus Consults the Pythia*, study for a pendentive in the Deputies' Library, Assemblée Nationale (Palais Bourbon), Paris, ca. 1838–42. Pastel on gray paper, 9⅝ x 12⅝ in. (24.5 x 32 cm). Musée du Louvre, Paris (RF 32259) (Johnson 1995, no. 9)

FIG. 45 *Hesiod and the Muse*, study for a pendentive in the Deputies' Library, Assemblée Nationale (Palais Bourbon), Paris, ca. 1838–47. Watercolor and gouache on brown paper, 8¹¹⁄₁₆ x 11 in. (22 x 28 cm). Musée du Louvre, Paris (RF 4773)

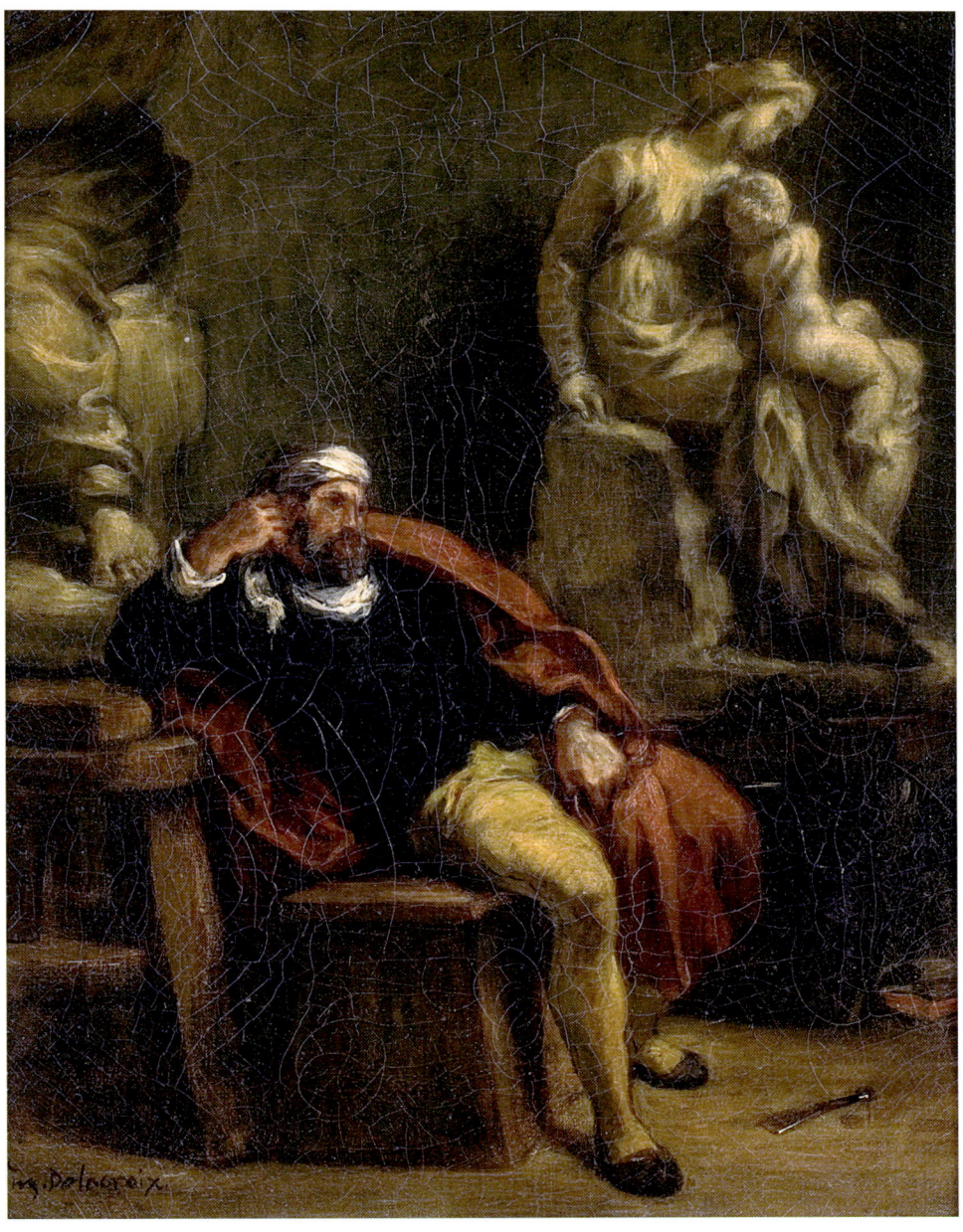

CAT. 114 *Michelangelo in His Studio*, 1849–50

Delacroix infused his designs with variety and at the same time forged a formal typology by giving each subject type a distinct compositional schema. For example, great men of virtue and sacrifice are represented as central, monumental figures (*Hippocrates Refusing the Gifts of the King of Persia, Archimedes Killed by the Soldier, The Death of Seneca, Cicero Accusing Verres, Demosthenes Haranguing the Waves, The Death of Saint John the Baptist*). Figures positioned on steps running the length of one side symbolize a link between spiritual and worldly power (*Alexander and the Heroic Poems of Homer, Herodotus Consults the Magi, Aristotle Describes the Animals,*

Ovid among the Scythians, and *Lycurgus Consults the Pythia* (see fig. 44), the meditative pose of which repeats that of Cleopatra in *Cleopatra and the Peasant,* cat. 95). Reclining figures shown one above another (*Numa Pompilius and the Nymph Egeria, Hesiod and the Muse,* see fig. 45) and figures partly superimposed (*Adam and Eve Driven from Paradise, Socrates and His Demon, Michelangelo and His Genius*) usually embody the inspiration that mysteriously unites the human and the divine.[37] He would continue to explore the themes embodied by such works, as he did in *Michelangelo in His Studio,* an easel picture undertaken in 1849–50 (cat. 114).

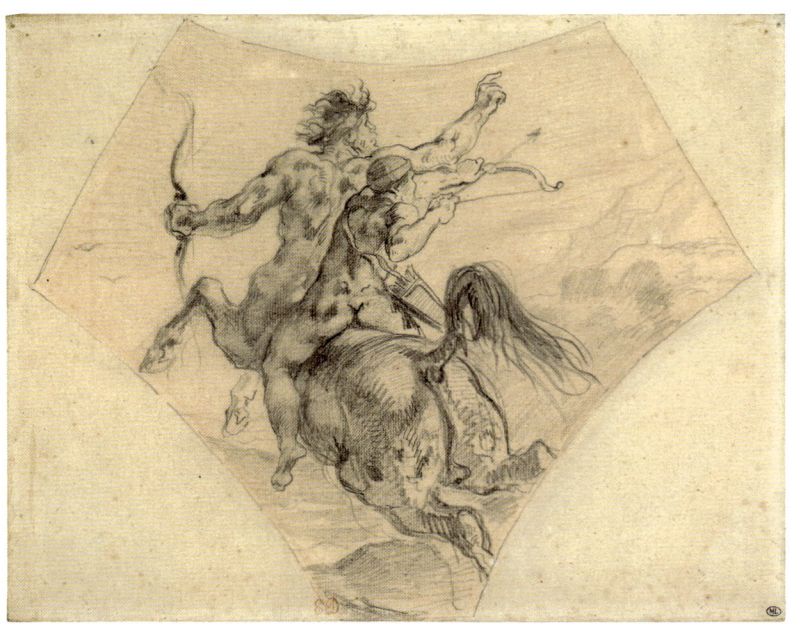

FIG. 46 *The Education of Achilles*, study for a pendentive in the Deputies' Library, Assemblée Nationale (Palais Bourbon), Paris, ca. 1838–47. Graphite on paper, 9⁷⁄₁₆ x 12 in. (24 x 30.5 cm). Musée du Louvre, Paris (MI 1079)

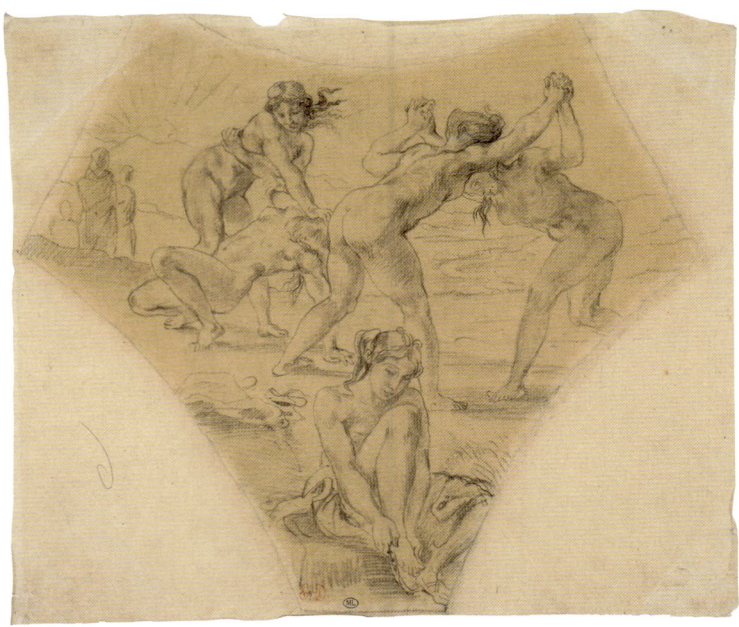

FIG. 47 *Spartan Girls Practicing Wrestling*, study for a pendentive in the Deputies' Library, Assemblée Nationale (Palais Bourbon), Paris, ca. 1838–47. Graphite on tracing paper, 8¹¹⁄₁₆ x 10½ in. (22 x 26.6 cm). Musée du Louvre, Paris (RF 3713)

Isolated formal inventions of a more audacious sort include a fantastic beast—the centaur Chiron—ridden by the young hero in *The Education of Achilles* (see fig. 46); the use of empty space to evoke the sublime (*The Chaldean Shepherds, Inventors of Astronomy*); and, to fill the composition, the choreographic division and dispersal of a figure group to the three arms of a pendentive. Exemplifying this last approach is *Spartan Girls Practicing Wrestling* (fig. 47), which anticipated by twenty years Edgar Degas's treatment of the same rarely encountered subject (National Gallery, London). The work was never completed, perhaps because it was judged to be ill suited to a studious, exclusively male setting. The extraordinary formal inventiveness applied in all the pendentives would later provide Delacroix with motifs that he would develop as easel paintings or pastels.

Yet *Cleopatra and the Peasant* (cat. 95) shows that another artistic influence was also at work in his studio practice, one that had nothing to do with the large decorative commissions in the Palais Bourbon. The vigorous chiaroscuro modeling of the figures, rendered half-length on a brown ground, reveals Delacroix's new orientation toward the Caravaggesque painters of the seventeenth century. The contrast between the queen's noble melancholy and the peasant's rustic charm suggests a link to the art of Valentin de Boulogne. *Last Words of Marcus Aurelius* (Musée des Beaux-Arts, Lyon), which Delacroix exhibited five years later, at the Salon of 1844, relied on the dark, austere style of Poussin's *Extreme Unction* (1638–40; Fitzwilliam Museum, Cambridge), thus confirming the turn Delacroix had taken.

Second Experiment: Concentration and Unity of Emotion

The succession of dark, spare, and intense religious scenes that Delacroix exhibited at the Salons in the late 1840s (*Christ on the Cross* in 1847, see cat. 103; *Christ at the Tomb* in 1848, see cat. 106) stands in stark contrast to the luminous robustness of *Saint Sebastian Tended by the Holy Women* from the Salon of 1836 (see cat. 90). Here again, a comparison with the large decorative projects sheds light on the experimentation—stemming from a different source—that led to these disparate results.

Like the Moroccan subjects, religious painting was not a monolithic genre within Delacroix's oeuvre but changed radically with the specific concerns of each commission.

After the unveiling of the Salon du Roi and the launch of the Deputies' Library project in 1838, the painter was entrusted, in 1840, with the decoration of the Chapel of the Virgin at the church of Saint-Denys-du-Saint-Sacrement (see fig. 48). This was Delacroix's second religious commission from the prefecture of the Seine, for which he had painted *Christ in the Garden of Olives* in 1824–26 (cat. 17). And it was the first involving a mural decoration, an opportunity Delacroix was not about to miss. Since the success of the first decorative paintings at the Palais Bourbon, he had been well aware that, when it came to secular decorations in civic buildings, he had earned the trust of the public authorities. They were still wary, however, about his paintings for churches. Delacroix knew that, from the administration's perspective, the project he was taking on at Saint-Denys was merely a consolation prize. Fifteen years later, he recalled the situation when, at a private gathering, he had run into the comte de Rambuteau, former prefect of the Seine, who had been dismissed following the revolution of 1848. Delacroix noted with some bitterness:

> The old ruffian! All the time he was prefect he never said a word to me except to warn me not to ruin his church of Saint-Denys-du-Saint-Sacrement. They had originally offered [Joseph-Nicolas] Robert-Fleury the commission for this thirteen-foot [*sic*] picture, at six thousand francs, but he did not feel inclined to accept it and suggested that I should do it instead, of course with the consent of the directors. Varcollier [head of the division of the Fine Arts at the prefecture], who at the time knew neither myself nor my pictures as well as he does now, consented rather contemptuously to this exchange of artists; but I always understood that the prefect was more difficult, owing to his lack of confidence in my meager talents.[38]

The prefectoral officials probably knew that the clergy had little appreciated the religious paintings by Delacroix that had been sent previously by the Ministère de l'Intérieur. The prospect of entrusting a chapel dedicated to the Virgin to such a painter may have raised fears of a particularly inopportune glorification of the flesh. The prefect might have recalled the tumultuous sensuality of the *Christ on the Cross* (cat. 85),

displayed at the Salon of 1835. That painting, however, was not intended to be placed in a church; rather, the artist conceived it as a reinterpretation of Rubens's *Christ on the Cross (The Coup de Lance)* (1620; Royal Museum of Fine Arts, Antwerp) even before seeing the original in Antwerp in 1839. Delacroix diverted attention from the pathos of the Virgin, who is supported by Saint John on the left, to the muscular, suntanned laborer carrying the ladder on the right. Mary Magdalene, her garments and hair disheveled, prostrates herself at the foot of the cross on which Christ hangs lifelessly; behind her, a crucified thief writhes in agony. As early as 1829, in an intimate painting for his mistress, Eugénie Dalton, Delacroix had explored the provocative, nearly licentious contrast between the dying Christ and the anguished sinner (Museum of Fine Arts, Houston).

At Saint-Denys-du-Saint-Sacrement, Delacroix was determined to be taken seriously as a religious painter (fig. 48). Inspired by the spatial configuration of the chapel and its dedication to the Virgin, he initially composed an Annunciation scene (fig. 49). Following famous examples by Raphael and Ingres, he imagined transforming the chapel into a theatrical space. Above the altar—the stage of the Christian drama—he placed two angels pulling back a large red curtain to reveal the scene. It unfolds in a simple room, its back wall punctuated by a half-open door that creates the illusion of extended space. While the room and its main furnishing, a large, green-canopied bed seen in central perspective, recall the Annunciations of the Flemish Primitives, the radiant glory of the Virgin and the clouds carrying the archangel Gabriel echo Baroque painting. Delacroix ultimately abandoned his initial idea in favor of a Pietà exalting the Virgin's suffering. He wavered about whether or not to keep the red draperies drawn open by angels (see cat. 100) before deciding on a more austere, rocky setting (see cat. 101), and he reversed the composition to adapt it to the lighting in the chapel. After many delays involving the clergy, he was finally able to paint the work on the chapel wall in the winter of 1843–44 with the help of his assistant Gustave Lassalle-Bordes.

The Baroque effect of a theatrical performance was replaced by the more archaic evocation of artificial caves or low, arched niches containing sculptural representations of the Entombment. The principal reference for the overall composition has been identified as a Pietà painted by Rosso Fiorentino about 1530–40 for Anne, duc de Montmorency, the Constable of France (see fig. 50). Delacroix transcribed

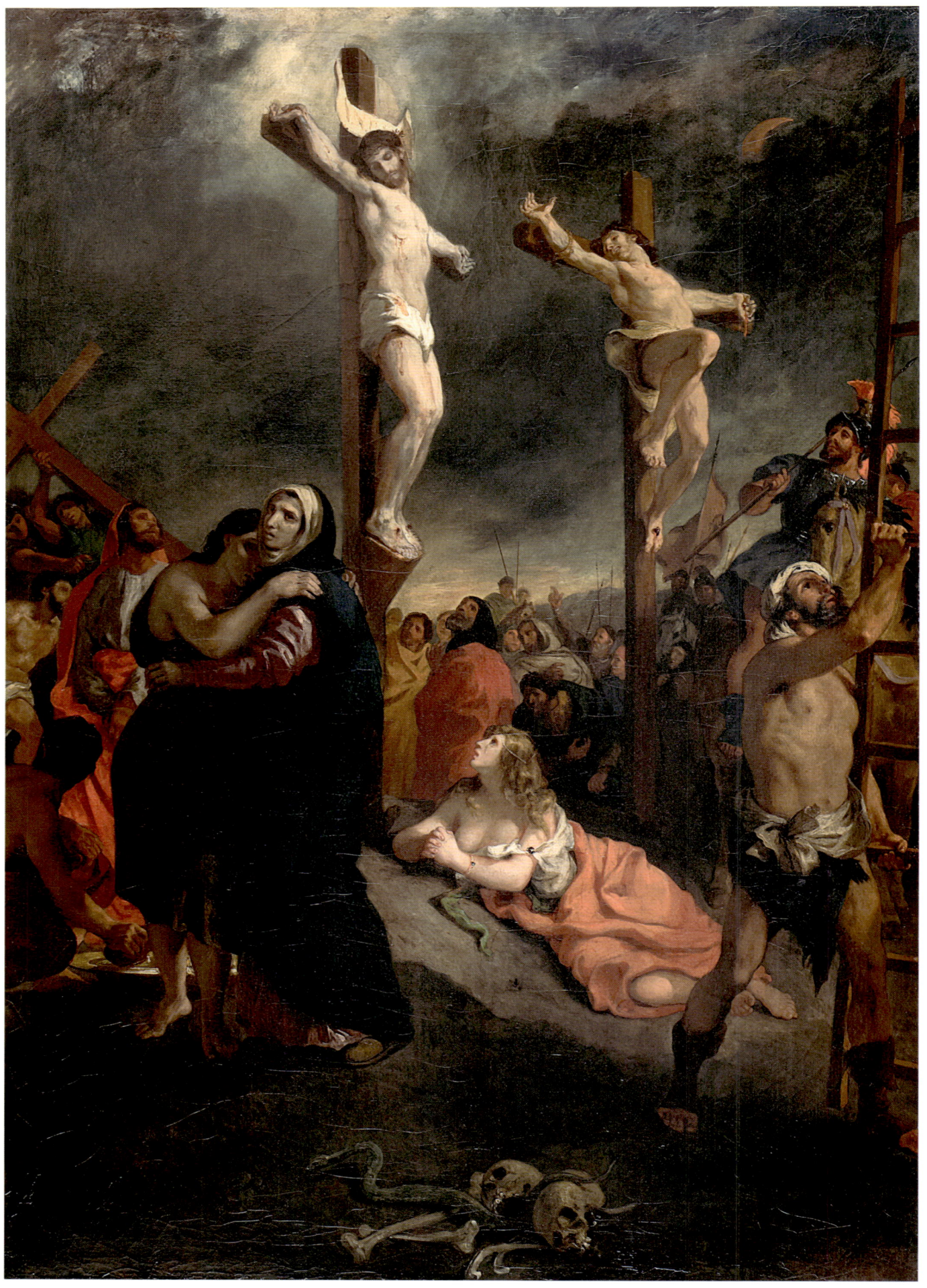

CAT. 85 *Christ on the Cross*, 1835

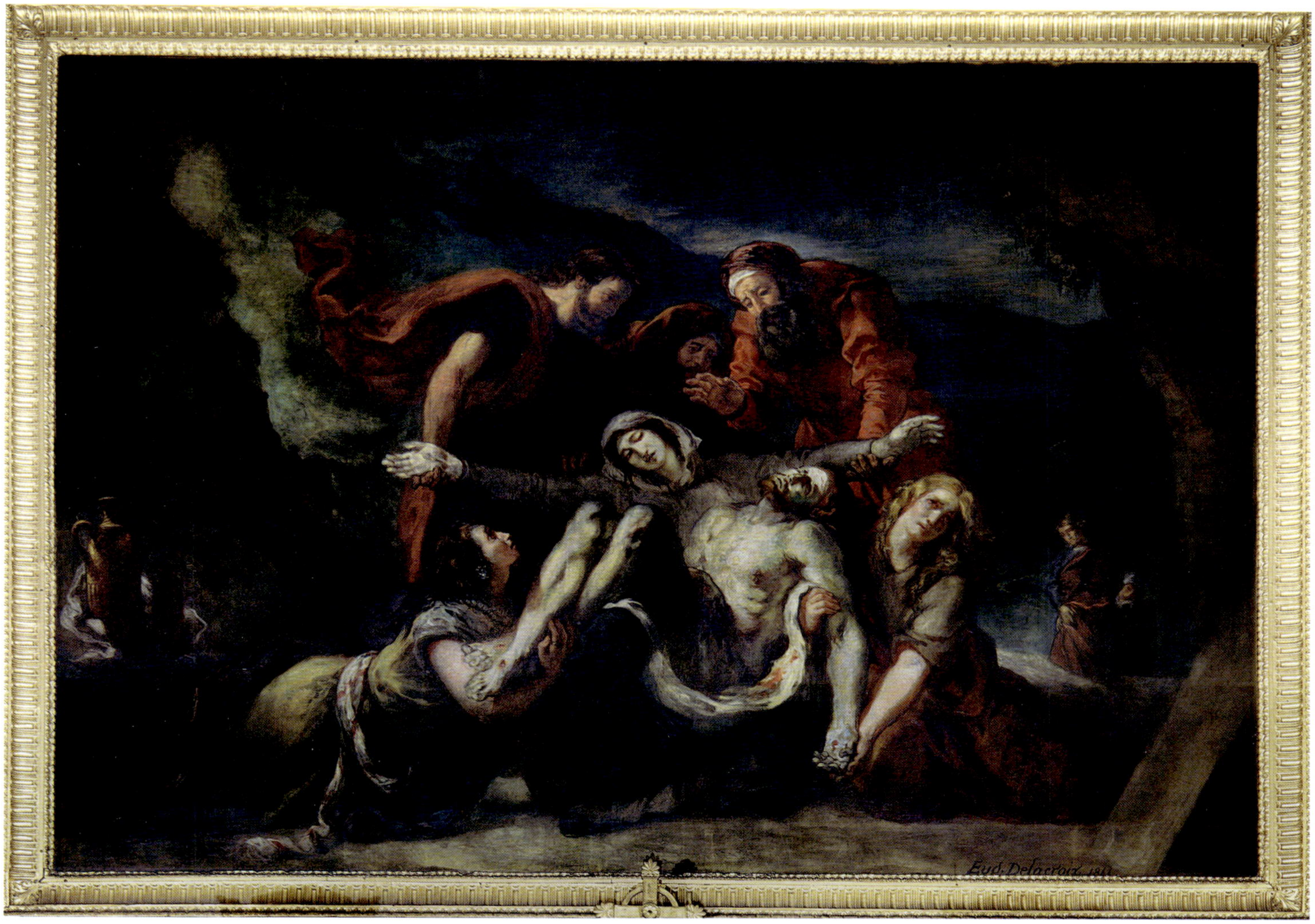

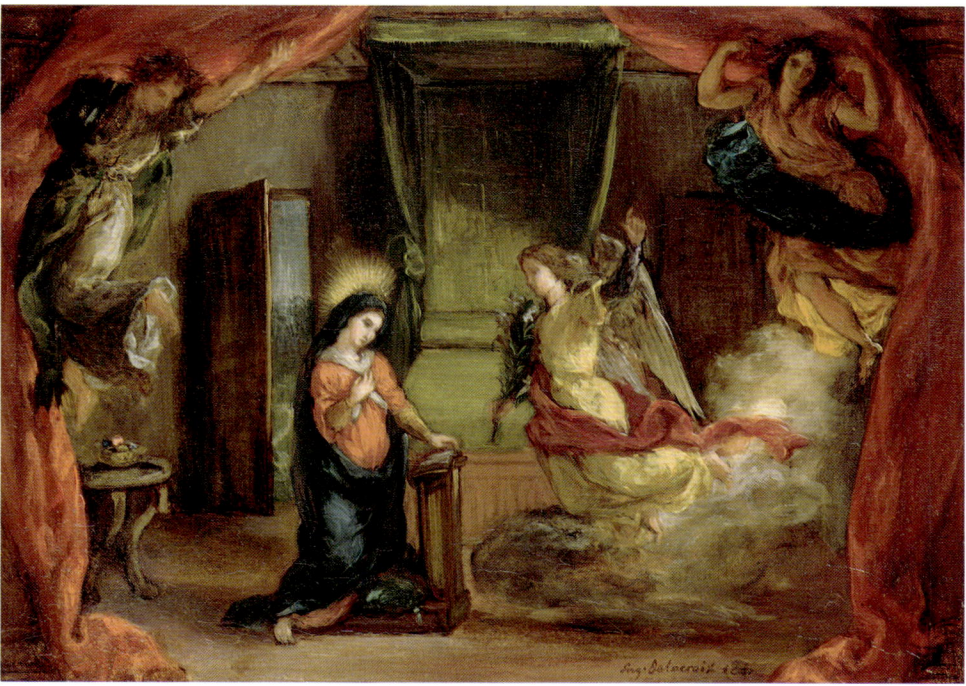

FIG. 48 *Pietà*, 1844. Oil and wax on plaster, 11 ft. 7¾ in. x 15 ft. 7 in. (3.5 x 4.7 m). Church of Saint-Denys-du-Saint-Sacrement, Paris (J 564)

FIG. 49 *The Annunciation*, 1841. Oil on paper, laid down on canvas, 12¼ x 17³⁄₁₆ in. (31.2 x 43.7 cm).
Musée National Eugène-Delacroix, Paris (inv. MD 1988–8) (J 425)

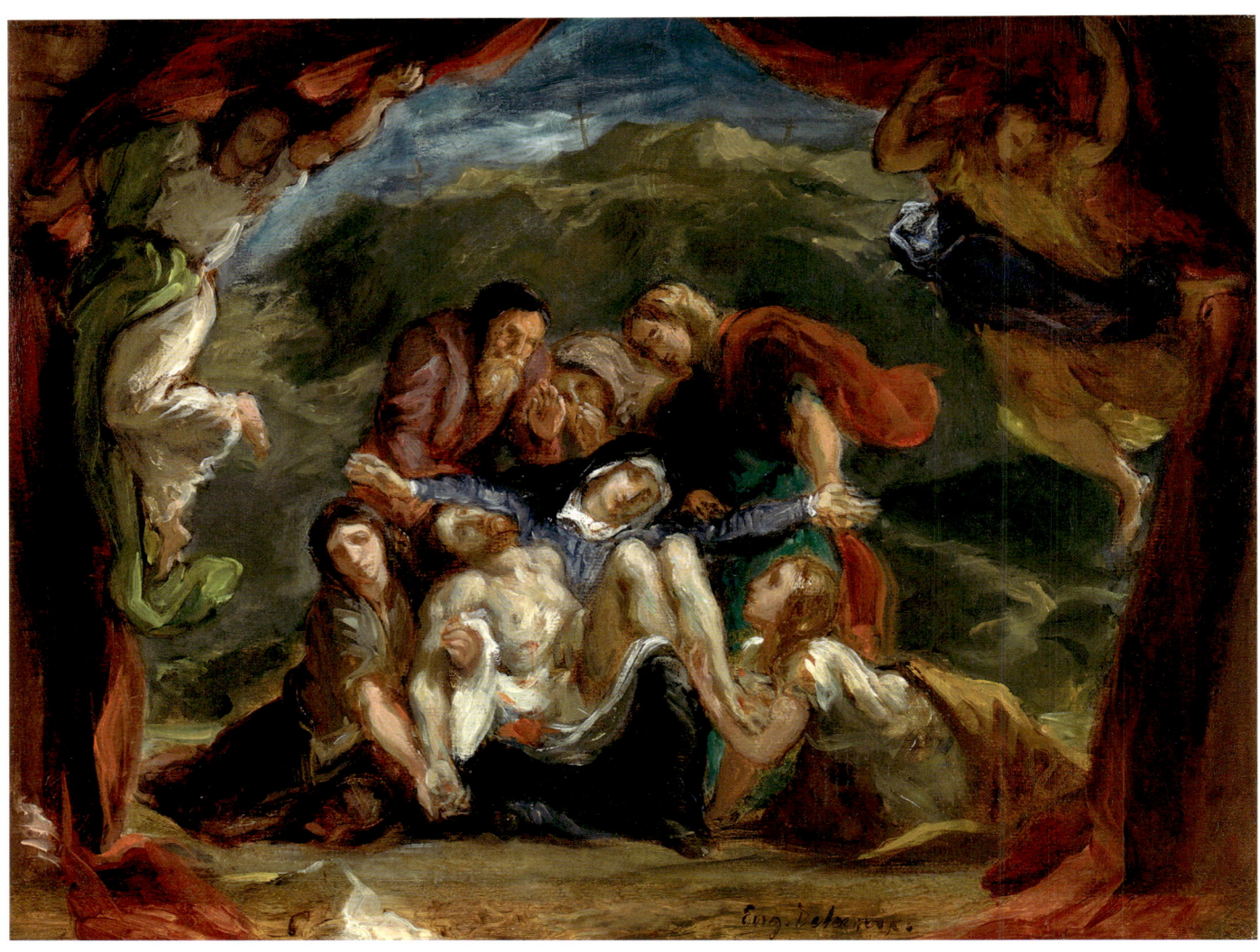

CAT. 100 *Pietà, first sketch*, by 1843

the key features of this work: the rocky setting in tight focus; the compact group of holy men (Nicodemus, Joseph of Arimathea, John the Evangelist) and women (Mary Magdalene, Mary of Clopas) forming a square around the Virgin; Mary Magdalene fervently grasping Christ's wounded feet, recalling their first encounter. The Italian master's ingenious inventiveness is faithfully rendered. The Virgin, head tilted and arms spread wide, assumes the pose of her son on the cross. Giving herself over to grief, she, too, appears to be dying; her gray and green flesh tones blend with those of the corpse resting against her. The union of mother and son in death is paired with a symbolic restaging of childbirth. Delacroix adopted the fetal pose of Il Rosso's Christ but replaced the model's Mannerist elegance with a stiffer posture.

Delacroix did not conceal his debt to Il Rosso's *Pietà*, probably confident in the knowledge that his own expressive

powers would successfully avert pastiche and guarantee the originality and unity of his composition. His experienced use of color to model flesh—understood as the vehicle for the expression of extreme suffering—served to energize the dry lines of his model. Exploiting the viscous consistency of oil mixed with wax, he gave material presence to the ravages of death and suffering, mimicking sweating skin, reddened eyes, bloody wounds, streaming tears, and decomposing flesh. The expressionist qualities imparted by that medium combine, however, with the solid grouping of the figures. The figures' cohesion is enhanced by their powerful contours and a concentric distribution of color: in the center, the fusion of the ashen bodies of Christ and the Virgin; surrounding them, the vivid reds of the mourners' flesh and attire; and framing all, the setting, which echoes, in darker shades, the blue and green harmonies of the central figures. It seems that Delacroix

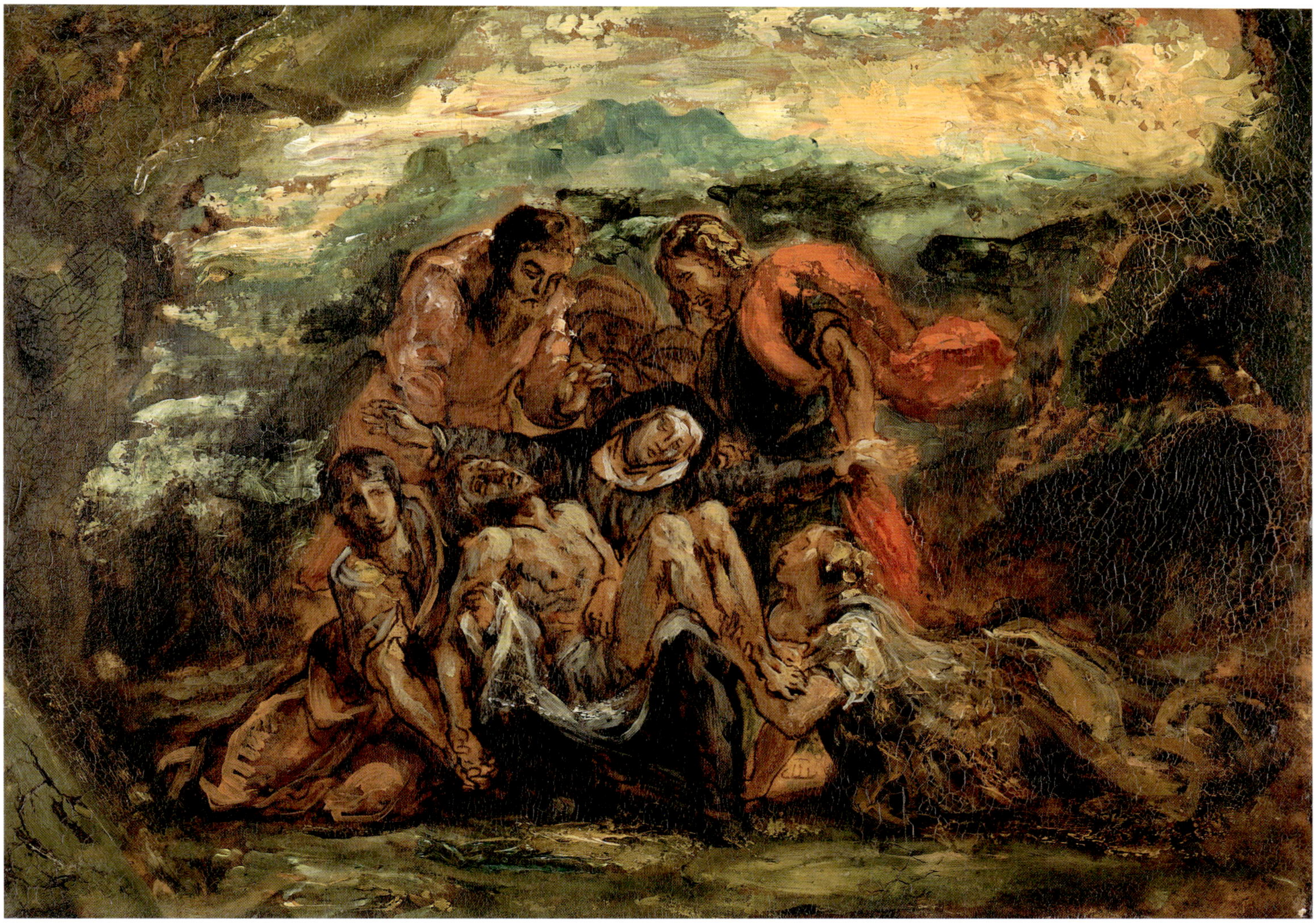

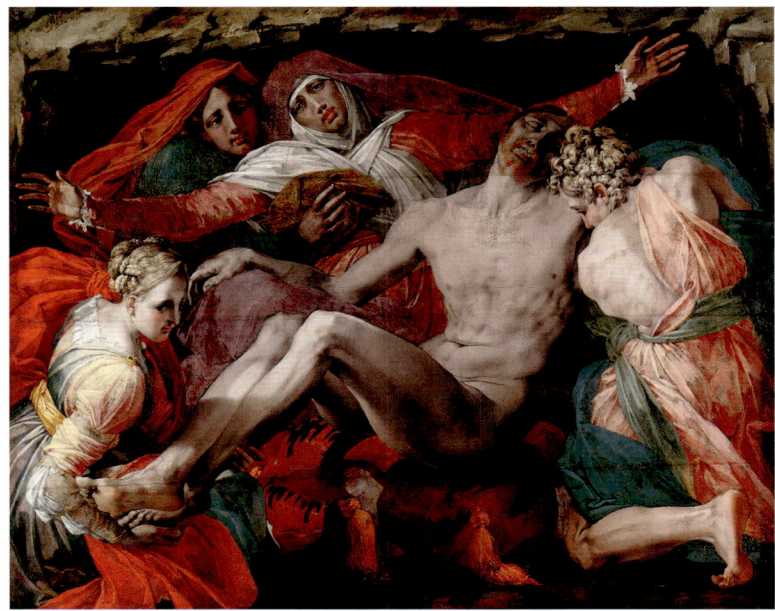

CAT. 101 *Pietà, second sketch,* by 1843

FIG. 50 Rosso Fiorentino (Italian, 1494–1540). *Pietà,* ca. 1530–40. Oil on wood, transferred to canvas, 50 x 64³⁄₁₆ in. (127 x 163 cm). Musée du Louvre, Paris (594)

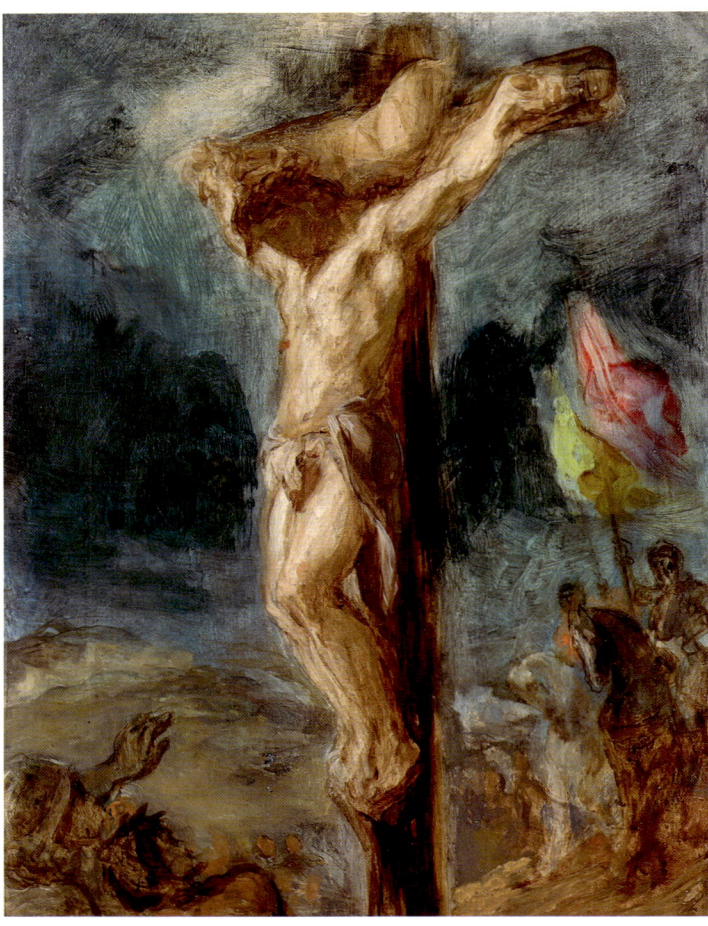

CAT. 102 *Christ on the Cross, sketch*, 1845

Despite the darkness of the chapel and the artist's dissatisfaction—Delacroix complained that he was denied the right to add his finishing touches—the painting's critical success allowed him to believe he had risen to the challenge and that other commissions for church decorations might follow. They were not long in coming. By January 1847, Edmond Cavé, director of the arts division at the Ministère de l'Intérieur, had led him to hope that he would be entrusted with the decoration for the transepts of Saint-Sulpice.[39] Delacroix thus had the opportunity to develop rapidly the expressive means he had employed in the *Pietà*. Only two years after completing that commission, he used the same principles in an even simpler, vertical composition: his most contemplative version of *Christ on the Cross* (cats. 102, 103). He modeled the work, an easel painting, on Pierre Paul Prud'hon's *Christ on the Cross* (1822; Musée du Louvre).[40] Initially commissioned for the cathedral of Strasbourg, Prud'hon's painting went instead to the Musée du Luxembourg—a particularly enviable fate in the eyes of Delacroix, who published a laudatory article on the elder painter during the same period.[41] In Delacroix's 1846 Crucifixion scene, the pallid body of Christ, whose face is obscured, rises up amid bluish shadows. When viewed from afar, it constitutes the primary source of light in the painting, as austere and solid in appearance as its neo-Caravaggesque model. Closer examination reveals blood streaming supernaturally from the figure's hands to its feet, even to the point of causing revulsion. Viscous and brilliant, the fluid is fashioned with multicolored strokes using the technique of *flochetage* over the entire length of the body. The flood of vermilion is augmented symbolically by the crimson banner of the Roman knight in the background and the coagulated coats of paint in the sunset on the horizon. Above Christ's head, the traditional sign bearing the charges against him is implausibly outsized, heavy, and limp, metamorphosed into the serpent of evil.

Christ on the Cross was followed directly by *Christ at the Tomb* (cat. 106), the beginnings of which were recorded in Delacroix's *Journal* in January 1847, under the title "Christ laid out on a stone, mourned by the holy women."[42] Delacroix, now more self-assured, departed from the closed schema of the *Pietà* of Saint-Denys-du-Saint-Sacrement (see fig. 48). Probably guided by the structure of an Entombment by Rubens of which he owned a painted copy—the original was then (as now) in Cambrai—he loosened the composition and let it breathe by dividing the figure group

was working on this scheme in the sketch now in the Louvre (cat. 101). The work began as a powerful line drawing in ink, over which the artist applied paint in colored masses, some thickly impastoed and laid down with a knife, others more fluid, applied with a brush. The chiaroscuro is exaggerated and the colors bold, but the structure holds together.

The painter has caught the beholder's gaze in a trap. Once drawn in by the *Pietà*'s concentric force, the viewer's gaze circles continuously within the virtuoso composition, picking up subtle echoes in the protagonists' faces, hands, and arms. Worshippers, caught up in the work's anguish, would be motivated to repeat their prayers. The *Pietà* thus marks Delacroix's return to the intense pathos of *Massacres at Chios,* but with one essential difference: the scattered, centrifugal composition of the painting of 1824 was succeeded twenty years later by the extreme concentration and dramatic unity of the religious mural.

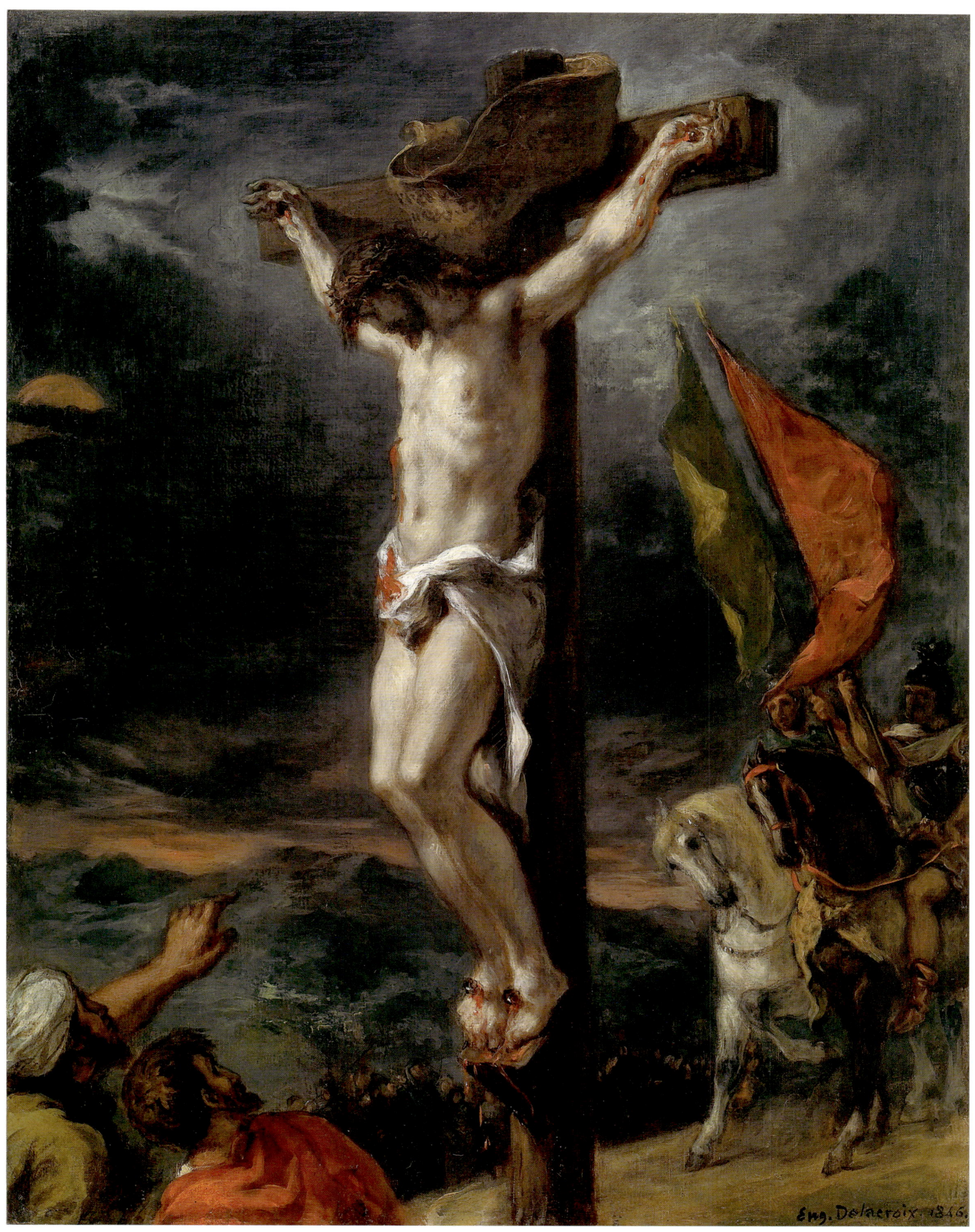

CAT. 103 *Christ on the Cross*, 1846

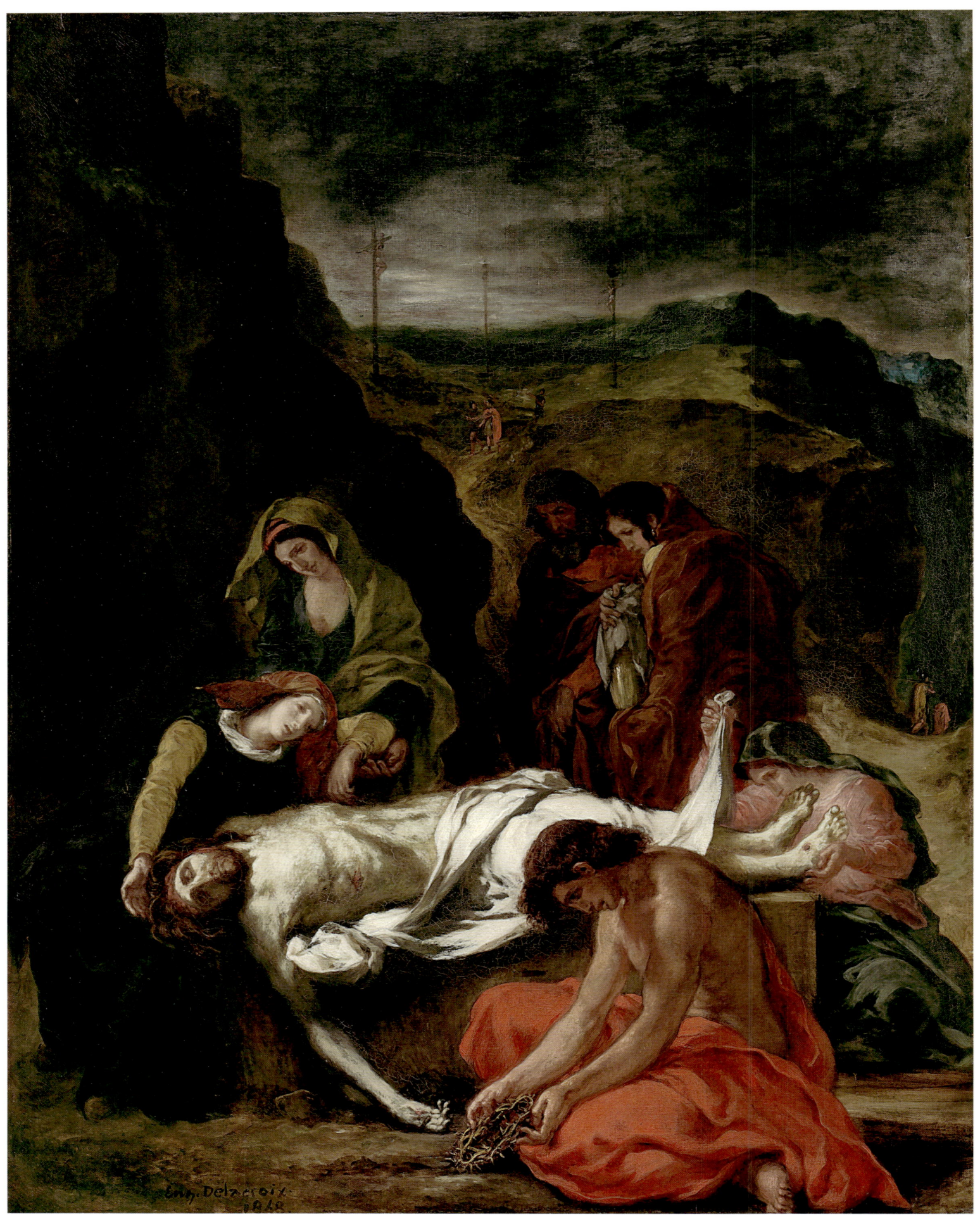

CAT. 106 *The Lamentation (Christ at the Tomb)*, 1847–48

into subgroups.[43] The Lamentation scene occupies the lower part of the frame; in the background, the desolate landscape of Mount Golgotha is punctuated with three crosses. The light, used with great economy, seems to emanate solely from the livid body and white shroud of Christ, laid out on the tomb. The other protagonists and the landscape are painted in varied but very muted tones; Saint John's bare chest, shaded by his bent head, is as dark as the other figures' clothing. The color notes in the artist's *Journal* indicate that earth tones (umber, green earth, burnt green earth) played a decisive role.[44] Christ's stiff corpse, its skeletal structure showing through under the pallid skin, is modeled in two tones (bluish-white and gray-green), which blend under the effect of chiaroscuro. Gore is represented discreetly. Abandoning Rubens and his sensual eloquence, Delacroix here seems deliberately to have followed in the footsteps of Jusepe de Ribera and Rembrandt, taking asceticism to a level unequaled in the rest of his oeuvre. He was inspired, perhaps, by the masterpieces in the Galerie Espagnole that Louis-Philippe established at the Louvre in 1838.

Delacroix derived lasting satisfaction from the high degree of dramatic and formal unity he achieved in *Christ at the Tomb*. The work even seems to have played a key role in his artistic experimentation. It is probably no coincidence that in January 1847, just as he was starting the painting, he began once more to keep a journal. For the first time since *Massacres at Chios* (painted between January and August 1824), Delacroix reported daily on the development of a painting he intended to show at the Salon. From the start, he used the *Journal* to reflect on his working process. He no longer seemed preoccupied with finding subject matter or inspiration; rather, he was concerned about mastering its execution. Determined this time to preserve the integrity of the whole as he originally conceived it, he invested a considerable amount of time in the *ébauche*, or preliminary laying-in of the composition:

> After lunch, I resumed work on the *Christ at the Tomb*: it is the third session on the ébauche; . . . I got it going again in a lively manner and prepared it for a fourth pass. I am satisfied with this ébauche; but how to preserve the overall impression that results from very simple masses while adding details? Most painters—and I did this too in the past—begin with the details and create the effect at the end.—Whatever regret you feel when you see the impression of simplicity in a beautiful

drawing vanish as you add details to it, a great deal more of that impression remains than you will manage to put into it if you proceed in the opposite fashion.[45]

Delacroix deliberately sought to reverse the creative process he had followed in his youth, notably, the one he had used for *Massacres at Chios*, which he was probably reminded of as he reread his *Journal* of 1824. This meant not rushing to the canvas and beginning with the particulars of each figure, a method that would necessitate creating unity after the fact, with highlights and glazes. On the contrary, the entire elaboration of the painting had to be grounded in the preparatory study's "tone and the effect"—its large, colored shapes, light, and shadows—with as little deviation as possible, because that method guaranteed unity. He returned to this subject in detail the very next day.

> One of the great advantages of [doing] a lay-in by tone and general effect, without worrying about the details, is that you need to put in only those that are absolutely necessary. Beginning by completing the backgrounds, as I have done here, I have made them as simple as possible so as to avoid their appearing overloaded beside the simple masses that still represent the figures. Conversely, when I come to finish the figures, the simplicity of the backgrounds will allow—even compel—me to put in only what is absolutely essential. Once the sketch has been brought to this stage, the right thing to do is to carry each part as far as possible, and to refrain from working over the picture as a whole, assuming, of course, that the effect and tone have been determined throughout. What I mean is, that when you decide to finish a particular figure among others as yet only laid in, you must be careful to keep the details simple, to avoid being too much out of harmony with figures that are still in the stage of a sketch.[46]

Delacroix thus formulated a system to prevent himself from working on all parts of a painting simultaneously. He set a level of completion not to be surpassed in one part of the composition (the background, in the present case), then applied that limit to the rest. When work proceeds on all elements at the same time and on the same level, "the eye becomes accustomed to details, when they are introduced gradually into one figure after another, and in all at the same sitting, and the painting never seems finished. First disadvantage of the method: the details smother the masses. Second disadvantage: the work takes much longer to do."[47] Delacroix invoked these precepts until the end of his life, though he was not always able to adhere to them. For example, in 1860 he wrote: "There are two things that must be learned: the first is that one must correct a lot; the second is that one must not correct too much."[48]

Christo at the Tomb was sold to comte Théodore de Geloës d'Elsloo even before it was shown at the Salon of 1848. Delacroix was pleased when he saw it again, as he reported in his Journal on February 16, 1850, after a visit to the collector's home in Paris.[49] He borrowed the painting for his retrospective at the Exposition Universelle of 1855 and, with the memory of the work still fresh in his mind, noted in December of that year his delight in the unity of the scene. "It inspires an emotion that astonishes even me. You can't pull yourself away, and not a single detail calls out to be admired or distract attention. It's the perfection of this art [painting], whose aim is to produce a simultaneous effect. If painting produced its effects in the manner of literature, which is but a series of successive scenes, there would be some justification for the detail to stand out."[50]

It is likely that the success of Christ at the Tomb encouraged Delacroix to develop his new approach to form by applying it to other subjects, including some taken from secular literary sources. The Death of Valentin (fig. 51), after Goethe's Faust, painted the same year and also exhibited at the Salon of 1848, would demonstrate this talent to the public. The scene depicts the aftermath of Valentin's fateful duel with Faust and Mephistopheles (depicted in plate 11 of the 1828 suite of lithographs; see cat. 50), as the collective lamentation for the murdered victim begins. But the pale, stiff silhouette that attracts the light in the center of the painting is not Valentin: it is Marguerite, his errant sister, consumed with remorse and condemned by the curses of her dying brother, who takes on the role of martyr. The dark cliffs of Christ at the Tomb are replaced by city buildings unified by their uniformly treated brown facades even as, sunlit in the distance, three pinnacles of the church replace the three crosses of Golgotha.

Such adaptations of a literary subject remained rare during this period. More often, he chose to represent Christian martyrs, a theme that he would take in a far more harrowing direction than he had in the Saint Sebastian at Nantua (see cat. 90), as the artist noted in his Journal on December 14, 1847, "Saint Stephen, after being stoned, gathered up by the

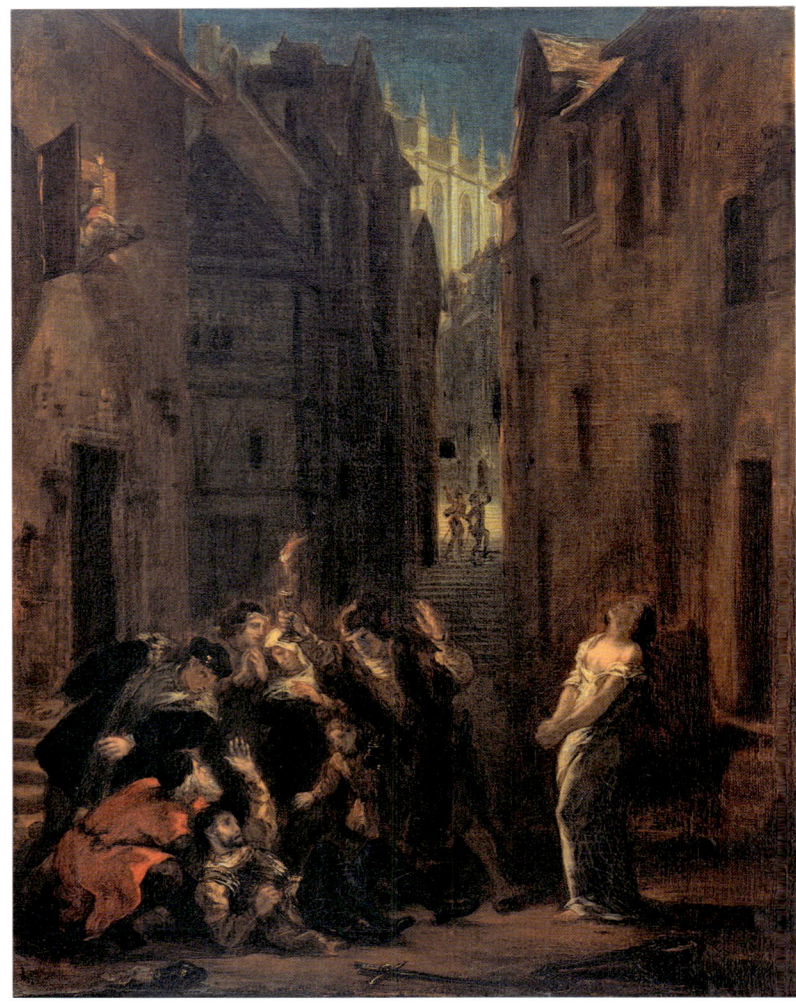

FIG. 51 The Death of Valentin, 1847. Oil on canvas, 32¼ x 25⁹⁄₁₆ in. (82 x 65 cm). Kunsthalle Bremen—Der Kunstverein in Bremen (inv. 552-1948/12) (J 288)

holy women and disciples."[51] Saint Stephen Borne Away by His Disciples was finally completed for the Salon of 1853 (cat. 130). The format and the main lines of the composition are similar to those of Christ at the Tomb, but the dark rocks have been replaced by the ramparts of Jerusalem, and Stephen's body faces right rather than left, like Christ's. The kneeling figure in the foreground is no longer a tearful Saint John meditating on the crown of thorns but a holy woman wiping the blood from the steps where the stones that killed Stephen still lie. The intense physicality of the two female figures in the foreground (both have vigorous bare arms, and one, an exposed bust) tempers the austerity of the scene. The entanglement of bodies is more complex and disjointed than in Christ at the Tomb, but the restricted palette, underscored by stark chiaroscuro effects, is even more severe than in the earlier work.

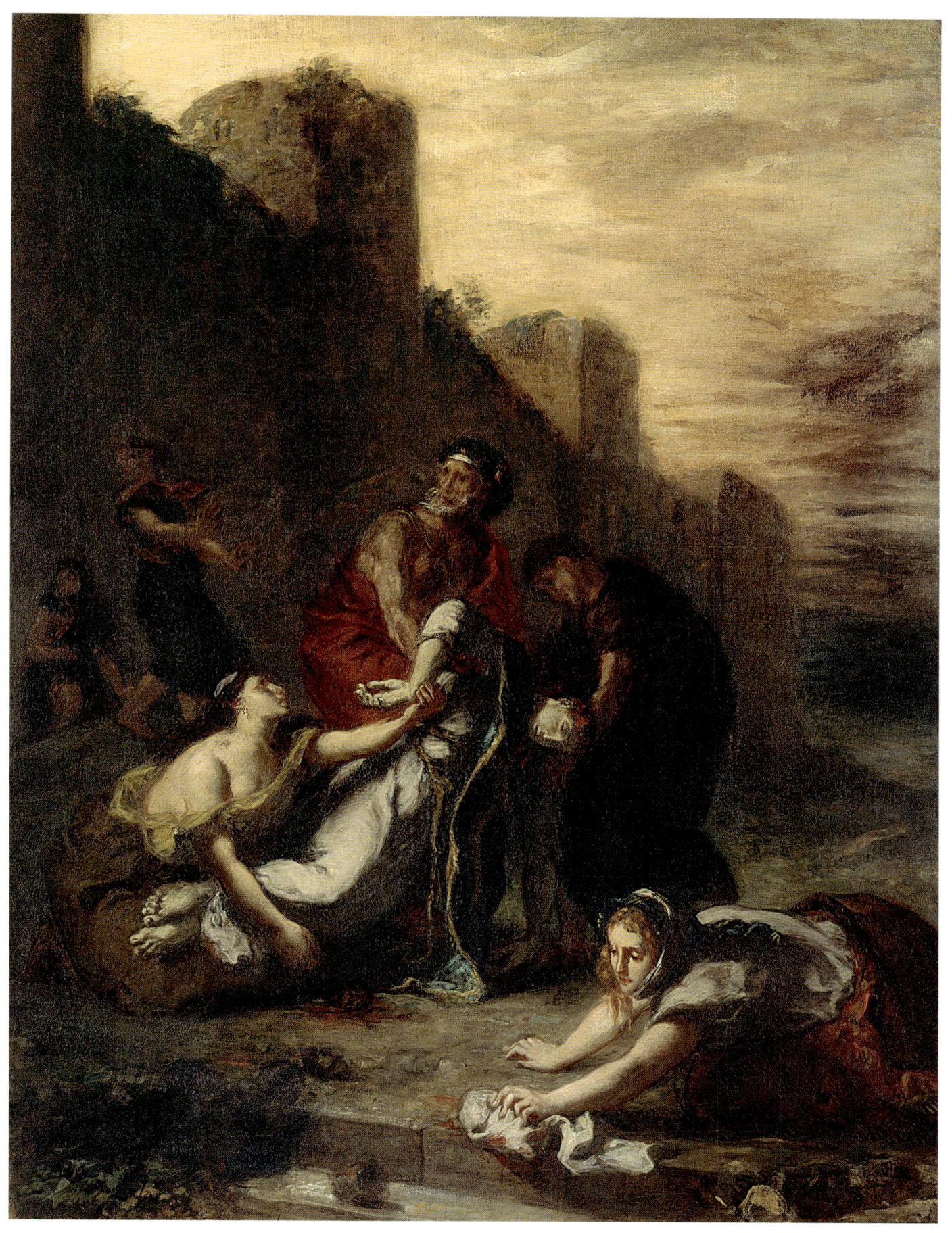

CAT. 130 *Saint Stephen Borne Away by His Disciples*, 1853

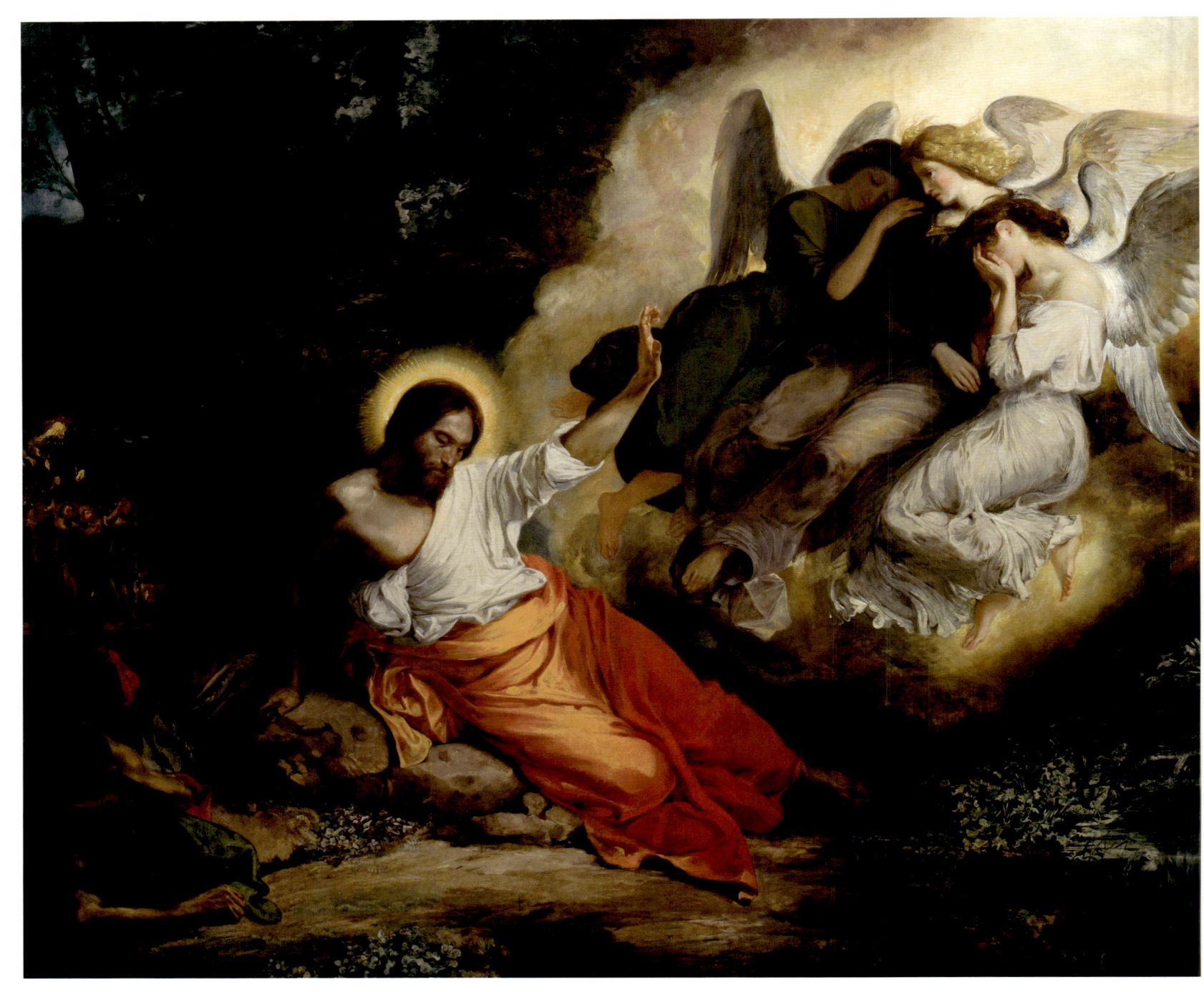

CAT. 17 *Christ in the Garden of Olives (The Agony in the Garden)*, 1824–26

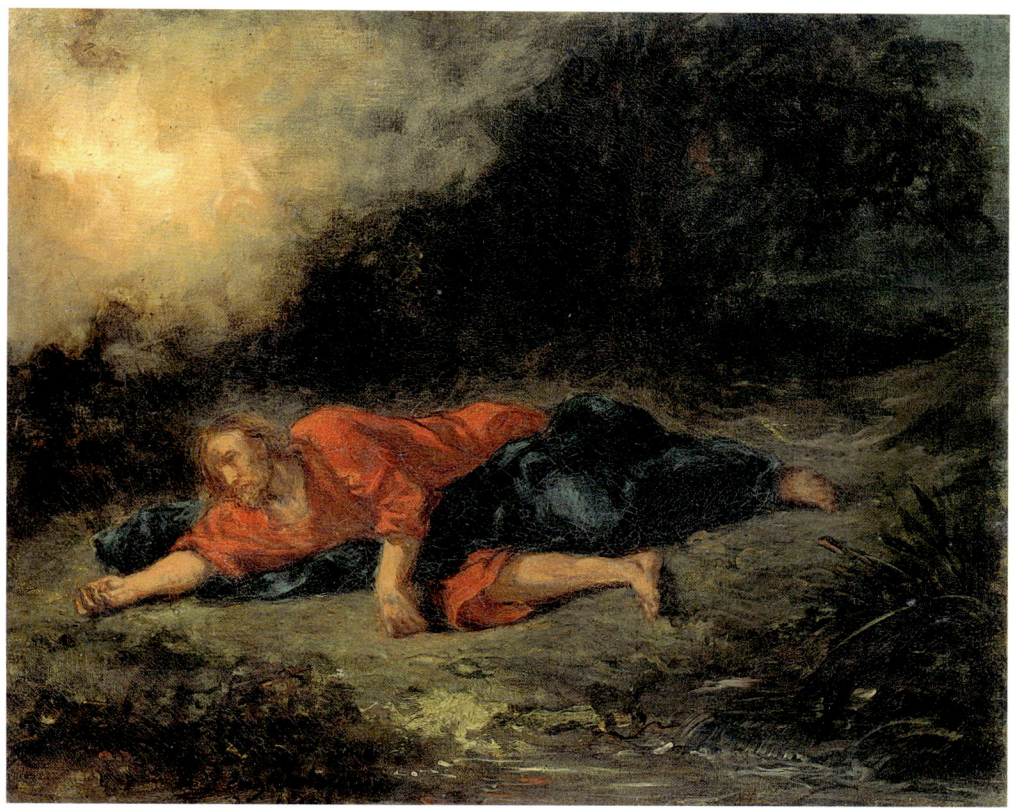

CAT. 125 *The Agony in the Garden*, 1851

In an atmosphere of red, earth-tone, and gray harmonies, the only precious luminous notes lie in the white dawn and the green chasuble fringed with gold falling from the saint's upper body. The naive, almost Symbolist character of the architectural setting echoes many other paintings by Delacroix: the sky with its long, glowing horizontal streaks is a distant revival of the skies in the much earlier *Massacres at Chios* (see fig. 5) and *Hamlet and Horatio in the Graveyard* (see cat. 86). The impenetrable opacity of the walls, composed of a series of cubes, is cast into relief by the rain of fire. Their shape derives from Delacroix's memory of the ramparts at Meknes, but their almost biblical simplicity is probably indebted also to theatrical sets, which the artist admired for their effectiveness:

> Saw *I Puritani* [by Vincenzo Bellini, at the Théâtre-Italien]. . . . The moonlight scene at the end is superb, like everything that the designer in this theater does.[52] I think he obtains his effects with very simple colours, using black and blue and perhaps umber, but they are well understood as regards the planes and the way in which one tint is placed above another. A very simple tone was used for the terrace at the top of the ramparts,

with brilliant touches of white to represent the lines of mortar between the stones. Tempera lends itself admirably to such simple effects because the colors do not blend together as they do in oil painting. Several towers or castellated battlements stand out against the very simply painted sky, and are detached from one another solely through the intensity of the tone.[53]

Delacroix was emboldened by the new mastery of emotion that he achieved by using a dark palette. He was no longer afraid to take on subjects that he would have judged unrewarding for their lack of moral ambiguity signified, in part, by the visually exuberant details that were a prominent feature of his early paintings. He no longer hesitated to paint the absolute solitude of Christ in extremis. Therefore, in the early 1850s, he returned to the subject of Christ on the Mount of Olives, which he had first painted in 1824–26 for the church of Saint-Paul-Saint-Louis (cat. 17). In contrast to that early composition, in which Jesus fends off the coming torture with a theatrical gesture, the later one shows him reduced by anguish to crawling on the ground, like a beast at bay (cat. 125). Any human companionship (sleeping apostles

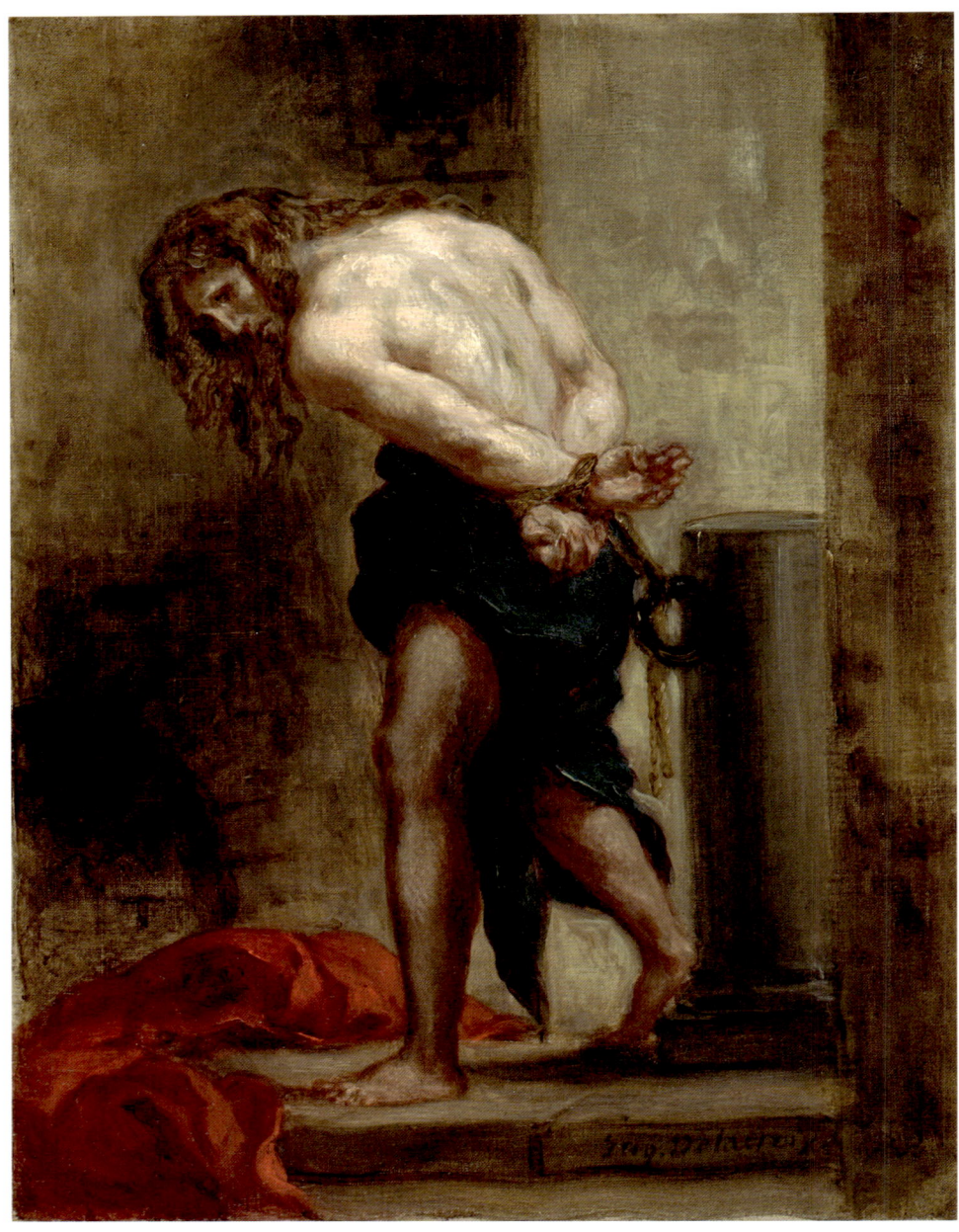

CAT. 112 *Christ at the Column*, probably 1849

or approaching soldiers), any visible supernatural presence (angels), is denied him.

Delacroix's new interest in Christ's solitary suffering may explain why the artist never painted the scene of his arrest, however dramatic its potential. It was the scene of Christ's flagellation that held his attention at the dawn of the 1850s. That motif would have struck a chord for any admirer of Rubens. Delacroix had been dazzled by the Flemish painter's *Flagellation* on his first visit to the church of Saint Paul in Antwerp in 1839 and again eleven years later, when he wrote: "The *Flagellation of Christ* . . . a masterpiece of genius if ever there was one. It is slightly marred by the big executioner on the left. It really

requires an incredible degree of sublimity for this ridiculous figure not to ruin the whole picture. . . . The blood-streaked back, the head, so wonderfully expressive of the fever of suffering, the one arm that can be seen, are all indescribably beautiful."[54] In keeping with these observations, Delacroix excluded any presence that would have competed with that of the martyr (cat. 112). He isolated Christ's figure in a bare stone setting and eliminated the realistic effects of whip marks and bloody wounds, which he symbolically transferred to the red draping at Christ's feet. The subject is reduced to a single motif: Jesus' throbbing, dripping back, rendered in a virtuoso weave of pink, green, white, and brown brushstrokes. In the second version

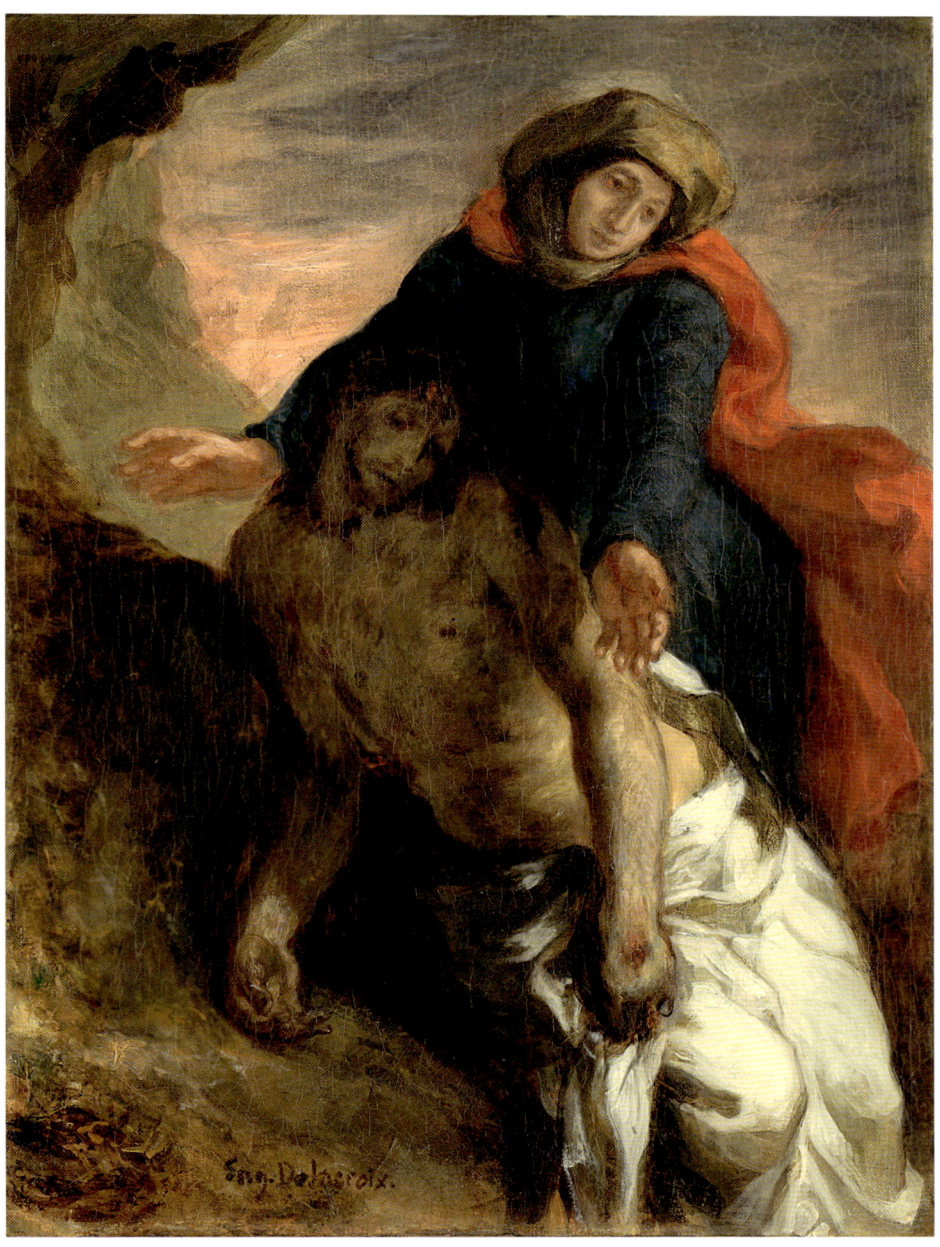

CAT. 124 *Pietà*, ca. 1850

(Musée des Beaux-Arts, Dijon), dated 1852, the silhouettes of a few soldiers appear under the vault in the lower left corner, but the light is reduced even more. The draping loses its brilliance, the column is darker, Christ's legs and face vanish in the shadows, and the rendering of his hair is no longer vibrant and refined. Light emanates solely from his tortured back and bound hands, their gleam accentuated by the contrast with the filth of the shirt and the notice plastered on the wall to the right. The picture's dramatic and formal intensity is radically distilled.

During this same period, Delacroix executed his most concentrated version of the Pietà (cat. 124). The vertical, tightly framed composition, featuring a compact arrangement of sinuous bodies in three-quarter profile, can probably be traced to the central panel of Rubens's *Christ on the Straw* (1618; Royal Museum of Fine Arts, Antwerp), a Lamentation Delacroix saw in the Cathedral of Our Lady in Antwerp during his visit there in 1850. The scene is considerably simplified in comparison to its counterpart at Saint-Denys-du-Saint-Sacrement (see fig. 48). It features the mouth of a cave, two figures, and a harmonious balance of three bright colors (blue, white, and red) amid cool tones (gray, green, and brown). The outstretched arms of the Virgin no longer recall those of Christ on the cross but extend toward her son as she leans to her left, her body's curve echoed by the cave's rocky

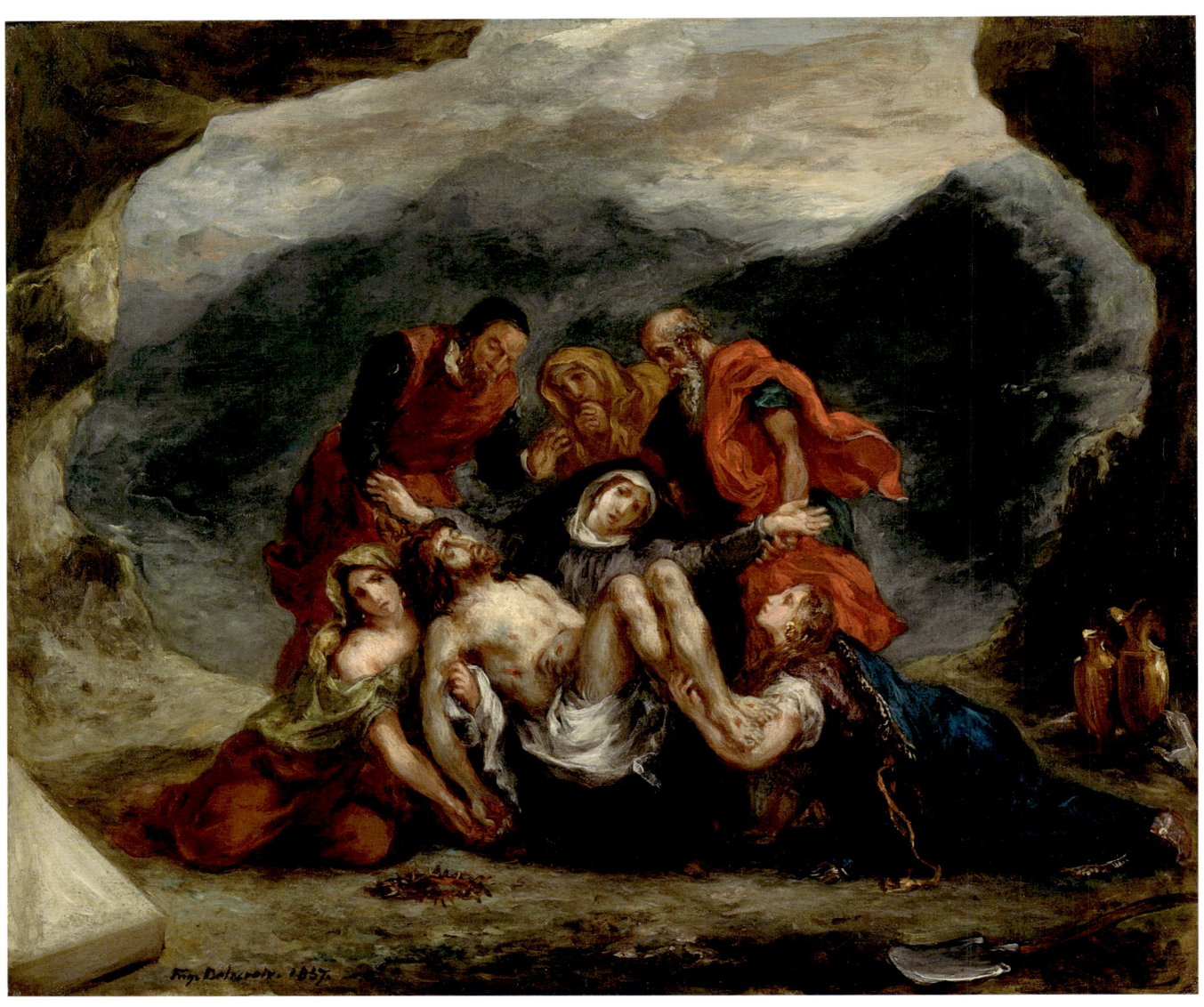

CAT. 140 *Lamentation over the Body of Christ*, 1857

profile. While her face is relatively inexpressive, her posture, nearly identical to that of the dead Christ, conveys her maternal suffering. She seems to want to protect her son from the world's hatred. In so doing, she shields him from the light; it touches only the white shroud, leaving his ashen face and torso sheltered in his mother's midnight-blue embrace.

That Pietà, Delacroix's simplest and most compact expression of the theme—a lithograph by Célestin Nanteuil after the painting would later captivate Vincent van Gogh—by no means exhausted the subject or achieved perfection in the painter's eyes (Van Gogh Museum, Amsterdam). He returned subsequently to the composition recorded in a sketch (see cat. 101) for the mural at Saint-Denys-du-Saint-Sacrement. He produced a new version with variations, less dramatic but

more luminous and brightly colored, probably at the request of the dealer Jean-Hector Bouruet-Aubertot in 1857 (cat. 140). The same is true for the subject of Christ on the Cross, to which Delacroix returned in 1853 at the instigation of another dealer, Adolphe Beugniet (fig. 52).[55] For this reprise, he reversed the composition of *Christ on the Cross* exhibited at the Salon of 1847 (see cat. 103) and replaced the dark atmosphere of that earlier work with the murky light of an overcast sky. The vaporous clouds have a lightness and clarity rivaling that produced by pastel, a medium he was using during this period for other versions of the same subject, but on paper.[56] Delacroix also made deliberate reference to earlier works. For example, in the 1847 picture Mary Magdalene recalls her role in the treatment of the theme exhibited at the Salon of 1835 (see

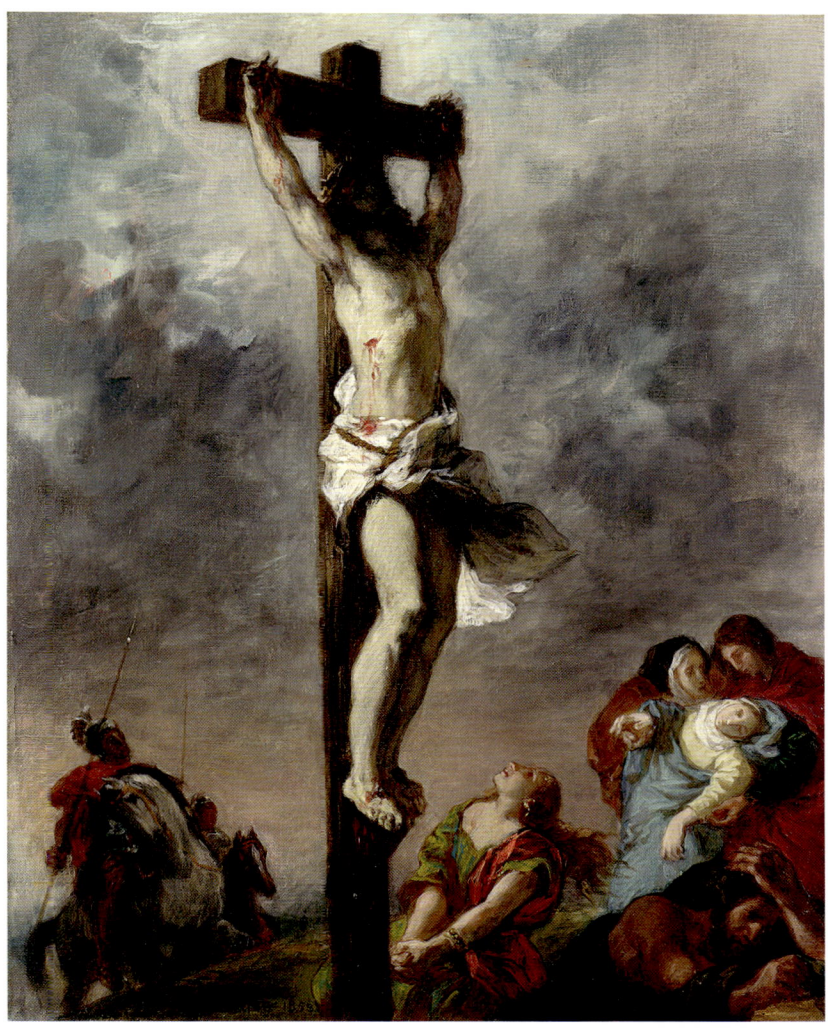

FIG. 52 *Christ on the Cross*, 1853. Oil on canvas, 28¹⁵⁄₁₆ x 23½ in. (73.5 x 59.7 cm). The National Gallery, London (inv. NG6433) (J 460)

cat. 85); the same might be said for the figures supporting the swooning Virgin in the later painting, who recall the Virgin supporting Saint John in the earlier one. Certainly the prostrate apostle with bronze flesh tones clothed in green drapery in the later work echoes his counterpart at the lower left of *Christ on the Mount of Olives* exhibited at the Salon of 1827–28 (see cat. 17).

What emerges is that the most compelling phase of Delacroix's religious painting occurred between 1847 and 1852, when it reached its expressive height. During these years, through the concentration of his compositions and the austerity of his palette, the painter demonstrated absolute mastery of his pictorial powers. And yet, during exactly the same period, he was exploring a path leading in the opposite direction, toward dynamism and rich decoration.

Third Experiment: Explosion and Whirlwind of Colors

At the turn of the 1850s, Delacroix achieved an astonishing, almost contradictory diversity in his painting. He had just distinguished himself at the Salon of 1848 with the extraordinary gravity of *Christ at the Tomb* (see cat. 106) and the dramatic tension of *The Death of Valentin* (see fig. 51) when, the next year, his submissions to the following Salon cast him in a completely new light. They included two large outdoor views of flowers and fruit and two sumptuous interiors, one lighthearted (*Women of Algiers,* fig. 32), the other tragic (*Othello and Desdemona*; see fig. 116). The luxury and sensuality in these paintings are striking when considered in the context of the workers' uprising of June 1848, the first French presidential campaign, the competition for the allegory of the Republic, and the honors and medals awarded for the first time to exponents of unvarnished rural realism—Théodore Rousseau, Rosa Bonheur, and Gustave Courbet. Delacroix's gesture was interpreted as a sign of retreat from the modern world, in line with the reactionary skepticism he was unafraid to display in his correspondence during the same period.[57] It is certain that the artist was deeply disturbed by the outbursts of violence that followed the events of February and June 1848. The sacking of the Palais Royal, which brought about the destruction of his *Cardinal Richelieu Saying Mass*, must have come as a hard blow.[58] But the Bonapartist sympathies of his lover Joséphine de Forget, a close friend of Charles-Louis-Napoleon Bonaparte, were rewarded when the latter was elected as the first president of France in December 1848. Beginning in January 1849, Delacroix was invited to soirées at the Palais de l'Elysée and to sit in the presidential loge at the Opéra.

It is risky to take the political reading of the large floral still lifes any further. However, there is good reason to consider them in the context of the artist's new commissions for large decorative projects. In 1846 and 1847, Delacroix had completed the mural paintings commissioned for the Palais Bourbon and the Palais du Luxembourg. As the reign of Louis-Philippe was collapsing, he thus found himself without a public project for the first time since 1833. Commissions were not long in arriving, however, owing to the good relations he enjoyed with the new government, headed by the Prince-President Louis Napoleon Bonaparte. He learned in April 1849, through his friend the curator Frédéric Villot, that his name had been put forward by the architect Félix Duban

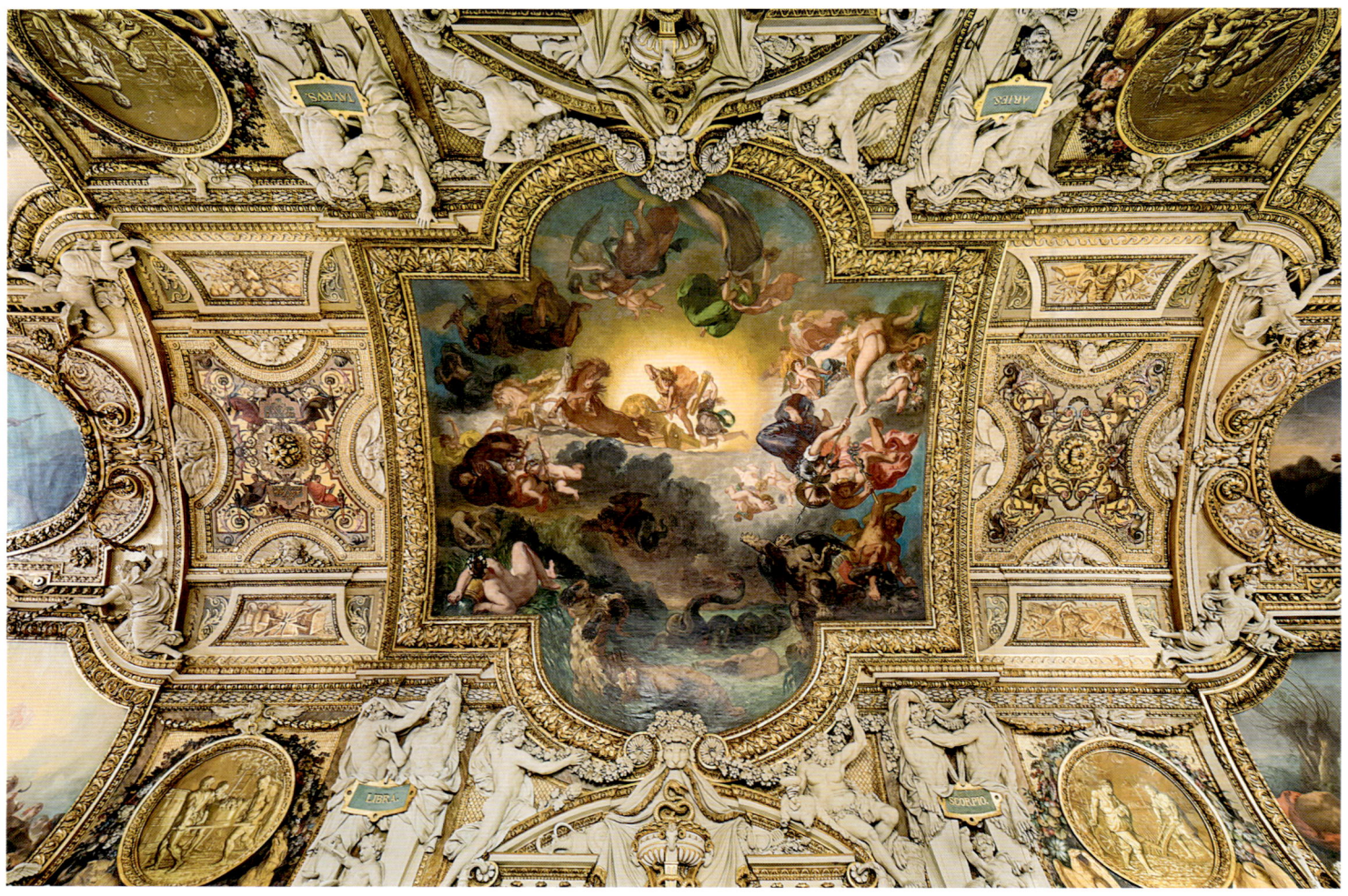

FIG. 53 *Apollo Slays the Python,* 1849–51. Oil on canvas, ceiling of the Gallery of Apollo, Musée du Louvre, 26 ft. 2¹⁵⁄₁₆ in. x 24 ft. 7¼ in. (8 x 7.5 m). Musée du Louvre, Paris (3818) (J 578)

for the project to complete the ceiling of the Gallery of Apollo.⁵⁹ The following month, the Ministère de l'Intérieur commissioned him to decorate a chapel in the church of Saint-Sulpice, a much larger and more prestigious religious site than Saint-Denys-du-Saint-Sacrement. The commission for the ceiling of the Gallery of Apollo was an extraordinary honor; it gave Delacroix the opportunity to occupy a central, permanent position in the most prominent area of the foremost museum in the world (fig. 53). These two projects would allow him to work for the first time in far more historic spaces. His previous commissions in the capital were associated with the completion of new spaces, both in a simplified and streamlined Neoclassicist style by the two architects Alphonse de Gisors and Etienne Hippolyte Godde. But at Saint-Sulpice as at the Louvre, Delacroix found himself in a princely Baroque

setting. He came into direct dialogue with the most illustrious masters of the French *grand goût:* the ornamentalist Gilles Marie Oppenord, who had produced the plans for Saint-Sulpice at the behest of the regent Philippe d'Orléans; the architect Louis le Vau; and the painter Charles Le Brun, who in the 1660s had done decorative work for Louis XIV in which he elaborated the prototype for the Royal Apartments at the Château de Versailles. Delacroix's new commissions were also part of a historicist movement that, following the burst of enthusiasm for Gothic art and the French Renaissance in the 1830s, gave new life to the styles of Louis XIV and Louis XV. That aesthetic, inspired by the restoration of the Château de Versailles and its opening as a museum, was taken up and adapted from the early 1840s by the architects and interior designers Jules de Joly and Eugène Lami; it was also favored

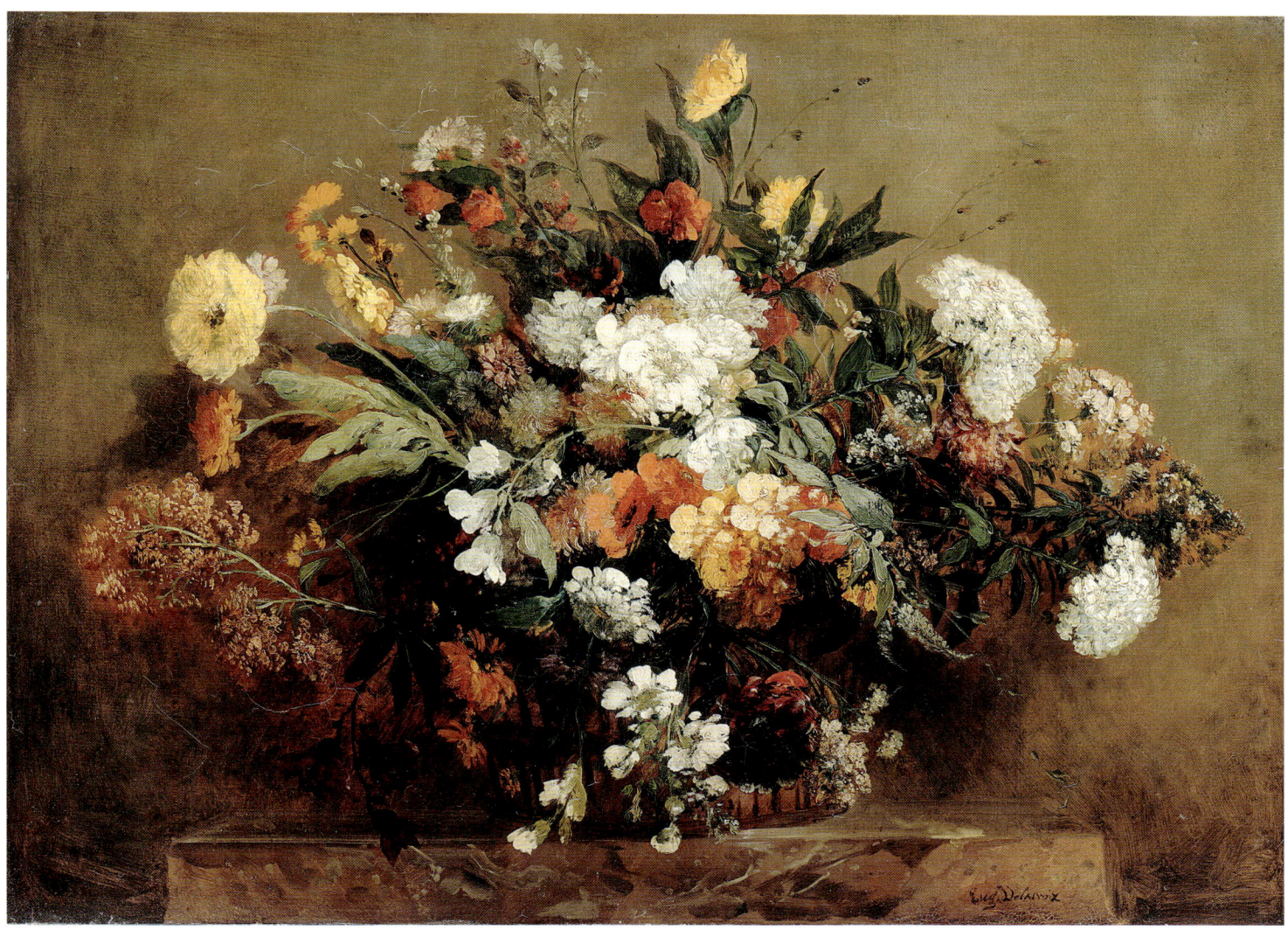

CAT. 111 *Basket of Flowers*, ca. 1848–50

by the great patrons of the arts who emerged at that time: James de Rothschild and the king's two eldest sons, Ferdinand Philippe, the crown prince, and Louis, duc de Nemours.

Delacroix began the large floral compositions in autumn 1848, basing them on studies of flowers and fruit he had done the previous summer.[60] He resumed working on five of them in mid-February 1849, with the intention of exhibiting them at the Salon, which opened on May 15. The paintings were, then, contemporaneous with the inception of the two most prestigious decorative commissions of his career as well as with the French revival of seventeenth-century court art. When the critics discovered them at the Salon, where two of the five were shown, they recognized immediately "the gravity of the style, the breadth of execution . . . the skillful arrangement."[61] These qualities distinguished Delacroix's

floral compositions from most other flower paintings of the day, heirs to the spirit of botanical science and its adherence to the illusionistic, limpid, and meticulous graphic description of each element. The deaths of Pierre Joseph Redouté, in 1840, and Louis Antoine Berjon, in 1843, left only Antoine Chazal and a few other specialized flower painters to perpetuate the Flemish tradition in Paris. Under attack by weary young critics scornful of the "vulgar, nit-picking florists" condemned to produce mere "dining room pictures," the practice was fading.[62]

Only the best-informed critics, such as Théophile Gautier, would identify the tradition that Delacroix had embraced, one that had been initiated by the seventeenth-century painter Jean-Baptiste Monnoyer.[63] After training in Antwerp, Monnoyer had introduced to France and then to

FIG. 54 *A Vase of Flowers*, 1833. Oil on canvas, 22¾ x 19³⁄₁₆ in. (57.7 x 48.8 cm). National Galleries of Scotland, Edinburgh (inv. NG 2405) (J 492)

England the art of the ceremonial still life pioneered by Jan Davidsz. de Heem. He gave the form unprecedented amplitude, adapting it to the decoration of the châteaux of Vaux-le-Vicomte and Versailles and to the design needs of the royal tapestry manufactories of Gobelins and Beauvais. Delacroix's painting of a rustic bouquet of syringa blossoms, wild rose, anemones, wallflowers, and white hydrangea (cat. III), possibly done in the summer of 1848, presents characteristics typical of Monnoyer.[64] Bursting forth from a modest wicker basket set on a front-facing table, the remarkably light, well-balanced arrangement is modeled in depth, with the result that certain flowers are lost in shadow. The artful, precise

composition marks a growing maturity in its departure from the spontaneity of Delacroix's early bouquets of 1833–34 (fig. 54), painted at Frédéric Villot's home, in Champrosay, and at George Sand's, in Nohant. Those earlier works, the vivacity of which betrays what must have been the messy reality of study sessions plagued by drooping stems, fallen leaves, wilted petals, and fruit rotting around the rustic stoneware pot, were elaborated in a far more fluid medium, perhaps in emulation of similar floral compositions by Paul Huet.

The large floral compositions that Delacroix elaborated over many months for the Salon of 1849 were the products of high ambition. Perhaps the artist had seen, displayed in the

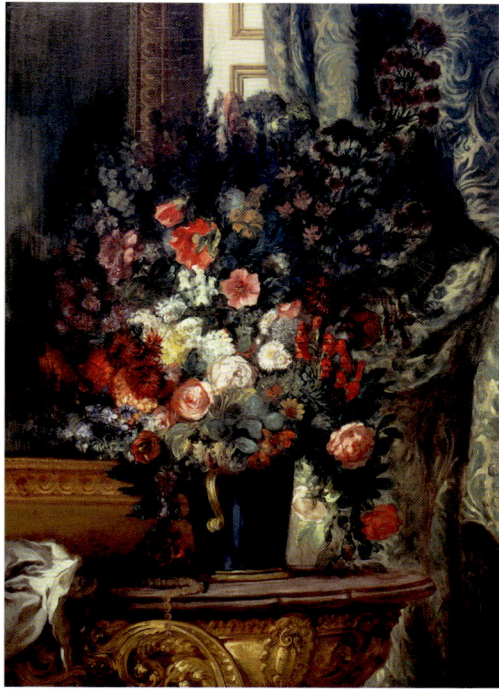

FIG. 55 Jean-Baptiste Belin, called Blin (or Blain) de Fontenay (French, 1653–1715). *Flowers in a Gold Vase, a Bust of Louis XIV, a Cornucopia, and Armor*, 1687. Oil on canvas, 74¹³⁄₁₆ x 63¾ in. (190 x 162 cm). Musée du Louvre, Paris (4464)

FIG. 56 *A Vase of Flowers on a Console*, 1848–49. Oil on canvas, 53⅛ x 40³⁄₁₆ in. (135 x 102 cm). Musée Ingres, Montauban (inv. MNR 162) (J 503)

Louvre, the reception piece that Monnoyer's successor and son-in-law, Jean-Baptiste Belin de Fontenay, had exhibited at the Académie Royale de Peinture et de Sculpture in 1687 (fig. 55). Belin's painting attests to the nobility and splendor acquired by the floral still life under Louis XIV: unprecedented in dramatic intensity, skillfully linked to sculpture and architecture, the still life acceded to the ranks of court art and large-scale decoration. Delacroix's *A Vase of Flowers on a Console* partakes in that tradition (fig. 56). The painting depicts the reception area of a palace or large Paris mansion decorated with gilded white woodwork, large mirror, heavy sheared-velvet curtain, and marble-topped gilt-wood console in the style of Louis XIV. Centered in the foreground, a porcelain vase with gilded bronze mount sends forth an explosion of flowers—a dense arrangement of roses, peonies, geraniums, marguerite daisies, gladioli, wallflowers, cinerarias, and poppies—that almost reaches the upper edge of the frame. The bouquet's full size is not immediately apparent, as its shaded, outer portions are camouflaged by the surroundings, swallowed up by the curtain's vegetal motif and the blurry reflection in the mirror. Evidently placed between two windows, the bouquet is modeled by these two sources of light: colorful, brightly illuminated flowers mass together in the lower portion, while the other half of the arrangement is greatly muted, seen in contre-jour against the incoming daylight.

In the end, *A Vase of Flowers on a Console* was not exhibited at the Salon of 1849; it was shown for the first time in 1855. Delacroix had originally wanted this aristocratic, city dweller's bouquet to be exhibited together with outdoor flower paintings. As he explained to his friend Constant Dutilleux, "I wanted to get away from the kind of template that seems to make all flower painters repeat the same vase with the same columns, or the same fantastic hangings that serve as background or foil. I have tried to render bits of nature as they appear in gardens merely by assembling the greatest possible variety of flowers inside the same frame and in a more or less probable manner."[65] However, owing to the setting Delacroix chose—a grand, English-style park bordered by tall trees—these floral compositions are both luxurious and implausible. *Basket of Flowers* (cat. 109) is luminous, evoking summer through the intense blue of the sky. The composition centers on a precious piece of basketwork artfully overturned to release a flood of flowers (asters, geraniums, dahlias, wallflowers, peonies) in warm colors. Above them, a strange arch of morning glories, in preparation for which Delacroix produced a splendid pastel study (cat. 108) its leaves disproportionately large in relation to the basket, rises from the left and unspools in the form of a gallows.

Basket of Flowers and Fruit (cat. 110), darker and in sharper contrast, takes autumnal opulence as its subject: against a late

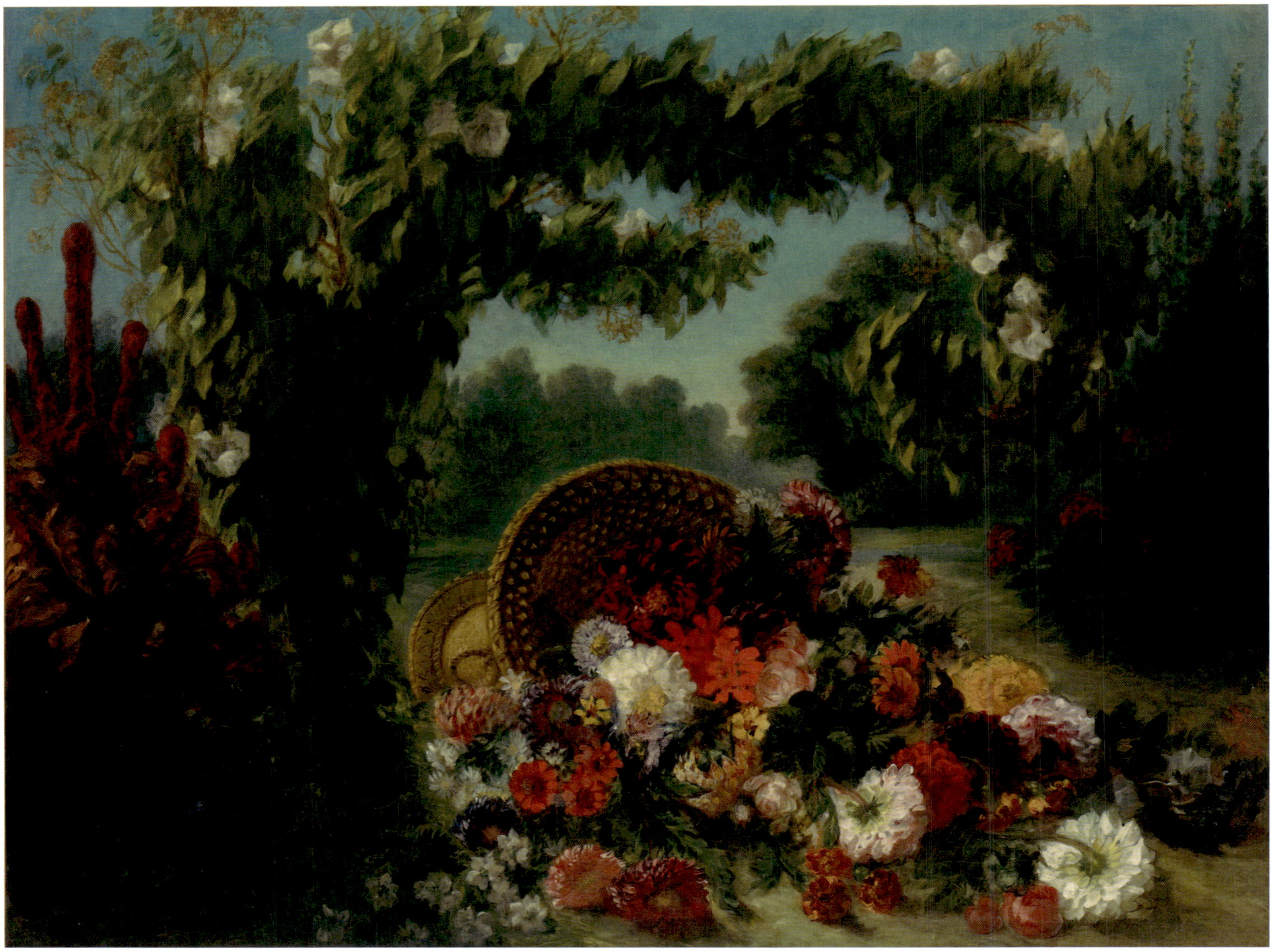

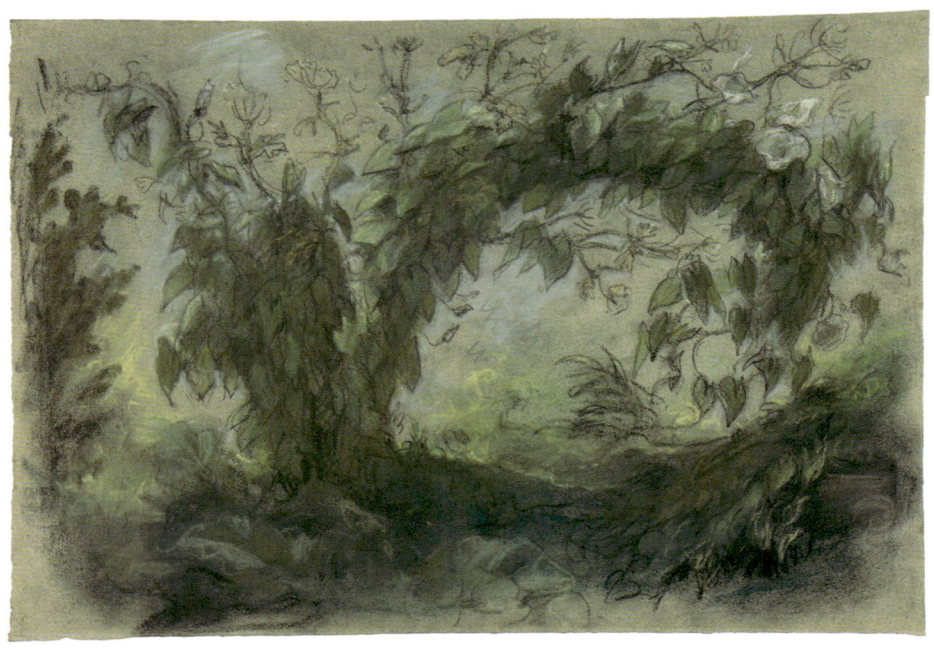

CAT. 109 *Basket of Flowers*, 1848–49

CAT. 108 *Arch of Morning Glories*, study for *"Basket of Flowers,"* 1848/49

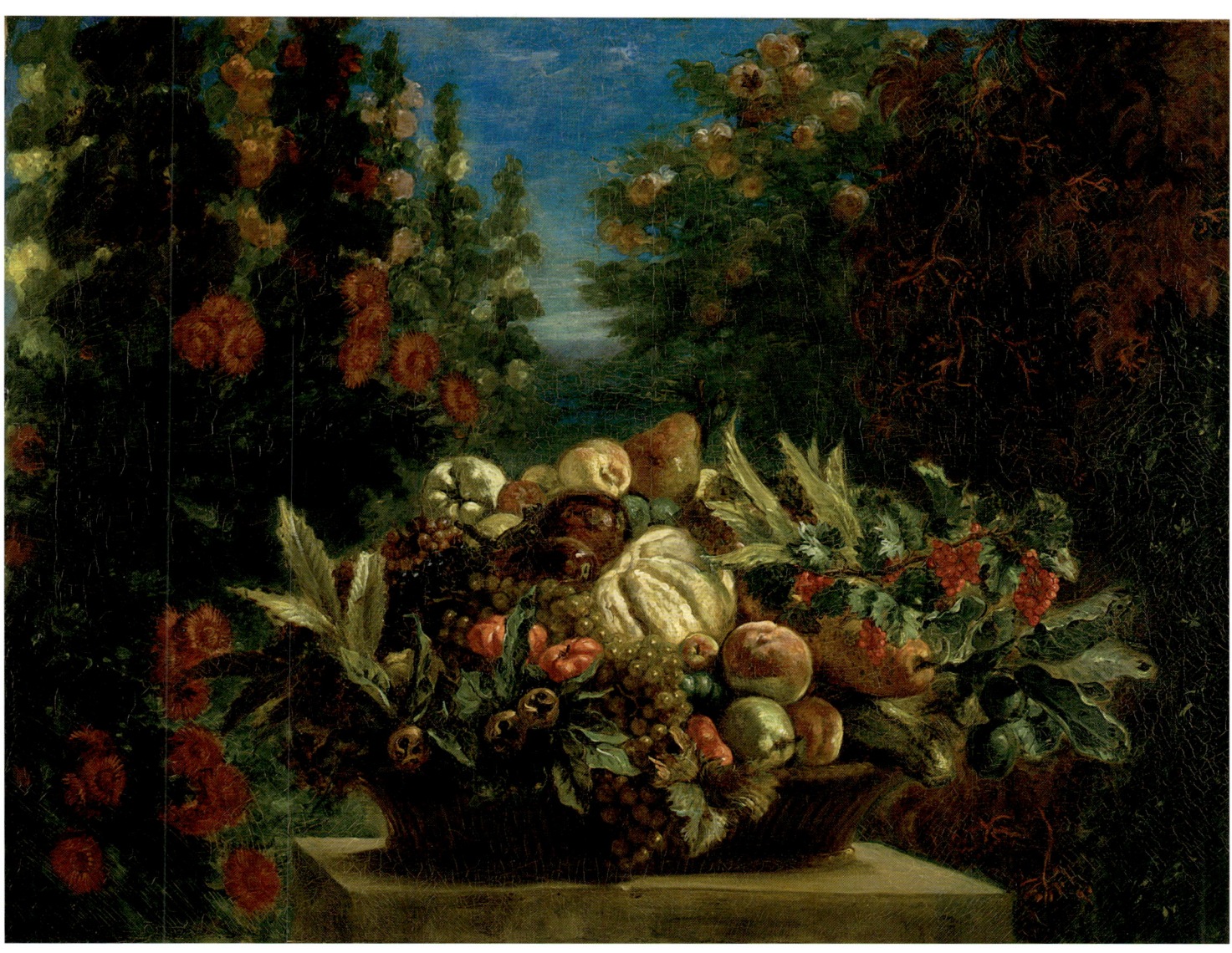

CAT. 110 *Basket of Flowers and Fruit*, 1849

afternoon sky, the basket seems to collapse under the weight of an impossible heap of fruits and vegetables: peaches, pears, melon, eggplants, grapevines, oxheart tomatoes, gooseberry and plum tree branches. As in *A Vase of Flowers on a Console*, Delacroix here used great skill in creating effects of contrast. The muted colors of the hollyhock bushes that frame the basket bring out the brilliance of the fruits in the foreground. The soft light emphasizes their smooth or rough textures, and a bright, hazy outline, traced with the brush, gives them a peculiar radiance. No debris or trace of decay sullies the stone table or the contents of the basket, which is protected by a vegetal honor guard. The viewer experiences an almost religious feeling before what looks like an offering on an altar dedicated to a

transcendent power, perceptible in the unreal light that bathes the scene. The atmosphere in these two outdoor still lifes is steeped in the marvelous and the fantastic; the plant kingdom asserts itself with such force that it seems to possess an autonomous power capable of making one forget that the compositions' highly artificial arrangements are human inventions.

The three large floral compositions were exhibited together at the Exposition Universelle of 1855 and remained in Delacroix's studio at his death. In all three, the painter seems to have been moved by the desire to saturate the surface, sometimes at the cost of an unlikely invasion. He also sought to produce an overall dynamic by carefully attending to the succession of forms and the contrasts of light. The whirlwind

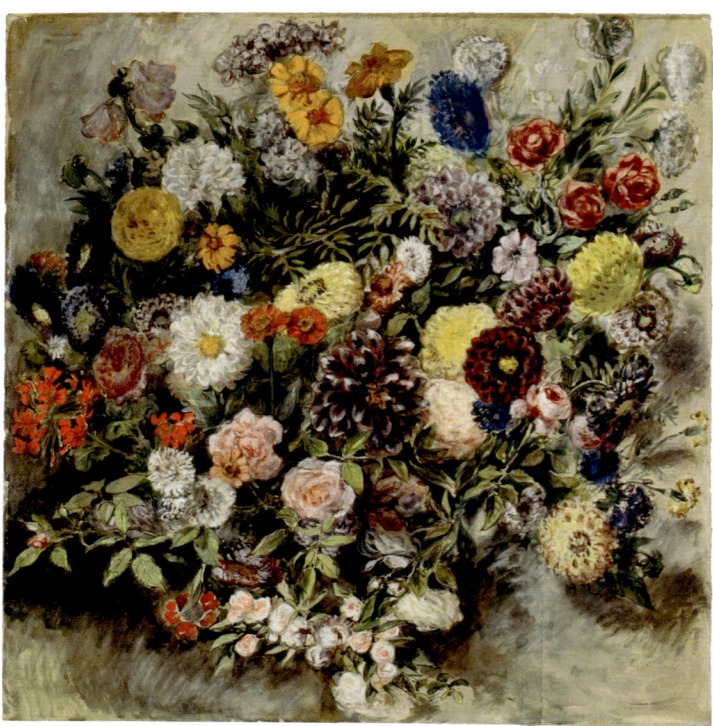

FIG. 57 *Bouquet of Flowers*, ca. 1848. Watercolor, gouache, and pastel highlights over graphite on two sheets of gray paper, joined vertically, 25⁹⁄₁₆ x 25¾ in. (65 x 65.4 cm). Musée du Louvre, Paris (RF 31719)

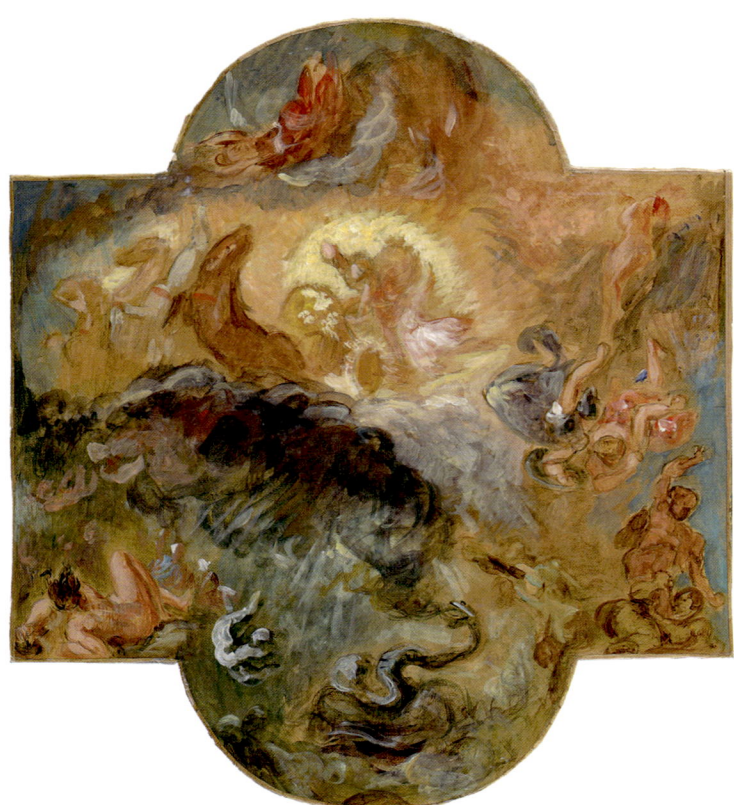

CAT. 122 *Apollo Slays the Python, sketch*, ca. 1850

motion that resulted is particularly vigorous in *Basket of Flowers* (cat. 109), but it is already present in certain studies, such as the large watercolor heightened with gouache and pastel formerly in the Choquet collection (fig. 57). In those works, Delacroix often chose not to represent the flowers' stems, but only the heads, rising up from all sides and defying gravity.

These characteristics are particularly interesting when linked to the challenges Delacroix faced the following year in the Gallery of Apollo. There, on the ceiling, he was tasked with depicting the battle between the Olympian gods and earthly forces; visible and comprehensible from all sides, the scene was to create the illusion that the gallery was open to the sky. These constraints meant that the composition had to be circular and would have to fill the entire surface allotted to it. He developed the composition in a series of drawings and oil sketches (cat. 122).[66] The final sketch, elaborated between April and June 1850 and presented as a *modello* for the approval of the architect Félix Duban, shows how Delacroix arrived at his formal solution.[67] Beginning with the original subject (Apollo slays the Python), placed in the center, he summoned a considerable number of secondary figures and established connections among them (cat. 123). The program was explained in a booklet that accompanied the invitation to the unveiling in October 1851:

> The god, mounted on his chariot, has already launched a portion of his arrows; his sister, Diana, flying behind him, presents him with her quiver. . . . The waters of the flood begin to subside and deposit the corpses of men and animals on the mountaintops, or carry them away. . . . The gods are outraged upon seeing the land abandoned to misshapen monsters. . . . Minerva and Mercury dash off to exterminate them, expecting eternal wisdom to repopulate the lonely universe. Hercules crushes them with his club; Vulcan, the god of fire, drives off Night and the impure vapors; and Boreas and the Zephyrs dry up the waters with their breath and disperse the clouds.[68]

To complete the circle, Delacroix added Victory holding a palm leaf; Iris, messenger of the gods; and finally, "more timid deities [who] contemplate this battle of the gods and the elements from a distance"—namely, Juno and Venus with her procession of cupids. The painter ordered the figures by size. Paradoxically, the most important, Apollo, is also the

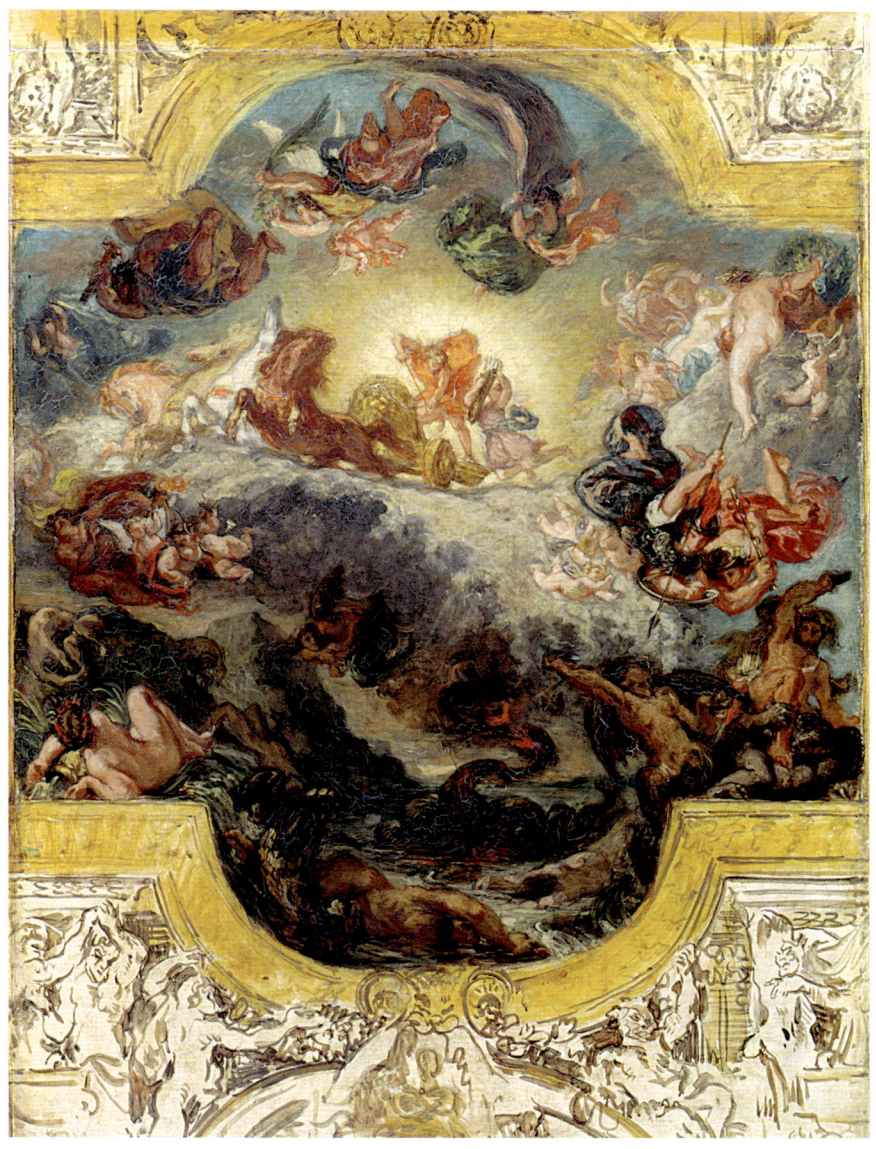

CAT. 123 *Apollo Victorious over the Serpent Python, sketch, ca.* 1850

smallest, because supposedly the farthest from the beholder, but his presence is augmented by the visual power of the golden halo that surrounds him. The figures nearest to the edges are the largest. In size and form, they relate to the atlantes, sculpted in stucco, that support the frame of the painted compartment. This continuity with the ceiling's sculptural decoration is particularly striking in the portrayals of the river gods, monsters, and giants at the bottom of the composition.

Delacroix also adapted his formal and iconographic repertoire to the ambience of the seventeenth century, known as the *Grand Siècle*. The chariot of the Sun is inspired by the fountain of the same name carved in 1670 by Jean-Baptiste Tuby for the pool at the west end of the Gardens of Versailles.[69] In addition, the painter appropriated elements from the

decorations Charles Le Brun had completed in the gallery before the project was suspended in 1679. From Le Brun's *Night*, Delacroix borrowed the billowing canopies of green and violet fabric, and from *Triumph of the Waters (Neptune and Amphitrite)*, the human figures plummeting from the sky. The figure of Diana escorting Apollo is a quotation from the more recent ceiling executed by Prud'hon in the nearby gallery of the Louvre, the Hall of Diana.[70]

The swirling, supernatural assemblage of figures in *Apollo Slays the Python*, unprecedented in Delacroix's history painting, owes a debt to his experiments the previous year with the flower and fruit compositions. No other subjects had allowed Delacroix to arrange his forms and colors with such freedom, specifically, a total disregard for the laws of gravity. The artist

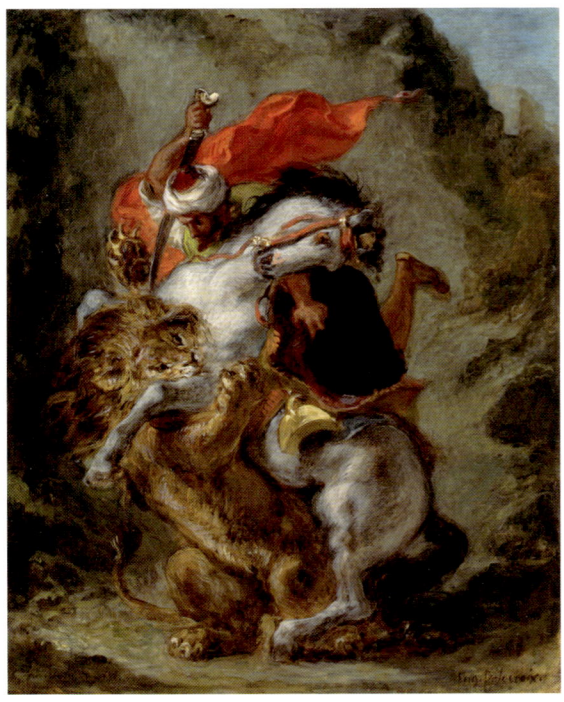

FIG. 58 *Arab Horseman Attacked by a Lion,* 1849/50. Oil on wood, 17¼ x 15 in. (43.8 x 38.1 cm). Art Institute of Chicago, Potter Palmer Collection (1922.403) (J 181)

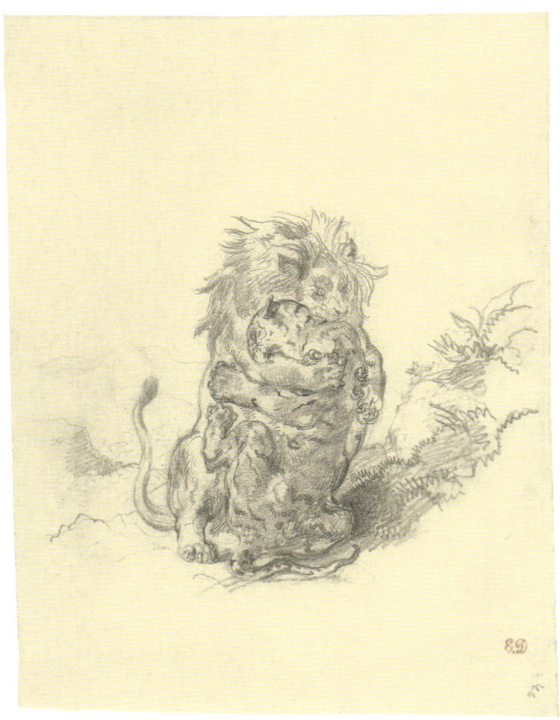

CAT. 133 *A Lion and a Tiger, Fighting,* ca. 1854

returned to the exercise four years later with a more contained subject, the lion hunt, which he had chosen for the state commission he had won for the Exposition Universelle of 1855. Delacroix had already tried his hand at the central group, composed of a hunter, his horse, and a big feline. After *Horseman Attacked by a Leopard,* which Lee Johnson dated about 1835–40 (Národní Galerie, Prague), Delacroix further developed the idea about 1849 with *Arab Horseman Attacked by a Lion* (fig. 58) and, after widening the frame, with *Tiger Hunt* in 1854 (Musée d'Orsay, Paris).[71] In those works, the painter discovered the ingredients of a master alchemist. The Arab costume and accessories were a perfect vehicle for swirling waves of dazzling fabric (red, white, blue) and shining goldwork. The lion's attack from below allowed him to entangle the figures and, by means of dramatic foreshortening, bring the three heads close together as the limbs radiated outward. Finally, the rocky setting, sober and mysterious, highlighted the savage splendor of the three-headed, twelve-limbed monster of fur, gold, and fabric.

Emboldened by these experiments, Delacroix opened up and replicated the figure group in numerous works (see, for example, cat. 133) in what would amount to a virtuoso performance. In *Lion Hunt* (cat. 135) he not only included two

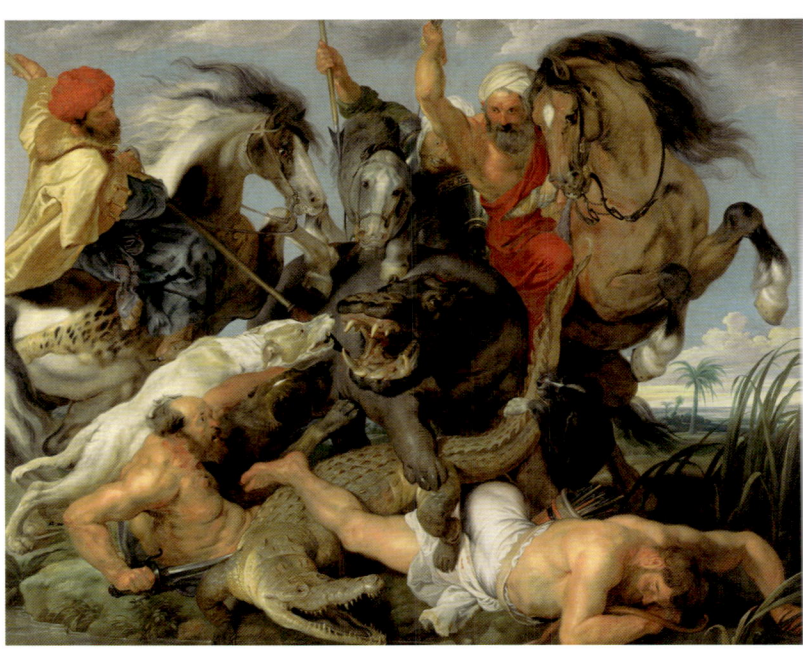

FIG. 59 Peter Paul Rubens. *Hippopotamus and Crocodile Hunt,* ca. 1616. Oil on canvas, 97⅝ in. x 10 ft. 6⅜ in. (2.5 x 3.2 m). Bayerische Staatsgemäldesammlungen, Alte Pinakothek, Munich (inv. 4797)

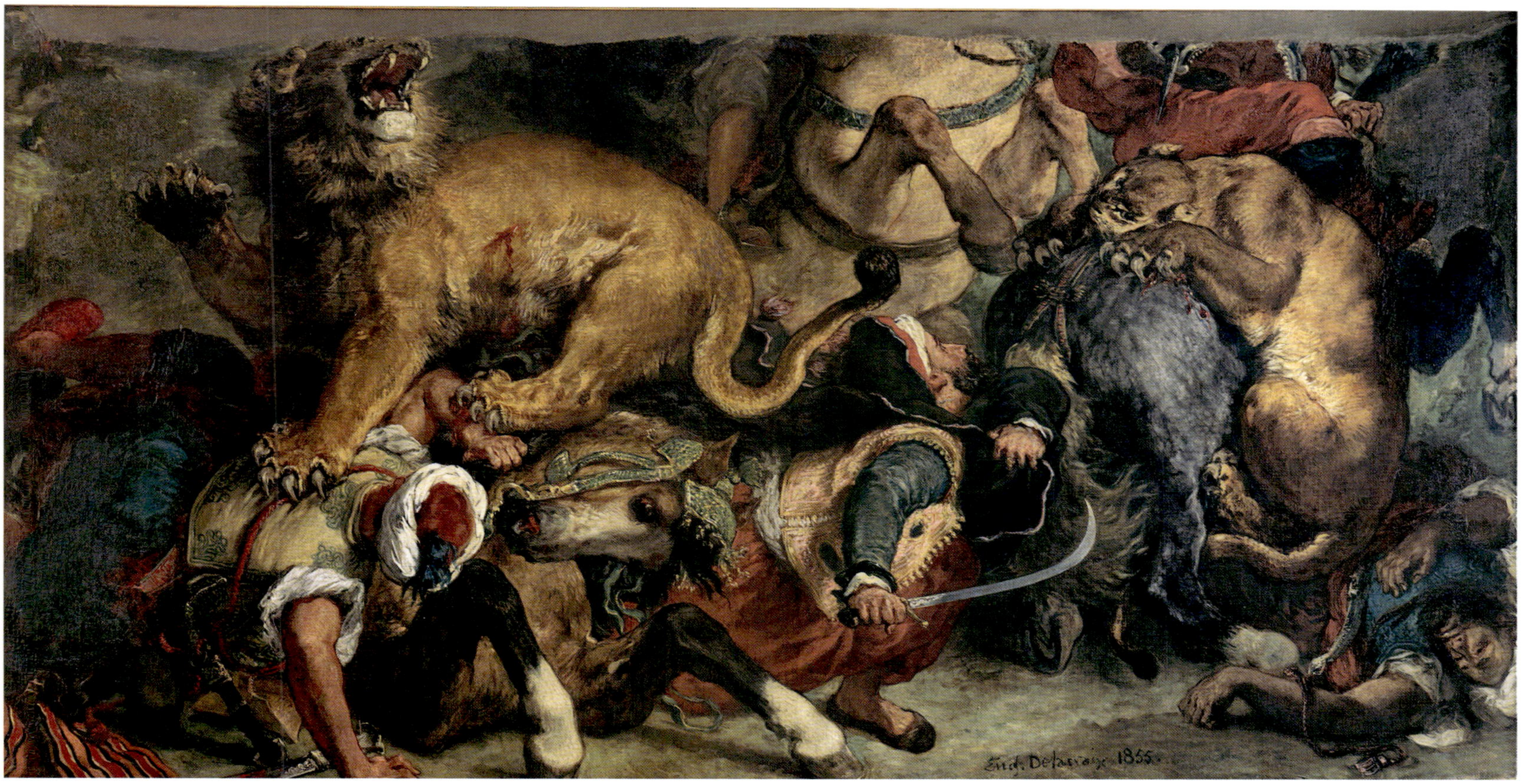

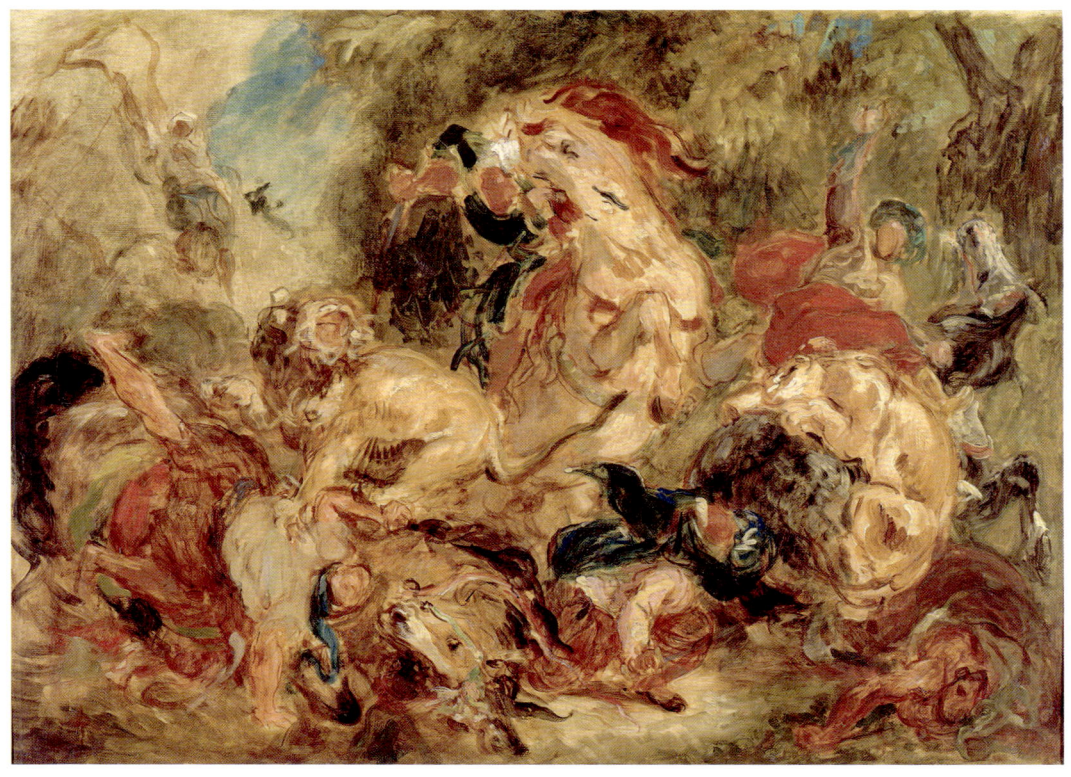

CAT. 135 *Lion Hunt (fragment)*, 1855

CAT. 134 *Lion Hunt, sketch*, 1854

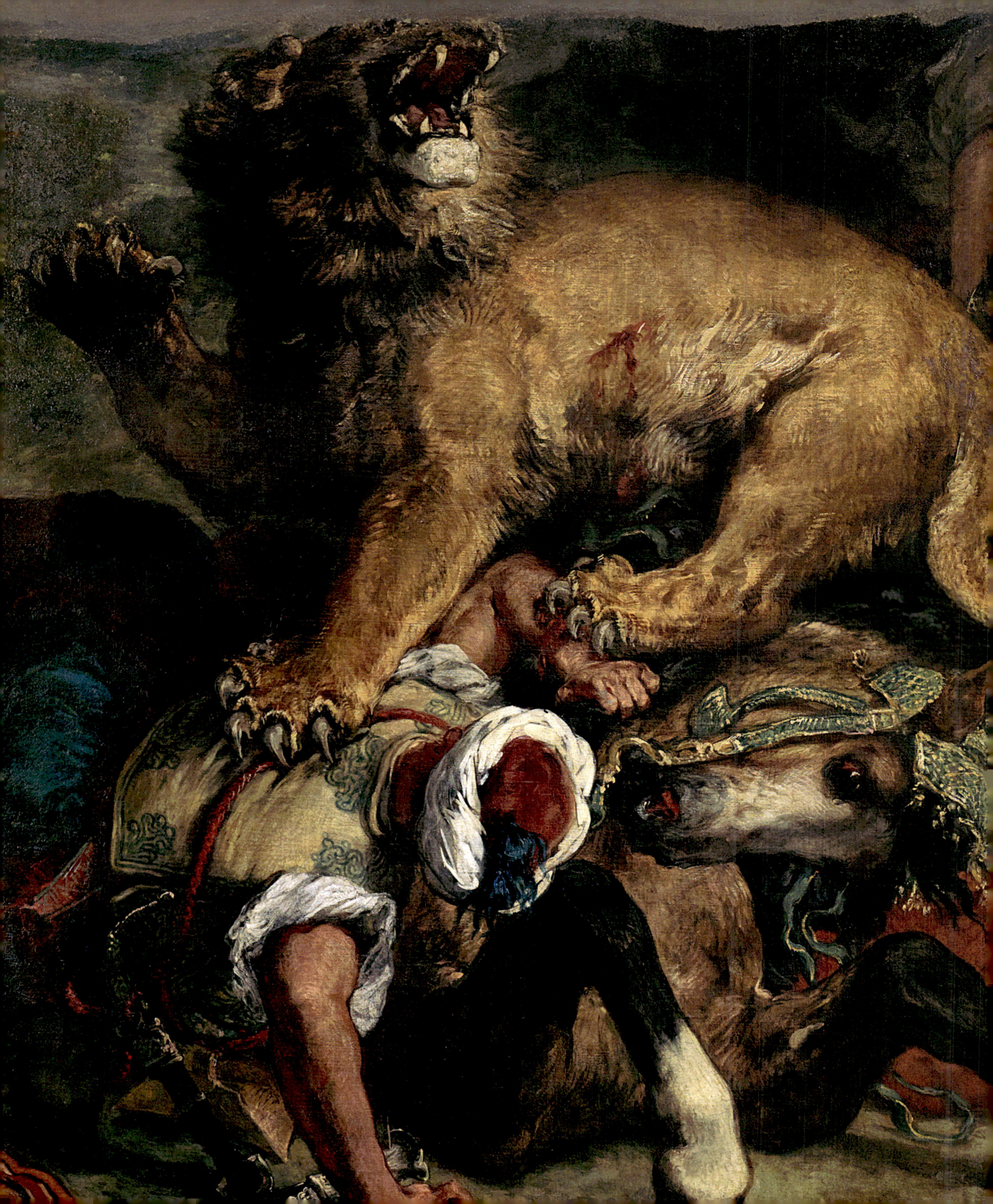

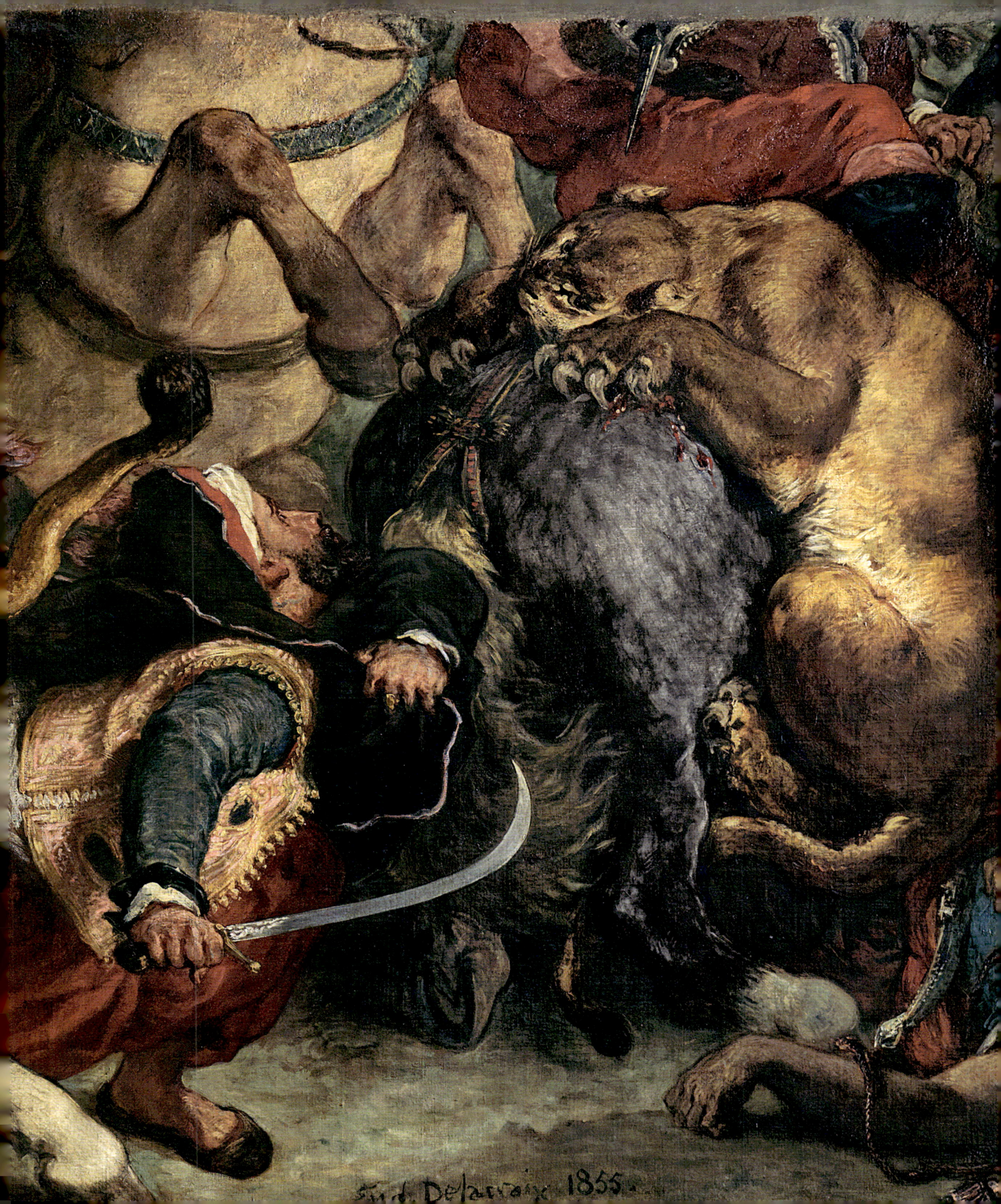

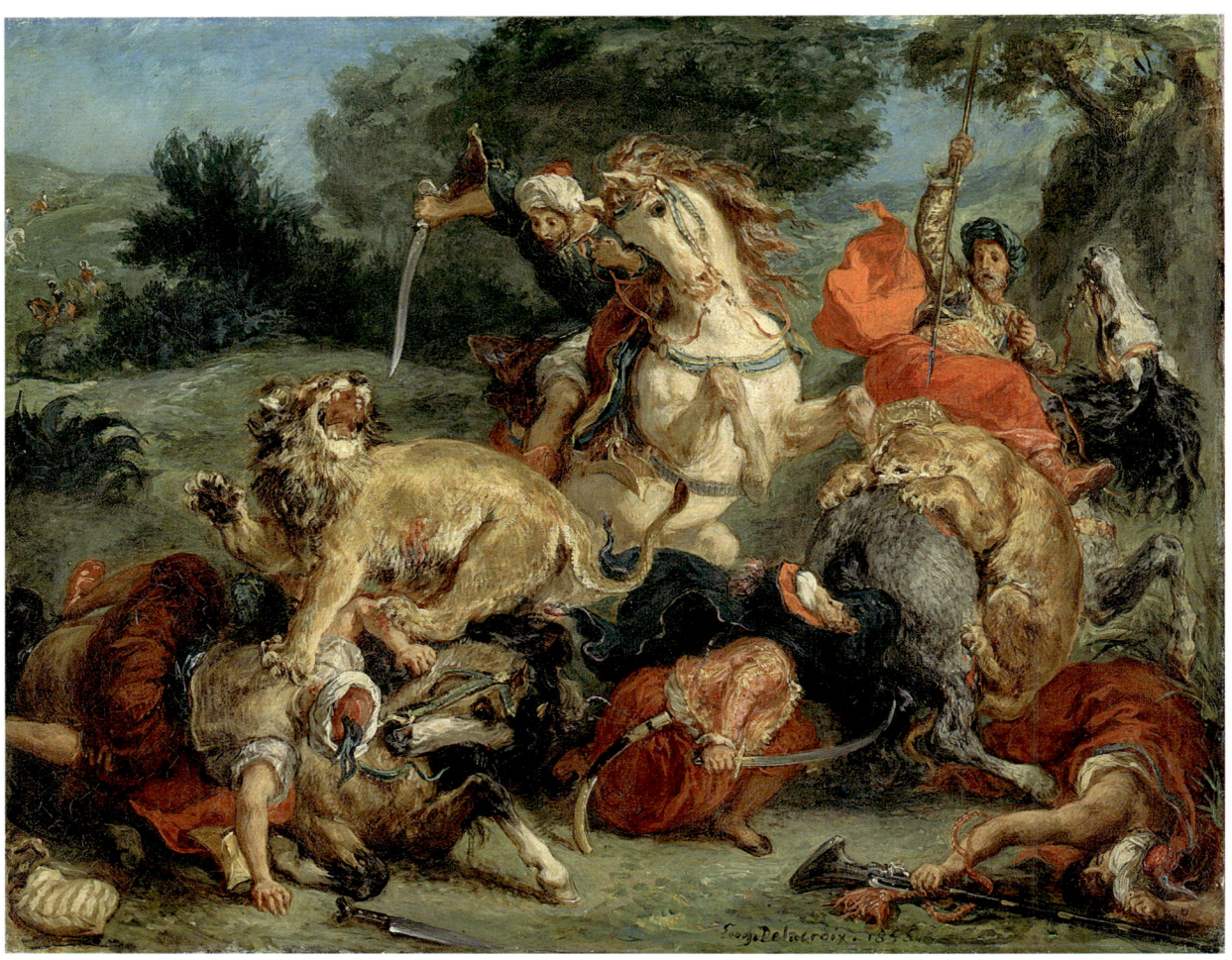

CAT. 136 *Lion Hunt,* 1855–56

great cats, three horses, and five hunters but also deliberately placed himself in direct competition with Rubens, who had painted four big-game hunting scenes for Maximilian I, elector (later prince-elector) of Bavaria, beginning in 1615. Delacroix had seen the Flemish artist's *Lion Hunt* during his visit to Bordeaux in 1845 (it would be destroyed in a fire in 1870). The others were unknown to him except through the engravings of Pieter Soutman, which he described in his *Journal* on January 25, 1847. Delacroix's favorite was the *Hippopotamus and Crocodile Hunt* (fig. 59), the composition of which he found particularly effective: "In the *Hippopotamus Hunt,* the amphibious monster occupies the center; the riders, horses, and hounds are all attacking it furiously. The composition is approximately in the shape of a Saint Andrew's cross. . . . One effect is beautiful beyond words; a great sheet of sky frames the whole on both sides . . . thus, the very simplicity of the contrast gives incomparable movement, variety, and unity to the whole picture."[72]

For his own *Lion Hunt,* Delacroix widened the scene and opted for a pyramidal rather than square composition, perhaps under the influence of Rembrandt's 1641 etching *The Great Lion Hunt.* With his first sketch (cat. 134), Delacroix moved the roaring animal to the left of center; he added a lioness and made the main hunter's rearing horse the central axis. The background reinforces this arrangement with a clump of trees in the center and the turquoise sky breaking through on either side. The painter attended closely to the harmonious tangle of forms, adding wounded hunters and horses. These figures, fallen to the ground, struggle to get back up, relaunching the action from bottom to top and establishing a circular movement. Like Rubens, Delacroix took up the challenge of imbuing a sense of abundance and triumph in that fight to the death.

The painting was completed just in time for the opening of the Exposition Universelle in May 1855. "The energetic and glowing painting" delighted Gautier and Baudelaire but put off a number of other critics, even young ones such as Paul

Mantz: "The composition is hard to understand, and it is only after long and intense effort that the eye, making order from disorder, finds its bearings in that confusion of entangled men and animals. The drawing is slack, the forms rumpled like old fabric. The lines flare up and twist about; it is the spectacle of force rather than force itself."[73] Maxime du Camp fumed about the painting, saying it "defies criticism. It is a vast logogriph rendered in colors for which no words can be found. It is a strange hodge-podge. . . . almost raving mad; even the harmony is slipshod, because all the colors have similar value."[74] Du Camp's opinion was echoed by Pierre Petroz: "This strange jumble lacks M. Delacroix's usual qualities completely. . . . The color is very bright, but it flickers, and that chaos of reds, greens, yellows, and violets, all with the same value, makes the *Lion Hunt* look like a tapestry."[75] These critiques were similar to the ones Delacroix had received in 1827–28 for *The Death of Sardanapalus,* which was not included in the retrospective of 1855 and which these young critics had never seen.[76] This time, however, the harshness was tempered by positive remarks about the painting's decorative character.

The painting was damaged in a fire at the Musée des Beaux-Arts, Bordeaux in 1870, resulting in the loss of the landscape with turquoise sky. (The missing portion of the work is visible in the second version, cat. 136, where there is more space between the figures.) This and other losses to the perimeter of the canvas have heightened the impression of chaos and density, but they have also accentuated the effect of material abundance that Delacroix sought to capture by juxtaposing lion's fur with gold embroidery, and glinting swords with gleaming fangs and claws. He used the same method of juxtaposition to invite a comparison between the musculature of human arms and horses' legs. Animality and humanity were paired in a ferocious choreography.

"The New Is Very Old": Redefining Originality

The amazing ease with which Delacroix glided from one pictorial genre to another, immersing himself in the heterogeneous traditions of Rubens, Monnoyer, Veronese, Ribera, and the School of Fontainebleau, and moving from the register of austere pathos to that of decorative exuberance, may be disconcerting. If his subjects were not new, and if his compositions were inspired by those of illustrious predecessors or taken from his own earlier work, wherein lies his originality?

This mutable quality, central to Romanticism, was associated with the assertion of the unique, creative self. Delacroix gave much thought to the concept of originality and deliberated on it in his *Journal,* which he resumed in 1847. There he was able not only to take stock of the passage of time, which gave perspective to the notion of the never-before-seen or reduced it to the latest fad, but also to look more critically, more intently, and with greater experience than before at his own work and that of his predecessors, owing to his deeper knowledge of art history.

The observations on originality that Delacroix recorded while designing the ceiling for the Gallery of Apollo are especially telling. The official confirmation of the commission had come in early March 1850. From the start, Delacroix understood that working on a historical monument would demand a level of respect and adaptation that could imperil his artistic freedom, compromise his originality, and open him to accusations of imitation. In the following months, as he worked on the project in earnest, he reflected on this matter.

> As I considered the composition for the ceiling . . . it struck me that a good picture is like a good dish. It is made of exactly the same ingredients as a bad one— the artist does everything! How many magnificent compositions would be worthless without a pinch of salt from the hand of the great cook? In Rubens, the power of this, whatever it may be, is astounding. It is incredible what his temperament, his *vis poetica,* can add to a composition without seeming to change it. Yet it is only a turn of his style. It is the way he does it that matters; what he works on is comparatively unimportant. The new is very old. You might even say that it is the oldest thing of all.[77]

A week later, commenting on writing and classical architecture, he added: "A great writer . . . takes expressions in everyday use and, by giving them a special twist, changes them into something new. . . . When an architect of genius copies a great monument of antiquity he knows how to modify it so as to make it original. . . . Ordinary architects are only able to make literal copies, with the result that they add to this humiliating evidence of their own lack of ability, a failure even to imitate successfully."[78]

In July 1850, while taking the waters at Bad Ems, in Germany, Delacroix read Thomas Medwin's *Conversations of*

Lord Byron with great interest. He lingered especially over the passages concerning the accusations of borrowing and plagiarism that were lodged against Byron. Happy to learn that one of his favorite authors was preoccupied with the same concerns that were vexing him, Delacroix copied out his words:

> I am taxed with being a plagiarist, when I am least conscious of being one; but I am not very scrupulous, I own, when I have a good idea, how I came into possession of it. . . . As to originality, Goethe has too much sense to pretend that he is not under obligations to authors, ancient and modern. . . . 'How difficult it is,' said he [Byron], 'to say any thing new!' . . . Perhaps all nature and art could not supply a new idea. . . . It is a bad thing to have too good a memory.[79]

Alongside his course of treatment, Delacroix visited Antwerp, Brussels, and Mechelen, experiences that revived his early enthusiasm for Rubens.[80] He quickly overcame his emotion upon seeing the paintings and focused on analyzing the master's methods, especially his halftone technique. Looking carefully at *The Raising of the Cross* (1610–11; Cathedral of Our Lady, Antwerp), which was being restored, he noted the precocious Antwerp master's debt to Michelangelo: "He [Rubens] is still young and trying to please the pedants. Full of Michelangelo. . . . [His mind] was imbued with sublime works; it cannot be said that he imitated. He had that side to him, along with others. . . . It is clear that he did not imitate; he is always Rubens. All this will be useful for my ceiling [*Apollo Slays the Python*]."[81] Delacroix reassured himself by comparing Rubens's early style to that of his own youth, which was also marked by Michelangelo's powerful magnetism. "I had that feeling when I began [my career?]. Perhaps I was indebted to others, too, for it. Painters of each generation in turn have been exalted and elevated by studying Michelangelo."[82]

When he returned from Belgium in mid-August 1850, work began on positioning the composition on the ceiling. Delacroix continued to consult paintings by Rubens and Veronese in nearby galleries of the Louvre, but less as a subordinate looking for artistic inspiration than as a colleague seeking expert technical advice. "I noticed how straightforward shadow and light are in P. Veronese's *Susanna* [*and the Elders*], even in the foregrounds. In a vast composition like the ceiling, that is all the more necessary. . . . The contours are also very pronounced, a new way of being clear from a distance. I experienced that with the cartoon as well after drawing almost dumb, uninflected contours around the figures."[83]

These reflections liberated Delacroix considerably in his relation to the old masters. He had acquired enough confidence in his own artistic worth to regard their genius as sustenance for his further development rather than as an overbearing or inhibiting influence. It was likely this sense of self-validation that underlies an allegorical drawing executed about 1849–51, *The Triumph of Genius over Envy* (cat. 117), which plumbs a theme that had preoccupied him since his early maturity. He therefore felt justified in taking up and interpreting his predecessors' subjects and compositions. He wrote with increasing freedom about them, establishing comparisons and bridges between artists from different eras and disciplines (musicians, painters, sculptors). He found virtue in certain of their "lapses," "imperfections," "disproportions," and "incompletions," factors that enhanced their charm, personality, the expressiveness and contrast of their works, and that "augmented the effect" of the whole. He caught himself feeling slightly bored by Mozart's graceful perfection, for example, and took a growing interest in the powerful and provocative irregularity of Beethoven, whom he had previously found unappealing.[84]

Delacroix's new preference for idiomatic pictorial language over "the priority of inventing certain ideas, certain striking effects," led him to disdain punctilious imitators of earlier styles, especially Ingres and his students Hippolyte Flandrin and Henri Lehmann, who had adopted the dry, linear manner of ancient Greek painting and the Italian and Flemish Primitives.[85]

> Our Primitives, our Byzantines, who are so mulish about style, their eyes always fixed on images from another time, take from them only their stiffness without adding qualities of their own. That mob of sad mediocrities is vast. . . . What can be found in those pictures of the true man who painted them?[86]

> Raphael's gestures are naïve in spite of the strangeness of his style. What is odious is when fools imitate his strangeness, and are false in gesture and intention into the bargain. Ingres, who has never learned to compose a subject as nature presents it, believes that he resembles Raphael because he apes certain forms which are characteristic of the master. These do actually give his work a kind of grace, reminiscent of Raphael, but with

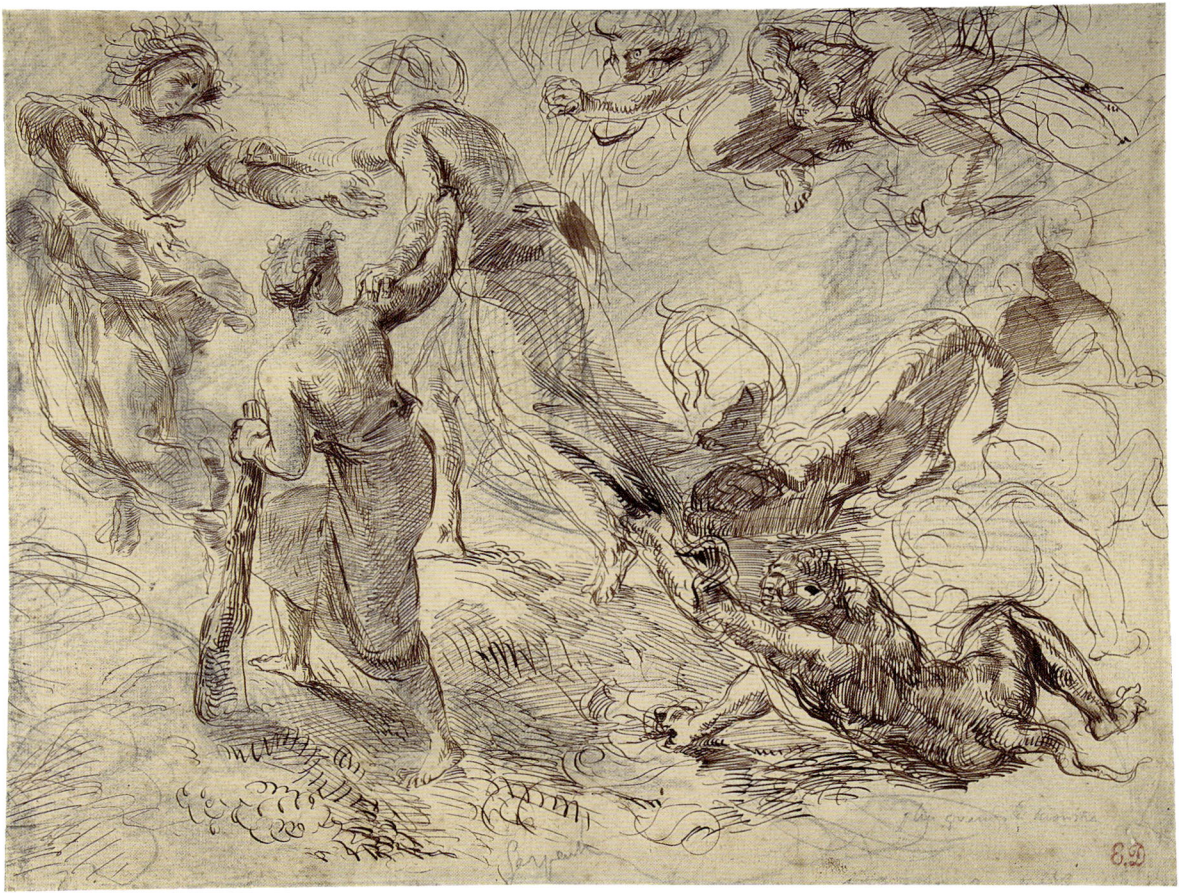

CAT. 117 *The Triumph of Genius over Envy*, ca. 1849–51

the latter you are very conscious that they come naturally and are not deliberately cultivated.[87]

Painters who pursue that primitive dryness, a practice quite natural in schools still feeling their way and drawing on almost backward sources, are like grown men who, in order to look ingenuous, would imitate children's speech and movements.[88]

Respect for the permanence of certain principles was not to be confused with the imitation of obsolete pictorial language. "True primitives are original talents. La Fontaine, who seems pure imitation, actually proceeds on the basis of his own genius."[89] "You can speak only in your own tongue, and also, only in the spirit of your own times. Those who hear you must be able to understand you, but above all, you must understand yourself."[90] Delacroix's own language distinguished his style from those of all others. Using a technique that involved the superposition, intermingling, and simultaneous contrast of colors, he applied oil paint in a free, vibrant,

and increasingly fluid manner. From tradition he borrowed compositional structures and chromatic harmonies, the effectiveness of which had been proved over generations. These he adapted and translated into his own idiom, which he undoubtedly esteemed to be of his time. His sources were not restricted to old master paintings. In the 1840s, Delacroix began to appropriate elements from certain of his own earlier works, and to modify and develop them further in new ones.

"I Am the Penitent": Reprises and Variations

Delacroix never stopped discovering new subjects and broadening his horizons.[91] At the end of his life, he took an interest in chivalric romances, Ovid's *Metamorphoses,* and stories from the Gospels that he had not already addressed in his work. At the same time that he was expanding his repertoire, he was also returning to subjects he had treated previously. There are several reasons for this reengagement. It was impelled in part

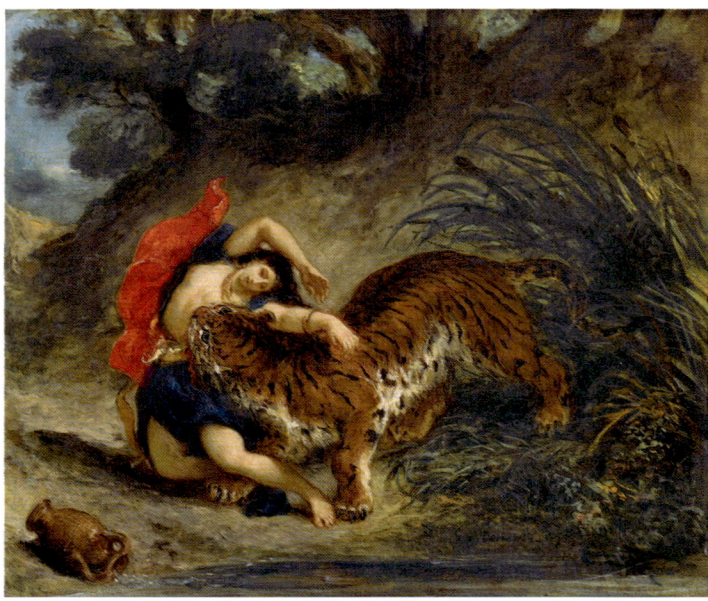

FIG. 60 *Young Woman Attacked by a Tiger (Indian Woman Bitten by a Tiger)*, 1856. Oil on canvas, 20¹⁄₁₆ x 24⅛ in. (51 x 61.3 cm). Staatsgalerie Stuttgart (inv. 2695) (J 201)

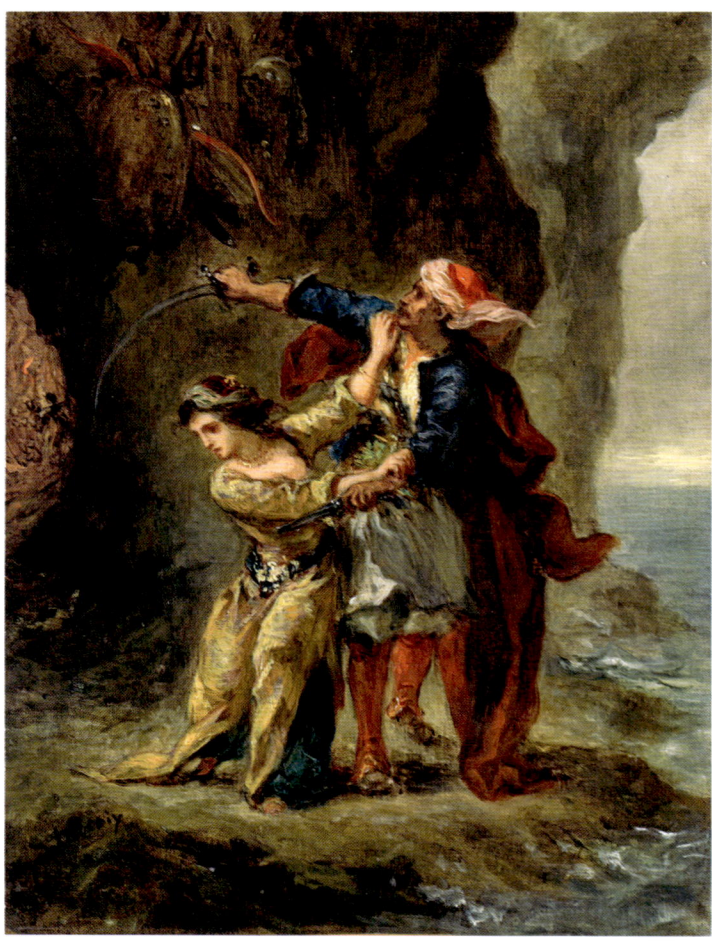

FIG. 61 *The Bride of Abydos*, ca. 1852–53. Oil on canvas, 14 x 10¹³⁄₁₆ in. (35.5 x 27.5 cm). Musée du Louvre, Paris (RF 1398) (J 311)

by the tradition, observed by many artists, of repeating compositions that had found an appreciative audience—of satisfying the demands of the market. Painted replicas of *Medea About to Kill Her Children* are a good example. Interest in *Medea* had been revived by the distribution of a beautiful, large lithograph by Emile Lassalle that was exhibited at the Salon of 1857. Delacroix was asked to do three new painted versions of the composition: the first, now destroyed, in 1859 for the art dealer and collector Jean-Hector Bouruet-Aubertot; the second in 1862 for the banker Emile Pereire, through the intermediary of Etienne François Haro; and the third the same year for the Société des Amis des Arts, Arras, represented by Constant Dutilleux.[92]

Reformulations of paintings could also result from the gradual evolution of a favorite motif, which Delcroix would explore in various configurations simultaneously or in succession. Such was the case with the hunter on his mount attacked by a great cat, a group that was perfected and multiplied until it reached a first culmination in oil: the large *Lion Hunt* (see cat. 135). The motif then evolved along a different course. No longer were new protagonists added; rather, a more spacious composition was created, along with a greater interplay of receding planes.[93] Parallel to these complex compositions, where the hunters on horseback lead the choreography, Delacroix worked on many scenes with two figures, in which a great cat is shown tearing its prey—human or animal—to pieces. *Lion Devouring a Rabbit, Lion Devouring an Arab,* and *Young Woman Attacked by a Tiger* (also known as *Indian Woman Bitten by a Tiger,* fig. 60) occupy cavernous landscapes filled with disturbing clumps of spiny plants (agaves or bulrushes).[94] The preliminary drawings for the tiger painting demonstrate the decisive role of the formal interplay of two tangled, undulating bodies, those of the feline and the young woman, perhaps inspired by the dryads (*salabhanjika*) of ancient Buddhist art.[95]

Another highly prized motif, that of the young woman who has fallen prey to male violence in a dark, rocky setting, was a topos of gothic romance and Romantic melodrama, genres that profoundly shaped the visual imaginary of Delacroix's generation. The motif proved so durable that it survived the literary genre that spawned it. Hence, the abduction of Rebecca by the Knight Templar outside the flaming Castle of Front-de-Boeuf, first painted in 1846 (see cat. 105), was reprised in 1858 (see cat. 141), well after Delacroix had lost his taste for Sir Walter Scott's historical novels.

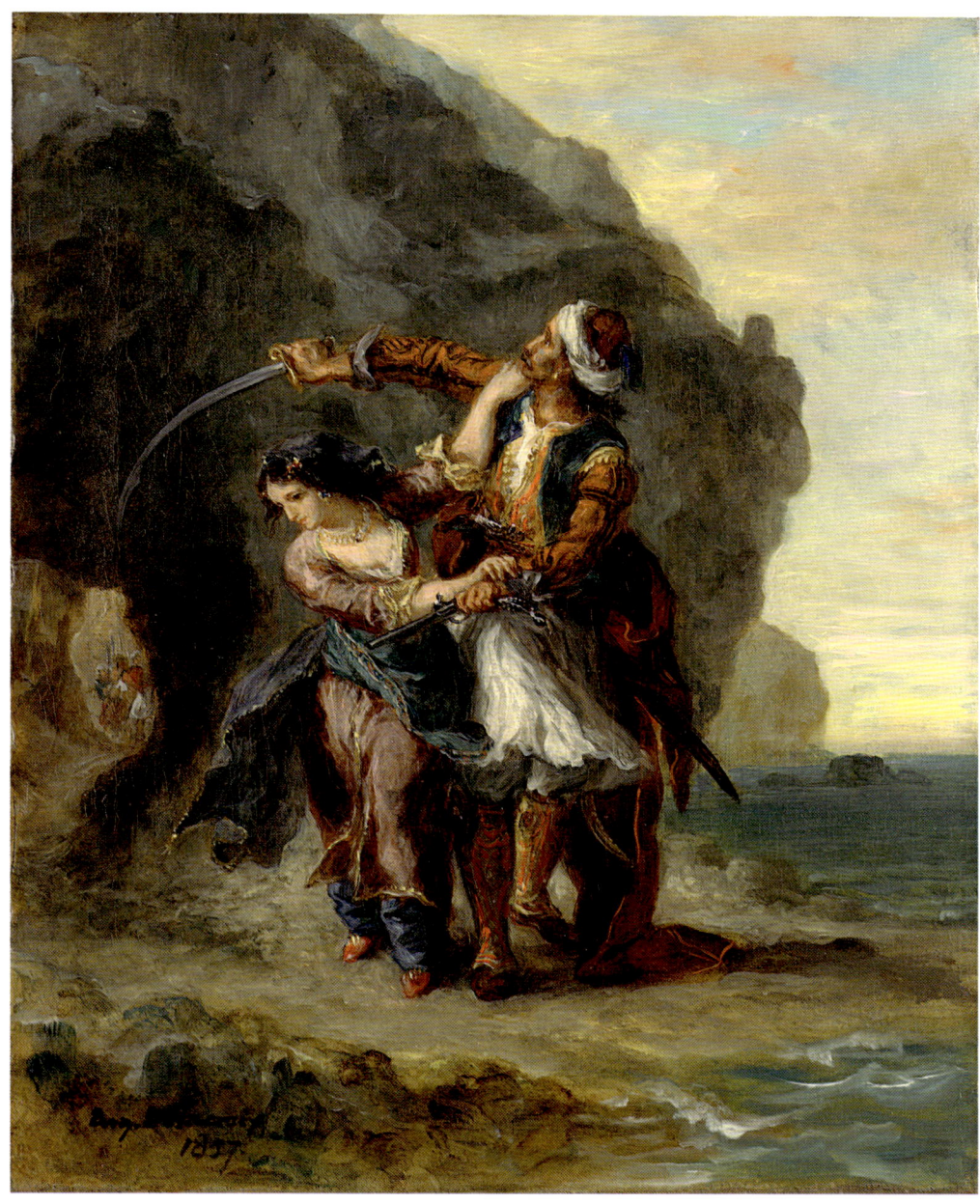

The Bride of Abydos (Selim and Zuleika), 1857

After 1849, the year Delacroix completed the last of his paintings based on Byron's epic poem *The Giaour*, Byron's poetry yielded up only one subject for the artist: that of the doomed lovers portrayed in *The Bride of Abydos*. The scene, set outside a cave on the banks of the Hellespont, shows the pirate Selim preparing to defend himself against the troops of Sultan Giaffir, sent to prevent him from running off with the sultan's daughter. Delacroix painted two initial versions of the episode: one about 1849 and another in 1852. He favored the third rendering (fig. 61), which he reiterated with chromatic variations in a fourth work made for his landlord, Jules Hurel, in 1857 (cat. 139).[96] In the 1852 version and its copy,

the pose of the young woman, who crouches and looks away as she attempts with one hand to hold back her lover's arm and with the other grips his shoulder, could easily be misinterpreted as a defensive one. However, close examination reveals that she is by no means Selim's target. Rather, she is trying to dissuade the cornered warrior from engaging in a futile fight against his assailants, who are barely discernible in the background. There is reason to believe that Delacroix was aware of the ambiguity of the woman's pose and intentionally fostered it. In *Desdemona Cursed by Her Father* (fig. 62), a painting exactly contemporaneous with the 1852 *Bride of Abydos* and with a nearly identical composition, he employed the same

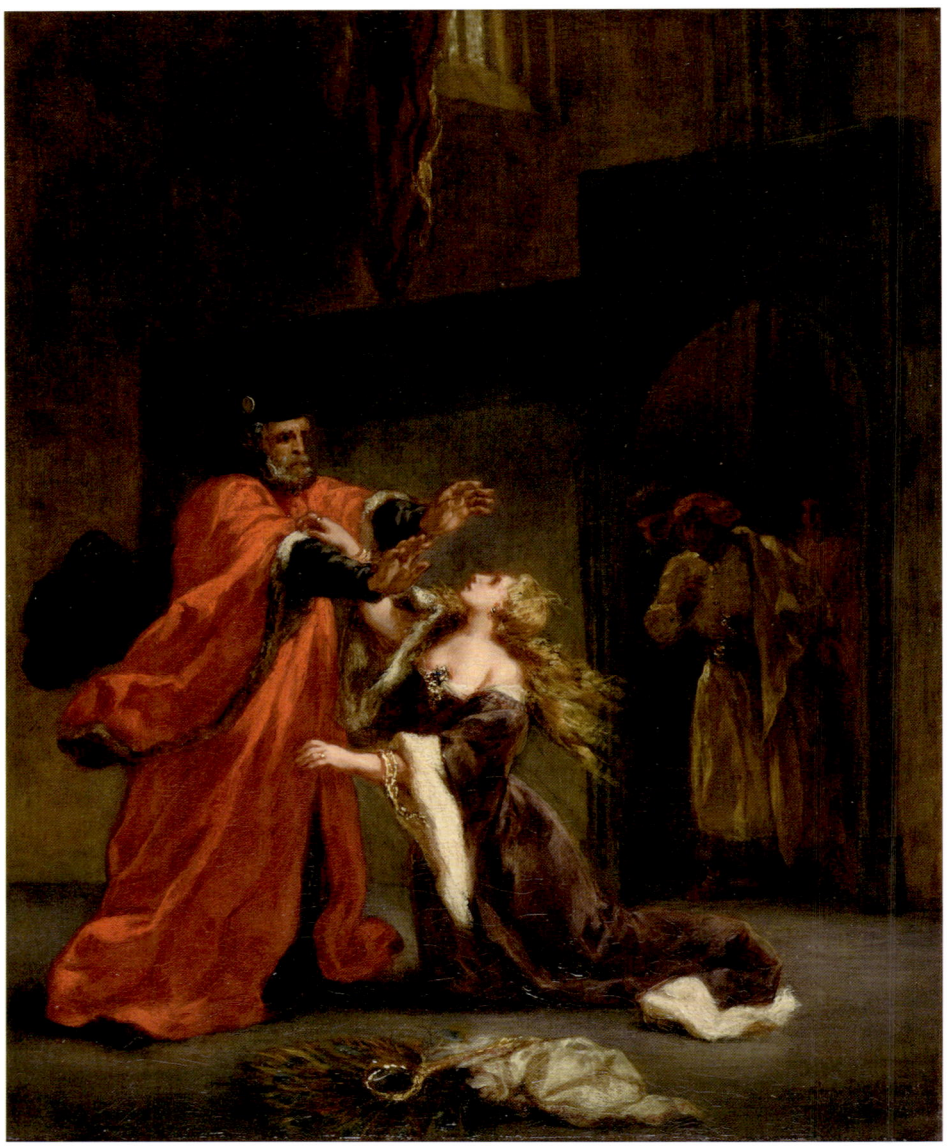

FIG. 62 *Desdemona Cursed by Her Father*, 1852. Oil on canvas, 23¼ x 19⁵⁄₁₆ in. (59 x 49 cm). Musée des Beaux-Arts, Reims (inv. 907.19.89) (J 309)

motif to portray a young woman as victim: Desdemona, shown kneeling before her onrushing father, raises her arms to his chest as he lashes out at her in anger.

The development of a motif could thus exceed the narrative confines of the original reference and circulate from one genre to another. Take, for instance, the topos of the reclining female nude observed by a male onlooker. In his youth, Delacroix had used this motif in small erotic pictures inspired by Pierre de Bourdeille Brantôme's titillating memoirs and eighteenth-century galante painting. *A Lady and Her Valet* (cat. 32), for example, features a seductively posed woman feigning sleep while a servant she fancies looks on.

Delacroix was soon dissatisfied with producing this type of light fare for art lovers to enjoy in private; he also rejected the idea of painting the female nude at the scale of history painting, in the manner of Ingres's *Odalisque*. He therefore moved away from the subject, preferring the ethnographic veracity of *Women of Algiers* (see cat. 83). Nearly twenty years later, through his memories of the Maghreb and his meditation on Rembrandt, Delacroix found his way back to the motif of the desirable reclining nude and enhanced it with a mysterious aura.

The small-format odalisques undertaken at the end of the 1840s (for example, fig. 63) lack the effrontery of the courtesans of the 1820s. Their nudity is in soft focus and

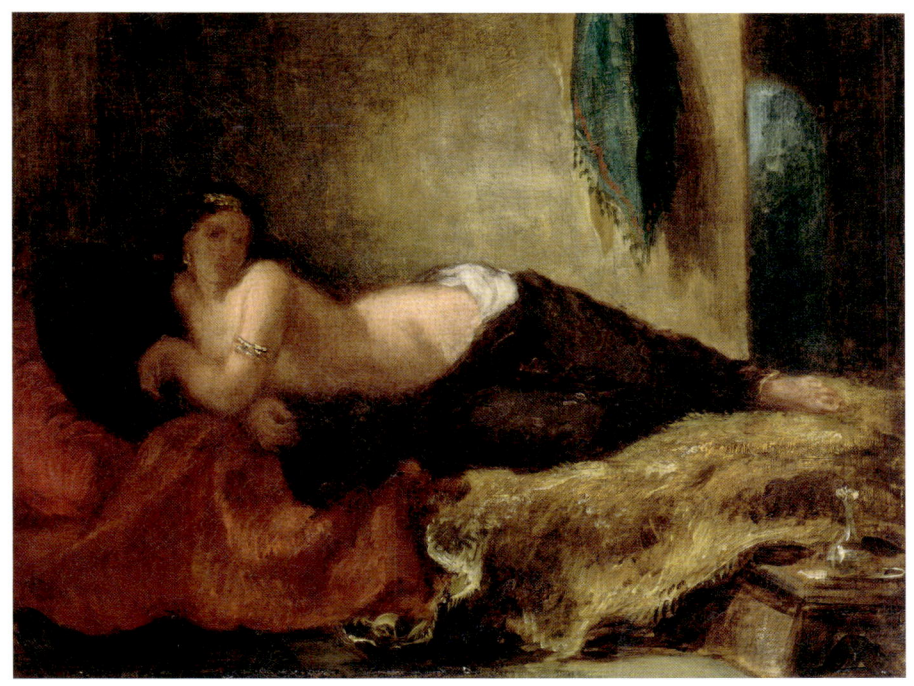

FIG. 63 *Odalisque,* ca. 1848–49. Oil on canvas, 9⁷⁄₁₆ x 12⁵⁄₈ in. (24 x 32 cm). Musée du Louvre, Paris (RF 1658) (J 381)

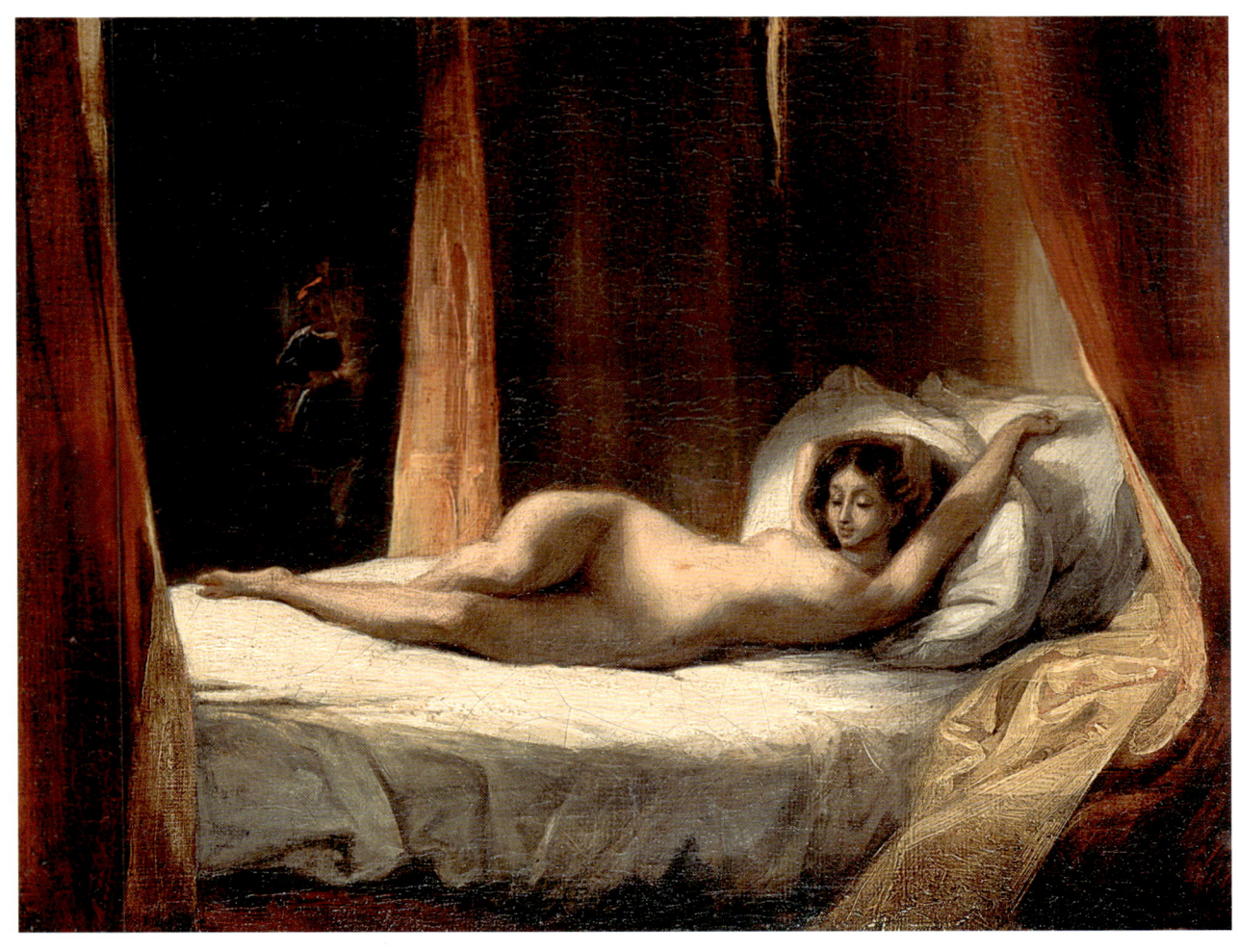

CAT. 32 *A Lady and Her Valet,* ca. 1826–29

relatively reserved, their accessories are more prominent, and shadows close in around them, creating a vague sense of menace. The second version of *Women of Algiers* (see fig. 32) and *Othello and Desdemona* (see fig. 116) were painted at the same time and were exhibited together at the Salon of 1849. By means of the works' shared theatrical props (heavy curtains, luxurious accessories) and mirror compositions (each has a standing figure on one side opposite a reclining female figure on the other), Delacroix demonstrated how different genres can enrich each other. In *Women of Algiers* he elevated a scene of manners to the rank of history painting not by means of format, as he had done in 1834, but through the dramatic expressiveness of light and shade; and in *Othello and Desdemona*, a great tragic scene inspired by theater and opera, he conjured a hushed, mysterious atmosphere through mastery of the decorative effects of textiles and goldwork.[97] The large red bed in *A Lady and Her Valet* (cat. 32), the contorted pose in *Odalisque* (fig. 63), and the coarseness of the attendant in *Cleopatra and the Peasant* (see cat. 95) are assembled and transcended in this staging of Desdemona's final moments. The art of the colorist and the theater director, along with the skillful interplay of resonating motifs, allowed Delacroix to break down the traditional divide separating genre painters from history painters, while avoiding the anecdotal.

Finally, the reprise of a theatrical subject could be induced not only by the expressive pleasure and formal free play associated with a motif, but also by developments in stage productions that Delacroix attended and by his evolving view of a favorite character—Hamlet, most notably, whom he usually portrayed with the skull of the jester Yorick, in the famous gravedigger scene. Delacroix probably saw a version of the play in Paris in his youth, with the actor François Joseph Talma playing the title character. Talma was a client of the young painter, and Hamlet was Talma's defining role from 1803 until his death in 1826. However, the version of the play he starred in, a highly altered, expurgated adaptation by Jean François Ducis, bore little resemblance to the original.[98] Delacroix was staying with his brother in Touraine in August–September 1822, when Samson Penley's troupe presented the first English-language production of *Hamlet* in Paris.[99] During the painter's visit to London three years later, he regretted not having the opportunity to see Edmund Kean's famous performance as Hamlet at the Drury Lane Theater.[100] It was not until September 1827, when Charles Kemble, manager of the Covent Garden Theater, brought *Hamlet* to the Théâtre de l'Odéon in Paris,

that the painter finally saw the play performed in English.[101] Although abridged, the production was the first in France to include the play's most violent scenes, previously censored or skirted: the appearance of the ghost in the first act, Ophelia's madness in the fourth, and the gravediggers scene in act 5.[102]

That experience probably triggered the proliferation of Hamlets in Delacroix's iconographic repertoire. Responding to the play, the painter wrote: "The English have opened up their theater. They are working wonders. . . . Our actors are learning from them; their eyes have been opened. The consequences of this innovation are incalculable."[103] Critics, the intelligentsia, and Parisian high society seemed to agree with Delacroix; all gave the English *Hamlet* an enthusiastic reception. The artist certainly saw the publication that was issued as a memento of the production. Published under the title *Souvenirs du théâtre anglais à Paris*, it comprised a series of illustrations by Achille Devéria and Louis Boulanger that conveyed the main lines of the set and poses struck by the leading actors.[104] Their costumes, which established the standard that held for the next seventy years, were far more precisely described.[105] Delacroix, too, adhered to this standard in his many representations of the protagonist, whose all-black attire changed very little over the decades: trunk hose (puffy, thigh-length breeches worn over long stockings), wide-sleeved cloak, cape worn over the shoulder, biretta with long plumes, and sword. The exception, found in the 1843 engraving showing Hamlet wearing Horatio's light-colored doublet, is also based on the 1827 production in Paris.

The same spirit of competition ("what has been said has not yet been said enough")[106] that led Delacroix to measure himself against Moritz Retzsch in the Faust series may well have spurred him to outdo Devéria and Boulanger's mediocre illustrations of *Hamlet*.[107] In a lithograph of 1828 (see fig. 64), he presented his personal interpretation of a scene that seems to have attracted him from the start, that in which Hamlet meditates on the skull of Yorick.[108] Based on a watercolor study, the print shows the three characters—Hamlet, Horatio, and one of the gravediggers—stylized to the point of caricature in a landscape far more ambitious than that of Devéria and Boulanger. The augmented setting permitted Delacroix to unite in a single image two successive scenes from the play: Hamlet's meditation on Yorick's skull and the departure of Ophelia's funeral cortege from Elsinore Castle. In the fantastical and grotesque spirit of *Faust*, Delacroix juxtaposed the gravedigger's physical deformity with the lugubrious and

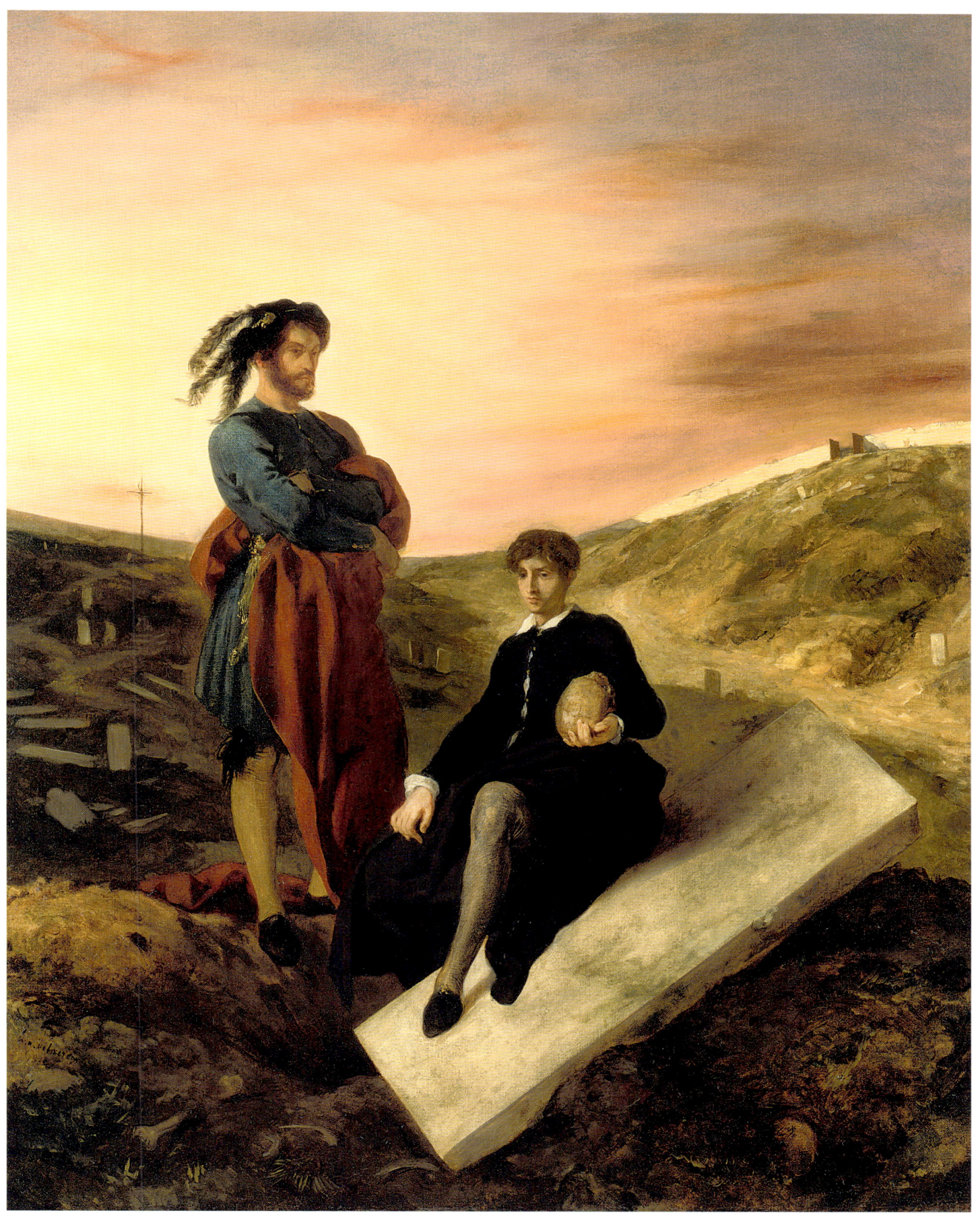

CAT. 86 *Hamlet and Horatio in the Graveyard*, 1835

somewhat frightening procession of hooded figures adapted from the witches' sabbath scene in *Faust*. The lithograph was an isolated effort. There is no way of knowing what prompted Delacroix to publish six years later, at his own expense, and independent of any text, a suite of lithographs based on *Hamlet*. Was he inspired by the new edition of Le Tourneur's translation, published by Henri Horace Meyer the same year?[109]

He executed six scenes in 1834 and 1835, omitting the gravediggers episode, which he reserved for an oil painting done for the Salon of 1835 (cat. 86). This was the first work with a Shakespearean motif that Delaroix produced with the Salon in view, and it was also the one that diverged the most from the text. Did he intend it to announce the publication of the lithographs? Should the painting be understood as a kind of frontispiece? The scene depicted does not correspond to any moment in the play: though it is set in the churchyard, the gravediggers are absent. Hamlet, wearing neither plumed hat nor sword—the distinguishing attributes of a gentleman—is seated with one foot in the grave. Backlit by a hot, late-afternoon sky, Horatio waits, impassive, lost in his own thoughts. The landscape, a vast, deserted wasteland enclosed by white-washed walls, might have been inspired by the artist's memories of Moroccan graveyards or of the old cemetery in Toulon, abandoned in 1829, which Delacroix described to his friend Jean-Baptiste Pierret when he returned from Morocco.[110]

The familiar scene of animated dialogue is replaced here by a majestic, static, silent tableau. Each character has withdrawn into himself. Whereas a preliminary drawing shows the two friends together, their faces lowered in communion as they contemplate Yorick's skull, in the finished painting they are separated, with faces raised.[111] Each looks straight ahead, absorbed in his own thoughts; the communication is broken. The representation of Hamlet follows the codes of posthumous portraiture seen in Delacroix's portrait of Rabelais (Musée de Chinon), completed the previous year. The prince is rendered full-length, with a gravestone for his throne, the court jester's skull as his celestial globe, and an abandoned graveyard as his kingdom. Lacking crown and scepter, he seems to be submitting to the sham of a sardonic royal portrait. The wobbly gravestone and foot disappearing into the muddy hole convey better than any struck pose the complexity of the character, whose indecisiveness and simulated buffoonery mask his profound disgust with the vanity of the world and his thoughts of suicide. This effigy of Hamlet as the prince of darkness, on the edge of the abyss of buried illusions,

scrambled the codes of specific genres. Delacroix, eschewing literary illustration and the theatricality of history painting, created an ambiguous work, one that is simultaneously a landscape painting, a *vanitas*, and a posthumous portrait.

That was probably the reason why the canvas was rejected by the jury for the Salon of 1836 and, consequently, heralded as a Romantic manifesto by proponents of artistic freedom. Shortly after the Salon opened, the painting was purchased by Achille Ricourt, director of the review *L'artiste*, who used it as the rallying point for a media campaign directed against what was judged to be the tyrannical interference of the Académie in the workings of the Salon and the jury's decision. In addition to many articles in defense of the painting by Gustave Planche, Alfred de Musset, Alexandre-Gabriel Decamps, Roger de Beauvoir, and others, the review published a lithograph of it followed by an homage in poetry by Louise Colet.[112] A wood engraving accompanied by a laudatory article was published the following year in *Le magasin pittoresque*.[113]

Encouraged by these demonstrations of support but eager to reach a compromise with the jury so that his favorite Shakespearean subject could be exhibited at the Salon, Delacroix executed a new oil painting for the Salon of 1839, simultaneous with a *Death of Ophelia*.[114] He reformulated the gravedigger scene, this time hewing close to the text and the theatrical context (cat. 96). The composition is far more narrative than the preceding one: the cynical gravediggers reappear, their animation and plebeian directness contrasting with the patrician reserve of the two gentlemen. Hamlet, his delicate white hand and gold ring highlighted against the deep black of his cloak, possesses the sober elegance of Titian's *Man with a Glove* (ca. 1520; Musée du Louvre). He reacts with a movement of revulsion to the skull brandished by one of the laborers. The characters are tightly framed, their attention concentrated on the skull, the focal point of the composition. The painting was accepted by the Salon jury in February 1839 and honored by the crown prince, who bought it.

That critical success was immediately followed by the publication of at least three different prints in illustrated magazines.[115] It wasn't until four years later, however, in 1843, that Delacroix finally executed his own lithograph of the scene, completing the suite he had initiated in 1834.[116] The composition of the print reverses that of the 1839 painting with only slight variation (fig. 65). Delacroix added prominent narrative details (the gravedigger's pickax, the churchyard cross, Elsinore Castle) and accentuated the hierarchy within

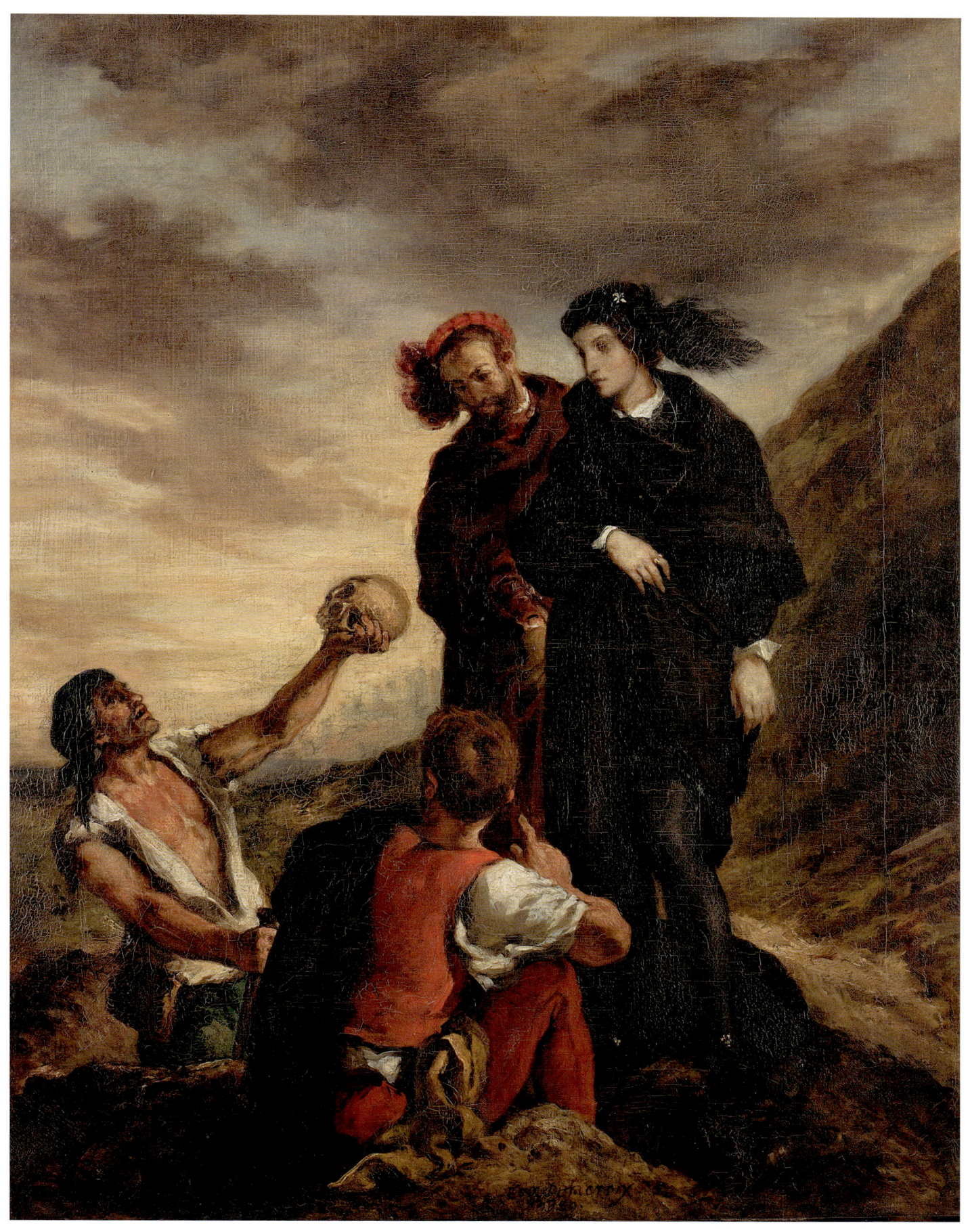

CAT. 96 *Hamlet and Horatio in the Graveyard*, 1839

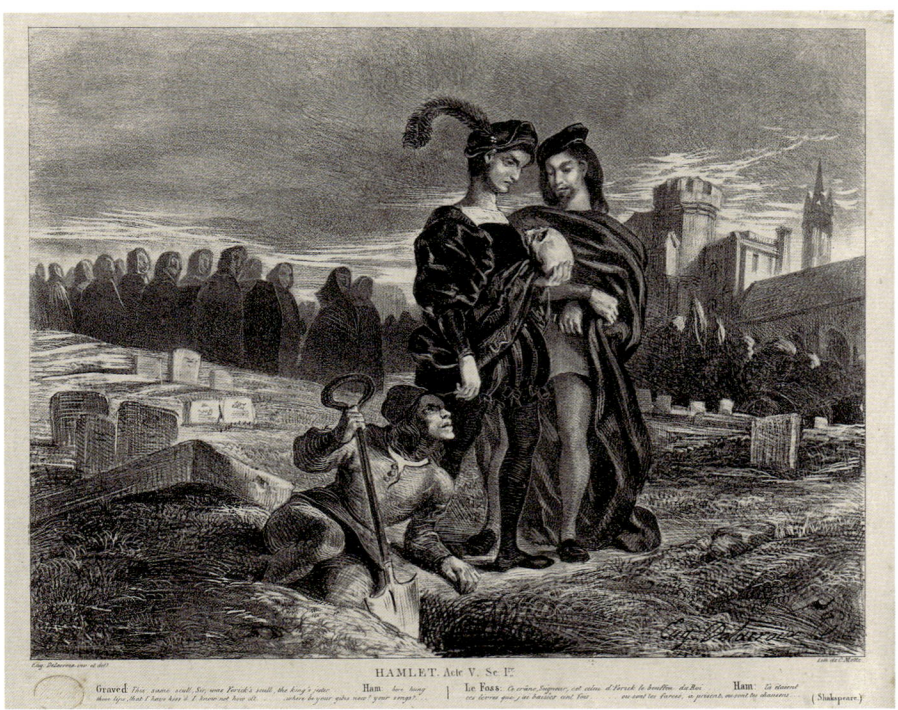

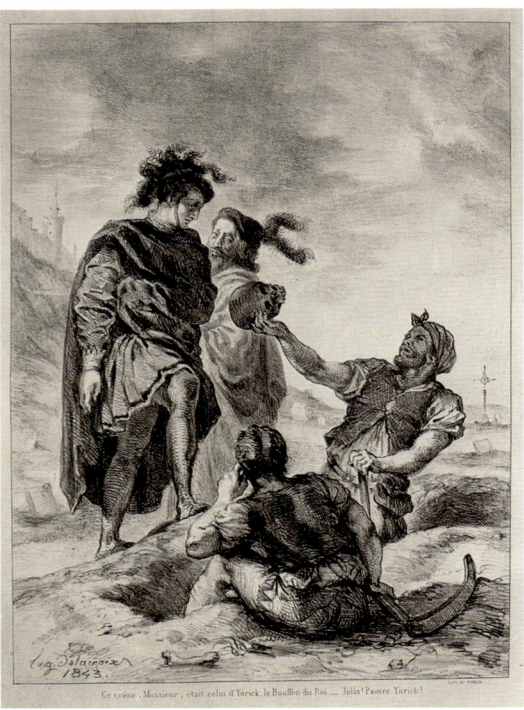

FIG. 64 *Hamlet Contemplating Yorick's Skull,* 1828. Lithograph with chine collé, third state of three, image 11⁹⁄₁₆ x 14⁷⁄₈ in. (29.3 x 37.8 cm), sheet 16⅝ x 19½ in. (42.2 x 49.5 cm). The Metropolitan Museum of Art, New York, The Elisha Whittelsley Collection, The Elisha Wittelsley Fund, 2018 (2018.79) (D-S 75)

FIG. 65 *Hamlet and Horatio with the Gravediggers,* 1843. Lithograph, second state of four, image 11¼ x 8¼ in. (28.5 x 21 cm), sheet 12½ x 9⁵⁄₁₆ in. (31.8 x 23.7 cm). The Metropolitan Museum of Art, New York, Rogers Fund, 1922 (22.56.16) (D-S 116)

the chiasma linking the two secondary characters (the grave-digger viewed from the back and a smaller Horatio) to the two principal characters. The gravedigger holding the skull has been moved closer to Hamlet, who, larger than Horatio and with his weight on his right leg, appears more assertive.

It would be natural to imagine that, having used the same formal solution in both the painting and the lithograph, Delacroix would feel no need to treat the gravedigger scene again. Nonetheless, in 1859 he returned to it, one last time in oil, in a manner that exemplifies his late creative process (fig. 66). In scrupulously replicating the composition of the lithograph of 1828, he returned to his original approach to the subject. He faithfully transposed all the elements present in the lithograph while enhancing it with new narrative elements: a liquor bottle planted in the overturned earth in the foreground, the second gravedigger in the middle ground, Ophelia's coffin and torches for the funeral procession. The blazing sky, a reminder of the 1835 painting (see cat. 86), bathes the scene in a glowing, unreal light that has no effect

on the coloration of the human figures or any other components of the foreground: seen in contre-jour, they should logically be very dark. This inconsistency must be responsible for the impression of preciosity and naïveté, which displeased the critics at the Salon of 1859. The transfer of the beard from Horatio's face to Hamlet's can be explained by the refashioning of the character of Hamlet on the French stage in 1846–47. The actor Philibert Rouvière played the lead role in a new version of the play that was adapted and translated by Alexandre Dumas and Paul Meurice. Baudelaire commented admiringly on the impassioned, tempestuous acting of Rouvière, who was immortalized in the role in a portrait by Edouard Manet (1866; National Gallery of Art, Washington, D.C.).[117]

An important aspect of the 1859 painting that has been little discussed is its reversal of two traditional practices. Typically, the painted rendering of a composition precedes the print version, which functions to disseminate the original image. The genesis of this *Hamlet and Horatio* can therefore be interpreted as a reversal of the traditional relationship of

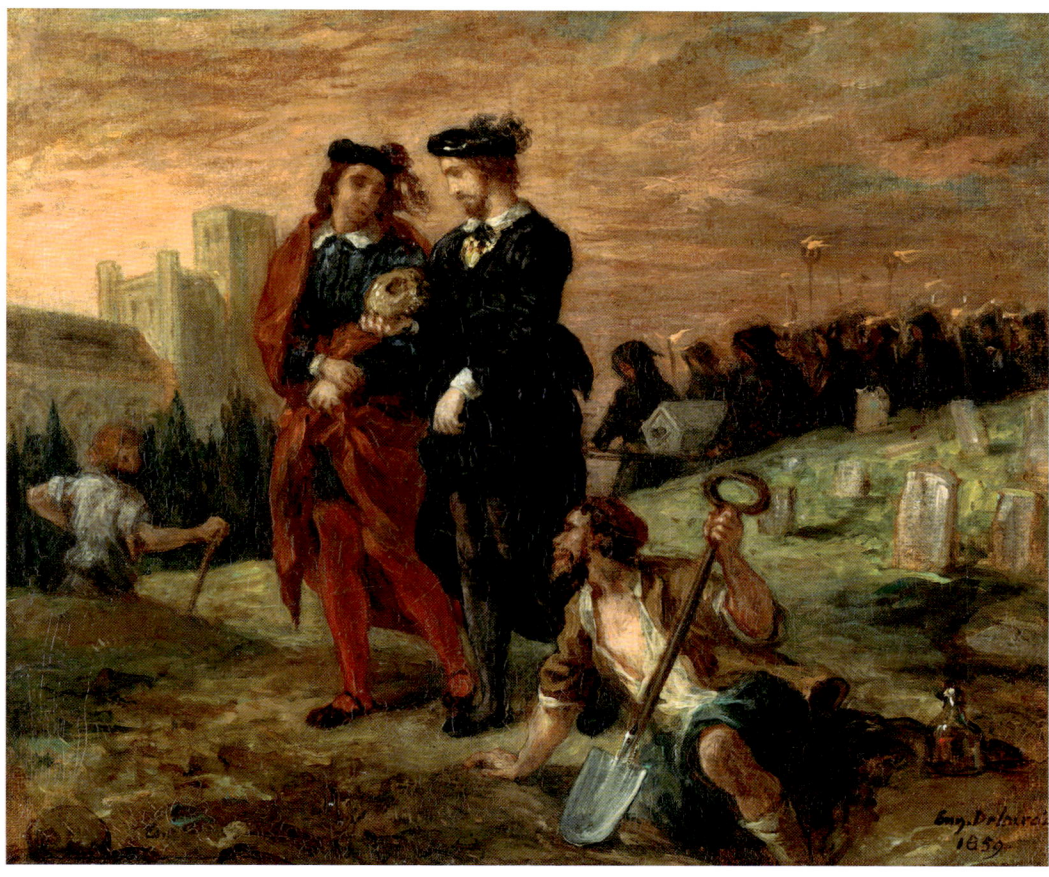

FIG. 66 *Hamlet and Horatio in the Graveyard*, 1859. Oil on canvas, 11⁷⁄₁₆ x 14³⁄₁₆ in. (29 x 36 cm). Musée du Louvre, Paris (RF 1399) (J 332)

anteriority and artistic hierarchy—the precedence of lithography over painting. Moreover, the dimensions of the painting are close to those of the lithograph, but the composition is reversed. As a rule, a reversal occurs when a painting is translated into a lithograph or other type of print, not when a print is used as the source of a painting. Perhaps Delacroix based the painting not on a print but on the original lithographic stone. Whether or not this was the case, the painting seems to reverse the flow of time. It is as if Delacroix re-created in 1859 a painted original that could have served as the model for the 1828 lithograph.[118]

Delacroix thus ventured to step into the shoes of the artist he had been thirty years earlier. He recalled the galvanizing experience of the production at the Odéon in 1827, of which he had recently been reminded: "[Caught up with] my old friend [Achille] Ricourt. . . . He spoke of what I used to be in those far-off days. He remembered the green coat, my long hair, my passion for Shakespeare, novelties, etc."[119] Even so, in his painting of 1859, Delacroix concealed neither the

theatrical metamorphosis Hamlet had undergone, as Kemble's character was replaced by Rouvière's, nor the evolution in his own style, which had become more fluid and vibrant, less precise and firm than in his youth. He was fully aware of this stylistic change: "Every original talent goes through the same stages in its development that art does in its various evolutions, namely, timidity and dryness at the beginning, and breadth or carelessness of details at the end (*Count de Palatiano* in comparison with my recent paintings). . . . That is how the talent of a single man, as he develops, passes through the different phases in the history of the art he practices."[120]

The complex, reflexive strategy of moving back and forth in time that Delacroix employed in his late work—notably applying it to the most famous memento mori dialogue in European literature—is similar to the one played out in his *Journal* during the same period. It reveals the interest the painter had in maintaining a connection between goings-on in the world of art and his own creative practice during the final decade of his life.

To be bold when doing so might compromise
your past is the greatest sign of strength.

—Delacroix's *Journal*, March 1, 1859[1]

The years 1853–63, the decade immediately preceding Delacroix's death, allowed the painter to reap the benefits of his career and overcome remaining obstacles. After his extended battle with the Académie des Beaux-Arts, he finally won official artistic recognition. In addition to continuing to receive public commissions, he enjoyed the honor of a solo retrospective exhibition in 1855 and was elected to the Institut de France in 1857. These two major events placed him on nearly equal footing with contemporaries already canonized early on by the academic system, namely Jean Auguste Dominique Ingres and Horace Vernet.

The various critical circles came to recognize that Delacroix had accomplished the rare feat of always remaining at the forefront of the Paris art scene. The first histories of nineteenth-century French painting were now being written, and Delacroix was the subject of a number of studies, essays, and magazine articles. He captivated the younger generation of art critics, museum curators, and the officials of the fine arts: Louis Clément de Ris, Philippe de Chennevières, Charles Baudelaire, Paul Mantz, Théophile Silvestre, Paul de Saint-Victor, Philippe Burty, Zacharie Astruc, and Ernest Chesneau. They saw that Delacroix, owing to the enlightened support of successive governments from the Restoration to the Second Empire, had circumvented the persistent hostility of the Académie while preserving his independence, refusing to submit to the propaganda of the time.

Delacroix was a fascinating case, but also a rather difficult one. The oeuvre he produced, though enormous and immediately recognizable, did not give rise to a movement taken up by a community of young artists. The critics struggled to name the artistic phenomenon he embodied. The adjective "Romantic" was no longer apropos: Romanticism had gradually come to be perceived as a historical movement of youthful rebellion associated with 1830, the year of political and theatrical revolution. Yet Delacroix's career and his art now extended far beyond that horizon. He had outdistanced a number of fellow artists of the so-called Romantic generation who in the 1820s might have given the impression that they could compete with him. In addition to those who had died young and been forgotten (Richard Parkes Bonington, Xavier Sigalon), some confessed early on that they had run out of originality (Eugène Devéria, Alexandre Colin, Charles-Emile Callande de Champmartin), while others such as Vernet, Paul Delaroche, and Léon Cogniet found success along more commercial lines. In the early 1830s, these three artists gave up trying to confront the problems raised by the materiality of painting, opting for a form of imagery adapted to mass production and ideologies then in fashion.

During the same period, by contrast, Delacroix chose to revive a form of painting that could not be easily transported or reproduced. He dedicated himself to monumental and allegorical decorative paintings in the tradition of the old masters, granting only a subordinate role to the Salons, even at the risk of weakening the bond he had established with the public early on and of being excluded from the artistic battles of his time. Attempts continued, however, to place him in the fray, if only artificially. During the 1840s members of the press, disoriented by the growing diversification of painting trends, tried to reenvision the art scene, no longer as a pyramid (since the French school was no longer one and indivisible), but as a field of opposing forces. They supported this view by positing a powerful "classical" pole, represented with relative ease (though against type) by Ingres and his accomplices, whom they deemed to be dogmatic. Delacroix, situated on the other side of the "golden mean" embodied by the Vernet-Delaroche dynasty, represented the other extreme and most valid alternative.

That paradigm crystallized at an exhibition—a retrospective of French painting from the 1770s to 1845—organized by Baron Taylor in 1846 at the Bazar Bonne-Nouvelle in Paris.

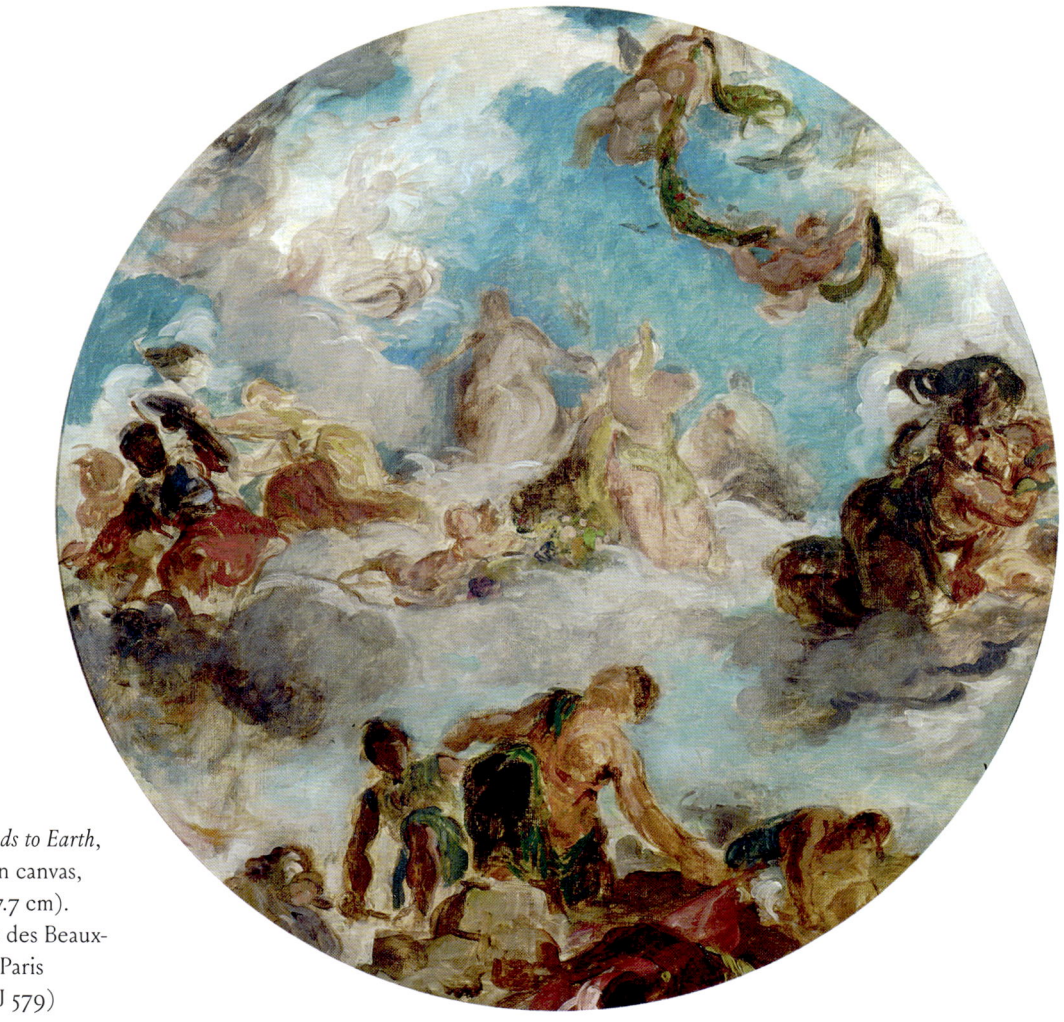

FIG. 67 *Peace Descends to Earth*, sketch, 1852. Oil on canvas, diam. 30⁹⁄₁₆ in. (77.7 cm). Petit Palais–Musée des Beaux-Arts de la Ville de Paris (inv. PPP04622) (J 579)

The critics took the opportunity to fabricate an artificial genealogy leading from David to Ingres[2] in opposition to the Other, Delacroix, who was that much easier to stereotype because he was not represented in the exhibition. The press looked for the appropriate term to define him. Because "Romantic" was now ambiguous and, it was suspected, outdated, Baudelaire invented a tautology. Sometimes he used the vague but powerful expression "leader of the present-day school" or "leader of the modern school." At other times he dehistoricized Romanticism, redefining it in terms of what Delacroix had become in the meantime: "Romanticism, to be precise, lies neither in the choice of subjects nor in the exact truth, but in the manner of feeling." Ultimately, Baudelaire merged the two definitions: "For me, Romanticism is the most recent, the most up-to-date expression of the beautiful."[3] Three years later, however, with the sudden rise of the austere realism of Gustave Courbet and the painters of the Barbizon school, Delacroix's "modernity" became difficult to define and defend.

In the early 1850s, most critics had to fall back on the age-old opposition between the proponents of drawing (called idealists or stylists) and the so-called colorists, represented, respectively, by Ingres and Delacroix, except that Ingres could still pass for a leader, whereas Delacroix appeared more like a solitary and indomitable figure of genius. Delacroix's singularity would now be systematically attributed to his ingenuity in the expressive use of color and his talent for large decorative paintings, gifts that Paul Signac erected into a myth at the end of the century. Decoration was ripe for apotheosis.[4]

1855: The Trap of Apotheosis

The first act played out in spring 1854 at the unveiling of the decorations that Delacroix had painted in the Salon de la Paix (fig. 67) of the Hôtel de Ville in Paris.[5] They were only a few feet from the Salon de l'Empereur, the ceiling decorations of which the municipality had entrusted to Ingres.

Clément de Ris, Théophile Gautier, and Gustave Planche took note of this new evidence of Delacroix's mastery of the demanding genre of large allegorical and mythological ceiling compositions: "M. Delacroix is one of the most inventive artists of our time; as such, he occupies a significant place in the French school. . . . Decorative painting suits him marvelously, it is truly where he reigns as master. It seems that his palette becomes richer as the space in front of him grows larger. He likes to handle large shapes, to mold them. . . . The duty of criticism is to encourage him on that path."[6] Falling in with that chorus of praise was Etienne Jean Delécluze, a traditionally harsh critic, uncompromising when it came to less than proficient drawing. At seventy-three, he still presided over the art criticism of the *Journal des débats*. Appreciating the grace, charm, and distinction of a piece that took its place respectfully within the architectural setting, Delécluze abandoned his usual reprimands: "This painter has the particular merit of loving and understanding color and of turning it to good account, because what he reproduces of the form is expressed neither by the stroke nor by the modeling but by the color. . . . It is a painted piece of music in which no striking melody can be discerned but which pleases the eye through a sequence of chords as artful as they are graceful."[7]

Planche declared a tie: "All men of real value seek a model and assistance from the tradition. In that respect, MM. Ingres and Delacroix are of the same opinion. . . . If they part ways when it comes to invention, it is not for us to complain, since they offer for our admiration two faces of art, which combine to create supreme beauty, the severity of line, and the spark of fantasy."[8] The next year, Charles Perrier concurred: "Variety is the sign of richness, just as union is the sign of strength, and no other country in the world can lay claim to a glory composed of so many heterogeneous and national elements. The people of this country know how to honor the Victor Hugos as they honored the Corneilles, and worship without distinction M. Delacroix and M. Ingres."[9]

This atmosphere of communion for the greater glory of French art did not occur by chance. The inaugural festivities for the new decorations at the Hôtel de Ville in the spring of 1854 were in fact the prelude to the Exposition Universelle of 1855, a grand display that the government had been planning since late 1853. The Great Exhibition of 1851 in London had caused the regime of Napoleon III to realize that France's artistic influence was now competing directly with that of other European powers (primarily the artistic hubs of London, Munich, Düsseldorf, and Milan). The government wished to federate French artists and transform internal quarrels into a mark of national wealth, creative vitality, and good taste. With the Exposition, which was to take place in Paris from May 15 to October 31, 1855, the emperor wished not only to showcase French excellence in the face of British competition but also to assemble great national artistic points of pride of the past several decades. Delacroix was invited in December 1853 to sit on the Exposition's fine arts commission. He was among the most privileged of artists, invited to display a selection of masterpieces representative of his career. On March 20, 1854, the state also commissioned a large composition on a subject of his choosing to be shown at the Exposition. Delacroix chose the theme of the lion hunt (see cats. 134–36). For more than a year, he had devoted considerable energy to finishing the decorations in the Salon de la Paix (completed in March 1854) and to painting new compositions for the Exposition. All the while, he expanded his research and made requests for loans and restorations, with the aim of presenting, not only to the public and the authorities, but also to the members of the Institut de France, a significant body of work spanning thirty-three years.

He succeeded in this aim, displaying an extraordinary set of paintings of the greatest importance, primarily large-format paintings that had been shown at the Salons between 1822 and 1848. Their Salon titles were: *Dante and Virgil* (Salon of 1822); *Scenes of the Massacres at Chios* (Salon of 1824); *Christ in the Garden of Olives*, *The Execution of the Doge Marino Faliero*, and *The Emperor Justinian* (Salon of 1827–28); *Battle of Poitiers* (1830); *Liberty Leading the People*, *Boissy d'Anglas*, and *The Murder of the Bishop of Liège* (Salon of 1831); *The Battle of Nancy* and *Women of Algiers* (Salon of 1834); *The Battle of the Giaour and the Pasha* and *The Prisoner of Chillon* (Salon of 1835); *Medea About to Kill Her Children* and *Convulsionists of Tangier* (Salon of 1838); *Hamlet and Horatio* (Salon of 1839); *The Justice of Trajan* (Salon of 1840); *Entry of the Crusaders in Constantinople*, *The Shipwreck of Don Juan*, and *Jewish Wedding in Morocco* (Salon of 1841); *Mary Magdalene in the Desert*, *Cumaean Sibyl*, and *Last Words of Marcus Aurelius* (Salon of 1845); *The Farewell of Romeo and Juliet* (Salon of 1846); *Christ on the Cross* (1847); *Christ at the Tomb* and *The Death of Valentin* (Salon of 1848); *Basket of Flowers and Fruit* (Salon of 1849); and a *Romeo and Juliet*, a *Tasso in Prison*, and the head of an old woman. Three new works were added: *Arab Family*,

The Two Foscari, and *Lion Hunt*. The public rediscovered *Liberty Leading the People*, unseen for two decades, but could not view *The Death of Sardanapalus*.

Barely a year after the unveiling of the decorations at the Hôtel de Ville, the immensity of Delacroix's achievement and the diversity of his talent were on full view; the critics were flabbergasted. Baudelaire aptly summed up the impression: "The proof is given, the question is forever settled, the result is there, visible, enormous, flamboyant. . . . M. Delacroix has treated every genre; his imagination and knowledge have covered every corner of the pictorial landscape. He has made . . . charming little paintings, full of intimacy and profundity; he has decorated the walls of our palaces, has filled our museums with vast compositions."[10] Gautier similarly observed: "The Exposition Universelle of 1855 has elevated M. E. Delacroix to great heights. . . . The education of the masses comes about gradually, and admiration gives way to sarcasm. Paradox becomes axiomatic: it is now a commonplace to praise M. Ingres and M. Delacroix."[11]

After the Exposition, on November 15, Delacroix received a fifth-place grand medal of honor[12] and was promoted to commander of the Legion of Honor. He thereby attained the same level of distinction that his father, Charles François Delacroix, and his elder brother, Charles Henry, had reached before him. Despite his fatigue, he was encouraged to present himself, for the eighth time, as a candidate for the Académie des Beaux-Arts, to fill the chair of Delaroche, who had died on November 4, 1856. Delacroix was elected on January 10, 1857, but he was denied the opportunity to teach at the Ecole des Beaux-Arts. As a result, what energy he still had was devoted primarily to moving to the studio he had built on rue de Furstenberg. He settled in at the end of 1857 to work on the decoration for the Chapel of the Holy Angels at the nearby church of Saint-Sulpice (completed in late July 1861) and to compile his *Dictionary of the Fine Arts*, through which he hoped to transmit ideas that the academic system had not sanctioned.

These circumstances might suggest that Delacroix's position was altogether assured, that his dominant place in the pantheon of French painting had become unassailable. And yet, a few years later, Delacroix risked a return to the Salon with paintings that blurred the lines between past and present, repetition and originality. He was met with incomprehension and endured the bitter experience of having outlived himself.

The Disaster of the Salon of 1859: "The Critics in Mourning"

It was with some surprise that the public saw the new member of the Institut de France, aged sixty-one, return to the arena of the Salon of 1859. The act of exhibiting after four years of absence, when such high honors had been bestowed on him, was in itself astonishing. Everyone was willing to forgive painters who had reached the pinnacle of their careers if they did not feel the need or desire to lay themselves open at the Salon, the site of cabals, mockery, and overstatement. Ingres and Delaroche had spared themselves the ordeal since the mid-1830s. Even in 1857, the critic Clément de Ris had commended Delacroix's eagerness to face the line of fire at the Salon: "This is the highest praise that can be given him. . . . The artist never backed away from publicity. Every Salon found him at the ready, responding to the attacks with new works, defending his flag with unshakable assurance, taking up the battle anew in all its forms, returning blow for blow, always hounded, never diminished, finally forcing his adversaries to admire his steadfastness if not his talent."[13]

Delacroix wished to bear witness to his restored vitality by exhibiting eight paintings in his favorite genres, both religious (*The Ascent to Calvary*, *Saint Sebastian*, *Christ Descended into the Tomb*) and literary. For the literary subjects, he had taken care to combine Baroque and Romantic references he had been fond of since his youth (Shakespeare and Sir Walter Scott) with classical references to ancient Roman history and sixteenth-century chivalric romances (fig. 68).

The result was disastrous. The critics, profoundly disappointed and cheerless, felt that they were dealing with an old and worn-out painter. They saluted a genius who had reached his twilight years. Mantz, though a fervent supporter, opened his article with a funeral oration:

M. Delacroix returns to us today, visibly tired but still valiant, uneven in his efforts but recognizable from afar by his brilliant touches and elegant grandeur. Should his recent works betray a certain lassitude (and that is in fact our belief), no one ought to be very surprised. . . . M. Delacroix has been at the ready since 1822. His oeuvre is infinite, enormous. . . . No one more than he would be entitled to take a rest. And if ever his failing hand were to betray his ideas, no one would be more deserving of the consolation of the critics in mourning.

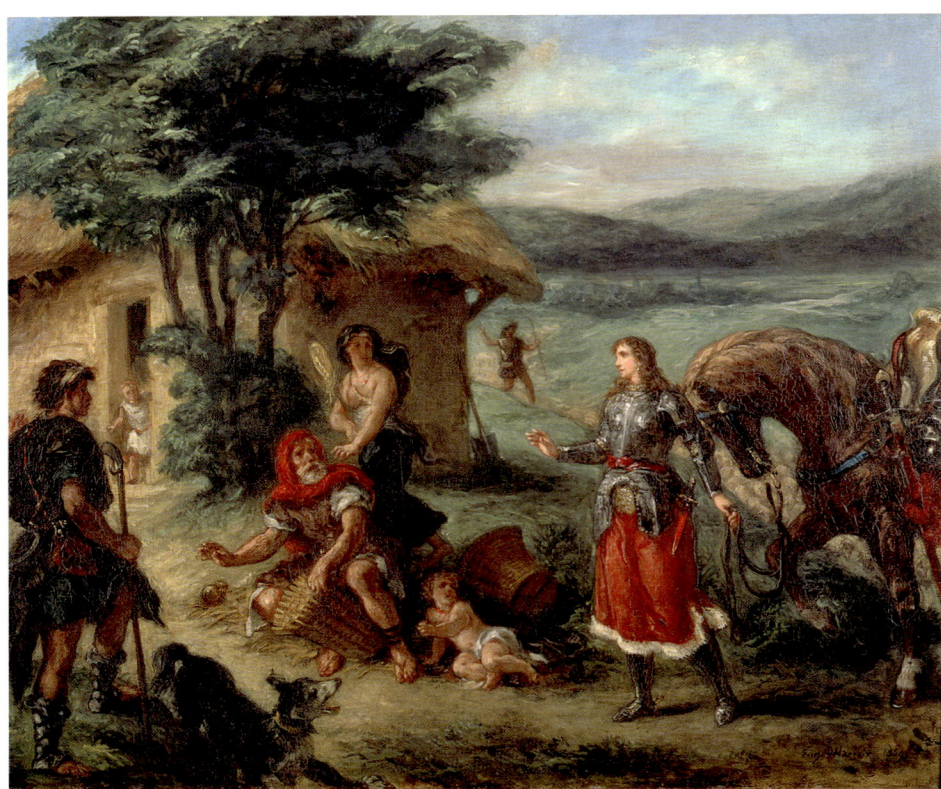

FIG. 68 *Erminia and the Shepherds* (from Torquato Tasso's *Gerusalemme Liberata*), 1859. Oil on canvas, 32⁵⁄₁₆ x 41⅛ in. (82 x 104.5 cm). Nationalmuseum, Stockholm (inv. NM 2246) (J 331)

He ended on a note of sad reverence: "We owed that loyal scrutiny to the glorious master, the skillful harmonist, the inexhaustible inventor. . . . Alas! A fateful law weighs heavy on genius, as it does on beauty. . . . Admirers become fewer and lovers depart."[14] Mantz was echoed by Saint-Victor for *La presse*: "It hurts us to have to fault, for the first time, the illustrious master who for thirty years has been the leader of the modern school."[15] Jean Rousseau followed suit. His review, "What Remains of Delacroix," began as follows: "Here is a painful sight. We are at the bedside of a genius approaching the end. . . . The time will soon come, if Delacroix does not recover, when all his exertions will be directed at pairing one tone with another, and without concern for representing something—and at making bouquets where no flowers can be found."[16] Maxime du Camp went so far as to reproach the artist for sabotaging his own apotheosis by becoming senile: "So has death struck M. Eugène Delacroix as well? By that I mean the anticipatory death that paralyzes the hand, closes the eyes, and steals from the mind the notion of the right and true. What are these paintings done by a ghost and exhibited under his name? . . . In the interest of his reputation, may he never come out of retirement again."[17]

It was now believed that the artist was putting his talent to the wrong use. Saint-Victor remarked:

Small paintings do not suit Eugène Delacroix's talent. It is subjected to microscopic analysis: his good qualities are cramped and his flaws fantastically magnified. His dramatic and uneven drawing needs to spread out over the vast field of a wall or canvas. Restricted to a small space, it often becomes unintelligible. . . . [The human figures,] hindered in their movements, impeded in their growth, break into pieces, writhe, miss the mark, and come to embody a delirious inaccuracy.[18]

Charles Perrier commented: "M. Delacroix's small paintings are absolutely unintelligible, unless they are viewed with the large ones in mind."[19] Further, the reprises of his previous compositions raised doubts about his capacity to innovate, since the proposed variants were held to be unconvincing. Mantz, for example, despised *Hamlet and Horatio in the Graveyard* (fig. 66), "a painting mediocre in its significance, a second crop of hay hastily mown in a field that once produced splendid harvests."[20] Saint-Victor considered *Abduction of Rebecca* (see cat. 141) merely an "unfortunate repetition of a subject already treated."[21] He suspected Delacroix of giving in to a facile mannerism:

It is that deliberate inaccuracy that I have been sorry to find for some time in Eugène Delacroix's small canvases; he repeats his Barbary types, his wild anatomies, his enormous flaws in physique. In these small dimensions, painting becomes for him a kind of hieroglyphic writing that eliminates the real rendering of objects, in favor of a rapid and cursory abbreviation of them. . . . The repetition [of these canvases] alerts me to the fact that they express a habitual procedure and not the first burst of ideas or a precipitous verve.[22]

The more elaborate paintings were disconcerting because of the limp forms, the neglect of proportions, the implausibility of the space, the illogical placement of the human figures and the resulting absence of hierarchy, as well as a certain affectation of gestures similar to the "sentiment and manner of the French decadent painters of the eighteenth century."[23] Not even the use of color, the artist's ultimate claim to fame, escaped this chorus of lament: "At least in the past, the color set ablaze that dross of forms; it captured them in a delightful impression of splendor or transparency. But for some time, the master seems to have snuffed out his sun. His figures, woven from reddish strands, begin to fray in a dull and muted setting. It remains harmonious, but at the expense of light. . . . *Erminia and the Shepherds* looks like a fading tapestry."[24] *Le figaro* echoed these words: "The eight scenes are all immersed in the same grayish tone. The eight scenes appear under the same overcast skies, at the same undefinable hour, which is neither the hour of dawn nor that of twilight. Delacroix snuffed out the sun that gave his previous color such caustic touches and such varied effects."[25]

Only four years after the triumph at the Exposition Universelle of 1855, the gap between Delacroix and his public had reopened. Saint-Victor aptly summed up the situation:

> The Exposition of 1855, in displaying his oeuvre in all its breadth, elevated Eugène Delacroix to great heights. The ridicule was silenced, the protests ended, the crowd itself felt the grandeur and range of that oeuvre without being able to measure it. May the master no longer risk his hard-won prize, may he have respect for his genius and the dignity of his rank. He can only compromise himself in exhibiting these insignificant, weak pieces, which disfigure him in the public's eyes. The diatribes are beginning again, negativity is resurfacing, jealousies are reawakening. . . . Why

gratuitously undermine a glory acquired at such great cost? Why enter the arena looking rumpled, when you can appear in a strong and splendid suit of armor?[26]

Delacroix was celebrated for his past works, but his present offerings were an occasion for surprise and confusion. Discernible in these reviews is a great deal of reticence, even guilt, at being obliged to criticize a master despite the respect due him. With the exception of Alexandre Dumas, Baudelaire, and Astruc, whose enthusiasm remained intact, the consternation was evident even among the younger art critics who had emerged in the *Revue des deux mondes*, *L'artiste*, or the new *Gazette des beaux-arts*. And yet their tastes had been formed by Delacroix, and they had made their mark defending him. To be polite yet without conviction, they attributed what they interpreted as "weakness" or "lassitude" to the artist's age. Their disappointment was especially strong because the Salon of 1859 sounded the death knell of religious and history painting at large, done in by the mixing of genres and the overwhelming dominance of landscape painting and genre scenes. In the absence of Ingres (who no longer exhibited his works) and Delaroche and Théodore Chassériau (both of whom had died in 1856), these critics were counting a great deal on Delacroix, the "last great painter,"[27] to display the dynamism of a highly imaginative mode of painting and to give the younger generations the courage to undertake *grandes machines*.[28] The master, isolated by the depletion of his imaginary repertoire, did not seem to understand the scope of the mission he had taken on. Hopes were dashed. The same impression can be found among such younger artists as Claude Monet, who told Eugène Boudin of his visit to the Salon: "[the artist] has painted better works than those he is showing this year. They are only indications, *ébauches*; but as always, he has verve, he has movement."[29]

The most prudent still hoped that the misunderstanding would dissipate in time. Chesneau, rejecting both sarcastic laments and blind accolades, admitted he was at a loss: "I know it seems inappropriate for a critic to be perplexed, much less admit to his perplexity; however, out of penitence for my many acts of summary and sometimes harsh judgment, I want to impose upon myself the humiliation of acknowledging that, for the moment, I am incapable of delivering a just verdict with regard to M. Delacroix. . . . If one day I broach publicly this sphinx of modern painting, it will be because that day I will have wrung his secret from him."[30]

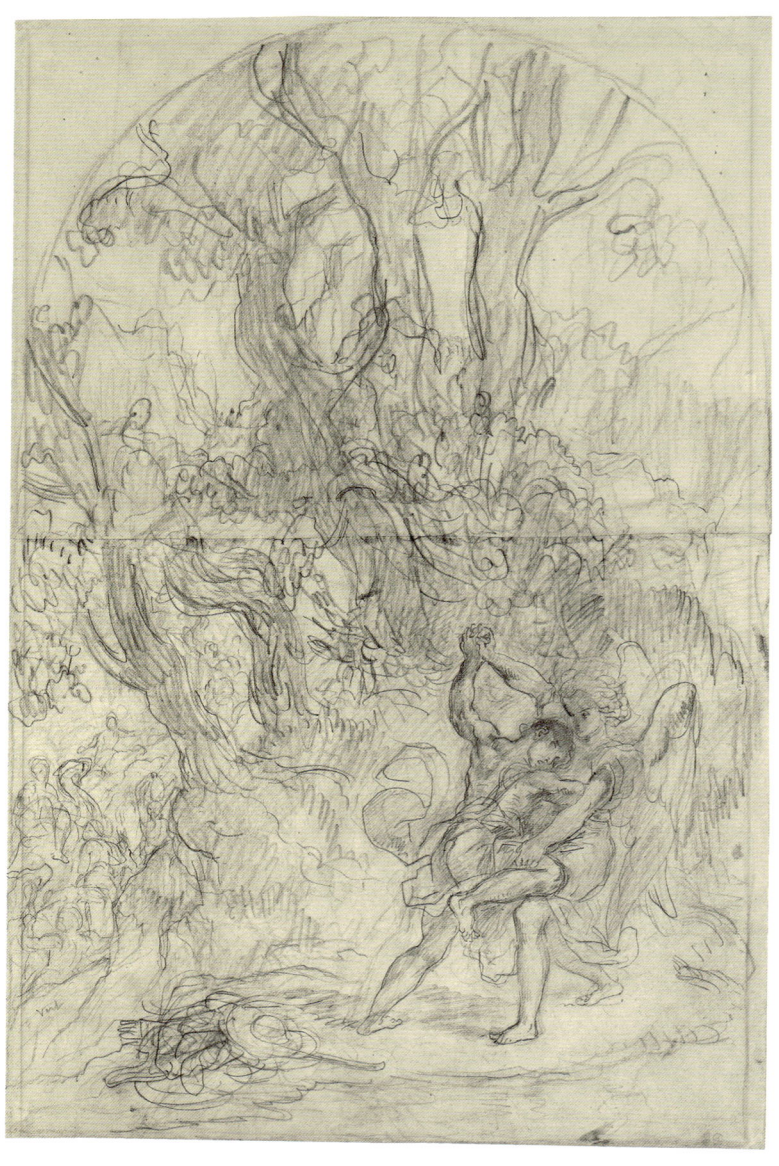

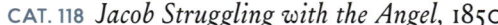

CAT. 118 *Jacob Struggling with the Angel*, 1850

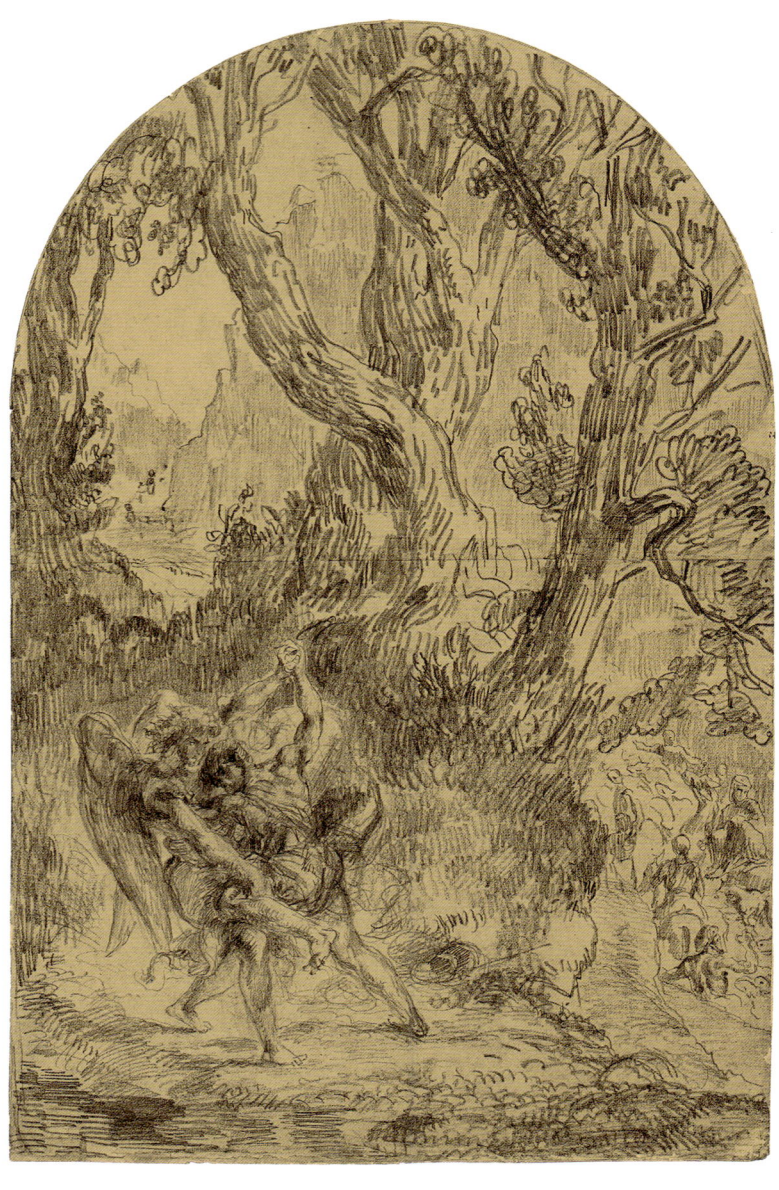

CAT. 119 *Jacob Wrestling with the Angel*, 1850

Delacroix was not the leader of the French school, which was now atomized, or of the Romantics, many of whom were now deceased. Neither was he the charismatic leader of a colorist movement, which lacked both substance and disciples. He belonged to no group. By his autonomy and his carefully staged solitude, he gave the impression of wishing to cultivate the myth of genius, of being unclassifiable and above the fray. Along the way, he seemed to have lost his connection to the public entirely, not only the masses but also the best-informed and most tolerant critics.

The disaster of 1859 was quickly forgotten. Delacroix's participation at the exhibition of modern artists at the Galerie Francis Petit in the spring of 1860[31] took on the appearance of a retrospective, combining works as old as *The Murder of the Bishop of Liège* (see cat. 64) with the latest works on the motif of Christ Asleep during the Tempest (see cat. 129). Owing to the lyricism of the landscape and eminently Romantic character of the subject (a boat in a storm), these compositions reassured journalists, who found that they conformed to the expectations the name Delacroix raised. The critical reception

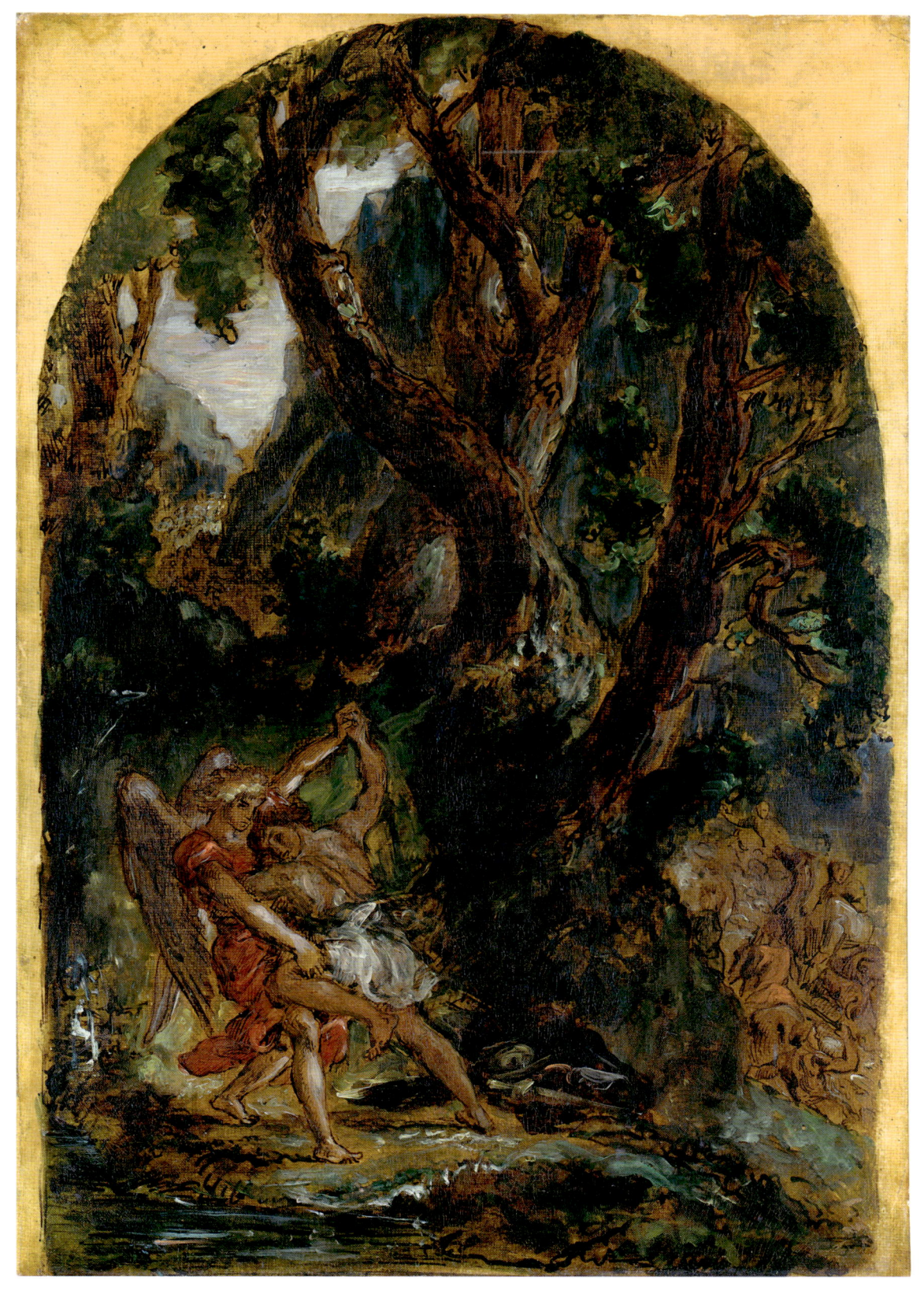

CAT. 120 *Jacob Wrestling with the Angel*, 1850

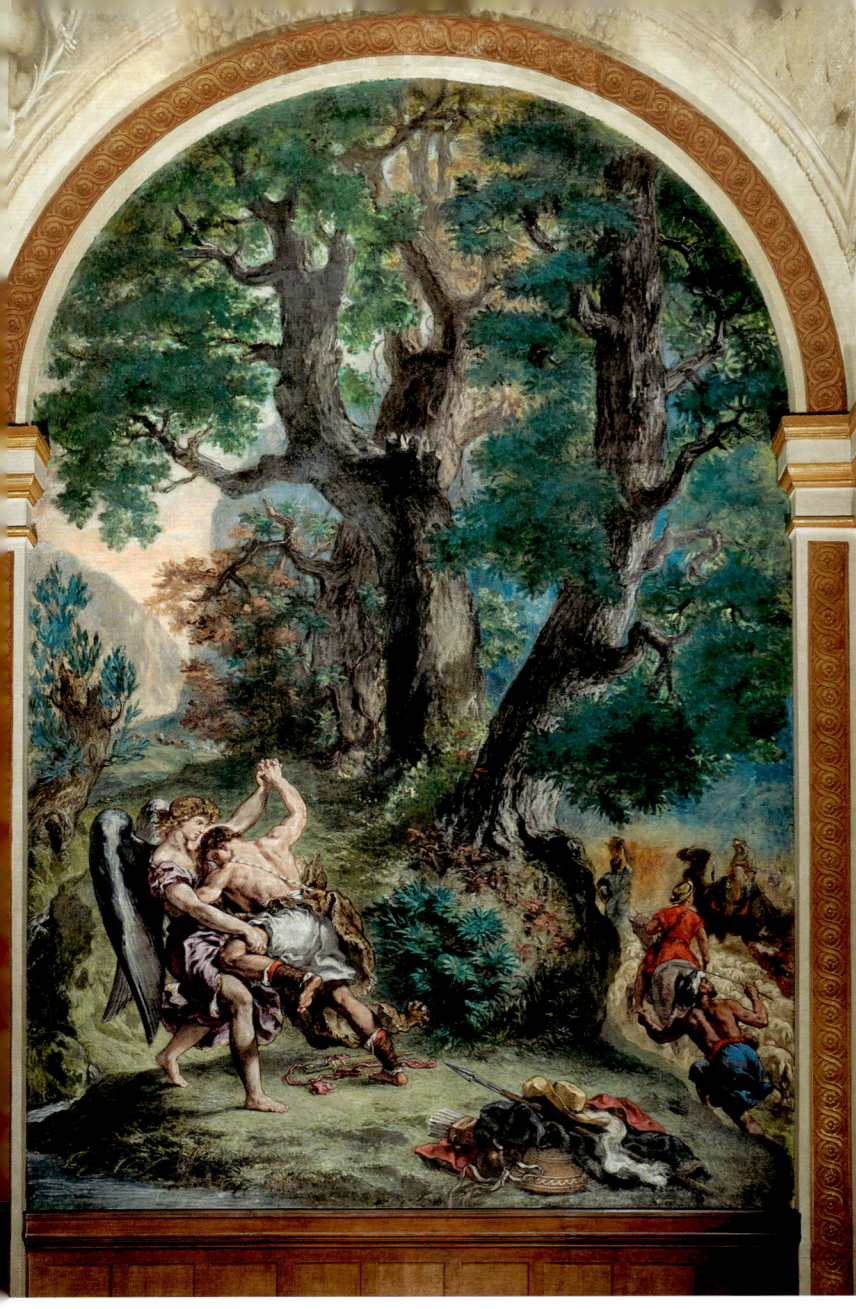

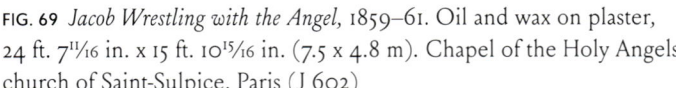

FIG. 69 *Jacob Wrestling with the Angel,* 1859–61. Oil and wax on plaster, 24 ft. 7¹¹⁄₁₆ in. x 15 ft. 10¹⁵⁄₁₆ in. (7.5 x 4.8 m). Chapel of the Holy Angels, church of Saint-Sulpice, Paris (J 602)

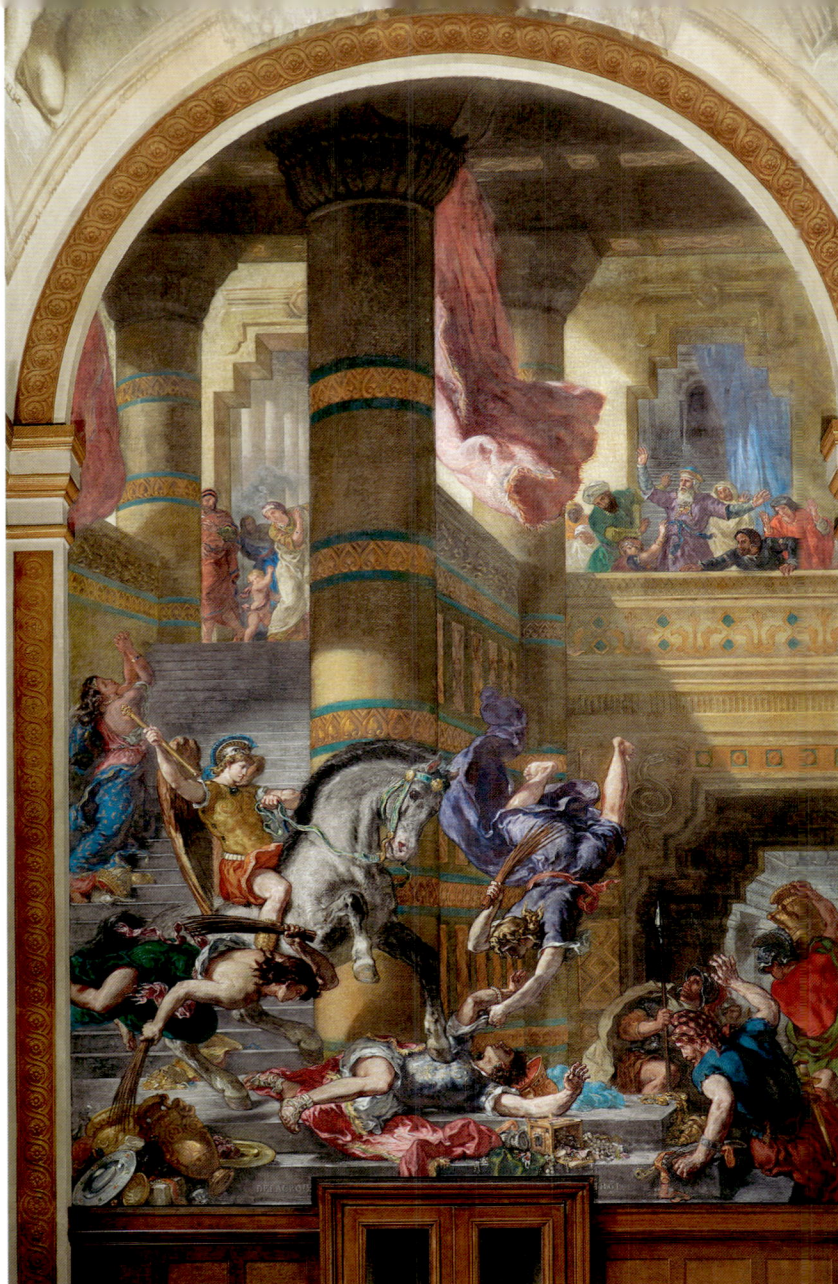

FIG. 70 *Heliodorus Driven from the Temple,* 1859–61. Oil and wax on plaster, 24 ft. 7¹¹⁄₁₆ in. x 15 ft. 10¹⁵⁄₁₆ in. (7.5 x 4.8 m). Chapel of the Holy Angels, church of Saint-Sulpice, Paris (J 601)

was equally favorable upon the unveiling of the sumptuous Chapel of the Holy Angels at Saint-Sulpice in 1861 (cats. 118– 20; figs. 69, 70), which reconfirmed Delacroix's ability to bring distinction to the genre of large decorative painting. Following the artist's death two years later, the sale of the contents of his studio was an extraordinary success, and many tributes followed.

The riddle of the Salon of 1859 was thus overshadowed but not solved. The doubt that had taken hold of well-informed visitors demands consideration. As we have seen, since the

1830s and 1840s the painter had sought to redefine the notion of originality and to argue the need for innovation, particularly to fend off the dangers of routine and the passage of time. This preoccupation resurfaced in his *Journal* just two months before the opening of the Salon of 1859, with a reflection on the idea of "boldness" in art, associated from the start with the problem of old age:

This is what makes all the more surprising the boldness displayed by the illustrious masters at an advanced stage in their careers. To be bold when doing so might compromise your past is the greatest sign of strength. . . . In the arts particularly, it takes a very profound sentiment to maintain the originality of your thought, in spite of the habits to which even talent inevitably falls prey. The artist, having spent a large part of his life accustoming the public to his genius, finds it very difficult not to repeat himself—to revitalize his talent in some sense—so as not to fall into the same banalities and commonplaces that are the weakness of men and of schools as they grow old.[32]

Yet everything suggests that Delacroix was persuaded he had avoided that pitfall, owing to his awareness of it. Not without pleasure, he admitted to pride on the eve of the Salon, believing that he had displayed a restored vitality through his many submissions. He was convinced of having achieved perfection: "I accomplished a real tour de force in finishing my paintings for the Salon. I have no fewer than *eight*. As you well know, I'm not someone who would improvise in such circumstances: they have all reached the point where every difficulty seems to be overcome."[33] A month later, he had lost his illusions: "I haven't had a spare moment or the courage to go to the Salon. I'm afraid the poor paintings there are not having the full effect that my paternal heart would have desired. In any case, they have been strikingly rebuffed by the critics."[34] He admitted to his cousin how deeply wounded he was: "If I was not turned away from the Salon, I was at least trounced by the critics. I console myself from their sting the best I can, but I'm afraid I've been attacked to the core of my being. Self-worth follows a stormy path."[35] By mid-June, when a rave review by Baudelaire finally appeared—though unfortunately in an obscure magazine about to go bankrupt[36]—the damage had been done: "You come to my aid at a time when I have been scolded and vilified by a rather large number of serious critics (or claiming to be so). . . . Having had the good fortune to please you, I am heartened and find their reprimands easier to take. You treat me the way that only the *noble dead* are treated."[37] That flash of wit may have had a bitter aftertaste, given the cruel funerary orations of Du Camp, Mantz, and Rousseau.

Delacroix was clearly not expecting such a debacle and was all the more affected by it. Discomfort and incomprehension were felt on all sides.

The Art of Indecision?

The chagrin produced by Delacroix's later compositions had to do primarily with the sense that their dramatic tension had dissipated, that their force had been dispersed and their forms dissolved. That impression was favored by a change in focus. In the compositions of the 1850s, whatever the subject treated—literary history, mythological fable, Moroccan memories—the relative size of the human figures diminished, and their forms grew less substantial. They blended into the setting amid accessories that, for their part, took on a more defined character, a greater refinement, and an increased narrative verve.

That change is easy to see if we compare the 1846 version of *The Abduction of Rebecca* (cat. 105) with the 1858 version displayed at the Salon in 1859 (cat. 141). The first version prominently features the Rubenesque tangle of struggling bodies (the overpowered Rebecca, the horse, and the two Saracen slaves). The group is situated on a bulging hillock, furnished with a few discreet war trophies, which establishes a solid foreground. In the middle ground, the figure of the Knight Templar, Brian de Bois-Guilbert, organizer of the assault, brings about an artful transition: the whirling movement of his white mantle and the gesture of his arm lead the beholder's eyes to the end of a tortuous path, where, in the background, the castle besieged by Front-de-Boeuf is burning. The fortress is a vague silhouette, vanishing into the sky in a burst of flames and smoke, thus casting into relief the solidity of the foreground group.

When Delacroix returned to the subject twelve years later, he completely changed the composition. This time, the action is composed of three moments. Rebecca has not yet been carried off on the white horse, which a Saracen holds in the foreground. She struggles in the arms of the Knight Templar striding in the middle ground, his retreat protected by an accomplice brandishing a shield against pursuers, who can be made out through a portal behind the principal figures. Discernible in the foreground to the left, amid a jumble of beams, stones, and crossbows, is the dying body of one of the besiegers. Instead of a compact group, as in the version of 1846, at least five dispersed characters now participate in the narrative. A sixth protagonist may be added: the architecture itself, which comes to life, imposing and moody. By means of a visual personification, Delacroix makes the towers howl and spit through their gaping maws. The exaggeratedly curved

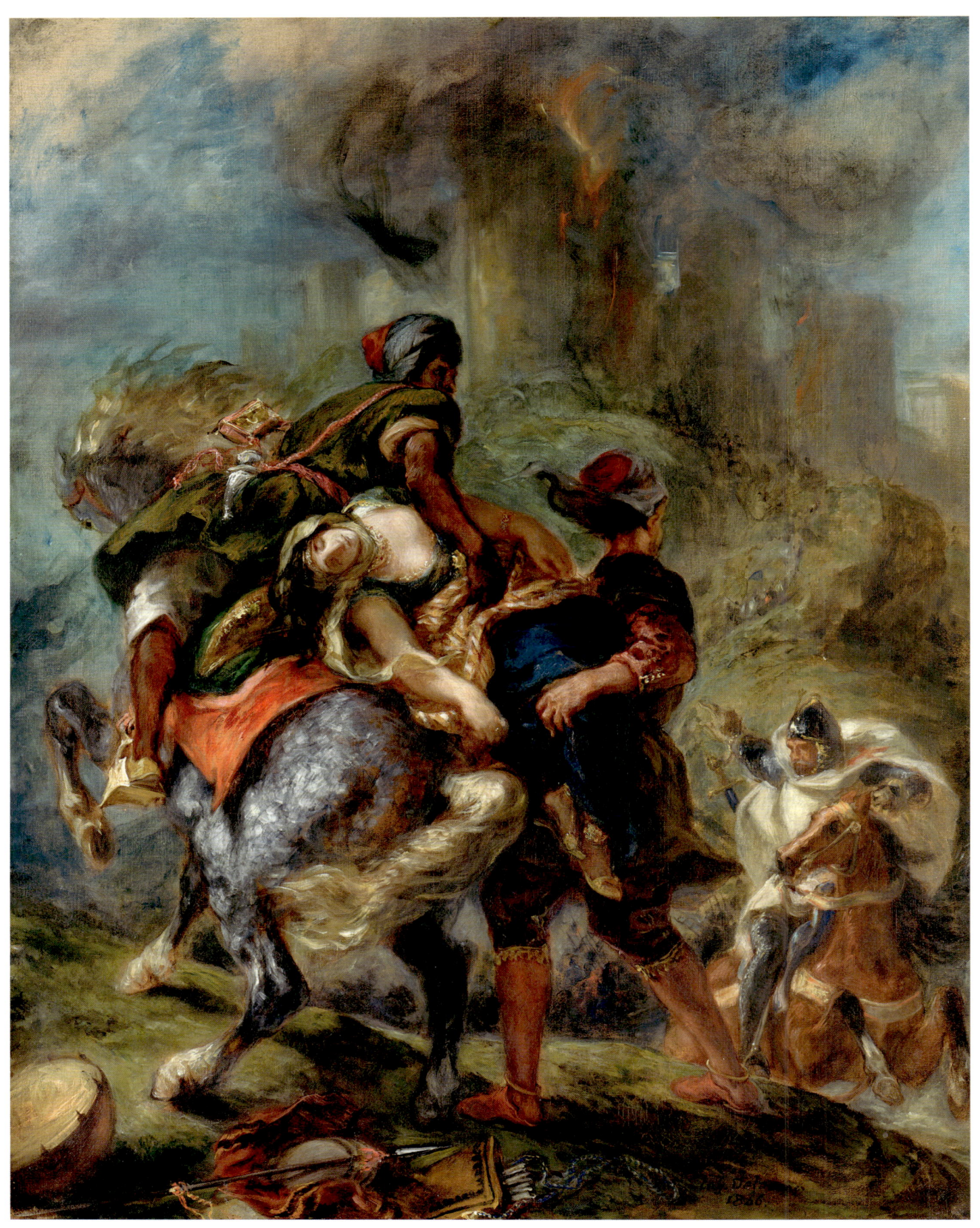

CAT. 105 *The Abduction of Rebecca*, 1846

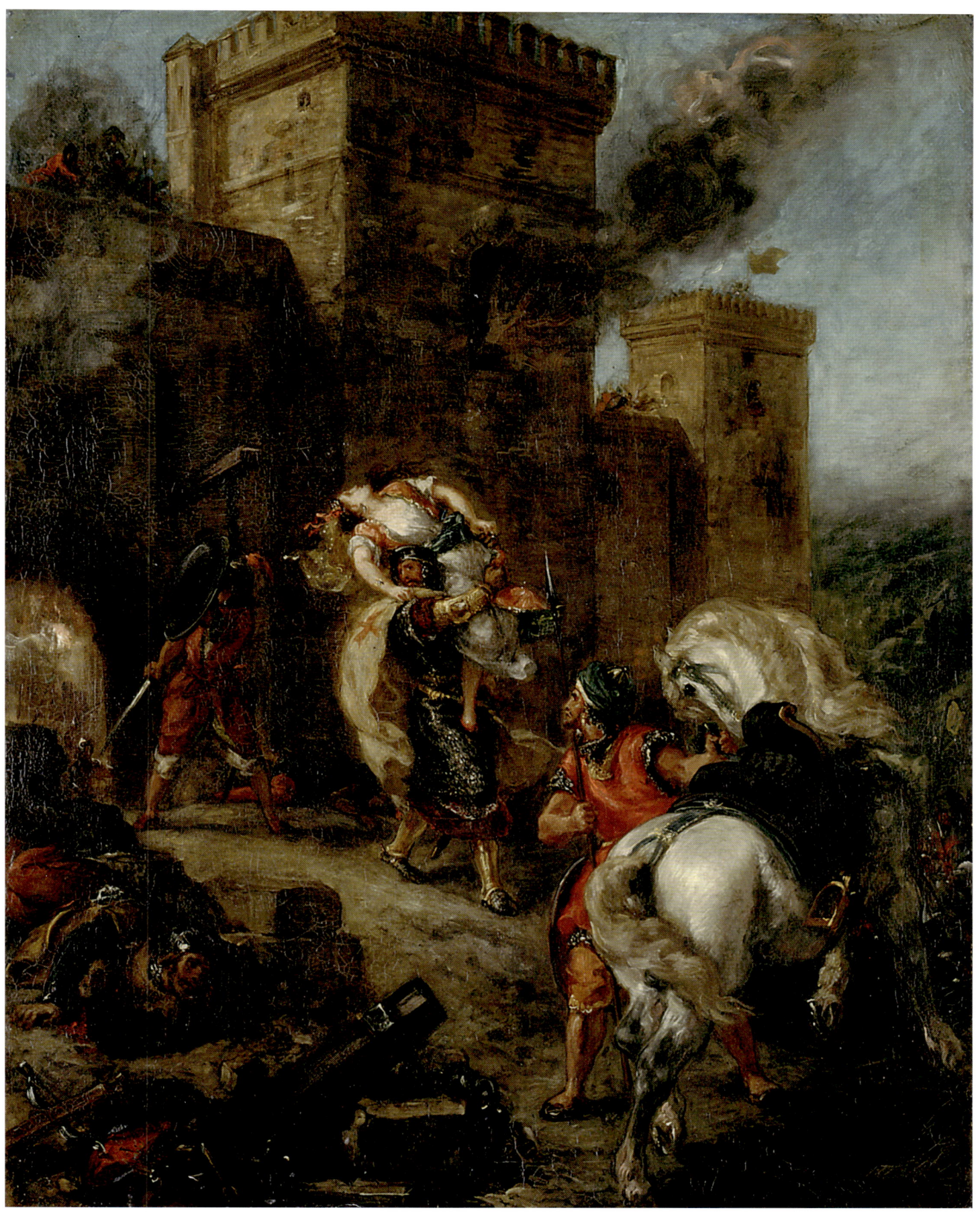

CAT. 141 *Abduction of Rebecca*, 1858

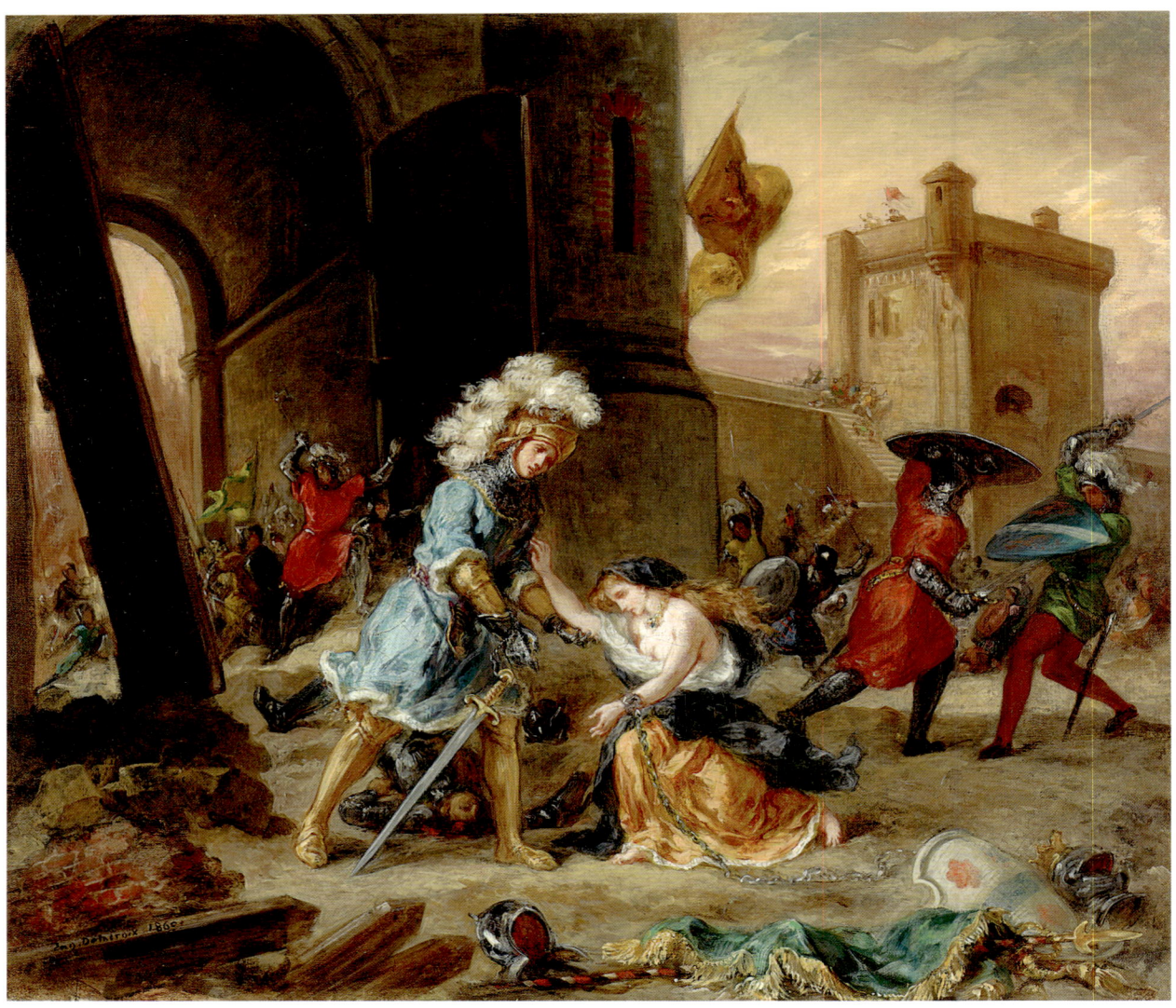

CAT. 143 *Amadis de Gaule Delivers a Damsel from Galpan's Castle*, 1859–60

path shortens considerably the distance between the planes, depriving the proportions of verisimilitude.

The impression of feigned naïveté emanating from the painting irritated critics at the Salon of 1859:

> Here, the *ébauche*, the sketch, has turned into *débauche*, debauchery. The figures have lost their limbs in the fight; they catch up to them and adjust them at random. Rebecca floats in her ravisher's arms like a dress snagged on the branches of a misshapen tree. The Knight Templar's slave stretches out a seven-league leg. The horse he is holding belongs to the bestiary of heraldic art. An oppressive light, as we might imagine the light of dead planets deprived of atmosphere, exacerbates the sadness of that gloomy scene.[38]

The half-light is offset by the gleam of the many metallic and embroidered accessories strewn about the painting, an effect achieved by thin brushstrokes of white or pure yellow. It accentuates the preciosity of the paintings, but it seems inappropriate to the dramatic tension required by the subject.

The composition *Amadis de Gaule Delivers a Damsel from Galpan's Castle* (cat. 143) has an even more naive set design. Painted the following year, it was inspired by *Amadis de Gaule*, a chivalric romance set down in writing in the early sixteenth century. Renouncing the foil figures still used in the second version of *The Abduction of Rebecca*, Delacroix placed only war trophies in the foreground. The two principal figures are shown in profile on a single plane parallel to the picture plane. In the background is a frieze of combatants in front of the fortified walls, seen in cavalier perspective. The saturated colors (golden yellow, royal blue, white, vermilion), the shallowness of the scene, and the codification of gestures accentuate the similarity to so-called primitive forms of European art. Delacroix seems to have updated scenes of a city's surrender, found in abundance in the French illuminated manuscripts of the fifteenth century, or to have reproduced the simplicity of *Jesus Handing the Keys to Saint Peter*, as Pietro Perugino formulated it for the Sistine Chapel in Rome during the same era.

A similar dispersal is evident in *Ovid among the Scythians* (see cat. 142). This was the only composition at the Salon of 1859 to be appreciated by reviewers, who thought they saw the mark of the master in it. Mantz hailed it as "one of the most beautiful, one of the most poetic landscapes ever transfigured by his dream." But he went on to note a number of inconsistencies, which ultimately led him to modify his first favorable impression and to see the work as a painful failure:

> This landscape would produce an even greater effect if the figures the artist placed in the foreground were better subordinated one to another, in observance of a more systematic hierarchy. Ovid, the protagonist of the drama from a moral perspective, is too small, too understated in the painting; accessory characters, even animals, absorb the beholder's initial attention and greatly attenuate the exiled poet's importance. Here, and this is a serious flaw, the episode masks the poem.[39]

Most shocking was the disproportionate size of the mare: "A gigantic beast that clutters up the foreground, the mare of the Trojan Horse, you might say," exclaimed Saint-Victor. He attempted to find a moral justification, however: "Perhaps the painter, by that structural exaggeration, wanted to depict the barbarian horse, the animal created by the primal forest and endowed by it with the necessary vitality to plow through the mud and wade powerfully through the swamps."[40]

Delacroix wished to inscribe his figures in an expansive setting, one that enveloped and interacted with them, at the risk of disturbing the fragile narrative equilibrium and the classic subordination of setting to actors. But the painter never went so far as pure landscape painting. Might Delacroix, ever on the alert for developments in the art of his time, have been torn, both captivated by the dominance of landscape painting but also unwilling to follow the artists of the Barbizon school, who had abandoned the traditional primacy of history painting?

Should that impression of instability be construed as a flaw? Does it reveal a hesitation, a resistance, even an incapacity to be of his own time?

The Vigor and Diversity of Landscape Painting in the 1850s

Delacroix, who for several years had been a member of the Salon jury, could not have failed to notice the vigor landscape painting had achieved since the late 1840s. The genre now exemplified the vitality of French painting. The Salon of 1859 had confirmed the shift. Jules Castagnary, a fervent supporter of Courbet and Jean-François Millet, was delighted by the "new revolution":

> Then the works of T. Rousseau, Corot, Daubigny, Troyon, and Millet came into being: works of force, melancholy, grace, or gloomy grandeur, which have made landscape painting the most important branch of the art of our time. And that is why the roles are now reversed: what was once minuscule is now in the forefront, what was at the pinnacle barely exists anymore, except in name. What have become of religious paintings and history paintings? What have become of architecture and the epic? They are dead, but they do not want to admit it. . . . The future lies with canvases of small dimensions, those that express the human and, as it were, the earthly side of life.[41]

The landscape genre was all the more vigorous for having undergone a profound reformation: the tradition of the composite historical landscape (*paysage composé*) had gradually died out (the Prix de Rome for historical landscape painting would be eliminated in 1863). Rousseau, Jules Dupré, Courbet, and Charles-François Daubigny, abandoning the harmonic compositions of Nicolas Poussin in favor of the animistic force of seventeenth-century Dutch landscape painting (that of Jacob van Ruisdael and Meindert Hobbema), gave prestige to the trees, springs, and rocks of what were reputed to be the intact territories of rural France. Vernacular modern landscape painting was obstinately rejected by the jury of the Salon, which under the July Monarchy was in the hands of the Institut. Nevertheless, it met with growing commercial success among dealers, art lovers, and collectors

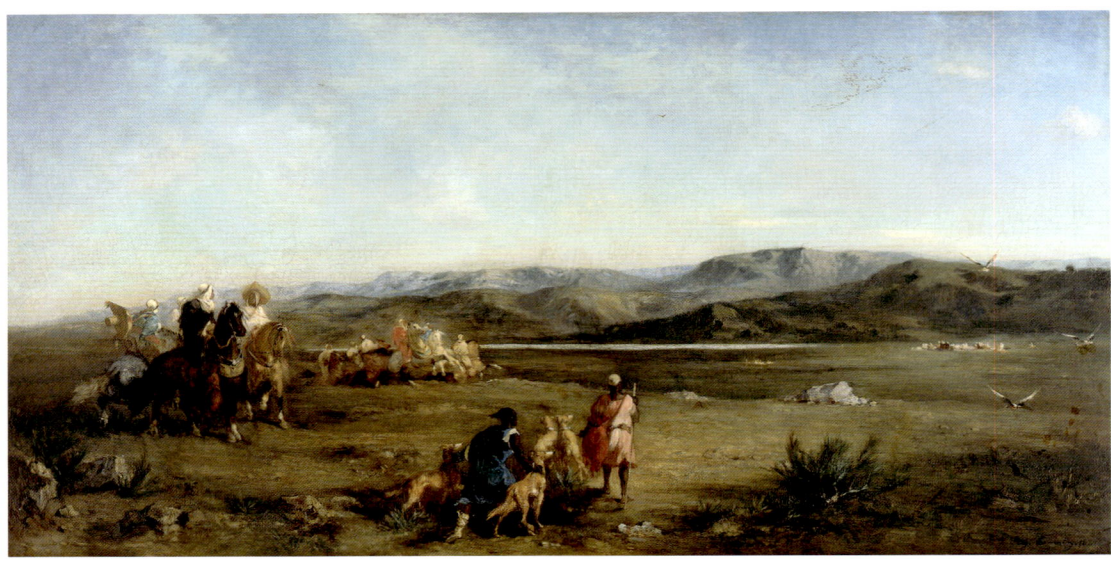

FIG. 71 Eugène Fromentin (French, 1820–1876), *Gazelle Hunt in the Hodna, Algeria*, 1856. Oil on canvas, 38⁹⁄₁₆ x 77³⁄₁₆ in. (98 x 196 cm). Musée d'Arts, Nantes (inv. 978)

throughout the 1840s, before finally receiving official honors after the 1848 Revolution. Delacroix closely followed that ascent. Through his friendship with Paul Huet, he was regularly in contact with the painters of the Barbizon school. He displayed a great admiration for the works of Théodore Rousseau, which he often recommended.⁴² He did not go so far as to support Rousseau and Dupré in their attempt to create an exhibition in 1847 that would have rivaled the Salon.⁴³ In 1850, however, when Rousseau took the risk of organizing a public sale of about fifty works, including studies, Delacroix twice went to see them on display at Galerie Durand-Ruel and admitted that he was "charmed by a number of extremely original pieces."⁴⁴ An advocate of retaining the presence of human figures in landscape paintings and of the primacy of the imagination, he followed with interest the art of Diaz, who was then reviving the genre of the fête galante. It is not impossible that he was also stimulated by the efforts of Courbet in the same genre. His *Young Ladies of the Village* (Metropolitan Museum), on view at the Salon of 1852 and later at the home of the duc de Morny, displays interesting similarities to *Ovid among the Scythians*, both in its composition and in its odd proportions.

The vitality of French landscape painting not only was evident in the representation of vernacular territories but also found expression in depictions of the French colonies of North Africa. In that regard, the name on everyone's lips in the late 1850s was Eugène Fromentin. Delacroix must have been moved by a young painter who had distinguished himself during three long stays in Algeria (1846, 1847–48, and 1852–53) and by his remarkable talent for description

in his travel narratives, *A Summer in the Sahara* (1854) and *A Year in the Sahel* (1859). Delacroix, encouraged by George Sand, read both books with interest.⁴⁵ Fromentin, awarded a second-prize medal in the landscape genre in 1849, came to the public's attention at the Salon of 1857 (fig. 71) and triumphed at the Salon of 1859.⁴⁶ From the start, some critics, foremost among them Baudelaire, established a connection between Fromentin and Delacroix: "Of the young celebrities, one of the most solidly established is M. Fromentin. . . . His painting in the strict sense, wise, powerful, and disciplined, obviously has its source in Eugène Delacroix, who also exhibits that artful and natural understanding of color." But might not Delacroix have been beholden to the younger painter's art as well? Although the heroic and classical interpretation of Maghrebian manners is indisputably a legacy of Delacroix, it is not unreasonable to think that he was in turn encouraged by the expansiveness of Fromentin's vast landscapes, which glorify the prairies and boundless skies of the Atlas Mountains. Baudelaire thought so when he contemplated Delacroix's *Ovid among the Scythians* (see cat. 142): "I am convinced that this painting has a quite particular charm for delicate souls. I would almost swear that, more than other paintings, it has pleased nervous and poetic temperaments—that of M. Fromentin, for example."⁴⁷ Zacharie Astruc, gazing at Fromentin's *Souvenir of Algeria*, exhibited at the Salon of 1859, imagined that "Delacroix must have applauded these proud horses in such a bold color."⁴⁸

The dynamic surrounding landscape painting at the time was thus echoed in Delacroix's practice, but it is difficult to

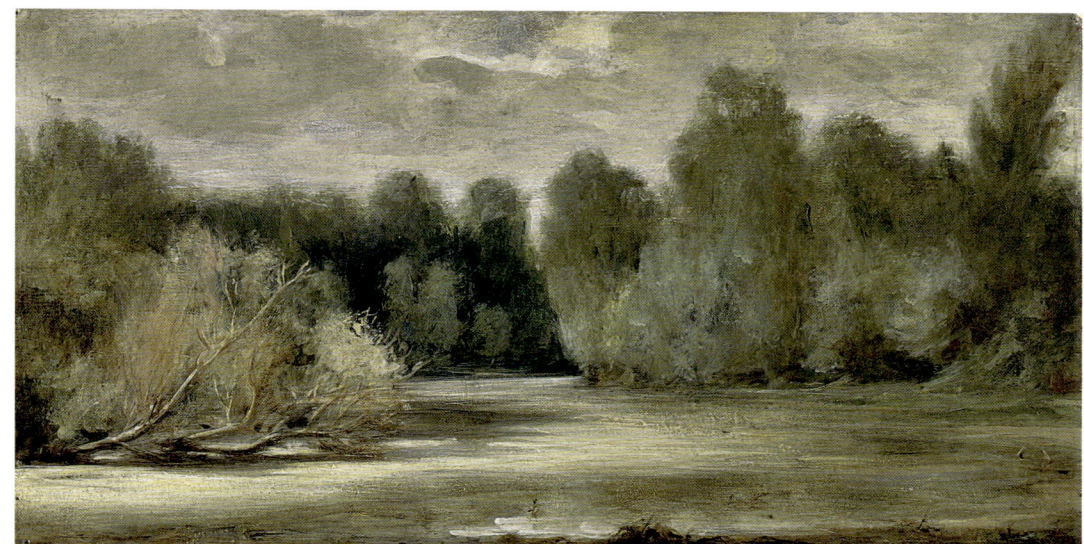

FIG. 72 *The Pond at Le Louroux,* ca. 1822–28. Oil on canvas, 11 x 21¼ in. (28 x 54 cm). Musée du Louvre, Paris, on deposit at the Musée National Eugène-Delacroix, Paris (MNR 232) (J L191)

judge the artist's position in the debate. In 1854 he wrote the words "On landscape" in his *Journal,* probably in view of an essay or an entry in his future *Dictionary of the Fine Arts,* though no entry was ever composed.[49] He returned to it four months later, in a notably brief definition: "On landscape, *as accompaniment to the subjects.*"[50] He took note of "the contempt of moderns for that interesting element," before quickly mentioning the more or less accomplished talent of Rubens, Titian, Rembrandt, and Watteau, in order to establish a connection between their figures and the landscapes in which they are inscribed. Delacroix took no more trouble formulating, in the introspective and serene context of the *Journal,* his personal definition of landscape painting. Was it for lack of interest, since his practice of landscape painting corresponded to the traditional habit of "accompanying" historical subjects? Or did it stem from his difficulty in knowing how to formulate a complex and shifting relationship with that genre of painting?

Landscape Studies: A Consistent Preliminary Exercise

Delacroix consistently and regularly practiced landscape painting. The activity seems to have corresponded to two widespread objectives among history painters of his time. Above all, it was a kind of training, yielding personal exercises not intended for exhibition but that might serve as a support (without ever being quoted literally) for the backgrounds of his historical compositions.

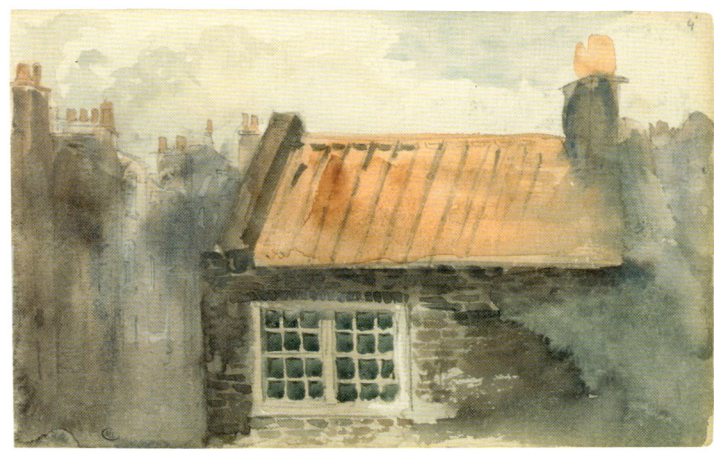

FIG. 73 *House with a Red Roof,* "English Sketchbook," folio 4 recto, 1825. Watercolor over graphite on paper, overall 5⅝ x 18½ in. (14.3 x 47 cm). Musée du Louvre, Paris (RF 9143)

When he visited his brother in Touraine in the 1820s, he rendered in oil, with great subtlety, the monochrome grays of the pond in Le Louroux under an overcast sky (fig. 72). While staying in England in the summer of 1825 and enjoying jaunts on the River Thames, he perfected his use of watercolor by painting the vast hilly perspectives of the English countryside. He also tried his hand—and this was far more unusual—at a few fragments of urban views, captured in watercolor or wash drawings from a window: a modest brick facade stands out against the forest of London chimneys (fig. 73); the towers of Saint-Sulpice jut out from the Faubourg Saint-Germain, observed from the garret occupied by his friend Thales Fielding.

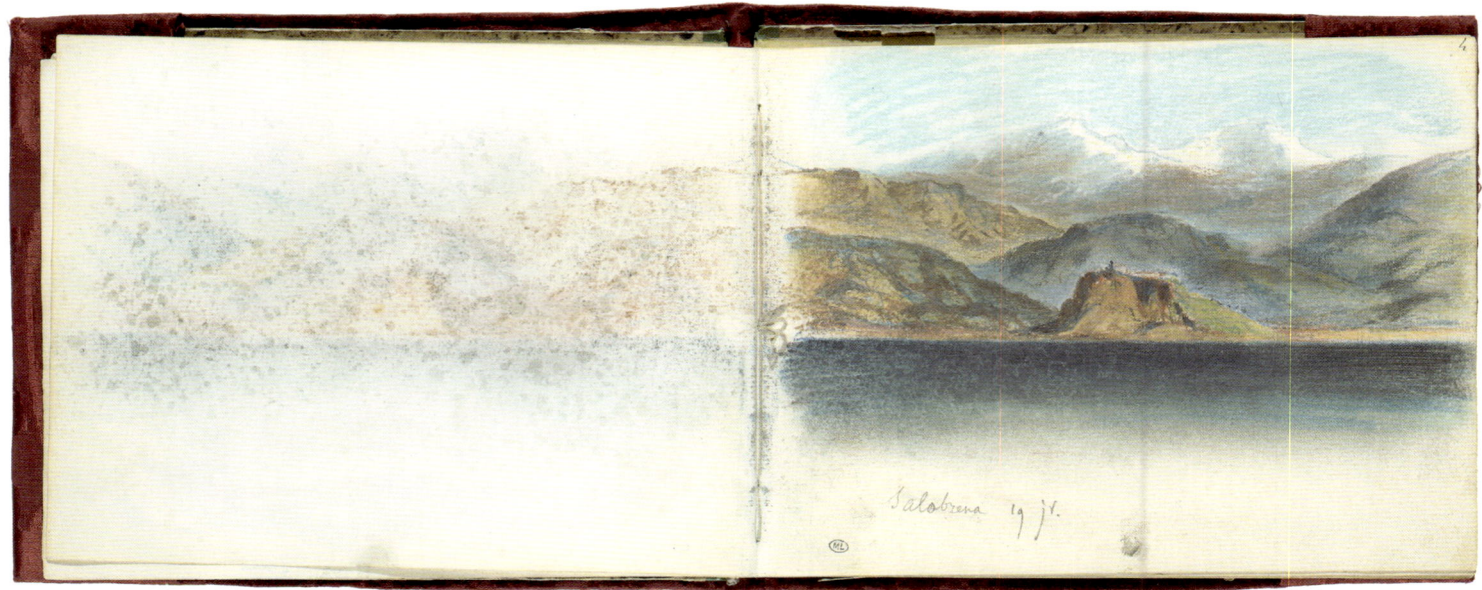

FIG. 74 *The Coast of Spain at Salobreña, January 19, 1832,* "North African and Spanish Sketchbook," folio 4 recto, 1832. Pastel on paper, overall 6¼ x 16¹¹⁄₁₆ in. (15.8 x 42.4 cm). Musée du Louvre, Paris (RF 9154) (Johnson 1995, no. 21)

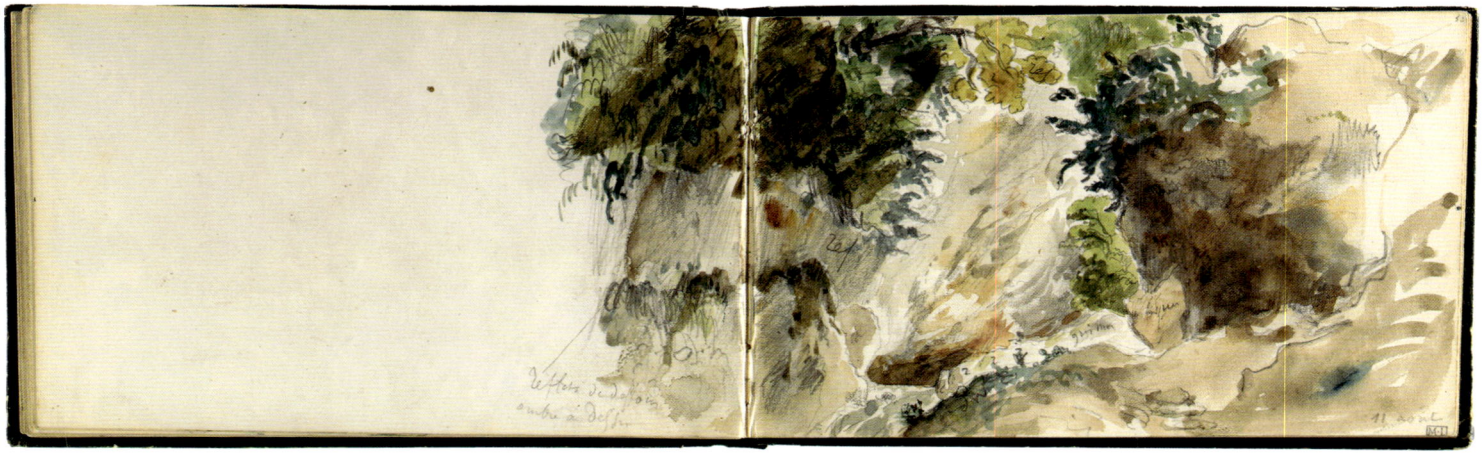

FIG. 75 *Torrent on the River Valentin, August 11, 1845,* "Pyrénées Sketchbook," folios 32 verso and 33 recto, 1845. Watercolor over graphite on paper, overall 4⁹⁄₁₆ x 15⁵⁄₁₆ in. (11.6 x 39.5 cm). Musée du Louvre, Paris (RF 52997)

The trip to Morocco was an opportunity to fill many notebooks with studies. For the first time, Delacroix saw mountain landscapes rushing down to the sea. Observing the Andalusian coast off Salobreña (fig. 74), he depicted the terraced mountains separated by veils of blue mist, from the promontory with the city clinging to it to the snow-covered peaks of the Sierra Nevada. More than the Alps, which he would never cross, it was the Pyrénées that acquainted

Delacroix with high mountains, owing to a stay at the spa village of Eaux-Bonnes in 1845. The Pyrénées notebook (fig. 75) is fascinating not only for its vast conventional panoramas but also for its depictions of torrents. The artist attempted to get as close to them as possible, in order to record their violence. The water, constricted by rocks and caressed by the wild grasses caught on them, slips out the narrow window of the notebook sheet and invades the

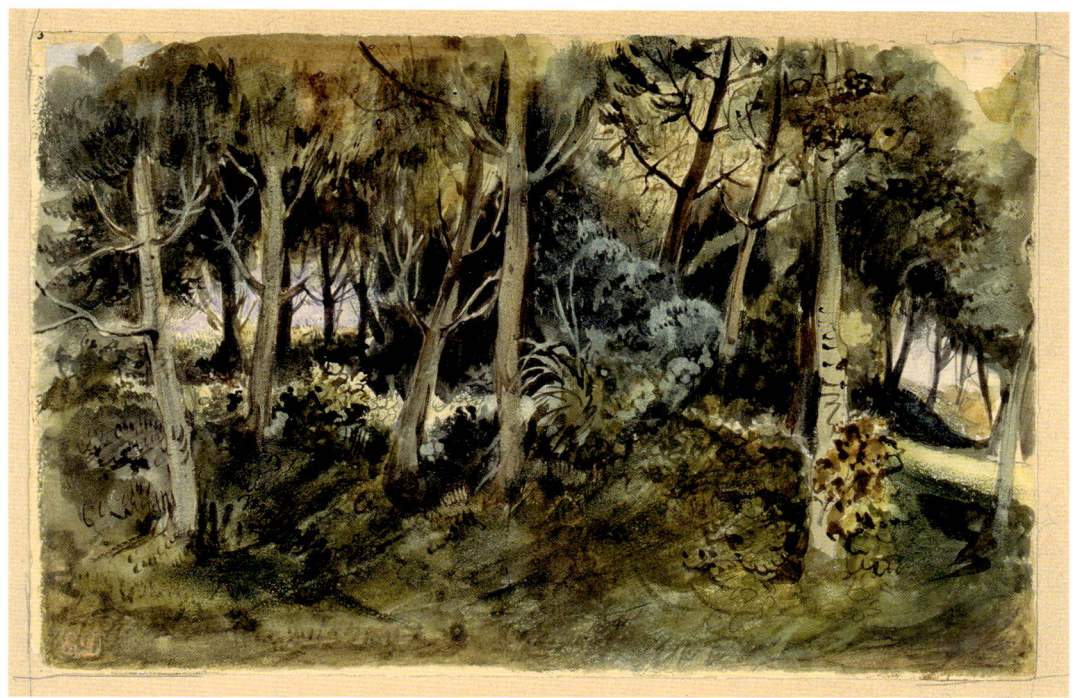

FIG. 76 *Interior of a Wood*, ca. 1842–46. Watercolor and gouache on paper, 6¹¹⁄₁₆ x 10⁷⁄₁₆ in. (17 x 26.5 cm). Maison de George Sand, Nohant-Vic, Centre des Monuments Nationaux (inv. NOH2009003907)

neighboring page. The frame is so tight and the forcefulness of the elements so centrifugal that it is not clear at first which is the top of the drawing and which the bottom.

Visits to George Sand's home in Berry were an occasion to study the foliage on the grounds of Nohant and the tangle of the surrounding woods (fig. 76). The challenge this time was to convey the soul of a clump of trees while striving to distinguish both the aspect of individual trees and the succession of receding planes. Ink or a dark wash allowed him to cast into sharp relief the principal branches, either with bright colors set against a mass of dark foliage or in silhouette, backlit by a portion of sky or a sudden shaft of light in a clearing.

His study of the landscape intensified from the late 1840s on. Studies done in oil and pastel were more numerous and more polished, and three themes recurred persistently: the contrasts in the sky at sunset, the interplay of clouds and waves on the sea, and the abundance and transparency of forest foliage.

Beginning in the summer of 1844, the artist made visits to a small country house he had rented in Champrosay, which he ultimately purchased and occupied regularly beginning in 1858. That new home base allowed him to take long walks in the surrounding area, which had "the advantage of being located between the meandering course of the Seine" and the forest

of Sénart), a "sumptuous and ancestral" massif, "as rich at the time in oak trees and rare essential oils as the vicinity of Fontainebleau and Barbizon" (cat. 116).[51] There Delacroix could contemplate at leisure the changes of the colors over the course of a day. He could set down his memories immediately on returning to his little country studio, either as drawings and paintings or in written form, trying to render visible phenomena in pictorial terms. Late afternoon and sunset greatly interested the painter, because the simultaneous contrasts of colors, especially the tension between orange and blue, reached their greatest intensity at that time of day. In autumn 1850 he noted,

> On that walk, we [he and his housekeeper, Jenny] observed some extraordinary effects. It was sunset. The chrome and lake tones were most brilliant on the side where it was light and the shadows were extraordinarily blue and cold. And in the same way, the shadows cast by the trees, which were all yellow, terre d'Italie, and reddish brown, and directly lit by the sun's rays, stood out against part of the gray clouds, which were verging on blue. . . . What made this effect appear so vivid in the landscape was precisely this law of contrast. I noticed the same phenomenon at sunset yesterday, November 3; it is more brilliant and striking than at

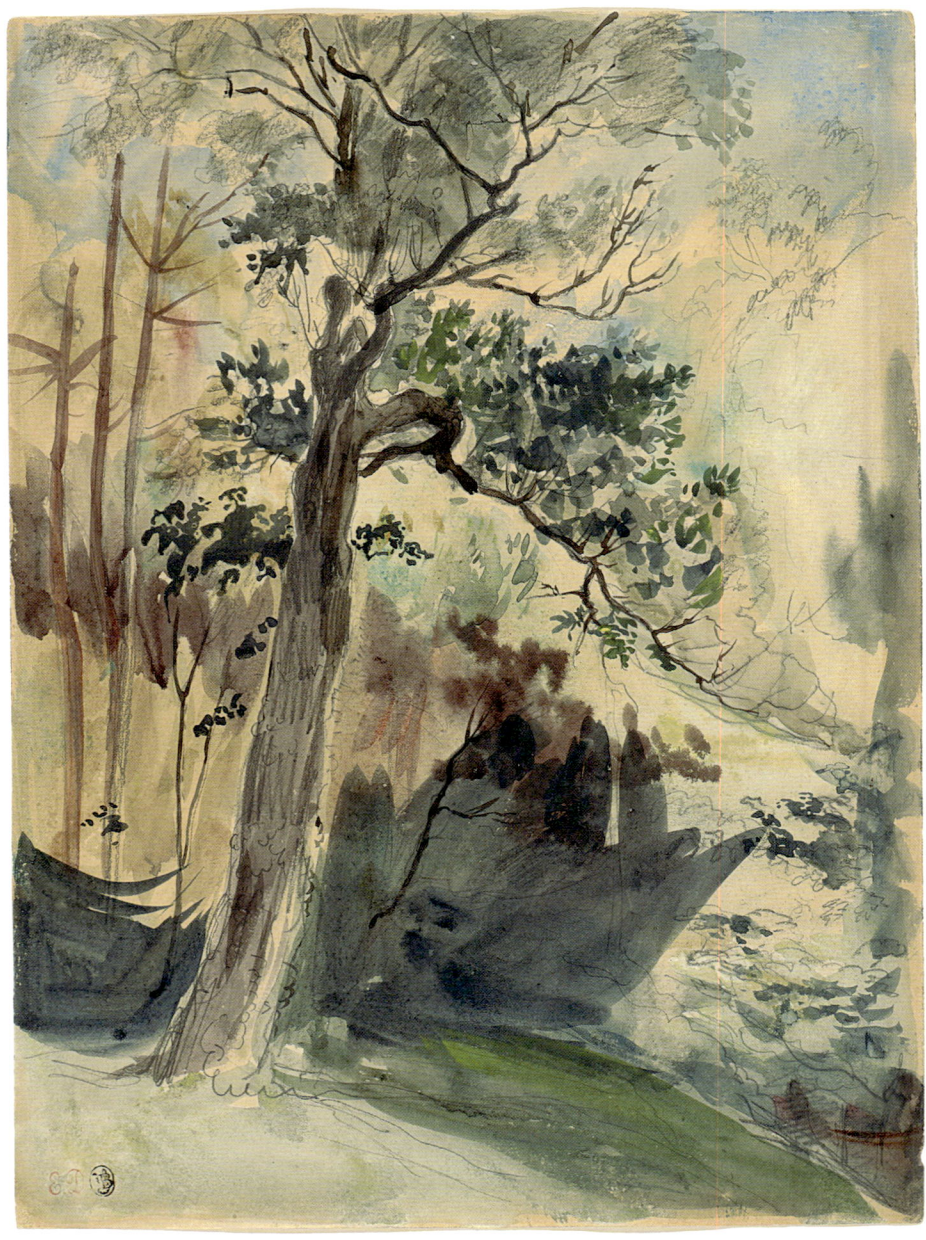

CAT. 116 *Forest View with an Oak Tree*, ca. 1849–50

midday only because the contrasts are sharper. The gray of the clouds in the evening verges on blue; the clear parts of the sky are bright yellow or orange. The general rule is: the greater the contrast, the more brilliant the effect.[52]

In his afternoon landscape study (cat. 113), Delacroix placed the horizon in the upper quarter of the composition in order to display, with the richness of a tapestry, the colored contrasts of the bocage: the warm colors of the fields accented by the

dwindling light alternate with the dark green of the hedges, the dense clumps of fruit trees in the foreground, and the shadows cast by tall poplars. He would explore the landscape at Champrosay with even greater freedom of brushwork in a somewhat later sketch now in a private collection (cat. 137).

Studies of the sky at twilight required working in full color and quickly, so as not to miss any part of the ephemeral spectacle and to replicate the contrasts and the strong luminosity of the sunset, even while correcting for the growing dusk. That no doubt explains the use of pastel in place of watercolor.

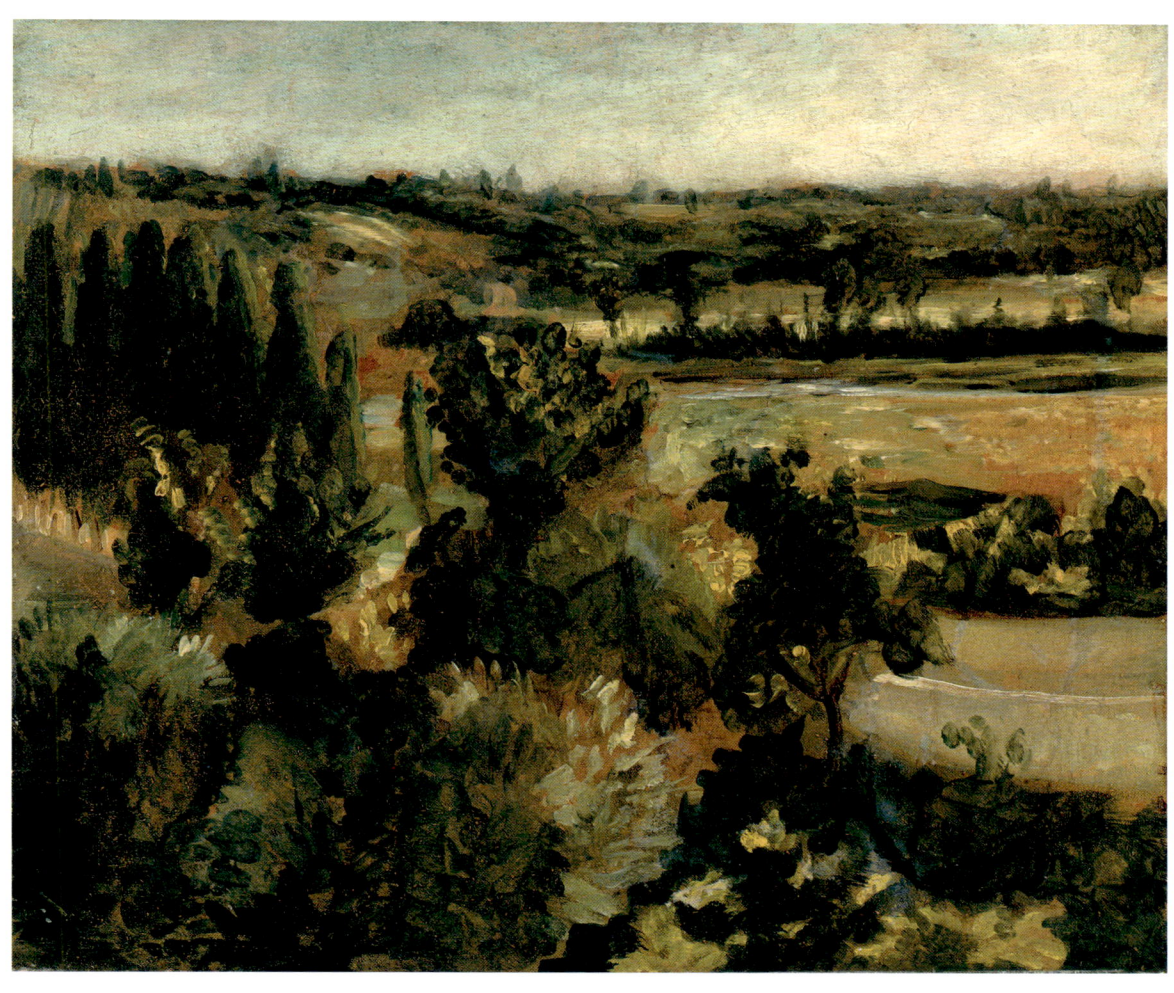

CAT. 113 *Landscape at Champrosay,* possibly 1849

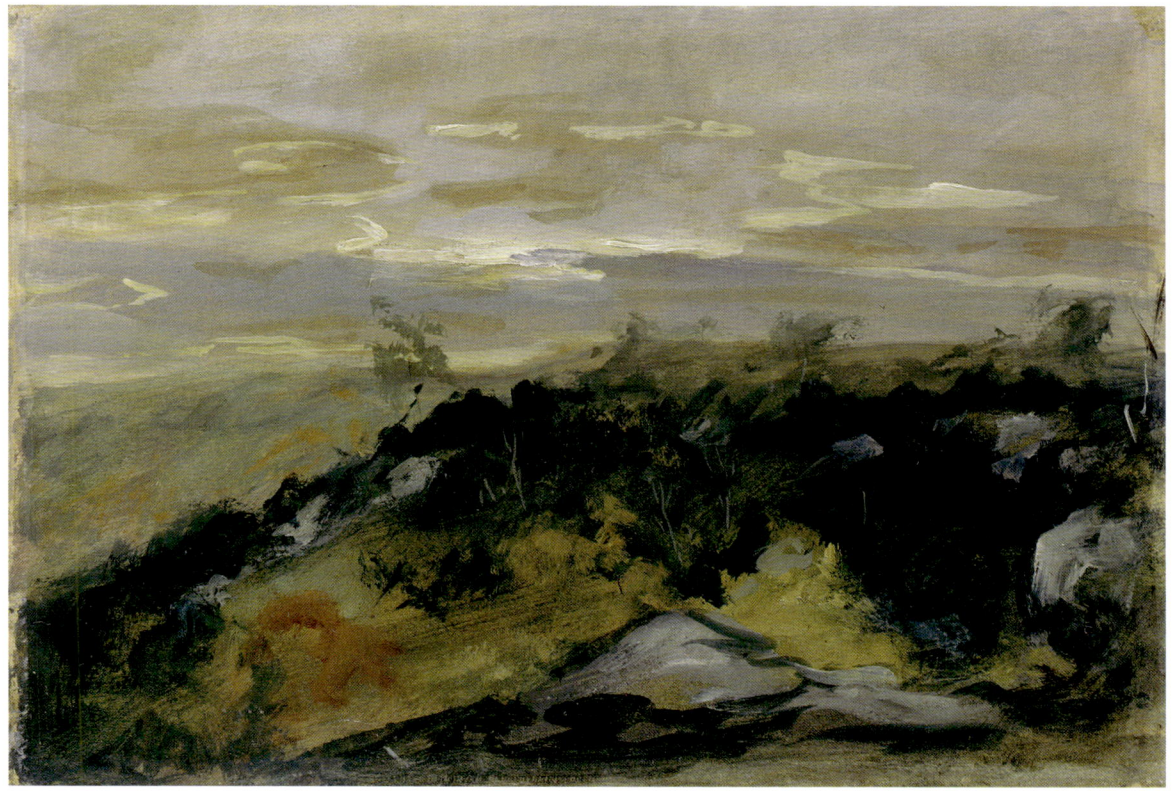

CAT. 137 *Hilly Landscape,* ca. 1855

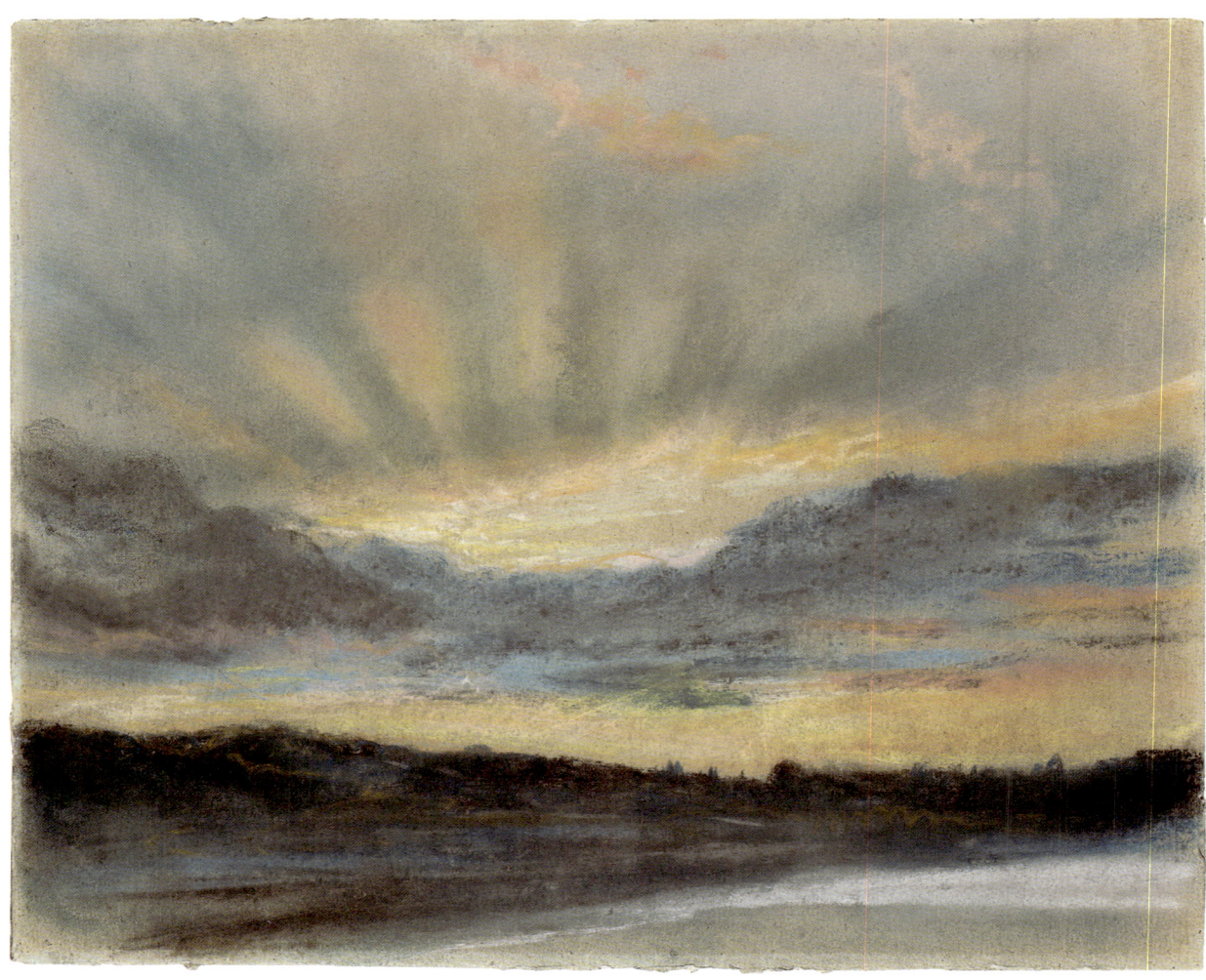

CAT. 121 *Sunset*, ca. 1850

Two sky studies in pastel illustrate the variety of Delacroix's practice. One shows a distinct gradation of warm tones in a cloudless sky;[53] the sensation of depth disappears, evoked solely by the ground, which takes on intense blue shades. The other shows a sky rendered in high relief and in perspective, sculpted by vast clouds that make the earth look rather flat and gray.[54] Elsewhere, too, Delacroix sought a mandorla effect, with the rays of the declining sun tracing beams of light through the clouds (cat. 121).

The aim of this research, conducted in summer and autumn 1850, was to execute not a landscape painting in oil or even the background for a historical scene but rather the ceiling of the Gallery of Apollo: "The view of the landscape at the bridge and while climbing [is] charming because of the springtime greenery and the effect of the shadows made by the clouds passing over everything. When I got home, I did a kind of pastel drawing of the effect of sunlight with an eye to my ceiling."[55] The abstract nature of the ceiling, the subject of which was Apollo Slays the Python, did not prevent Delacroix from feeling the need to turn to natural phenomena for the structure and tones best suited to represent the god of the sun and of civilization. If the ceiling (see fig. 53) is examined without regard for the human figures, it becomes clear that the composition is entirely structured by a landscape. A slash mark made of black clouds divides the image in two: the lower part is of water and stone, the upper half illuminated by the Apollonian sun, the golden rays of which gradually dissipate into blue. A month after rendering in pastel the effects of the sun in Champrosay, the painter, having returned to Paris, pulled everything together: "I have been pleased with my ceiling composition . . . only since yesterday, after making the alterations to the sky with pastel."[56]

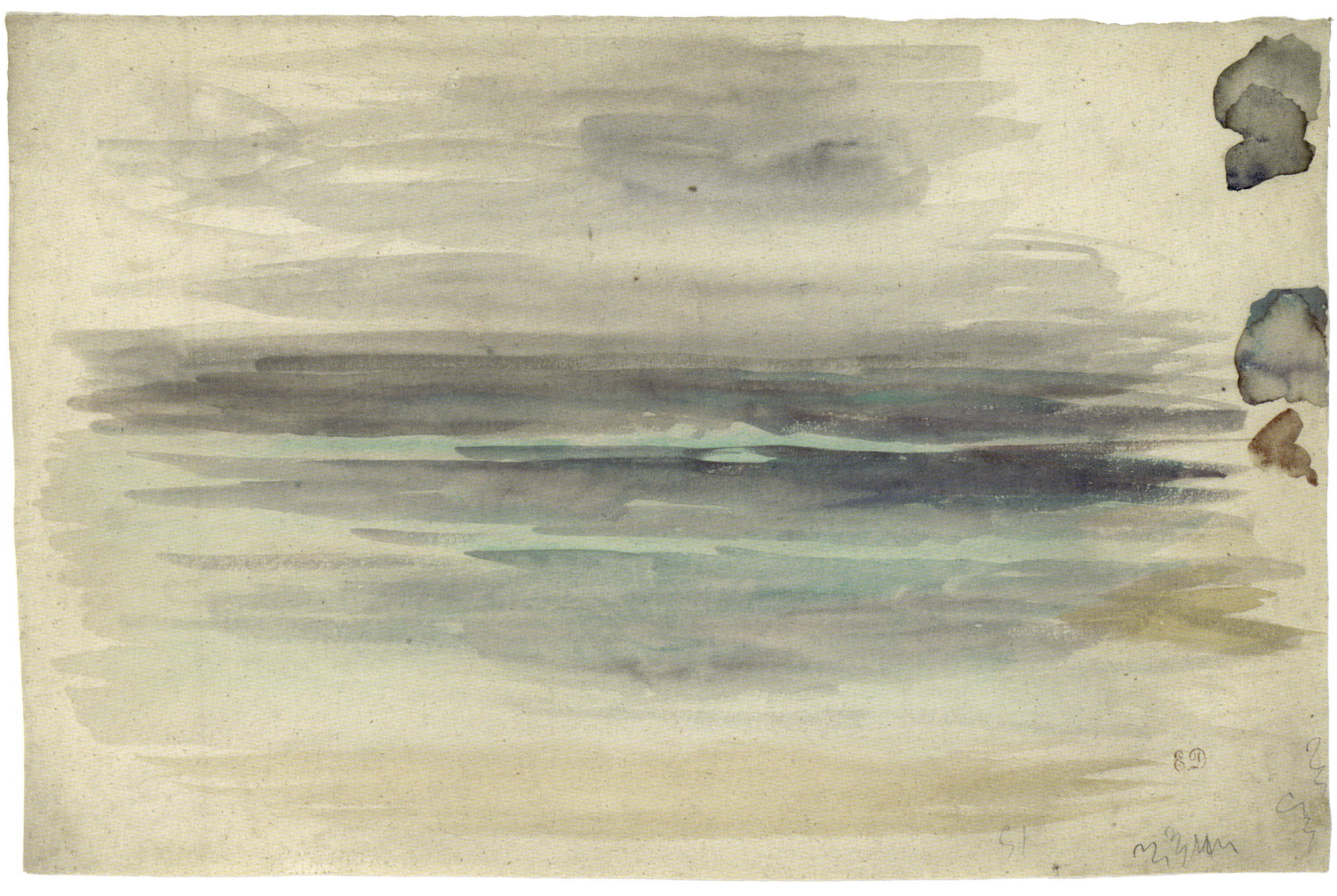

CAT. 126 *Study of the Sea*, 1851(?)

The Sea, Antechamber to the Underworld

Seascapes were another motif that occupied Delacroix in the 1840s and 1850s (cat. 126). He had returned to the home of his cousin Bataille at Valmont Abbey, near Fécamp, in September 1838, then again in 1840, before visiting Trouville in September 1841, where he regularly swam in the sea. After another stay in Valmont in October 1849, at which time he made an excursion to Etretat, he arranged to stay in Dieppe during his subsequent summer visits. Between 1851 and 1860 he stayed at a hotel that looked out on the quai Duquesne, allowing him to see the activities of the port in all kinds of weather. Walking along the jetty, on the beach, and to the foot of the cliffs, the painter did many studies, in written form and as drawings. A typical example is a notation in his *Journal*,

dated August 25, 1854, regarding the effect of the morning sun on the sea in Dieppe:

> On my walk this morning, I spent a long time studying the sea. The sun was behind me, and thus the face of the waves as they rose up in front of me was yellow, and the side turned toward the bottom reflected the sky. Cloud shadows passing over all this produced charming effects: at the bottom, where the sea was blue and green, the shadows appeared violet; a violet and golden tone extended over the nearer part as well when shadow covered it. The waves were like agate. In these shaded parts, you get the same relationship between the yellow waves, facing the sun side, and the blue and metallic patches reflecting the sky.[57]

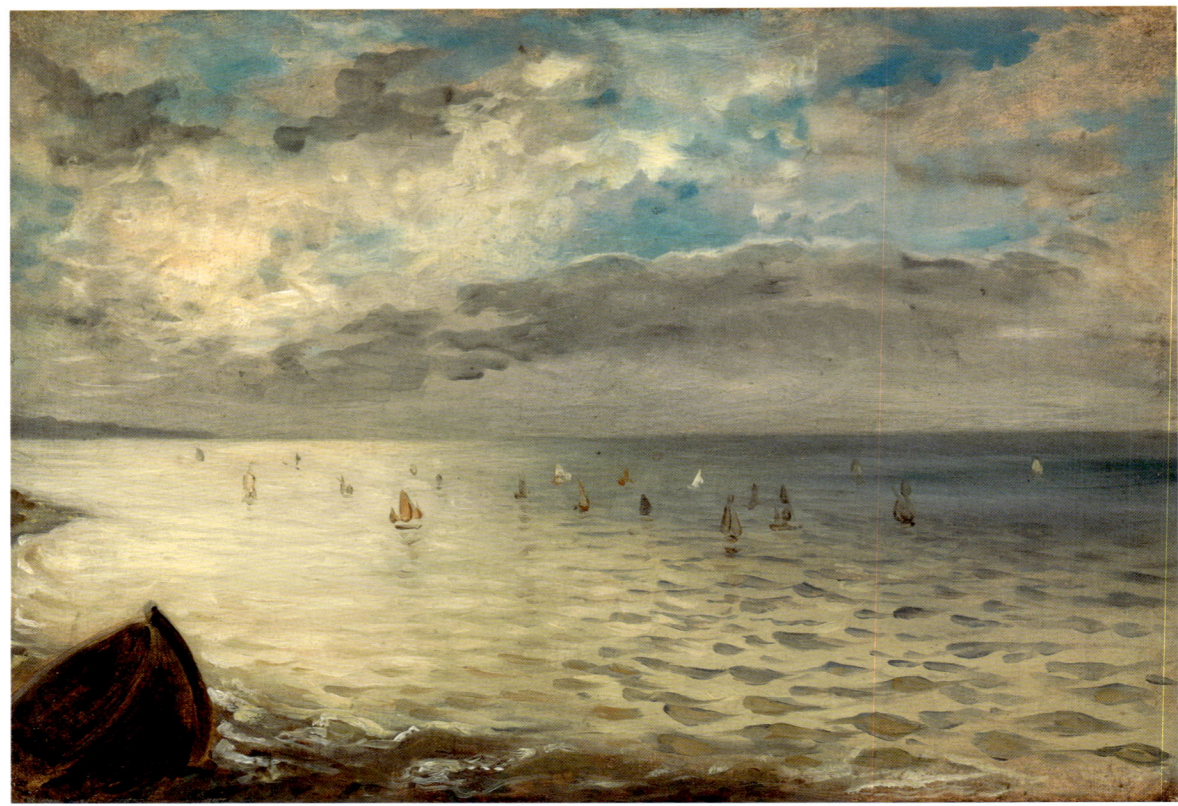

CAT. 128 *The Sea at Dieppe*, 1852

The precision of these observations can be linked to an oil study of the sea in Dieppe. Brilliant in its concision and accuracy, the work was found in the studio after the artist's death (cat. 128). It is painted on cardboard, probably of the same type offered ready-made to traveling painters by the art supply trade (especially in Britain). This view may have reproduced an impression he had of the sea in the late afternoon, perhaps in Dieppe in mid-September 1852: "At about three o'clock, I went down to take my last look at the sea. It was perfectly calm, and I have seldom seen it more lovely. . . . The sketch I made from memory was of this sea: golden sky, boats waiting to return with the tide."[58] As in the notation of August 1854, the attention is drawn to the modulation of the sea: blue and green in the shadow of the clouds on the right, dazzling directly below the sun on the left, and gray in the foreground. The waves are carved into facets simply through a juxtaposition of greenish-gray brushstrokes (to which a greater or lesser quantity of ocher had been added), applied on a smooth ground of pale gray. A few pointed brush marks symbolizing the boats indicate the scale and depth.

The artistic challenge of representing waves is the primary subject of the brilliant watercolor in the Albertina (fig. 77), which also passed through the studio sale. Delacroix sculpted in three dimensions the first four rows of waves, depicted as gray crests, the intensity of which increases as they rise. They are separated by light-colored furrows where the white paper is left visible, merely punctuated by small strokes of sky blue. The artist, abandoning the artifice of heightening in white gouache, managed to make the metallic gleam of the waves perceptible simply by manipulating watercolor and the reserve of the paper. This is indicated by an annotation in graphite in the lower right-hand corner: "On the tips of the waves directly under the sun, luminous / specks in a very / circumscribed space." He made similar inscriptions on other such studies (cat. 132).

These studies must be linked to several paintings with a maritime setting that he produced from 1840 on, though it is not possible to determine which influenced the other: Were the compositions sparked by the studies done during visits to the coast? Or was the aim of these experiments to cultivate the preexisting desire to do historical compositions located on the water? The connection is difficult to establish because, between his studies and the final compositions, the painter introduced a radical change of register, the important work of

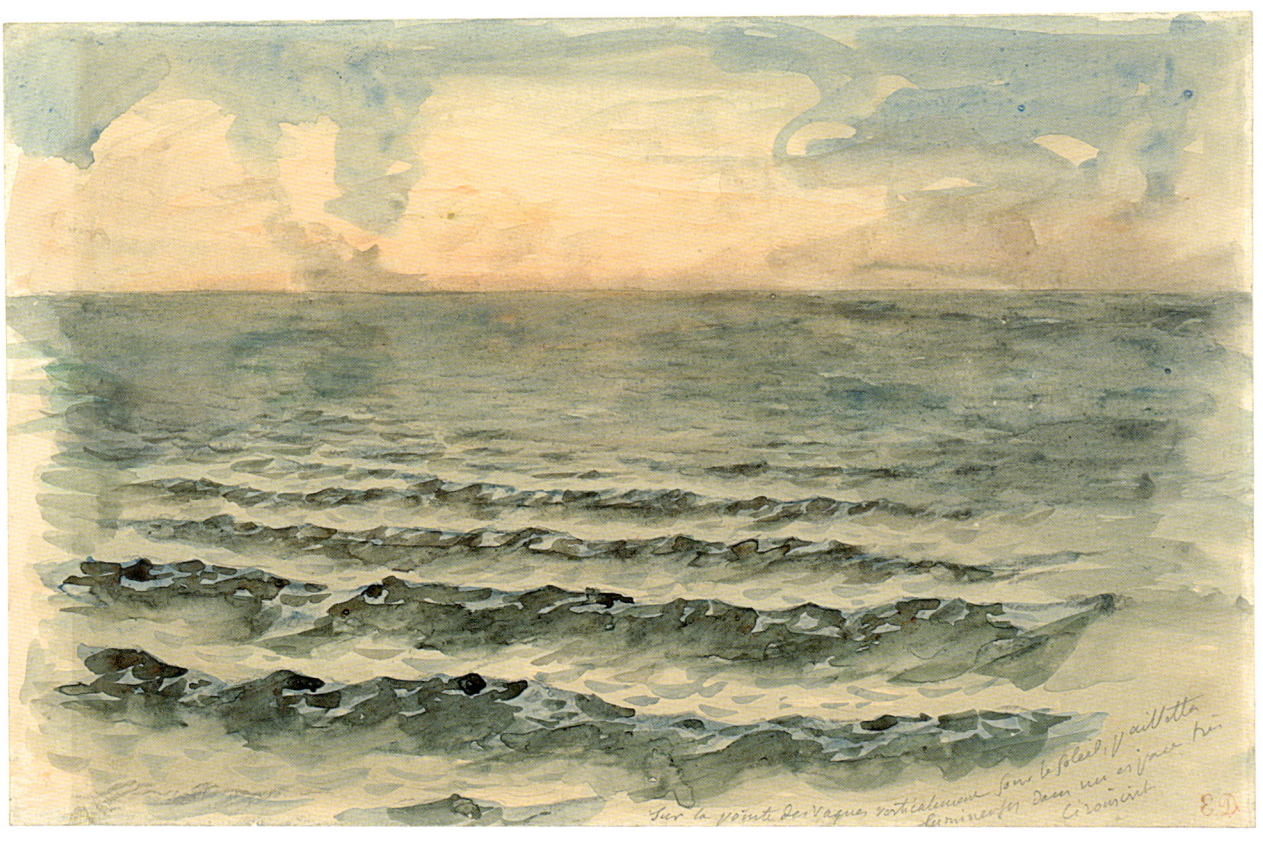

FIG. 77 *Sunset on the Sea, Dieppe,* ca. 1852–54. Watercolor over graphite on paper, 9 x 13⅞ in. (22.8 x 35.2 cm). The Albertina Museum, Vienna (inv. 24099)

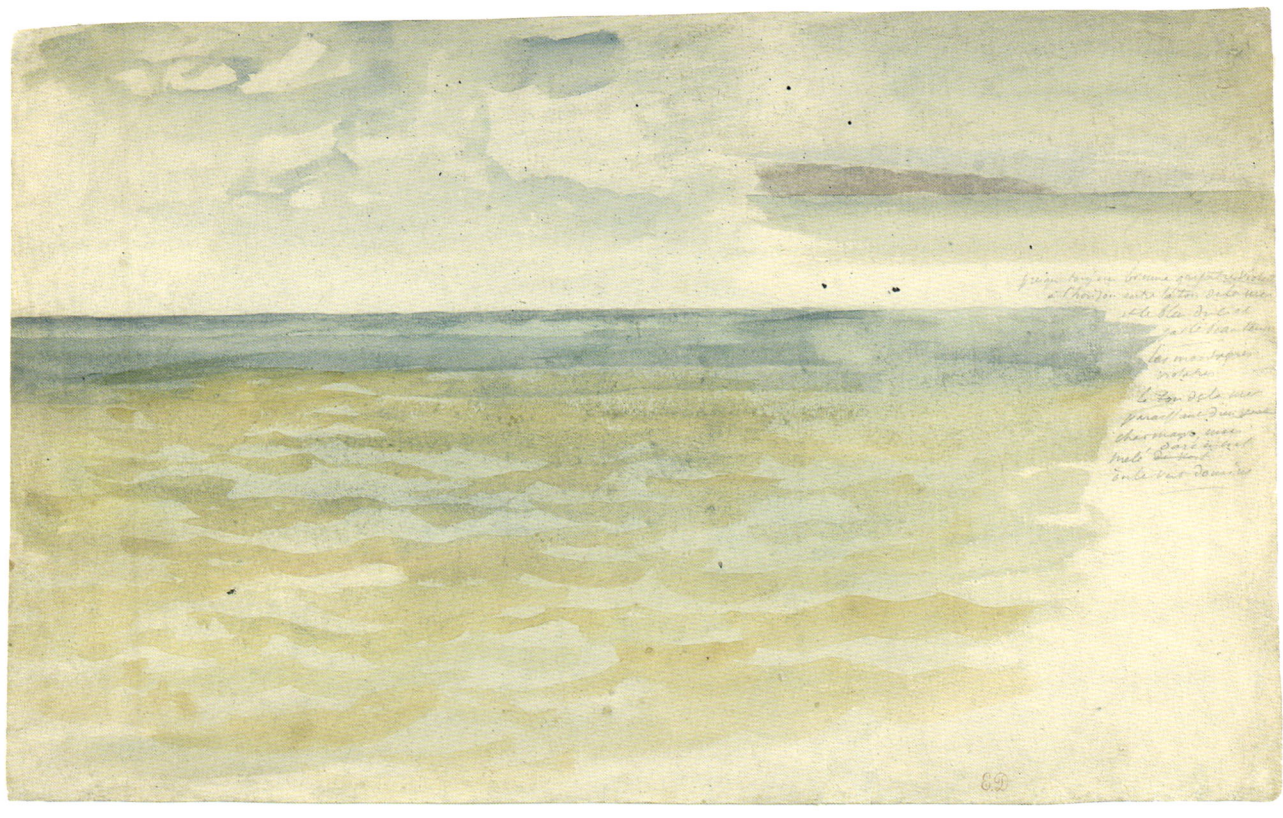

CAT. 132 *The Sea at Dieppe,* probably 1854

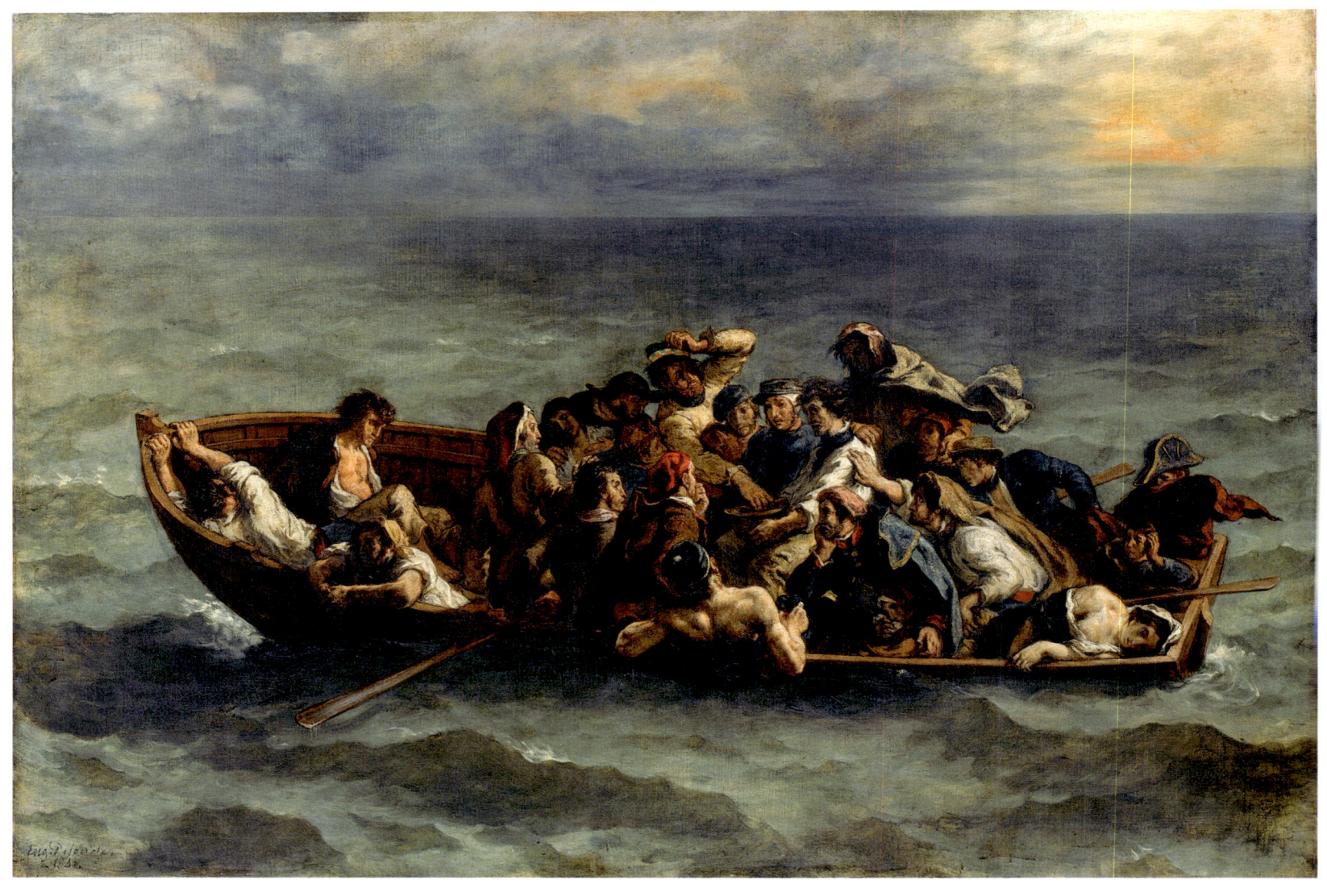

CAT. 98 *The Shipwreck of Don Juan*, 1840

the imagination. The studies were often done in clear and calm weather, whereas the painted compositions, on literary or religious subjects, are always full of pathos and sometimes tragedy:

> Sea, seascapes . . . Seascape painters do not generally represent the sea well. The same reproach can be made of them as of landscape painters. They want to display too much science: they do portraits of waves, just as landscape painters do portraits of trees, ground, mountains, etc. They do not concern themselves enough with the effect on the imagination, which too many details, even when they are correct, divert from the principal spectacle of immensity or depth, an idea that may be conveyed by a certain style.[59]

When the sea returns to Delacroix's paintings, therefore, it reanimates the infernal visions of his first success, *The Barque of Dante* (see fig. 2).

The first of Delacroix's seascape compositions is a tragedy unfolding in a compressed space, *The Shipwreck of Don Juan* (cat. 98). When Delacroix first exhibited it at the Salon of 1841 he made no mention of its literary source. The subject is taken from canto 2 of Lord Byron's poem *Don Juan*, first published in 1819, which well-informed critics recognized. Obliged to flee Spain after an adultery scandal, the seducer crosses the Mediterranean aboard a ship that founders after several storms. The crew drifts in a boat for more than a week under a scorching sun. Delacroix chose the moment when, having exhausted their food supply, including Don Juan's spaniel, the shipwrecked men and women make the decision to sacrifice one of their own by drawing lots, in the hope of surviving by eating him. Don Juan refuses; in the end he will be the only survivor, the others having hastened their deaths through cannibalism. The tragic situation of their collective damnation, cast into relief by the writer's black humor, provided a choice subject for Romantic sensibilities: it therefore found its way into the *Journal* in the spring of 1824. The recent death of Gericault, whose *Raft of the Medusa* had deeply affected Delacroix and had formed his artistic temperament, may have both liberated him and sparked a desire to test his mettle against the illustrious elder painter. While working on *Massacres at Chios*, Delacroix had noted in his *Journal* that he again had "the desire to do Lord Byron's Shipwrecked." It is important to pay attention to what follows, however: "but to do it at the seaside, at the scene."[60] What are we to conclude? Did the prod of literary inspiration prove insufficient for that particular subject? Was Delacroix afraid that he would not adequately master the depiction of his subject unless he came face-to-face with the sea? Did he wish to distinguish himself or improve on Gericault by giving a greater narrative and plastic aspect to the sea, which in Gericault occupies only a peripheral place? Are we to think that the artist postponed the execution of the oil on canvas for fifteen years because he was unable to spend long periods of time by the sea until the late 1830s?

The project did remain on hold for many years, as attested by early drawings, one of the earliest of which probably dates to the second half of the 1820s (fig. 78). Lee Johnson rightly noted its sharp lines and the profiles stylized to the point of caricature, which are comparable to those in the Faust series. There are also effects of high contrast similar to those in *The Murder of the Bishop of Liège* (see cat. 64).[61] Delacroix, fascinated by the fate of the shipwrecked crew, was at first concerned primarily with the infernal circle formed by them. The sea is suggested only laconically, and the study has not yet reached the level of development seen in the finished painting.

About 1840, then, at a time coinciding with his first prolonged visits along the English Channel, Delacroix seems finally to have tackled the painted composition. Of his stay in Valmont in September 1838, he wrote: "I have seen quite a bit of the landscape, a great deal of the sea, which I now know by heart."[62] He added that he was not working, but the success of *The Shipwreck of Don Juan* is difficult to explain without the intermediate studies done directly from nature or executed from memory a few minutes after the artist had observed maritime phenomena. It is not unreasonable to wonder

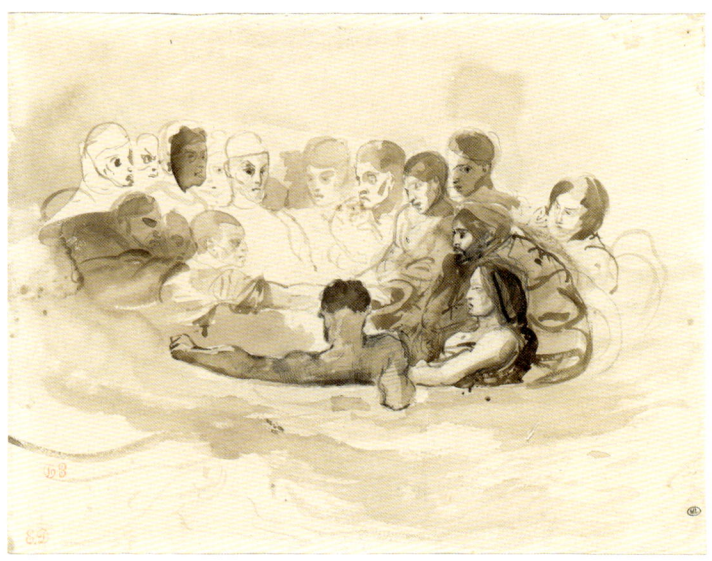

FIG. 78 *Study for Don Juan,* possibly ca. 1825–30. Brown ink and brown wash over pencil on paper, 9⅟₁₆ x 11¹³⁄₁₆ in. (23 x 30 cm). Musée du Louvre, Paris (RF 6743 recto)

whether the study of waves in the Albertina (fig. 77) is linked to this period, since it has many points in common with the completed painting: the parallel arrangement and firm drawing of the waves in the foreground; the placement of the horizon line in the upper two-thirds of the frame; and an orange glow suggesting the setting sun. The intentionally blurry and fluid treatment of the oil paint used for the sky and water conveys the desire to preserve the watercolor effect of the study on paper.

The time elapsed between the plan and its execution also led to changes in the conception of the subject, which strayed further from Byron's text. Gautier noted:

> if you reread the passage in Byron's poem from which the artist drew his subject for *The Shipwreck of Don Juan,* you may be surprised that he did not place his boat between a sea smooth as glass and a sky of a pitiless blue, which increase the horror of the scene by the irony of the contrast. But the resources of poetry are not the same as those of painting: a blue sky and a calm sea might not have given as good an idea of the danger faced as these heavy, churning waves under clouds of a sinister lividity.[63]

That artistic license also applied to the protagonists. Delacroix reduced the number of shipwrecked individuals

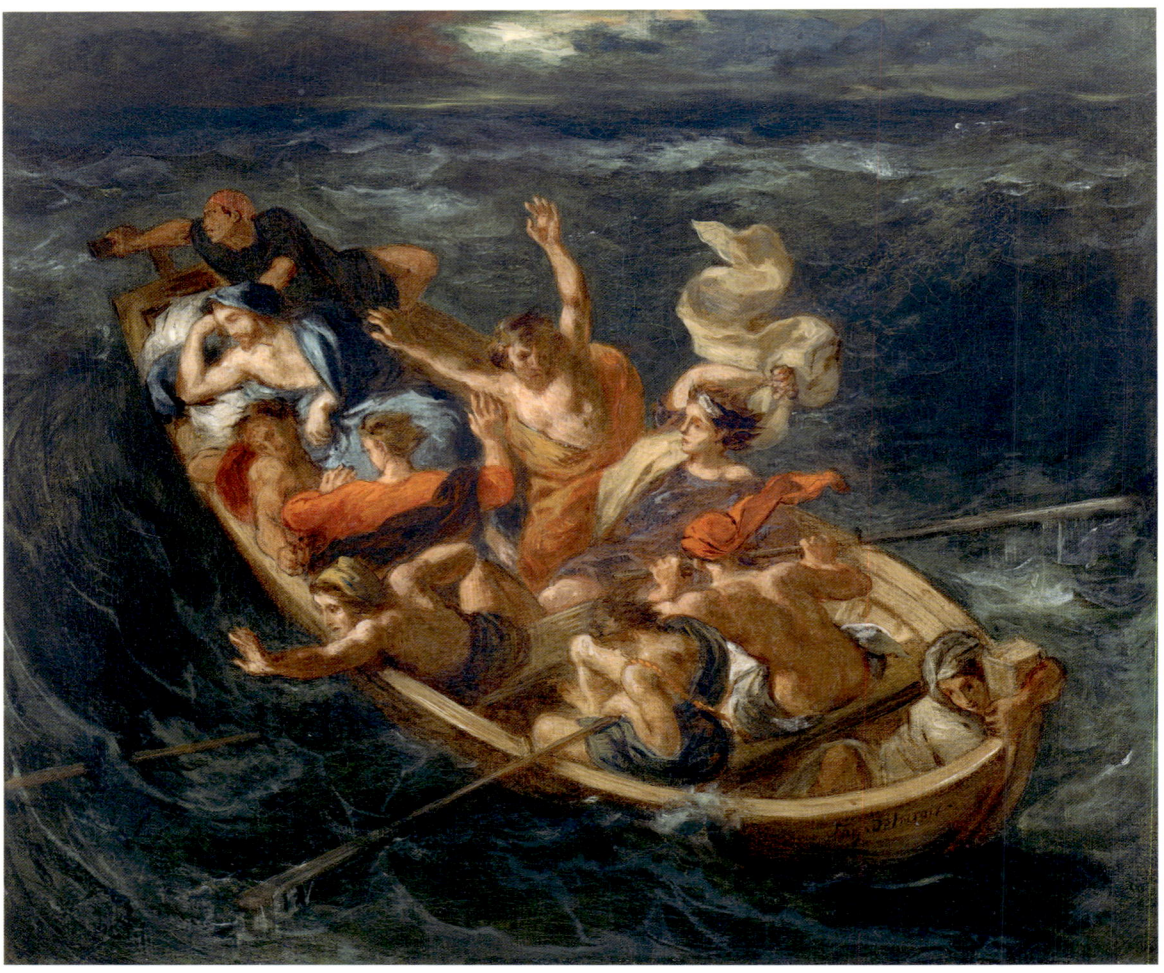

CAT. 99 *Christ on the Lake of Genesareth*, ca. 1841

from about thirty in Byron's text to about twenty; he also broadened the frame, introducing more space and a greater dynamism into the composition by separating some figures from the group. In the boat's bow are three prostrate young men, while visible in the stern are a dying woman, a melancholy child, and a man wrapped in a mantle, his hat pulled over his eyes (perhaps Don Juan himself, revulsed and resistant). This last figure, placed discreetly on the rim, registers only belatedly with the beholder, whose eyes are caught up in the complex light effects produced by the artful combination of the other figures. Rendered by means of chiaroscuro, they are sculpted by the light of a storm that takes place beyond the picture frame, somewhere, it is suggested, behind the beholder's right shoulder. If the orange spot on the horizon is interpreted as the setting sun, then its light is not based in reality. Yet it is more than a mere theatrical device: it is responsible for the fantastic atmosphere of this ambiguous scene, where the sea is all but indistinguishable from the waters of the Underworld. The picture is, in addition, an

homage, in the guise of a quotation, to Gericault's *Raft of the Medusa*, since it reproduces in reverse that painting's two sources of light, emanating from both the left foreground and the horizon. Another point of confluence is the clothing: although Don Juan lived during the ancien régime, the costumes here clearly derive from nineteenth-century, which is to say, modern, civilian and military dress. It is therefore easier to understand what Delacroix may have been suggesting when he first presented his painting to the public under the generic title "A Shipwreck." It was a wink to the timid "Shipwreck Scene," the title Gericault used at the Salon of 1819 for *The Raft of the Medusa* to evade censorship.

It was probably in the early 1840s as well that Delacroix had his first ideas for the dramatic scene Christ Asleep during the Tempest (cats. 99, 129, 131). The iconography of the subject had been wildly popular in Mannerist and Baroque painting, particularly in Flanders and Holland, from Pieter Bruegel the Elder to Ludolf Backhuysen. Delacroix chose not the moment in the Gospel account when Jesus rebukes the

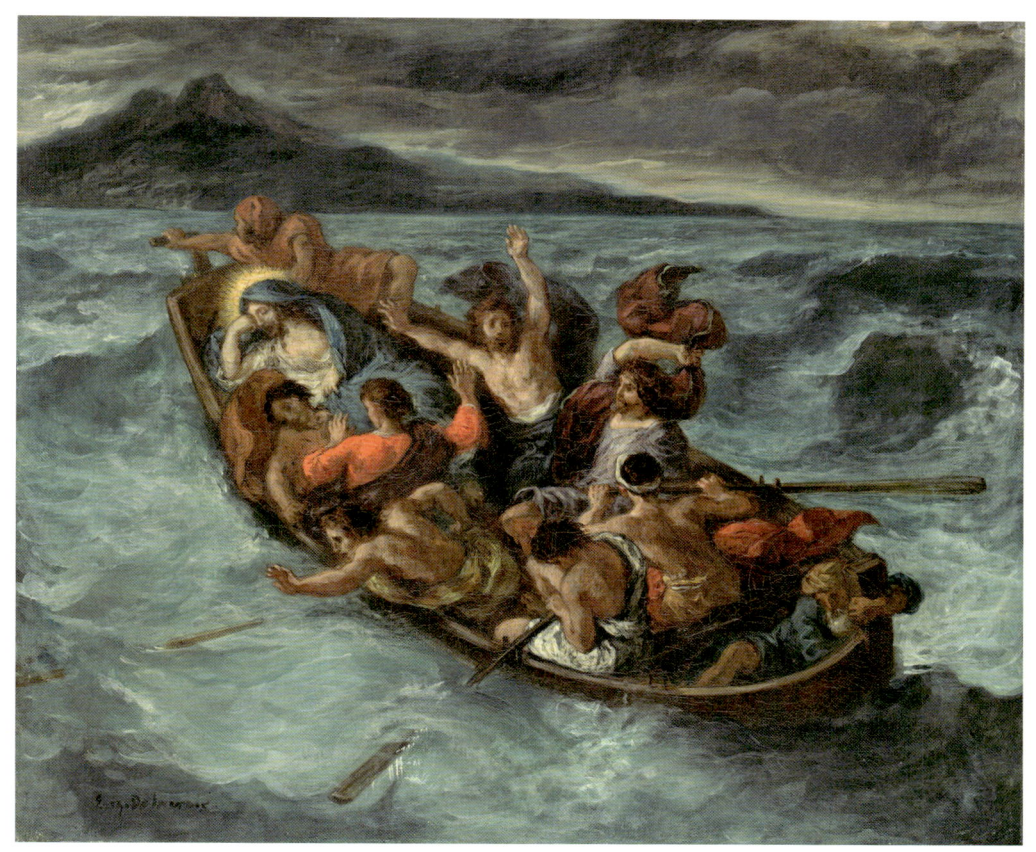

CAT. 129 *Christ Asleep during the Tempest*, ca. 1853

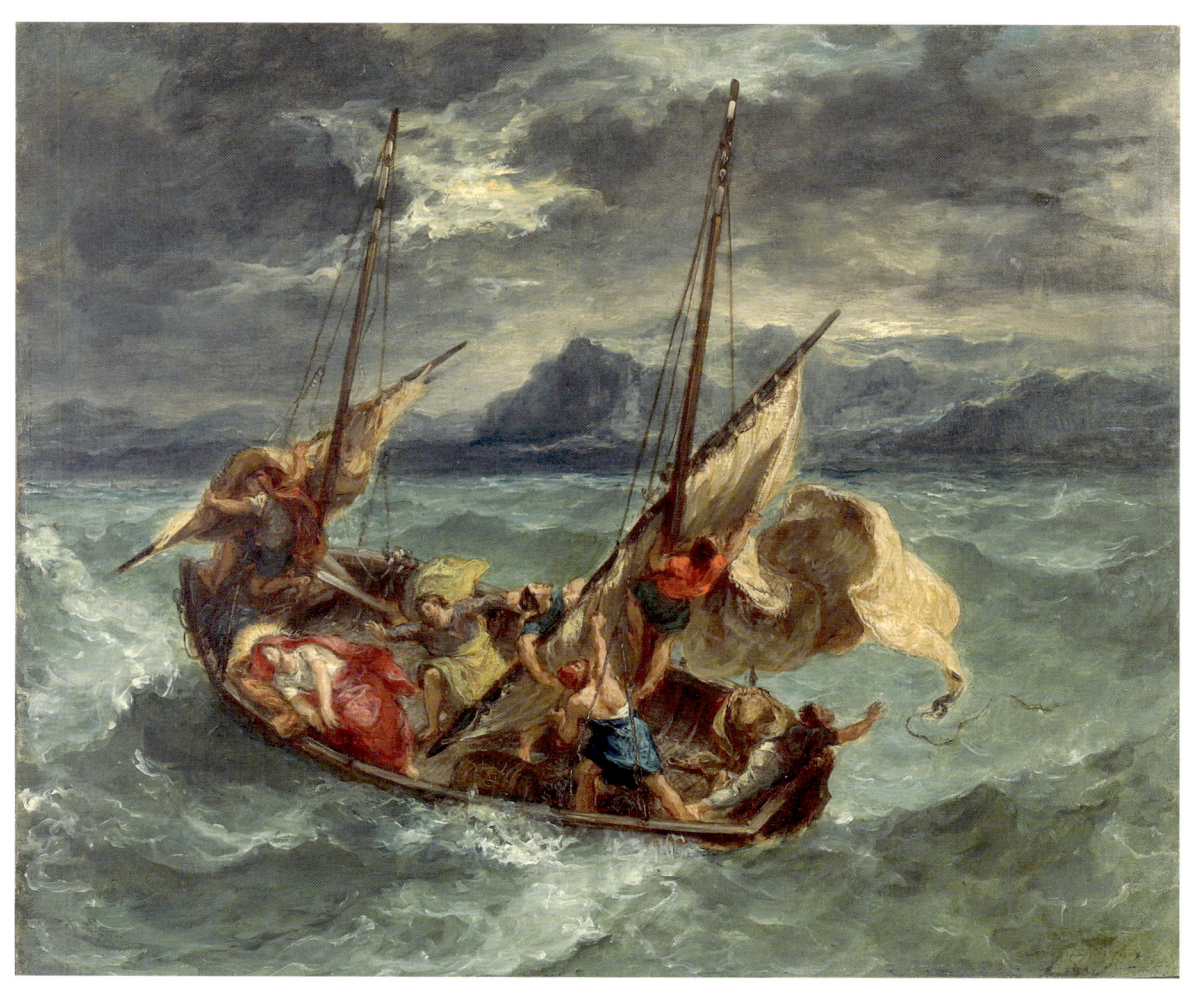

CAT. 131 *Christ on the Sea of Galilee*, 1854

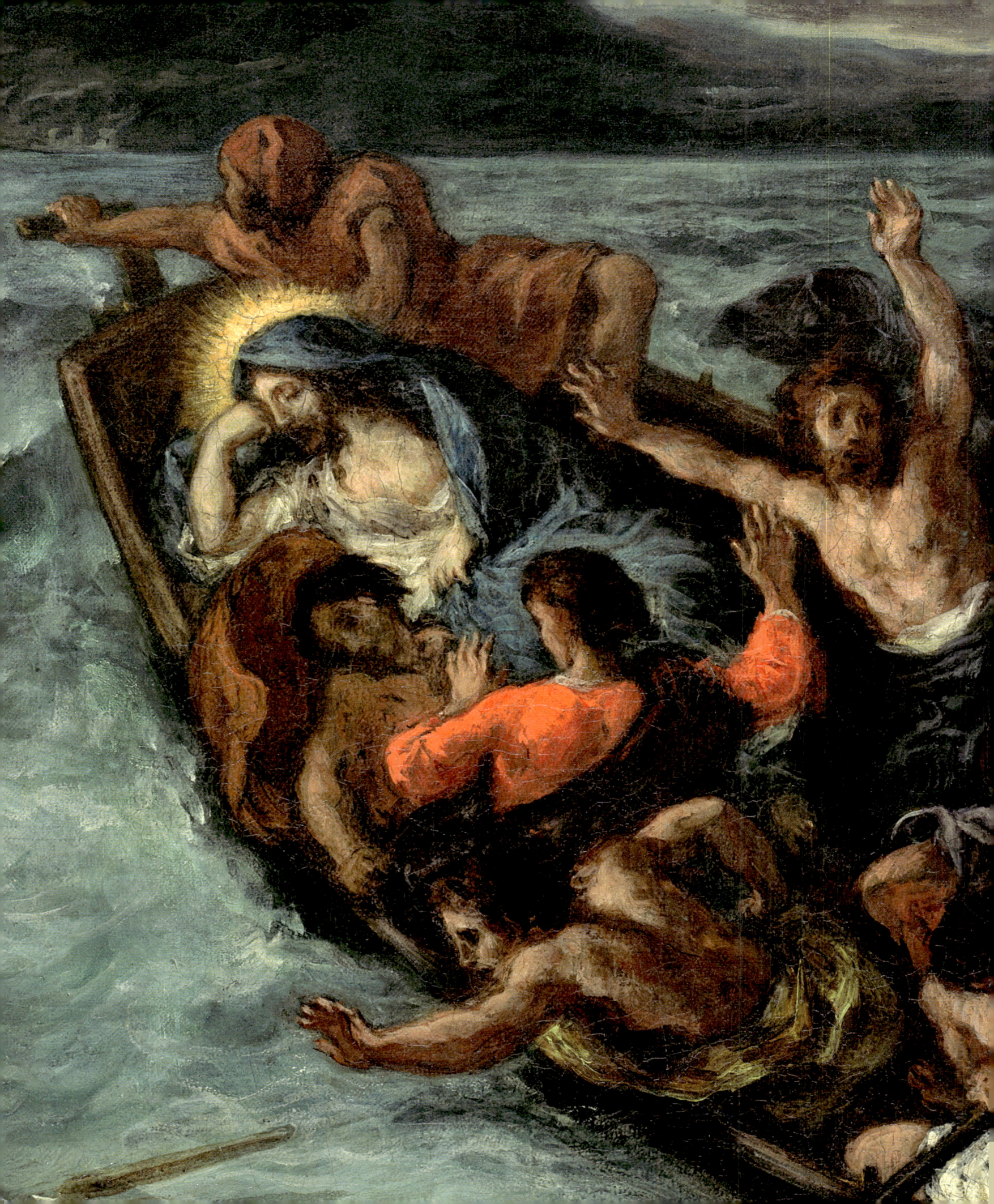

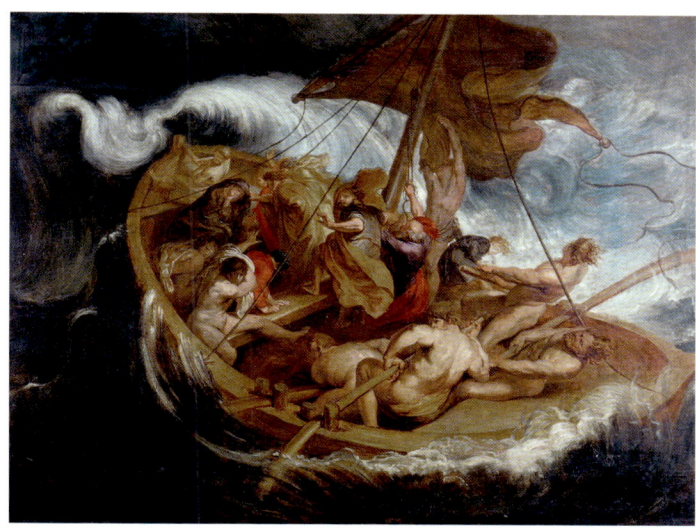

FIG. 79 Peter Paul Rubens. *Christ Calming the Sea*, ca. 1608–9. Oil on wood, 39³⁄₁₆ x 55½ in. (99.5 x 141 cm). Gemäldegalerie Alte Meister, Dresden (inv. Gal.-Nr. 1001)

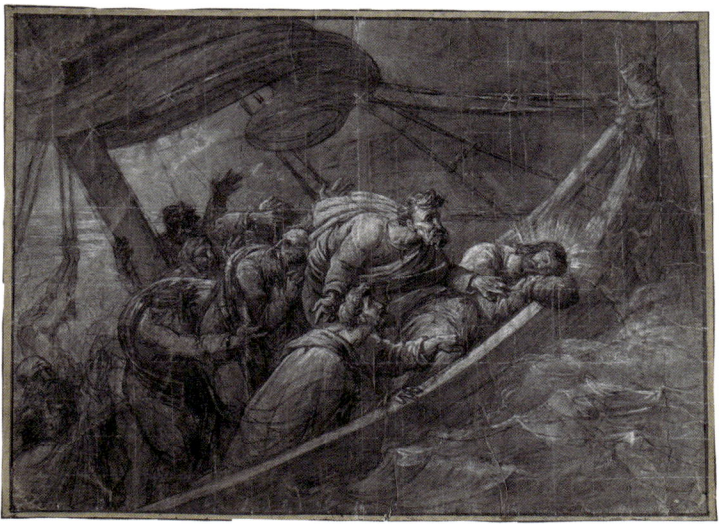

FIG. 80 François Joseph Heim (French, 1787–1865). *Christ on the Lake of Genesareth*, ca. 1810–20. Chalk and black conté crayon on brown paper, 17³⁄₄ x 24⁷⁄₁₆ in. (45 x 62 cm). Musée Jean-Jacques Henner, Paris (inv. JJHD2008-0-2)

wind to calm the storm but the previous moment, when he is still sleeping, oblivious to the danger. Meanwhile, the apostles are terror-stricken, as the vessel takes on water on all sides. As indicated by the version at the Metropolitan Museum (cat. 129), Delacroix constructed his composition based on a work by Rubens, previously attributed to Jacob Jordaens (fig. 79). Delacroix probably knew it through an engraving. As in the Rubensian model, in his painting the horizon line is placed extremely high, almost along the upper edge of the picture, and imprisons the protagonists inside the raging waters. The ship, seen from above, is tipped forward and crosses the picture field on the diagonal. Clearly wishing that no element should extend beyond the frame, Delacroix eliminated the mast. It is replaced symbolically by two apostles, one with his arms raised, the other with a mantle wafting like a sail. Had Delacroix noticed the incoherence of the position occupied by Rubens's rowers, who have their backs to the stern? In any event, he reversed the direction of the boat, restoring the logical placement of the rowers, backs to the prow. Jesus, dozing and wrapped in a blue tunic, is near the helm. Blessed and close to heaven, he is in Manichaean opposition to the bare-chested rowers struggling against the material world in the lower foreground. As they lean forward, their musculature is evident and evokes that of Phlegyas, the ferryman who guided

CAT. 129 *Christ Asleep during the Tempest*, ca. 1853, detail

Dante and Virgil through the dark waters of the Lake of Dis, in the composition of 1822 (see fig. 2).[64]

More recent sources, which may have influenced Delacroix's ideas for successive versions, should not be underestimated. One might think especially of the Dutch painters Rembrandt and Backhuysen, who placed the action in the more realist context of a fishing boat and opened up the painting. Delacroix may also have drawn on references dating to his youth. Perhaps he remembered *Saint Thomas Aquinas Preaching His Confidence in God during a Tempest* (Petit Palais, Paris), commissioned from Ary Scheffer by the prefecture of the Seine for the church of Saint-Thomas-d'Aquin in Paris and exhibited to great acclaim at the Salon of 1824. Could he have known about a planned work by François Joseph Heim, probably from the 1810s or 1820s, for which sketches survive (fig. 80)? The version painted by Delacroix in 1853, now in Zürich, has the same orientation.[65] As in Heim's work, the golden aureole around Jesus' head, a detail absent in the Dutch and Flemish sources, evokes the art of the "Primitives." These two works have a third point in common: Delacroix represents distinctly the moment when two apostles touch the arm of the Messiah to wake him.

The painter seems to have derived pleasure from producing a series of variations for dealers (Beugniet, Petit) and enlightened art lovers (comte Grzymala), as well as for his own enjoyment, as indicated by the two versions still in his studio when he died.[66] The image, at first simple and highly symbolic, became more complex and increasingly elaborate as Delacroix reprised it.

The first versions radically contrast, in the manner of the Symbolists, the warm colors of the human world (bronze flesh tones, red and brown tunics, the wood of the ship) and the turquoise-blue of water and sky. Only the blue-and-white tunic wrapped around the sleeping Jesus seems to establish a connection to nature and to anticipate his imminent mastery of the waves. In the New York version (see cat. 129), the artist even placed a mountain peak directly above Jesus' head: that sculptural effect, which is not apparent at first glance, symbolizes with great effectiveness the steadfastness and loftiness of faith. As in the case of *The Shipwreck of Don Juan* (see cat. 98), Delacroix rendered the various passions gripping the apostles by highly demonstrative gestures: arms held out to call for help, to seize the helm, to grab a mantle that is flying off, or to cry out one's distress. Then there is the most unexpected detail, a sick or terrorized apostle curled up in the prow. The compact cluster of figures contained in the mandorla formed by the ship allowed Delacroix to counterbalance the disorder and to keep the composition very simple.

In the later version, in Baltimore, which dates to 1854 (cat. 131), the palette is less systematic and more varied: Christ has traded his blue mantle for a raspberry-pink drapery, which complements the emerald color of the water and corresponds to the mauve and blue accents of the overcast sky and the mountain chain in the background. Many little cream-colored curls heighten the brilliance of the waves, the subtle swelling of the sails, and the glow of the sky, broken here and there by a ray of sunlight. The beholder's eye, previously caught up in a circular movement, is now attracted simultaneously to different points in the painting. A radical change has also come over the protagonists: the apostles have become experienced sailors, fitted out with the trousers and caps typical of a bargeman in eighteenth- and nineteenth-century Europe. Far from giving in to paralysis and fear, each attends to the most urgent matter as the storm threatens, coordinating with the other protagonists to lower the yards and gather in the sails. The boat, generic and rustic in the first versions, has been replaced by a two-masted fishing vessel similar to a yawl, large fleets of which could be found along the Atlantic seaboard in the fishing harbors of the nineteenth century. The rigging of the two masts probably originated in a study from nature that Delacroix did in the port of Dieppe in September 1854.[67] The

many drawings executed on that occasion indicate his curiosity and enthusiasm.

Yet that infatuation does not mean that the modern world had suddenly burst forth in Delacroix's art. The sailing ships he observed were already considered archaic in the 1850s, and he looked at them critically, as a man of his time: "How cumbersome and inefficient all that masting is most of the time: until the advent of steam, which changed everything, that art had not advanced a single step in two hundred years."[68] Although he was doubtless aware of the anachronism of inserting an eighteenth- or nineteenth-century yawl into a scene from the Gospels, in his view the motif was picturesque enough not to break the spell of a painting with a biblical subject. These studies, then, in undoing his own expectations, were ultimately useful to him. What remains to be fully understood are the reasons for this affirmation of pure art. And why, in the last versions of *Christ Asleep during the Tempest*, are the boat and the sailors emancipated from the narrative account? We may propose a formal rationale: the masts of the yawls allowed Delacroix to balance a composition that had become more expansive because the frame had been widened. Compared with the first versions of the subject, the horizon is lower, so that, classically, it divides the seascape into two equal halves, leaving more room for the mountainous shore and the sky than for the lake. Formally speaking, the masts connect the sky and the lake, creating a poetic analogy between the sails flapping in the wind and the shreds of bright clouds that seem to cling to the masting.

To that formalist explanation we may add a second hypothesis: Delacroix's imagination was invested in the motif. A reflection made in Dieppe the following year is enlightening:

> It strikes me more forcibly even than last year, as I
> watch the scenes in this seaside town, the ships, and
> the interesting types of people, that not enough has
> been made of such subjects. Even ships do not play a
> large enough part in marine paintings. I would like to
> see them the heroines of the scene. I adore them; they
> give me an impression of strength, and grace and
> picturesqueness, and the more disheveled they look,
> the more beautiful I find them. Marine painters render
> them every which way: as long as they keep the proportions correct, and the rigging conforms to the
> principles of navigation, they feel their job is done.
> They do the rest with their eyes closed.[69]

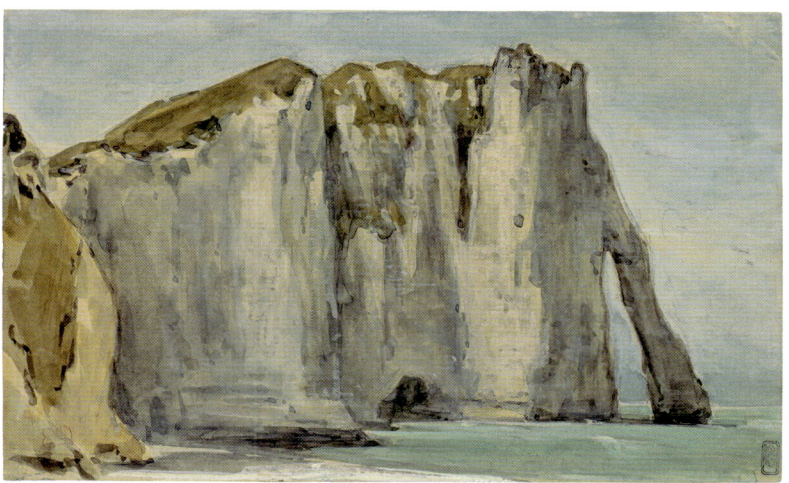

FIG. 81 *Cliffs at Etretat,* ca. 1849. Gouache over light traces of black chalk on blue paper, 5¹¹⁄₁₆ x 9⁷⁄₁₆ in. (14.5 x 24 cm). Museum Boijmans Van Beuningen, Rotterdam (formerly Koenigs Collection) (inv. F II 163 [PK])

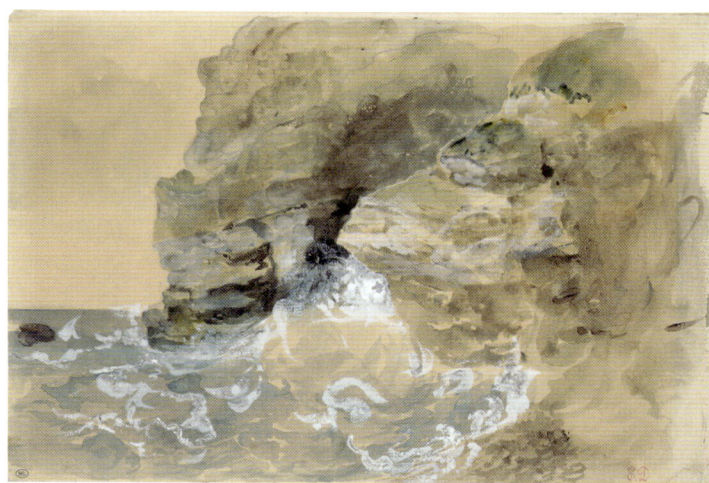

FIG. 82 *Waves Breaking against a Cliff,* ca. 1849. Watercolor and touches of gouache over graphite on paper, 8³⁄₈ x 12³⁄₈ in. (21.3 x 31.5 cm). Musée du Louvre, Paris (RF 4654 recto)

In Delacroix's imagination, the boat and the sailors fighting the elements have an antiquity, a heroism, a picturesque quality (in the original, strong sense of "picturesque") that lifts them above the anecdotal. In that respect, they have a legitimate place in religious history painting. The feeling that the discourse is disrupted in the last version of *Christ Asleep during the Tempest* can therefore be attributed to the depiction in the same space of two complementary but competing heroic figures: first, the sleeping Jesus, imperturbably trusting in divine protection; and second, the sailors and their ship, negotiating the raging elements with strength and intelligence. The heroism of faith stands side by side with the heroism of action. The discourse, far from being impoverished or dissipated, has thus been enriched by the moral and pictorial elaborations Delacroix pursued following his seaside observations.

Rocks and Forest, Epic and Erotic Places

Parallel to his studies of waves, Delacroix devoted himself to observing rocks. During strolls along the coast of Normandy in October 1849, he made various study drawings and paintings of the cliffs of Etretat. Handily combining gouache, watercolor, and chalk to evoke the consistency of the cliff and its glinting qualities (fig. 81), he anticipated by twenty years the point of view and layout chosen by Courbet at the end of

the Second Empire. But Delacroix did not use that motif for large compositions in oil. His sensibility instead guided him to close-up views that allowed him to depict the waves crashing against the rock in a sublime and Homeric battle. *Waves Breaking against a Cliff* (fig. 82), though now severely washed out by exposure to light, remains a powerful example. The foam is conveyed by highlights in white gouache; the rock, evoked solely by a fine interweaving of watercolor, appears strangely fluid and insubstantial in the face of the sea's power. The artist was probably thinking of the manner of his friend Huet from the Académie Suisse. Huet, whom Delacroix had known since the early 1820s, would exhibit *Breakers at Granville Point* at the Salon of 1853 (Louvre).

Delacroix may have also remembered a visit he made on October 18, 1849, during a low tide with a high tidal range, to the caves—one of which was nicknamed "Trou-au-Chien" (dog hole)—at the foot of the cliffs of Cape Fagnet, north of Fécamp:

> We had some trouble reaching the pillars, which resemble Romanesque architecture and support the cliff, leaving an opening underneath.—Then two magnificent amphitheaters with several tiers. . . . In one of them, I believe, is that deep cave, which looks like the retreat of Amphitrite. . . . Beneath the great arch, the ground seemed to be furrowed by the wheels of chariots, like the ruined streets of some ancient city.[70]

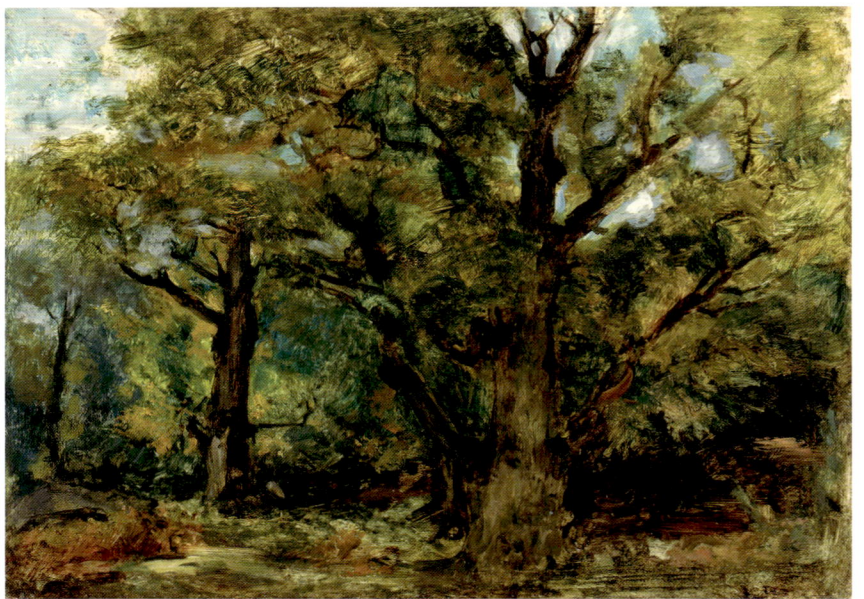

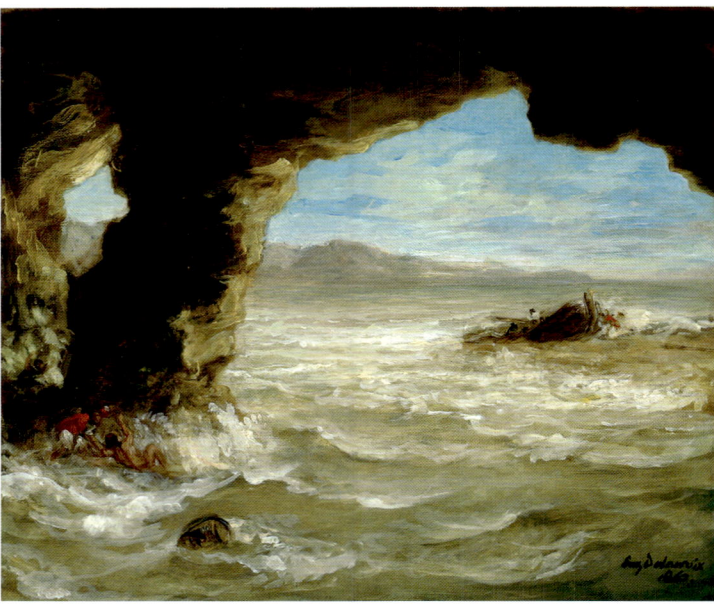

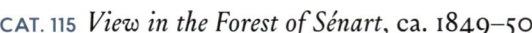
CAT. 115 *View in the Forest of Sénart*, ca. 1849–50

CAT. 145 *Shipwreck on the Coast*, 1862

As during his trip to Morocco, the artist filtered reality through ancient history to convey the sensations of the sublime that the place elicited in him. The epic wind, produced by the natural architecture of rocks constantly assailed by the sea, naturally found its pictorial formulation in the *Shipwreck on the Coast* (cat. 145), inspired by Giovanni Battista Piranesi's compositions. Rocks also appear often in scenes of young women being ravished or rescued: for example, the scene of a woman's abduction by African pirates, possibly inspired by Victor Hugo's *Orientales* (fig. 83),[71] and mythological scenes of the deliverance of Andromeda.[72]

Delacroix first treated the subject of Andromeda on canvas under the influence of Rubens.[73] At the time, the rock served only to display to advantage the young woman's robust anatomy and oily, glistening flesh tones, enhanced by tawny glints and muted greens. The composition of the second *Andromeda*, painted for the market between 1850 and 1853,[74] clearly alludes to a painting by Veronese (Musée des Beaux-Arts, Rennes).

In Delacroix's pictorial geography, the earthly complement to the sea could only be an equally mysterious and wild place: the forest. After the studies in Frépillon (on the edge of the forest of Montmorency) in the 1830s and in Nohant during the following decade, the forest of Sénart offered him the best training ground, easily accessible from the house in

Champrosay. His study of the nearby forest of Sénart (cat. 115) is striking for its powerful contre-jour effects and its tight focus: the dense network of branches invades almost the entire painted surface (see fig. 76). In that composition, contemporaneous with Camille Corot's and Karl Bodmer's studies of trees,[75] Delacroix had the audacity to place the tree trunk in the center, forcing the beholder's gaze toward the periphery. The study is distinguished by vigorous colors and remarkable effects of transparency. Although the branches form a firmly drawn and opaque armature, the foliage is merely suggested by rapid strokes of glaze in various green and russet tones, which let the white undercoat show through, evoking the transparency of the leaves filtering the light.

The seascape studies, the majority executed during calm weather at sunset, served as a prelude to tragic scenes of storms and shipwrecks. Conversely, in Delacroix's later works the role of the forest is both to protect and to display to advantage. The dark green harmony of the forest, heightened with glints of light and water, cast into relief the richness of the flesh tones of Jacob's powerful muscles as he wrestles the angel and of the voluptuous *Bathers*. The mysterious divine power of the oak tree shades Jacob wrestling with the angel (see cats. 118–20; fig. 69), while the forests in *The Bathers* (see fig. 85) and in *Marphise* (see cat. 127) are complemented by erotic and feminine imagery.

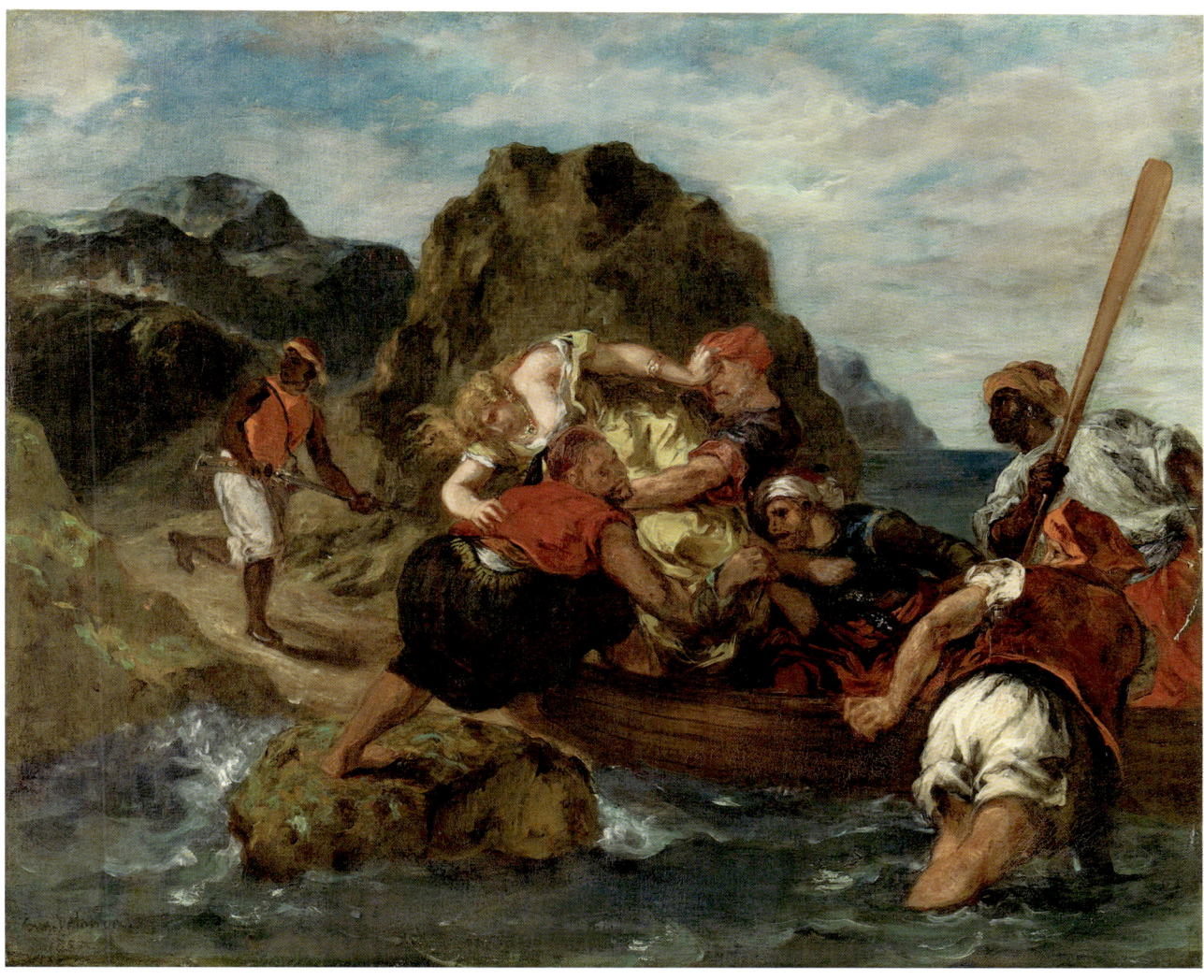

FIG. 83 *African Pirates Abducting a Young Woman on the Mediterranean Coast*, 1852. Oil on canvas, 25⁹⁄₁₆ x 31⁷⁄₈ in. (65 x 81 cm). Musée du Louvre, Paris (RF 1965-9) (J 308)

Against the Grain of Realism?

The important role of the landscape studies, but also the many filters the artist inserted between them and his finished compositions, is thus evident. The only spurs to Delacroix's imagination were the natural environments least marked by modern human exploitation: the sea, rocks and cliffs, mountains, forest. The only buildings that appear belong to remote eras and allude to an imaginary feudalism. In his many travels around the French provinces, Delacroix was impervious to modern architecture, but he noticed the ruins of the Château de Turenne, saying that he was struck by them during his stay in Corrèze in 1855.[76] On the coast of Normandy in 1854, he freely expressed his loathing of the Château d'Eu, modernized by Fontaine for King Louis-Philippe; conversely, he

appreciated the austere Château de Dieppe.[77] What Delacroix selected from his visual environment no longer had the aim, as it had in his early works, of bringing the pathos and bitter flavor of the real to his historical compositions. It was now only a catalyst, one that could not aspire to compete or interfere with the work of the imagination.

Once this is taken into account, Delacroix's objective distance from the art of his time seems less surprising. Realist, rural, and vernacular tendencies largely prevailed in the practice of landscape painting, with settings that ranged from Courbet's native Doubs to Adolphe-Pierre Leleux's picturesque Brittany to Millet's Brie. Delacroix left no room for that world in his paintings. At first he looked unkindly on the reality of the peasant world, as indicated by this judgment, formulated in the early 1840s:

The most beautiful provinces of France, once you have seen Holland, for example, seem like sorrowful places laid waste by plague and war. The ruined aspect of our villages in Picardy and the Paris region inspires a mortal sadness, and it seems they must be inhabited only by the poorest and most unhappy people in the world. The horrible clothing of our peasant men and women, and the tasteless, shapeless rags that cover them, do not give a better impression of their condition.[78]

In his mature years, however, he came to appreciate the authenticity of the rural world, as he took stock of the artificiality of the zone where city and country met. At the home of his cousins in Argonne in 1862, he confided to the duchesse Colonna: "I take delight in everything I see, I'm really in the country here. Champrosay is a village straight out of comic opera: all you see are stylish people or peasants who look like they have groomed themselves backstage. Nature itself seems to be wearing makeup. I am offended by all those little houses and gardens done up by Parisians."[79]

Except for a few picturesque thatched cottages in Normandy, sketched when he was young, even in the copious notebooks of drawings Delacroix shows no artistic interest in French villages or the figures of agricultural labor. There are none of the plowmen, sowers, reapers, gleaners, shepherds, or shepherdesses of which the Barbizon painters were so fond. Delacroix looked askance at Millet, whose art of ennobling the peasant world he considered artificial and pedantic, a vaguely dangerous undertaking because of the social issues it raised:

> They brought Millet to my studio this morning. . . . He spoke of Michelangelo and the Bible, which, he says, is almost the only book he reads. This explains the rather pretentious look of his peasants. Moreover, he is himself a peasant and boasts of it. He truly belongs to the constellation of bearded artists who made the revolution of 1848 or encouraged it, thinking, apparently, that it would bring equality of talent as well as equality of wealth. But Millet himself seems to me to be above this level, and the small number of rather similar paintings by him that I have seen show a deep though pretentious feeling struggling to reveal itself through an execution that is either dry or confused.[80]

Labor was not the subject of any of Delacroix's paintings, not even in Morocco: there is hardly more than a blacksmith or a few orange vendors or jewelry salesmen in his repertoire.

He also had a bias against the modern urban setting. Delacroix's moral judgment of that environment was contemptuous, particularly after long visits to the provinces. Having returned from Dieppe, he exclaimed: "I find that I dislike Paris as much as ever."[81] Three years later, just back from Strasbourg, he wrote: "So far, I've gone out only once into the streets of Paris: I was horrified by the faces of all those schemers and prostitutes."[82] He denigrated the very thing that the painters of modern life would make their subject a decade later, for example, the cafés on the *grands boulevards*: "Lazily, and with a kind of philosophical pleasure, I enjoyed watching the life of the sordid little place, the men playing dominoes and all the vulgar details of that crowd of automatons, the smokers, beer drinkers, and waiters."[83] Composing the entry "Flesh color" for his dictionary, he bypassed the subject that would give rise to Gustave Caillebotte's masterpiece twenty years later (Musée d'Orsay, Paris): "The effect I noticed . . . in the man planing wood in the gallery opposite my window: how strongly colored the half-tints of the flesh were compared with lifeless objects."[84] Delacroix's aversion to painting genre scenes, whether taken from French urban or rural life, never diminished. For the entry "Subject" in his dictionary, he noted that "modern subjects [are] difficult to treat, given the absence of the nude and the poor quality of the clothing."[85]

His judgments, not only aesthetic but moral, about his social and physical environment invite us to interpret his resistance to pictorial realism as foremost a movement of aristocratic affirmation. This tendency can be understood as both a retreat from the economic and social reality of his time and an effort to rise above it. He was reacting against urban modernity, characterized by immorality and ennui, and against the agricultural world, defined by the pursuit of profit through the exploitation of natural resources.

The Fête Galante and the Chivalric Romance: A Space for Aristocratic Freedom

In his mature years, Delacroix developed a profound affinity with the aristocratic ethos in his choice of reading material, the new subjects of his paintings, his moral and social ideas, and even, episodically, his way of life.[86]

That affinity took shape, first, in his growing interest in the Renaissance literature of chivalry. The first references to Ludovico Ariosto and Torquato Tasso appeared in his *Journal* in 1824, but he began to write down the subjects drawn from their works only in the late 1840s. Delacroix was probably spurred on by the illustrated editions published in Paris in the mid-nineteenth century such as the publisher Mallet's 1841 *Jérusalem délivrée*. In 1845 Delécluze published an encyclopedic work titled *Roland, ou la chevalerie*. In 1840 the publisher and bookseller Ruel Aîné brought out an edition of Ariosto's *Orlando furioso* in the translation by the comte de Tressan, richly illustrated with ninety engravings after drawings by Karl Girardet. On reading these works, Delacroix began to look closely at the paintings, both earlier ones and those of his own time, related to the literary world. In 1849, returning from a visit to the Louvre and probably inspired by the love story of Rinaldo and Armida—as painted by François Boucher, Domenichino, or Anthony Van Dyck—he wrote down subjects drawn from *Jérusalem délivrée* and encouraged himself to reread the book.[87] Two series of subjects were also recorded in 1858 and 1860.[88]

These books probably reminded Delacroix of the gothic romances he had read in his youth, but devoid of the terror that had characterized them. Tasso's and Ariosto's romances combined the breathlessness of the romance of adventure with the chivalrous ideal of the medieval courtly romance (to which they were beholden), alongside a whiff of modernity provided by Renaissance humanism: libertine eroticism, burlesque comedy, a complicity between the narrator and the reader. Castles, gardens, mountains, seas, and forests are the setting where a mischievous, spirited, and magnificent epic poem unfolds, in contrast to the prosaic realism of cities and farms, the locales for picaresque romances and modern social novels. Tasso's and Ariosto's romances thus offered a sense of time and place that provided the nineteenth-century reader the illusion of a simple and enchanted world where aristocratic freedom could thrive in its absolute form and where erotic fantasies could be satisfied.

At annual gatherings he greatly enjoyed, Delacroix thought that this ideal was within his grasp. From 1854 to 1862, the painter was invited every spring or fall to the Château d'Augerville, a vast seventeenth-century residence renovated at great expense by Antoine Pierre Berryer, a distant cousin on his father's side.[89] As a lawyer, Berryer defended the great generals of the Empire during the Restoration, and Delacroix

deeply admired him for the courage of his convictions. Beginning in 1848, Berryer was also the leader of the royalist and legitimist party. A connoisseur of music and literature who was elected to the Académie Française in 1854, he hosted a salon in both Paris and Augerville, welcoming the best singers, composers, artists, and writers of the time. In Augerville, the guests, selected from the aristocracy of talent as well as that of birth, were received sumptuously by a gentleman farmer who was pleased to have them savor the aroma of the ancien régime.

> It is a visit arranged by him, full of the old things I am so fond of. I know nothing more enchanting than an old country house. In towns, people have lost touch with the old-fashioned way of living, but here, old portraits, old paneling, turrets, pointed roofs, everything, even the very smell of the old house, warms the heart and imagination. I found some old prints tucked away that used to amuse us when we were children; they must have been new then.[90]

Charmed by the social and aesthetic atmosphere of the locale, its poetry and harmony, Delacroix allowed himself to imagine that he was experiencing a bucolic, aristocratic, and self-sufficient ideal, based on a sense of intimacy between the lord and his peasants in an idyllic community.

The pleasures of conversation were not devoid of small talk. Delacroix evoked in a humorous vein the little comedies of desire played out between him and the wealthy Hermance Marchoux, comtesse de Caen.[91] With a rare sense of delight, Delacroix depicted an eighteenth-century world of the fête galante, where reality is reenchanted and conforms to the compositions of Watteau.[92] The imaginary world of chivalric romances blended with that of the gallant eighteenth century: such was the aesthetic and literary atmosphere that Delacroix enjoyed from 1850 on. That world gave rise to a proliferation of scenes of deliverance, taken from *Orlando furioso* (*Roger Freeing Angelica*, *Angelica and the Wounded Medor*), *Jérusalem délivrée* (*Clorinda Frees Olindo and Sophronia*), and *Amadis de Gaule* (see cat. 143), as well as from the *Golden Legend* (*Saint George Killing the Dragon*) and Ovid's *Metamorphoses* (*Perseus and Andromeda*). All feature desirable female nudes offered up to an ambiguous hero.

One of the most spectacular examples dates to 1852: *Marphise* (cat. 127). Taken from canto 20 of Ariosto's *Orlando*

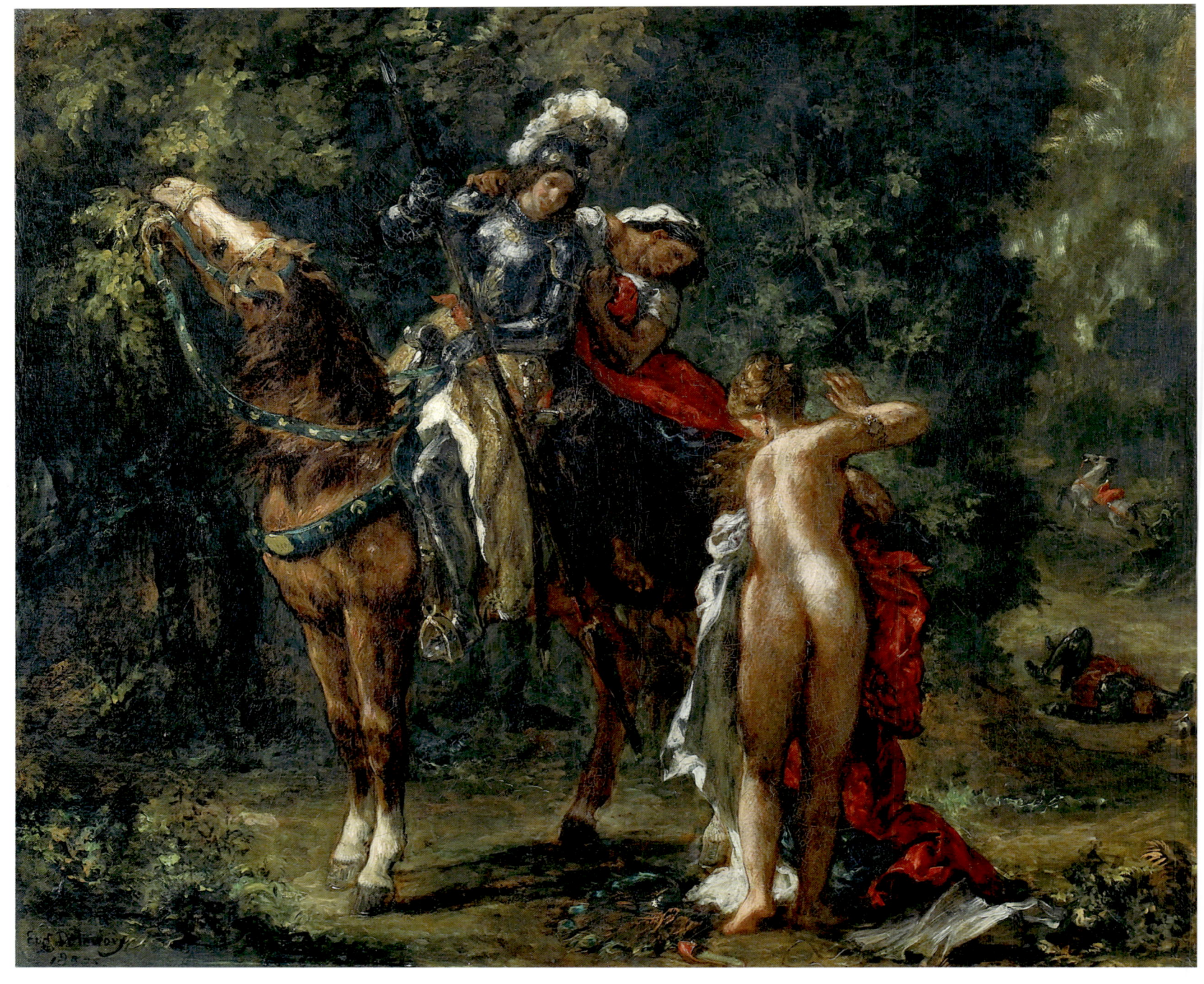

CAT. 127 *Marphise*, 1852

furioso, the episode is typical of the author's deliciously biting humor in that it reverses all the chivalric codes. The valiant knight Marphise (a woman in disguise) has generously allowed Gabrina to ride behind him on his horse. Gabrina is not a beautiful maiden but an ugly old woman, who asked for Marphise's help in crossing a ford. By chance they come across the proud knight Pinabello, accompanied by a pretty young woman, elegant but arrogant. The taunts fly, leading to a confrontation that turns to Pinabello's disadvantage. Delacroix had taken note of the episode about 1825–30,[93] and it is likely that the new Ruel edition of *Orlando* in 1850 prompted him to reread the text and savor the moment immediately following the confrontation. He had previously explored it in a few watercolor drawings but never in paint. Once Pinabello is thrown from his horse, the impertinent beauty accompanying him is punished for her pridefulness.

Ariosto, without describing the scene in detail, recounts that Marphise forces her to exchange her rich attire for Gabrina's rags before continuing on his way. Delacroix, a connoisseur of Ariosto's humor and erotics, filled in the blank left by the writer and imagined a striptease in the middle of the forest.

At the heart of the composition, constructed in slightly curvilinear perspective in the manner of the Flemish primitives, is the opposition between the fully armed lady knight and the defenseless beauty. Delacroix seems to have relied on Flemish references for both figures. Sara Lichtenstein, following René Huyghe, has rightly linked the composition and the figure of Marphise to Van Dyck's *Saint Martin Dividing His Cloak*.[94] Delacroix possessed a copy of it, painted by Gericault, and therefore had before his eyes the powerful harmonies of red and white that frame the main character's resplendent armor. That reprise is a parody, because the act of generosity has been replaced by a taking by force. The young woman, her back bare, may be a quotation of Rubens's *Judgment of Paris* (1632–35; National Gallery, London).[95] The goddess Juno has a similar hairstyle in that painting, and she is wrapped in a sumptuous purple cloak and a piece of white cloth, a peacock walking at her feet.[96] Or perhaps Delacroix simply adapted to a vertical format the pose and flesh tones of his own *Study of a Woman Viewed from Behind*, etched in 1833 (fig. 84). The accentuated *flochetage* of the painted nude may have been inspired by the crisscrossing of small ink strokes that model the flesh tones in the etching. Delacroix felt a legitimate pride in this remarkable bit of painting and wrote down the recipe:

> The underpainting for the *Impertinent Woman* was made with a very thick impasto and in a very warm and above all, a very red tint. On this [I] laid a glaze of terre verte with perhaps a little white. This produced the halftone of iridescent opal-gray, and over it I simply touched in the lights with the extremely good tone of Cassel earth, white, and a little vermilion followed by a few orange tones, strong in places. All this was still merely an underpainting, but an exceedingly subtle one.[97]

The iridescent flesh of the impertinent woman, the sparkling texture of the fabrics, and the horse's silky coat are highlighted by the green harmony of the forest, like a piece of gold jewelry in its setting. What captures the drama of the scene is less the faces, which are inscrutable, immersed in

shadow, or rendered in receding three-quarter profile, than the harmonic contrast, combined with the choreography of the bodies.

Delacroix planned to paint a similar scene: it was never realized but is known through a drawing of 1853 that provides a glimpse of its composition.[98] In the heart of the forest, two knights in armor turn away from nude bathers. As indicated by the annotations, the subject corresponds to canto 15 of Tasso's *Jérusalem délivrée*, when the knights Ubaldo and the Dane, approaching Armida's enchanted palace, discover a delicious spring:

> O'er-arch'd by trees that lent perpetual shade,
> But still so limpid, that its waters show
> Whate'er of beauty lies conceal'd below;
> While rising high the tempting stream beside,
> The grass-clad turf a soft, fresh couch supplied.
> There, on the bank, they found a costly board,
> With viands rare, in rich abundance stor'd
> And wantoning amid the crystal flood,
> Two prattling maids their frolic play pursued.[99]

The author is describing the erotic ballet of the two captivating nymphs, from whom the knights, albeit tempted, conceal

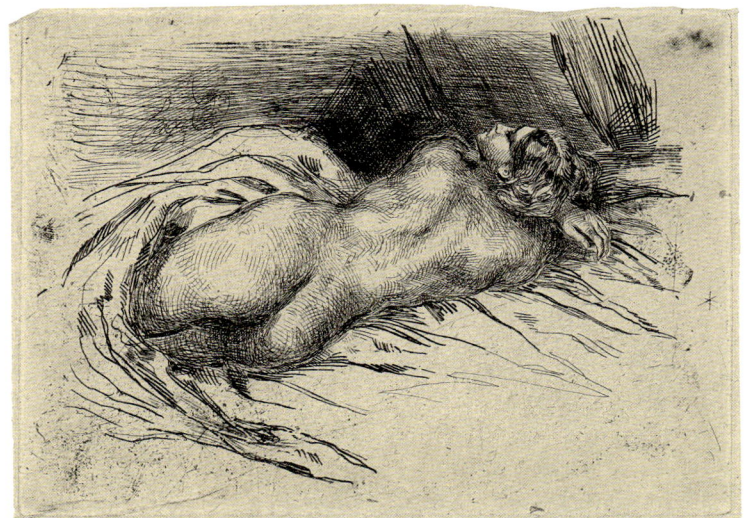

FIG. 84 *Study of a Woman Viewed from Behind*, 1833. Etching on chine collé, second state of four, plate 4⁷⁄₁₆ x 6⁵⁄₁₆ in. (11.2 x 16.1 cm); chine: 4½ x 6⁷⁄₁₆ in. (11.4 x 16.4 cm), support sheet 8⁷⁄₈ x 12⁵⁄₁₆ in. (22.6 x 31.3 cm). The Metropolitan Museum of Art, New York, Rogers Fund, 1922 (22.60.12) (D-S 21)

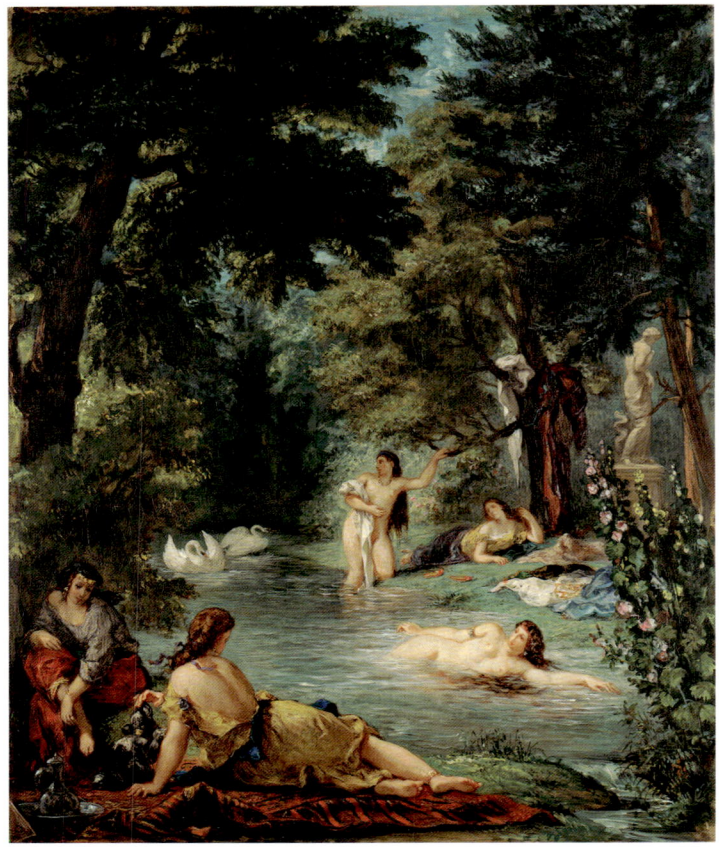

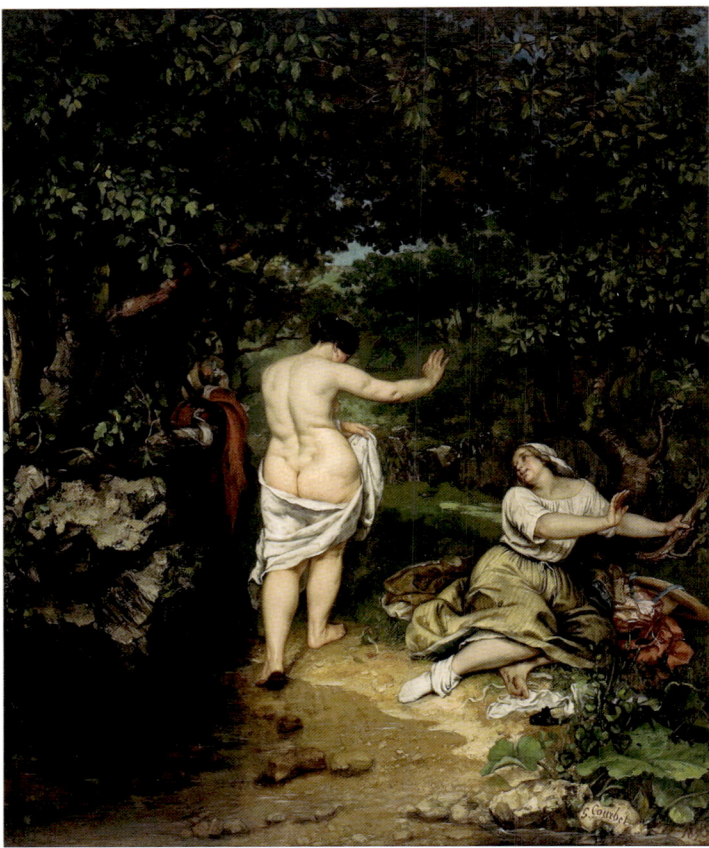

FIG. 85 *The Bathers*, 1854. Oil on canvas, 36¼ x 30½ in. (92.1 x 77.5 cm). Wadsworth Atheneum Museum of Art, Hartford, The Ella Gallup Sumner and Mary Catlin Sumner Collection Fund (1952.300) (J 169)

FIG. 86 Gustave Courbet (French, 1819–1877). *The Bathers*, 1853. Oil on canvas, 89⅜ x 76 in. (227 x 193 cm). Musée Fabre, Montpellier (inv. 868.1.19)

themselves on a magician's advice. In the margin of the sketch for the composition, Delacroix indicates all the studies from nature he would need: "The pastel done in the Jardin des Plantes this spring for the plan[ts] in the water—Also flowers reflecting in the water—Sept. 1853—Trees in bloom—See the sketch back view of woman that I etched [in 1833; see fig. 84]—Sky [repeated]—flowers."[100] The idea for the subject had already been indicated in the *Journal* under the date of June 2, 1849.[101] It reappeared on June 28, 1854, when Delacroix finished *The Bathers*: "Think about asking [Léon] Riesener for my study of trees on paper. Borrow . . . studies from him of landscape of Frépillon [country residence of the Rieseners, near Pontoise] and others, for the freshness of the colors. Also of Valmont [Abbey] for the subject of *Two Knights and Nymphs*, from *Jerusalem* [*Delivered*]."[102] Delacroix mentioned it again on January 2, 1855, when he once more indicated his intention to use the etching of the reclining female nude of 1833.[103]

If the plan never came to fruition, it was not for lack of interest but probably because a commission on a similar subject had in the meantime deprived the theme of its originality, making its execution less urgent. The work in question was *The Bathers* (fig. 85), commissioned in March 1854 by a private collector under restrictive conditions. In addition to the dimensions of the canvas, the price, the timetable for delivery, and the subject, the patron not only detailed the number of bathers and their different activities and imposed a "chaste intent, with the figures dressed in draperies around their waists," but also recommended that the artist seek inspiration in the painting by "Diaz, *The Bathers*" (fig. 87).[104] Delacroix later wrote that *The Bathers* was a painting he was not proud of, "having done it under conditions that [did] not please [him]."[105] Although his financial situation would have permitted him to turn it down, he not only agreed to do it but also respected the terms of the commission, even going so far as to pastiche Diaz's *Bathers*.

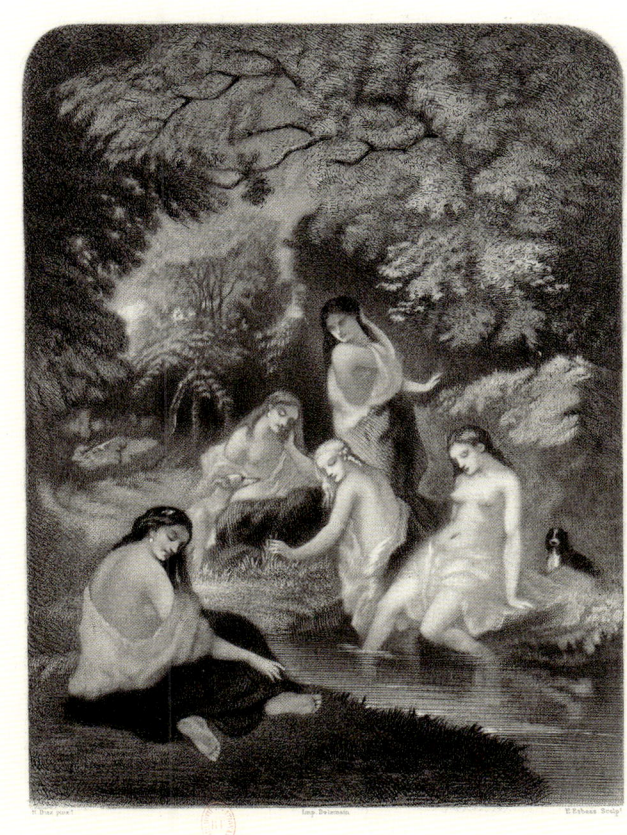

Delacroix liked Diaz, whom he had known since at least the early 1840s.[106] In 1853 he declared that he had even praised "the forest painting of Diaz."[107] For about a decade Diaz had specialized in small paintings depicting voluptuous nymphs and bathers from bygone times, often accompanied by children, in verdant undergrowth derived from his studies done in the forest of Fontainebleau. He thus satisfied the new vogue for the vernacular modern landscape, enlivened by an anecdotal narrative and the delights of the nude. That hybrid genre also corresponded to a revival of the fête galante of eighteenth-century France, as depicted by Watteau, Nicolas Lancret, and Jean Baptiste Pater. The tone was set by the major collectors of the time: the duc de Morny, comte Anatole Demidoff, William Wallace, and Doctor Louis La Caze. The Louvre, through its painting curator, Frédéric Villot, a friend of Delacroix's, contributed to the reassessment of that genre of painting in 1852, when it acquired Boucher's *Diana Leaving Her Bath*. Delacroix faithfully replicated the

composition of Diaz's *Bathers* (five women and a dog, on either side of a pond) and improved on his fellow painter by locating the scene in a much more luxurious rocaille setting. The Persian carpet, the tableware, and the many Oriental jewels evoke Charles Amédée Van Loo's *Sultan Served by Her Eunuchs*, while a statue adopting the Venus Pudica pose can be seen in the background. That motif is characteristic of the fêtes galantes by Watteau and his followers, who liked to display their wit by creating a formal interplay between the idleness of the characters and the animation of the sculptures.

With these Bathers, Delacroix also seized the opportunity to position himself resolutely in the camp opposing Courbet, whose *Bathers* (fig. 86) had caused a stir at the Salon the previous year. Delacroix had seen the painting as it was developing, during a visit to Courbet's studio before the exhibition opened:

> I was amazed at the strength and relief of his principal painting, but what a painting! What a subject! The vulgarity of the forms is nothing; it's the vulgarity and futility of the idea that are abominable! . . . There seems to be some exchange of thought between the two figures, but it is quite unintelligible. The landscape is extraordinarily vigorous, but Courbet has merely enlarged a study that can be seen near his canvas. It seems evident that the figures were added later, with no connection to their surroundings. This raises the question of harmony between the accessories and the principal object, a harmony lacking in the majority of the great painters.[108]

This is a decisive passage from the *Journal* that reveals what Delacroix understood realism to be, in a more spontaneous and less doctrinaire manner than in his famous entry in the *Dictionary of the Fine Arts*, written seven years later ("Realism—*Realism* should be defined as the exact opposite of art. It is perhaps even more detestable in painting and sculpture than in history and the novel").[109] Delacroix experienced that genre of painting as a veneer (further on, he used the term "marquetry"[110]) of raw, unstylized fragments of the visible world, superb in their wit and truth, but producing no narrative. Courbet did not try to connect the fragments logically or to support them with any literary, historical, or moral reference. The beholder of this monumental scene is not provided with a key to decipher the plot or any real-world context whatsoever. Delacroix therefore interprets Courbet's painting as an unschooled and underhanded art, in which the misleading transparency of the visible realities ultimately produces a strange and disagreeable sensation of opacity. That explains his recurrent sense of a "pointlessness of the idea," something that antagonized him.

In 1855, when he visited Courbet's Pavilion of Realism, his impression was more favorable. There, he again saw *A Burial at Ornans* and also discovered *The Painter's Studio* (see fig. 119). He did not conceal his admiration for them, directed primarily at the "superb details" and "the creditably executed parts," a judgment that once again concerned the fragmentation that he believed was characteristic of realist painting. Although he "discovered a masterpiece in [Courbet's] rejected painting,"[111] he did not explain why it was a masterpiece. Symptomatically, Delacroix confined himself to bestowing praise as a fellow practitioner of painting and never offered an opinion about the idea behind that "real allegory," though it is obvious and remarkably complex. Might he have understood, without admitting it to himself, that he stood before a cosmogony of modern art, which mimicked the tradition (especially the layout of the Last Judgment) only to better supplant it? Delacroix, the humanist painter par excellence, may have taken the measure of everything that separated his own notion of originality from that of Courbet, whose paintings were not part of a preexisting mythological, artistic, and literary continuum but claimed to be a founding myth in and of themselves. Ultimately, however, the two extremes came together and mirrored each other: the proud Courbet, with his "Assyrian" beard,[112] re-creating the world and painting through pigments spread in manly fashion with a knife, styled himself the brother of King Sardanapalus, who, in an orgy of brushwork, contemplated the destruction of his city and of art. Delacroix, too, had painted a scandalous studio picture, assembling on an enormous surface all the fantasies of flesh and paint that inhabited his crucible (real or metaphorical), before provoking the public by deliberately throwing the painting in its face.[113]

Memory to the Rescue of Painting

Delacroix's paradoxical experience of looking at Courbet's paintings—he saw both a fascinating landscape and an enigmatic opacity—probably had the advantage of strengthening his private conviction that painting did not achieve its full expression and its meaning unless it was practiced as an art of the imagination, an "ingenious artifice."[114] It was likely not by chance that the years 1853–55, when Delacroix was in closest contact with Courbet's painting, were also those when he set out to define what the imagination is. His major discovery was that the imagination has to be linked to the work of memory, both the painter's and the beholder's. Imagination should not be understood as a reflex that embellishes the visible data in a conventional way or as an automatic repetition of forms learned by heart: in that respect, Delacroix distinguished it from "style" and "practice."[115] The work of an artist with the gift of imagination is to distill and combine, to sacrifice and connect, activities that link everything to the harmony of the painting and the explicit rendering of the narrative it supports. And that exercise of the imagination is more natural, liberating, and properly creative because it is based on the freedom of the brushstroke and on memory. In response to the pointlessness of mechanically imitating reality and the sterility of adhering to academic conventions, Delacroix placed all his trust in memory. It has the advantage of pruning away the useless and emphasizing the essential (defined as what is pleasing and expressive), while at the same time being governed by a personal, singular, and inimitable principle. A recollection is the most faithful reflection of its bearer. "I firmly believe that we always mingle something of ourselves in the emotions that seem to arise out of objects that impress us. And I think it probable that these works delight me so much only because they echo feelings that are also my own. And since they give me the same degree of pleasure even though they are dissimilar, the source of the kind of effect they produce lies within myself."[116]

Step by step, Delacroix became aware of what recollection added to creativity. First, he came to realize that the places he liked to visit were all associated with childhood memories. He appreciated the particular density that the passage of time and a warmth of feelings gave to certain landscapes: the Valmont Abbey in the Pays de Caux, near the home of his cousin Bornot; the Château de Croze in the Causses du Quercy, where his Verninac cousins lived; or Argonne, the birthplace of the Delacroix family, though he did not visit it until 1856.[117] The first sensation he felt was a painful nostalgia. In September 1838, for example, Valmont reminded him of his vacations with his mother and sister in the summer of 1813:

This place is a former abbey of rich monks, with a superb church in ruins and ravishing waters and gardens. It makes me a little sad. You find yourself terribly defenseless against a host of emotions, which the surrounding noise helps you to combat in Paris. There are even ghosts in the garden, everyone believes in them; but the actual ghosts are too real for me, though they are in my imagination. These are dear ghosts in petticoats, whom I expect at any moment to see in the recesses of dark avenues and along rushing streams that are worthy of Ariosto's copses. Never was a place more likely to pierce you with stings that don't kill but which aggrieve.[118]

Seven years after his brother Charles Henry's death, which left him the sole survivor of his family, Delacroix had the Proustian experience of a well-being produced by involuntary memory. That memory, conveyed by the senses, revived the dead with an incomparable intensity and clarity. The sea spray inhaled during his first solo stay in Dieppe, in 1852, returned him to his adolescence in Valmont, a few miles farther south and four decades earlier. Returning from a walk on the beach, he wrote: "I think the greatest appeal of things we enjoy lies in the memories they awaken in the heart or mind, but especially in the heart. . . . Especially at low tide, the smell of the sea—which is perhaps its keenest charm— has an almost incredible power to take me back among those beloved people and those precious times that are gone forever."[119] He revisited that charm a year later, this time under poplars in Champrosay:

These poplars, and especially the poplars of Holland turning yellow in the autumn, have an inexpressible charm for me. I lay down on the ground to see them silhouetted against the blue sky with their leaves blowing off in the wind and falling all about me. Once again, the pleasure they gave me lay in my memories, in the recollection of seeing such things at a time when I was surrounded by the people I loved. This feeling accompanies all our pleasure in the spectacle of nature; I felt it last year in Dieppe when I was looking at the sea.[120]

Also in Dieppe, he strolled the hills to draw the castle and the hinterland:

I set up in a field that had just been harvested, to have a view of the castle and the surrounding countryside— not because it was particularly interesting, but to preserve the memory of this exquisite moment. The scent of the fields and the newly cut wheat, the birdsong, the purity of the air, put me into one of those moods when I can remember nothing but the days when I was young and my soul was easily stirred by such delicious sensations. I think that nowadays I can almost coax myself into being happy by remembering how happy I used to be in similar circumstances.[121]

In 1855, the artist's visit to the Château de Croze with his relatives, the Verninac family, elicited particularly rich emotions. His sister Henriette de Verninac and nephew Charles de Verninac had died more than twenty years before:

How to describe what I find charming about this place? It is a mixture of all the sensations that are lovely and pleasant to our hearts and imaginations. It makes me think of those places where I had so much quiet happiness when I was young; I think of old friends as well, of my brother, dear Charles, and of my sister. Alone as I am at present, it seemed to me, in this place so near the south, that I was once more with those dear ones in Touraine, in Charente, places that are so lovely to me, so dear to my heart.[122]

Alongside these experiences sparked by his travels, Delacroix felt the positive virtues of the passage of time simply by assembling his memories of his trip to Morocco ten years later, with the intent of writing an article. He took his time in a long preamble, where he pondered the best form to give to a travel narrative, one that would satisfy both readers, eager for an experience of exoticism and picturesque anecdotes, and the author himself: "Is it possible to recount to one's own satisfaction the various events and emotions experienced on a journey? Satisfying others, painting for them, is a matter of talent; but will someone who paints, whatever talent he may have, rediscover in his own painting the precise lines and delicate nuances of his impressions?"[123] He opted to abandon any painstaking accuracy: "Describing is not painting. A particular phrase by a great master in the art of writing, a choice, a consonance of syllables, creates a totality, a tableau in the mind. The first effect of a long description is weariness and certainly confusion. Description is the plague of literature."[124] The liberating and selective virtue of memory became clear:

> That journey is already long [eleven years] past. The very thing that would have prevented me from writing about it a few years ago is precisely what gives me the courage to do so today. I now see as if through a cloud a host of circumstances that once caught my attention. Many of them appear like so many dreams. Great quantities of notes taken on the fly appear unintelligible. By contrast, I see clearly in my imagination all the things that were not necessary to write down, the only things, perhaps, that deserve to be preserved in memory.[125]

Delacroix was discovering the paradox of material and immaterial relationships to the past: the truth of a past experience is revealed more easily by the virtual sensations of memory than by concrete notes in a travel log.

That exercise may have awakened Delacroix's desire to theorize the effect of time. An isolated sheet, which Michèle Hannoosh proposes to date to 1843, contains a reflection on the coloring that emotional memory gives to facts:

> An event is nothing, because it passes away. Only the idea of it remains. And really, it does not even exist in the idea, because the event gives the idea a certain coloring, imagines it by coloring it in its own way, in accordance with the mood of the moment. Why is the recollection of past pleasures infinitely sharper than lived experience? Why does the mind linger with such indulgence on places we will never see again, places where we experienced happiness? Why does . . . even the memory of the friends we miss enhance them once we have lost them? What happens in the mind when it remembers the emotions of the heart is also what happens when the creative faculty seizes hold of thought to animate the real world and draw from it imaginary pictures. The mind composes, which is to say, it idealizes and chooses. Thought cannot occur without idealization.[126]

In the end, it was the alchemy of the *Journal*, resumed in 1847, that allowed Delacroix to pursue his reflections. His recurrent personal experiences prompted him to draw

parallels with his artistic practice. He returned first to the liberation that came from distancing himself from the living model. It was October 1853, and Delacroix was in Champrosay:

> Jean-Jacques [Rousseau] was right when he said that the joys of liberty are best described from a prison cell, and that the way to paint a fine landscape is to live in a stuffy town where one's only glimpse of the sky is through an attic window above the chimneypots. When a landscape is in front of my eyes and I am surrounded by trees and pleasant places, my own landscape becomes heavy, overworked, perhaps truer in its details but out of harmony with the subject.[127]

Memory has the property of establishing an arbitrary relation of dependency—but one that becomes almost necessary—between an entity and the environment in which it appeared the last time, especially when both have vanished. The unity of the painting, the harmonious connection between the figures and the ground, had become an obsession for Delacroix. The connection formed naturally and powerfully through the work of memory proved invaluable to him. The unifying property of memory may have given him greater insight into the second version of *The Education of the Virgin*, on which he was then working.

The first version had been painted in Nohant in 1842. Delacroix had been touched by a reading lesson given under the trees by the farmwife of Nohant to her daughter. He observed it in secret during a walk and transposed the scene into a religious context (fig. 88).[128] Eleven years later, Delacroix painted a new version (fig. 89), the genesis of which is mentioned in the *Journal*:

> During the day, worked . . . on the little *Saint Anne*. Repainting the background from the trees I drew two or three days ago, on the edge of the forest near Draveil, has changed the whole painting. This little piece of nature, taken from life, fits in with the rest and has given it character. In the same way, for the figures, I took up the sketches I did from life in Nohant for the painting of Mme Sand. I have gained in freshness and firmness through simplicity.—Such is the effect that must be obtained through the use of the model and of nature in general.[129]

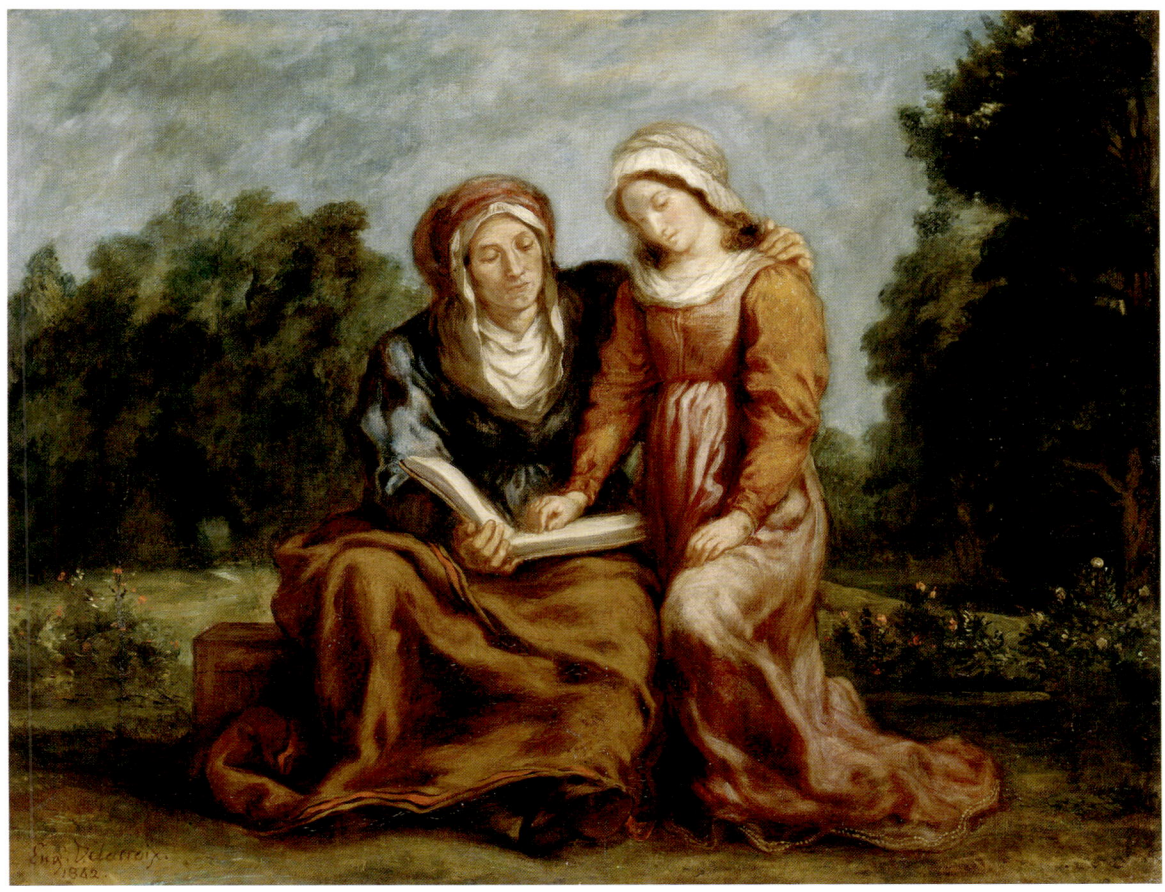

FIG. 88 *The Education of the Virgin*, 1842. Oil on canvas, 37⅜ x 49³⁄₁₆ in. (95 x 125 cm). Musée National Eugène-Delacroix, Paris (inv. MD 2003-8) (J 426)

A few lines later, the artist congratulated himself for having abandoned studies from the living model: "It is therefore far more important for an artist to come near to the ideal which he carries in his mind, and which is characteristic of him, than to be content with recording, however strongly, the fleeting ideal that nature may offer."[130]

It is evident at first glance that Delacroix accentuated the expressiveness of the two women, contrasting the vigor of Saint Anne (reminiscent of women he observed in Morocco, and whose costume evokes Jewish women of Algiers) and the pale fragility of Mary (a memory of Faust's Marguerite?). But it is hardly clear what "character" he gave the scene, placed in the center of an English garden with its requisite accessories. The spaniel, the cluster of ferns behind the bench, and the wicker basket filled with roses evoke the horticulture of Berry more than the ancient Holy Land. Delacroix had not stayed in Nohant since 1846; Sand's separation from Frédéric Chopin, followed by the composer's death, pushed those memories back to a bygone time. In rediscovering the sketches of Saint Anne in

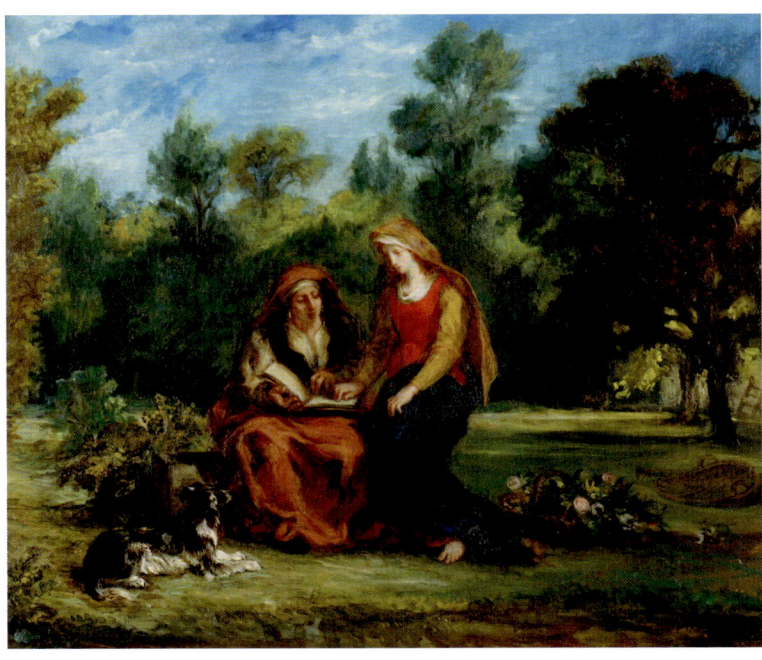

FIG. 89 *The Education of the Virgin*, 1853. Oil on canvas, 18⅛ x 21⅞ in. (46 x 55.5 cm). The National Museum of Western Art, Tokyo (inv. P.1970-1) (J 461)

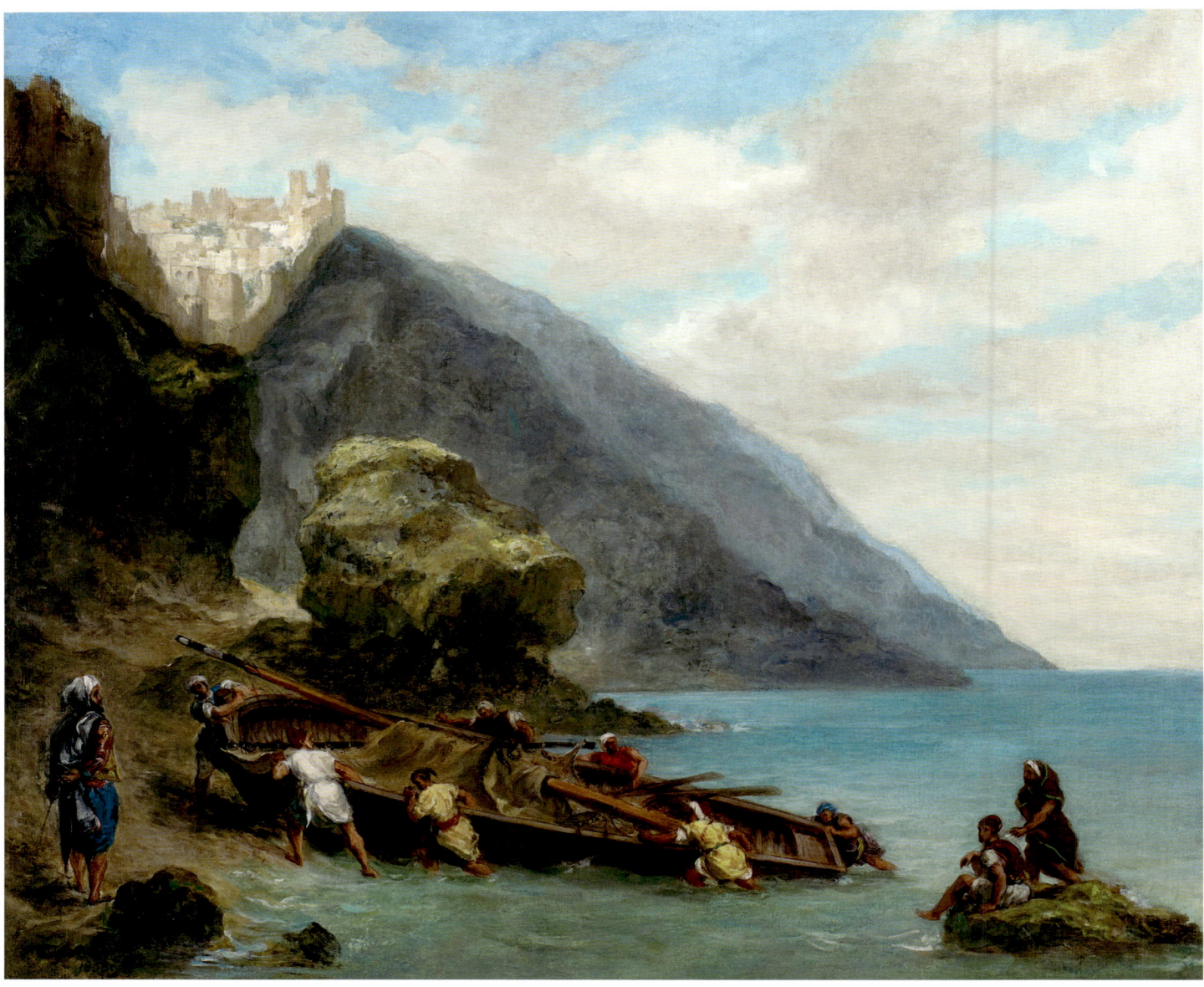

FIG. 90 *View of Tangier from the Shore*, 1858. Oil on canvas, 31¹⁵⁄₁₆ x 39⁵⁄₁₆ in. (81.1 x 99.8 cm). Minneapolis Institute of Art, Gift of Mrs. Erasmus C. Lindley in memory of her father, James J. Hill (49.4) (J 408)

his studio in 1853, he must have remembered the first painting's genesis. Are we therefore to imagine that the new version of *The Education of the Virgin* had its beginnings in the physical and emotional environment in which the subject was first conceived and that this environment had attached itself to the motif and slipped in around it? The landscape is no longer simply a setting from a plastic standpoint, nor is it merely a contextualization required by the needs of history. It also maintains a necessary connection to the subject in the artist's memory.

Delacroix shored up his line of reasoning by returning to the way he had used the unique experience of Morocco: "I began to make something acceptable of my African journey only after I had forgotten the trivial details and remembered nothing but the striking and poetic side of the subject. Up to that time, I had been haunted by this passion for accuracy that most people mistake for truth."[131] Delacroix thus established a clear distinction. Exactitude is to be understood as a relation of imitation that legitimates the painted work based on its fidelity to appearances in the visible world or to ethnographic knowledge of a past or distant world. Truth in art, by contrast, comes into play only within the autonomous world of the painted work, without external interference. Delacroix echoed that reflection two years later, after an observation about the lack of imagination of seascape painters: "It is the exactitude of the imagination that I demand. . . . Color and form must combine to achieve the effect I desire. My kind of accuracy would consist . . . of strongly sketching in only the principal objects, but in such a way as to show their essential functions in relation to the figures. As for the rest, I look for the same qualities in marine paintings as I do in any other kind of subject."¹³²

To attain the truth of a painting, Delacroix did not trouble himself with ethnographic coherence. In his later compositions, therefore, he freely combined French and Moroccan memories. The idealized memories of Morocco allowed him to ennoble a trivial scene he had seen in France. Conversely, the studies from life done in France gave a particular savor

and a harmonic envelope to Moroccan scenes, when the mere recollection of them was too insubstantial. Take, for example, a rare case when Delacroix indicated that a phenomenon he had observed in his everyday surroundings was of interest for a painting. In Dieppe, he said:

I noticed a good subject for a painting: a dinghy bringing fish ashore from a small boat that could be seen in the distance. The men [were] carried to land on the shoulders of others who had waded into the water to bring in baskets of fish to a group of women. The dinghy [was] dragged up on to the beach by two or

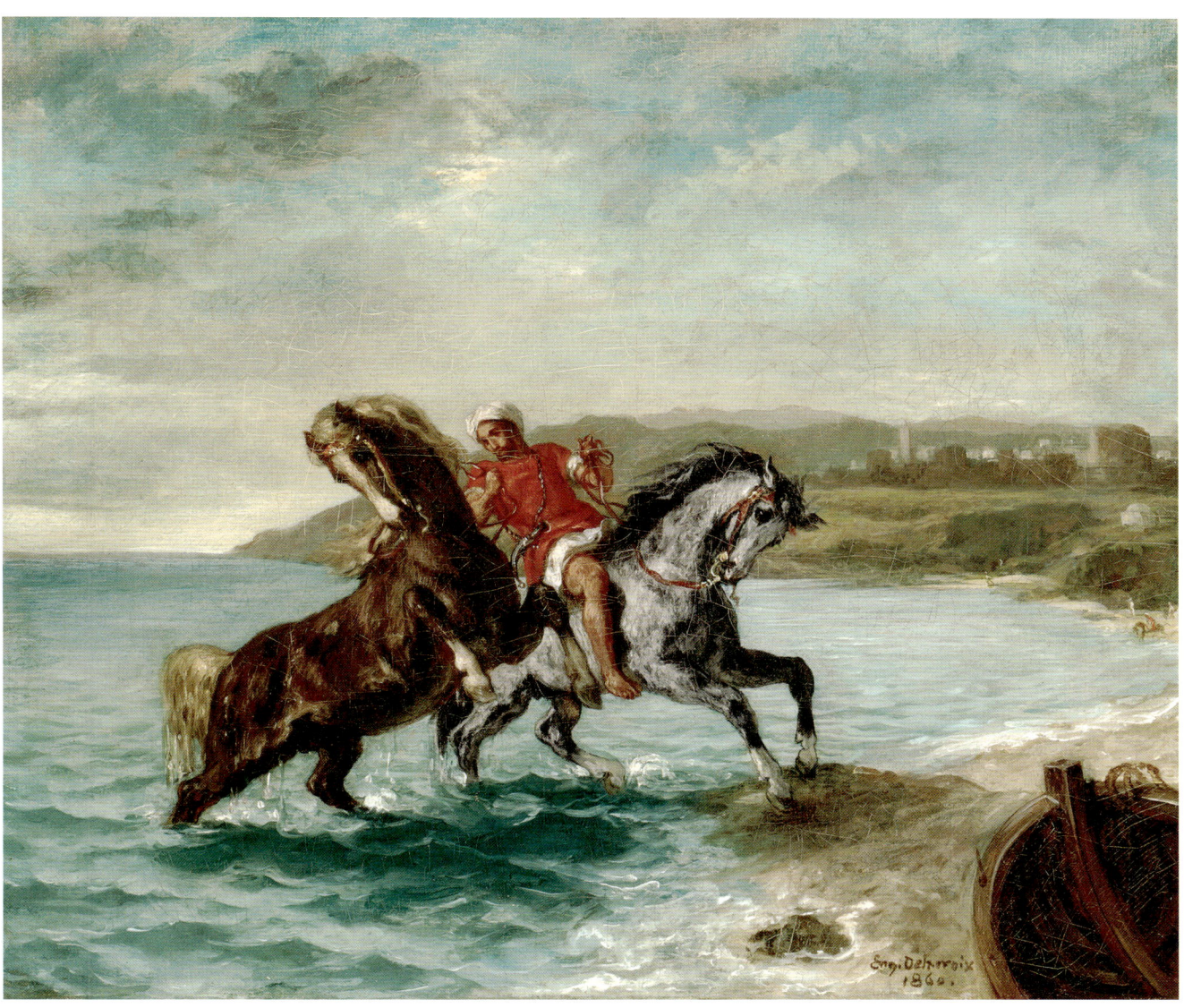

FIG. 91 *Horses Coming Out of the Sea*, 1858–60. Oil on canvas, 20¼ x 24¼ in. (51.4 x 61.6 cm). The Phillips Collection, Washington, D.C. Acquired 1945 (J 414)

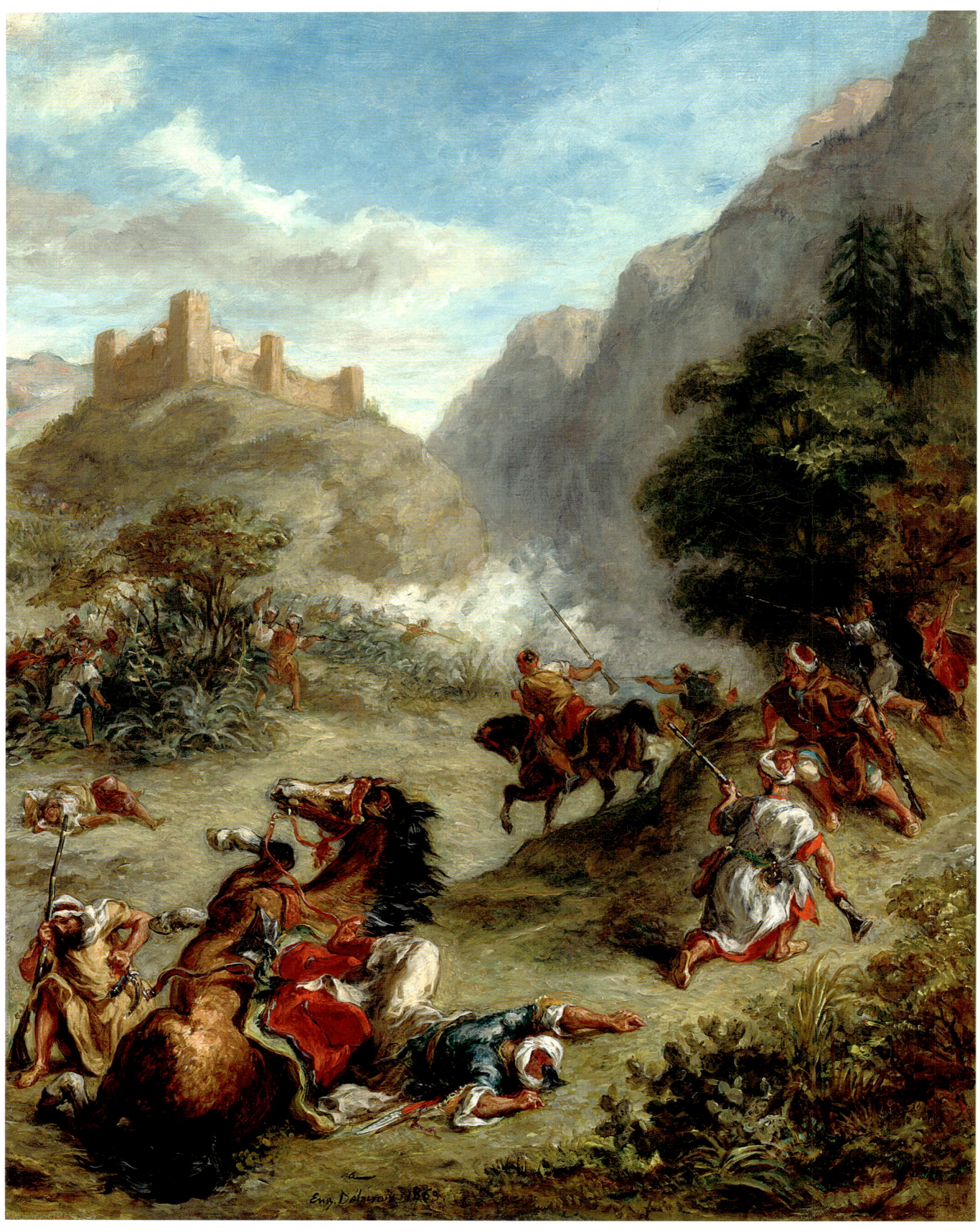

FIG. 92 *Arabs Skirmishing in the Mountains,* 1863. Oil on canvas, 36⁷⁄₁₆ x 29⁵⁄₁₆ in. (92.5 x 74.5 cm). National Gallery of Art, Washington, D.C. Chester Dale Fund (1966.12.1) (J 419)

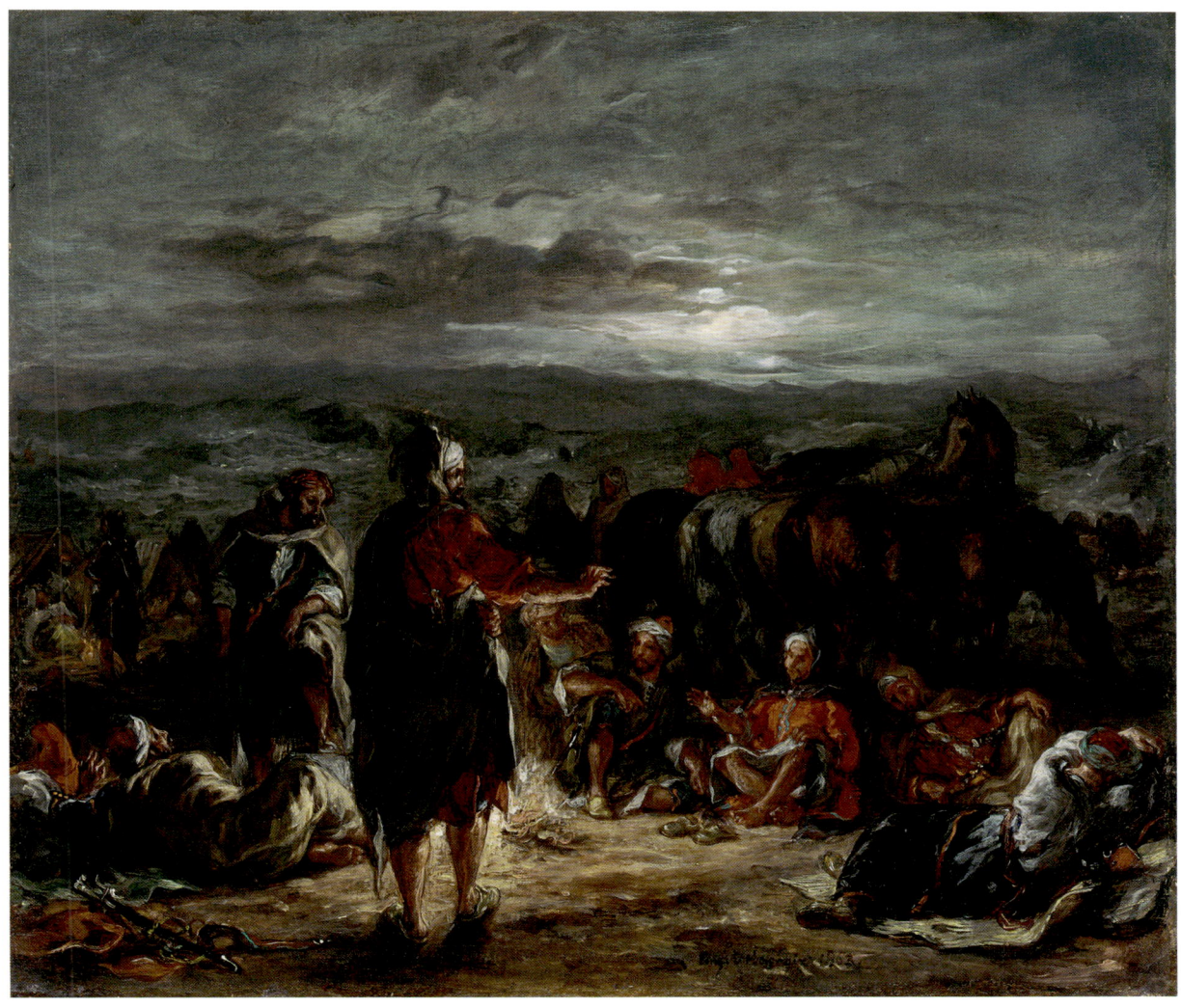

FIG. 93 *An Arab Camp at Night*, 1863. Oil on canvas, 21⅝ x 25⁹⁄₁₆ in. (55 x 65 cm). Szépművészeti Múzeum, Budapest (inv. 72.7.B) (J 418)

three little ship's boys and was then launched again with oars upright, the morning sun streaming down on the whole scene.[133]

In his mind, that "pretty subject" was only a starting point. The painter seems to have begun to elaborate a composition based on it a few years later (fig. 90), but at the cost of numerous adjustments that make the original unrecognizable. The fishermen and the baskets of fish are forgotten: all that remains is the boat pushed by young men in Arab costume. The Dieppe beach is metamorphosed into a steep bank modeled by imposing rocks (inspired by the rocky coast of Normandy or the grounds of Augerville). A path leads the beholder's eye to a mountaintop, crowned with ramparts enclosing a Moroccan city—a memory of Tangier.

We see clearly the scope of the delocalization in space and time that Delacroix applied to a motif taken from life to make it worthy of a painting, and the extent to which he broadened the frame, which led him to convert into a landscape what was originally the subject of a genre painting.[134] That expansion of the motif may have come about through an association of images favored by memory: superimposed on the fortified castle of Dieppe, framed by cliffs, is the analogous image of the crenellated ramparts of Tangier towering over the rocks. *Horses Coming Out of the Sea* (fig. 91) follows a similar procedure, but in the opposite direction. The motif is a memory of the journey from Tangier to Meknes, when the artist saw two horses crossing the Sebou River or fighting in the water. Yet the painting is set on the beach of Dieppe, as indicated by the tip of a washed-up boat in the foreground,

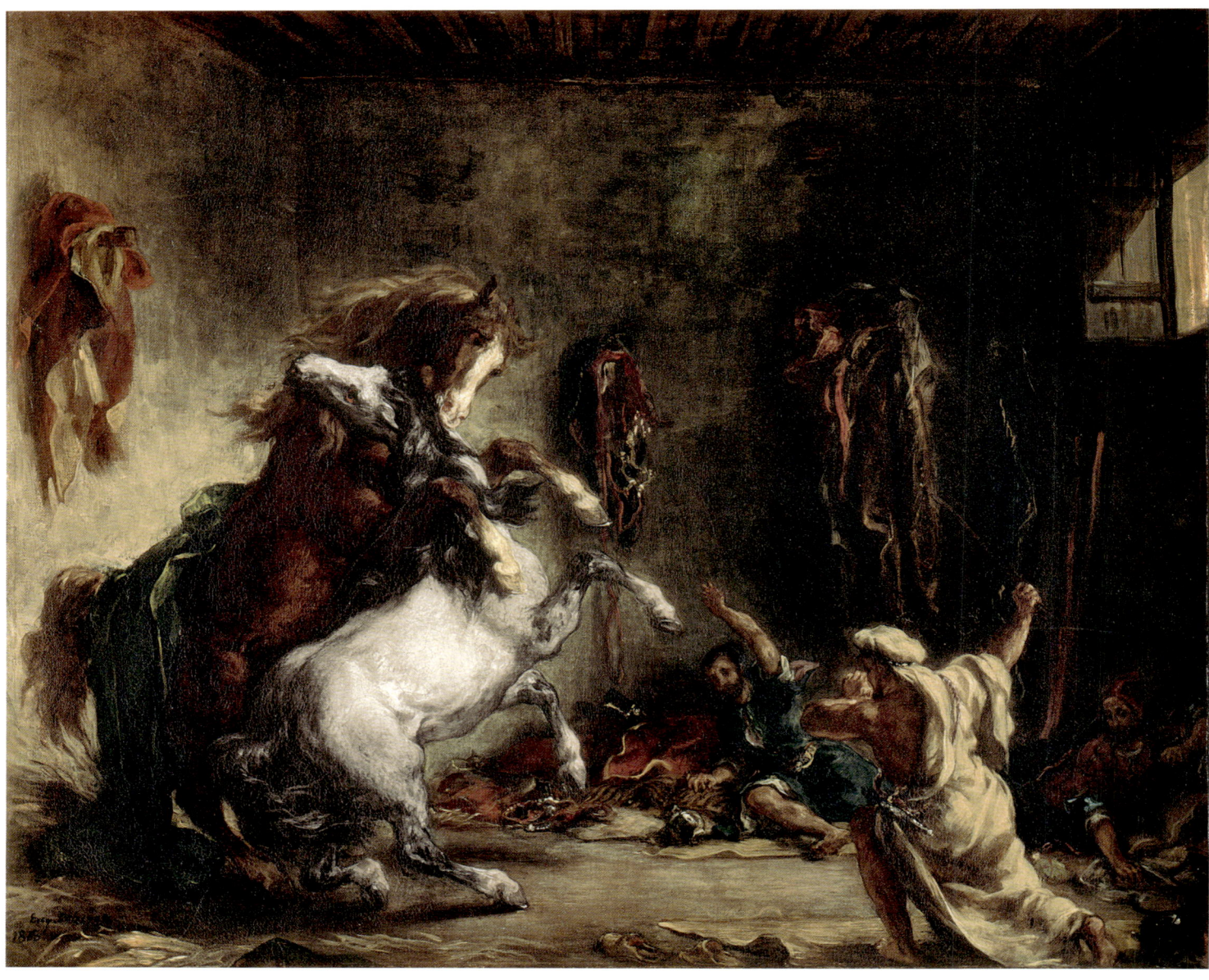

CAT. 144 *Arab Horses Fighting in a Stable*, 1860

taken directly from his oil study of the sea there (see cat. 128). Recognizable in the background is a view of the verdant coast of the Pays de Caux, between Dieppe and Fécamp. The artist noted in his *Journal* on March 10, 1858, that he was working on a "view of Dieppe with the man coming out of the sea with the two horses."[135]

If we are to believe an incidental remark Delacroix made in Le Tréport in 1854, that bridge of the imagination, which freely connected the coast of Normandy to the Moroccan coast in his mental geography, apparently did not end with the landscape. Observing the costume of the women of Le Tréport, which he found "charming," he detailed, among other

characteristics, the "sleeves of the wide shirts, down to the elbows." This comment is accompanied by a sketch—very rare in the *Journal*—immediately followed by an abrupt association of images: "the ease of movement of the Jewish women of Tangier."[136] It is also probable that the very steep and green setting of *Arabs Skirmishing in the Mountains* (fig. 92) was more indebted to the artist's journey in the Pyrénées (1845) and the area around the Château de Turenne in Corrèze (1855) than to Morocco itself. The action was inspired as much by the capture of fortresses in the novels of Scott or in Ariosto as by the few skirmishes Delacroix observed during the trip from Tangier to Meknes. *An Arab*

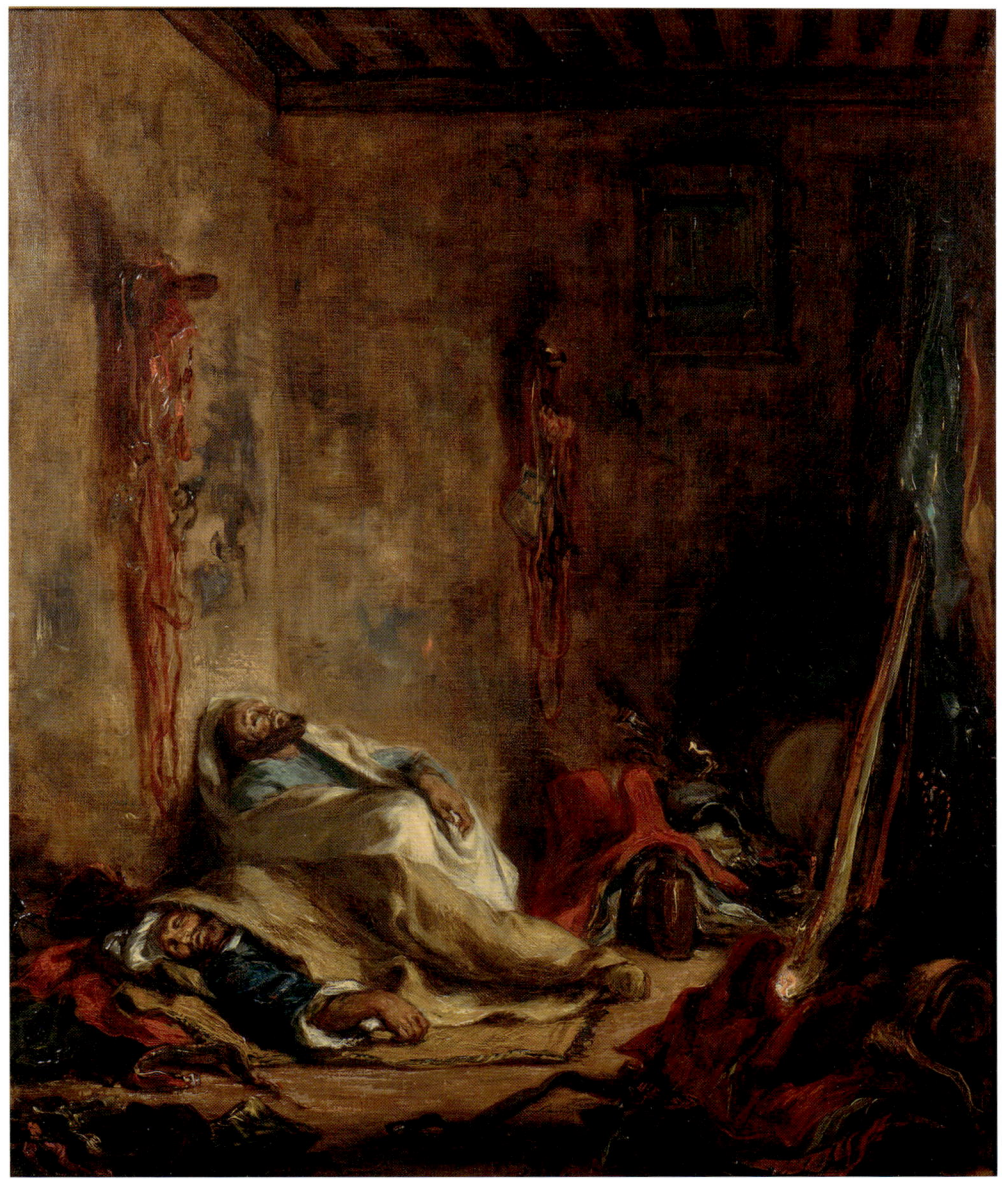

FIG. 94 *Guard-Room at Meknes,* 1846. Oil on canvas, 25¹³/₁₆ x 21⁷/₁₆ in. (65.5 x 54.5 cm). Von der Heydt Museum, Wuppertal (inv. G 1297) (J 374)

Camp at Night (fig. 93) displays few of the picturesque elements noted in the sketchbooks, such as the tents, which Delacroix relegated to the darkness in the middle ground to the left. The scene focuses on the stories favored at the bivouac around the fire. Its brightness rivals that of the moon, the light of which passes through bands of clouds. That phenomenon was based on observations of the night sky that Delacroix had made in Champrosay or on stage sets he had seen at the opera.¹³⁷

The liberating effect of memory on the artist took yet another path in the form of *Arab Horses Fighting in a Stable* (cat. 144), which depicts a fight to the death between two stallions, the recollection of an actual event described in his

Morocco sketchbooks. Twenty-eight years later, the actual outdoor setting where this event took place was replaced by an indoor one, the same one he devised for an earlier picture, *Guard-Room at Meknes* (fig. 94).

His reflections continued in 1854, again owing to the calm of Champrosay. A notation written the morning of April 28, 1854, after a moment of synesthetic grace as he was falling asleep, proved decisive:

As I awakened [in Champrosay], my thoughts turned to pleasant and sweet moments in my memory and my heart, moments I spent near my good aunt [Riesener]

in the countryside [of Frépillon near Pontoise]. . . . While reflecting on the freshness of memories and on their power to lend enchantment to the distant past, I have been marveling at the way in which our minds involuntarily suppress and brush aside anything that spoiled the charm of those happy moments when we were actually living them. I have been comparing this kind of idealization, for such it is, with the effect that great works of art have on the imagination. A great painter concentrates interest by suppressing details that are useless, offensive, or foolish. His mighty hand orders and prescribes, adding to or taking away from the objects in his paintings and treating them as his own creatures. He ranges freely throughout his kingdom and gives you a feast of his own choosing. With a second-rate artist, you feel he is master of nothing; he wields no authority over his accumulation of borrowed materials. Indeed, what possible order could he establish in a work where everything dominates him? All he can do is invent timidly and copy slavishly. Instead of suppressing the uglier aspects, as the imagination does, he gives them equal if not greater importance by the slavishness of his imitation.[138]

Having returned to Champrosay six months later, Delacroix completed his thought, this time adopting the beholder's point of view: "Painters who simply reproduce their studies never give the beholder a living sense of nature. The beholder is moved because he sees nature through the eye of his memory while he looks at your painting. Your painting must already be beautified, idealized, if you are not to seem inferior to the conception of nature formed by the ideal, which memory thrusts willy-nilly into all our recollections."[139] Although the last part of the sentence seems garbled, Delacroix was bringing to light the need for a reciprocity of the imagination—but also the problem it raises—if the artistic virtue of the work is to be fully operative. The added value of the recollection can be appreciated only if the beholder looks at the painting through a prism similar to the painter's. If he expects from Delacroix's painting only a mimetic reproduction, he will necessarily be disappointed.

It was this sharing of imaginative predispositions that Delacroix recalled in 1857, when he tried to define the imagination in his *Dictionary*: "Imagination.—It is the foremost quality of the artist. It is no less necessary to the art lover. . . .

But, though this may seem strange, most people are without it."[140] He returned again to the question a few pages later: "The principal source of interest [in the artwork] comes from the soul, and it goes irresistibly to the beholder's soul. Not that every interesting work strikes equally every beholder simply because he is supposed to have a soul: only a subject endowed with sensibility and imagination can be moved. These two faculties are as indispensable to the beholder as to the artist, though to different degrees."[141] That discriminating, even aristocratic definition of a public endowed with imaginative capacities on the same level as the artist's foreshadowed Delacroix's painful experience at the Salon of 1859 two years later. In exhibiting such unusual and demanding art to masses largely sensitized to the protorealist aesthetic of contemporary painting and photography, he necessarily exposed himself to the risk that his paintings would be widely misunderstood.

Delacroix contrasted the laborious and cumulative process of realism, which leads only to vain and "indiscreet abundance,"[142] to the force of memory, which purifies, enchants, combines, reconnects, and powerfully reorganizes the visible data. He willingly accepted the artifice of that mode of creation: "Cold precision is not art; skillful invention, when it is pleasing or when it is expressive, is art itself. The so-called conscientiousness of the majority of painters is nothing but a laboriously rendered perfection resulting in an art of the boring."[143] In that trust in memory as the essential driving force of his artistic activity at the end of his life, Delacroix maintained a profound affinity with Corot, one final indication of the parallelism of their careers. The two artists belonged to the same generation (Corot was two years older), one originally trained in the Neoclassical craft of painting; both emancipated themselves from that training at a very young age. After many years of struggle, they were able to receive public and official recognition as a result of their sustained and innovative activity, but that activity also exposed them to the risk of being left behind by the realist revolution. Corot and Delacroix therefore proposed an art based on the nostalgic and serene reminiscence of an intimate pictorial imagination, constantly reborn in new combinations in the crucible of their studios.

When Delacroix visited Corot in his studio on March 14, 1847, Corot, significantly, encouraged him to trust his instinct, to "let myself go a little and to allow myself to take things as they come."[144] In the 1850s the method shared by Corot and Delacroix, the two living monuments of French painting, was to set off on an adventure without leaving the studio, to combine constantly the treasures of their vast mental and emotional picture libraries. Such healthy work habits allowed them to continue creating as painters and to cultivate carefully their uniqueness in a world where the accelerated production and circulation of images were scrambling all codes and placing originality in peril.

The New Pantheon of the Old Masters

The distorting filter of personal memory, though it assumed increasing importance in Delacroix's art, must not allow us to forget the persistence of references to the old masters. The painter implicitly established correspondences among motifs, subjects, and a certain tradition. We have already seen the connection between rocks and the scenes of deliverance inspired by Veronese. In the same way, Delacroix wrote, returning from a nocturnal stroll in Champrosay: "The sight of the stars shining through the trees gave me the idea to do a painting that would show this poetic effect, which is difficult to render in painting because of the darkness of the whole: *Flight into Egypt.* Saint Joseph leading the donkey and illuminating a small ford with a lantern; that weak light would suffice for the contrast."[145] For Delacroix, then, the motif of the starry night was not to be rendered for its own sake; rather, it would serve as a framework for a subject drawn from the Gospels, in a layout that, according to Delacroix's cursory description, was developed in the late sixteenth century by Adam Elsheimer.[146]

His relationship to the masters is subject to intriguing lines of inquiry. Rubens still held a central place in his pantheon, but he was reclassified in response to Delacroix's new concerns in the last decade of his life. The painter, leaving aside somewhat the quest for the sublime, pathos, and the rendering of flesh, looked more critically at Michelangelo and Rubens. Conversely, his admiration grew for Titian, Veronese, and Rembrandt, three painters renowned for their attention to the unity and harmony of compositions, a constant concern of Delacroix's in his final years. He found the broad strokes of these painters akin to his own. When his friend Paul Chenavard praised engravings after Michelangelo's *Last Judgment*, Delacroix voiced his disagreement: "I see only striking details, details that strike like a punch; but the unity, the interest, the continuity of it all is absent. . . . Titian—now there is a man made to be enjoyed by those who are growing

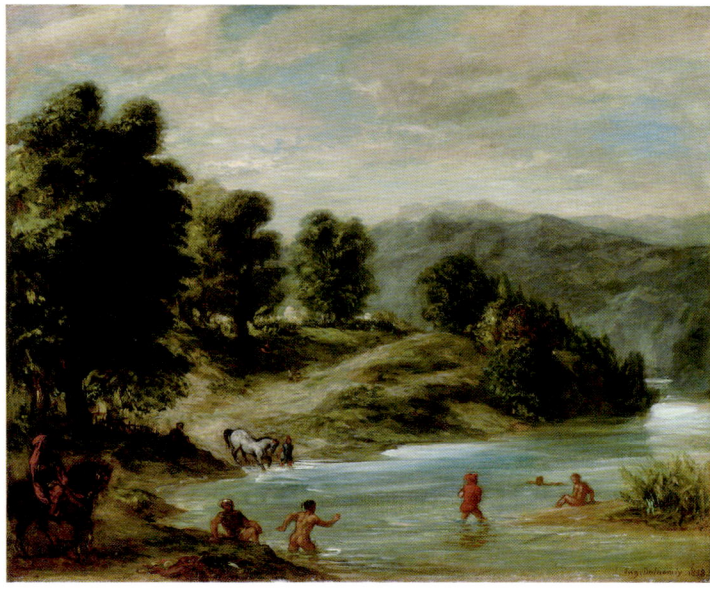

FIG. 95 *The Banks of the River Sébou*, 1858. Oil on canvas, 19½ x 23¾ in. (49.6 x 60.3 cm). Pérez Simón Collection, Mexico (J L169)

old. I confess I had no appreciation for him during the time when I greatly admired Michelangelo and Lord Byron."[147]

Three years later, in a plan for a project "In Praise of Titian," Delacroix argued that the Venetian master "can be considered the creator of landscape painting. He brought to it the same breadth of treatment that he gave to the rendering of figures and draperies.—We stand amazed at the power and fertility, the universality of those men of the sixteenth century."[148] A few days later he added:

> If we lived to be a hundred and twenty, we should end by preferring Titian above everyone. He is not a young man's painter. He is the least mannered and therefore the most varied of artists. . . . Titian originated that breadth of handling that broke sharply away from the dryness of his predecessors and is the very perfection of painting. . . . This breadth of Titian's is the final aim of painting and is as far removed from the dryness of the primitives as from the monstrous abuse of touch and the soft slickness of painters in decadent periods.[149]

Delacroix placed Veronese alongside Titian: "There is one man who produces brightness without violent contrasts, who produces the open air, which we have repeatedly been told is impossible: Paul Veronese. In my opinion, he is probably the

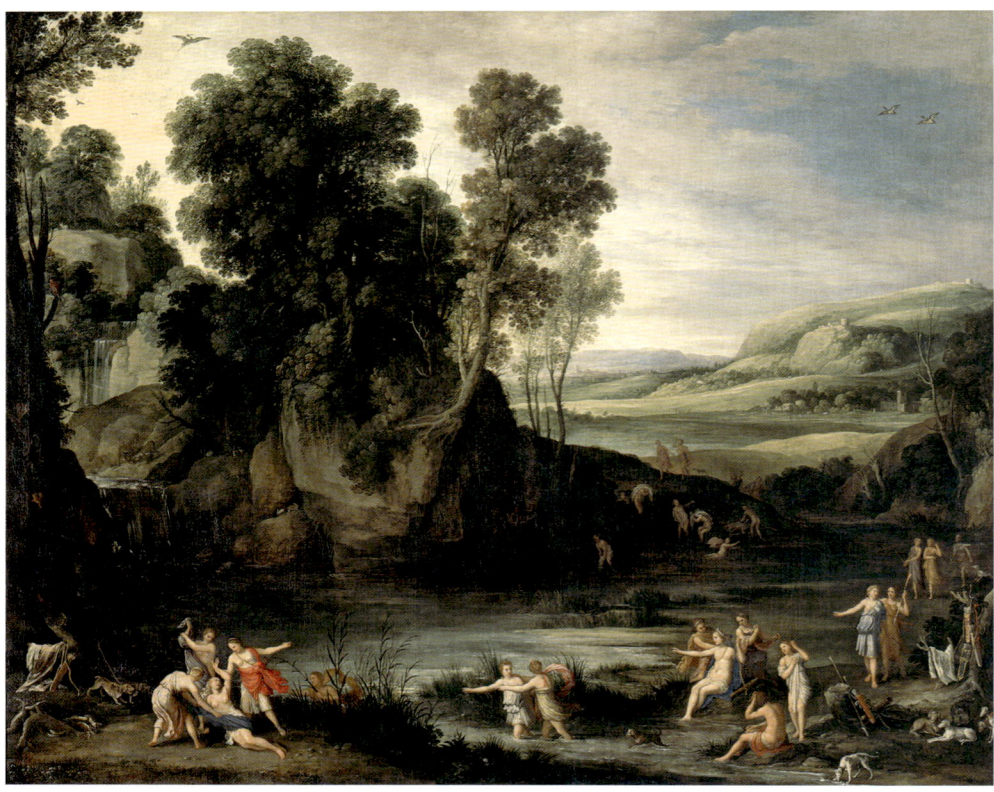

FIG. 96 Paul Bril (Netherlandish, 1553/54–1626). *Diana Discovering Callisto's Pregnancy*, 1615–20. Oil on canvas, 63⅜ x 81⅛ in. (161 x 206 cm). Musée du Louvre, Paris (207)

only one who captured the full secret of nature."[150] These words were written in April 1859, a few weeks before Delacroix exhibited *Ovid among the Scythians* (see cat. 142), its emerald and turquoise harmony similar to that of the final compositions of the Venetian master.

The influence also comes through in a work exhibited under the title *The Banks of the River Sebou* (*Kingdom of Morocco*) at the Salon of 1859 (fig. 95).[151] The landscape painting was linked to an episode that occurred during the expedition between Tangier and Meknes in 1832.[152] The naïveté of the landscape hardly fooled the critics. Mathilde Stevens made fun of that "Norman Africa," while Mantz was reminded of the landscape paintings of Rubens.[153] Yet it seems the conjunction between the Flemish and the Italian traditions of painting the landscape at the dawn of the seventeenth century served as Delacroix's model. At the Louvre, he was able to see the landscapes of Domenichino and Paul Bril. In addition to the motif of bathers in the foreground, Bril's *Diana Discovering Callisto's Pregnancy* (fig. 96) displays unusual similarities to *Banks of the River Sebou*, in both its composition and its color scheme.

In the entry he planned for the *Dictionary of the Fine Arts* "on Landscape, *as accompaniment to the subjects*," Delacroix noted "the ignorance of almost all the great masters of the

effect that could be drawn from it." Even Rubens was reproached for not establishing a close enough relationship between his figures and the landscape. Conversely, "the landscapes of Titian, Rembrandt, and Poussin are generally in harmony with the figures.—In Rembrandt—and this is perfection itself—the background and figures are one. The interest is everywhere, nothing is separate. It is like some lovely natural scene where everything combines to please."[154] "It is really not until Rembrandt that you see the beginning of that harmony between the details and the principal subject, which I consider to be one of the most important elements, if not the most important element, in a painting."[155]

His admiration for these painters was directed primarily at their mastery of harmony in complex compositions. They were able, smoothly and easily, to assemble and articulate in the space of a single landscape a complex, poetic, and universal discourse. They thus offered a response to Delacroix's principal aesthetic concern in his final years. He believed that, in the evolution of the painting of his time, the excesses of realism and eclecticism led to fragmentation, dissonance, and the absence of meaning. Moreover, he disapproved of the unevenness of his own early works and wished to increase the unity of his painting, even while continuing to treat complex historical and philosophical subjects.

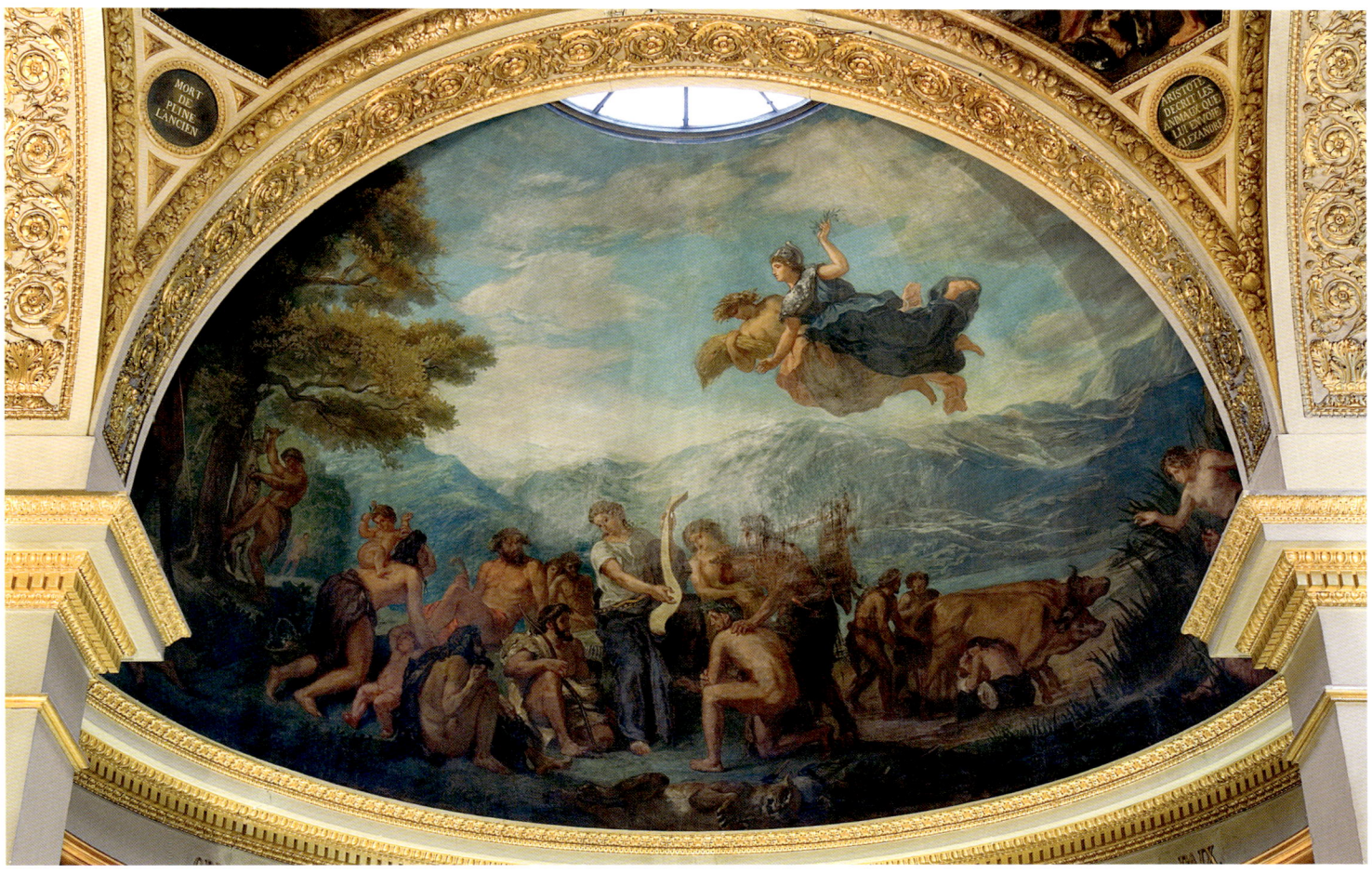

FIG. 97 *Orpheus Civilizes the Greeks and Teaches Them the Arts of Peace,* 1845–47. Oil and wax on plaster, 24 ft. 1⅜ in. x 36 ft. ¼ in. (7.3 x 11 m). Half-dome, Deputies' Library, Assemblée Nationale (Palais Bourbon), Paris (J 540)

Painting as Microcosm: The Painter "Moves about His Domain and Gives You a Feast to His Own Liking"

In the first half of the nineteenth century, painting had a pronounced tendency to embrace an encyclopedic ambition. The development of the history of the arts, the sciences, and philosophy fostered a progressive, global, and hierarchical vision of civilization. It also encouraged increasingly ambitious efforts to synthesize, by means of the image, the most productive and beneficial things European culture had created for itself and for the rest of humanity. In the wake of Ingres's *Apotheosis of Homer* (1827; Musée du Louvre), plans were elaborated for Panthéons (by Delaroche) and Palingeneses (by Chenavard), facilitated by public commissions. Delacroix participated in the movement through his library decorations. His historical discourse, at first fragmented into a series of decorated pendentives and

apses for the library of the Palais Bourbon, would come together in a single space in the cupola of the library of the Palais du Luxembourg (see fig. 40). At the time, he experienced and confronted the tensions between the encyclopedic ambition of the discourse and the necessary unity of the image. Villot recounted the genesis of the iconographic program:

> The evening when he came to share with us the news [of receiving the commission], he found me reading Dante's *Inferno,* and he had hardly finished his invariable question in such cases—What ought to be put there?—than I told him: 'I have just the thing: two admirable subjects that naturally go hand in hand.' Then I read him the passage in which Dante tells of his arrival in the Elysian Fields, the welcome given him by Horace, Ovid, Lucan, and Homer.

Villot also advised Delacroix to add "various episodes that could be brought into the composition, which would allow you to introduce women and men—nude or draped—animals, and a magnificent landscape."[156] The difficulty, of course, lay in making a motley collection of illustrious philosophers, artists, poets, lawmakers, generals, and war heroes hold together, at the risk of creating a heterogeneous and off-putting juxtaposition of "great men." The solemnity and studious atmosphere of the space below the cupola also precluded a violently agitated composition of sharp contrasts. The required clarity and serenity could give rise to tedium. The aesthetic solution lay, first, in the suggestion of Dante and his visit to the Elysian Fields as the subject and, second, in Poussin's poetics of painting.

Poussin's *Inspiration of the Poet* (ca. 1629–30; Musée du Louvre) gave Delacroix a brilliant encapsulation of all the ingredients that would allow him to link idea and action, history and myth, even while guaranteeing smooth connections between the figures, to create a narrative with diverse light sources, colors, and gestures that would break the monotony. Taking Poussin as his model, Delacroix laid out arcadian landscapes in a bluish atmosphere, with myrtle bushes and laurel trees. He introduced women in the guise of nymphs, muses, and poetesses, and scattered about nude children and winged genies (one brings Cincinnatus his helmet, another offers water to Dante from the Hippocrene spring, while a third bestows the palm leaf on Socrates), as well as symbolic animals: the swan of Apollo, a doe and a leopard near Orpheus. The challenge was met with panache, as critics pointed out at the unveiling of the cupola:

> M. Delacroix's genius is essentially complex: it embraces every horizon where the human soul can lose its way. . . . What impressed us no less is the extreme deftness with which all the heroes are arranged into groups. Disseminated, in appearance, under the dense shade of the myrtles, on the green mounds of the prairie, they obey the imperious law of the group and are connected to one another by lighting effects, a trick of color, an artful unevenness of the terrain, and almost always as well by the idea.[157]

"The colorist's reputation is assured, but the reputation of the composer and the poet will certainly be further enhanced by the publicity afforded by the paintings at the Luxembourg."[158]

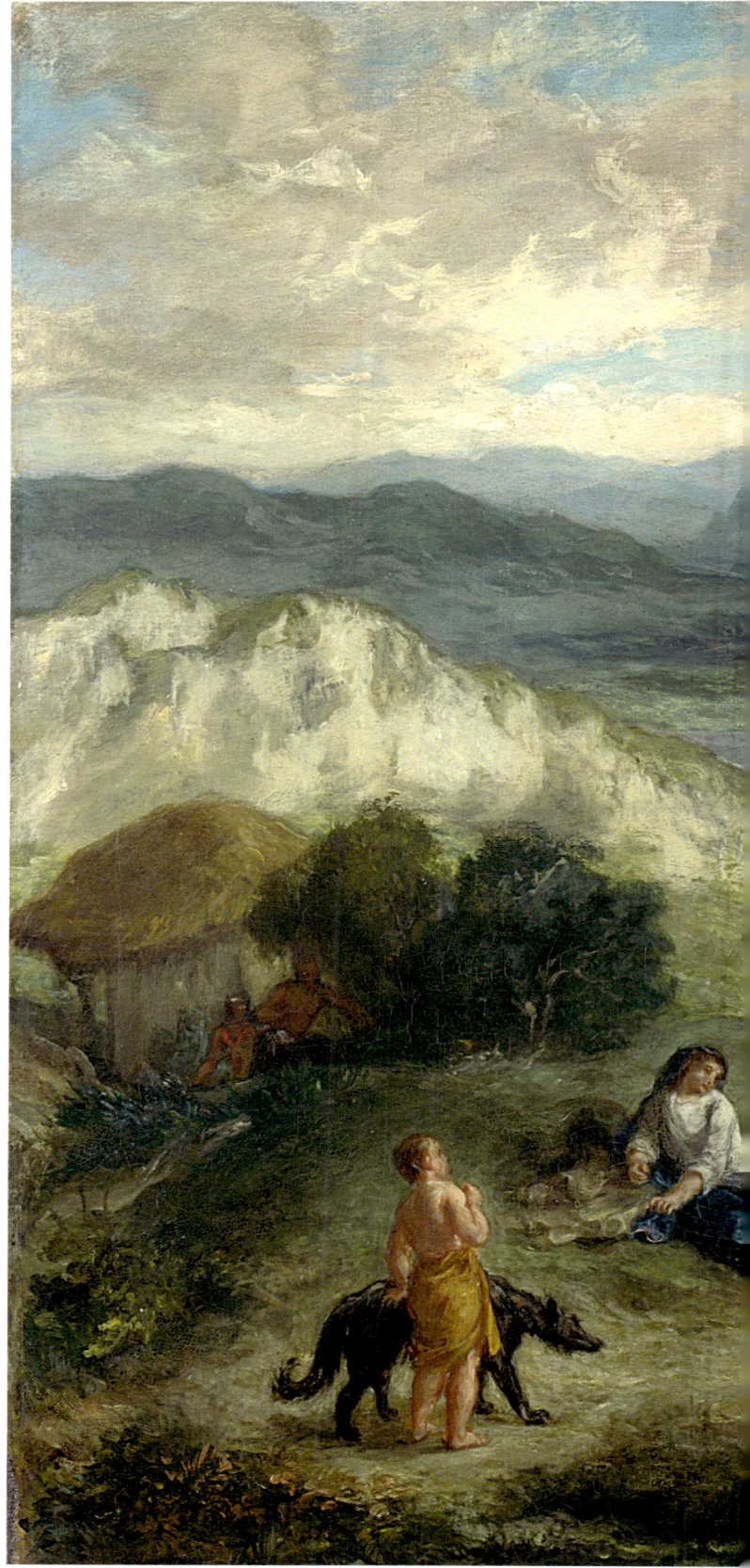

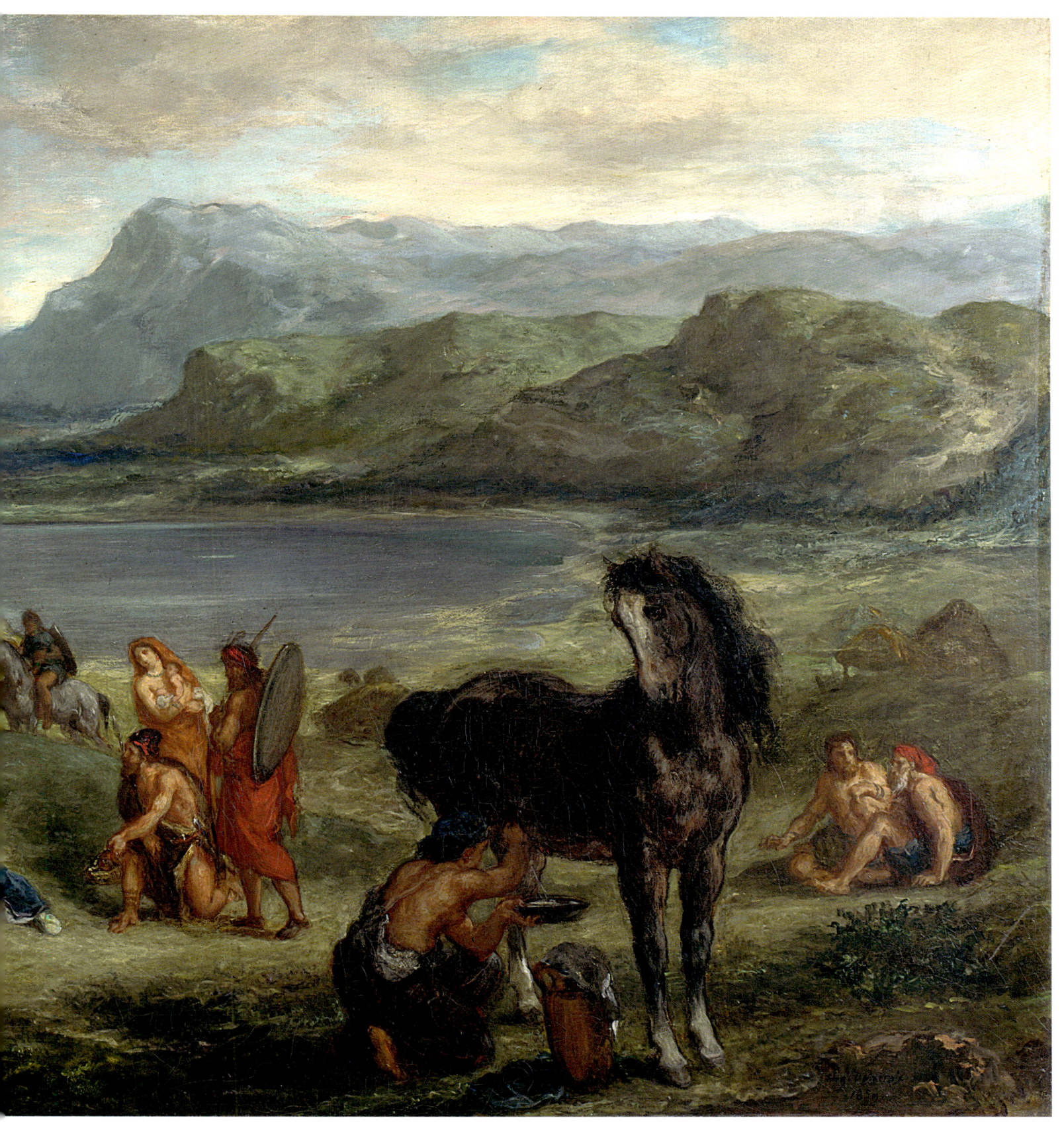

CAT. 142 *Ovid among the Scythians*, 1859

During this period, Delacroix had painted an identical composition for the half-dome in the library of the Palais Bourbon: *Orpheus Civilizes the Greeks and Teaches Them the Arts of Peace* (fig. 97). It represents the felicitous birth of civilization; its extinction was painted in the opposing apse, in the form of *Attila and His Hordes Overrun Italy and the Arts*. With *Ovid among the Scythians* (cat. 142) about ten years later, Delacroix seems to have wished to rework that same program on the scale of a large easel painting to be exhibited before the public. As Henri Loyrette noted, the artist did not adopt the plaintive tone of Ovid's *Tristia*. Rather, he turned to the description of the Scythians by the Greek geographer Strabo, who remarked on their communal and harmonious social model, the simplicity of their economy, their frugality, and their innocent ways.[159] The positive vision of an ignorant and barbarian society, but one that was peaceful and spared from corruption, agreed with a reflection Delacroix had inscribed in the *carnet héliotrope*: "Framework for the history of an ailing heart and imagination, that of a man who, having lived a worldly life, finds himself a slave among the barbarians, or cast onto a desert island like Robinson Crusoe, forced to employ his bodily strength and his industry—which makes him return to natural feelings and calms his imagination . . . *Ovid among the Scythians*."[160] The subject, though represented a first time on one of the many pendentives in the library of the Palais Bourbon, was far from exhausted in Delacroix's opinion. In 1849 he had expressed the need to rework "the subject of *Ovid in Exile*, composed in a larger format."[161]

Ovid among the Scythians, as it was conceived and painted between 1855 and 1859, can be considered a kind of summation, in the sense that it represents Delacroix's most intimate philosophical thoughts and deeply personal pictorial motifs. The situation of the banished poet Ovid, welcomed with generosity and respect by the barbarians—they kneel before him and share their humble meal—allowed Delacroix to synthesize the ideas he had developed about the inevitable fate of great civilizations (a drift toward authoritarianism, moral decadence, social disintegration) and great geniuses (incomprehension, slander, exile). But he also introduced the hope of a possible regeneration, permitted by the Rousseauist credo of precivilized man's intuition of the beautiful, but also by the great man's tolerance, which ought to prevail over his contempt for ignorance. That revived optimism comes through in an article published two years earlier: "The man of London and Paris may be farther from a proper sense of

beauty than the uneducated man who lives in regions where nothing is known of the pursuits of civilization. We see the beautiful only through the imagination of poets and painters; the savage encounters it with every step of his nomadic life. . . . In this the Siberian resembles the Greek [of the Archaic period] and the Berber."[162] From a formal perspective, Delacroix took the details provided by Strabo on Scythian landscapes and the people's ways (for example, the importance of mare's milk as the basis of the Scythian diet) as an opportunity to recapitulate all the beautiful bits of painting he had perfected through study and the use of his memory over a decade: horses, dogs, children, nude or draped men and women, prairies and mountains, expanses of water and clouds.

Finally, the meditation on what ought to survive civilization in general and his own oeuvre in particular may have led Delacroix to reflect from a distance on his artistic and social career. Having attained the serenity of a career crowned with honors, but also protected from intrigues, did he remember the uproarious and almost self-destructive audacity that had guided him as a young artist? A discreet inverted quotation of *The Death of Sardanapalus* (see cat. 104) can in fact be detected in *Ovid*. In each of these compositions, the hero of the scene is a small figure enveloped in a white tunic, reclining in the middle ground, his weight resting on his left arm; a horse occupies the foreground. After the final orgy of a tyrant who embodies civilization at its most inhumane and corrupt, the artist depicts a return to the most ingenuous state of a human community, which seems to recognize instinctively the superiority and respect that poetic genius inspires.

At the risk of a biographical interpretation, we may also detect an even more personal resonance in the theme and framework of Ovid's exile. The landscape of *Ovid among the Scythians* displays a striking similarity to a landscape study Delacroix kept in his studio until his death.[163] The study is said to have been painted in the 1820s, as a recollection of the Vienne Valley, south of Touraine. A comparison between it and the *Ovid* decoration is unsettling, not only because of the format and the depth, evoked by the staggered rows of mountains slightly eroded by the river, but also because of the close resemblance between the skies in the two works and the overall balance of the color scheme. The fact that Delacroix could base himself on that old study in 1856–57, more than thirty years after its execution, raises a question: Was it purely by chance, or should we attribute a meaning to the act of borrowing, one having to do with the theme of exile common to the two works? Delacroix discovered Touraine in his youth precisely because his family was exiled: he passed through it many times when returning to Charente, where his elder sister, Henriette—bankrupted by bad investments—had taken refuge to avoid the high cost of living in Paris. His brother Charles Henry, a baron who received his title during the Empire and a general on half-pay, also lived in Touraine. Forced to get by on his wits after the fall of Napoleon and the death of his protector, Eugène de Beauharnais, Charles Henry had to accept very humble accommodations in the area around Tours. At the time, Eugène Delacroix, young and on the threshold of success, had felt a mixture of shame and compassion for the wretched situation of his elder brother, a "tired libertine" who concealed his loss of social status while living "surrounded by roughnecks and riff-raff."[164]

Thirty years later, the suffering and dissension were forgotten; what remained was the pleasure, on returning to the family's roots in familiar landscapes, of reviving the memory of loved ones he had lost. In 1855, during his stay with the Verninacs in Corrèze, he was pleased to imagine himself once more "with these dear ones in Touraine and Charente, places that are beautiful to me, beautiful to my heart." The enchanting filter of past time and memory metamorphosed the land of forced exile into an earthly paradise, where the aged artist, having lost his illusions about the world, more willingly consented to retire.

It is possible that the unifying ambition that seems to have guided Delacroix in *Ovid among the Scythians* (see cat. 142) and its testamentary nature might have taken a different form or found an even richer, complementary outlet. In 1855, the year Delacroix came up with the first sketch for *Ovid*,[165] he wrote of another project, rather similar formally, taken from Genesis. "A magnificent subject: *Noah's Sacrifice with His Family after the Flood*. The animals are spreading out over the earth, the birds into the air—the monsters, condemned by divine wisdom, lie half buried in the mud; the dripping branches reach toward the sky."[166] Nearly two years later, while Delacroix was working on *Ovid* (its execution was commissioned by Benoît Fould), the idea of that "magnificent subject" came back to him and was faithfully recopied.[167] It reappeared two weeks later, then once again in 1860, when he was rereading the *Journal* of 1855. Delacroix formulated his idea a third time and this time completed it: "The clouds run along the horizon; Eurus and Notus disperse them. The sun

returns, radiant: everything seems to be reborn and to sing a hymn to the Lord."[168] The subject probably interested Delacroix for the same reasons as Ovid: it was a moment of restored peace and union among human beings, animals, and nature within a vast lakeside landscape. The sacrifice of Noah also would have allowed him to evoke the aftermath of cataclysm in the landscape and to depict the repopulation of the earth by humans and animals. Delacroix's entire bestiary could have flourished there in a lavish display. Finally, the painter could certainly have engaged in a dialogue with the great masters, primarily Michelangelo but also Jacopo Bassano, Baldassare Castiglione, Bruegel, and Rubens.

That testamentary exercise of synthesis, which occurred about 1855, can be explained in part by the context. Not only was Delacroix at the height of his career, but he was also granted the rare privilege (no doubt unprecedented in the history of French painting) of a vast retrospective exhibition during his lifetime. The event was not just for the benefit of the public and the critics but for himself as well. Regrettably, he did not express what he felt on seeing his body of work reassembled in a single space. It is possible to imagine that such an experience could have sparked the desire to produce a final summation and to bequeath to posterity a key to understanding his most profound artistic aspirations. The same mechanism may have been at work in Ingres, another beneficiary, in 1855, of a solo retrospective, who was engaged during the same period in a synthesis of his motifs in *The Turkish Bath* (1852–59, modified 1862; Musée du Louvre).

When Delacroix reintroduced himself to the public at the Salon of 1859, he did not do so only with the microcosm of *Ovid*, the reprise of a subject for a large decorative painting, enriched with the landscapes, populations, fauna, and flora of ancient Scythia. He also included: *Erminia*, a microcosm of the Renaissance world of chivalry; the second version of *The Abduction of Rebecca* (cat. 141), which conveys the sparkling medieval imagination of Sir Walter Scott; *The Banks of the River Sebou*, with its procession of memories of Morocco; the fifth version of *Hamlet and Horatio in the Graveyard*, which summed up his long engagement with Shakespeare's works; and the golden and bloody legend of Christianity, with *Saint Sebastian* (sixth reprise) and *The Ascent to Calvary* (the initial idea for the decoration of Saint-Sulpice). The juxtaposition of these concentrated worlds, covering in appearance a small surface but delving deep into time and the spaces the artist had passed through over nearly forty years, allowed Delacroix to give a form to the enormous pictorial galaxy constructed in the twilight of his career. That world grew out of his understanding of the great books and his mastery of all the genres of painting. It was later revitalized by an uninterrupted dialogue with the great painters of the past and the successive challenges of the large decorative paintings. And it was finally enriched by his awareness of the passage of time and the creative force of memory. The artist thus demonstrated the maturity, autonomy, and fertility of his pictorial imagination, the definition of which he had finally set down in writing: "The artist's imagination does not merely represent objects of one kind or another: it combines them for the end it wishes to achieve; it makes pictures, images that it composes as it likes."[169] To borrow his own terms, Delacroix was finally ranging freely throughout his entire kingdom and giving, to all eyes willing to linger there, "a feast of his own choosing."[170]

The public and the art critics were accustomed to glorifying Delacroix as a painter of *grandes machines* and large decorative works. But, with the exception of Baudelaire and Astruc, they did not understand what was being played out in these little worlds. Not until ten years after Delacroix's death did Gautier look back and seem to have taken their measure:

> Delacroix was not one of those painters who liked to close himself off in a narrow specialization and represent only a small number of objects, always the same. His vast talent embraced nature as a whole, and everything that had life, form, and color was within the ken of his palette. With a spirit remarkably harmonious in its apparent disorder, he made a world of his own, a microcosm where he reigned as master, composing and decomposing its elements depending on the effect he wanted to produce. All the images of nature floated in it, not copied but conceived and transformed, used like words to express ideas and, especially, passions. In the slightest sketch as in the largest painting, the sky, the earth, the trees, the sea, and the factories participate in the scene they surround. They are stormy or clear, smooth or turbulent, leafless or verdant, calm or convulsive, ruined or magnificent, but always they seem to embrace the wrath, the hatred, the sorrow, and the sadness of the characters. It would be impossible to detach the figures from the landscape. They themselves have meaningful costumes, draperies, weapons, and accessories that could not be used by others. Everything ties together, everything is tied up to form a magic whole, from which no part could be removed or transposed without making the entire edifice collapse. In art, we know of only Rembrandt who has that same unity, profound and indissoluble. That is because these two great masters created their works by an inner vision of sorts. They had the gift of making it perceptible with the means they possessed, rather than through an immediate study of the subject. Rembrandt, like Delacroix, had his architecture, his changing room, his arsenal, his museum of antiques, his types and forms, his light and darkness, his ranges of colors, which do not exist elsewhere and from which he knows how to extract marvelous effects, rendering the fantastic truer than reality.[171]

CAT. 98 *The Shipwreck of Don Juan*, 1840, detail

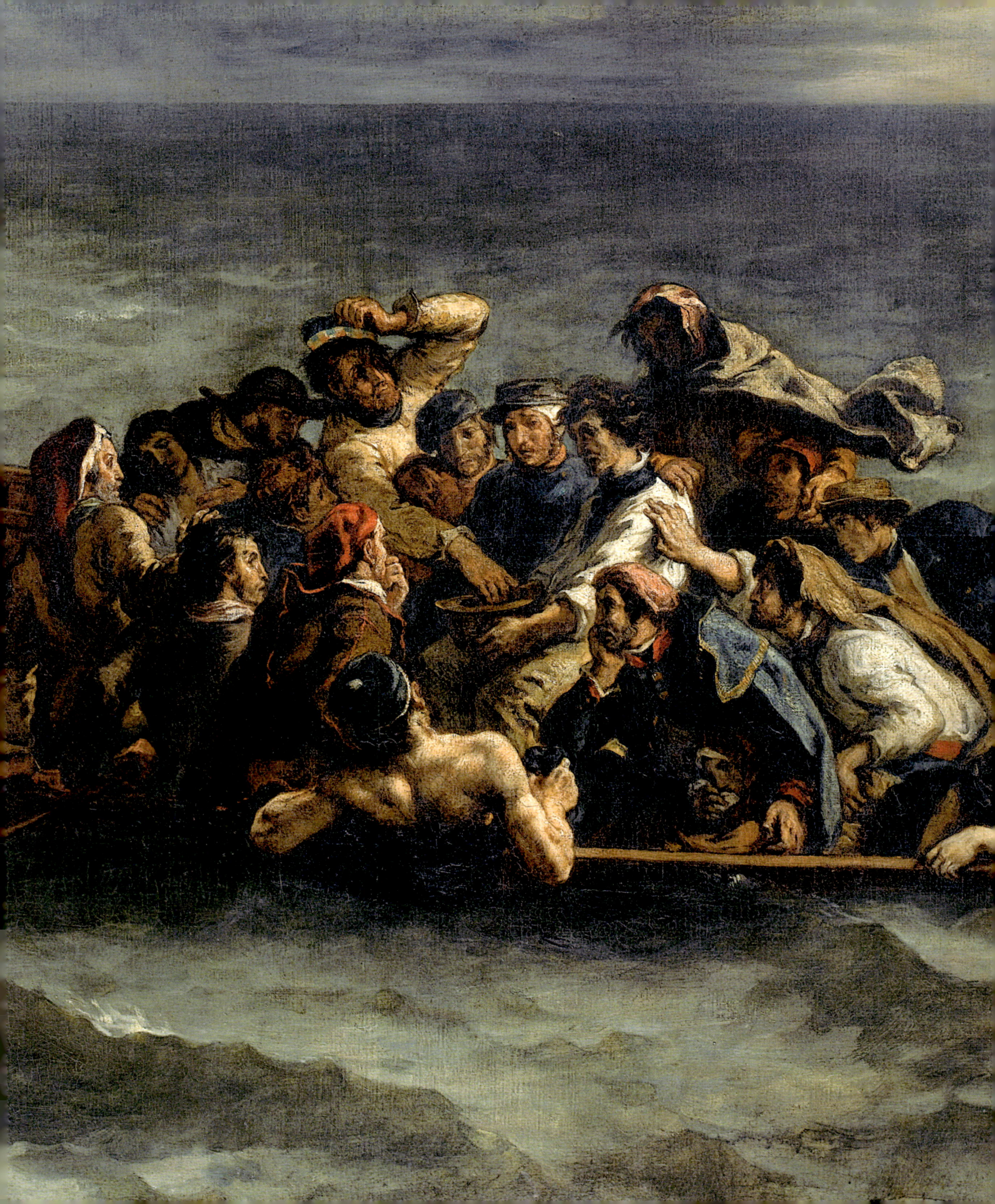

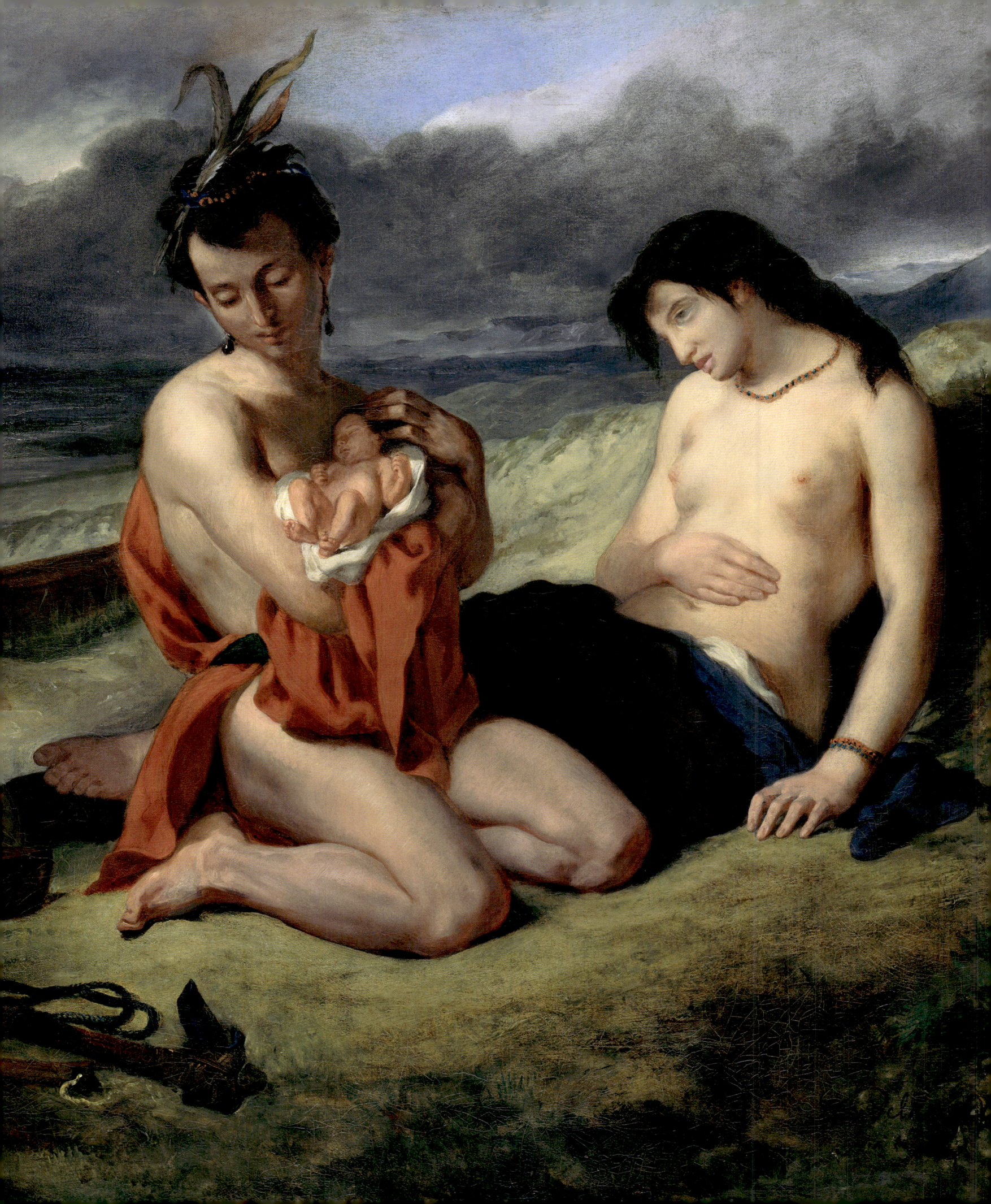

The Act of Looking in Delacroix's Early Narrative Paintings

ASHER MILLER

Sometime in 1824 or 1825, on a leaf of paper crammed with jottings and sketches, Delacroix noted to himself, "look for a subject."[1] Delacroix's imagination was galvanized by an active dialogue between visual and literary stimuli. To realize his paintings, the artist drew from a vast store of pictorial sources, most immediately, the holdings of the Louvre. And a passion for reading, encompassing the Bible and the latest novels of Sir Walter Scott, catalyzed his creative process. Distinctive among the subjects he chose to paint were narrative historical scenes in which the protagonists' act of looking was crucial to the unfolding of the story. The focus of this essay is Delacroix's particular attraction to subjects that enabled him to stage the act of looking in his paintings. Delacroix sought to engage his viewers by portraying a trail of gazes that they could follow with their own eyes, even if they were unfamiliar with the literary source depicted. The following account of his treatment of the theme of sight during the 1820s will shed light on his larger aims as he sought to build an audience through the display of paintings of varying size and ambition at the Salon during the opening decade of his career.

As the decade opened, Delacroix was a young art student who had yet to produce a major painting. On May 1, 1820, in a letter to his sister, Henriette de Verninac, Delacroix described the activities that made up his daily routine. "I rise fairly early," he wrote, explaining, "I practice my harpsichord

a little or read. Then I eat a frugal lunch . . . Next I go to work either at the Museum or at M. Guérin's." Following dinner, "I go to my [drawing class] three times a week, which takes up the better part of my evenings."[2] After quitting Pierre Narcisse Guérin's studio he wrote to Henriette again, on May 30, adding a detail in connection with his afternoon work at the Louvre, ". . . which I wouldn't miss because I've paid for a very expensive scaffold. . ."[3] Many years later, Delacroix's friend Charles Soulier would recall finding the aspiring twenty-two-year-old painter, apparently on June 10, 1820, "perched at the top of an immense ladder in the Grand Salon of the Louvre, copying heads in Paul Veronese's *Marriage at Cana*" (fig. 98).[4]

Close study of masterpieces, especially by means of copying, was a core practice of artistic training. Veronese's picture—then as now the largest in the Louvre—was considered exemplary not only for its vivid color, dynamic brushwork, and drama, but also for its deployment of some 130 figures in a thoroughly unified and harmonious composition. From its arrival at the museum in 1798, *Cana* was central to the revival of the Venetian school's prestige, which took hold especially during the Romantic period. Delacroix's copy (cat. 3) reproduces two bearded heads seen in left profile, a detail no more or less remarkable than any other he could have selected in the original painting. Perhaps most notable are the impressive

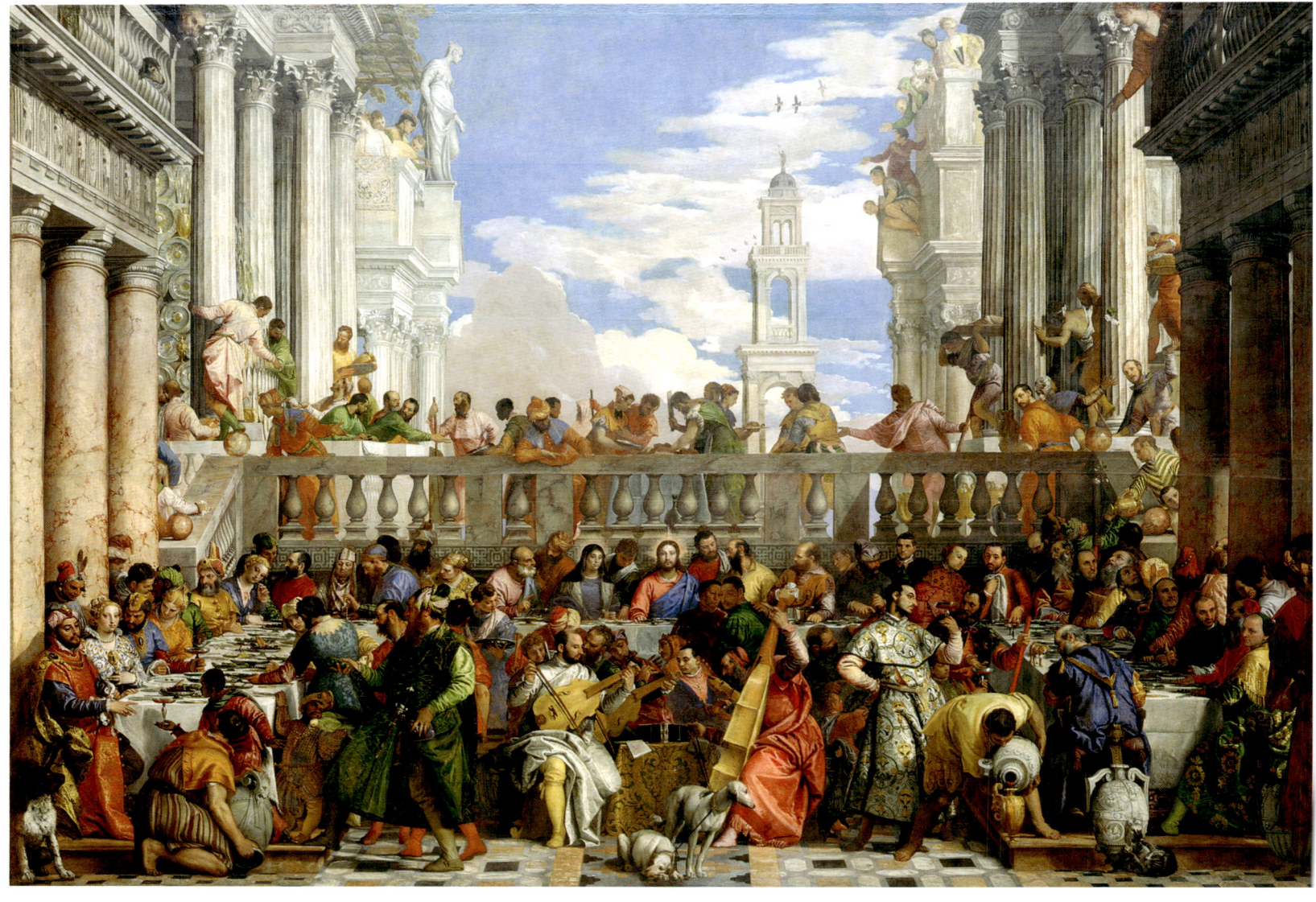

FIG. 98. Paolo Veronese (Italian, 1528–1588). *The Marriage at Cana*, 1563. Oil on canvas, 22 ft. 3 in. x 32 ft. (6.8 x 9.8 m). Musée du Louvre, Paris (142)

dimensions of the copy, which, at sixty-four centimeters in height by eighty-two in width, is executed on the same imposing scale as its source. By employing a scaffold, Delacroix was able to produce an aide-mémoire for his studio based on close study of Veronese's brushwork.

Delacroix's selection of these figures may have been suggested by a similar copy, one made by his somewhat older friend and mentor Théodore Gericault (fig. 99).[5] Gericault's copy, of similar size, features the same two figures, but it also includes seven others, as well as the shoulder of an eighth seen from behind—and a parrot. Gericault took certain liberties, introducing subtle shifts in position that turn the grouping into a veritable ring of heads. One consequence of pulling multiple figures closer together was to link them; the dwarf's

glance, for example, now connects more directly with the central bearded figure.[6] The result holds together almost as an independent composition, if not precisely a "complete" work of art. Whether Delacroix saw Gericault's creative copy before he painted his own is a matter of conjecture, but he eventually came to own it, possibly acquiring it after Gericault's death on January 26, 1824, at his atelier sale. Rather than forge a new context for the two bearded figures, as Gericault had done, Delacroix simply excised them from their original setting, rendering it impossible to identify the object of their gaze.

In Veronese's picture, the bearded men are stewards of the house of Cana, and they address the bride and groom, who are found at the far left of the vast painting. The bride, in

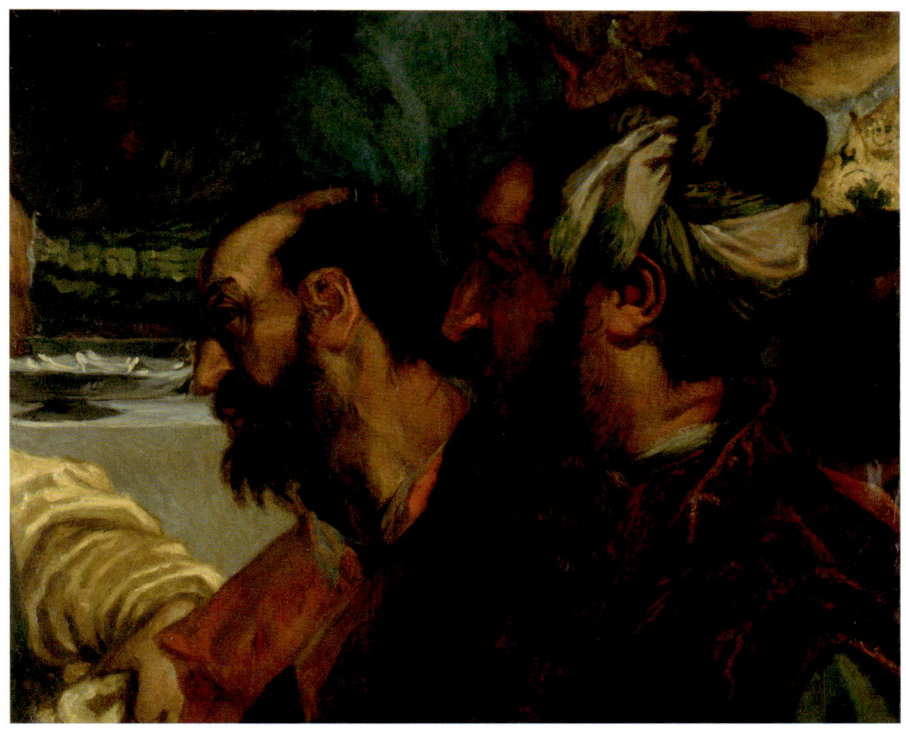

CAT. 3 *Two Bearded Heads, after Veronese*
(detail from "The Marriage at Cana"), 1820

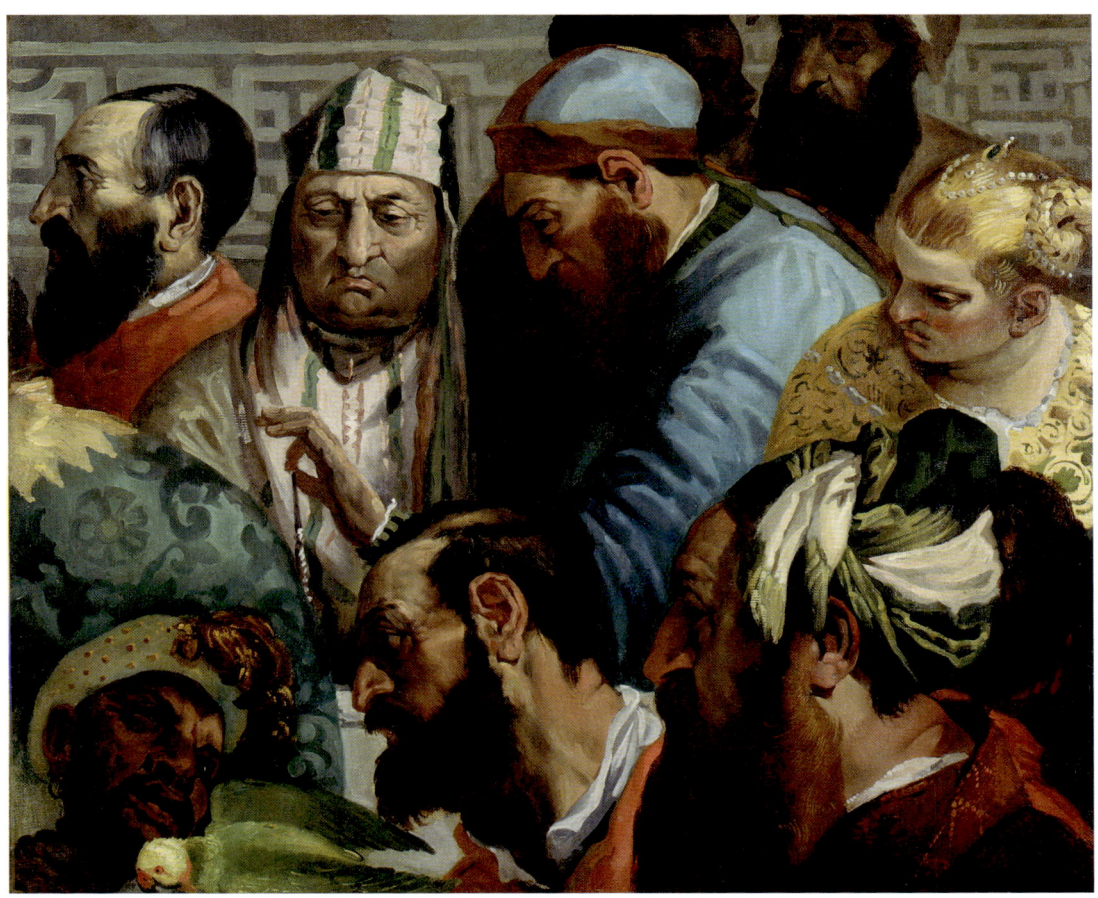

FIG. 99. Théodore Gericault. *Study after Veronese* (detail from *The Marriage at Cana*), ca. 1810(?). Oil on canvas, 25³⁄₁₆ x 32⁵⁄₁₆ in. (64 x 82 cm). Museum Folkwang, Essen

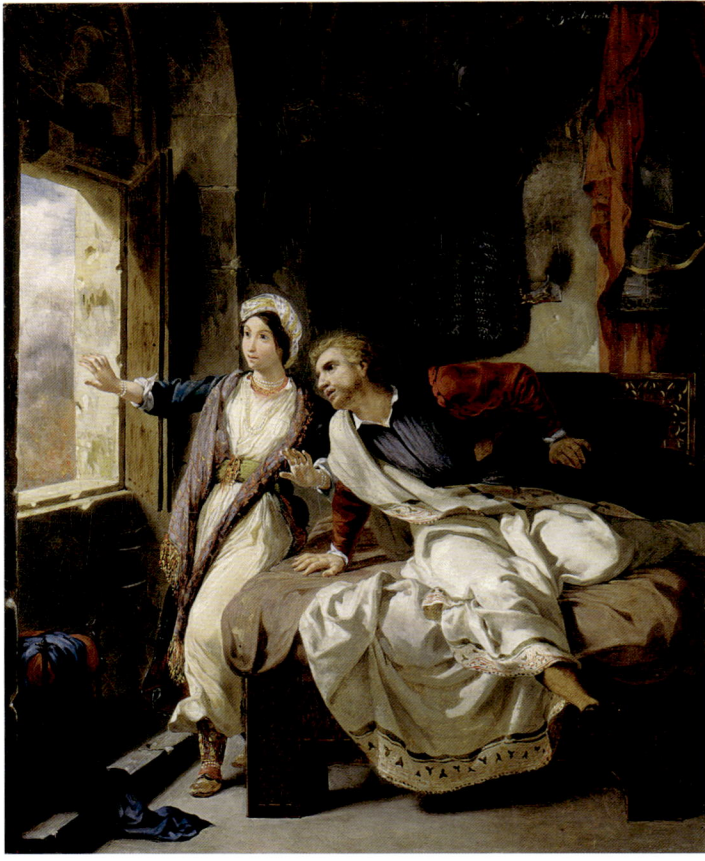

FIG. 100. *Rebecca and the Wounded Ivanhoe*, 1823. Oil on canvas, 25⅜ x 21⅛ in. (64.5 x 53.7 cm). Signed (upper right): *Eug. Delacroix*. Mrs. Charles Wrightsman, New York (J 243)

turn, looks directly out of the picture to meet the gaze of the viewer, impassively and without a hint of solicitousness. Thus is completed a triangular circuit of gazes, one that originates and concludes with the viewer. In his framing of the two bearded figures, Delacroix (as both beholder and painter) was reproducing, or underscoring, a single node of this circuit. Delacroix made other copies after *The Marriage at Cana*. One of these copies, which reproduces the bride and groom plus four further heads (private collection), has at various times been identified as a work by Delacroix, and as such would have made a curious pendant to *Two Bearded Heads*, which is of the same or similar dimensions.[7] Although the figures in *Two Bearded Heads* are extracted from their original context in Veronese's complex composition, the copy bears a more than vestigial relationship to the whole because in it resides the potential for the viewer to complete the greater circuit of gazes of which it forms one part. Many years later Delacroix commented on the viewer's role to the part as it relates to the whole, writing, "Perhaps the only reason why the sketch for a

work gives so much pleasure is that each beholder can finish it as he chooses."[8]

The interval between spring 1820 and spring 1822 was a gestational period for Delacroix, culminating in the exhibition of his first masterwork at the Salon, *The Barque of Dante* (fig. 2). Based on *Inferno*, from Dante Alighieri's early fourteenth-century epic poem *The Divine Comedy*, it shows the great Florentine poet crossing the lake surrounding the walled city of Dis with his imagined guide, the Roman poet Virgil, and it helped to establish Delacroix's reputation as a painter of a literary cast. In the autumn of 1822, following its acquisition by the state and subsequent installation at the Musée du Luxembourg, Delacroix noted reflectively in his *Journal*:

> When I have painted a fine picture I have not given expression to a thought. That is what they say. What fools people are! They would strip painting of all its advantages. A writer has to say almost everything in order to make himself understood, but painting builds a kind of mysterious bridge between the soul of the characters and that of the spectator. We see the figures outside us but we reflect within ourselves; the true thinking that is common to all men.[9]

Delacroix's statement makes explicit the terms of the relationship between the painter, the figures he depicts, and the viewer—and it does so in terms that proclaim the advantages of painting over literature, reiterating in personal terms a topos with Renaissance origins.

As far as is known, the first literary subject Delacroix completed after *The Barque of Dante* in 1822 was *Rebecca and the Wounded Ivanhoe*, which he painted in 1823 (fig. 100).[10] This would also be Delacroix's first treatment of a scene from Sir Walter Scott's widely read historical novels, and his first drawn from contemporary literature.[11] *Ivanhoe* was initially published in English in 1820, and it was translated into French the following year. Delacroix's picture may even be the very first visualization by a French artist of a novel by Scott.

The scene Delacroix chose to depict comes from chapter 29, in which Wilfrid of Ivanhoe and the Jewish heroine Rebecca are imprisoned in Torquilstone, the castle of Reginald Front-de-Boeuf, which is under siege by forces including the disguised Richard the Lionheart. Because Ivanhoe is wounded, he is confined to bed. For this reason,

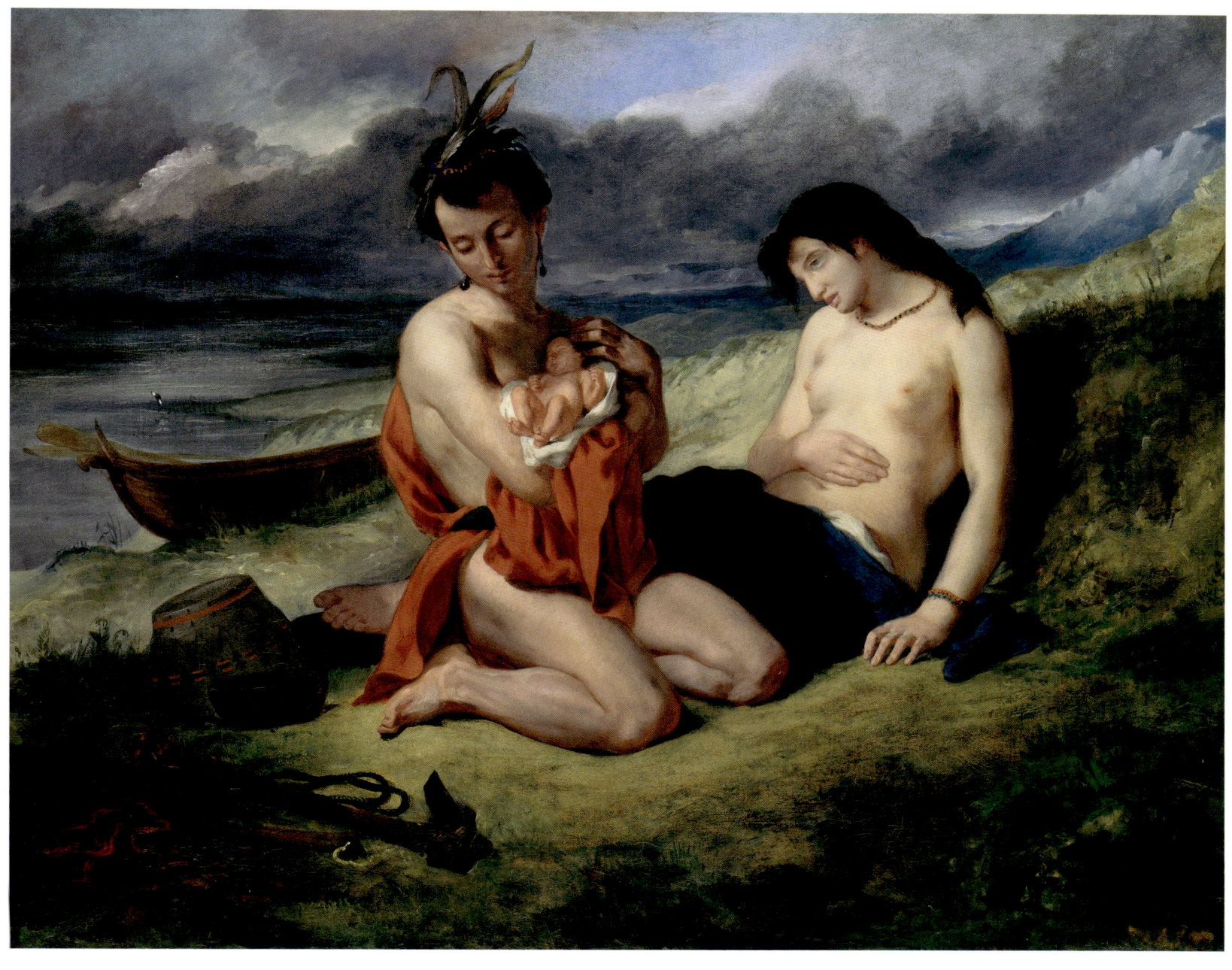

CAT. 84 *The Natchez,* 1823–24 and 1835

Rebecca, who is secretly in love with Ivanhoe, must describe the battle taking place outside the window. Rebecca is appalled by the violence she chronicles because military combat is alien to her experience. Her reaction is contrasted to that of Ivanhoe, whose chivalric ethos leads him to strain to see what she sees, and to be frustrated that he can neither see nor participate in the bloodletting. His reply to her makes explicit their divergent cultural perspectives: "Thou art no Christian, Rebecca." The action that underlies the scene is witnessed by Rebecca alone; the subject of the painting is predicated on her act of seeing, and, secondarily, Ivanhoe's response to her reaction to what she sees.

Rebecca and the Wounded Ivanhoe was the first painting on a literary theme that Delacroix completed after *The Barque of Dante,* but it was not the only one in progress at the time he sold it in the final days of December 1823, directly from his studio, to the collector Louis Joseph Auguste Coutan.[12] As early as October 1822, Delacroix noted his thought to paint a subject quite different from *Ivanhoe:* "A young Canadian traveling through the wilderness with her husband is taken by labor pains and lies down; the father enfolds the newborn in his arms."[13] This idea would eventually find an outlet in *The Natchez* (cat. 84), the subject of which, set on the banks of the Mississippi River, is a fictionalized episode from the French and Indian War of the 1760s, drawn from François René de Chateaubriand's 1801 novella *Atala*.[14] The painting was under way by December 1823: "I'm working on my savages."[15] For reasons that will soon be addressed, however, progress on *The Natchez* ceased in early 1824, and the picture would remain incomplete until 1835, when it was finally exhibited in the Salon. Delacroix would then include an explanatory note in the *livret*: "Fleeing the massacre of their tribe, two young savages traveled up the Méschacébé [Mississippi River]. During the voyage, the young woman was seized by labor pains. The moment is that when the father holds the newborn in his hands, and both regard him tenderly (CHATEAUBRIANT [sic], scene from *Atala*)."

At first glance, the mother's expression may be read as one of physical exhaustion, befitting a woman who has just given birth. Indeed, the overriding effect of the scene, taking into account the disposition of the figural group, the landscape setting, and the narrative moment predicated on an escape from danger, is that of a Holy Family in traditional depictions of the Flight into Egypt. Seen in this light, which is consistent with *Atala*'s Christian theme, the mother's expression can be understood as revealing an intimation of her child's tragic fate. Yet even as Delacroix relates the spirit of the text, the painting diverges from it in significant ways. At the time Chateaubriand introduces the infant to the reader, the child has already died; the father returns soon afterward to find the mother preparing funerary rites. Delacroix thus takes the death of the child into account by means of the mother's expression, while diverging significantly from the textual source. In *The Natchez*, the nature of the parents' gazes, which is more than a simple tender regard on the mother's part, to use the artist's words, gains additional resonance when the early history of the painting is taken into account together with that of yet another stripe, *Scenes from the Massacres at Chios* (see fig. 5).

Massacres at Chios is based on the tragic siege of the Aegean island in early 1822, during the Greek War of Independence from the Ottoman Empire. Delacroix first thought to paint the subject in May 1823,[16] and work on the immense canvas commenced in the middle of January 1824. The origins of *Chios* interwine with those of *The Natchez*, yet this is not obvious from their respective styles, in part owing to the fact that Delacroix set aside *The Natchez* in order to devote himself more assiduously to the larger and far more ambitious *Chios*, only to return to the smaller picture a decade later. The chronology of the preparatory studies that relate to the two pictures is unclear, but their genesis is closely linked. A watercolor study for *Chios* (see fig. 6) shows that an early stage of the composition already featured the prominent cleft between the two main figural groupings in the foreground that was present in *The Natchez* from its inception.[17] In the *Chios* watercolor, the mother at the right sits on the ground with her knees bent to her right in a position which mirrors that of the father in *The Natchez*. She looks down to her dead infant, who lies beside her. Attention to two mothers—one whose child is dead (*Chios*) and one whose child is soon to die (*Natchez*)—evidently stretched the artist's capacity to infuse both pictures with commensurate emotional power, and Delacroix is likely to have reached an impasse about how to proceed with both works simultaneously. He would find a solution with the aid of a report from Chios, the account given by Olivier Voutier in his *Mémoires du Colonel Voutier sur la guerre actuelle des Grecs*: "A traveler who witnessed the disasters at Chios told me that nothing had ever produced a more painful impression on his soul than the sight of the cadaver of a young woman whose child still pressed her withered breasts with its eager hands."[18] This book was published in Paris in December 1823, and Delacroix met its author soon afterward, on January 12, 1824, the day he began to paint *Chios*.[19] The stricken mother and uncomprehending child cited by Voutier undoubtedly summoned to Delacroix's mind the motif he eventually employed, that of the dead mother with its living child, with which he was certainly already familiar from such works as Marcantonio Raimondi's engraving after Raphael's *Plague at Phrygia*, of about 1515–16, and Poussin's *Plague at Ashdod* of 1630–31.[20] The figure of the mother in the *Chios* watercolor was transformed in the final painting into the elderly woman who looks up and to her left, with an expression of resignation on the heels of fear. In the painting, where she sits beside the dead mother and the uncomprehending infant, she assumes the role of matriarch in a group that signifies the Three Ages of Man, violently ruptured. It was probably the adoption of this three-figure grouping in *Chios*, in place of the earlier one showing only the mother with her dead child, that prompted Delacroix to cease work on *The Natchez* in 1824.

Because he had intensified the morbidity of the larger picture, the imperative of bringing the smaller one to a conclusion must have lost urgency in 1824. Yet when Delacroix resumed work on *The Natchez* in 1835 in order to complete it for the Salon, the experience of having transformed the relevant passage of *Chios* could not have been remote from his thoughts, even if the layers of association behind the gazes in the *Natchez* family group were not evident to the public. The conjunction between two subjects bound by charged relationships between a mother and her children extended to a third that Delacroix first noted at the time he was working on those pictures: on March 4, 1824, he noted summarily, "I'm preoccupied by *Medea*," another subject he would develop into a painting in the 1830s, one in which the principal figure's gaze plays a dominant role in conveying the effect (see cats. 91, 94).[21]

Delacroix's penchant for literary subjects that stage the act of looking lies behind his investigation of the possibilities of the gaze in disparate and sometimes even mischievous paintings that he produced throughout the 1820s, giving credence to his notion of a "bridge between the spirit of the persons in the picture and the beholder." A cabinet picture in the Troubador mode, *The Duke of Orléans Showing His Lover* (cat. 24) is based on an episode in *Les vies des dames galantes*, by Pierre de Bourdeille, called Brantôme, which was first published in 1666 and reissued in 1822. The author recounts a story about Louis I, duc d'Orléans, who had taken the wife of one of his vassals as his mistress. When the husband enters Louis's bedchamber, Louis raises the woman's skirt, putatively to mask her face and preserve her modesty, but thereby revealing her nudity. For not recognizing his wife, neither above nor below, the husband is thus twice the cuckold. In this complex game of who-sees-what, the viewer alone sees all. The possibilities suggested by its licentious theme were extended in *A Lady and Her Valet* (cat. 32), which is probably also based on a scene from Brantôme. Here, a woman asleep—or seemingly so—in a canopy bed is presented nude for the viewer's delectation. Only secondarily is the viewer likely to notice that the reclining woman's valet has just entered the shadowy depths of the room, and only afterward that the valet is a potential rival for the woman's attention.[22]

A more high-minded subject, depicted in *Milton Dictating "Paradise Lost" to His Daughters* (Salon of 1827–28), attracted numerous Romantic painters.[23] Here, the blind English poet's inability to see is presented alongside manifestations of other senses that he retained in force: touch, by

means of his hand on the carpet that covers the table; smell, by means of the flowers; and hearing, by means of the mandolin held by one of the daughters. It has often been noted that a painting within the painting, a copy of Raphael's *Expulsion of Adam and Eve from Paradise* fresco in the Vatican, which appears at the upper left of the composition, conveys the subject of Milton's poem, but it may also be understood as standing in for the act of copying as representing the primacy of sight.[24]

Another, slightly later, English subject is *Cromwell at Windsor Castle* (1828/30; private collection). Drawn from an episode in Sir Walter Scott's *Woodstock*, it shows the Lord Protector glowering at a portrait of his nemesis, Charles I (by Anthony Van Dyck, according to Scott). A cavalier called Wildrake, in the author's words, "stood a silent, inactive, and almost a terrified spectator, while Cromwell, assuming a firm sternness of eye and manner, as one who compels himself to look on what some strong internal feeling renders painful and disgustful to him, proceeded, in brief and interrupted expressions, but yet with a firm voice, to comment on the portrait of the late King." It is quite possible that the subject was realized as the result of a conversation with its first owner, Charles's descendant Edouard, duc de Fitz-James.[25]

The paintings under consideration to this point have been presented chronologically but selectively. Indispensable to Delacroix's literary imagination was a writer not yet addressed here, Lord Byron. The British adventurer-poet was responsible for texts that inspired a number of Delacroix's most ambitious paintings of the 1820s, and the author would remain a touchstone to Delacroix for the rest of his life (see, for example, *The Shipwreck of Don Juan* and *The Bride of Abydos [Selim and Zuleika]*; cats. 98, 139). Among these were two works exhibited at the Salon of 1827–28, *The Execution of Doge Marino Faliero* (1825–26; see fig. 25) and *The Death of Sardanapalus* (1826–27; see fig. 20).[26] The earlier painting is based on act 5 of the dramatic poem *Marino Faliero, Doge of Venice* (1820), which tells the story of the fourteenth-century leader who led a failed coup d'état against the Republic's aristocratic regime.[27] The picture shows the decapitated former doge at the bottom of a staircase, which provides a conspicuously empty center to the composition. On the steps and the balcony above are gathered the leaders of Venice, among whom Faliero had stood moments earlier; one of them raises the bloody sword, while the executioner himself stands to the right of the corpse. The commoners with whom Faliero had conspired surge into the scene at the bottom right. It has often been observed that the painting departs from Byron's text.[28] The gazes of the figures in *Marino Faliero* do not orient the viewer in the same directed way as many of the signal figures in paintings discussed elsewhere in this essay, and neither does the mise-en-scène. Yet Delacroix arguably found ample cues in Byron's text that prompted him to approach the picture according to terms laid out here. When the sentence is delivered to the disgraced Faliero and he is told that his would-be tomb among those of other doges of Venice will be empty save for its inscription, "This place is of Marino Faliero, / Decapitated for his crimes," Faliero's initial reply concludes with these lines:

> Decapitated for his crimes?— *What* crimes?
> Were it not better to record the facts,
> So that the contemplator might approve,
> Or at the least learn *whence* the crimes arose?
> When the beholder knows a Doge conspired,
> Let him be told the cause–it is your history.

The text raises questions that address the relationship between author and audience, questions surrounding what one sees and who makes that determination, and the way in which still-unfolding events will be recounted after they have concluded, far in the future. Further on one reads, "the Ten, the Avogadori / The Giunta, and the chief men of the Forty / Alone will be the beholders of thy doom"; and still later, as if in response, one of the citizens deep in the crowd outside the gates of the Ducal Palace states, "Let us hear at least, since sight / Is thus prohibited unto the people / Except the occupiers of those bars." In Byron's text, because any view of Faliero is blocked by the city leaders who surround him, from that moment onward partial updates are called out by the various citizens who are able to catch a glimpse of the beheading. The poem ends with the line, "The gory head rolls down the Giants' Steps!"

The similarly violent *The Death of Sardanapalus* (see fig. 20) is based on Byron's dramatic poem first published in 1821. In this massive picture, the action unfolds at the instigation of the protagonist, the final king of Assyria, who has ordered the ultimate visual spectacle: the destruction by fire of all that he possesses, which he will observe until he too is immolated. Not only is the subject drawn from Byron, but it is a painting in a Byronic mode, because Delacroix employs the writer's strategy of compressing the action into a time frame that is both limited and elastic.

Byron's writings stimulated and challenged Delacroix to produce some of his most ambitious paintings. Yet the relationship between the viewer and the figures in these paintings is more complicated, ambiguous, and diffuse than in the others. The shift is subtle, yet a clue is to be found in later iterations of his initial 1822 credo.[29] The next time Delacroix is known to have committed it to writing, in his *Journal* in 1850, it appears as: "I've told myself a hundred times that painting, materially speaking, is only the pretext, the bridge between the mind of the painter and that of the spectator. Cold precision is not art; skillful invention, when it is *pleasing* or when it is *expressive*, is art itself."[30] In the original formulation, it is the souls of the characters within the painting and the viewer Delacroix aimed to bridge, but in the latter version, the material painting itself has become the bridge between the mind of the painter and that of the spectator. Taking the artist at his word, the point of emphasis in the tripartite circuit of looking has shifted.[31]

The shift is perceptible in a work executed in 1846, when, over two decades after he painted *Rebecca and the Wounded Ivanhoe* (see fig. 100), Delacroix was inspired to take up the very next scene in Scott's novel. (There is no written evidence that he had previously contemplated it.) The subject of the *Abduction of Rebecca* (see cat. 105), exhibited at the Salon of 1846, is the battle that Rebecca had been describing to Ivanhoe moments before in the earlier picture. Now, having fainted, she is being carried off by two Saracen slaves commanded by the villainous knight Brian de Bois-Guilbert. Gone are the period details—the mail and armor, the finely patterned fabrics and beaded jewelry, and the Gothic décor brought to enamel-like finish—the exceptionally punctilious brushwork of which probably contributed to the artist's self-deprecatory reference to the picture as "my execrable painting."[32] Conspicuously absent in the later picture, too, is the reliance on the act of seeing and facial expression that impart maximal charge to the earlier one; one might even cite the rejection of active looking in the dormant figure of Rebecca herself. In their place is energetic, gestural painting anticipated, perhaps, by the jumble of paint strokes immediately surrounding and to the left of Rebecca's right hand in *Rebecca and the Wounded Ivanhoe*.

The figures who constitute the main group in the *Abduction of Rebecca* interlock in a fashion that is difficult to apprehend at a glance, particularly as their complex and fluid movements compete for the viewer's attention; they are, as it were, suspended in a very complicated state of animation.

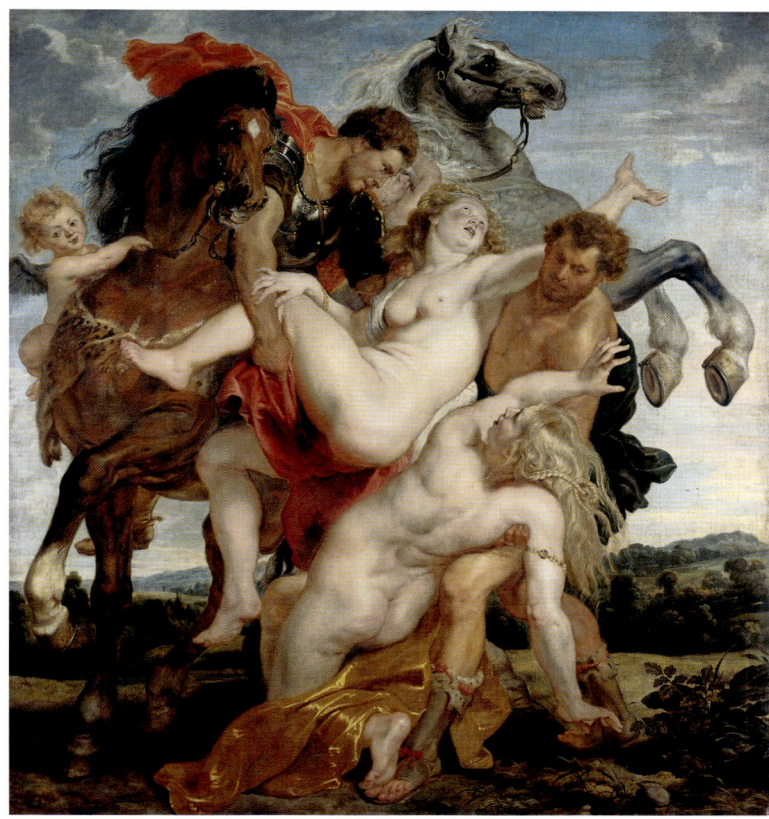

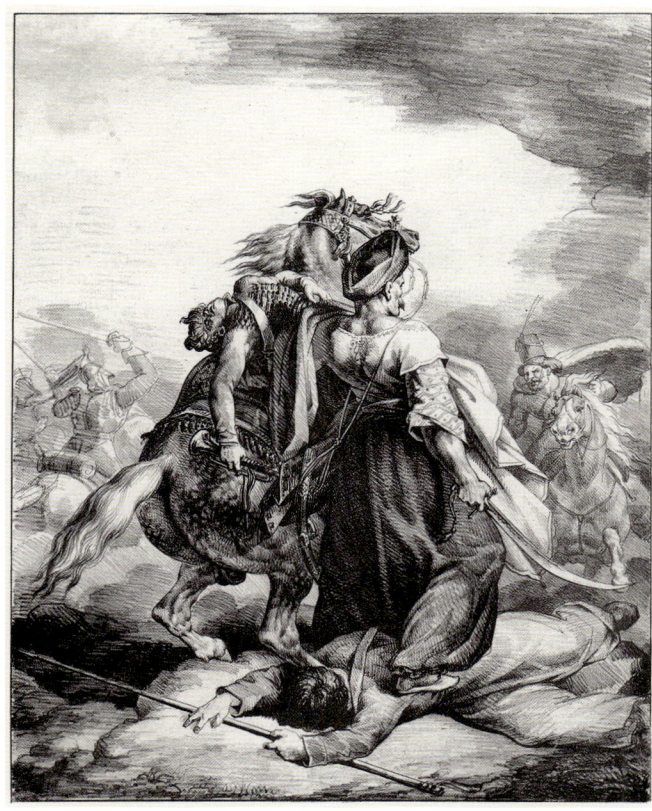

FIG. 101. Peter Paul Rubens. *Abduction of the Daughters of Leucippus*, 1618. Oil on canvas, 88³⁄₁₆ x 82⁷⁄₈ in. (224 x 210.5 cm). Alte Pinakothek, Munich (inv. 321)

FIG. 102. Théodore Gericault. *Mameluck of the Imperial Guard Defending a Wounded Trumpeter from a Cossack*, 1818. Lithograph, image 13⁷⁄₁₆ x 10¹⁵⁄₁₆ in. (34.2 x 27.8 cm), sheet 16 x 11⁷⁄₈ in. (40.7 x 30.2 cm). The Metropolitan Museum of Art, New York, H. O. Havemeyer Collection, Bequest of Mrs. H. O. Havemeyer, 1929 (29.107.123)

And yet, their volume and firm silhouette are a counterpoint to the vaporous form of the flaming fortress behind them. Although Delacroix had rehearsed the composition in preparatory drawings, he improvised directly on the canvas: no underdrawing is evident, and the brushwork is constructive, varied, sketch-like.[33] The result is an effusion of painting, representing half a lifetime of visual memory projected onto the canvas. The figural group as a whole is a reimagining of Rubens's *Abduction of the Daughters of Leucippus* (fig. 101) and Gericault's *Mameluck of the Imperial Guard Defending a Wounded Trumpeter from a Cossack* (fig. 102).[34] Rebecca's upper body in the 1823 painting is transfigured into the pose of her tormentor Bois-Guilbert in the 1846 painting. Ivanhoe's blue doublet with red sleeves is reconceived as the one worn by the Saracen on the right in the later picture, and Rebecca's white-and-gold-striped kerchief is restyled as the shawl hiked up around her waist.

Delacroix ceaselessly investigated new possibilities of pictorial representation, drawing from a tradition that extended back through Gericault, through Guérin to David and beyond—to a truly broad swath of European art encompassing Rubens to the north and Veronese to the south. Time and again, in the course of his readings from literature and history, the narrative moment that would strike him as a compelling subject to transpose into paint was one that revolved around the faculty of sight. This idea unites paintings from the formative decade of the 1820s that are disparate in terms of subject and tenor, date and décor; and Delacroix's pursuit of it in a variety of pictorial contexts helped to set the stage for his later production. "Look for a subject" is a simple phrase, but a revealing statement that goes to the heart of his pictorial practice. To look, to observe, to gaze upon something or someone was a form of action that grasped Delacroix's attention and upon which he ruminated, with novel results.

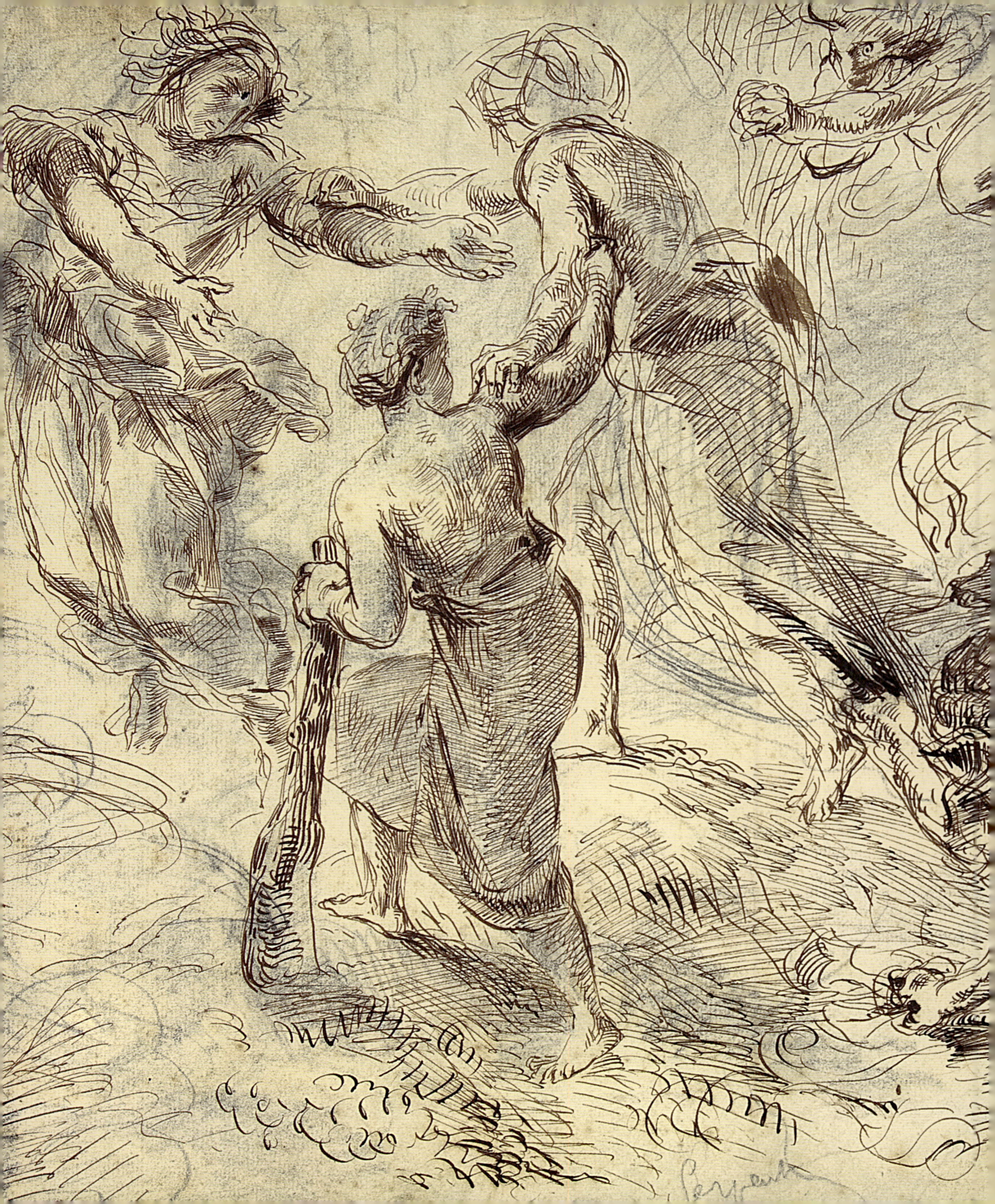

"Painting His Thoughts on Paper": Delacroix and His *Journal*

MICHÈLE HANNOOSH

"Just as he was confident about *writing* what he thought on a canvas, so he worried about not being able to *paint* his thoughts on paper": as the poet Charles Baudelaire suggested in 1863, painting and writing were for Delacroix interrelated activities.[1] Painting was literary, a means of expressing his ideas through color and form; writing was pictorial, giving depth, shape, and density to immaterial thought. Baudelaire based his remarks on Delacroix's then-published essays on art and artists, and on his printed descriptions of some of his paintings. Baudelaire did not know Delacroix's greatest experiment in writing, which would become one of the major works in the literature of art history and one of the painter's most original contributions: his *Journal*.

A long tradition defining painting as a manual, rather than intellectual, art has made the corpus of writings by artists relatively small: Leonardo da Vinci's notebooks, Michelangelo's poetry, Joshua Reynolds's *Discourses*, Vincent van Gogh's correspondence, to name the salient examples. The *Journal* occupies a prominent place within this select group. In these pages, Delacroix discusses matters ranging from practical information to abstract ideas, from small details to momentous events. The *Journal* provides a unique perspective on his life, thought, and work, and on a society undergoing the rapid and sometimes tumultuous changes of modern life. Perhaps most of all, it raises the question of why writing mattered to him,

as a painter, at all. For it did matter: not only did Delacroix spend a considerable amount of his time writing—the text of the *Journal* occupies more than one thousand pages of print—but the result is a resolutely literary work, containing only a handful of drawings. Not just another sketchbook with notes, the *Journal* was the repository and crucible of Delacroix's thoughts, a space of experimentation for ideas and expression, and, as such, absolutely essential to him as an artist.

The *Journal* begins in 1822 when Delacroix was twenty-four and continues for two years. It then falls silent for more than two decades, resuming only in 1847, after which it proceeds fairly regularly until his death in 1863. In the long interval between these two phases, he filled many notebooks, including the resplendent ones that he brought back from North Africa and southern Spain in 1832, recording places visited, sights seen, and people encountered.[2] The *Journal*, in contrast, was a long, sustained conversation with himself—his thoughts, emotions, readings, observations, and memories. And its two phases are significantly different from each other, serving distinct purposes.

Tuesday, 3 September 1822—I am carrying out the plan, which I have made so often, of keeping a diary. What I most keenly desire is not to lose sight of the fact that I am writing for myself alone; thus I will be truthful, I hope; I will become the better for it. This paper will reproach me for my variability (fig. 103).[3]

This is a momentous time in Delacroix's life. The *Journal* opens on the anniversary of his mother's death—"may her spirit hover over me as I write it, and may she never have cause to blush for her son."[4] He has also just learned that his first major painting, *The Barque of Dante*, purchased by the French government at the Salon of 1822, has been installed in the Musée du Luxembourg, at the time the museum of contemporary art.[5] This first professional success might have inspired a sense of confidence and self-assurance; instead, as the New-Year's-resolution quality of the first lines implies, it did not. The young Delacroix is worried about his fickleness, weakness of character, falseness to himself, the need to "become better." Indeed the early diary bears witness to a life in chaos. His financial affairs, his emotional state, even his memory have gotten away from him: "My memory disappears so much from one day to the next that I'm no longer in control of anything: neither of the past which I'm forgetting, nor of the present, when I'm almost always so obsessed with one thing that I lose sight . . . of everything else; nor even of the future, since I'm never sure of whether I might have already committed myself to something. . . . A man without memory does not know what he can count on—everything betrays him."[6]

The regular exercise of writing the *Journal* is meant to establish control, present him with a record of failings to rectify, calm his agitation, impose order on his ideas and behavior, and testify to experiences that his faulty memory has forgotten: "I have just read the preceding pages. I deplore the gaps. It seems to me that I am still master of those days that I wrote about, even though they have passed. But those days that these pages do not mention, it's as though they never existed."[7]

The early *Journal* has the character of this tumultuous, slightly bohemian life of a young man in the full fervor of his emotions and on the threshold of his career. It records his enthusiasm for Byron and Dante, Velázquez and Michelangelo; it registers the passions and disappointments of his love life as he makes advances to his studio models or carries on a liaison with his best friend's lover while the friend is away. It contains drafts of his love letters to this woman, with their rather fatuous, self-serving reasoning: "Tell me, my love, that he and I are equally dear to you. Why should you be embarrassed about that? Are women made differently from us men? Do *we* have any scruples about wooing someone we fall for momentarily?"[8]

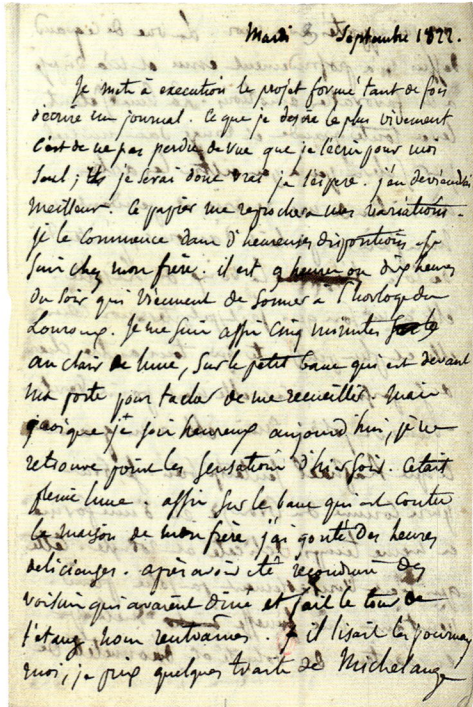

FIG. 103. *Journal*, September 3, 1822. Ink on paper, each page 6⅞ x 4½ in. (17.6 x 11.5 cm). Institut National d'Histoire de l'Art, Bibliothèque Jacques Doucet, Paris (Ms 247, cahier 1, fol. 1 recto)

Here, too, are the comings and goings of his band of friends as they move freely in and out of one another's homes, sharing paints, food, drink, and lovers, discussing genius, glory, friendship, and the soul.[9] Self-exhortations recur throughout:

Wretch! how can you ever do anything great when you spend all your time with lowly things? Concentrate on the great Michelangelo. Nourish yourself with the grand, austere beauties which feed the soul. I am always turned away from them by foolish distractions. Seek out solitude. If your life is orderly, your health will not suffer from your isolation.

Go to bed early and get up likewise.

Steel yourself against your first impressions: keep your composure.

Order in your ideas is the only route to happiness.

Work calmly and unhurriedly. As soon as you begin to work up a sweat and your blood begins to boil, beware. Careless painting is the painting of the careless.[10]

Among the possible subjects for paintings that Delacroix notes in these years are the most grandiose allegories, reflecting the Romantic extravagance and ambition of the debutant—"Blind destiny dragging the supplicants who vainly try, through their cries and prayers, to arrest its inflexible arm"; "On the edge of the abyss, Time struggles against Chaos"; "The man of genius at the gates of death. . . . He throws himself into the arms of Truth, the supreme deity; . . . he leaves error and stupidity behind"; "Barbarism dancing around the pyre of civilization."[11] And sometimes, peeking through the bathos and the bombast, are his first philosophical thoughts on painting:

> Painting builds a kind of mysterious bridge between the soul of the characters and that of the spectator. We see the figures outside us but we reflect within ourselves. . . . The art of the painter is all the closer to the human heart for being more material. . . . The soul finds something stirring in objects which only strike the senses.

> What is most real for me are the illusions that I create in my painting.

> This silent power . . . first speaks only to the eye and then takes hold of all the faculties of the soul.[12]

In some ways, the unevenness and freedom of the early *Journal*, its lurching from one subject to another, its dramatic ups and downs, its youthful exaltation and moroseness, its spurts of energy, visible even in the handwriting, are reminiscent of the drawings from these years with their wild, fluid line, their drama and energy, their centrifugal movement and force (figs. 104, 105). "I now see that my mind in its first thoughts must get worked up, undo things, try them a hundred different ways, before reaching the goal which burns in me. . . . If I haven't writhed like a serpent in the hands of a priestess, I come out cold."[13]

When the *Journal* resumes in 1847, Delacroix is nearly fifty years old. Age has tempered some of the passion and energy. The grandiose allegories have been embedded in stories and realized in paintings: "Barbarism dancing around the pyre of civilization" has become the powerful *Attila and His Hordes Overrun Italy and the Arts*, in the library of the Assemblé Nationale; "On the edge of the abyss, Time struggles against Chaos" will soon become *Apollo Slays the Python*

on the ceiling of the Gallery of Apollo in the Louvre (see fig. 53). The debutant has become a famous artist, still contested and shunned by some, but nevertheless secure in his success. He has not touched his *Journal* in twenty-three years.

The 19th of January may be considered a fairly typical day. He paid visits to the architect Alphonse de Gisors to discuss a possible commission, and to an engraver who was to reproduce one of his paintings. He also stopped at a colleague's place to discuss plans for an independent exhibition to rival the Salon. Entering the Panthéon, he observed the paintings in the cupola by Antoine Jean Gros, about which he would write an article the following year. From there he visited the studio of one of his students who was painting a Prometheus, and then arrived at the Muséum National d'Histoire Naturelle.[14]

> Natural history museum, open to the public Tuesdays and Fridays. Elephants, rhinoceroses, hippopotamuses . . . I was gripped, upon entering this collection, by a feeling of happiness. As I advanced further, this feeling increased; it seemed to me that my very being

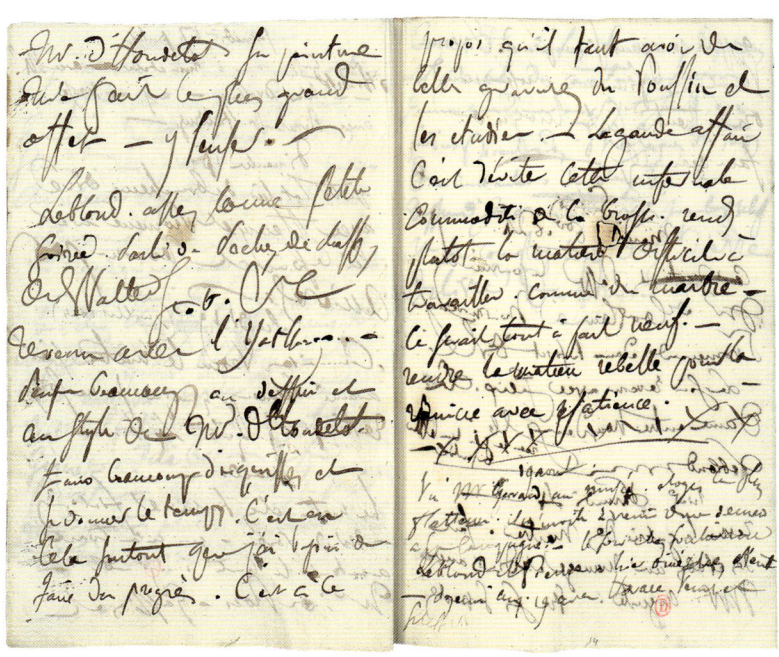

FIG. 104. *Journal*, July 20, 1824. Ink on paper, each page 8 x 5 in. (20.2 x 12.7 cm). Institut National d'Histoire de l'Art, Bibliothèque Jacques Doucet, Paris (Ms 247, cahier 5, fol. 13 verso and fol. 14 recto)

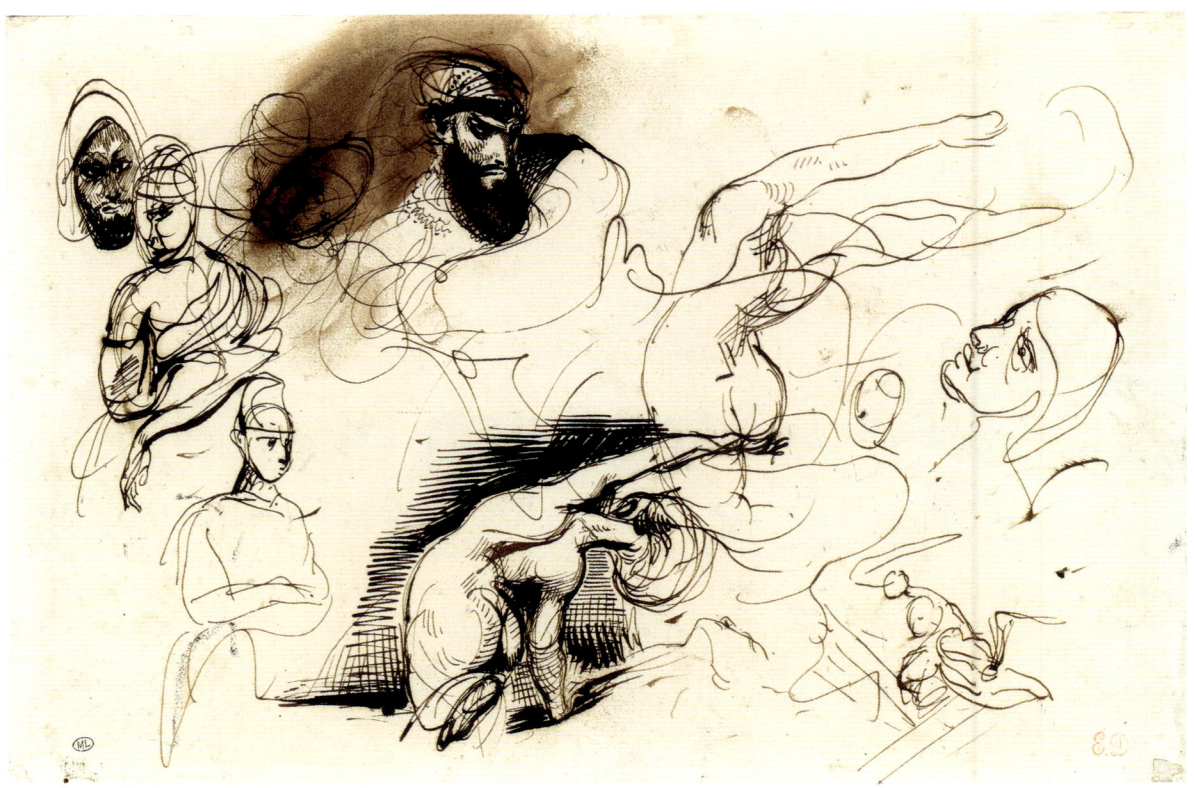

FIG. 105. *Study for The Death of Sardanapalus*, 1827–28. Pen and brown ink, brown wash, 8⅛ x 12⅜ in. (20.5 x 31.4 cm). Musée du Louvre, Paris (RF 5277 recto)

rose above the trivialities, the petty ideas and worries of the moment. What a prodigious variety of animals, and what variety of species, forms, functions, *raisons d'être*. At every moment, what we take to be deformity alongside what we consider gracefulness. Here, the herds of Neptune: seals, walruses, whales, immense numbers of fish with their vacant eyes, their mouths gaping senselessly; crustaceans, spider crabs, turtles. Then the hideous family of snakes: the boa with its enormous body and tiny head, its elegant coils entwined around the tree; the ugly dragon, the lizards, crocodiles, alligators, the monstrous gharial whose jaws suddenly taper and end at its nose with a strange projection.[15]

After two pages naming the extraordinary multiplicity of species, Delacroix concludes:

Why did I feel such emotion in seeing all of that?— It's because I was taken out of my ordinary ideas, which are my whole world; out of my street, which is my universe. How necessary it is to shake yourself up from time to time, to stick your head out of doors. . . . As I

left, the trees themselves came in for their share of admiration, and they played their part in the feeling of pleasure that this day gave me. I came back by way of the far end of the garden, along the quay. . . . I am writing this by the fireside, delighted to have stopped, before coming home, to buy this diary, which I am beginning on a good day. May I often continue to write down my impressions in this way. In doing so, I will see all that can be gained from noting and probing our impressions, when they are recalled.[16]

The difference between this beginning and that of the early *Journal* is striking. The earlier effort at resolve, self-mastery and self-possession, the attempt to get hold of himself and gain control of the wild mobility of his thoughts and emotions, has here become the opposite. The purchasing of the diary and the breaking of the long silence are motivated by the dizzying variety of species and forms in the museum's displays, rich testimony to worlds beyond his own. The later *Journal* is born when Delacroix ventures outside of himself and his petty ideas and worries, escaping the narrow confines of habit. The result is happiness and enthusiastic creativity—he takes pleasure in describing what he saw, running on for pages with a kind of delight in language—and also a sense that something momentous has happened. As he notes, he stopped and bought the *Journal* on the way home; and he preserved the receipt from this purchase, which was found among his papers 150 years later.

The later *Journal* reflects this openness of spirit: Delacroix tries not to restrain his imagination, as he had done earlier, but gives it free rein; he tries not to control his impressions, but fleshes them out, letting his mind wander, and following his thoughts in their meanderings and peregrinations. He engages with a host of subjects—art, literature, music, nature, politics, society, history, and humankind. As time goes on, he rereads his old diaries and adds comments, making some entries a collection of observations from different periods; he cross-references the entries, creating rich thematic networks on topics such as unity, imitation, and the sublime (fig. 106). In 1857 he conceived the project of a *Dictionary of the Fine Arts*, which he never finished but which he drafts in the *Journal*.[17] It is effectively a retrospective of the *Journal*, as Delacroix extracts the themes discussed there and provides a reference to the relevant date, themes ranging from "academies" to "varnish," "Homer" to "Chopin," "fresco" to "photography," and "on the fragility of painting" to "how to succeed in an art." The writing is essayistic, based on the style of his avowed master, the philosopher Michel de Montaigne, which Delacroix characterized as "the moving picture of a human imagination . . . all the liveliness of impressions expressed at the moment they are felt."[18] Such writing—improvisatory, expansive and wide-ranging, advancing and reversing course, posing and counterposing—reflects an intellectual and moral complexity: "One is always surprised at the diversity of opinion among different people; but a man of healthy mind himself conceives of all possibilities, he places himself . . . at all points of view"; "Subtle minds . . . see all the different sides of things."[19]

The American abstract expressionist Robert Motherwell credited "Delacroix's alert and cultivated mind constantly rolling, like an ever-changing tide, over the rocky questions of *l'art moderne*" with being "a sustaining moral force in my inner life," a model for painters who were "preoccupied, when not making art, with thinking about what it *is*."[20] Painting is certainly a primary subject of the *Journal*. Delacroix comments on his own paintings, those of his contemporaries and of past masters, but also on the distinctive power of painting, its

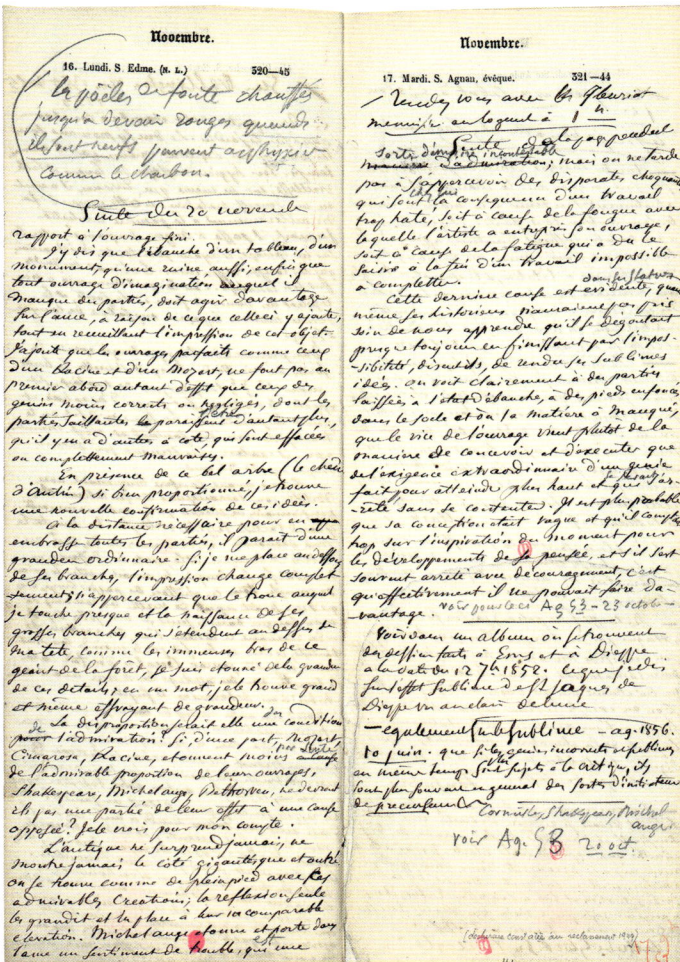

FIG. 106. *Journal*, November 16–17, 1857. Ink and pencil on paper, each page 14¾ x 5⅛ in. (37.5 x 13 cm). Institut National d'Histoire de l'Art, Bibliothèque Jacques Doucet, Paris (Ms 253 [6])

difference from the other arts and especially from literature. "The first merit of painting is to be a feast for the eye," he writes in the very last diary entry, a remark much quoted by later painters.[21] But for Delacroix the visual feast is a bearer of *thought*. The art of painting imparts a double pleasure, for the eye and the mind; its material forms have meaning in themselves as well as for the thoughts they inspire, thus complicating and enriching the aesthetic experience. They are both a reality and a representation:

> [In painting], you delight in the *representation* of real objects as though you were actually seeing *them*, and at the same time the *meaning* that the images hold for the mind moves and transports you. These figures, which strike you at one level as being the thing itself, are like a solid bridge linking the imagination to the deep and

mysterious sensation of which they are the sign; but a sign very different from the coldness of printed characters on a page. . . . [Painting is] a hundred times more expressive, since, independent of the idea, the visible sign . . . is *itself* a source of the most lively pleasure. . . . Those who think that when they have written "a foot" or "a hand" they have inspired in my mind the emotion I feel when I see a lovely foot or a lovely hand are strangely mistaken. Success in the arts lies in amplifying and prolonging sensation, by all means possible.[22]

As a spatial, atemporal art, painting can be seen in one glance; its effect is concentrated and captivating; it would take volumes to describe what a picture conveys in an instant.[23] Unlike writing, which demands to be read in a certain order, painting allows the viewer the freedom to experience the work at will, to come and go among its parts and across its surface, offering multiple and varied perspectives. Delacroix describes it using the analogy of a climber on a hilltop who surveys in one glance a vast expanse of landscape. Writing, in contrast, sets the climber on a single path, to encounter only one or another of the many natural beauties available; it may even bypass the most important or interesting sights.[24] The *Journal*'s essayistic writing is in this sense pictorial, reproducing in words and in the movement of text the qualities of the painted image: a writing adequate to painting, to a pictorial vision of the world.

But painting, in the *Journal*, is not just a subject; it is a passion. "How I adore painting! Just remembering certain paintings fills me with a feeling that moves my whole being, even when I am not seeing them."[25] Soon after, Delacroix extends the metaphor: "I set to work the way others run to their mistress, and when I leave it, I carry away . . . a delightful memory which resembles but little the agitated pleasure of lovers."[26] Perhaps the most moving instance of this fervor occurs at the beginning of 1861. After more than ten years at work on his murals in the church of Saint-Sulpice (see figs. 69, 70), Delacroix greeted the year with this entry:

> I began the year by pursuing my work at the church, as usual. I paid no visits except by leaving cards . . . and I went to work for a whole day. Oh, happy life, what a divine compensation for my supposed isolation! . . . Painting harasses me, indeed torments me, in a thousand ways like the most demanding of mistresses; for

the last four months I have fled at daybreak and have run to this enchanting work, as though to the feet of the most cherished lover; what from afar appeared to me easy to overcome in fact presents me with horrible and incessant difficulties. But how is it that this eternal struggle, instead of beating me down, raises me up, and instead of discouraging me, consoles me and fills my moments after I have left it? What a happy compensation for what the good years have carried off forever; what a noble use of my old age, which already besieges me from a thousand directions, but leaves me still the strength to surmount the pains of the body and the afflictions of the soul.[27]

Written a few months before the chapel was completed and just two years before Delacroix died, the entry has something of the ardor and passion of the youthful *Journal*. Moreover it bears witness to an identification between the artist and his subject: it applies to his own enterprise the metaphors of the paintings in the chapel. Painting is the struggle that uplifts, like Jacob wrestling with the angel; it is the strength that raises up the artist besieged on all sides, like Heliodorus, by old age and death, exalting him through the "horrible and incessant difficulties" with which it confronts him, and which he must overcome in a Jacob-like struggle with the divine.

Such sustained personal and aesthetic reflection is interwoven with a fascinating portrait of nineteenth-century French society. Even on the material level, the *Journal* preserves the details of daily life: press clippings, advertisements, addresses, train schedules, recipes, dried flowers or feathers. Delacroix's distinctive position in that society—on the one hand, accepted by official circles, awarded important state commissions for public buildings, and elected in 1857 to the Académie des Beaux-Arts; on the other, a radical painter, a close acquaintance of scandalous artists like Baudelaire, the caricaturist Honoré Daumier, and the novelist George Sand—brought him into contact with an extraordinary range of personalities. For ten years he served on the Paris Conseil Municipal over which Baron Haussmann presided, and in which the daily life of the capital, including the famous program of public works, was debated, usually to his dismay: "The place de la Concorde has been completely dug up. They are talking about removing the Obelisk of Luxor. Périer claimed this morning [at the Council] that it blocked the view! . . . When we are a little more like the Americans they will try to sell the Tuileries gardens, for being a vacant lot which serves no purpose."[28] He frequented artists, critics, and intellectuals: visiting Camille Corot's studio and discussing the value of an "improvisational" method, attending a private reading of the libretto to Hector Berlioz's opera in progress, *Les Troyens*, at the composer's house, ruminating on old age with the effervescent Alexandre Dumas, and walking around the Jardin des Plantes looking at flowers for his paintings with the botanist Adrien de Jussieu (cats. 110, 111).[29] He was entertained at the soirées of the bourgeoisie, complete with the séances and "turning tables," or proto-Ouija boards, that were all the rage. He chatted with his color merchant, settled bills with his suppliers, and took a walk in the country with his peasant housekeeper. He recorded nearly all his conversations with his friend Frédéric Chopin, whom he revered: "What a loss," he wrote when the composer died. "So many ignoble scoundrels walk the earth, while this beautiful soul has been snuffed out."[30]

Delacroix hears about the strange music and radical political ideas of the newcomer composer Richard Wagner. He comments on the rise of mass transit, the mechanization of labor, the influence of religion in public affairs, the politics of consumerism and commercialism, and the benefits and dangers of technology.

> I read . . . in the paper that at Harvard they are experimenting with photographing the sun, the moon and even the stars. They have obtained from the star Alpha, in the constellation Lyra, an imprint the size of a pinhead. The letter which announces this result makes an observation as correct as it is strange: that since the light of the photographed star took twenty years to reach Earth, the ray that was fixed on the photographic plate had left its celestial sphere long before Daguerre had discovered the means by which they captured it.[31]

The discrepancy between cosmic and human time suggested here brings out the disjunction between nature and technology, between the long, slow temporality of the universe and the frenetic pace of modernity, with its credo of speed.[32] Elsewhere he frets about the excesses of the free market, about changes in the climate, about growing old.

One of the *Journal*'s most interesting aspects is the many reading notes that fill its pages. Delacroix was an avid reader, from the great classics ancient and modern to the daily papers,

perusing anything that came his way: "You must always read pen in hand. Not a day goes by that I don't find in the most worthless rag something interesting to note down."[33] The notes are not just a record, but part of the very fabric of the diary: reading is an exercise in self-discovery, as Delacroix interrogates, confirms, and revises his opinions through the texts of others. For example, in 1856 while reading Edgar Allan Poe's "Tales," translated by Baudelaire, Delacroix is at first intrigued, but nevertheless skeptical. He sees Poe's fantastic and otherworldly stories as alien to the French imagination, which prefers "classical" values of reason, moderation, and verisimilitude. As he continues, however, he comes to a different position. First he quotes lines from "Ligeia": "In beauty of face no maiden ever equaled her. . . . Yet her features were not of that regular mould which we have been falsely taught to worship in the classical labors of the heathen. '*There is no exquisite beauty,*' says [Bacon], Lord Verulam . . . *without some strangeness in the proportion.*'"[34] Delacroix underlines the latter sentence as though to signal his agreement. He then comments: "Reading this awakens in me the sense of mystery that used to concern me more in my painting, and which I think has been neglected in my monumental paintings, my allegorical subjects, etc. Baudelaire says in his preface that my work is the painterly expression of that peculiar sense of the ideal that takes pleasure in the terrifying. He is right. . . ." This is a remarkable admission.

Baudelaire had made a rather outlandish comparison between Delacroix and Poe, who "animate their figures against violet or greenish backgrounds that give off the phosphorescence of putrefaction and the whiff of a storm," whose scenes translate the heightened sensations of an opium trance, and, "bursting with light and color," open up onto shimmering perspectives of Oriental cities and architectures "in a shower of golden sunlight."[35] One might have expected the reserved, cerebral Delacroix to object to this odd comparison between himself and the provocateur Poe, who had been found dead, seemingly from drink, in the gutter in 1849; nor would he normally admire its extravagant, overblown language. Yet he agrees with Baudelaire, ultimately understanding something about the evolution of his painterly style that he had not previously considered: the sense of mystery and terror, of brooding or luminous settings, of the supernatural in nature that had infused his earlier paintings but been abandoned in his recent public commissions. The receding depths of *The Battle of Nancy* and the intensity of Cleopatra's gaze in *Cleopatra and the Peasant* come to mind as examples of this mystery and drama (cats. 69, 95). But Delacroix's remark also corresponds to a striking feature of his late work: his clear interest in, if not a sense of mystery per se, at least an impression of grandeur and sublimity in nature. In the turbulent seas of *Christ Asleep during the Tempest* or *Shipwreck on the Coast* (cats. 129, 145), the vast landscapes and imposing mountains of *Ovid among the Scythians* (cat. 142), *Arabs Skirmishing in the Mountains* (fig. 92) or *View of Tangier from the Shore* (fig. 90), the dramatic skies of the *Lamentation over the Body of Christ* (cat. 140) or *An Arab Camp at Night* (fig. 93), the luminous background of the 1851 *Agony in the Garden* (cat. 125), nature dominates the action and conveys an impression of the sublime.

The *Journal* is replete with observations about nature, especially the sea, sky, trees, and mountains. One senses the painter's eye that perceives via color and form. In Dieppe in 1854 Delacroix writes: "On my walk this morning I spent a long time studying the sea. The sun being behind me, the side of the waves that rose up before me looked yellow and the part that looked down reflected the sky. The shadows of clouds passed over all that and produced delightful effects; in the background, where the sea was blue and green, the shadows looked almost violet. . . ."[36] His remarks bring out the philosophical aspects of these material or sensual qualities. For example, walking in the forest near his country cottage in Champrosay, twelve miles south of Paris, he notices from afar a large oak tree (figs. 107, 108):

> At the distance necessary to take in all its parts, it seems of an ordinary size. If I stand under its branches, the impression changes completely: perceiving only the trunk which I am almost touching, and the beginning of its thick branches which stretch over my head like the immense arms of this giant of the forest, I am astonished at the size of these details; in a word, I find it grand and even frightening in its grandeur. Does this mean that disproportion is a condition of our admiring something? If, on the one hand, Mozart, Cimarosa, and Racine cause less surprise because of the admirable proportion of their works, do not Shakespeare, Michelangelo, and Beethoven owe some of their effect to the opposite cause? For my part I do think so.[37]

Delacroix's whole theory of the sublime is in this remark—the grandeur that comes from disproportion, from a view close-up; accordingly, the entry on the sublime for the *Dictionary of the Fine Arts* cross-references it. Color, form, light, shadow, and perspective: these aspects of vision, these tools of the painter, had philosophical implications that he explored through writing.

Delacroix's commitment to writing, the prominence of the *Journal* in his life, even its sheer length, all raise the question of why it mattered for this painter to write at all.

> *November 8, 1857.* When he really wanted to get clear on his ideas, Napoleon put them on paper, *knowing like all men who have thought a lot about things, that to write out your ideas is to probe them more deeply.*

> *November 10, 1857.* Voltaire wrote the following about the notes he took on his readings: they are an account that I take for myself of my readings, the only way of truly learning and of getting clear on your ideas.[38]

As these entries indicate, and the *Journal* attests, writing was a source of ideas and an aid to reflection, allowing Delacroix to record his thoughts, then interrogate, refine, and revise them. But there is perhaps a more existential reason too:

> I'm reading a *Life of Leonardo da Vinci.* . . . I'm especially struck by the disappearance of almost all his works— paintings, manuscripts, drawings, etc. There is no one who has produced so much and left so little.[39]

Writing was a means of self-preservation, a hedge against oblivion. Delacroix was conscious of the ease with which works of art could be destroyed, and was especially aware of the destruction of art during times of social upheaval. In a list that he made of some of his paintings, he noted next to *Cardinal Richelieu Saying Mass*: "the picture destroyed in the Palais Royal," that is, in the revolution of 1848.[40]

Moreover for Delacroix, a painter who wrote made a special contribution to society. A passage about Joshua Reynolds that he transcribed from an article is telling: "Men gifted with the faculty of producing works which seem alive are rarely capable of the deep, sustained reflection of which the philosophical mind alone seems capable, as though action excluded thought or at least limited it."[41] Delacroix sought to disprove this rarity, and to embody the coexistence of action and thought. Their mutual exclusion was in his view dangerous, leading to barbarism (action without thought) or empty ideology (thought without action), which the turbulent

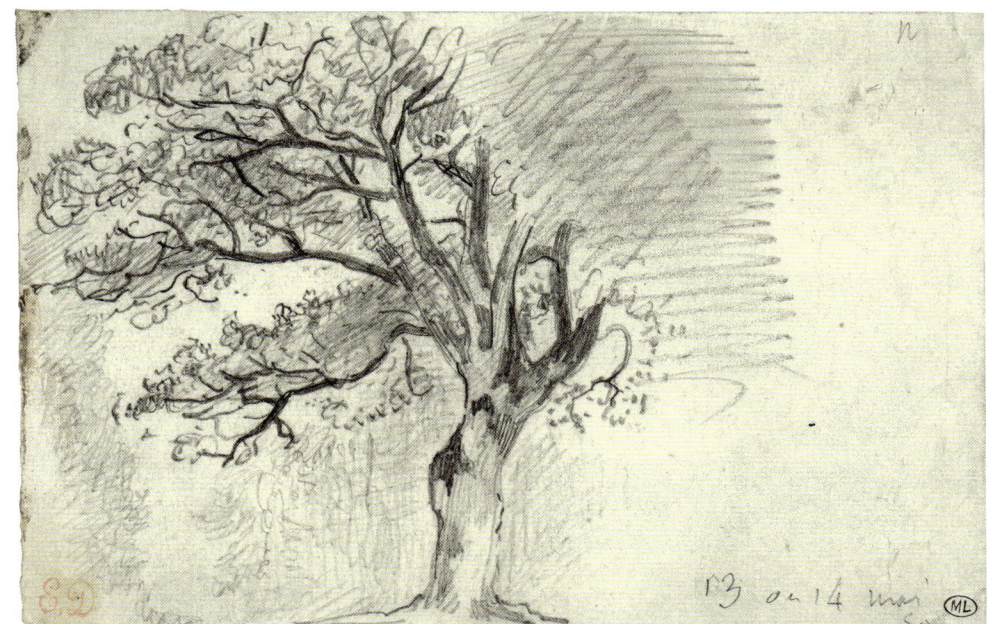

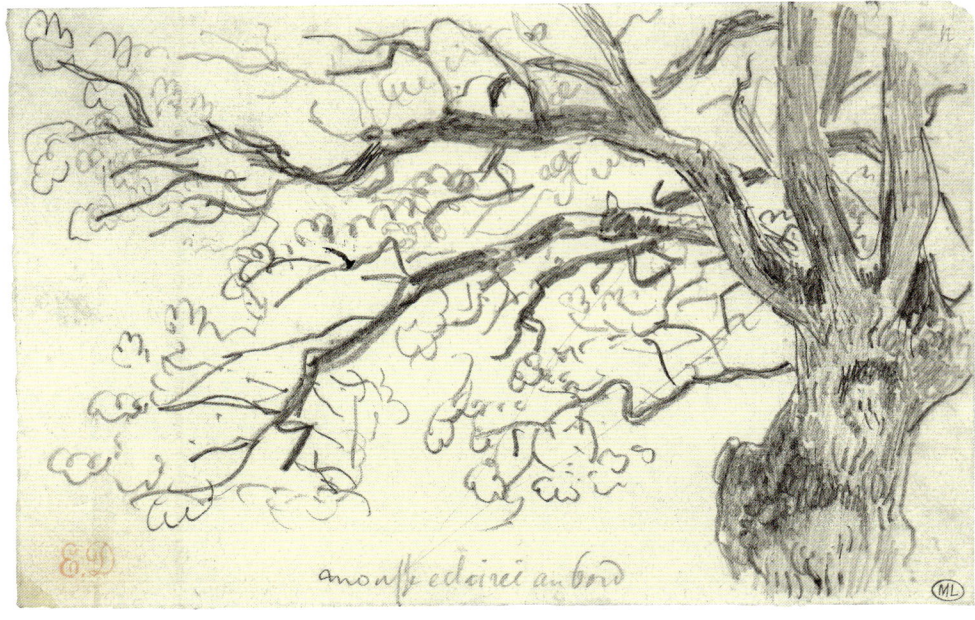

history of his own time had made all too clear. A painter-writer, in contrast, affirmed the compatibility of action and meditation, material and abstract, painting and philosophy.

In the end, all diaries are about time: passing time, recording time, reflecting on time. Delacroix's assiduous engagement with writing the *Journal* may have been an answer to his oft-expressed dread of too much time, time without value, what he calls "ennui." The "terrible enemy," ennui is a languor, a torpor, a spiritual emptiness that foreshadows death: "All my life I have found time too long."[42] The only antidote

to it is work, and specifically "the mind constantly at work."[43] Earlier he had stated: "The secret of avoiding ennui, for me at least, is to have ideas. Thus I cannot look hard enough for ways to generate them."[44] Along with painting, the *Journal* was Delacroix's primary means for the generation of ideas—the mind at work, freed from the domination of time and from an anxiety about time by making it valuable. After a near lifetime of diary writing, a simple sentence perhaps sums up best what Delacroix sought in this activity most of all: "The purpose of work is not just to produce things; it is to give value to time."[45]

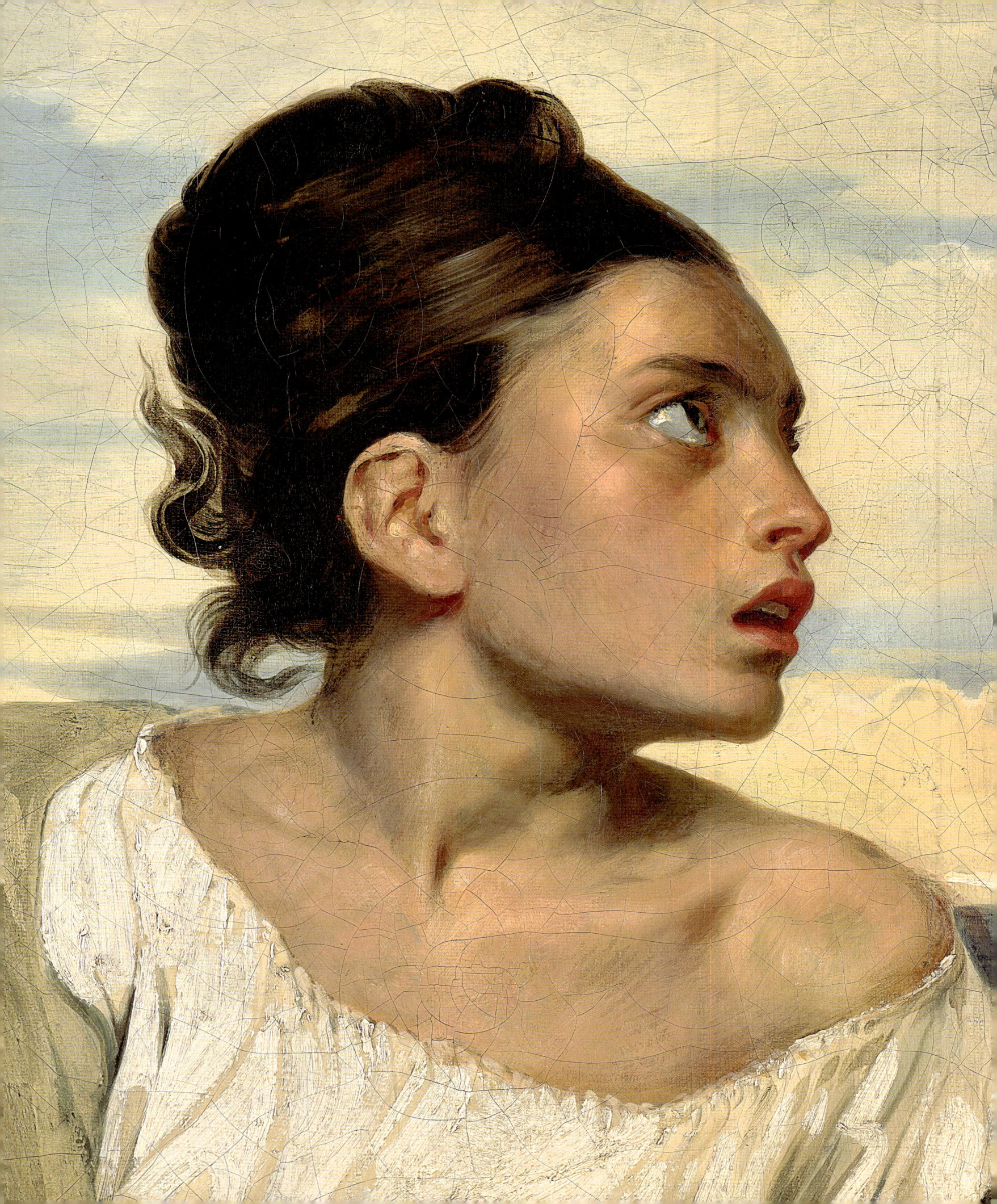

Eugène and His Masters: Becoming Delacroix

MEHDI KORCHANE

In an homage to Delacroix written shortly after the painter's death in 1863, Charles Baudelaire ventured an opinion that, thirty years earlier, in the era of triumphant Romanticism, would have seemed like a provocation to that movement's supporters, who were eager to see the school of Jacques Louis David supplanted. "However different he may be from his master Guérin in his method and color," Baudelaire wrote, "he inherited from the great republican and imperial school a love of the poets and a kind of furious rivalry with the written word. David, Guérin, and Girodet were impassioned by the writings of Homer, Virgil, Racine, and Ossian. Delacroix movingly translated Shakespeare, Dante, Byron, and Ariosto. A great resemblance, a slight difference."[1] Baudelaire placed subject matter over execution; not long before, an artist's manner of painting had seemed to be the gauge for evaluating his art and appraising his innovation. Thus, within the space of two generations, standards of critical judgment were inverted, and Delacroix, who had launched Romanticism in the 1820s, was named the heir to those whose fall he had precipitated.

In rehabilitating David and his followers by extolling their literary sensibility, Baudelaire showed himself to be aligned with a movement that opposed the doctrinal drift of the naturalistic aesthetic developed by Champfleury.[2] But the cursory way in which he established the resemblance between Delacroix and his elders obscured all complexity. To preserve the singularity of the great Romantic painter—his idol—Baudelaire took care not to posit any direct lineage, nor did he mention the young Delacroix's elective affinities. Just a few years earlier, in fact, Delacroix had confided to Théophile Silvestre that from the age of fifteen he had preferred Pierre Paul Prud'hon and Antoine Jean Gros to Pierre Narcisse Guérin and Anne Louis Girodet-Trioson.[3]

It is known that Delacroix was inclined to revise his own history when addressing posterity. To be sure, his attachment to Prud'hon's art, his admiration of Gros, and his veneration for Gericault were genuine, but his memories cannot be taken at face value if we are to understand how he arrived in the world of the arts and the debt he owed to his master Guérin and other representatives of the "republican and imperial school." Furthermore, however appealing Baudelaire's assertion may be, it is too reductive to be accepted without careful investigation.

Delacroix and Guérin (1815–22)

Guérin's influence on Delacroix's development as a revolutionary painter has never been considered particularly important; indeed, the matter has never been studied in depth. The aging Delacroix chose to remember his master "with fond respect."[4] However, in reporting to his old friend Louis-Désiré Véron the moment when he and Guérin had gone their separate ways, he intimated only a distant relationship: "I don't know if he perceived any promise of talent in me, but he never encouraged me. In 1822, when I did *Dante and Virgil,* my first painting [for the Salon], I asked M. Guérin, out of deference, to come to my place and give me his opinion. He rarely offered me anything but criticism; I could never get him to support my wish to submit my first painting to the [Salon] exhibition."[5] There is no evidence to suggest that Delacroix and Guérin communicated with each other once Delacroix left Guérin's studio, much less to a relationship. Guérin excluded his former pupil from his will, in which he bequeathed the contents of his studio to nine of his other former students. These two pieces of information support the idea of a rift between the two men. A reconsideration of the facts will yield a more nuanced view, however. Although it would be pointless to try to prove that Guérin and Delacroix were at all close, certain factors show that the master's teaching did indeed leave its mark.

The principal evidence, the importance of which must be weighed carefully, is the young Delacroix's long affiliation with Guérin's studio, which lasted seven years, from October 1815 to 1822. The fledgling artist probably produced his first studies under the master even earlier, beginning in 1813.[6] The reasons for such constancy can be attributed as much to Delacroix's personal relationships as to his art. Friendship was vital to him: his parents had died by 1814, leaving him with only two immediate family members, a brother and a sister, both much older, who lived in the provinces. The emotional support of his circle of lycée schoolmates, who would accompany him throughout his life, would be complemented by that of his friends from Guérin's studio: Charles-Emile Callande de Champmartin, Léon Cogniet, Théodore Gericault, and Ary Scheffer. Open to students all day long, the studio was a place of camaraderie and stability for the uprooted Delacroix and a place where, in lean times, he could go to get warm, do odd jobs to earn a little money, and compose his correspondence.[7] That he frequented the studio over many years, even irregularly, necessarily meant that master and student were well acquainted.

With respect to Delacroix's apprenticeship, Guérin seems to have offered the best guarantee of success to the aspiring history painter. Henri François Riesener, Delacroix's uncle, understood this and encouraged his nephew to join Guérin's studio. This master was, after all, the foremost dramatic painter of his day; he was also young, had a reputation as a cultivated, worldly man, and, above all, as an authority in the teaching of art. The year 1816 appears to have been pivotal for Guérin: he turned down the position of director of the Académie de France in Rome, offered to him by King Louis XVII, in order to devote himself to his studio and consolidate his position at the Salon. When Delacroix enrolled in the Ecole des Beaux-Arts on March 23, on Guérin's recommendation, his master had just filled the seat previously held there by David.[8] Guérin assumed a decisive role at the restored Académie des Beaux-Arts, becoming the intellect behind the painting section. In his report on the students' submissions from Rome that year, he proposed a new vision for the academy's doctrine, one that emphasized the study of nature over the imitation of antique models—the latter a practice he felt had degenerated into sterile imitation.[9] The imitation of nature, by contrast, would prevent all pitfalls, whether of wooden style, the "craze for making paintings with paintings" by copying ancient masters without discernment, or the oddity and bad taste that result from misguided inspiration.[10] As Guérin sought not to found a school but, rather, to develop the talent of each student by giving him the capacity to reflect on his own art—this was "the moral or intellectual part" of his teaching—and perfect his techniques, it is easy to appreciate the benefit a candidate for the Prix de Rome could draw from his lessons.[11] It was from Guérin that Delacroix acquired his lifelong practice of working each day from the live model, substituting photographs for posing sessions when necessary so as not to miss what he called his "daily prayer."[12]

Initially, discipline of this sort must have seemed off-putting to the young artist-in-training. The scarcity of early academic drawings by Delacroix and the glimpse his writings give of how he used his time during his first years of study reveal indecisiveness about his apprenticeship. Letters he exchanged with his friends Achille Piron and Félix Guillemardet during his months-long holiday in Charente show him to be, at an age when students aiming for the Prix de Rome typically redoubled their efforts, a hunter, a voracious reader, and a translator of English and Italian, but they make no allusion to art.[13] The novels and plays he wrote between 1813 and 1819—*Alfred, Les dangers de la cour, Victoria*—show the fervor with which he dedicated himself to writing and how much that activity must have encroached on his art practice, notwithstanding his capacity for hard work.[14] Indeed, when financial problems arising from his family's bankruptcy compelled him to economize by living in the provinces for long periods of time, thus keeping him away from the studio, it was not through drawing that he channeled his need to create. He seems to have wanted to prolong his woolgathering years, to give himself over entirely to his imagination, and to postpone the moment when he would need to focus on a single pursuit. Such is the adolescent whose portrait Gericault painted about 1815 or 1816 (fig. 109).[15]

It was not until September 1818 that Delacroix expressed certainty about his future as an artist, and even then he showed reluctance: "In truth, I can't think without a heavy heart of the long years I will be spending in Italy, far from anyone who could take an interest in me."[16] Such sentiment helps to explain why Guérin might have questioned the abilities of the erratic and independent student, as compared to those of Guillaume Bodinier, who practiced life drawing morning and evening, with the intention of doing so "for a long time yet." Bodinier acknowledged "the impossibility of doing anything without that" and rejoiced that he was being led by "an infallible guide" without whose advice he "did not want to take a single step."[17] Guérin's opinion of his students was surely affected by the ardor they showed for their work; in 1816, Bodinier no doubt held a higher place in the master's esteem than did Delacroix.

Several things contributed to the young man's change of heart about 1818–19. Among them is an experience that has become a famous episode in Delacroix mythology: his observation of Gericault up close, in the heat of creating *The Raft of the Medusa*, which would soon cause a sensation at the Salon of 1819. Delacroix even participated in the work by posing as a model for one of the figures. Gericault's painting gave the young artist the first major aesthetic jolt of his life and hastened his recognition of the inferiority of his own literary efforts, at least insofar as his career was concerned. These experiences set him on the path to maturity and enabled him to implement the means for ensuring his success as an artist. His determination was strengthened both by his need to support himself and by an awareness that he had fallen behind friends such as Scheffer and Champmartin, who were already being awarded public commissions. Nevertheless, it was not until 1822 that Delacroix set about launching himself as a professional.

While training under Guérin, Delacroix seized on the opportunity to execute a large painting for the cathedral in Nantes. The commission for *The Virgin of the Sacred Heart* had

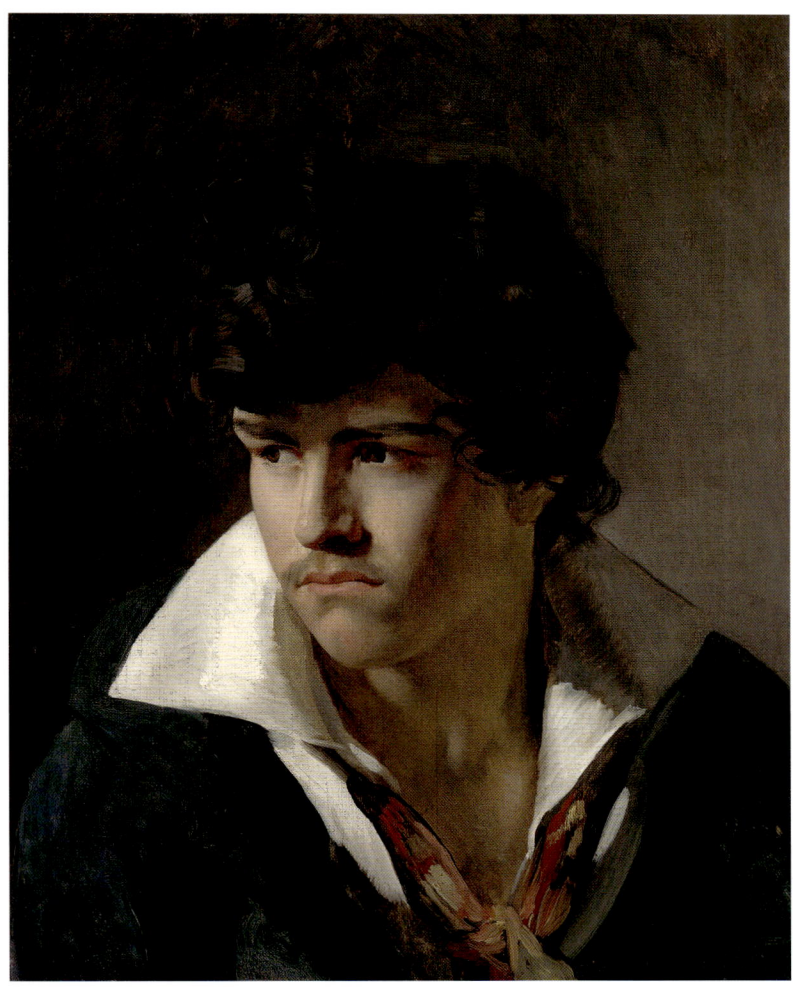

FIG. 109. Théodore Gericault. *Presumed Portrait of Eugène Delacroix*, ca. 1815–16. Oil on canvas, 21¼ x 17¾ in. (54 x 45 cm). Jean-Luc Baroni Ltd., London

been awarded initially to Gericault, who, loath to fulfill it, subcontracted the work to Delacroix in 1820 (fig. 110). Gericault's role in Delacroix's formation as a painter is well known.[18] It should be noted, however, that the import of Gericault's influence has exerted an outsize sway over modernist critics, who, in omitting Guérin from their web of references and quotations, have somewhat obscured Delacroix's debt to him. Though the composition of *The Virgin of the Sacred Heart* owes a great deal to the model Gericault provided, it was in Guérin's repertoire that Delacroix found a motif for his own addition to the composition.[19] Dropped into the lower right-hand corner are two male figures in profile that likely derive from a drawing by Guérin related to *Clytemnestra*, a painting that had caused a sensation

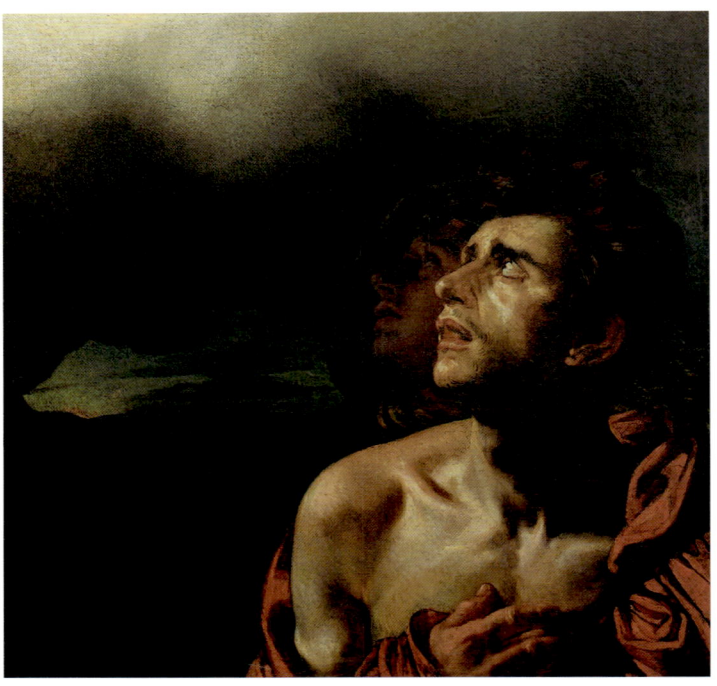

FIG. 110. *The Virgin of the Sacred Heart* (detail), 1821. Oil on canvas, overall 8 ft. 5⅝ in. x 59 in. (258 x 152 cm). Cathedral of Our Lady of the Assumption, Nantes (J 153). The two figures in the painting's lower right corner probably derive from Pierre Narcisse Guérin's *Studies for the Head of Aegisthus,* shown in fig. 111

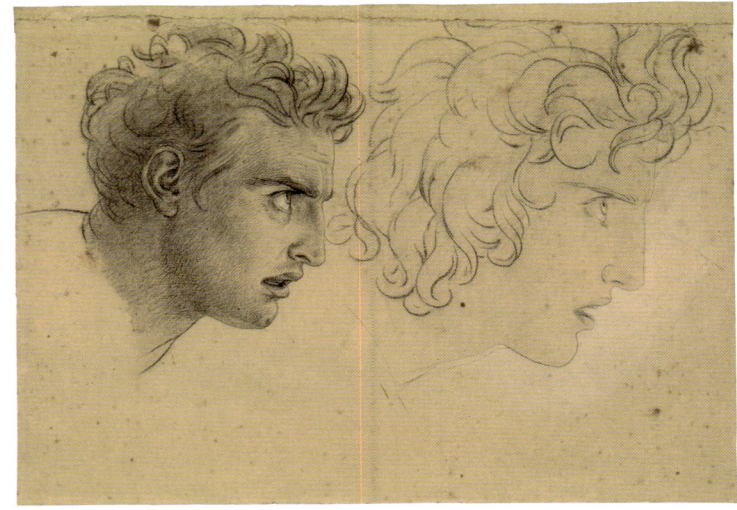

FIG. 111. Pierre Narcisse Guérin (French, 1774–1833). *Studies for the Head of Aegisthus,* before 1813. Black pencil and traces of white chalk on beige paper, 14¾ x 21¼ in. (37.5 x 54.1 cm). Musée des Beaux-Arts, Angers (inv. MBA 226 1 [1881] D). The drawing was made in preparation for the figure of Aegisthus in Guérin's *Clytemnestra Hesitating before Killing the Sleeping Agamemnon,* seen in fig. 112

at the Salon of 1817 (fig. 112). From that double study, which shows the process Guérin employed in idealizing human physiognomy, Delacroix chose only the head on the left, vigorously copied from life. With close attention, he imitated the volume of the eyeball and the gleam of light that intensifies the gaze. In the years that followed, he was among the students of Guérin—the others were Gericault, Cogniet, and Scheffer—who most perfectly assimilated the art of communicating the passions, which their master was acknowledged to possess to a high degree. The means for making the lustrous eye the epicenter of expression acquired a masterful force of persuasion in Delacroix's *Head of an Old Greek Woman* (cat. 7) and *Orphan Girl in the Cemetery* (fig. 9). In December 1823, the artist visited the exhibition of Lucien Bonaparte's collection to examine Guérin's *Return of Marcus Sextus* (1799; Musée du Louvre), "thinking I had only that one painting to see." Undoubtedly, he believed he still had a lesson to learn from it.[20]

Of the advice that Guérin dispensed to his students, that relating to dissections has thus far gone unnoticed. The defender of the beau ideal might have been expected to shy away from such procedures and to be more inclined to share the purist Ingres's reservations about cadavers, confining himself to recommending the study of art treatises on anatomy rather than the direct study of the human body. On the contrary, Guérin not only counseled his students to observe dissections in operating theaters—Paris provided several for art students—but he also encouraged them to carry out the dissections themselves, as Bodinier reported in 1816: "After the hour of life drawing . . . I want to work dissecting at the school of medicine until dinner. M. G[uérin] recommends that I do it every day."[21] The evidence of these instructions provides an objective argument against the prevailing saturnine interpretation of Gericault's anatomical still lifes as an influence on Delacroix and helps to account for the large number of *écorché* studies by him.[22] It can be deduced from Bodinier's statement that all Guérin's students must have been encouraged in the practice by their master's demand for truth. Although it has been shown that none of Gericault's known anatomical drawings were realized during a dissection, many

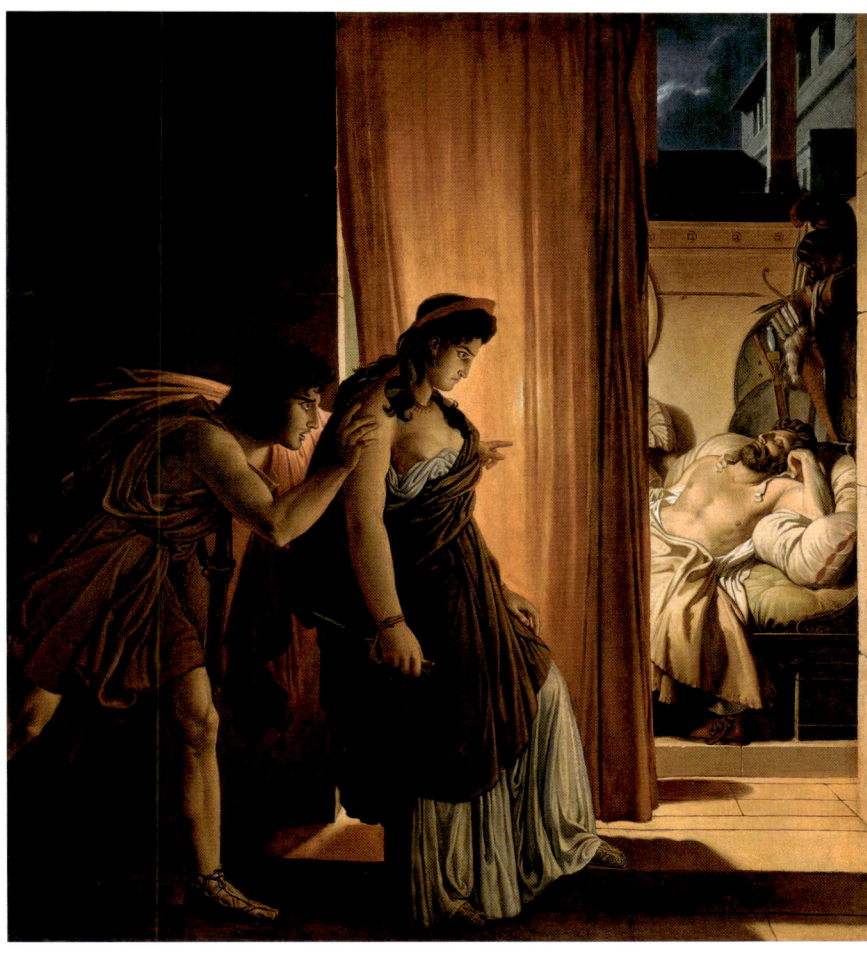

FIG. 112. Pierre Narcisse Guérin. *Clytemnestra Hesitating before Killing the Sleeping Agamemnon*, 1817. Oil on canvas, 11 ft. 2¾ in. x 10 ft. 8 in. (3.4 x 3.2 m). Musée du Louvre, Paris (5185)

of Delacroix's sketches were.[23] Guérin warned, however, that this relation to the natural and to the truth of the human body could also encourage too keen an attachment to the real, particularly among young artists accustomed throughout their youth to imagery like that found in Gros's monumental, cadaver-strewn depictions of the Napoleonic Wars. Gericault, in elaborating *The Raft of the Medusa* by means of life studies of anatomical fragments, developed aesthetically what had been, under Guérin's training, merely a utilitarian exercise; and Delacroix, far more under Gericault's influence than Guérin's, would explore in his early years the iconoclastic path of representing the macabre, which in 1824 would culminate in his *Massacres at Chios* (fig. 5).[24] Nonetheless, after completing *The Barque of Dante* in the spring of 1822, Delacroix was "deferential" toward Guérin, according to Véron, and sought his advice.[25]

It is certain that Delacroix, together with Champmartin, was one of Guérin's "most disruptive" students, whose departure at the end of that year was welcomed by Guérin's servant.[26] Yet they and other defenders of the aesthetics of excess

in Guérin's studio were not driven off by their master, as Maurice Quai and his followers had been by David.[27] It has not been sufficiently emphasized that, notwithstanding Delacroix's predilection for Gros's art, the void created by the departure of Guérin, who was preparing to take over the directorship of the Académie de France in Rome, encouraged Delacroix to turn to the other master. As he reported in his *Journal* on September 12, 1822, "In the last few days I have resolved to go to M. Gros's studio, and that idea is very much on my mind—agreeably so."[28]

Delacroix and Gros (1822)

Although Delacroix continued to hold Gros in the highest esteem throughout his life, accounts that have come down to us indicate that their relationship was as brief as it was intense. Delacroix's surge of warm feeling ended in cruel disillusionment caused by the loss of a myth cherished since youth. Gros zealously developed the cult of David after the

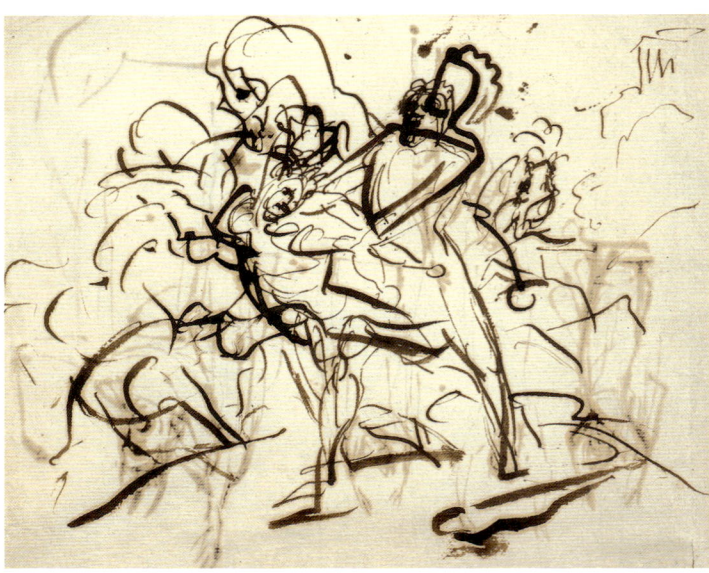

FIG. 113. Antoine Jean Gros. *Study for Hercules and Diomedes,* ca. 1835. Pen and brown ink, heightening with reed pen, 7⅛ x 8⅞ in. (18 x 22.5 cm). Private collection

latter was exiled in 1816, perpetuating his pedagogy by taking over his studio. As Delacroix aptly analyzed the situation in an article of 1848, those efforts precipitated the decline of the painter of *Napoleon Visiting the Plague Victims of Jaffa,* resulting in the self-loathing and annihilation of personality that led him, in 1835, to suicide.[29] In a famous letter of 1820, David ordered Gros to abandon the modern subjects that had made him famous and to paint "what is called a true history painting."[30] In the fifteen years that elapsed between that moment and Gros's death, Gros strove to model his manner on the master's beau ideal and, through the training of students, to extend his legacy. Gros's *David Playing the Harp for King Saul* (private collection), painted for the duc d'Orléans and exhibited at the Salon of 1822, was the first fruit of that forced and backward-looking effort.[31] Gros definitively abandoned the primacy of color adopted from Rubens in favor of a conception of localized color more consistent with the classical tradition—that is, color subordinated to drawing. Inspired by Guérin's *Clytemnestra,* Gros focused his audacity on the crimson chiaroscuro effect without managing to achieve the unity, harmony, or dramatic concentration of that painting. Drawing was the only area in which Gros gave free rein to his innate tendencies, as indicated to the very end by his brisk sketches made with an ink-filled brush (fig. 113). He allowed himself this liberty precisely because his drawings remained private. Those works are now seen to betray his

constant effort, during his Davidian years, to dissimulate his true nature.

Gros's enthusiasm for the young painter of *The Barque of Dante* was a dissonant episode in the otherwise reactionary late stage of his career. In a well-known account from 1853, Delacroix described the master's effusive response to his first Salon painting and in doing so revealed the chink in the armor that the doctrinaire painter had forged for himself:

> I idolized Gros's talent, which is for me, as I write you and after everything I've seen, still one of the most notable in the history of painting. I encountered Gros by chance, and he, learning that I was the one who had created the painting in question, paid me compliments with an incredible warmth. These have made me impervious to all flattery for life. In the end, after pointing out its merits, he told me that it was "Rubens refined." For this man, who worshiped Rubens and had been brought up in the strict school of David, that represented the greatest praise. He asked if he could do anything for me. I asked immediately if he would let me see his famous paintings of the Empire, which were at that moment hidden away in his studio and could not be shown in broad daylight because of the times [the Bourbon Restoration] and the subjects. He allowed me to remain there four hours, with him and alone, amidst his sketches and preparatory studies; in a word, he displayed toward me the greatest confidence, and Gros was a very anxious and suspicious man. Personal motives on the great painter's part may perhaps have been mingled with that complete approval: I thought I detected later on, through a certain sharpness in Gros's dealings with me, that he had thought to take me under his wing at his school to help me win the Prix de Rome. Although unassuming, I had by that time traced out my path in another direction, and I declined his patronage. Later on, however, when his students, apparently to flatter him, criticized my paintings in front of him, he cut them off, not by defending my talent, but saying that I was a perfectly upright young man and a good student.[32]

In his *Journal* of 1822, Delacroix expressed in crueler terms his grounds for turning away from Gros: "The torso and painting by [Auguste-Hyacinthe] Debay, a student of Gros's, a prize-winning student, filled me with disgust for his master's school, and just yesterday I wished it!"[33] But clearly, Gros, the rigid academician and staunch opponent of the new school, seems to have had no desire to harm the painter of *Massacres at Chios*.

The Delacroix Effect: The Masters' Reaction (1824–1833)

Eighteen twenty-four was the year of the Romantic revolt at the Salon, bookended by the deaths of Gericault and Girodet. It was a year of crisis in the fine arts. Although an entire generation was making its mark, Delacroix was perceived as the one responsible for fomenting revolution. His *Massacres at Chios*, which combined the aesthetics of excess with pictorial virtuosity, riveted attention even as it elicited disgust and horror.[34] From that moment on, Delacroix effectively crystallized the generational divide. His importance was measured by the yardstick of his imitators—Eugène Devéria, Alexandre Colin, Gillot Saint-Evre, Joseph Guichard—and by the amount of confusion his example sowed in the minds of students, including the *pensionnaires* at the Académie de France in Rome, heirs to a now-threatened tradition.[35]

The history of Delacroix's critical reception in the 1820s is well known.[36] Of relatively recent vintage, by contrast, are studies of established masters' reactions to the new manner of painting, which many regarded as licentious, and the crisis of legitimacy its rise provoked in the academic regime.[37] Gros's attitude toward the innovators was signaled in his invective against Horace Vernet, whom he likened, in an impromptu speech at Girodet's funeral, to a hack. François Gérard, the *premier peintre* to Louis XVIII, was much more indulgent, having lavished his congratulations and connections on Delacroix, welcoming him into his society in 1824.[38] Gérard had assigned himself a strategic role in assembling all the elites of society at the Salon. By modernizing his style and presenting himself as open-minded, he hoped not only to win the admiration of the younger generation but also to retain the esteem of the wider public. Two sketches recently brought to light show that he experimented with Romantic vocabulary using a freedom of brushwork that he might not have attempted without Delacroix's example. Even so, it is not accidental that these sketches, *Horses Frightened by the Surf* (fig. 114) and *Sea Study,* feature a crepuscular sky.[39] In choosing this light, which had announced a new, pre-Romantic sensibility in his

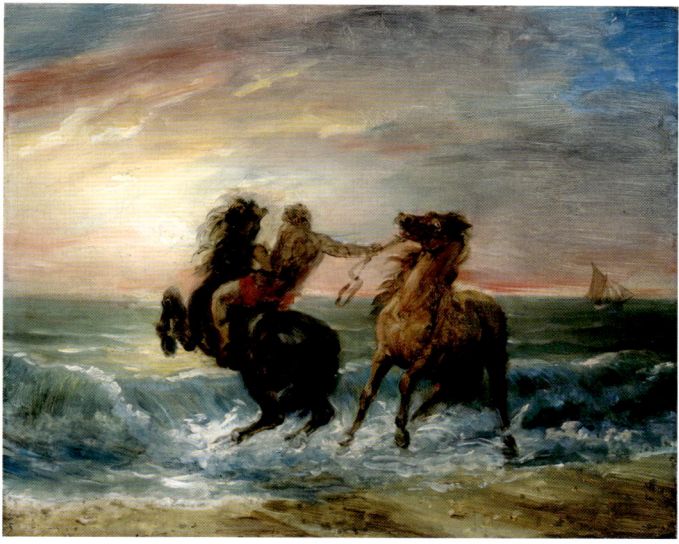

FIG. 114. François Gérard (French, 1770–1837). *Horses Frightened by the Surf,* 1830s. Oil on canvas, 12¹³⁄₁₆ x 16 in. (32.5 x 40.5 cm). Private collection

Belisarius (location unknown) at the Salon of 1795, Gérard reminded viewers that he, too, was a precursor.

The warmth toward Delacroix of another senior academician, Guillaume Guillon Lethière, did not survive the exhibition of *The Death of Sardanapalus* at the Salon of 1827–28. He is said to have boasted the following year that he had driven a student from his studio for imitating Delacroix's manner.[40] Lethière was among the masters who intended to respond to the innovators with creations of their own, but he was unable to complete his *Death of Virginia* in time for the Salon of 1827–28. He sent that enormous work, which he painted in three years on the basis of a thirty-year-old design, to be displayed at the Egyptian Hall in London for two years, as had been done earlier with *The Raft of the Medusa*. Lethière was therefore able to exhibit *The Death of Virginia* at the Salon of 1831 crowned with the success it had been accorded by the British, whose culture was greatly admired by the Romantics. Lethière's painting is an example of the forceful return of so-called classic Romanticism characterized by the representation of a violent antiquity, frenetic pantomime, exaggerated shadows, and a drawing style that was more vigorous than idealizing. But that "Romantic of thirty years ago"— Charles Lenormant's caustic epithet for Lethière—could not win the battle for public opinion in a critical arena split by partisanship; the voices of the two camps canceled each other out.[41]

In Rome, Guérin had no direct contact with Delacroix (nor do they seem to have corresponded) but was nonetheless

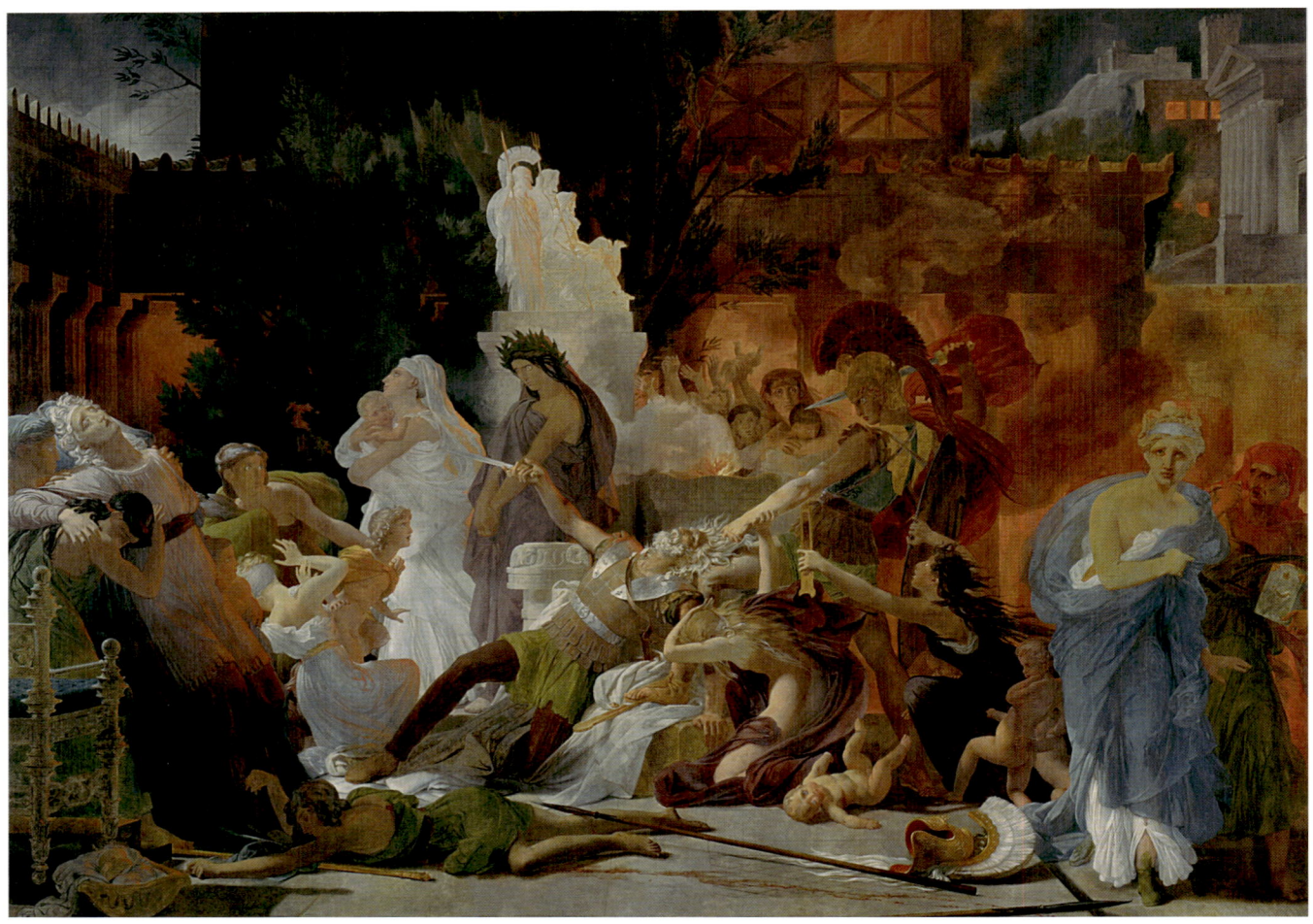

FIG. 115. Pierre Narcisse Guérin. *The Death of Priam*, or *The Last Night of Troy*, 1830–32. Oil on canvas, 14 ft. 4¾ in. x 20 ft. 7¾ in. (4.4 x 6.3 m). Musée des Beaux-Arts, Angers (inv. MBA J 79 [J 1881] P)

affected by the negative publicity surrounding his former student. After the Salons of 1824 and 1827–28, the master attempted to contain the Romantic fever overcoming his charges at the Villa Medici—all of them Prix de Rome winners. They were dragging their feet more than ever in completing their assignments at a moment when young independent artists were monopolizing the Salon's attention. Although their rivals, unburdened by academic obligations, aroused envy, it was Delacroix, above all, who gave them pause, as evinced in a letter by *pensionnaire* Larivière late in 1827: "Is it the manner of the great Delacroix or that of the cold David that we must follow?"[42] At this time, however, Guérin was far less preoccupied with Delacroix's disturbing art than with the mediocrity of his own poorly trained and easily influenced *pensionnaires*. He referred to them as "spineless talents, weak athletes who burden the profession without being able to succeed at it"—products of an academic

education in decline and ineffective government policy for encouraging artistic endeavor.[43]

Guérin formed his idea of Delacroix's "School of the Ugly" while in Rome, at second hand.[44] It was only upon returning to France, in the autumn of 1829, that he discovered for himself Delacroix's trailblazing works and the extent of his influence. From that point on, Guérin envisioned *The Death of Priam*, a project he was then in the process of reviving after a six-year cessation of his artistic practice, as a retort to those of his students who had wandered off onto the path of Romanticism (fig. 115).[45] In fact, only exponents of the aesthetics of excess and Delacroix, the man who inspired them, were the targets of his corrective undertaking. Léon Cogniet and Ary Scheffer, despite their association with the new school of painting, were among Guérin's nine former students who inherited the contents of his studio, an indication that the master considered them to be his artistic heirs. *The Death of*

Priam was conceived not only as the summation of its maker's pictorial convictions, an encapsulation of his highest qualities shown to best advantage, but also as a way to surpass David and do battle with Delacroix. It was to be a rebuttal to David's *Intervention of the Sabine Women* (1799; Musée du Louvre)— seen by detractors of the academy as the epitome of degenerate classicism—and of Delacroix's *Death of Sardanapalus*.[46] Color is the primary criterion that distinguishes Guérin's work from those of his two antagonists. From Guérin's perspective, their mistake was to emancipate color from its purely descriptive function: David, on the basis of an imagined Greek purity; and Delacroix, by making "pictures with pictures," that is, through an overwrought imitation of the great colorists of the past. In *The Death of Priam,* the artist carefully managed color and chiaroscuro with the aim of exciting the senses and thrilling the spectator; the work's dramatic effect and colossal scale were intended to amplify its impact on the public.

But Guérin died in 1833 before completing the painting, and his student heirs hastened to secrete it away, probably less from fear of its critical reception than from apprehensions about how it would be received politically by the July Monarchy. It would not have been wise to exhibit an image of the execution of a king before the eyes of Louis-Philippe, a monarch embarrassed by its revolutionary origin.[47] Had *The Death of Priam* been displayed to the public, it most likely would have met with the same generational prejudices that greeted Lethière's *Death of Virginia* two years before.

Delacroix paid homage to Gros in an article acknowledging him as one of the "most notable" talents "in the history of painting."[48] But what did he retain from Guérin? From an ethical perspective, it is no small paradox that Guérin, out of respect for the individuality of his students, refused to make them his imitators or to employ them in executing his commissioned works, whereas Delacroix, first of the Romantics, after receiving major mural commissions, opened a studio with the sole aim of training assistants in whom he stifled all personal ambition.[49] Although Delacroix's artistic practice differed greatly from Guérin's, and though during his long artistic maturation he turned to successive models, his *Othello and Desdemona,* for example, suggests that he was capable of emulating his master's poetic invention when he chose to (fig. 116). This Shakespearean painting from the late 1840s is

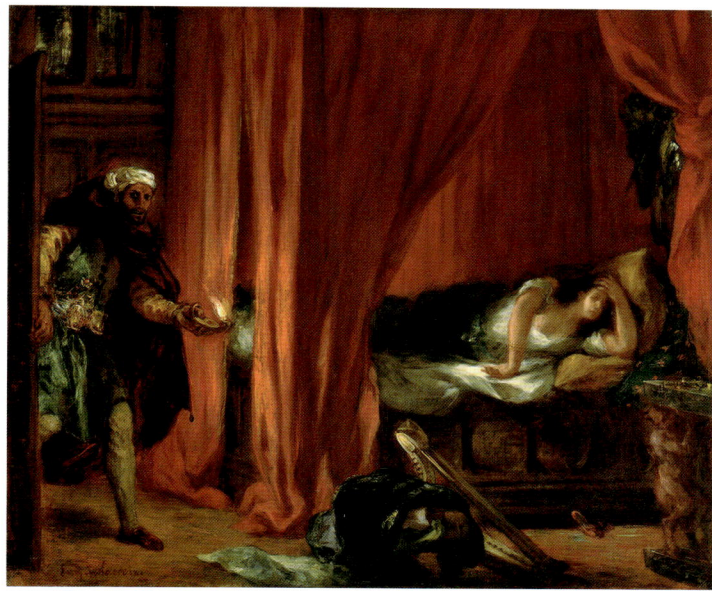

FIG. 116. *Othello and Desdemona,* ca. 1847–49. Oil on canvas, 20 x 24½ in. (50.8 x 62.2 cm). National Gallery of Canada, Ottawa (inv. 15700)

an explicit reformulation of Guérin's *Clytemnestra,* a work that, by virtue of its crimson chiaroscuro and its brutal subject— the bloody assassination of Agamemnon—was in Delacroix's youth the most audacious history painting in the antique genre to be produced by the modern school. Also of note are the resemblances, perhaps slight but nonetheless intriguing, in the two men's personalities. The traits they shared may have made Delacroix the student of Guérin's who was most like his master: frail silhouette, delicate health, elegant bearing, good manners, a fondness for writing, the love and practice of music (qualities and skills that made both artists sought after in the social world), moderate political opinions, and the choice to remain single, free from the contingencies of family life that could have distracted them from art, to which they devoted themselves exclusively. Like Guérin, Delacroix had the ambition, perhaps illusory, to belong to the Académie in order to change its way of teaching and contribute to the progress of the art of his century. The resemblance Baudelaire identified went beyond the field of literary inspiration. And in the end, it was in the natural order of things that this resemblance increased when Delacroix was no longer young, or an innovator.

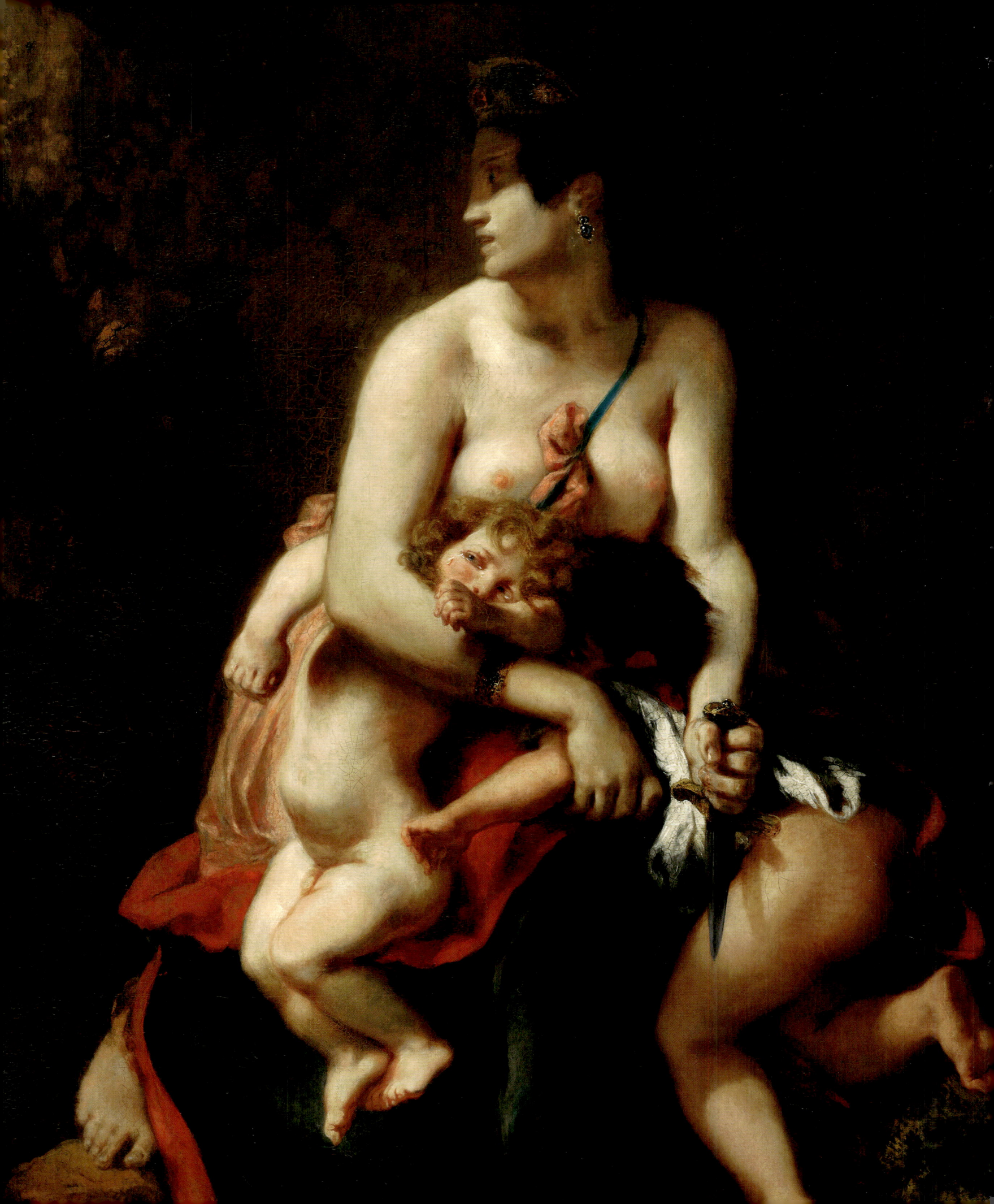

Delacroix and the Exposition Universelle of 1855

DOMINIQUE DE FONT-RÉAULX

In 1854, at the conclusion of an article on the sense of the beautiful—*le beau*—and on critics' ability to define it—the author signed his name "Eugène Delacroix, of the Academy of Amsterdam."[1] The same year, although Delacroix had been honored as recently as 1849 with commissions to adorn monuments of his nation and his city of Paris, the Académie des Beaux-Arts once again denied him membership. A long letter he wrote in 1849 to the engraver Jacques Edouard Gatteaux, then president of the Académie, reveals his dismay at already having been refused admission three times and his fierce desire to highlight his accomplishments up to that point. While showing deference toward the masters who were affiliated with the renowned institution, Delacroix let it be known that his artistic production amply qualified him to be accepted as one of them:

> I ask you, and them, to bear in mind a certain number of history paintings, including, among others, *Dante and Virgil,* the *Massacre of Chios, Christ in the Garden of Olives, The Justice of Trajan, The Entry of the Crusaders into Constantinople,* and *Medea.* I was also called upon to decorate the dome of the library of the Palais du Luxembourg, the vault and both ends of the library of the Palais de l'Assemblée Législative, and, before that, the Throne Room in the same building. I take the liberty of adding to this list several paintings in a *genre secondaire* (a relatively minor genre), such as the *Bishop of Liège, Marino Faliero,* the *Women of Algiers in Their Apartment, A Shipwreck,* and a *Jewish Wedding.*[2]

Delacroix did not mention *The Death of Sardanapalus* (fig. 20), knowing the scandal caused by that painting was still fresh in the minds of many academicians. He claimed that, far from disdaining the models of the past, as he had been reproached for doing, he greatly admired them, as he had shown and continued to show by taking the same liberties that the earlier masters had allowed for themselves.

The question of the validity of artistic judgment, of recognition granted or refused, of present or future glory, had long preoccupied Delacroix.[3] Ever since his debut at the Salon of 1822, he had felt it necessary to be singled out and commended, if not appreciated.[4] As the years went by, his desire for recognition increased. The painter feared he would be unable to complete projects already under way because he tired quickly; his concerns about his health sharpened his perception of the passage of time, feeding his doubts and anxieties. Delacroix also worried that without critical and official support he would become an old man before his time, one whose audacity would pale next to that of the younger generation of artists wishing to make their names on the art scene.

Even so, the outlook was auspicious at the very end of 1847, when, nearing fifty, Delacroix finally finished the decoration of the library of the Chamber of Deputies in the Palais Bourbon (which he referred to as the Palais de l'Assemblée Législative in his letter to Gatteaux), a commission awarded ten years before.

Scarcely more than a month later, in February 1848, he was deeply shaken by the events that put a violent end to the reign of King Louis-Philippe. Delacroix feared the disorder that, in all likelihood, would follow. It seemed to him that, as in 1830, the hopes that had accompanied the street demonstrations would be dashed, and disappointment would bring new difficulties. He cautioned George Sand, who had contemplated getting involved with the new regime, and wrote to his childhood friend Charles Soulier one of his most deeply moving letters.[5]

> Dear friend, I have not written you and yet I have not forgotten you. Your letter, when it reached me, heartened me a little. We had just been witnessing a terrible upheaval, and for nearly a month I felt as if an entire house had fallen on my head.[6] I am now resigned to it. I have buried the man I was, with his hopes and dreams for the future, and now I can come and go with a certain semblance of calm over the tomb in which I have shut all that away, as if I were a different person. . . . How old we are, and how much this will age us! I have seen some of these zealots, and they were young.[7]

Like those close to him and other creative people of his time, Delacroix was keenly aware of having once belonged to a new generation, and he realized that the Revolution of 1848 would give rise to yet another generation.[8] In addition, and more immediately, he was afraid that the political unrest would distract him from painting, a risk he was unwilling to take. Yet, despite his anxieties, the short-lived Second Republic was not unfavorable toward him. Napoleon Bonaparte's rise to power in 1848 and his proclamation of empire in 1852 boded well for Delacroix, whose family had loyally served the new ruler's uncle.

France, Mother of the Arts

By 1852, Napoleon III had conceived the plan for a grand Exposition Universelle in response to the pomp of the Great Exhibition held in London in 1851.[9] A series of decrees issued in 1853 stipulated that a universal exposition of agricultural and industrial products, open to all nations, was to be held. The emperor also wished to accord a prominent place to the fine arts, which had been consigned to lesser status in London. He wanted to show off the talents of French artists to the nations gathered together for the occasion and to celebrate France as the Mother of the Arts. Originally, the Exposition Universelle—the first ever held in Paris—was to take place in 1854. It finally opened its doors on May 1, 1855, and closed five months later, on September 30.

The emperor seems to have personally chosen the artists to whom he would give special honors. Delacroix took full advantage of this support in a letter to Georges-Eugène Haussmann, prefect of the Seine, requesting to borrow the large painting *Christ in the Garden of Olives (The Agony in the Garden)* (see cat. 17) from the church of Saint-Paul-Saint-Louis for display at the Exposition. "The Emperor's very express intention, which he did me the honor of conveying personally, is for French artists to appear at the Exposition with all the works they deem appropriate to withstand competition from the foreigners."[10] The support of Emilien de Nieuwerkerke, a close friend of the imperial family who had been named director of museums in 1849, was undoubtedly invaluable. Delacroix knew him and saw him on a regular basis. He had written to Nieuwerkerke on March 2, 1855, asking him to intercede with the fine arts museums in Nancy and Rouen so that they would lend *The Battle of Nancy* (cat. 69) and *The Justice of Trajan* (see fig. 35) to the Exposition.[11] Delacroix was beholden to Nieuwerkerke for the commission of a large painting, *Lion Hunt* (cat. 136), painted specifically for the Exposition. Furthermore, it was by claiming to have the emperor's authorization that Delacroix was able to exhibit *Liberty Leading the People*, known as his *Barricade* for commemorating the July Revolution of 1830 (fig. 26). The work had been displayed at the Salon of 1831 and acquired by the state, only to be placed in storage after demonstrations in 1832 were violently repressed by Louis-Philippe's so-called July Monarchy. Afterward, the painting was returned to the artist, who lamented that it could not be shown.

Delacroix took great care in choosing each picture he would exhibit at the Exposition's Palais des Beaux-Arts. He wished to assemble the key works of his career, beginning with his first success at the Salon in 1822, *The Barque of Dante* (see fig. 2). His selection included not only paintings that had been acquired by the state but also works in private hands. Those inspired by his stay in Morocco—*Women of Algiers in Their Apartment* (fig. 32) and *Jewish Wedding in Morocco* (fig. 31)—hung next to *Liberty Leading the People*, *Entry of the Crusaders into Constantinople* (fig. 36), and *The Justice of Trajan* (fig. 35). Delacroix also accorded a place for works of more modest dimensions, such as *Mary Magdalene in the Wilderness* (fig. 122), which he had shown at the Salon of 1845, as well as two of the flower paintings he had exhibited at the Salon of 1849 (cats. 109, 110). Through its diversity, the selection showed to advantage his achievements over the course of thirty years, confirming Delacroix's status as one of the most important painters of his time. Finally, there was the special state commission for the exhibition, the monumental *Lion Hunt*, an homage to Rubens that affirmed Delacroix's ability to master an extremely complex composition. Charles Baudelaire celebrated this new feat by his favorite painter in the following terms: "The *Lion Hunt* is a veritable *explosion* of color (this word is intended in its positive sense). Never have more beautiful, more intense colors penetrated the soul through the channel of the eyes!"[12]

Certain works were missing, however—among them, the large painted decorations that could not be removed from walls and ceilings for the occasion. Also missing was *The Death of Sardanapalus*, which had been acquired nearly ten years earlier by a Scottish industrialist based in France.[13] Whether or not the large canvas could have been borrowed, it had provoked the lasting indignation of the academic critics when it was shown at the Salon of 1827–28.

The installation of the exhibition caused problems for Delacroix. He was one of four living artists—the others were Jean Auguste Dominique Ingres, Horace Vernet, and Alexandre-Gabriel Decamps—who were to have major retrospectives, but the space allotted to Delacroix's works did not correspond to what he had been promised. He complained to Frédéric de Mercey, general curator of the exhibition:

> I should like it very much if you would be good enough to find a time at your earliest convenience to go to the Exposition. I will be there myself, with the aim of obtaining from you a space suited to my paintings. I was blandished with the possibility of having a

place in the rooms that are now allotted *in their entirety* to Messieurs Ingres and Vernet. Age and talent confer privileges that I do not dispute. But I am not a young man or an unknown. I would not have drawn these large paintings from the provinces, which entailed a great deal of trouble and cost, in order to exhibit them here in an unfavorable light.[14]

Delacroix expressed his point of view with great composure. A note in his *Journal*, dated March 24, 1855, shows that he was far more disappointed than he admitted. He turned to writing for the solace that the company of his contemporaries did not provide. "In my current state of lethargy, which has truly reached a critical phase, when I see the time I have left to finish my paintings slipping away, I am very despondent at how indifferent the people at this exhibition are about helping me. But then I take pleasure in withdrawing into myself and, unable to get much assistance from the affection other people have for me, I seek sustenance in the memory of my own feelings."[15] Delacroix retained the force of his conviction, and he knew how to be persuasive despite his emotional distress and fragile health.[16] Although he failed to secure a room dedicated solely to his own works, he managed to have them installed in one of the two grand salons located at the entrance to the Palais des Beaux-Arts, where they benefited from good light (figs. 117, 118). He had written to Mercey: "I returned yesterday to the Exposition and, after looking again, asked whether my paintings could be placed in *the smaller of the two grand salons devoted to French artists, in the part facing the entrance, together with the right-hand corner. . . .* I ask this of you, assuring you in advance of the satisfaction I would feel from the proper effect my paintings would have as a result."[17] Delacroix appears here in his full complexity: ready to ardently defend his works; tenacious and practical in achieving his ends; urbane and extremely refined in his choice of words. He was all these things despite being plagued by anxiety, which nothing could mollify.

Delacroix's retrospective exhibition of 1855 was a success: the many visitors to the Paris event greatly admired his paintings; he was named or promoted to Commander of the Legion of Honor; and the critics were unanimous in hailing his talent. Baudelaire was enthusiastic and full of praise, as he had been since 1845, when he first reviewed a Salon in which Delacroix exhibited. Despite the critic's penchant for contrarianism, his opinion was fully shared in 1855. Baudelaire

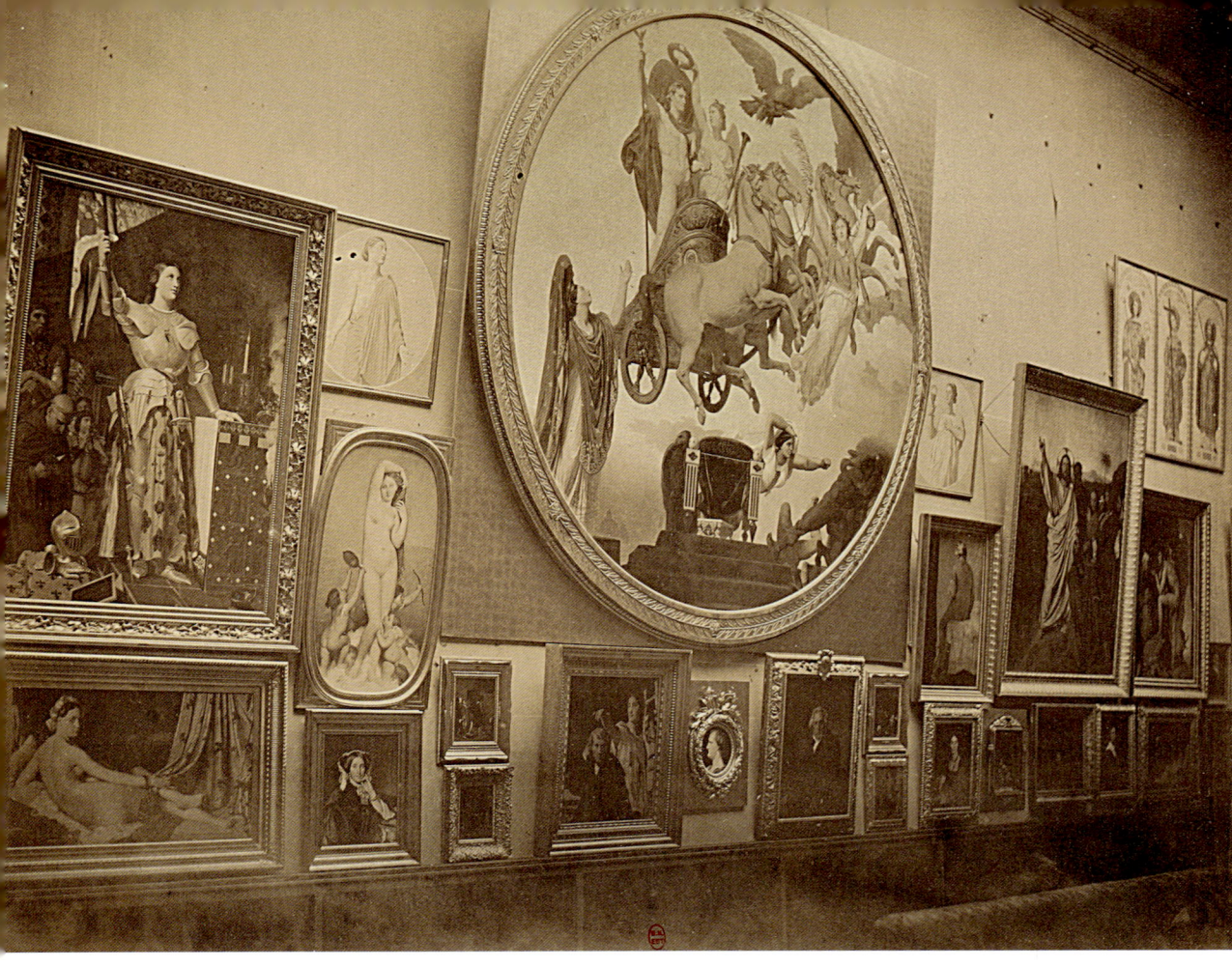

had read Théophile Silvestre's remarkable articles on living artists, notably the one on Delacroix that had appeared in the *Revue des deux mondes* in 1854.[18] Like Silvestre, Baudelaire closed his essay with a reference to posterity, celebrating Delacroix's place—the one the painter himself wished for—as a man of genius within a prestigious pictorial tradition:

> How will M. Delacroix stand with Posterity? What will that righter of wrongs have to say of him? He has now reached a point in his career at which it is already easy to give the answer without finding many who disagree. Posterity will say, as we do, that he combined the most astonishing faculties: like Rembrandt, he had a sense of intimacy and a profoundly magical quality; like Rubens and Lebrun, a feeling for decoration and for combination; like Veronese, an enchanted sense of color, etc. But that he also had a quality all his own, a quality indefinable but itself defining the melancholy and the passion of his age—something quite new, which has made him a unique artist, without ancestry, without precedent, and probably without successor—a link so precious that it could in no wise be replaced; and

that by destroying it—if such a thing were possible—a whole world of ideas and sensations would be destroyed, and too great a gap would be blasted in the chain of history.[19]

The Question of Modernity

Delacroix's recognition was complete, but perhaps too perfect. The young man who could "run across the rooftops," as François Gérard reportedly described Delacroix at his Salon debut in 1822, and who on the same occasion was singled out for the originality of his talent by the painter Antoine Jean Gros, had, in 1855, become a celebrated painter elevated to the rank of model artist and awarded the highest national distinctions.[20] Owing to his masterful retrospective exhibition, Delacroix now seemed to be accepted without reservation for his singular manner—the primacy of color in his work, the freedom of his brushstroke, the variety of his subjects. In the eyes of his contemporaries, he was a painter defined by a complex body of work, the themes of which required extensive literary and historical knowledge in order to be

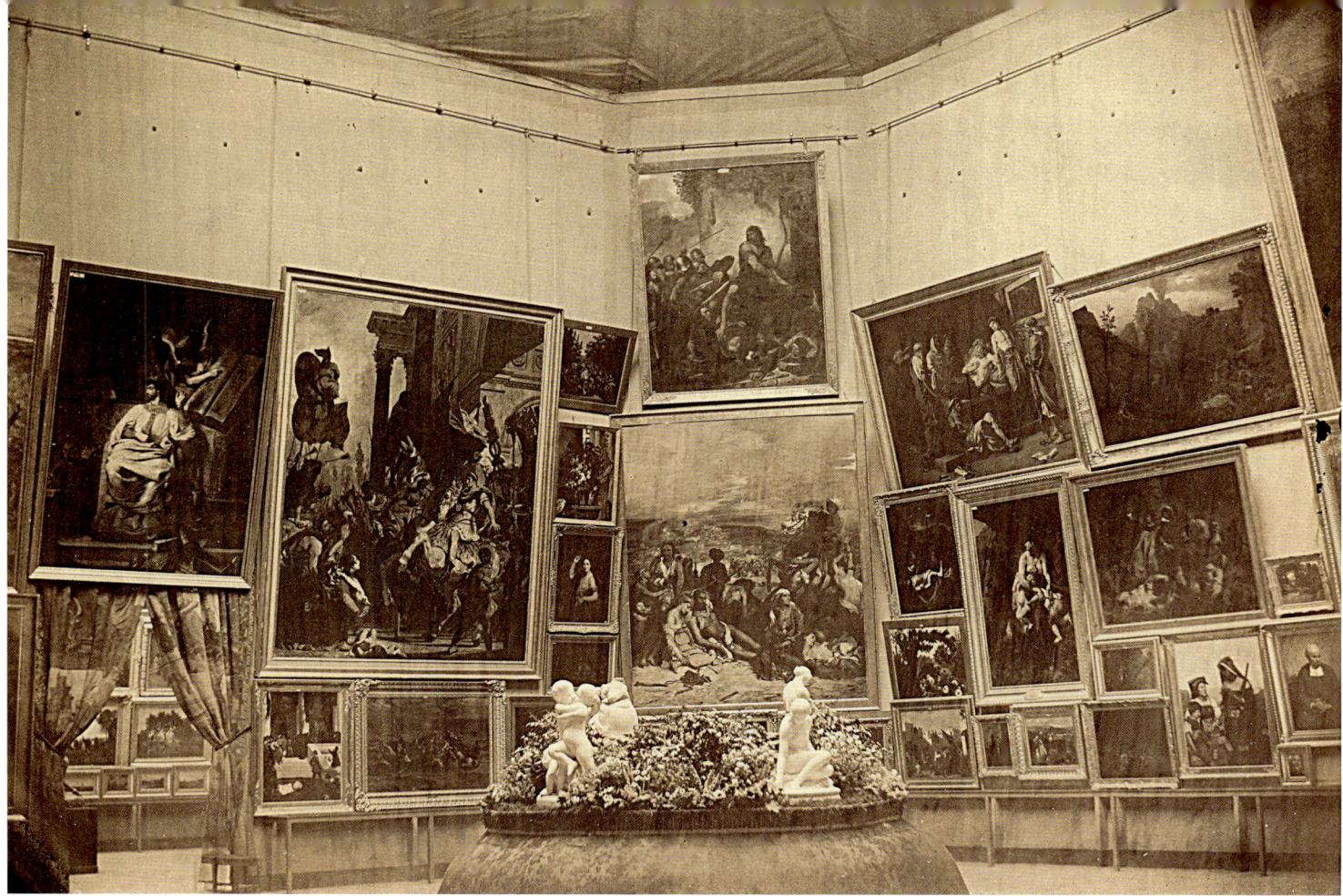

understood. He no longer seemed so audacious a representative of his day. Comparisons with his rival, Ingres, no longer offered the point and counterpoint that had fueled the passions of opposing factions during the Salons of the 1820s. Ingres, too, was celebrated, honored, and rewarded in 1855. Despite Baudelaire's admiration for Delacroix, which was absolute, the critic, in his review of the Exposition Universelle, opened the section devoted to the artist not by contrasting him to the painter of *The Apotheosis of Homer,* as he had done in other texts, but by recognizing both men as essential actors on the art scene of their time. "MM. Eugène Delacroix and Ingres share between them the support and the antipathy of the public. It has been a long time since popular opinion first drew a cordon around them, like a pair of wrestlers. But without acceding to this childish and vulgar love of antithesis, we must begin with an examination of these two French painters."[21] The lines Baudelaire devoted to Ingres's retrospective exhibition were no less positive than those he had written about Delacroix; indeed, they came first: "But today we are faced with a man of an immense and incontestable renown whose work is much more difficult to understand and explain."[22] Obviously, one could not confuse the two

painters. But despite Ingres's seniority—he was born in 1780—and central position in academic circles from his earliest years, Delacroix no longer faced off against him as either a young man or a rebel. A look at how they chose to present themselves at the Exposition Universelle reveals that it was Delacroix who claimed to be the great history painter, able to take on the *grand sujet,* with Ingres once more proving himself a portraitist of genius. Delacroix's talent was remarkable, but he appeared in 1855 as an artist whose *modernity,* at a time when it was necessary to be *modern,* seemed difficult to define.

Delacroix and Courbet

That year, the novelty—the brio—came from another painter, one a generation younger than Delacroix. Gustave Courbet had succeeded not only in getting eleven of his paintings accepted to the Salon of the Palais des Beaux-Arts but also in convincing Alfred Bruyas, a patron of the arts from Montpellier and a collector of Delacroix's, to finance the construction of an independent pavilion, the Pavilion of Realism, devoted entirely to a solo exhibition of his work.[23] Courbet's art had

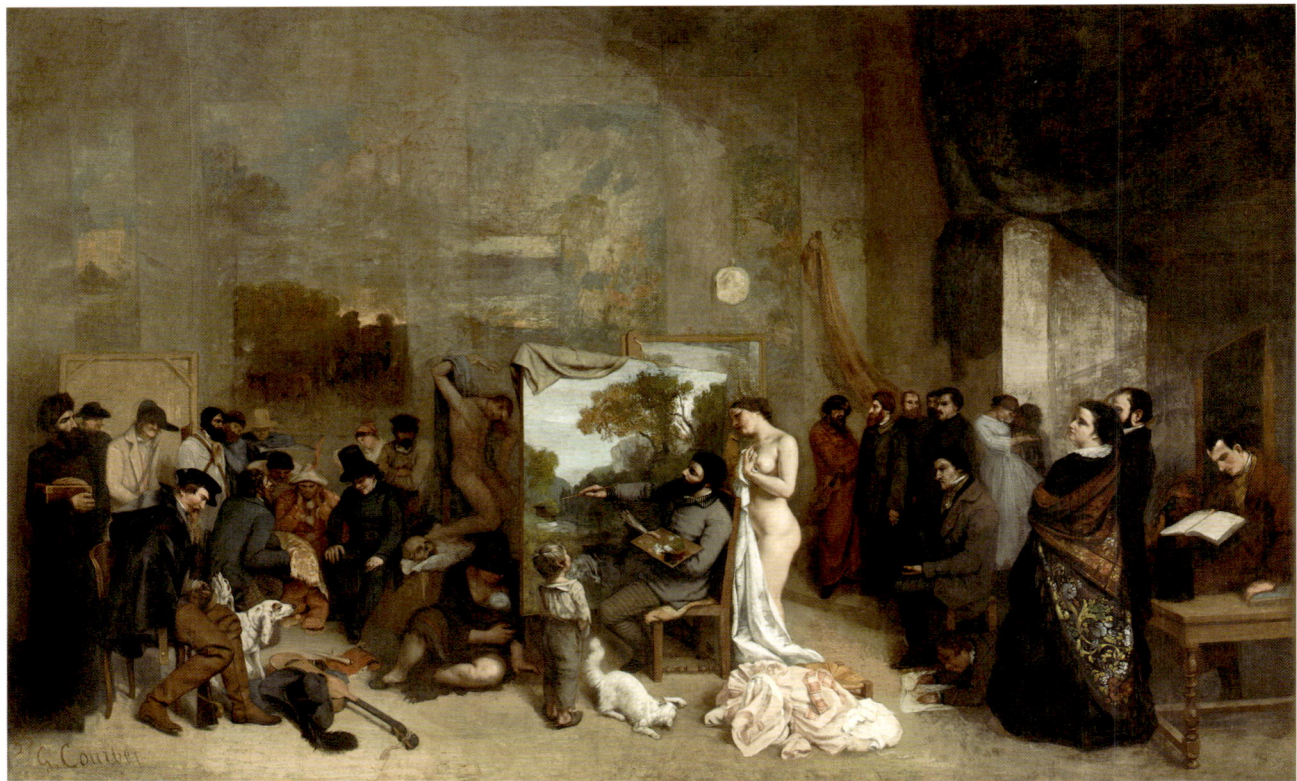

FIG. 119. Gustave Courbet. *The Painter's Studio* (after restoration), 1855. Oil on canvas, 13 ft. 8¼ in. x 21 ft. 5½ in. (4.2 x 6.5 m). Musée d'Orsay, Paris (RF 2257)

been admitted to the Salon for the first time in 1844. In 1849, his *After Dinner at Ornans* was awarded a gold medal, affording him the privilege of displaying any works of his choice at the following Salon.[24] But the exhibition of his monumental canvas *A Burial at Ornans* at the Salon of 1850–51 incurred the wrath of the critics, triggering a reaction reminiscent of the one that had erupted over Delacroix's *Sardanapalus* twenty-three years before.[25] And in 1855, Courbet's outcry at the rejection of his outsize work *The Painter's Studio* (fig. 119) from the Salon of the Exposition Universelle—even though his contribution to the exhibition was far more extensive than what had been granted to the majority of painters of his generation—recalled the way the young Delacroix had complained at having been snubbed from 1827 onward, despite his many public commissions.[26]

Delacroix was not unappreciative of Courbet's talent, but he nevertheless kept a certain distance. On April 15, 1853, he noted in his *Journal* that he been to the Salon to see the younger artist's paintings and proceeded to write lengthy ruminations on them.[27] His critique of *The Bathers* was ambivalent, in part owing to ambiguities in the work. While he recognized the force of the painter's talent and especially

admired the beauty of his treatment of the landscape, he remained highly circumspect about the unexpressed connections between the two women, the large bather seen from the back, undressed, and her companion, a servant or attendant. The gesture that the bather directs toward her companion has an expansiveness somewhat reminiscent of Christ's *Noli me tangere* to Mary Magdalene; in an 1840 painting by Delacroix, Hamlet employs the same gesture toward Ophelia.[28] Of the Courbet, Delacroix wrote: "She is making some meaningless gesture, and another woman, presumably her maid, is seated on the ground taking off her shoes and stockings. You see the stockings; one of them, I think, is only half removed. There seems to be some exchange of thought between the two figures, but it is quite unintelligible. The landscape is extraordinarily vigorous."[29]

In 1855, Delacroix visited Courbet's Pavilion of Realism, where he once again saw *The Bathers*, among the other works on display. By his own admission, he spent a long time admiring *The Painter's Studio*, which was too large and had been submitted too late for inclusion in the Exposition Universelle. The painting's rejection is what prompted Courbet to have a space built solely for his own works. Delacroix wrote:

Afterwards I went to the Courbet exhibition. He has reduced the price of admission to ten sous. I stayed there alone for nearly an hour and discovered a masterpiece in the picture which they rejected; I could scarcely bear to tear myself away. He has made enormous strides, and yet this picture has taught me to appreciate his *Burial*. In this picture [*The Burial*] the figures are all on top of one another and the composition is not well arranged, but some of the details are superb, for instance, the priests, the choirboys, the vessel for holy water, the weeping women, etc., etc.— In the later picture [*The Painter's Studio*], the planes are well understood, there is atmosphere, and in some passages the execution is really remarkable, especially the thighs and hips of the nude model and the breasts—also the woman in the foreground with the shawl. The only fault is that the picture, as he has painted it, seems to contain an ambiguity: it looks as though there were a real sky in the middle of the painting.—They have rejected one of the most remarkable works of our time; but [Courbet] is not the type to be discouraged by so little.[30]

Such elaborate recognition and praise are rare in Delacroix's writings. He had been an attentive visitor to the Exposition; in a letter to Paul Huet, he warmly congratulated his friend for the choice of the works exhibited, especially his large *Flood at Saint-Cloud* (1855).[31] "I hope you will be pleased by what everyone tells you," he wrote, "because my judgment is the same as what I heard from everyone who saw them."[32] He went several times to the section devoted to the English school; he had not forgotten his early years under British influence, which he always remembered with a nostalgia-tinged pleasure that elated him. Delacroix appreciated that in the works of the English artists "nearly every object is depicted with the attention it deserves."[33] He was particularly enthusiastic about *Our English Coasts 1852 (Strayed Sheep)* by the Pre-Raphaelite artist William Holman Hunt: "I spent until about noon examining the paintings by English artists, which I admire a great deal; I am truly amazed by Hunt's *Sheep*" (fig. 120).[34]

Conversely, Courbet, in the letters he wrote to his friends and loved ones, betrayed a certain cruelty of judgment toward Delacroix. Driven by a fierce determination to make his mark, Courbet was aware that he was implicitly assuming

what had been Delacroix's role in the renewal of painting; sharply intuitive, he undoubtedly knew that he was adopting the audacious manner that the Romantic painter had himself chosen. In 1852, writing to his family about his fellow artists' unfavorable reactions to *Young Ladies of the Village* (1851–52; Metropolitan Museum), shown at that year's Salon, he railed against what he presumed to be Delacroix's attitude: "The painters are furious, they hadn't taken it [my art] seriously. They don't come to see me [my work] as they did last year. They feel they have been taken in and that I have got the better of them. Even Delacroix went to the ministry to knock my painting (this comes from Romieu). The man is amazed that he is less talked about than he used to be."[35] Writing to the poet Victor Hugo after the scandal of *The Return from the Conference*, a painting widely disparaged and refused even by the Salon des Refusés of 1863, Courbet, associating Hugo with the recently deceased Delacroix, emphasized that he belonged to a generation different from theirs. "When Delacroix and you were in your prime, you did not have, as I do, an empire to say to you, 'Outside of us there is no salvation.' . . . Delacroix never saw soldiers force themselves into his home on a minister's orders and pour turpentine over his paintings. . . . He did not have that pack of mongrels howling at his heels, in the service of their mongrel masters. The battles were about art, about questions of principle; you were not threatened with banishment."[36] Exaggeration, whether of the criticisms directed at him or the abuses heaped

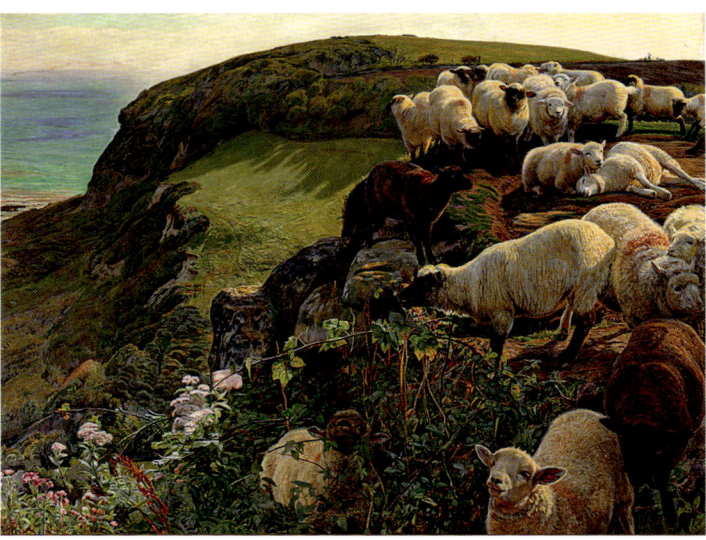

FIG. 120. William Holman Hunt (English, 1827–1910). *Our English Coasts 1852 (Strayed Sheep)*, 1852. Oil on canvas, 17 x 23 in. (43.2 x 58.4 cm). Tate Britain, London, Presented by the Art Fund, 1946 (inv. No5665)

upon him, was a common rhetorical tactic of Courbet's, as was, conversely, pompous boasting of his successes.[37] His aim was to set himself apart as a unique figure, one whose battles were more difficult, more complex, and waged with more courage and talent than those of the artists who had preceded him—Delacroix above all. Even so, Courbet evidently regarded the painter of *Sardanapalus* as a role model in his strategy of provocation and scandal.

Although Courbet said nothing about it, Delacroix served him on several occasions as an artistic role model as well. If, unlike the older painter, Courbet did not reveal his own response to the Exposition Universelle, it is nevertheless certain that he not only saw Delacroix's assembled works there, but also that he observed them carefully and admired them. Delacroix's influence on Courbet's painting, beginning in the late 1850s, is clearly evident. This topic has not yet been the subject of in-depth study, but the few reflections that follow will, it is hoped, stimulate focused attention. The remarkable flower pictures exhibited by Delacroix in 1849 (cats. 109, 110) and again in 1855 surely captivated Courbet by their freedom of composition, vibrant and loaded brushstrokes, and

the beauty of their colors. Courbet may have had the opportunity to admire Delacroix's still lifes once again in May 1862, when they were exhibited at the Galerie du Cercle des Beaux-Arts, before he left Paris for a sojourn in Saintes, near Bordeaux.[38] Once there, Courbet would paint *The Trellis, or Woman with Flowers* (fig. 121), in which he infused the interlacing flowers that a young girl is arranging on a lattice with an exuberance that rivals the older painter's.

Like Delacroix, Courbet paid close attention to form and color and to relations between the two to arrive at a dazzling floral palette. He painted bouquets or groups of flowers several times during the 1860s, creating a group within his corpus that remains little studied but whose echo of Delacroix is distinct.[39] In 1871, during Courbet's imprisonment at Sainte-Pélagie and in the months that followed, his references to Delacroix were perhaps more personal and even painful. Just as the Romantic painter, anxious about the events of 1848 and frightened by the passage of time, had chosen to paint flowers, an ostensibly uncontroversial subject that kept both reality and history at bay, Courbet, at the most tragic moment of his life, produced the moving series of still lifes with fruit and

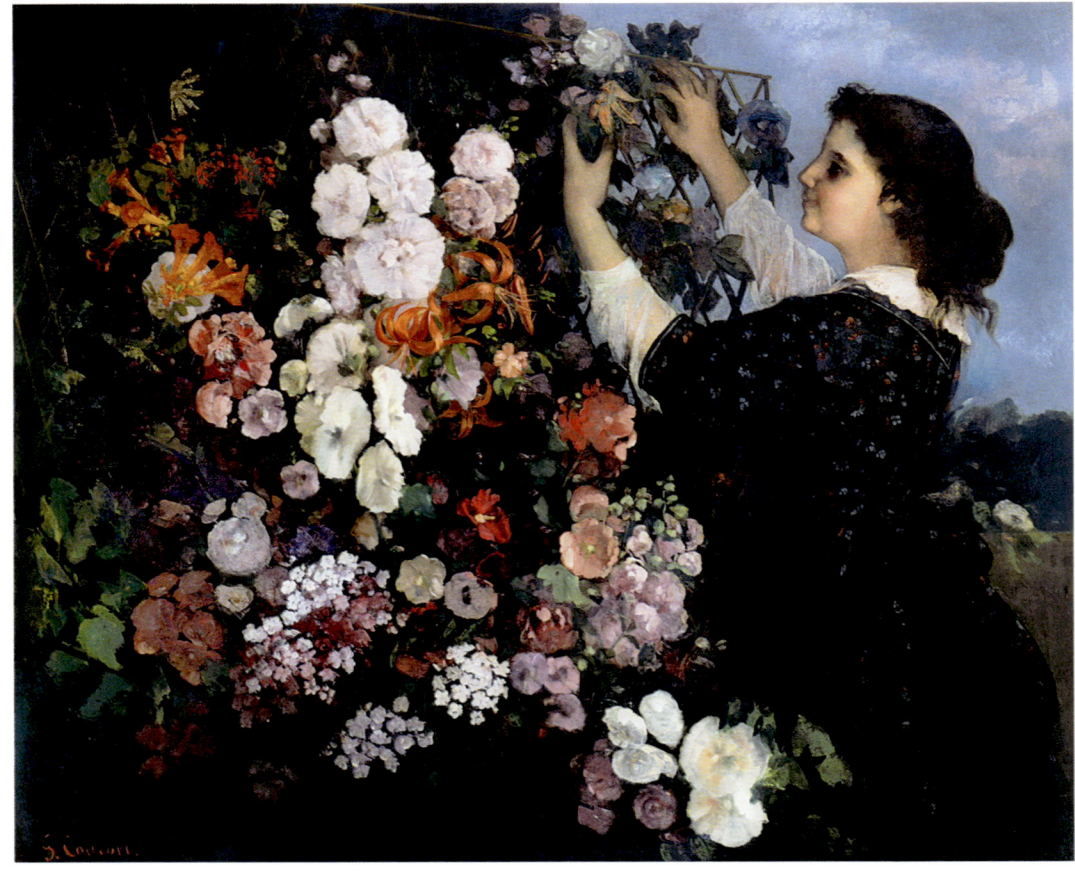

FIG. 121. Gustave Courbet. *The Trellis, or Woman with Flowers*, 1862. Oil on canvas, 43¼ in. x 53¼ in. (109.9 x 135.3 cm). Toledo Museum of Art, Purchased with funds from the Libbey Endowment, Gift of Edward Drummond Libbey (1950.309)

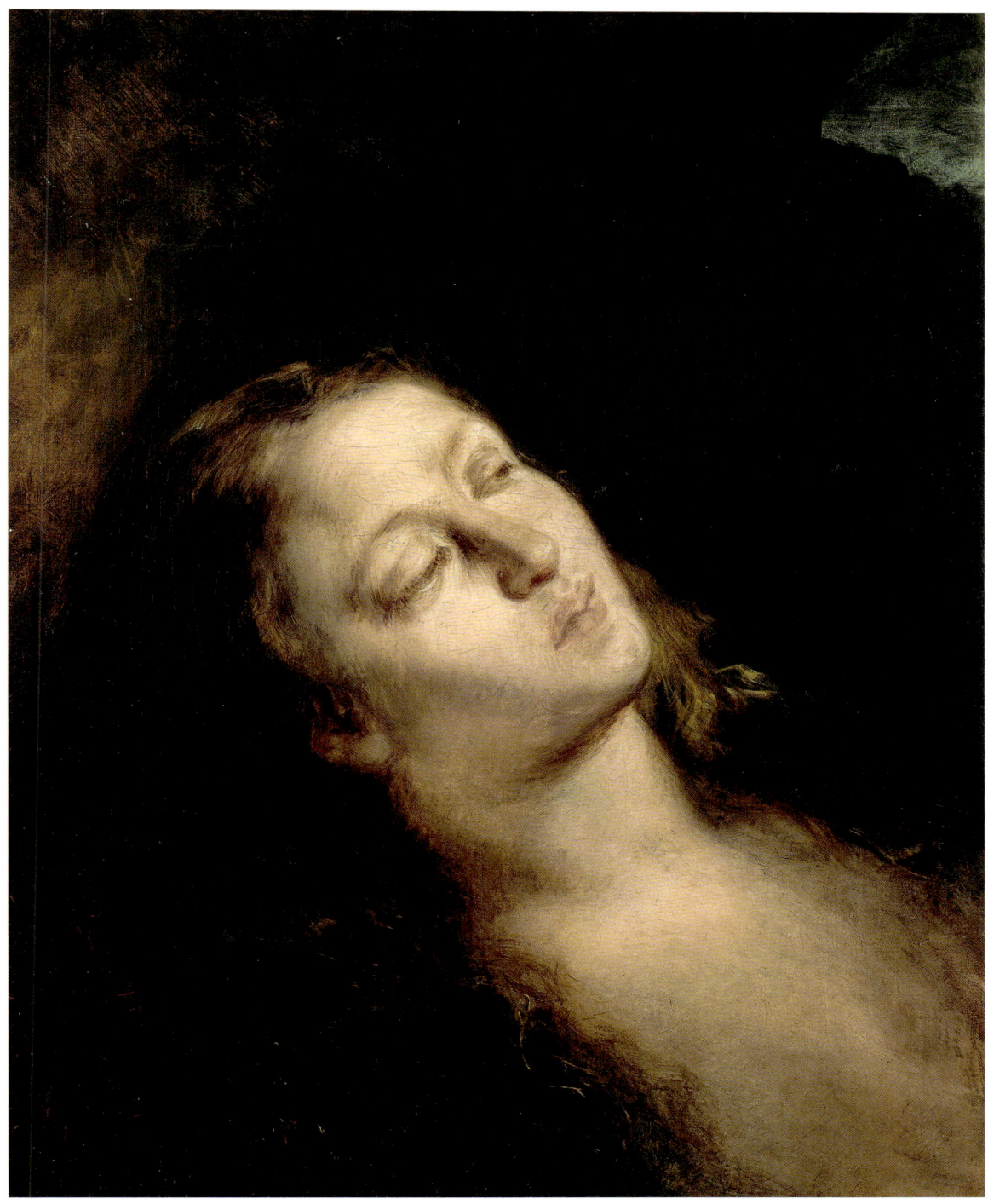

FIG. 122. *Mary Magdalene in the Wilderness*, 1845. Oil on canvas, 21⅞ x 17¾ in. (55.5 x 45 cm). Musée National Eugène-Delacroix, Paris (inv. MD 1990-4)

flowers—cut flowers, splendid and colorful, but condemned to a brief life, caught up in an ineluctable decay, a reflection of the artist's own desolation.[40]

Mary Magdalene in the Wilderness (fig. 122), "with her strange, mysterious smile, and so supernaturally beautiful that you cannot tell whether she has been transfigured by death or

beautified by the spasms of divine love," as Baudelaire describes her with both sensitivity and bombast, certainly intrigued Courbet.[41] In this painting, Delacroix invented a resolutely unique variation on a theme that painters had seized upon since the Renaissance, a pretext to flaunt the female nude under the guise of a religious subject. Unlike his

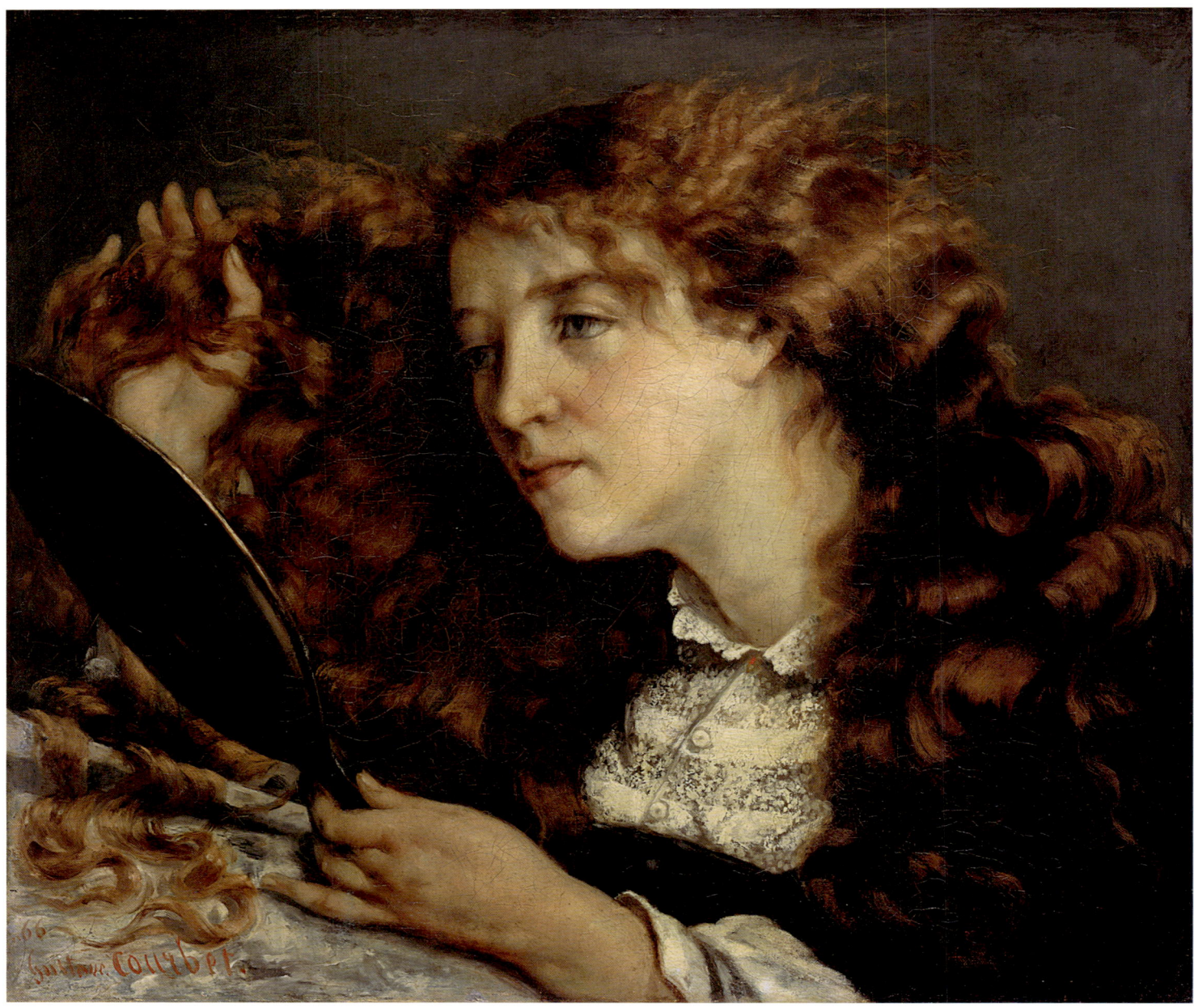

FIG. 123. Gustave Courbet. *Jo, La Belle Irlandaise*, 1865–66. Oil on canvas, 22 x 26 in. (55.9 x 66 cm). The Metropolitan Museum of Art, H. O. Havemeyer Collection, Bequest of Mrs. H. O. Havemeyer, 1929 (29.100.63)

predecessors, the artist avoided the sensual nudity typical of the sinner-saint by painting only her head and upper torso, albeit falling backward in a kind of lover's swoon, spirited away by religious ecstasy, perhaps abandoned in death. He played cannily on the character of Mary Magdalene, harlot and holy woman, combining in the description of her face, with its harmonious features, the signs of sensuality—the fleshy mouth; heavy, half-closed eyelids; voluminous loose hair— and those of the sacred, including the straight nose, well-defined arch of the eyebrows, and high forehead synonymous

with genius. Only the title, provided by Delacroix himself when the painting was first exhibited at the Salon of 1845, identified her as Mary Magdalene, Christ's beloved. Just a bit of blue sky in the upper part of the canvas reveals that she really is in the desert, having come to die, according to legend, in a cave in Sainte-Baume, in the South of France. Delacroix's Magdalene appears to be a severed head, which suggests the possibility of violence.

In 1865, when Courbet painted *Jo, La Belle Irlandaise* (fig. 123), modeled after Joanna Hiffernan, the mistress of his friend James Abbott McNeill Whistler, he clearly remembered the woman depicted by Delacroix. Jo shares with Mary Magdalene the abundant flowing hair, heavy eyelids, straight nose, and elegantly arched brow. The composition truncates the young woman's body just as Delacroix's does Mary Magdalene's. Courbet retained the Romantic painter's audacious metonymic procedure. His beautiful, distant lover is entirely absorbed in observing her face in a mirror. Like the elder painter, Courbet, through the representation of youth and charm, played on the evocation of a memento mori.

To Each His Own Delacroix

By 1822, Delacroix had shown artists a new path of self-affirmation outside academic circles, a freedom of choice in subject matter and pictorial manner. He was the first to have put up resistance in the face of criticism, but the path he helped to blaze opened up new avenues that he did not take. Until the end of his life, he remained faithful to literary, religious, and historical subjects, themes that had been his choice from the outset. The paintings he exhibited at what would be his final Salon, in 1859, especially *Ovid among the Scythians* (cat. 142), were harshly criticized, especially by Maxime du Camp. It seemed that Delacroix, aware of the revolutions in landscape painting to which this Salon gave its blessing, had opted for a classical tradition that linked the representation of nature to mythological and historical subjects.[42] Although sometimes defying this tradition and often transcending it—as was the case in the two large paintings he was then executing in the church of Saint-Sulpice, *Jacob Wrestling with the Angel* and *Heliodorus Driven from the Temple* (figs. 69, 70)—Delacroix remained faithful to a pictorial heritage he knew perfectly.[43] In Saint-Sulpice, Delacroix succeeded brilliantly at synthesizing his own works, which provided inspiration for the three paintings in the chapel, with those of the masters he admired, especially Raphael, Titian, Rubens, and Claude Lorrain. There, his mature talent combined with the desire for a new challenge, in which the painter, now in his sixties, recovered the passion of his youth.

The successes of the Exposition Universelle of 1855 and the threat of a new, up-and-coming generation spurred him on. He therefore managed to impose a singular vision of the themes he had chosen, composing a modern, aesthetic, and intimate struggle. By their power and determination, the two men facing off in *Jacob Wrestling with the Angel* evoked combatants of antiquity, Theseus and Herakles; they also seemed to echo Gustave Courbet's *Wrestlers* (1853; Szépművészeti Museum, Budapest), which Delacroix had seen at the Salon of 1853. The older artist thus showed the younger one that he had lost none of his vigor or his talent for transcending painted scenes. Hardly more than a few weeks after Delacroix's death, however, Henri Fantin-Latour, in a tribute to the older artist, began a masterly canvas that has come to be regarded as a manifesto of the modern pictorial tradition: *Homage to Delacroix* (1864).[44] This group portrait is also an homage to the talent of the young representatives of the "new painting," such as Edouard Manet and James Abbott McNeill Whistler, and to the audacity of the critics of the time, namely Charles Baudelaire, Champfleury, and Edmond Duranty. Evoking Velázquez, Goya, and Courbet, Fantin painted himself at work, implicitly transforming what is otherwise an indeterminate place into an artist's studio. In celebrating the genius of Delacroix, he endeavored to glorify the legacy attached to the Romantic artist's prestige and bearing, which Fantin's generation had assumed as its own. In his *Homage*, Fantin endowed the theme of artistic transmission with the significance of history painting itself, exalting the status of his models, among whom he figured as well. This homage to Delacroix was followed by many more: Paul Cézanne, Aimé-Jules Dalou, Odilon Redon, and Maurice Denis, among others, composed works celebrating the artist they admired. Few artists have ever stirred such a passionate response following their deaths. Delacroix, having died without students, nevertheless did have heirs. The diversity of the tributes that his followers paid him points to the freedom that his oeuvre—triumphantly summed up at the Exposition Universelle of 1855—offered to those who appreciated it.[45]

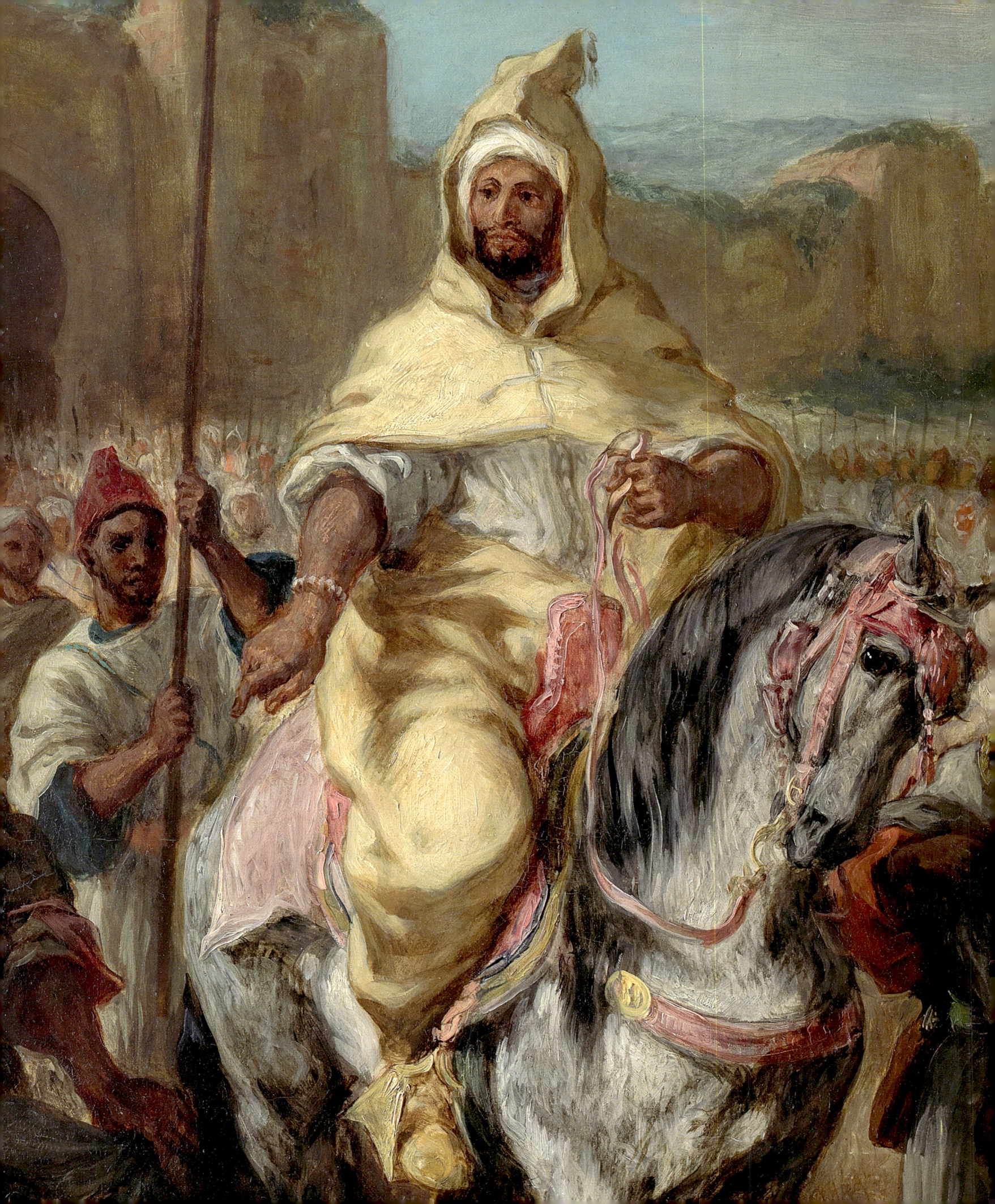

Notes

Abbreviations
INHA (Institut National d'Histoire de l'Art)
BnF (Bibliothèque nationale de France)

Some paintings are identified by their catalogue raisonné number in Johnson 1981–2002, abbreviated as "J" followed by the number.

**Sébastien Allard and Côme Fabre,
The Sphinx of Modern Painting
"Fame Is Not an Empty Word": 1822–32**

1. Charles Henry Delacroix, the artist's elder brother, owned a small estate in Le Louroux, about 170 miles southwest of Paris.
2. Thiers 1822, p. 4; Etienne Jean Delécluze in *Le moniteur universel,* May 8, 1822.
3. Delacroix 2009, vol. 1, p. 150 (April 29, 1824); translation adapted from Delacroix 1995a, p. 36.
4. Delacroix 1954, p. 38 (letter to Achille Piron, November 11, 1815).
5. "Think about strengthening your principles. Remember your father and overcome your flightiness." Delacroix 2009, vol. 1, p. 83 (September 12, 1822); translation adapted from Delacroix 1995a, p. 4.
6. Delacroix 1935–38, vol. 5, pp. 119–21 (letter to his sister, Henriette, May 13, 1822, Bibliothèque de l'INHA).
7. Delacroix 1954, p. 38 (letter to Piron, November 11, 1815).
8. Eugène Delacroix, "Cahier de classe," INHA, Bibliothèque Jacques Doucet, Ms 246-10, fol. 9 recto.
9. Delacroix 2009, vol. 1, p. 84 (September 19, 1822).
10. See the essay by Mehdi Korchane in the present volume.
11. See Chaudonneret 1999.
12. David had voted in favor of the execution of Louis XVI.
13. See Allard and Chaudonneret 2010.
14. Auguste de Forbin, in Néto 1995, p. 70 (letter to François Marius Granet, May 31, 1821).
15. Delacroix 1935–38, vol. 5, p. 91 (letter to his sister, Henriette, July 26, 1821).
16. See Le Men 2018.
17. Delacroix 1935–38, vol. 5, pp. 51–54 (letter to his sister, Henriette, May 30, 1820).
18. Ibid., vol. 1, pp. 125–30 (letter to Charles Soulier, April 30–July 30, 1821).
19. Ibid., vol. 1, pp. 119–24 (letter to Soulier, March 30, 1821).

20. See Louvre, 5180.
21. The Gericault painting is Louvre, 4885.
22. See Allard 2005, pp. 19–20.
23. See the essay by Mehdi Korchane in the present volume; and see Allard and Chaudonneret 2010, pp. 116–22.
24. Delacroix 1935–38, vol. 1, p. 141 (letter to Soulier, April 15, 1822).
25. Ibid., vol. 1, p. 132 (letter to Soulier, September 15, 1821).
26. Louvre, 4884.
27. See Allard and Chaudonneret 2010, pp. 52–55.
28. Delacroix 1935–38, vol. 5, pp. 106–7 (letter to his sister, Henriette, February 9, 1822).
29. Ibid., vol. 1, p. 141 (letter to Soulier, April 15, 1822).
30. See Marie Philippe Coupin de La Couperie's *The Ill-Fated Love of Francesca da Rimini* (Napoleon Museum Thurgau, Schloss und Park Arenenberg, Salenstein), exhibited at the Salon of 1812.
31. Ms 246 (15), Bibliothèque de l'INHA.
32. Translation of Dante's *Inferno*, canto 3, and *Charon Rowing His Oars to Gather Up the Souls of Cowards to Force Them across the River Acheron.* From untitled sketchbook, folios 34 verso and 35 recto, ca. 1818–22. Louvre, RF 23356.
33. Delacroix 1954, p. 78 (letter to Félix Guillemardet, September 23, 1819).
34. On the genesis of the work, see Paris 2004.
35. Delacroix 1954, p. 108 (letter to Guillemardet, November 2, 1819).
36. Hugo's text would come to be regarded as a manifesto of the Romantic movement.
37. See Louvre, RF 23356, fols. 34 verso and 35 recto.
38. See Allard 2010.
39. Delacroix 1935–38, vol. 1, p. 31 (letter to Jean-Baptiste Pierret, November 6, 1818).
40. Ibid., vol. 1, p. 78 (letter to Pierret, October 2, 1820).
41. Letter from Delacroix to Piron, August 20, 1815.
42. [Arnold Scheffer] (unsigned), "Salon de 1827," *Revue française* 1 (1828): 197.
43. Musée du Louvre, Paris, Département des Arts Graphiques, RF 23356; see fols. 34v and 35r.
44. Etienne Jean Delécluze in *Le moniteur universel,* May 3, 1822.
45. Thiers 1822.
46. Delacroix 2009, vol. 1, p. 138 (April 11, 1824); translation adapted from Delacroix 1995a, p. 31.
47. Yale University Art Gallery, 1962.25; Louvre, 20369.
48. Bruyas 1876, p. 361.

49. Delacroix 2009, vol. 2, p. 1738; see also Allard in Paris 2004, p. 83.
50. Thiers 1822, p. 4.
51. Allard and Chaudonneret 2006, p. 86.
52. Delacroix 2009, vol. 1, p. 137 (April 11, 1824); translation adapted from Delacroix 1995a, p. 31.
53. See Allard 2011, p. 53.
54. Delacroix 2009, vol. 1, p. 137 (May 11, 1824); translation adapted from Delacroix 1995a, p. 40.
55. Delacroix 2009, vol. 1, p. 90 (October 8, 1822); translation from Delacroix 1995a, p. 7.
56. Delacroix 2009, vol. 1, p. 102 (May 24 or 31, 1823); translation adapted from Delacroix 1995a, p. 15.
57. Delacroix 1935–38, vol. 1, p. 132 (letter to Soulier, September 15, 1821).
58. Delacroix 2009, vol. 1, p. 113 (January 12, 1824).
59. Ibid., vol. 1, p. 132 (April 3, 1824).
60. Ibid., vol. 1, p. 136 (April 9, 1824); translation adapted from Delacroix 1995a, p. 29.
61. Delacroix 2009, vol. 1, pp. 155–57 (May 7, 1824); translation adapted from Delacroix 1995a, p. 39.
62. Fraser 1998.
63. Letter from Forbin to Sosthène de La Rochefoucauld, September 6, 1824; Archives Nationales, O³ 1413.
64. See Chaudonneret 1999, p. 136.
65. Delacroix 1846, p. 437.
66. Marie Mély-Janin in *La quotidienne,* September 12, 1824.
67. See Allard 2010.
68. Chauvin 1825, p. 13.
69. Pierre Ange Vieillard said as much in his review (1825, p. 15): "The last salon was no less commendable for the choice of subjects displayed by our history painters than for the merit of their execution."
70. Stendhal 2002, p. 93.
71. Thiers 1824, p. 27.
72. See Louvre, 5064.
73. Thiers 1824, p. 27.
74. Landon 1824, p. 54.
75. Delacroix 2009, vol. 1, p. 114 (January 18, 1824).
76. Ibid., vol. 1, p. 116 (January 24, 1824); translation adapted from Delacroix 1995a, pp. 21–22.
77. Delacroix 2009, vol. 1, p. 118 (January 26, 1824).
78. Ibid., vol. 1, p. 124 (March 3, 1824); translation adapted from Delacroix 1995a, p. 26.
79. Delacroix 2009, vol. 1, p. 125 (March 5, 1824).
80. Ibid., vol. 1, p. 143 (April 18, 1824); translation adapted from Delacroix 1995a, p. 33.
81. Delacroix 2009, vol. 1, p. 154 (April 20, 1824).
82. Ibid., vol. 1, p. 163 (May 28, 1824).

83. See the study of the model known as Le Polonais, who is depicted standing, with his hand on his heart, his head turned, and wearing an expression of indignant anger. Louvre, on deposit at the Musée National Eugène-Delacroix, RF 1953-40.

84. See the X-radiographic studies by Elisabeth Ravaud in Paris 2004, pp. 108–9.

85. Delacroix 2009, vol. 1, p. 154 (May 7, 1824); translation adapted from Delacroix 1995a, p. 39.

86. Delacroix 2009, vol. 1, p. 1176 (October 4, 1857): "For the Aspasie to the waist, lifesize, see a good sketch in an album of the time."

87. Some authors contend that Delacroix was sexually attracted to models of color, basing their arguments on an entry in his *Journal* dated May 1824, in which he mentions a "chiavatura" with "una nera." The word *nera* can designate a black woman and also a brunette.

88. See Grigsby 2002.

89. Thiers 1824, p. 28.

90. Jal 1824, p. 13.

91. See Louvre, MR 1803. Generally known as the *Horses of Marly*, two pendant sculptures by Guillaume Coustou I (1677–1746) are each officially titled *Horse Restrained by a Groom*.

92. Quoted in Johnson 1981–2002, vol. 1, p. 103.

93. François Joseph Navez, in Charleroi–La Chaux-de-Fonds–Coutances 1999–2000, p. 80 (letter to Louis Léopold Robert, December 11, 1824).

94. Delacroix 2009, vol. 1, p. 157 (May 9, 1824); translation adapted from Delacroix 1995a, pp. 38–39.

95. National Gallery, London, NG 1207.

96. Silvestre 1859, p. 60; see also Michèle Hannoosh in Delacroix 2009, vol. 1, pp. 170–71, n. 334.

97. Quoted in Johnson 1981–2002, vol. 1, pp. 104–5.

98. Delacroix 2009, vol. 1, pp. 173–74 (July 20, 1824).

99. Landon 1827, p. 70.

100. Location unknown (J 88).

101. Villa Vauban, Musée d'Art de la Ville de Luxembourg (J 38).

102. Neue Pinakothek, Munich (J 53).

103. Delacroix 1935–38, vol. 1, p. 196 (letter to Soulier, September 28, 1827).

104. The biographical argument serves to refute the hypothesis that the painting represents Hamlet.

105. Quoted in Johnson 1981–2002, vol. 1, p. 36, no. 59.

106. Taine 1905, p. 360.

107. Louvre, RF 6860 recto.

108. Landon 1827, p. 74.

109. Thénot 1839, p. 18, quoted in Alliez 2007, p. 93.

110. Vitet 1828, p. 253.

111. Delacroix 2009, vol. 1, p. 121 (February 27, 1824).

112. Ibid., vol. 1, pp. 415–16, n. 31.

113. Delécluze 1828a, p. 1.

114. See Musée des Beaux-Arts, Bordeaux, Bx E 61.

115. See Louvre, 3690.

116. See Louvre, 3691.

117. See the reports made to the Société Royale des Sciences, Lettres et Arts de Nancy by MM. Caumont, de Haldat, and Laurent (Service de Documentation du Musée des Beaux-Arts, Nancy).

118. Jal 1828, p. 111.

119. Vitet 1826, p. 372.

120. Corbin, Courtine, and Vigarello 2011, p. 222.

121. Gautier 1856–57, p. 177.

122. See Metropolitan Museum, 17.50.37.

123. Delacroix 1991, pp. 16–17 (letter to Charles de Verninac, August 17, 1830).

124. Corbin, Courtine, and Vigarello 2011, p. 224.

125. See Duprat 1997.

126. See Paris 1982–83.

127. See Allard 2010.

128. Delacroix 1935–38, vol. 1, p. 319 (letter to Jean-Baptiste Pierret, February 29, 1832).

129. Delacroix 2009, vol. 2, p. 1412 (June 22, 1863); translation adapted from Delacroix 1995a, p. 444.

130. Cantaloube 1864, p. 27.

131. Delacroix 1935–38, vol. 1, pp. 318–20 (letter to Pierret, February 29, 1832).

132. Delacroix 2009, vol. 1, p. 121 (February 27, 1824); Delacroix 1935–38, vol. 3, pp. 264–66 (letter to Mme Cavé, June 8, 1855).

133. See Allard in Paris 2004, pp. 90–91.

134. Blanc 1870, p. 564.

135. See Hannoosh in Delacroix 2009, vol. 1, p. 319 ("Notes et brouillons des *Souvenirs*").

136. Delacroix 2009, vol. 1, p. 399 (October 8, 1847).

137. Cantaloube 1864, p. 28.

138. Ibid., p. 27.

139. Ibid.

140. Delacroix was invited to the wedding by his interpreter, Abraham Ben-Chimol, who worked for the French consulate in Tangier.

141. Fernand Khnopff, in Houyoux and Sulzberger 1964, pp. 183–84 (letter to Léon Houyoux, 1877).

142. Blanc 1870, p. 573.

143. Planche 1834, pp. 58, 59, quoted in Paris (Mémorial) 1963, p. 149, no. 201.

144. Quoted in Bruyas 1876, p. 333.

145. Baudelaire 1846 (1976 ed.), vol. 2, p. 440.

146. Vauday 2006.

147. Signac 1911, pp. 41–42.

148. Decamps 1834, p. 60.

149. Planche 1834, p. 59.

150. Du Camp 1882, p. 253.

151. Frédéric Villot, preface, in Delacroix sale 1865, p. vi.

152. Cézanne in Gasquet 1921, p. 108.

153. Blanc 1876, p. 49.

154. Ibid., p. 74.

155. See Alliez 2007, pp. 102–7.

156. Eugène Delacroix, "Album de voyage en Espagne, au Maroc et en Algérie," Musée Condé, Chantilly. See Roque 1997, pp. 201–2.

157. Gautier 1841, p. 160.

158. Gautier 1838, p. 3.

Driven to Greatness: 1833–54

1. Gautier 1838, p. 3.

2. Planche 1836 (1855 ed.), pp. 23–24.

3. Delacroix 1935–38, vol. 2, p. 4 (letter to Charles Rivet, February 15, 1838).

4. Ibid., vol. 5, p. 180.

5. The *Journal du commerce* of January 11, 1828, reported, "for three or four days, the public will be granted entry to the halls of the Conseil d'Etat: it is a favor we must hasten to take advantage of. The doors will probably close on the fifteenth; the Council will resume its sessions behind closed doors." See Johnson 1981–2002, vol. 1, p. 113, n. 1, no. 123.

6. Delacroix 1935–38, vol. 4, pp. 222–23 (letter to Achille Fould, 1860).

7. Thoré 1837, part 1.

8. Delacroix 1935–38, vol. 5, pp. 194–95 (letter to the priest of the church of Saint-Paul-Saint-Louis, April 5, 1855).

9. Paris (Mémorial) 1963, pp. 184–85, no. 245.

10. Delacroix 1935–38, vol. 2, pp. 95–96 (letter to Edmond Cavé, April 5, 1843 [not 1842]).

11. Ibid., vol. 2, p. 219 (letter to Cavé, June 30, 1845).

12. Delacroix 2009, vol. 1, pp. 457–58 (Ecoublay, September 1, 1849).

13. Ibid., vol. 1, pp. 685–86 (Champrosay, October 12, 1853).

14. Ibid., vol. 1, p. 786 (Paris, June 27, 1854).

15. Paris 2004, p. 23.

16. Baudelaire 1863 (1976 ed.), vol. 2, p. 769.

17. Delacroix 1846, p. 440.

18. Delacroix 2009, vol. 1, p. 397 (Paris, October 5, 1847).

19. Delacroix 1935–38, vol. 2, p. 4 (letter to Rivet, February 23, 1838).

20. Tardieu 1837.

21. In an article devoted to the painter Prud'hon, whose "true genius, domain, and empire is allegory," Delacroix (1846, p. 445) noted, "allegory is tedious when the painter, who ought to have wings to carry us to loftier regions, timidly clings to the details of imitation and dares not leave the down-to-earth aspect of his subject."

22. Delacroix 1935–38, vol. 1, pp. 303–4 (letter to Jean-Baptiste Pierret, January 8, 1832).

23. The drawing is in the library of the Assemblé Nationale. See Paris 1995, p. 117, no. 28.

24. Gautier 1836, p. 2.

25. Alexandre-Gabriel Decamps in *Le national*, November 15, 1838.

26. Planche 1846, p. 154.

27. Gautier 1847a, p. 1.

28. Planche 1836 (1855 ed.), vol. 2, pp. 21–22.

29. Anon. 1836, pp. 77–78.

30. Planche 1838 (1855 ed.), vol. 2, pp. 107–8.

31. Gautier 1838, p. 3.

32. "Medea killing her two children," inscribed

ca. 1820, Delacroix album no. 17, folio 8, Musée du Louvre (RF 9153). The comment is from Delacroix 2009, vol. 1, p. 124 (March 4, 1824).

33. Victoria & Albert Museum, London, inv. S.2026-2009.

34. Virginie Bernast in Paris 2001, pp. 38–39.

35. *Liberty Leading the People* was on Delacroix's mind at the time. Having become an embarrassment to the regime of Louis-Philippe, the painting had been returned to the artist by the Musée du Luxembourg.

36. Delacroix may have been replying to the somewhat pretentious sublime of Paul Delaroche's *Children of Edward*, shown at the Salon of 1831, another scene of children anticipating their own murder, but one evoked much more elliptically. See Louvre, 3834.

37. *Michelangelo and His Genius* was not executed but exists as a pastel sketch. See Musée Fabre, Montpellier; see also Johnson 1995, p. 54, no. 8.

38. Delacroix 2009, vol. 1, p. 881 (January 30, 1855); translation adapted from Delacroix 1995a, pp. 287–88.

39. See Delacroix 2009, vol. 1, pp. 330–31 (January 22 and 23, 1847). The Saint-Sulpice commission, confirmed two years later by the republican regime, was for a chapel at the church entrance and not for the transepts.

40. Théophile Gautier (1847b) was the first to remark on this connection.

41. Delacroix 1846. He makes only passing mention (p. 449) of *Christ on the Cross* in his homage to the elder artist, which begins with a critique (p. 432) directed more at Ingres than at David: "The pedantry of the contour, the taste for archaism in place of the antique, a bizarre hatred of the picturesque: such were the shackles against which Prudhon waged his victorious struggle."

42. Delacroix 2009, vol. 1, p. 329 (January 21, 1847).

43. See Johnson 1981–2002, vol. 1, pp. 218–19, no. D4.

44. Delacroix 2009, vol. 1, p. 356 (March 2, 1847).

45. Ibid., vol. 1, p. 356 (March 1, 1847).

46. Ibid., vol. 1, p. 358 (March 2, 1847); translation adapted from Delacroix 1995a, p. 71.

47. Delacroix 2009, vol. 1, p. 358 (March 2, 1847); translation adapted from Delacroix 1995a, p. 71.

48. Delacroix 2009, vol. 2, p. 1332 (March 8, 1860).

49. Ibid., vol. 1 (February 16, 1850).

50. Ibid., vol. 1, p. 732 (December 11, 1855 [under the date December 30, 1853]). Delacroix wrote the entry while studying a lithograph by Jules Laurens after a second version of the painting.

51. Ibid., vol. 1, p. 401 (December 14, 1847).

52. Domenico Ferri (1795–1878) was appointed the principal set designer of the Théâtre-Italien in 1829.

53. Delacroix 2009, vol. 1, pp. 358–59 (March 3, 1847); translation adapted from Delacroix 1995a, p. 72.

54. Delacroix 2009, vol. 1, p. 519 (July 8, 1850); translation adapted from Delacroix 1995a, p. 130.

55. See Johnson 1981–2002, vol. 3, p. 240, no. 460; Delacroix 2009, vol. 1, p. 674 (June 28, 1853).

56. Johnson 1995, pp. 130–33, nos. 35 and 36.

57. Clark 1982, pp. 126–41.

58. Delacroix 2009, vol. 1, p. 411 (January 14, 1849): "At midday, appointment with the Commission at the Palais Royal. . . . Appalling devastation; galleries transformed into warehouses, financial traders' offices set up, and so on. . . . Then to the Tuileries . . . signs of dilapidation, and revolting smells everywhere." Translation adapted from Delacroix 1995a, pp. 89, 90.

59. Delacroix 2009, vol. 1, p. 441 (April 13, 1849).

60. Johnson 1981–2002, vol. 3, pp. 261–64, nos. 501–3.

61. Haussard 1849. The authors thank Aude Gobet for her research on flower painting in France in the mid-nineteenth century and have based the following lines on her scholarship.

62. The first quoted phrase is from Gautier 1849; the second is from Baudelaire 1845 (1976 ed.), vol. 2, p. 395.

63. Gautier 1849, p. [2].

64. Delacroix's painting bears comparison with Monnoyer's *Still Life with Basket of Flowers*, Art Gallery of South Australia, Adelaide, 855P13.

65. Delacroix 1935–38, vol. 2, pp. 372–73 (letter to Constant Dutilleux, February 6, 1849).

66. The mostly highly elaborated drawing related to the ceiling composition is Louvre, RF 1927 recto.

67. See Louvre, RF 1927 recto.

68. Sérullaz 1963, p. 118.

69. Delacroix had sketched the motif of the celestial chariot drawn by whinnying horses in a drawing for the allegory of War for the Salon du Roi at the Palais Bourbon (Louvre, RF 29664). See Sérullaz et al. 1984, vol. 1, p. 123, no. 180.

70. For a comprehensive monograph on the Gallery of Apollo, see Bresc-Bautier 2004.

71. See also Musée d'Orsay, Paris, RF 1814 (J 194).

72. Delacroix 2009, vol. 1, pp. 333–34 (January 25, 1847); translation adapted from Delacroix 1995a, p. 60.

73. The first quotation in this paragraph is from Gautier 1855b; the second is from Mantz 1855, p. 172.

74. Du Camp 1855, pp. 115–16.

75. Petroz 1855, p. [2].

76. Petroz was born in 1819, Mantz in 1821, and Du Camp in 1822.

77. Delacroix 2009, vol. 1, p. 514 (June 8, 1850); translation adapted from Delacroix 1995a, p. 127.

78. Delacroix 2009, vol. 1, p. 516 (June 14, 1850); translation adapted from Delacroix 1995a, p. 128.

79. Medwin 1824, pp. 168–71, 244, 246. For the excerpt copied by Delacroix into his *Journal*; see Delacroix 2009, vol. 1, pp. 525–26.

80. See Delacroix 1935–38, vol. 3, pp. 113–14 (letter to Soulier, August 3, 1850).

81. Delacroix 2009, vol. 1, pp. 542–43 (Antwerp, August 10, 1850); translation adapted from Delacroix 1995a, p. 142.

82. Delacroix 2009, vol. 1, p. 542 (Antwerp, August 10, 1850); translation adapted from Delacroix 1995a, p. 142.

83. Delacroix 2009, vol. 1, p. 546 (Paris, August 18, 1850).

84. Compare, for example, his negative impressions after the concerts of April 7, 1849, and February 7, 1850 (ibid., vol. 1, pp. 439 and 485), with the note of June 29, 1854 (ibid., vol. 1, p. 788), and the article "Questions sur le beau" (Delacroix 1854, p. 310): "I will side with him [Beethoven] against even my own feelings, believing this time, as on many other occasions, that one must always bet on genius."

85. *Dictionnaire des beaux-arts*, s.v. "Originalité"; see Delacroix 2009, vol. 2, p. 1104.

86. Delacroix 2009, vol. 1, p. 911 (Champrosay, June 17, 1855).

87. Ibid., vol. 2, p. 1243 (May 26, 1858); translation adapted from Delacroix 1995a, p. 408.

88. Delacroix 2009, vol. 1, p. 1060 (1857 [under the date of January 5]).

89. Delacroix 1857, p. 919. Jean de La Fontaine (1621–1695) was the author of *Fables* (1668–1694).

90. Delacroix 2009, vol. 1, p. 729 (December 24, 1853); translation adapted from Delacroix 1995a, p. 231.

91. Delacroix 1935–38, vol. 4, pp. 90–91 (letter to Dutilleux, April 2, 1859).

92. The second copy of *Medea About to Kill Her Children* is in the Louvre (RF 1402); the third, also from 1862, is in a private collection. An impression of the lithograph by Emile Lassalle is in the Musée National Eugène-Delacroix (inv. S.E.D. 1950-1); see Paris 2001, no. 54.

93. See the 1858 version at the Museum of Fine Arts, Boston (95.179), and the 1860–61 version at the Art Institute of Chicago (1922.404).

94. *Lion Devouring a Rabbit*, Louvre, RF 1394; *Lion Devouring an Arab,* Nasjonalgalleriet, Oslo, inv. NG.M.01178.

95. See Louvre RF 10022.

96. The earlier of the two circa 1849 versions is in the Musée des Beaux-Arts, Lyon; the second, owned by the Fitzwilliam Museum, Cambridge, is on loan to King's College.

97. Delacroix had seen Rossini's *Othello* again at the Théâtre-Italien in spring 1847. See Delacroix 2009, vol. 1, p. 369 (March 30, 1847).

98. Ducis refashioned the play in 1769 from a French translation.

99. Penley used David Garrick's adaptation of *Hamlet* for this production, which was staged in a small theater on the rue Chantereine.

100. He did see Kean play Richard III and Othello, however. See Delacroix 1935–38, vol. 1, pp. 161–63 (letter to Pierret, London, June 27, 1825).

101. See Phelps Bailey 1964, pp. 53–63.

102. However, after the first few performances of the Kemble production, French police put a stop to the churchyard scene.

103. Delacroix 1935–38, vol. 1, p. 197 (letter to Soulier, September 25, 1827).

104. *Souvenirs du théâtre anglais à Paris* 1827.
105. See Montier 2017.
106. Delacroix 2009, vol. 1, p. 163 (May 15, 1824).
107. The German artist Friedrich Moritz Auguste Retzsch was born in Dresden in 1799 and died at Hoflossnitz in 1857.
108. BnF, Dc 183n. Rés.
109. Le Tourneur 1835, vol. 2.
110. Delacroix 1935–38, vol. 1, p. 333 (letter to Pierret, July 5, 1832).
111. The preliminary drawing is in a private collection.
112. The lithograph, by Bernard de Frey, appeared in *L'artiste* 11, no. 6; the poem, "À M. Eugène Delacroix sur son tableau de Hamlet," dated August 1836, was published in *L'artiste* 12, no. 8, pp. 91–92.
113. "Hamlet," *Le magasin pittoresque,* ann. 5 (December 1837): 385–86; there is an impression in the Metropolitan Museum: 34.36.552. In 1845 the dealer Paul Durand-Ruel commissioned Delacroix to make a new lithograph (Durand-Ruel 1845, pl. 6).
114. Neue Pinakothek, Munich, inv. 12764 (J 264).
115. See Johnson 1981–2002, vol. 3, p. 87, no. 267.
116. See BnF, Dc 183n. Rés.
117. Baudelaire 1859a (1976 ed.). For the portrait by Manet, see *The Tragic Actor (Rouvière as Hamlet)*, National Gallery of Art, Washington, D.C., 1959.3.1.
118. It should be noted that Delacroix may have executed a painted version of *Hamlet and Horatio in the Graveyard* in the 1830s. A horizontal painting of the subject, attributed to him, appeared at a sale in 1840. The work not been published since that time. See Johnson 1981–2002, vol. 3, no. L140.
119. Delacroix 2009, vol. 1, p. 717 (November 28, 1853); translation adapted from Delacroix 1995a, p. 226.
120. Delacroix 2009, vol. 1, pp. 802–3 (August 5, 1854); translation of first part is adapted from Delacroix 1995a, p. 240.

From the Last of the Romantics to the Genius of Color: 1855–63

1. Delacroix 2009, vol. 2, p. 1270 (March 1, 1859).
2. Allard and Chaudonneret 2006, pp. 40–45.
3. Baudelaire (1976 ed.), vol. 2, p. 419.
4. See Signac 1911 and Ratliff 1992.
5. The decoration is composed of a circular ceiling, *Peace Descends to Earth*, eleven tympana depicting the labors of Hercules, and eight caissons showing the gods of Olympus. It was unveiled for a ball on February 21, 1854. That decoration vanished sixteen years later in the fire at the Hôtel de Ville caused by the Communards on the night of May 24, 1871.
6. Planche in *Revue des deux mondes*, April 15, 1854, quoted by Sérullaz 1989, p. 326.
7. Delécluze in *Journal des débats*, March 17, 1854, quoted by Sérullaz 1989, p. 320.
8. Planche in *Revue des deux mondes*, April 15, 1854, quoted by Sérullaz 1989, p. 327.

9. Perrier 1855.
10. Baudelaire 1855 (1976 ed.), pp. 591–92.
11. Gautier 1856–57, pp. 167–68.
12. The first- to fourth-place winners were Horace Vernet, Jean Auguste Dominique Ingres, Alexandre-Gabriel Decamps, and François Joseph Heim.
13. Clément de Ris 1857, p. 414.
14. Mantz 1859, pp. 136–39.
15. Saint-Victor 1859, pp. 1–2.
16. Rousseau 1859, p. 4.
17. Du Camp 1859, pp. 12–13.
18. Saint-Victor 1859, p. 2.
19. Perrier 1859, p. 293.
20. Mantz 1859, p. 136.
21. Saint-Victor 1859, p. 2.
22. Ibid.
23. Du Pays 1859.
24. Saint-Victor 1859, p. 2.
25. Rousseau 1859, p. 4.
26. Saint-Victor 1859, p. 2.
27. Castagnary 1892, vol. 1, p. 69.
28. See the overview of the Salon of 1859 by Henri Loyrette in Paris–New York 1994–95, pp. 3–27.
29. Claude Monet, in ibid., p. 23 (letter to Eugène Boudin).
30. Chesneau 1859, quoted by Arlette Sérullaz in Paris–Philadelphia 1998–99, p. 42.
31. See Delacroix 2009, vol. 2, p. 1333. See also Paris 1860.
32. Ibid., vol. 2, 1270 (March 1, 1859).
33. Delacroix 1935–38, vol. 4, pp. 90–91 (letter to Dutilleux, April 2, 1859).
34. Ibid., vol. 4, pp. 98–99 (letter to Dutilleux, May 12, 1859).
35. Ibid., vol. 4, pp. 106–7 (letter to Auguste Lamey, June 11, 1859).
36. His "Salon de 1859" appeared in the issues of June 10, June 20, July 1, and July 20 of the *Revue française*, which went under after that last issue. "Because it was in the *Revue française,* the Salon de 1859 [by Baudelaire] was hardly read" (Claude Pichois in Baudelaire 1976, vol. 2, p. 1384).
37. Delacroix 1935–38, vol. 4, p. 111 (letter to Charles Baudelaire, June 27, 1859).
38. Saint-Victor 1859, p. 2.
39. Mantz 1859, p. 137.
40. Saint-Victor 1859, p. 2.
41. Castagnary 1892, p. 72.
42. For example, Delacroix encouraged the Ministère de l'Intérieur to acquire *The Avenue of Chestnut Trees* (Delacroix 1991, pp. 100–101 [letter to Edmond Cavé, July 26, 1840]), but in vain. Seven years later, visiting the framer and gilder Souty, he was happy to see the painting again (Delacroix 2009, vol. 1, p. 376 [April 30, 1847]).
43. Delacroix 2009, vol. 1, pp. 340–41 (February 2, 1847).
44. Ibid., vol. 1, pp. 490, 492 (February 25 and March 1, 1850).

45. After a furtive meeting in 1846, Fromentin and Delacroix truly established contact in 1859. See ibid., vol. 1, p. 1148, and vol. 2, p. 2201.
46. On that occasion, Fromentin received a first-place medal and was awarded the Legion of Honor. See Paris–New York 1994–95, p. 386.
47. Baudelaire 1976, p. 296. Fromentin does not seem to have harbored unconditional admiration for Delacroix, as attested in *Notes sur le genre dans la peinture:* "It is not difficult to prove that even in his large so-called history paintings, Delacroix is only a genre painter" (Fromentin 1984, p. 921).
48. Astruc 1859, p. 296.
49. Delacroix 2009, vol. 1, p. 741 (March 22, 1854).
50. Ibid., vol. 1, p. 797 (July 29, 1845).
51. Vincent Pomarède, in Madrid–Barcelona 2011–12, p. 308.
52. Delacroix 2009, vol. 1, p. 551 (Champrosay, November 3 and 4, 1850); translation adapted from Delacroix 1995a, pp. 145–46.
53. Louvre, RF 9770.
54. Louvre, RF 23315.
55. Delacroix 2009, vol. 1, p. 508 (Champrosay, May 8, 1850); translation adapted from Delacroix 1995a, pp. 124–25.
56. Delacroix 2009, vol. 1, p. 514 (Champrosay, June 8, 1850); translation adapted from Delacroix 1995a, p. 127.
57. Delacroix 2009, vol. 1, p. 815 (Dieppe, August 25, 1854); translation adapted from Delacroix 1995a, p. 262.
58. Delacroix 2009, vol. 1, p. 603 (September 14, 1852); translation adapted from Delacroix 1995a, p. 169.
59. Delacroix 2009, vol. 1, pp. 1078–79 (1857).
60. Ibid., vol. 1, p. 124 (March 3, 1824). See also the sheet dated 1824–25 (INHA cartoon 120, autog. 1397/15): "Shipwreck of Don Juan. Scenes on the vessel.—The shipwrecked look ferociously at one another. The licentiate Pedrillo extends his throat and wrist to the surgeon." See Delacroix 2009, vol. 2, pp. 1451–53 (sheet).
61. Johnson 1981–2002, vol. 3, p. 102, no. 276.
62. Delacroix 1935–38, vol. 2, pp. 19–20 (letter to Pierret, Valmont, September 5, 1838).
63. Gautier 1856–57, p. 187.
64. Lee Johnson hypothesizes that the artist was simultaneously alluding to *The Death of Sardanapalus* (Johnson 1981–2002, vol. 3, p. 233).
65. Fondation Emil G. Bührle Collection, Zürich, inv. 125.
66. Paris–Philadelphia 1998–99, p. 279.
67. Louvre, RF 9466. See Sérullaz et al. 1984, vol. 1, p. 430, no. 1177, ill. p. 429.
68. Delacroix 2009, vol. 1, p. 821 (Dieppe, September 4, 1854).
69. Ibid., vol. 1, p. 963 (Dieppe, October 10, 1855); translation adapted from Delacroix 1995a, pp. 324–25.
70. Ibid., vol. 1, pp. 470–71 (Valmont, October 18, 1849); translation adapted from Delacroix 1995a, p. 111.

71. See Johnson 1981–2002, vol. 3, p. 129, no. 308.
72. Museum of Fine Arts, Houston, 85.1; Staatsgalerie Stuttgart, inv. 2636.
73. Dated by Lee Johnson to approximately 1852, it may actually have been undertaken much earlier as an *Ariadne,* contemporaneous with the *Odalisque* (Fitzwilliam Museum, Cambridge), which is similar to it. It is probable that Delacroix, who kept the work until his death, reprised and completed the work subsequently, turning it into Andromeda.
74. Staatsgalerie Stuttgart, inv. 2636.
75. Pomarède in Paris–Philadelphia 1998–99, p. 140, no. 38.
76. "This castle, perched on the rock like a pedestal, is altogether extraordinary" (Delacroix 2009, vol. 1, p. 942 [September 13–15, 1855]).
77. Ibid, vol. 1, p. 830 (September 11, 1854).
78. Ibid., vol. 1, p. 279 (Souvenirs du Maroc, 1843–44).
79. Delacroix 1991, pp. 87–88 (letter to the duchesse Colonna [Adèle d'Affry], Ante, September 23, 1862).
80. Delacroix 2009, vol. 1, pp. 633–34 (April 16, 1853); translation adapted from Delacroix 1995a, pp. 182–83.
81. Delacroix 2009, vol. 1, p. 843 (September 26, 1854); translation adapted from Delacroix 1995a, p. 278.
82. Delacroix 2009, vol. 1, p. 1173 (September 3, 1857); translation adapted from Delacroix 1995a, p. 395.
83. Delacroix 2009, vol. 1, p. 916 (June 20, 1855); translation adapted from Delacroix 1995a, p. 305.
84. Delacroix 2009, vol. 1, p. 1084 (1857 [under the date of January 23]); translation adapted from Delacroix 1995a, p. 364.
85. Delacroix 2009, vol. 1, p. 1080 (1857 [under the date of January 20]).
86. Ibid., vol. 1, p. 668 (May 29, 1853).
87. Ibid., vol. 1, p. 449 (June 2, 1849).
88. Ibid., vol. 2, pp. 1241–43 (May 23, 1858), 1327–28 (February 29, 1860).
89. With the exception of 1858 and 1860, see ibid., vol. 2, pp. 2110–11.
90. Ibid., vol. 1, p. 767 (May 20, 1854); translation adapted from Delacroix 1995a, p. 245.
91. Delacroix 2009, vol. 1, p. 859 (October 30, 1854).
92. Delacroix often mentioned Watteau's paintings, from the time he first saw one (no doubt *Rendez-vous de chasse,* currently in London, Wallace Collection) at the home of the duc de Morny: "He has a magnificent Watteau. I was struck by the wonderful skill it displayed. Flanders and Venice are united in this painting." (Delacroix 2009, vol. 1, p. 371 [April 3, 1847]); translation adapted from Delacroix 1995a, p. 77.
93. An oil on canvas on this subject came up for sale at the gallery of Sayn-Wittgenstein Fine Art, Inc., New York, in 1992.
94. Lichtenstein 1979, p. 131.
95. National Gallery, London, NG194.
96. A possible memory or quotation of Rubens's Juno may be found in the peacock feather fan that Delacroix painted at the feet of the beauty stripped bare on Marphise's order: having fallen to the ground along with a mule slipper and an unlaced corset, it also symbolizes the young woman's humiliated pride.
97. Delacroix 2009, vol. 1, p. 563 (May 13, 1851); translation adapted from Delacroix 1995a, p. 149.
98. Louvre, RF 9972.
99. Tasso 1825, vol. 2, p. 139.
100. Sérullaz et al. 1984, vol. 1, p. 259, no. 549.
101. Delacroix 2009, vol. 1, p. 448 (June 2, 1849).
102. Ibid., vol. 1, p. 787 (June 28, 1854).
103. Ibid., vol. 1, p. 871 (January 2, 1855). A similar subject, taken from canto 18 of *Jerusalem Delivered,* reappeared among sketches of trees that Delacroix filled in during his stays at the Château d'Augerville in October 1854 and 1855. See ibid., vol. 2, p. 1762 (January 2, 1855).
104. See the engraving in *L'artiste,* November 1, 1852; see also Paris–Philadelphia 1998–99, p. 253, no. 102.
105. Delacroix 2009, vol. 1, p. 809 (August 12, 1854).
106. On seeing one of Diaz's paintings at the Galerie Durand-Ruel in 1847, he felt that "everything came out of the painter's imagination, but . . . the memories are faithful, [there is] life, grace, abundance" (ibid., vol. 1, p. 399 [October 7, 1847]).
107. Ibid., vol. 1, p. 687 (October 12, 1853); translation adapted from Delacroix 1995a, p. 208.
108. Delacroix 2009, vol. 1, pp. 632–33 (April 15, 1853); translation adapted from Delacroix 1995a, pp. 181–82.
109. Delacroix 2009, vol. 2, p. 1323 (February 22, 1860); translation adapted from Delacroix 1995a, p. 424.
110. Delacroix 2009, vol. 1, p. 691 (October 17, 1853).
111. Ibid., vol. 1, p. 929 (August 3, 1855).
112. The term "Assyrian" became a topos in physical descriptions of Courbet, popularized in 1856 by Théophile Silvestre.
113. *The Death of Sardanapalus* and *The Painter's Studio* also shared the same fate: major works by their respective artists, they were long rejected by museums, passing through many hands before entering the Louvre at about the same time (in 1921 and 1920, respectively), where they coexisted for more than fifty years.
114. Delacroix 2009, vol. 1, pp. 528–29 (July 21, 1850).
115. "For Watteau, trees are painted according to a formula: they are always alike and remind one more of theater sets than of trees in the forests" (ibid., vol. 1, p. 797 [July 29, 1854]; translation adapted from Delacroix 1995a, p. 253). "Everything after Lebrun, and especially the eighteenth century as a whole, is commonplace and formulaic." (Delacroix 2009, vol. 1, p. 1175 [September 13, 1857]).
116. Delacroix 2009, vol. 1, p. 695 (Champrosay, October 20, 1853); translation adapted from Delacroix 1995a, p. 213.
117. "Went to see Givry (I was about to say 'see again'). That place, which I knew only through the accounts of all those I loved, awakened fond memories of them." Delacroix 2009, vol. 1, p. 1038 (Ante, October 8, 1856).
118. Delacroix 1935–38, vol. 2, pp. 21–22 (letter to George Sand, Valmont, September 5, 1838).
119. Delacroix 2009, vol. 1, p. 601 (Dieppe, September 11, 1852); translation adapted from Delacroix 1995a, p. 167.
120. Delacroix 2009, vol. 1, p. 701 (Champrosay, October 27, 1853); translation adapted from Delacroix 1995a, p. 218.
121. Delacroix 2009, vol. 1, p. 818 (Dieppe, August 30, 1854); translation adapted from Delacroix 1995a, p. 265.
122. Delacroix 2009, vol. 1, p. 941 (Croze, September 13–15, 1855); translation adapted from Delacroix 1995a, pp. 314–15.
123. Delacroix 2009, vol. 1, p. 264 ("Souvenirs d'un voyage dans le Maroc").
124. Ibid., vol. 1, p. 266.
125. Ibid., vol. 1, p. 267.
126. Ibid., vol. 2, pp. 1598–99, appendix 27.
127. Ibid., vol. 1, p. 691 (Champrosay, October 17, 1853); translation adapted from Delacroix 1995a, p. 210.
128. Johnson 1981–2002, pp. 215–16, no. 426.
129. Delacroix 2009, vol. 1, p. 686 (October 12, 1853); translation adapted from Delacroix 1995a, p. 207.
130. Delacroix 2009, vol. 1, p. 688 (October 12, 1853); translation adapted from Delacroix 1995a, pp. 208–9.
131. Delacroix 2009, vol. 1, p. 691 (Champrosay, October 17, 1853); translation adapted from Delacroix 1995a, p. 210.
132. Delacroix 2009, vol. 1, p. 963 (Dieppe, October 10, 1855); translation adapted from Delacroix 1995a, p. 325.
133. Delacroix 2009, vol. 1, p. 831 (Dieppe, September 12, 1854); translation adapted from Delacroix 1995a, p. 272.
134. The titles the painter used to designate his completed work attest to this: *Landscape of Tangier by the Sea* or *Seaside of Tangier.* See Johnson 1981–2002, vol. 3, p. 206, no. 408.
135. Delacroix 2009, vol. 2, p. 1228 (March 10, 1858).
136. Ibid., vol. 1, p. 839 (Dieppe, September 20, 1854).
137. "Saw *I Puritani* [by Bellini]. . . . The moonlight scene at the end is superb, like everything the designer in this theater [the Théâtre-Italien] does. I think he obtains his effects with very simple colors, using black and blue and perhaps umber, but they are well understood with regard to the planes and the way in which one tint is placed above another." Delacroix 2009, vol. 1, p. 359 (March 3, 1847); translation adapted from Delacroix 1995a, p. 72.
138. Delacroix 2009, vol. 1, p. 759 (Champrosay, April 28, 1854); translation adapted from Delacroix 1995a, p. 242.
139. Delacroix 2009, vol. 1, p. 851 (Champrosay, October 12, 1854); translation adapted from Delacroix 1995a, pp. 282–83.

140. Delacroix 2009, vol. 1, p. 1098 (1857 [under the date of February 1]).

141. Ibid., vol. 1, p. 1102 (1857 [under the date of February 6–7]).

142. Ibid., vol. 1, p. 1188 (October 29, 1857).

143. Ibid., vol. 1, p. 1093 (1857 [under the date of January 29]).

144. Ibid., vol. 1, p. 365 (March 14, 1847); translation adapted from Delacroix 1995a, p. 75.

145. Delacroix 2009, vol. 1, p. 852 (sheet inserted under the date of October 15, 1854).

146. At the Louvre, Delacroix could see a *Holy Family Fleeing Egypt* (1765) by an anonymous pasticher, who combined Elsheimer's composition with the group conceived by Rubens for the Flight into Egypt.

147. Ibid., vol. 1, p. 847 (October 4, 1854); translation adapted from Delacroix 1995a, pp. 279–80.

148. Delacroix 2009, vol. 1, p. 1057 (1857 [under the date of January 1]); translation adapted from Delacroix 1995a, pp. 347–48.

149. Delacroix 2009, vol. 1, pp. 1059–60 (1857 [under the date of January 5]); translation adapted from Delacroix 1995a, p. 349.

150. Delacroix 1935–38, vol. 4, p. 94 (letter to Pérignon, April 18, 1859).

151. Sale, Christie's, New York, October 25, 2006, no. 159.25

152. On March 12, 1832, then again on April 6–7, Delacroix had traveled alongside and across the Sebou River. Delacroix 2009, vol. 1, pp. 231–32 (Meknes notebook).

153. Mantz 1859, p. 137.

154. Delacroix 2009, vol. 1, p. 797 (July 29, 1854); translation adapted from Delacroix 1995a, pp. 252–53.

155. Delacroix 2009, vol. 1, p. 791 (July 5, 1854); translation adapted from Delacroix 1995a, pp. 249–50.

156. Frédéric Villot, quoted in Jobert 1997, pp. 205–6 (letter to Alfred Sensier).

157. Mantz 1847, p. 219.

158. Théophile Thoré in *Le constitutionnel,* January 10, 1847.

159. Loyrette 1995.

160. Delacroix 2009, vol. 2, p. 1552.

161. Ibid., vol. 1, p. 440 (April 10, 1849).

162. Delacroix 1857, p. 911.

163. J 157a. Sale, Fraysse & associés, Paris, June 4, 2008, no. 17.

164. "Poor brother!—You don't admit to yourself your sad position, and your friends cannot offer a remedy." Delacroix 2009, vol. 1, pp. 84–86 (September 19, 1822).

165. Johnson 1981–2002, vol. 3, p. 139.

166. Delacroix 2009, vol. 1, p. 878 (January 9, 1855).

167. Ibid., vol. 1, p. 1048 (December 7, 1856).

168. Ibid., vol. 1, p. 1334 (March 15, 1860).

169. Ibid., vol. 1, p. 1098 (1857 [under the date of February 1]).

170. Ibid., vol. 1, p. 851 (Champrosay, April 28, 1854).

171. Gautier 1874, pp. 214–15.

Asher Miller
The Act of Looking in Delacroix's
Early Narrative Paintings

1. New York 1991, pp. 118–19, no. 51 (as private collection).

2. Delacroix 1935–38, vol. 5, pp. 48–49 (letter to his sister, Henriette, May 1, 1820). Three nights a week, Delacroix would attend life classes or study plaster casts of ancient sculptures at the Ecole des Beaux-Arts; see Johnson 1981–2002, vol. 1, p. xvi.

3. Delacroix 1935–38, vol. 5, p. 51.

4. See Johnson 1981–2002, vol. 1, pp. 12–13, no. 14; vol. 2, pl. 11.

5. See Bazin 1987–97, vol. 2, pp. 430–31, no. 312.

6. On the sheet of *Notes and Figure Studies* cited in note 1 above (New York 1991, p. 118), Delacroix wrote, "Make drawings after Rubens's heads / . . . or those of Veronese . . . / with strong features / in the vein of the jester [dwarf] in the marriage at / Cana."

7. See Johnson 1981–2002, vol. 1, p. 13 (under no. 14); vol. 1, p. 218, no. D2; vol. 2, pl. 163. The copy showing the bride and groom is known to the author in reproduction only.

8. Delacroix 2009, vol. 1, p. 637 (April 20, 1853); translation by Lucy Norton in Delacroix 1995a, p. 183.

9. Delacroix 2009, vol. 1, p. 90 (October 8, 1822). According to Hannoosh, this is the first trace of this idea in Delacroix's writings; see Hannoosh in Delacroix 2009, vol. 1, p. 528 n. 263; translation adapted from Norton's version in Delacroix 1995a, pp. 6–7.

10. As noted in Johnson 1981–2002, vol. 1, p. 203, L94.

11. Although in his *Self-Portrait* of about 1819 Delacroix assumes the guise of Ravenswood (**cat. 4**), the painting is not based on a specific narrative incident in Scott's *The Bride of Lammermoor,* first published in 1819 and translated into French the same year.

12. Delacroix 2009, vol. 1, p. 110 (December 30, 1823).

13. Delacroix 2009, vol. 1, p. 88 (October 5, 1822).

14. Chateaubriand subsequently included *Atala* in *Le génie du Christianisme* in (1802) and *The Natchez* (1826).

15. Delacroix 2009, vol. 1, p. 109 (December 22 or 23, 1823).

16. Delacroix 2009, p. 102 (May 24 or 31, 1823).

17. Another sheet, with a study for *The Natchez* (Louvre, RF 9219) on the recto that includes most of the key features of the definitive composition, has on its verso a graphite study for *Chios,* in which the group on the right still includes the mother with the dead infant, further evidence that work on *The Natchez* began before *Chios* was well advanced.

18. Voutier 1823, p. 251 n. 1.

19. Delacroix 2009, vol. 1, pp. 112–13 (January 12, 1824).

20. The painting by Poussin was then, as now, in the Louvre (7276). The author thanks Andrea Bayer for sharing her thoughts about these sources.

21. Delacroix 2009, vol. 1, p. 124 (March 4, 1824).

22. See Johnson 1981–2002, vol. 1, pp. 8–9, no. 8.

23. Kunsthaus Zürich, 1988/28 (J 128]).

24. See Johnson 1981–2002, vol. 1, pp. 123–26, no. 128.

25. See ibid., vol. 1, pp. 126–27, no. 129. *Woodstock* was first translated into French in 1826.

26. *Marino Faliero* was previously shown at the *Exposition au profit des Grecs,* held at Galerie Lebrun in the summer of 1826.

27. It was first translated into French in 1821.

28. See Johnson 1981–2002, vol. 1, pp. 98–102, no. 112; vol. 2, pl. 98.

29. See note 9 above.

30. Delacroix 2009, vol. 1, p. 528 (July 18, 1850). Cf. Allard 2011, p. 53.

31. Most immediately, he was prompted by a reading of *Le dessin sans maître,* the manual written by his friend Marie-Elisabeth Cavé, which was first published in 1850; see Cavé 1850; Hannoosh in Delacroix 2009, vol. 2, pp. 2132–33.

32. Delacroix 2009, vol. 1, p. 110 (December 30, 1823).

33. Four drawings are listed in the catalogue of the artist's 1864 estate sale (under no. 354), probably Louvre, RF 3704, RF 3705, RF 9530, and Palais des Beaux-Arts, Lille, inv. Pluchart 1261.

34. Delacroix made a sketch after the Rubens work about 1837 (see Johnson 1981–2002, vol. 3, p. 267, no. L117, vol. 7, p. 16 and pl. 16); the first to draw a connection between these *enlèvements* was Thomas Lederballe: see Lederballe 2000.

Michèle Hannoosh
"Painting His Thoughts on Paper":
Delacroix and His *Journal*

1. Baudelaire 1863 (1976 ed.), vol. 2, p. 754.

2. See Louvre, RF 39050-22 and 39050-23; RF 1712*bis.*

3. Delacroix 2009, vol. 1, p. 77. All translations of Delacroix's writings in this essay are by Michèle Hannoosh.

4. Ibid., vol. 1, p. 80 (September 5, 1822). Victoire Delacroix, née Oeben, died on September 3, 1814.

5. Louvre, RF 3820.

6. Delacroix 2009, vol. 1, p. 116 (January 25, 1824).

7. Ibid., vol. 1, p. 135 (April 7, 1824).

8. Ibid., vol. 1, p. 106 (November 10, 1823).

9. Louvre, RF 9140, fol. 31.

10. Delacroix 2009, vol. 1, pp. 111 (January 4, 1824); 98 (April 15, 1823); 98 and 99 (May 16, 1823); 108 (December 22, 1823).

11. Ibid., vol. 1, pp. 147 (April 25, 1824); 154 (May 4, 1824); 100 (May 16, 1823).

12. Ibid., vol. 1, pp. 90 (October 8, 1822); 121 (February 27, 1824); 156 (May 7, 1824).

13. Ibid., vol. 1, p. 156 (May 7, 1824).

14. INHA, Ms 253-1.

15. Delacroix 2009, vol. 1, pp. 326–27 (January 19, 1847).

16. Ibid., vol. 1, p. 327 (January 19, 1847).
17. Ibid., vol. 1, p. 1056, n. 35 (January 1, 1857).
18. Ibid., vol. 2, p. 1605 (1844).
19. Ibid., vol. 2, p. 1226 (February 23, 1858; in fact February 28, 1860); vol. 1, p. 841 (September 23, 1854).
20. Motherwell 2007, p. 286.
21. Delacroix 2009, vol. 2, p. 1412 (June 22, 1863).
22. Ibid., vol. 1, p. 696 (October 20, 1853).
23. Ibid., vol. 2, p. 1579 (December 16, 1843).
24. Ibid., vol. 2, p. 1649.
25. Ibid., vol. 1, p. 694 (October 20, 1853).
26. Ibid., vol. 1, p. 717 (November 30, 1853).
27. Ibid., vol. 2, p. 1380 (January 1, 1861).
28. Ibid., vol. 1, p. 766 (May 10, 1854).
29. See also *Basket of Flowers* (cat. 109); and *Bouquet of Flowers* (1848–49) in the Louvre (RF 31719 recto).
30. Delacroix 2009, vol. 1, p. 472 (October 20, 1849).
31. Ibid., vol. 1, pp. 544–45 (August 13, 1850).
32. Ibid., vol. 1, p. 816 (August 26 and 27, 1854).
33. Ibid., vol. 1, p. 1153 (May 12, 1857).
34. Ibid., vol. 1, p. 1019 (May 30, 1856).
35. Baudelaire 1856 (1976 ed.), vol. 2, pp. 317–18.
36. Delacroix 2009, vol. 1, p. 815 (August 25, 1854).
37. Ibid., vol. 2, p. 1726 (May 9, 1853).
38. Ibid., vol. 1, pp. 1189, 1191–92.
39. Ibid., vol. 2, p. 1339 (April 3, 1860).
40. Ibid., vol. 2, p. 1634.
41. Ibid., vol. 1, p. 1627 (1844).
42. Ibid., vol. 1, p. 807 (August 11, 1854).
43. Ibid., vol. 1, p. 684 (October 9, 1853).
44. Ibid., vol. 1, p. 524 (July 14, 1850).
45. Ibid., vol. 2, p. 1257 (August 19, 1858).

Mehdi Korchane
Eugène and His Masters:
Becoming Delacroix

1. Baudelaire 1863 (1976 ed.), p. 746.
2. The aesthetic break between Baudelaire and Champfleury crystallized in Baudelaire's critique of the realistic imitation of nature, a practice he identified as "positivism." Baudelaire developed this argument in his review of the Salon of 1859.
3. "I admit not only that I am a Romantic, but also that I have been one since I was fifteen; I already preferred Prud'hon and Gros to Guérin and Girodet" (Silvestre 1856, p. 61).
4. Du Camp 2002, p. 230.
5. Véron 1853–55, vol. 1, p. 234.
6. Delacroix 1878, p. 8 (letter to Jules Allard, August 25, 1813, erroneously dated 1815 by Philippe Burty on p. 7): "I went to M. Guérin's studio this morning to bid him farewell. There I admired the beautiful paintings he will exhibit at the next Salon. I regret not being able to study with him this year, but, when I'm no longer at this lycée, I want to spend some time there [in Guérin's studio] to have at least a little talent as an amateur."

7. "[I am writing you] from M. Guérin's studio. You can guess the reason: so as not to have to light the fire at my own place." Delacroix 1935–38, vol. 5, p. 20 (letter to his sister, Henriette, January 5, 1820).
8. David was expelled from the Académie des Beaux-Arts in March 1816 for his role in the Reign of Terror. The Académie des Beaux-Arts is one of five academies administered by the Institut de France, the preeminent organization of French scholars and artists. The main function of the Académie des Beaux-Arts is the teaching of art by its members, at the Ecole des Beaux-Arts.
9. Korchane 2005a, pp. 90–92; Korchane 2005b; Korchane 2018, chap. 21.
10. Pierre Narcisse Guérin and Antoine Jean Gros, report on the submissions from Rome in 1816, read aloud at the Institut de France during the sessions of September 28 and October 12, 1816, Institut de France, Paris, A.B.A. 5E 8, fol. 3; see Korchane 2018.
11. See Lapauze 1924, vol. 2, pp. 122–23.
12. For Delacroix's use of photographs and their effect on his art, see Damisch 2001 and Paris 2008–9.
13. See Delacroix 1995b.
14. These three manuscripts are being prepared for publication by Dominique de Font-Réaulx; see Font-Réaulx 2017.
15. Delacroix specialists are divided on the identity of the model for this portrait, which resurfaced in 2015. I share the opinion of Bruno Chenique and Philippe Grunchec, who corroborate its identification as Delacroix. Chenique 2015, pp. 24–26; Baroni 2016, pp. 52–57.
16. Delacroix 1995b, p. 46 (letter to Félix Guillemardet, September 1818). A course of study in Rome was considered an essential part of a successful artist's training.
17. Guillaume Bodinier, in Angers 2011, p. 258 (letter to his father, November 27, 1816).
18. See Chenique 2015, esp. pp. 30–37.
19. A pencil study by Gericault for the painting was discovered by Louis-Antoine Prat in 1981. See Metropolitan Museum, 2002.481; see also Bazin 1987–97, vol. 7, p. 285, no. 2776, ill.
20. Delacroix 2009, vol. 1, p. 109 (December 30, 1823). See Louvre, 5180.
21. Guillaume Bodinier, in Angers 2011, p. 259 (letter to his father, November 27, 1816).
22. See Debord 1997.
23. See Sérullaz et al. 1984, vol. 1, pp. 352–58, nos. 938–66.
24. Responding to the painting when it was exhibited that year, a journalist identified as *L'amateur sans prétention* (The Unpretentious Art Lover) wrote: "I arrive eagerly; what a surprise! I feel repelled not by the horrors of the subject matter but by the hideous aspect of the painting. . . . Cadavers already marked with the stamp of destruction and the livid color that signals the second, disfiguring, phase of death; living bodies that resemble them" (Anon. 1824, p. 199).

25. Véron 1853–55, vol. 1, p. 234.
26. Victor Bodinier, in Angers 2011, p. 264 (letter to his brother Guillaume, November 22, 1822). Before departing for Rome, Guérin entrusted his students and studio to François-Edouard Picot. According to a note written by Guérin's servant in November of that year, "there remained twenty-one students, five of whom were new. Happily, the most disruptive had gone."
27. The critic Etienne Jean Delécluze linked the Romantic painters to the Primitives when he compared the former to "a sect of spiritualist artists." Delécluze 1828b, p. 250.
28. Quoted in Delacroix 2009, vol. 1, p. 82. Upon being named director of the Académie de France in Rome on April 13, 1822, Guérin devoted himself full-time to preparing for that assignment. He left Paris on October 15, 1822, and assumed his duties in Rome on January 1, 1823. See Le Normand-Romain, Fossier, and Korchane 2005.
29. Delacroix 1848.
30. David, in Wildenstein and Wildenstein 1973, p. 219 (letter to Gros, June 22, 1820). For Gros's conversion to Davidian painting, see Allard and Chaudonneret 2010, pp. 67–71.
31. Allard and Chaudonneret 2010, p. 70; Bordes 2012, p. 39. The painting resurfaced at the Pierre Bergé and Yves Saint-Laurent sale, Christie's, February 24, 2009, lot 88.
32. Quoted in Delacroix 2009, vol. 2, p. 1738.
33. Ibid., vol. 1, p. 87 (October 5, 1822).
34. The hostile comments of Victor Bodinier, Guillaume's brother and a student of Ingres, should be added to the list: "M. Delacroix is making his own revolution. People are talking about nothing but his new painting, *Scene of the Massacres at Chios: Greek Families Awaiting Death or Slavery.* I find some energy in it. But it disgusts me. Here are men, women, and children who look as if they are dying of starvation, plague, gangrene, every malady that can turn the body livid (and which, if I were an artist, I would always consider myself unfortunate to represent): it's a horror! I confess that I do not like the painting, which frightens and disgusts me." Victor Bodinier, in Angers 2011, pp. 273–74 (letter to his brother Guillaume, Paris, September 13, 1824).
35. Korchane 2003, pp. 107–15.
36. See the essay by Sébastien Allard and Côme Fabre in the present volume.
37. Korchane 2005b; Korchane 2018, chaps. 23–24; Allard and Chaudonneret 2010, pp. 121–27; Angers 2012, pp. 112–16.
38. Delacroix 2009, vol. 1, p. 174 (August 19, 1824); vol. 2, pp. 1741, 1742, 1744–46 (autobiographical notebook).
39. *Horses Frightened by the Surf* and *Sea Study* remained in the possession of Gérard's family until the Pescheteau-Badin sale, Paris, December 12, 2013, lots 23 and 24.

40. Lethière's name appears on the list of visitors to the Salon of 1827–28; see Delacroix 2009, vol. 2, p. 1469. The anecdote was reported by Henri Monnier, June 4, 1828; see Delacroix 2000, p. 110.

41. Angers 2012, pp. 115–16.

42. Charles Philippe Larivière, in Loddé 2003, p. 86 (letter to his father, Rome, December 4, 1827).

43. Pierre Narcisse Guérin, in Le Normand-Romain, Fossier, and Korchane 2005, p. 54, no. 45 (letter to Quatremère de Quincy, September 11, 1823). See also Guérin in ibid., pp. 202–3, no. 414 (letter to Quatremère de Quincy, March 15, 1829).

44. Letter from Guérin to Paul Lemoyne, March 22, 1828. INHA, box 16, painter Pierre Guérin.

45. Angers 2012, pp. 112–15.

46. For Guérin's inversion of the principles of David's *Intervention of the Sabine Women*, see Angers 2012, p. 122, and Korchane 2018, p. 278.

47. Angers 2012, pp. 50–52.

48. Quoted in Delacroix 2009, vol. 2, p. 1738.

49. This paradox is discussed in Larue 1996.

Dominique de Font-Réaulx
Delacroix and the Exposition Universelle of 1855

1. Delacroix 1854, p. 315. The painter had been elected a member of the Koninklijke Academie van Beeldende Kunsten of Amsterdam in February 1854.

2. Delacroix 1935–38, vol. 2, pp. 411–12 (letter to the president of the Académie des Beaux-Arts, December 7, 1849). Léon Cogniet, a former fellow student from Guérin's studio, was admitted as a member of the Académie that year.

3. Delacroix 2014, pp. 248–49.

4. See Paris 2004.

5. For Delacroix's communication to George Sand, see Delacroix 1935–38, vol. 2, pp. 349–50 (letter to George Sand, [May] 28, 1848).

6. Delacroix was probably alluding here to the various demonstrations held by supporters of the leftist slate, whose manifestations were broken up several times by the National Guard, more closely aligned with the bourgeois slate.

7. Delacroix 1935–38, vol. 2, pp. 347–48 (letter to Charles Soulier, May 8, 1848); translation adapted from Jean Stewart's version in Delacroix 2001, pp. 281–82.

8. Allard 2005.

9. Titled "The Great Exhibition of the Works of Industry of All Nations," the London exhibition, held in the spectacular Crystal Palace, was dedicated primarily to the progress of industry. The share granted to the fine arts was limited, and the works were displayed only in the pavilions of the various nations. Great Britain, which had set aside two-thirds of the space for itself, chose not to display works of art.

10. Delacroix 1935–38, vol. 3, pp. 248–49 (letter to Baron Haussmann, prefect of the Seine, March 21, 1855).

11. Ibid., vol. 3, pp. 245–46 (letter to the "Ministre d'Etat," March 2, 1855).

12. Baudelaire, "Eugène Delacroix," in Baudelaire 1855 (1976 ed.), vol. 2, p. 594; translation adapted from Jonathan Mayne's version, in Baudelaire 1981, p. 141.

13. Daniel Wilson acquired *The Death of Sardanapalus* in 1846. See "Correspondance d'Eugène Delacroix" (letter to Philippe-Eugène Pelouze, December 28, 1861), http://www.correspondance-delacroix.fr/correspondances/bdd/correspondance/102.

14. Delacroix 1935–38, vol. 3, pp. 250–51 (letter to Frédéric de Mercey, March 26, [1855]).

15. Delacroix 2009, vol. 1, pp. 890–91 (March 24, 1855).

16. Delacroix 1935–38, vol. 3, p. 253 (letter to Alexandre Dumas, April 6, [1855]): "I was later held back by all sorts of minor ailments and mishaps."

17. Ibid., vol. 3, p. 251 (letter to Frédéric de Mercey, March 31, 1855).

18. Silvestre planned to publish biographical essays on one hundred great artists of his time, from Ingres to Courbet, illustrated with photographs of the creators and their works, in successive issues. But only the first few, devoted to Corot, Ingres, and Delacroix, appeared in the form he intended; these and others were published as *Histoire des artistes vivants* in 1856; see Silvestre 1856.

19. Charles Baudelaire, "Eugène Delacroix," in Baudelaire 1855 (1976 ed.), vol. 2, pp. 596–97; translation adapted from Mayne in Baudelaire 1981, p. 143. Delacroix warmly thanked Baudelaire in a letter dated June 10, 1855; see Delacroix 1935–38, vol. 3, p. 266.

20. Gérard's quote is cited in Baudelaire 1846 (1976 ed.), vol. 2, p. 429.

21. Baudelaire 1855 (1976 ed.), vol. 2, p. 590; translation adapted from Mayne, in Baudelaire 1981, pp. 135–36.

22. Baudelaire, "Ingres," in Baudelaire 1855 (1976 ed.), vol. 2, p. 584; translation adapted from Mayne in Baudelaire 1981, p. 130.

23. Bruyas owned the following works by Delacroix: cats. 10, 78, 114 in the present volume.

24. *After Dinner at Ornans*, Palais des Beaux-Arts, Lille, inv. P 522.

25. See Paris–New York–Montpellier 2007–8, pp. 174–81.

26. "Cahier autobiographique," in Delacroix 2009, vol. 2, pp. 1742–43.

27. Courbet exhibited three paintings at the Salon that year: *The Bathers* (see fig. 86), *The Wrestlers* (Szépművészeti Múzeum, Budapest), and *The Sleeping Spinner* (Musée Fabre, Montpellier).

28. Louvre, RF 2638.

29. Delacroix 2009, vol. 1, p. 633 (April 15, 1853); Norton translation in Delacroix 1995a, p. 182. See also Paris–New York–Montpellier 2007–8.

30. Delacroix 2009, vol. 1, p. 929 (August 3, 1855); translation adapted from Norton in Delacroix 1995a, pp. 308–9.

31. Louvre, RF 96.

32. Delacroix 1935–38, vol. 3, p. 257 (letter to Paul Huet, April 21, [1855]).

33. Delacroix 2009, vol. 1, p. 910 (June 17, 1855).

34. Ibid., vol. 1, p. 918 (June 30, 1855).

35. Courbet 1996, p. 100 (letter to his family, June 15, 1852); translation adapted from Chu's version in Courbet 1992, p. 107. Auguste Romieu was the director of fine arts (comparable to today's minister of culture) at the time. No mention has been found in Delacroix's *Journal* or correspondence to support Courbet's remark.

36. Courbet 1996, pp. 222–23 (letter to Victor Hugo, November 28, 1864); translation adapted from Chu's version in Courbet 1992, p. 249. Hugo was in exile in Guernsey at the time. Courbet had not yet suffered at the hands of the police, but this letter may be seen as foreshadowing his arrest after the Commune in 1871, his conviction, and the exile that followed.

37. On this matter, see the forthcoming publication of the colloquium "La Correspondance de Courbet, 20 Ans Après," held at the Musée d'Orsay, Paris, January 2017. The conference was dedicated to research that has emerged since the invaluable publication of Courbet's *Correspondance* by Petra ten-Doesschate Chu (Courbet 1996).

38. See Delacroix 1935–38, vol. 4, pp. 315–16 (letter to Francis Petit, May 2, 1862), and p. 320 (letter to Petit, June 23, 1862); see also Hannoosh in Delacroix 2009, vol. 2, p. 1397 n. 31.

39. See Paris 2012–13; Minneapolis–London 2015–16.

40. See Paris–New York–Montpellier 2007–8.

41. Baudelaire, "Eugène Delacroix," in Baudelaire 1855 (1976 ed.), vol. 2, p. 593; translation by Mayne in Baudelaire 1981, p. 139.

42. See Paris–New York 1994–95, pp. 9–10, 380–81.

43. See Paris 2018.

44. Musée d'Orsay, Paris, bequest of Etienne Moreau-Nélaton, RF 729. See Paris 2011–12.

45. See Paris 2017.

Checklist

Compiled by Asher Miller

All works are by Eugène Delacroix and exhibited in Paris and New York, unless otherwise noted. Paintings are identified by their catalogue raisonné number in Johnson 1981–2002, abbreviated as "J" followed by the number. Pastels are identified by their number in Johnson 1995; and prints by the number in Delteil and Strauber 1997, abbreviated as "D-S" followed by the number. Citations to Delacroix's *Journal* are identified by their page numbers in Delacroix 2009.

Unless otherwise noted, the stamp *ED* found on many drawings in the catalogue is the one described in Frits Lugt, *Les marques de collections de dessins & d'estampes* (http://www.marquesdecollections.fr/), as no. 838a.

CAT. 1

Male Academy Figure: Half-Length, Side View
ca. 1818–20
Oil on paper laid down on canvas
15¾ x 13⅜ in. (40 x 34 cm)
The Metropolitan Museum of Art, New York, Promised Gift from the Karen B. Cohen Collection of Eugène Delacroix, in memory of Arthur G. Cohen
J 1
New York only
repr. p. 24

PROVENANCE: the artist's estate sale, Hôtel Drouot, Paris, February 17–29, 1864, part of no. 200; possibly Théophile Thoré (from 1864); possibly H. Vever; [A. Vuillier, Paris, until 1897; sold in February to Mercier]; Monsieur Mercier, Lausanne (from 1897); by descent to H. E. Lombardet, Lausanne (until 1966; his sale, Lausanne, February 3, 1966); C. Sfezzo, Lausanne (until 1987; sale, Christie's, London, November 27, 1987, no. 51, to London dealer); [London art market, 1987–88]; Karen B. Cohen, New York (from 1988)

SELECTED EXHIBITIONS: New York 1991, no. 1; New York 2000–2001, no. 23; Paris 2009–10, no. 83

CAT. 2

Female Academy Figure: Seated, Front View (Mademoiselle Rose)
ca. 1820–23
Oil on canvas
32⅛ x 25⅝ in. (81.5 x 65 cm)
Staatliche Museen zu Berlin, Nationalgalerie (inv. NG 53/86)
J 4
repr. p. 26

PROVENANCE: the artist's estate sale, Hôtel Drouot, Paris, February 17–29, 1864, part of no. 200, to Thoré; Théophile Thoré (from 1864); Paul Lacroix; Maurice Du Seigneur (d. Feb. 1892); F. Vieussa (in 1893); [Georges Bernheim et Cie, Paris, ca. 1925]; Dr. Georges Viau, Paris (1926–d. 1939; acquired in November 1926); his estate (1939–48; first estate sale, Hôtel Drouot, Paris, December 11, 1942, no. 98, but unsold because it was then in the U.S.; third estate sale, Galerie Charpentier, Paris, June 22, 1948, no. 4, to Bader); Bader, New York (from 1948); comte Philippe de La Rochefoucauld, Château de Beaumont, Montmirail (until 1951; his sale, Parke-Bernet, New York, May 19, 1951, no. 56, to Nicholas Acquavella for Pagliali); Bruno Pagliali, Mexico City (from 1951); [E. V. Thaw & Co., New York, 1985]; [Galerie Schmit, Paris, 1986; sold to Alte Nationalgalerie]

SELECTED EXHIBITIONS: Karlsruhe 2003–4, no. 50; Madrid–Barcelona 2011–12, no. 4

CAT. 3

Two Bearded Heads, after Veronese (detail from "The Marriage at Cana")
1820
Oil on canvas
25³⁄₁₆ x 32⁵⁄₁₆ in. (64 x 82 cm)
Tubacex S.A.
J 14
New York only
repr. p. 227

PROVENANCE: the artist's estate sale, Hôtel Drouot, Paris, February 17–29, 1864, no. 155, to Haro; Haro, Paris (from 1864); Monsieur Démellette (by 1927); Charles Lefèvre Démellette, Paris (by 1952); private collection, Paris; Sylvie Rosenfeld-Panissol, Paris; [Salander-O'Reilly Galleries, New York, 1986–at least 1992]; Tubacex S.A.

SELECTED EXHIBITIONS: Paris 1864b, no. 59; Zürich–Frankfurt 1987–88, no. 29

CAT. 4

Self-Portrait as Ravenswood
ca. 1821–24
Oil on canvas
16⅛ x 12¹¹⁄₁₆ in. (40.9 x 32.3 cm)
Musée du Louvre, Paris, Département des Peintures (RF 1953-38), on deposit at the Musée National Eugène-Delacroix
J 64
repr. p. 41

PROVENANCE: gift of the artist to Joseph-Auguste Carrier (until d. 1875; his estate sale, Hôtel Drouot, Paris, May 5, 1875, not in catalogue, to art dealer); [art dealer, Paris, 1875; sold on May 6 to Robaut]; Alfred Robaut, Paris (from 1875); Paul-Arthur Chéramy, Paris (bought by 1885–1908; his sale, Galerie Georges Petit, Paris, May 5–7, 1908, no. 165, to Vedel, possibly for Chéramy); Vedel (in 1908); Paul-Arthur Chéramy, Paris (until d. 1912; his estate sale, Hôtel Drouot, Paris, April 14–16, 1913, no. 26, to Jamot); Paul Jamot, Paris (1913–d. 1939; his bequest to Société des Amis de Delacroix, Paris; transferred in 1953 to Louvre; on deposit at the Musée National Eugène-Delacroix since 1994)

SELECTED EXHIBITIONS: Paris 1885, no. 179; Zürich–Frankfurt 1987–88, no. 1; Paris–New York 2002–3, no. 108; Marseilles–Rovereto–Toronto 2009–10, no. 88 (Marseilles and Rovereto only); Madrid–Barcelona 2011–12, no. 5; Leipzig 2015–16, no. 25

Edgar Ravenswood is the male protagonist of Sir Walter Scott's historical novel *The Bride of Lamermoor*, first published in 1819.

CAT. 5

Nereid, after Rubens, detail from "The Landing of Maria de Medici at Marseilles"
ca. 1822
Oil on canvas
18⁵⁄₁₆ x 14¹⁵⁄₁₆ in. (46.5 x 38 cm)
Kunstmuseum Basel – Öffentliche Kunstsammlung, Gift in Memory of Prof. Friedrich Rintelen, by His Friends, 1933 (inv. 1602)
J 16
repr. p. 13

PROVENANCE: the artist's estate sale, Hôtel Drouot, Paris, February 17–29, 1864, no. 172, to Burty; Philippe Burty, Paris (1864–d. 1890; his estate sale,

Hôtel Drouot, Paris, March 2–3, 1891, no. 10); sale, Hôtel Drouot, Paris, November 20, 1922, no. 45; Georges Aubry, Paris (until 1933; his sale, Hôtel Drouot, Paris, March 11, 1933, no. 80, to Kunstmuseum)

SELECTED EXHIBITIONS: Zürich–Frankfurt 1987–88, no. 131; Paris 2004, no. 16

Rubens's cycle of paintings depicting scenes from the life of the French queen, the second wife of Henri IV, was commissioned for the Luxembourg Palace in 1621; they were moved to the Louvre in 1816.

CAT. 6

Studies of a Damned Man, for "The Barque of Dante"
1822
Pen, brown ink, black wash over black chalk and graphite on laid paper
10½ x 13¼ in. (26.7 x 33.7 cm)
Stamped (lower left): *ED*
The Metropolitan Museum of Art, New York, Rogers Fund, 1961 (61.23)
New York only
repr. p. 9

PROVENANCE: the artist's estate sale, Hôtel Drouot, Paris, February 17–29, 1864, possibly part of no. 305; possibly Pierre-Jules Mêne, Paris (until d. 1879); possibly his heirs (1879–99; P.-J. Mêne sale, Hôtel des Commissaires-Priseurs, Paris, February 20–21, 1899, part of no. 52, to Degas); Edgar Degas, Paris (1899?–d. 1917; his estate sale, Galerie Georges Petit, Paris, November 15–16, 1918, no. 97b, to Daragnès); Jean-Gabriel Daragnès, Neuilly (d. 1950); [Jacques Seligmann, New York, by 1960–61; sold to MMA]

SELECTED EXHIBITIONS: Paris (Mémorial) 1963, no. 31; New York 1991, no. 20; New York 1997–98, no. 283

This is a study for fig. 2.

CAT. 7

Head of an Old Greek Woman
1824
Oil on canvas
16⁵⁄₁₆ x 13⅛ in. (41.5 x 33.3 cm)
Musée des Beaux-Arts, Orléans (inv. 96.2.1)
J 77
New York only
repr. p. 25

PROVENANCE: gift of the artist to Frédéric Leblond (until d. 1872); his widow (from 1872); their nephew, Dr. E. Gebauer, Cléry-Saint-André (by 1885–1904; his sale, Cléry-Saint-André, May 31, 1904, no. 15); Madame Albert Esnault-Pelterie, Paris (probably from

1904; died ca. 1938); her granddaughter, Madame Jacques Meunier, née Popelin; her family, by descent; Musée des Beaux-Arts, Orléans (from 1995)

SELECTED EXHIBITIONS: probably Paris (Salon) 1824, part of no. 451; Paris 1864b, no. 102; Paris 1885, no. 88; Paris (Mémorial) 1963, no. 54; Orléans 1997–98, no. 203; Rouen 1998, no. 9; Paris–New York 2002–3, no. 110 (New York only); Madrid–Barcelona 2011–12, no. 10

This work and *Orphan Girl in the Cemetery* (fig. 9) are thought to have been exhibited together at the Salon of 1824 under no. 451, as "Studies, same number" (*Études, même numéro*), that is, as studies related to the prior painting in the catalogue, no. 450, *Massacres at Chios* (fig. 5).

CAT. 8

Tasso in the Hospital of St. Anna, Ferrara
1824
Oil on canvas
19¹¹⁄₁₆ x 24¼ in. (50 x 61.5 cm)
Signed (upper left): *E. Delacroix*
Private collection, Courtesy Nathan Fine Art, Potsdam/Zürich
J 106
repr. p. 70

PROVENANCE: painted for Monsieur Formé (see Moreau 1873, p. 92); [Susse, Paris, until ca. 1833; sold to Dumas]; Alexandre Dumas père, Paris (from ca. 1833; sold to Arago); Etienne Arago (sold to Susse); [Susse, Paris; resold to Dumas]; Alexandre Dumas père, Paris (sold to Petit); Monsieur Petit (sold to Dumas); Alexandre Dumas fils (until 1865; his sale, Hôtel Drouot, Paris, March 28, 1865, no. 2, to Delaroche); [Delaroche, in 1865]; Khalil Bey, Paris (until 1868; his sale, Hôtel Drouot, Paris, January 16–18, 1868, no. 18, to Haro); Haro, Paris (from 1868); Carlin (until 1872; his sale, Hôtel Drouot, Paris, April 29, 1872, no. 5, to Candamo); J. C. Candamo (from 1872); Monsieur C. G. de Candamo (until 1933; his sale, Galerie Charpentier, Paris, December 14–15, 1933, no. 10, to Clark); Sir Kenneth Clark, London (1933–54; sold to Marlborough); [Marlborough Fine Arts Ltd., London, 1954]; Emil Bührle, Zürich (until d. 1956); his daughter, Hortense Ande-Bührle, Zürich (1956–at least 1981); private collection

SELECTED EXHIBITIONS: Paris (Salon) 1824, not in catalogue; Paris 1830c, no. 40; Paris 1846a, no. 97; Paris 1855, no. 2929; Paris 1860, supp. no. 346; Paris 1864b, no. 16; Paris 1885, no. 110; Zürich–Frankfurt 1987–88, no. 9; Rouen 1998, no. 145; Karlsruhe 2003–4, no. 22; Winterthur 2008, no. 5; Madrid–Barcelona 2011–12, no. 11; Leipzig 2015–16, no. 54

The melancholic Italian poet Torquato Tasso (1544–1595), author of the epic poem *Gerusalemme Liberata* (1581), was confined to an asylum from 1579 to 1586 by his patron Alfonso II d'Este, duke of Ferrara. This was the subject of Lord Byron's poem *The Lament of Tasso* (1817).

CAT. 9

Turk Mounting His Horse
1824
Aquatint; first state of two
Image 8⁹⁄₁₆ x 10⅜ in. (21.8 x 26.4 cm); sheet 9⁵⁄₁₆ x 11³⁄₁₆ in. (23.6 x 28.4 cm), trimmed within plate
The Metropolitan Museum of Art, New York, Purchase, The Elisha Whittelsey Collection, The Elisha Whittelsey Fund and Arthur Ross Foundation Gift, 1990 (1990.1113)
D-S 11
New York only
repr. p. 56

PROVENANCE: Adolphe Moreau fils, Paris (d. 1882); probably his son Etienne Moreau-Nélaton (d. 1927); [Libby Howie, London, until 1990; to MMA]

SELECTED EXHIBITIONS (this impression): New York 1991, no. 74

CAT. 10

Portrait of Aspasie
ca. 1824
Oil on canvas
31⅞ x 25⁹⁄₁₆ in. (81 x 65 cm)
Musée Fabre, Montpellier Méditerranée Métropole (inv. 868.1.36)
J 79
repr. p. 27

PROVENANCE: the artist's estate sale, Hôtel Drouot, Paris, February 17–29, 1864, no. 192, to Andrieu; Pierre Andrieu, Paris (1864); Alfred Bruyas, Montpellier (by August 1864–68; his gift to the city of Montpellier)

SELECTED EXHIBITIONS: Paris 1864b, no. 302; Paris (Mémorial) 1963, no. 43; Karlsruhe 2003–4, no. 53; Richmond–Williamstown–Dallas–San Francisco 2004–5, no. 38; Madrid–Barcelona 2011–12, no. 14

CAT. 11

Sketch after Goya's "Caprichos"
ca. 1822–24
Pen and brown ink on off-white laid paper, laid down
8¾ x 7⅛ in. (22.1 x 18 cm)
Harvard Art Museums/Fogg Museum, Cambridge, Mass., Bequest of Frances L. Hofer (1979.110)
New York only
repr. p. 54

PROVENANCE: Louis Dimier, Paris (?until 1921; his sale, December 15, 1921, no. 31, as by Goya); Léon Voillemot, Paris (possibly until 1946/49); Alfred Strölin, Paris (sold to Hofer); Philip and Frances L. Hofer, Cambridge, Mass. (until 1979; her bequest to Harvard)

SELECTED EXHIBITIONS: Frankfurt 1987–88, no. A 2; Paris–New York 2002–3, no. 117 (New York only)

This sheet features details from five of Goya's *Caprichos*, including, at the upper right, the bowing male figure Delacroix rendered in cat. 14.

CAT. 12

Study of Babouches
ca. 1823–24
Oil on cardboard
6½ x 8⅟₁₆ in. (16.5 x 20.5 cm)
Musée du Louvre, Paris, Département des Peintures, Bequest of Carle Dreyfus, 1953 (RF 1953-4)
J 26
repr. p. 56

PROVENANCE: the artist's estate sale, Hôtel Drouot, Paris, February 17–29, 1864, part of no. 221, to Calonne; Monsieur de Calonne (to Ricard); Gustave Ricard (until d. 1873; his estate sale, Hôtel Drouot, Paris, June 20, 1873, no. 37, to Sensier); Alfred Sensier, Paris (1873–d. 1877; his estate sale, Hôtel Drouot, Paris, December 10–15, 1877, no. 3, to Gauchez, probably for Wilson); John Waterloo Wilson, Paris (until 1881; his sale, 3 Avenue Hoche, Paris, March 14–16, 1881, no. 147, to Malinet); Malinet (from 1881); Auguste Courtin (until 1886; his sale, Hôtel Drouot, Paris, March 29, 1886, no. 38, to Chéramy); Paul-Arthur Chéramy, Paris (until 1908; his sale, Galerie Georges Petit, Paris, May 5–7, 1908, no. 153, to Wedel (for Chéramy?); ?Wedel (from 1908); Paul-Arthur Chéramy (until d. 1912; his estate sale, Hôtel Drouot, Paris, April 14–16, 1913, no. 22, to Schoeller); [Schoeller; from 1913; sold to Dreyfus]; Carle Dreyfus (1913–d. 1952; his bequest to Louvre)

SELECTED EXHIBITIONS: Madrid–Barcelona 2011–12, no. 16; Chantilly 2012–13, no. 11; Paris 2014–15, no. 18

CAT. 13

Thales Fielding (1793–1837)
ca. 1824–25
Oil on canvas
12⅝ x 9⅟₁₆ in. (32 x 25 cm)
Musée National Eugène-Delacroix, Paris (inv. MD 2009-1)
J 70
New York only
repr. p. 38

PROVENANCE: the artist's estate sale, Hôtel Drouot, Paris, February 17–29, 1864, no. 75, to Piron; Achille Piron (1864–d. 1865; his estate sale, Hôtel Drouot, Paris, April 21, 1865, no. 8, to Rivet); baron Charles Rivet (1865–d. 1872); his daughter, Madame Lajudie; by descent to private collection, Paris (until at least 1981); private collection, New York (by 2003–at least 2004); [New York art market, 2008; sold to Musée Delacroix]

SELECTED EXHIBITIONS: London–Minneapolis–New York 2003–4, no. 2

Delacroix befriended the English artist Fielding when the latter was living in Paris in 1823 and 1824. Fielding painted a reciprocal portrait of Delacroix, which he exhibited at the Royal Academy, London, in 1827 (now in the Musée National Eugène-Delacroix).

CAT. 14

Studies of Bindings, an Oriental Jacket, and Figures after Goya
ca. 1822–26
Oil on canvas
19⅟₁₆ x 24 in. (50 x 61 cm)
Musée National Eugène-Delacroix, Paris (inv. MD 2011-1)
J L34
repr. p. 54

PROVENANCE: the artist's estate sale, Hôtel Drouot, Paris, February 17–29, 1864, possibly part of no. 189; Philippe Burty, Paris (until d. 1890; his estate sale, Hôtel Drouot, Paris, March 2–3, 1891, no. 7, to Chéramy); Paul-Arthur Chéramy, Paris (1891–1908; his sale, Galerie Georges Petit, Paris, May 5–7, 1908, no. 188, to Langweil); Florine Ebstein Langweil, Paris (from 1908; d. 1958); her daughter, Berthe Langweil Noufflard (d. 1971); by descent to private collection, France; sale, Beaussant & Lefèvre, Paris, December 10, 2003, no. 64; [Jean-François Heim, Basel, until 2011; sold to Musée Delacroix]

SELECTED EXHIBITIONS: Rouen 1998, no. 113; Madrid–Barcelona 2011–12, no. 6; Chantilly 2012–13, no. 8

The objects depicted are (clockwise, from upper left): partial studies of two Carolingian missal bindings, the *Gospel of Metz*, possibly ca. 835–45, and the *Gospel of Drogon*, ca. 845–55 (both Bibliothèque nationale de France, Paris, inv. Latin 9383 and Latin 9388; as recognized by Charles T. Little in 2016); a fragment of a Suliot jacket or vest; and a print by Francisco Goya, *Which of them is the more overcome? (Quien mas rendido?)*, etching, aquatint and drypoint, plate 27 from *Los Caprichos*, 1799.

CAT. 15

Study of an Oriental Vest
ca. 1822–26
Graphite on paper
14⅟₅₁₆ x 16⅛ in. (37.9 x 41 cm)
Inscribed: *velours Rouge*; stamped (lower left): *ED*
Private collection, New York
New York only
repr. p. 55

PROVENANCE: [Arezzo Arts, Inc.]; private collection

SELECTED EXHIBITIONS: Paris 2009–10, no. 48

For very probably the same garment, see cat. 14.

CAT. 16

Study of Greek Costumes
ca. 1823–26
Graphite on paper
12 x 9 in. (30.5 x 22.9 cm)
The Metropolitan Museum of Art, New York, Promised Gift from the Karen B. Cohen Collection of Eugène Delacroix, in honor of Asher Ethan Miller
New York only
repr. p. 54

PROVENANCE: Marcel Guérin, Paris (d. 1948); David Daniels, New York; [Arezzo Arts, Inc.]; Karen B. Cohen

SELECTED EXHIBITIONS: Paris 2009–10, no. 47

CAT. 17

Christ in the Garden of Olives (The Agony in the Garden)
1824–26
Oil on canvas
9 ft. 1⁷⁄₁₆ in. x 11 ft. 3¹³⁄₁₆ in. (2.8 x 3.4 m)
Church of Saint-Paul-Saint-Louis, Paris; lent by the Conservation des Oeuvres d'Art Religieuses et Civiles de la Ville de Paris and the Direction Régionale des Affaires Culturelles d'Ile-de-France (inv. COA-PLO18/132)
J 154
repr. p. 132

PROVENANCE: commissioned from the artist by the Prefect of the Seine in 1824 for the church of Saint-Paul-Saint-Louis, Paris

SELECTED EXHIBITIONS: Paris (Salon) 1827–28, no. 293; Paris 1855, no. 2908; Paris 1864b, no. 13; Paris 1885 no. 25; Paris (Mémorial) 1963, no. 89

CAT. 18

Reclining Female Nude: Back View
ca. 1824–26
Oil on canvas
13 x 19½ in. (33 x 49.5 cm)
Private collection
J 6
repr. p. 23

PROVENANCE: Frédéric Leblond (until d. 1872); presumably his widow, Madame Leblond (from 1872); their nephew, Dr. E. Gebauer, Cléry-Saint-André (by September 1, 1881–1904; his sale, Cléry-Saint-André, May 31, 1904, no. 17); Jules Strauss, Paris (by 1926–32; his sale, Galerie Georges Petit, Paris, December 15, 1932, no. 38, to Weisweller); Weisweller (from 1932); [Brame et Lorenceau, Paris, 1987]; sale, Sotheby's, New York, November 10, 1998, no. 58; private collection

SELECTED EXHIBITIONS: Paris 1885, no. 85; Zürich–Frankfurt 1987–88, no. 15

CAT. 19

Macbeth Consulting the Witches
1825
Lithograph; third state of five
Image 12⁹⁄₁₆ x 9⅞ in. (31.9 x 25.1 cm); sheet 19¾ x 13⅞ in. (50.2 x 35.2 cm)
The Metropolitan Museum of Art, New York, Rogers Fund, 1922 (22.63.19)
D-S 40
New York only
repr. p. 69

PROVENANCE: [Maurice Le Garrec, Paris, until 1922; sold to MMA]

SELECTED EXHIBITIONS (this impression): New York 1991, no. 79

This print, based on a scene in Shakespeare's play, bears the caption: "MACBETH. / Toil and trouble / Fire burn, and cauldron bubble."

CAT. 20

Studies of Seven Greek Coins
1825
Lithograph; first state of five
Image 11⁷⁄₁₆ x 9⅛ in. (29 x 23.2 cm); sheet 13⅜ x 10⁵⁄₁₆ in. (34 x 26.2 cm)
The Metropolitan Museum of Art, New York, Harris Brisbane Dick Fund, 1931 (31.77.27)
D-S 45
New York only
repr. p. 57

PROVENANCE: Adolphe Moreau fils, Paris (d. 1882); probably his son Etienne Moreau-Nélaton (d. 1927); [Neuville & Vivien, Paris, until 1931; sold to MMA]

SELECTED EXHIBITIONS (this impression): Frankfurt 1987–88, no. A 8; New York 1991, no. 81

This work and cat. 21 are two of five lithographs based on antique coins that Delacroix produced in 1825; the others are D-S 43, 44, and 46. See Howell 1994.

CAT. 21

Studies of Twelve Greek and Roman Coins
1825
Lithograph; second state of four
Image 9⁵⁄₁₆ x 12 in. (23.6 x 30.5 cm); sheet 11⅝ x 15⁷⁄₁₆ in. (29.6 x 39.2 cm)
The Metropolitan Museum of Art, New York, Harris Brisbane Dick Fund, 1931 (31.77.24)
D-S 47
New York only
repr. p. 57

PROVENANCE: Adolphe Moreau fils, Paris (d. 1882); probably his son Etienne Moreau-Nélaton (d. 1927); [Neuville & Vivien, Paris, until 1931; sold to MMA]

SELECTED EXHIBITIONS (this impression): New York 1991, no. 82

CAT. 22

Mortally Wounded Brigand Quenches His Thirst
ca. 1825
Oil on canvas
12¹³⁄₁₆ x 16 in. (32.5 x 40.7 cm)
Signed (lower right): *Eug. Delacroix*
Kunstmuseum Basel – Öffentliche Kunstsammlung (inv. 1726)
J 162
repr. p. 36

PROVENANCE: Alexandre du Sommerard, Paris (1825–d. 1842; his estate sale, Hôtel rue des Jeûneurs, no. 16, Paris, December 11–13, 1843, no. 22); Monsieur A. Dugléré (by 1848–53; his sale, Hôtel des Ventes Mobilières, Paris, February 1, 1853, no. 43); Monsieur Bruissin (in 1864); Monsieur Dupont, Orléans (in 1884); sale, Hôtel Drouot, Paris, March 29, 1893, no. 14, bought in; Alfred Beurdeley, Paris (by 1900–d. 1919; his estate sale, Galerie Georges Petit, Paris, May 6–7, 1920, no. 33, to Stang); J. B. Stang, Oslo (1920–at least 1930); [Eugène Blot, Paris, in 1937]; Kunstmuseum Basel (purchased 1939)

SELECTED EXHIBITIONS: Paris (Salon) 1827–28, no. 297; Paris 1885, no. 75; Paris (Mémorial) 1963,

no. 97; Zürich–Frankfurt 1987–88, no. 16; Karlsruhe 2003–4, no. 56

At a time when contemporary Italian brigands began to appear in paintings exhibited at the Salon by artists such as Léopold Robert, Delacroix adopted the subject of this picture from canto 2, verse 16, of Byron's poem *Lara*, which is set in the Middle Ages. See Bandiera 1980.

CAT. 23

Charles VI and Odette de Champdivers
ca. 1825
Oil on canvas
14 x 10¾ in. (35.5 x 27.3 cm)
Signed (lower right): *Eug. Delacroix*
Pérez Simón Collection, Mexico (inv. 30957)
J 110
repr. p. 16

PROVENANCE: Pierre Duval le Camus, Paris (until 1827; his anonymous sale, Paris, April 17–18, 1827, no. 38); Frédéric Leblond (by 1832–d. 1872); Dumas-Descombes (in 1885); by descent to comtesse Théobal de Vigneral, Paris (by 1963–at least 1981); private collection, Paris (in 1991); [Stair Sainty Matthiesen Gallery, London and New York, April 1991]; [Richard L. Feigen, New York]; private collection, New York; sale, Heritage Auctions, Dallas, November 9–10, 2006, no. 24070, bought in; [Salander-O'Reilly Galleries, New York; to private collection]; private collection (until 2007; sale, Sotheby's, New York, October 23, 2007, no. 71); Pérez Simón Collection, Mexico City

SELECTED EXHIBITIONS: Paris 1885, no. 73; New Orleans–New York–Cincinnati 1996–97, no. 12; Rouen 1998, no. 55; London–Minneapolis–New York 2003–4, no. 62; Madrid–Barcelona 2011–12, no. 22

The French king Charles VI (r. 1380–1422) was prone to fits of madness and violence but could sometimes be calmed by his mistress, Odette de Champdivers (1390–1425). He was the subject of an 1826 play by Alexandre-Jean-Joseph de La Ville de Mirmont.

CAT. 24

The Duke of Orléans Showing His Lover
ca. 1825–26
Oil on canvas
13¾ x 10¹⁄₁₆ in. (35 x 25.5 cm)
Signed (lower left, on bed): *EUG. DELACROIX*
Museo Thyssen-Bornemisza, Madrid (inv. 127; 1977.19)
J 111
repr. p. 17

PROVENANCE: Frédéric Leblond (in 1832); sale, Schroth, Paris, March 6, 1843, no. 30; Frédéric Villot, Paris (until 1864; his sale, Hôtel des Commissaires-Priseurs, Paris, January 25, 1864, no. 12); Napoléon-Jérôme Bonaparte, prince de Montfort; comte Duchâtel (in 1885); Alfred Beurdeley (by 1912–d. 1919; his estate sale, Galerie Georges Petit, Paris, May 6–7, 1920, no. 34, to Nunès et Fiquet for d'Héricourt); Monsieur Schwob d'Héricourt (from 1920); [Paul Brame, Paris, 1967]; Mr. B. E. Bensinger, Beverly Hills, Calif. (in 1968); [Reid & Lefevre, London, by 1974–77; sold to Thyssen-Bornemisza]; Thyssen-Bornemisza Collection, Lugano (from 1977); Museo Thyssen-Bornemisza, Madrid (from 1992)

SELECTED EXHIBITIONS: Paris 1832, no. 145; Paris 1885, no. 71; Zürich–Frankfurt 1987–88, no. 18; Rouen 1998, no. 54; Madrid–Barcelona 2011–12, no. 23

CAT. 25

Count Demetrius de Palatiano (1794–1849) in Suliot Costume
ca. 1825–26
Oil on canvas
13⅜ x 10¼ in. (34 x 26 cm)
Signed (lower left): *E.D.*
Národní Galerie, Prague (inv. O 11446)
J 81a (in vol. 7, not vol. 3); see also J L80
repr. p. 40

PROVENANCE: A. Vidmann Sedlnitzý, Jaroměřice Castle (until 1955) and Národní Galerie, Prague (1955–63; placed on deposit by the Czech Commission of Historical Monuments); Národní Galerie, Prague (from 1963)

SELECTED EXHIBITIONS: Paris (Salon) 1827–28, no. 292 (probably this picture)

CAT. 26

Greece on the Ruins of Missolonghi
1826
Oil on canvas
82⁵⁄₁₆ x 57⅞ in. (209 x 147 cm)
Signed (lower left): *Eug. Delacroix.*
Musée des Beaux-Arts, Bordeaux (inv. Bx E 439)
J 98
repr. p. 72

PROVENANCE: the artist, Paris (until 1852; sold in February to Musée des Beaux-Arts, Bordeaux)

SELECTED EXHIBITIONS: Paris 1826a, not in catalogue; London 1828, no. 15; Paris 1829a, no. 7; Paris 1829b, no. 138; Paris 1830a, no. 90; Paris 1830b, no. 195; Paris (Mémorial) 1963, no. 111; Nantes–Paris–Piacenza 1995–96, no. 64; Bordeaux–Paris–Athens 1996–97,

no. 29; Rouen 1998, no. 147; London–Minneapolis–New York 2003–4, no. 8 (London and Minneapolis only); Madrid–Barcelona 2011–12, no. 28

This allegory was inspired by the catastrophic siege of the city of Missolonghi by Ottoman forces, between April 1825 and April 1826, a major event in the Greek War of Independence.

CAT. 27

Combat of the Giaour and Hassan
1826
Oil on canvas
23½ x 28⅞ in. (59.7 x 73.3 cm)
Signed (lower left): *Eug. Delacroix*
Art Institute of Chicago, Gift of Bertha Palmer Thorne, Rose Movius Palmer, Mr. and Mrs. Arthur M. Wood, and Mr. and Mrs. Gordon Palmer (1962.966)
J 114
repr. p. 33

PROVENANCE: Alexandre Dumas père (ca. 1827–May 1848); Charles Mahler (May 1848–at least 1885); Potter Palmer, Chicago (by 1889–d. 1902); his widow, Mrs. Berthe Honoré Palmer (1902–d. 1918; apparently kept at the Palmers' Paris address between 1892 and at least 1910); their son Potter Palmer Jr. (until d. 1943); his widow, Mrs. Pauline Kohlsaat Palmer (1943–d. 1956); her heirs and their spouses (1956–62; their gift to the Art Institute of Chicago)

SELECTED EXHIBITIONS: Paris 1826b, no. 44; Douai 1827, no. 94; rejected by the jury of the Paris Salon of 1827–28; Paris 1829b, no. 107; Paris 1846a, no. 98; Paris 1860, supp. no. 345; Paris 1864b, no. 78; Paris 1885, no. 135; New York 1991, no. 2; Rouen 1998, no. 116; London–Minneapolis–New York 2003–4, no. 76; Madrid–Barcelona 2011–12, no. 29; Paris 2014–15, no. 40

The subject of this painting (and cat. 87) is drawn from Lord Byron's poem *The Giaour*, first published in 1813.

CAT. 28

Justinian Drafting His Laws, sketch
1826
Oil on canvas
22¹⁄₁₆ x 18½ in. (56 x 47 cm)
Musée des Arts Décoratifs, Paris (inv. 27987)
J 120
repr. p. 36

PROVENANCE: the artist's estate sale, Hôtel Drouot, Paris, February 17–29, 1864, no. 53, to Corot; Camille Corot (1864–d. 1875); Alfred Robaut (until 1885;

sold in May to Chéramy); Paul-Arthur Chéramy, Paris (1885–d. 1912; his sale, Galerie Georges Petit, Paris, May 5–7, 1908, no. 175, unsold; his estate sale, Hôtel Drouot, Paris, April 14–16, 1913, no. 25, to Koechlin); Raymond Koechlin (1913–d. 1931; his bequest to Musée des Arts Décoratifs)

SELECTED EXHIBITIONS: Paris 1885, no. 175; Paris (Mémorial) 1963, no. 76; Zürich–Frankfurt 1987–88, no. 23; Rouen 1998, no. 148

The Byzantine emperor Justinian (r. 527–65) is shown drafting the set of laws known as the Justinian Code. The painting for which it was a study was commissioned by the state in 1826 for the Conseil d'Etat in the Palais du Louvre; in 1832 it was moved to the Palais d'Orsay, where it was destroyed during the Commune in 1871. It can be glimpsed in fig. 118.

CAT. 29

Baron Schwiter (Louis Auguste Schwiter, 1805–1889)
1826
Lithograph; only state
Image 8⅝ x 7⅞ in. (21.9 x 20 cm); sheet 11⅝ x 8¾ in. (29.6 x 22.3 cm)
The Metropolitan Museum of Art, New York, Purchase, Derald H. and Janet Ruttenberg Gift and The Elisha Whittelsey Collection, The Elisha Whittelsey Fund, 1983 (1983.1170)
D-S 51
New York only
repr. p. 38

PROVENANCE: [R. M. Light & Co., Santa Barbara, Calif., until 1983; sold to MMA]

SELECTED EXHIBITIONS (this impression): New York 1991, no. 84

CAT. 30

Louis Auguste Schwiter (1805–1889)
1826–27
Oil on canvas
85¾ x 56½ in. (217.8 x 143.5 cm)
Signed (lower left): *Eug. Delacroix.*
The National Gallery, London, Bought, 1918 (inv. NG3286)
J 82
repr. p. 39

PROVENANCE: the sitter (until d. 1889; his estate sale, Hôtel Drouot, Paris, March 26–28, 1890, no. 4, to Montaignac; [Montaignac, Paris, 1890–June 1895; sold to Degas in exchange for three of his pastels]); Edgar Degas, Paris (1895–d. 1917; his estate sale, Galerie Georges Petit, Paris, March 26–27, 1918, no. 24, to National Gallery)

SELECTED EXHIBITIONS: rejected by the jury of the Paris Salon of 1827–28; Paris (Mémorial) 1963, no. 75; New York 1997–98, no. 192; London–Minneapolis–New York 2003–4, no. 52; Madrid–Barcelona 2011–12, no. 39; Minneapolis–London 2015–16, no. 4

CAT. 31
Death of Sardanapalus, sketch
1826–27
Oil on canvas
31⅞ x 39⅜ in. (81 x 100 cm)
Musée du Louvre, Paris, Département des Peintures, Bequest of comtesse Paul de Salvandy, née Eugénie Rivet, 1925 (RF 2488)
J 124
repr. p. 51

PROVENANCE: gift of the artist to baron Charles Rivet (by 1849–d. 1872); his widow, baronne Rivet (1872–at least 1885); their daughter Eugénie, comtesse Paul de Salvandy (until 1925; her bequest to Louvre)

SELECTED EXHIBITIONS: Paris 1864b, no. 144; Paris 1885, no. 8; Nantes–Paris–Piacenza 1995–96, no. 65; London–Minneapolis–New York 2003–4, no. 78; Winterthur 2008, no. 9; Madrid–Barcelona 2011–12, no. 30; Leipzig 2015–16, no. 56

This is a sketch for fig. 20, of which cat. 104 is a replica.

CAT. 32
A Lady and Her Valet
ca. 1826–29
Oil on canvas
9⅝ x 12¹³⁄₁₆ in. (24.5 x 32.5 cm)
Private collection, courtesy of Art Cuéllar-Nathan
J 8
repr. p. 157

PROVENANCE: the artist's estate sale, Hôtel Drouot, Paris, February 17–29, 1864, no. 72, to Haro; Haro, Paris (from 1864); baron Joseph Vitta (in 1926); ?Roger de la Palme; sale, February 1963, possibly to Dubourg; [Jacques Dubourg, 1963; sold to Nathan]; Dr. Peter Nathan, Zürich (1963–d. 2001); his estate; private collection

SELECTED EXHIBITIONS: Zürich–Frankfurt 1987–88, no. 26; Karlsruhe 2003–4, no. 54

CAT. 33
Woman with a Parrot
1827
Oil on canvas
9⅝ x 12¹³⁄₁₆ in. (24.5 x 32.5 cm)
Signed and dated (upper left): *Eug. Delacroix. 1827.*
Musée des Beaux-Arts, Lyon, Gift of Monsieur Couturier de Royas, 1897 (inv. B-566)
J 9
repr. p. 92

PROVENANCE: Louis Joseph Auguste Coutan, Paris (until 1829; his anonymous sale, Paris, March 9–10, 1829, no. 50); Frédéric Leblond (by 1832–d. 1872); Couturier de Royas (until 1897; his gift to Musée des Beaux-Arts, Lyon)

SELECTED EXHIBITIONS: Paris 1832, no. 141; Paris (Mémorial) 1963, no. 109; Zürich–Frankfurt 1987–88, no. 27; Tokyo–Nagoya 1989, no. 34; Madrid–Barcelona 2011–12, no. 44

CAT. 34
Seated Turk (possibly Paul Barroilhet, 1805–1871)
ca. 1827–30
Oil on canvas
18⁵⁄₁₆ x 14¹⁵⁄₁₆ in. (46.5 x 38 cm)
Musée du Louvre, Paris, Département des Peintures (RF 1953-37), on deposit at the Musée National Eugène-Delacroix
J D13
New York only
repr. p. 56

PROVENANCE: Gérard (in November 1879); P. Tesse; Gérard fils (until 1892; sold in February to Bernheim); [Bernheim-Jeune, Paris, 1892–93; sold in February to Chéramy], Paul-Arthur Chéramy, Paris (1893–1908; his sale, Galerie Georges Petit, Paris, May 5–7, 1908, no. 163, to Vitta); baron Vitta, Paris (1908–ca. 1934; gift to the Atelier Delacroix, Paris; transferred in 1953 to Louvre)

SELECTED EXHIBITIONS: Madrid–Barcelona 2011–12, no. 46; Chantilly 2012–13, no. 10

CAT. 35
A Greek and a Turk in an Interior
late 1820s
Watercolor on paper
6¹¹⁄₁₆ x 9⁷⁄₁₆ in. (17 x 24 cm)
Signed (lower right): *Eug. Delacroix*
Private collection
New York only
repr. p. 15

PROVENANCE: Georges Petit, Paris (until 1921; his sale, Galerie Georges Petit, Paris, March 4–5, 1921, no. 9); [possibly Wildenstein, New York, 1944]; T. Edward Hanley, Bradford, Pa. (by 1961–d. 1969); his widow, Tullah Innes Hanley (1969–at least 1970); private collection (from early 1970s)

SELECTED EXHIBITIONS: Zürich 1987–88, no. 16

CAT. 36
Faust
Book by Johann Wolfgang von Goethe, translated from the German by Philipp Albert Stapfer
18 lithographs by Delacroix, including frontispiece portrait of the author and 17 illustrations
Printed and published by Charles Motte, Paris, 1828
Overall: 16³⁄₁₆ x 10⅝ x 1¹⁵⁄₁₆ in. (41.1 x 27 x 3.3 cm)
The Metropolitan Museum of Art, New York, Rogers Fund, 1917 (17.12)
D-S 57–74
New York only (not illustrated)

PROVENANCE: [E. Weyhe, New York, until 1917; sold to MMA]

SELECTED EXHIBITIONS (this copy): New York 1991, no. 85; Paris–New York 2002–3, no. 120 (New York only)

This epic tragedy, written in 1808 in the form of a drama in verse, recounts the corruption of Faust by the demon Mephistopheles, who has made a bet with God that he can win the protagonist to his side.

CAT. 37
Mephistopheles Flying over the City (Study for "Faust," plate 1)
ca. 1825–27
Pen and brown ink on wove paper
9¹³⁄₁₆ x 7½ in. (25 x 19 cm)
Houghton Library, Harvard University, Cambridge, Mass., Bequest of Philip Hofer (TypDr 815.D320.28f [6]Sz 3)
New York only
repr. p. 64

PROVENANCE: the artist's estate sale, Hôtel Drouot, Paris, February 17–29, 1864, possibly part of no. 391; said to have been in the Villot, Forgier, Sensier, and Doria collections (without documentation); [Nicolas Rauch, Geneva, until 1960; sold to Hofer]; Philip Hofer, Cambridge, Mass. (1960–d. 1984; his bequest to Houghton)

SELECTED EXHIBITIONS: Frankfurt 1987–88, no. E 2

CAT. 38
Faust, plate 1: Mephistopheles Aloft
1826/27
Lithograph on chine collé; first state of seven
Image $11\frac{15}{16}$ x $9\frac{13}{16}$ in. (30.4 x 25 cm); sheet $21\frac{1}{2}$ x $14\frac{1}{4}$ in. (54.6 x 36.2 cm)
Petit Palais, Musée des Beaux-Arts de la Ville de Paris, Collection Dutuit (inv. GDUT1821)
D-S 58
New York only
repr. p. 64

PROVENANCE: Eugène Dutuit (until d. 1886) and his brother Auguste Dutuit, Paris (until d. 1902); their bequest to the city of Paris; Musée du Petit Palais, Paris (from December 11, 1902)

CAPTION, introduced in the second state: . . . De temps en temps j'aime à voir le vieux Père, / Et je me garde bien de lui romper en Visière . . . (I like to see the Old Man now and then, and take good care to keep on speaking terms.)

CAT. 39
Faust, plate 2: Faust in His Study
1826/27
Lithograph; first state of eight, with remarques
Image $9\frac{11}{16}$ x $7\frac{1}{16}$ in. (24.6 x 18 cm); sheet $14\frac{3}{4}$ x $11\frac{3}{16}$ in. (37.5 x 28.4 cm)
Petit Palais, Musée des Beaux-Arts de la Ville de Paris, Collection Dutuit (inv. GDUT1822)
D-S 59
repr. p. 64

PROVENANCE: see cat. 38

CAPTION, introduced in the third state: Pauvre crâne vide que me veux tu dire avec ton grincement hideux? (You empty skull, why do you bare your teeth at me?)

CAT. 40
Faust, plate 3: Faust and Wagner
1826/27
Lithograph; first state of seven, with remarques
Image $7\frac{11}{16}$ x $10\frac{5}{16}$ in. (19.6 x 26.2 cm); sheet $10\frac{5}{8}$ x $14\frac{3}{8}$ in. (27 x 36.5 cm)
Petit Palais, Musée des Beaux-Arts de la Ville de Paris, Collection Dutuit (inv. GDUT1832)
D-S 60
New York only
repr. p. 64

PROVENANCE: see cat. 38

CAPTION, introduced in the third state: Faust—Heurex qui peut conserver l'espérance de surnager sur cet océan d'erreurs! . . . / . . . l'esprit a beau deployer ses ailes, le corps, hélas! n'en a point à y ajouter. (Faust—Happy the man who can still hope to swim to safety in this sea of errors! . . . Alas! it is so hard to find corporeal wings that match those of the human mind.)

CAT. 41
Faust, plate 4: Faust, Wagner, and the Poodle
1826/27
Lithograph; first state of four
Image $9\frac{3}{16}$ x $8\frac{1}{16}$ in. (23.3 x 20.4 cm); sheet $18\frac{1}{8}$ x $12\frac{3}{16}$ in. (46 x 31 cm)
Petit Palais, Musée des Beaux-Arts de la Ville de Paris, Collection Dutuit (inv. GDUT1828)
D-S 61
New York only
repr. p. 65

PROVENANCE: see cat. 38

CAPTION: Il grogne et n'ose vous aborder: Il se couche sur le ventre: / Il remue la queue. . . . (It snarls and hesitates, lies down on its belly, it wags its tail. . . .)

CAT. 42
Faust, plate 5: Mephistopheles Appearing to Faust
1826/27
Lithograph; first state of five
Image $10\frac{1}{4}$ x $8\frac{3}{8}$ in. (26 x 21.3 cm); sheet $13\frac{5}{16}$ x $10\frac{7}{16}$ in. (33.8 x 26.5 cm)
Petit Palais, Musée des Beaux-Arts de la Ville de Paris, Collection Dutuit (inv. GDUT1823)
D-S 62
New York only
repr. p. 65

PROVENANCE: see cat. 38

CAPTION, introduced in the second state: Meph: Pourquoi tout ce vacarme? que demande Monsieur? qu'n a-t'il pour son service? (Mephistopheles: What's all the noise? Sire, how can I be of service?)

CAT. 43
Faust, plate 6: Mephistopheles Receiving the Student
1826/27
Lithograph; first state of two
Image $10\frac{3}{8}$ x $8\frac{11}{16}$ in. (26.4 x 22 cm); sheet $12\frac{3}{8}$ x $10\frac{1}{8}$ in. (31.4 x 25.7 cm)
Petit Palais, Musée des Beaux-Arts de la Ville de Paris, Collection Dutuit (inv. GDUT1824[B])
D-S 63
New York only
repr. p. 65

PROVENANCE: see cat. 38

CAPTION: Meph: Ce que vous avez de mieux à faire, c'est de jurer sur la parole du maître . . . / . . . tenez vous en aux mots: vous êtes sur d'entrer par la grande porte au temple de la vérité. (Mephistopheles: Here, too it's best to listen to a single teacher and swear by every word he utters. Make it a principle to give your word of allegiance! You then will enter by the one safe gate into the temple of certitude.)

CAT. 44
Faust and Mephistopheles in the Tavern (Study for "Faust," plate 7)
1825/26
Ink wash in shades of gray to black over graphite on wove paper
$10\frac{5}{8}$ x $8\frac{11}{16}$ in. (27 x 22 cm)
Houghton Library, Harvard University, Cambridge, Mass., Bequest of Philip Hofer (TypDr 815.D320.28f [2] Sz 3)
New York only
repr. p. 66

PROVENANCE: the artist's estate sale, Hôtel Drouot, Paris, February 17–29, 1864, probably no. 386; Albert Pontremoli, Paris (until d. 1923; his estate sale, Hôtel Drouot, Paris, June 11, 1924, no. 19, to Petit); [Georges Petit, Paris, from 1924]; Georges Aubry, Paris (until 1933; his sale, Hôtel Drouot, Paris, March 11, 1933, no. 66); Maurice Gobin, Paris (until ca. 1935; sold to Hofer); Philip Hofer, Cambridge, Mass. (ca. 1935–d. 1984; his bequest to Houghton)

SELECTED EXHIBITIONS: Frankfurt 1987–88, no. E 13

CAT. 45
Faust, plate 7: Mephistopheles in Auerbach's Tavern
1826
Lithograph; first state of six
Image $10\frac{5}{8}$ x $8\frac{3}{4}$ in. (27 x 22.3 cm); sheet $18\frac{9}{16}$ x 12 in. (47.1 x 30.5 cm)
Petit Palais, Musée des Beaux-Arts de la Ville de Paris, Collection Dutuit (inv. GDUT1827)
D-S 64
New York only
repr. p. 66

PROVENANCE: see cat. 38

CAPTION, introduced in the second state:—Au feu, à l'aide, l'enfer s'allume.—Sorcellerie! jettez vous sur lui . . . son affaire ne sera pas longue. (I'm burning! I'm on fire! It's black magic! Stab him! The fellow is outside the law!)

CAT. 46

Faust, Marguerite, and Mephistopheles in the Street (Study for "Faust," plate 8)
ca. 1825–27
Pen, pencil, and brown wash on wove paper
9⁷⁄₁₆ x 7½ in. (24 x 19 cm)
Houghton Library, Harvard University, Cambridge, Mass., Bequest of Philip Hofer (TypDr 815.D320.28f [3] Sz 3)
New York only
repr. p. 66

PROVENANCE: the artist's estate sale, Hôtel Drouot, Paris, February 17–29, 1864, probably no. 387; Albert Pontremoli, Paris (until d. 1923; his estate sale, Hôtel Drouot, Paris, June 11, 1924, no. 18, to Godefroy); Godefroy (from 1924); Philip Hofer, Cambridge, Mass. (until d. 1984; his bequest to Houghton)

SELECTED EXHIBITIONS: Frankfurt 1987–88, no. E 15

CAT. 47

Faust, plate 8: Faust Trying to Seduce Marguerite
1826/27
Lithograph; first state of seven
Image 10½ x 8½ in. (26.7 x 21.6 cm); sheet 13⁹⁄₁₆ x 10¾ in. (34.5 x 27.3 cm)
Petit Palais, Musée des Beaux-Arts de la Ville de Paris, Collection Dutuit (inv. GDUT1825)
D-S 65
New York only
repr. p. 66

PROVENANCE: see cat. 38

CAPTION, introduced in the second state: Faust—Ma belle Demoiselle, oseraisje vous offrir mon bras et vous reconduire chez vous? (Faust: My lovely young lady, may I perhaps venture to give you my arm and be your escort home?)

CAT. 48

Faust, plate 9: Mephistopheles Introduces Himself at Martha's House
1827
Lithograph; first state of seven, with remarques
Image 9⁷⁄₁₆ x 7¹⁵⁄₁₆ in. (24 x 20.2 cm); remarques 16 x 12⅝ in. (40.7 x 32 cm); sheet 17 x 12⅞ in. (43.2 x 32.7 cm)
Petit Palais, Musée des Beaux-Arts de la Ville de Paris, Collection Dutuit (inv. GDUT1826)
D-S 66
New York only
repr. p. 47

PROVENANCE: see cat. 38

CAPTION, introduced in the third state: Meph: Il est bien hardi à moi de m'introduire aussi brusquement chez ces Dames, je leur en demande un million de pardons. . . . (Mephistopheles: I know I am intruding, unannounced, and I hope you ladies will pardon me. . . .)

CAT. 49

Faust, plate 10: Marguerite at the Spinning Wheel
1826/27
Lithograph; first state of six, with remarques
Image 8¾ x 7¹⁄₁₆ in. (22.2 x 18 cm); sheet 13¼ x 9¹⁵⁄₁₆ in. (33.7 x 25.3 cm)
Petit Palais, Musée des Beaux-Arts de la Ville de Paris, Collection Dutuit (inv. GDUT1829)
D-S 67
New York only
repr. p. 67

PROVENANCE: see cat. 38

CAPTION, introduced in the second state: Sans lui l'existence / N'est qu'un lourd fardeau / Ce monde si beau / N'est qu'un tombeau / Dans son absence. (Where he is not, is like the grave, and all my world is turned to gall.)

CAT. 50

Faust, plate 11: Duel between Faust and Valentin
1826/27
Lithograph; first state of six, with remarques
Image 9¹⁄₁₆ x 11⁷⁄₁₆ in. (23 x 29 cm); sheet 11 x 14¹⁵⁄₁₆ in. (28 x 38 cm)
Petit Palais, Musée des Beaux-Arts de la Ville de Paris, Collection Dutuit (inv. GDUT1830)
D-S 68
New York only
repr. p. 67

PROVENANCE: see cat. 38

CAPTION, introduced in the third state: Meph:—Pousse . . . Val.— oh! . . . Meph:— Voila mon rustaud apprivoisé. (Mephistopheles: Now strike! . . . Valentine: What pain! . . . Mephistopheles: There, we have tamed that lout! Night.)

CAT. 51

Faust, plate 12: Mephistopheles and Faust Fleeing after the Duel
1826/27
Lithograph; second state of seven, with remarques
Image 10⅜ x 8⅞ in. (26.3 x 22.5 cm); sheet 13⁵⁄₁₆ x 11³⁄₁₆ in. (33.8 x 28.4 cm)
Petit Palais, Musée des Beaux-Arts de la Ville de Paris, Collection Dutuit (inv. GDUT1831)
D-S 69
New York only
repr. p. 67

PROVENANCE: see cat. 38

CAPTION: Meph:—Il nous faut gagner promptement au large. (Mephistopheles: We must make ourselves scarce at once.)

CAT. 52

Faust, plate 13: Marguerite in Church
1826/27
Lithograph; second state of five
Image 10⅝ x 8⅞ in. (27 x 22.5 cm); sheet 13¼ x 10½ in. (33.7 x 26.7 cm)
Petit Palais, Musée des Beaux-Arts de la Ville de Paris, Collection Dutuit (inv. GDUT1833)
D-S 70
New York only
repr. p. 67

PROVENANCE: see cat. 38

CAPTION: Marg:—Malheureuse! ah! si je pouvais me soustraire aux pensées qui se succedent en tumulte dans mon âme et s'elévent contre moi / Le mauvais Esprit.—La colère de Dieu fond sur toi! la trompette sonne . . . Malheur à toi. / Choeur.—Judex ergo sum sedebit, / Quid quid latet apparebit. / Nil inultum remanebit. (Marguerite: Alas! Could I but escape these thoughts that come at me from every side, do what I will! Spirit: Feel God's wrath! Hear the trumpet sound . . . your heart brought back again to burn in torment. . . . Choir: When the Judge will sit, that which is hidden will appear. Nothing will remain unpunished.)

CAT. 53

Faust, plate 14: Faust and Mephistopheles in the Harz Mountains
1826/27
Lithograph; first state of seven, with remarques
Image 9½ x 8¼ in. (24.2 x 21 cm); sheet 14⁵⁄₁₆ x 10¹³⁄₁₆ in. (36.3 x 27.5 cm)
Petit Palais, Musée des Beaux-Arts de la Ville de Paris, Collection Dutuit (inv. GDUT1834[A])
D-S 71
New York only
repr. p. 68

PROVENANCE: see cat. 38

CAPTION, introduced in the third state: Meph:—Nous sommes encore loin du terme de notre course. (Mephistopheles: This way, it's too long until we reach our destination.)

CAT. 54
Faust, plate 15: Marguerite's Ghost Appearing to Faust
1826/27
Lithograph; first state of six, with remarques
Image 10⅞ x 13¹³⁄₁₆ in. (27.7 x 35.1 cm); sheet 12¹⁄₁₆ x
17⅛ in. (30.7 x 43.5 cm)
Petit Palais, Musée des Beaux-Arts de la Ville de
Paris, Collection Dutuit (inv. GDUT1835)
D-S 72
New York only
repr. p. 68

PROVENANCE: see cat. 38

CAPTION, introduced in the third state: Meph: Laisse
cet objet, on ne se trouve jamais bien de le
regarder . . . tu as bien entendu raconter l'histoire de
meduse? Faust: Assurément ce sont là les yeux d'un
mort, qu'une / main amie n'a point fermés; c'est-là le
sein que Marguerite m'a livre, c'est le corps charmant
que j'ai possédé. (Mephistopheles: Leave that
alone—it can only do harm! . . . You've surely heard
about Medusa! Faust: I know those are the eyes of
someone dead, eyes that no loving hand has closed.
That is the breast which Gretchen let me press, that
the sweet body which give me joy.)

CAT. 55
*Faust, plate 16: Faust and Mephistopheles Galloping
on Walpurgis Night*
1826
Lithograph; first state of five, with remarques
Image 8⅜ x 11⁷⁄₁₆ in. (21.2 x 29 cm); sheet 10¹¹⁄₁₆ x
13⁷⁄₁₆ in. (27.2 x 34.1 cm)
Petit Palais, Musée des Beaux-Arts de la Ville de
Paris, Collection Dutuit (inv. GDUT1836)
D-S 73
New York only
repr. p. 68

PROVENANCE: see cat. 38

CAPTION, introduced in the second state: Faust:—
Que vois-je remuer autour de ce gibet? . . . / . . . ils
vont et viennent, ils se baissent et se relevent. Meph:
— C'est une assemblée de Sorciers. Faust: — Ils
sèment et consacrent. / Meph:—En avant! (Faust:
What are you doing by that stone block?. . . . They
soar up, and then down; they are bending and
bowing. Mephistopheles: A witches' coven. Faust:
They strew and consecrate. Mephistopheles: On!
Hurry on!)

CAT. 56
Faust, plate 17: Faust with Marguerite in Prison
1826/27
Lithograph; first state of seven
Image 9¹³⁄₁₆ x 8¹⁄₁₆ in. (25 x 20.5 cm); sheet 13³⁄₁₆ x
10¹³⁄₁₆ in. (33.5 x 27.5 cm)
Petit Palais, Musée des Beaux-Arts de la Ville de
Paris, Collection Dutuit (inv. GDUT1837)
D-S 74
New York only
repr. p. 68

PROVENANCE: see cat. 38

CAPTION, introduced in the second state: Faust—
Reviens à toi! un seul pas et tu es libre . . . /
Meph:— . . . Que de paroles inutiles! que de delais et
d'incertitudes! / mes chevaux frissonnent: l'aube
blanchit l'horizon. (Faust: Be sensible, I beg you! One
step, just one! and you'll be free . . . Mephistopheles:
Futile faintheartedness! Delaying and prattling! My
horses are trembling; there's a first glimmer of dawn.)

CAT. 57
Wild Horse Felled by a Tiger
1828
Lithograph with chine collé; first state of four
Image 8¾ x 11¼ in. (22.2 x 28.6 cm); sheet 8¹¹⁄₁₆ x
10¹³⁄₁₆ in. (23 x 27.4 cm)
The Metropolitan Museum of Art, New York, Rogers
Fund, 1922 (22.63.43)
D-S 77
New York only
repr. p. 44

PROVENANCE: [Maurice Le Garrec, Paris, until 1922;
sold to MMA]

SELECTED EXHIBITIONS (this impression): Frankfurt
1987–88, no. I 18; New York 1991, no. 89; New York
2000–2001, no. 36

CAPTION, introduced in the second state: *Cheval
sauvage terrassé par un tigre*

CAT. 58
Wild Horse Felled by a Tiger
1828
Watercolor and gouache over pen and ink, with
touches of gum arabic on wove paper
5⁵⁄₁₆ x 7¹⁵⁄₁₆ in. (13.5 x 20.1 cm)
Signed (lower left): *EugDelacroix* [*g* and *D* in ligature]
The Metropolitan Museum of Art, New York,
Promised Gift from the Karen B. Cohen Collection
of Eugène Delacroix, in memory of Alexandre P.
Rosenberg
New York only
repr. p. 44

PROVENANCE: [Brame & Lorenceau, Paris, until
1986]; [Paul Rosenberg & Co., New York, 1986];
Karen B. Cohen, New York (from 1986)

SELECTED EXHIBITIONS: Frankfurt 1987–88, no. I 17;
New York 1991, no. 88; London–Minneapolis–New
York 2003–4, no. 173 (Minneapolis and New York
only); Paris 2009–10, no. 76

CAT. 59
Wild Horse
1828
Lithograph; first state of two
Image 9 x 9¼ in. (22.9 x 23.5 cm); sheet 12³⁄₁₆ x
10¼ in. (31 x 26 cm)
The Metropolitan Museum of Art, New York,
Harris Brisbane Dick Fund, 1931 (31.77.20)
D-S 78
New York only
repr. p. 45

PROVENANCE: Adolphe Moreau fils, Paris (d. 1882);
probably his son Etienne Moreau-Nélaton (d. 1927);
[Neuville & Vivien, Paris, until 1931; sold to MMA]

SELECTED EXHIBITIONS (this impression): New York
1991, no. 90

CAT. 60
Studies of a Lion, from *Sketchbook with Views of Tours,
France and Its Environs*, ca. 1824–29
Graphite on wove paper
4¹⁵⁄₁₆ x 7¹¹⁄₁₆ in. (12.5 x 19.5 cm)
Dated (lower left): *jeudi 12 février*
The Metropolitan Museum of Art, New York, Gift of
Alexander and Grégoire Tarnopol, 1969 (69.165.2)
New York only
repr. p. 43

PROVENANCE: the artist's estate sale, Hôtel Drouot,
Paris, February 17–29, 1864, probably part of
no. 664; Alexander Tarnopol and his brother
Grégoire Tarnopol, New York (until 1969)

SELECTED EXHIBITIONS: New York 1991, part of
no. 72; Tours 1998, part of no. 15

Delacroix used the sketchbook from which this sheet
derives during a visit to his elder brother Charles
Henry at Tours, from late October to early
November 1828. But the date on this study, Thursday,
February 12, must refer either to 1824 or to 1829, after
the artist returned to Paris.

CAT. 61

Sketches of Tigers and Men in Sixteenth-Century Costume
ca. 1828–29
Watercolor, pen and iron gall ink, and graphite on ivory laid paper with blue fibers discolored to buff
15⅝ x 20¹⁄₁₆ in. (39.7 x 51 cm)
Art Institute of Chicago, David Adler Memorial Fund (1971.309R)
New York only
repr. p. 46

PROVENANCE: [Otto Wertheimer, until 1971; sold to Art Institute of Chicago]

SELECTED EXHIBITIONS: Frankfurt 1987–88, no. I 9

CAT. 62

Nineteen Studies of Heads and Skulls of Lions
ca. 1828–30
Graphite on paper
12 x 18½ in. (30.5 x 47 cm)
The Metropolitan Museum of Art, New York, Promised Gift from the Karen B. Cohen Collection of Eugène Delacroix, in memory of Charles C. Bassine
New York only
repr. p. 43

PROVENANCE: de Vallière (late 19th century); [Georges Ambroselli, Paris]; [Saint Germain Arts, Ltd]; Karen B. Cohen, New York

SELECTED EXHIBITIONS: Frankfurt 1987–88, no. I 8; Paris 2009–10, no. 79

CAT. 63

Tiger Lying at the Entrance of Its Lair
ca. 1828–30
Etching, drypoint, and roulette; between fourth and fifth states
Image 5½ x 3⁹⁄₁₆ in. (14 x 9 cm); sheet 9¹⁄₁₆ x 8¼ in. (23 x 20.9 cm)
The Metropolitan Museum of Art, New York, Harris Brisbane Dick Fund, 1927 (27.10.7)
D-S 24
New York only
repr. p. 43

PROVENANCE: John Waterloo Wilson, Paris (d. 1883; his estate sale, Sotheby's, London, April 22–23, 1887, no. 5); [Arthur H. Harlow & Co., New York, until 1927; sold to MMA]

CAT. 64

The Murder of the Bishop of Liège
1829
Oil on canvas
35¹³⁄₁₆ x 45¹¹⁄₁₆ in. (91 x 116 cm)
Musée du Louvre, Paris, Département des Peintures (RF 1961-13)
J 135
repr. p. 61

PROVENANCE: Ferdinand Philippe, duc d'Orléans (1831–d. 1842); his widow (1842–53; her sale, Hôtel des Ventes, Paris, January 18, 1853, no. 17, to Villot); Frédéric Villot (1853–66; his sale, Hôtel des Commissaires-Priseurs, Paris, February 11, 1865, no. 1, bought in; sold on August 19, 1866, to Durand-Ruel); [Durand-Ruel, Paris, from 1866; sold to Bey]; Khalil Bey, Paris (until 1868; his sale, Hôtel Drouot, Paris, January 16–18, 1868, no. 17, to Durand-Ruel); [Durand-Ruel, 1868; sold in April to Francis Petit for Cassin]; Madame de Cassin, later marquise Landolfo Carcano (1868–1912; her sale, Galerie Georges Petit, Paris, May 30–June 1, 1912, no. 23, to Tauber); Léonard Tauber, Paris (1912–d. 1944); Tauber heirs (1944; sold to Gérard); Gérard (from 1944); Léon Salavin (until 1961; to Louvre)

SELECTED EXHIBITIONS: Paris 1829b, no. 108; Paris 1830a, no. 58; London 1830, no. 328; Paris (Salon) 1831, 3rd supplement, no. 2949; Paris (Mémorial) 1963, no. 136; Rouen 1998, no. 59

The subject is drawn from Sir Walter Scott's historical novel *Quentin Durward*, first published in 1823.

CAT. 65

Royal Tiger
1829
Lithograph; second state of five
Image 12¹⁵⁄₁₆ x 18⁷⁄₁₆ in. (32.8 x 46.9 cm); sheet 13¹⁄₁₆ x 18⅝ in. (33.2 x 47.3 cm)
The Metropolitan Museum of Art, New York, Bequest of Susan Dwight Bliss, 1966 (67.630.7)
D-S 80
New York only
repr. p. 44

PROVENANCE: Susan Dwight Bliss, New York (until d. 1966)

SELECTED EXHIBITIONS (this impression): New York 1991, no. 92

CAPTION, introduced in the third state: TIGRE ROYAL

Royal Tiger and *Lion of the Atlas Mountains* (cat. 66) were published as pendants by Gaugain, Paris, in January 1830.

CAT. 66

Lion of the Atlas Mountains
1829–30
Lithograph; probably second state of four
13 x 18⅜ in. (33 x 46.7 cm)
The Metropolitan Museum of Art, New York, Bequest of Susan Dwight Bliss, 1966 (67.630.13)
D-S 79
New York only
repr. p. 45

PROVENANCE: Susan Dwight Bliss, New York (until d. 1966)

SELECTED EXHIBITIONS (this impression): New York 1991, no. 91

CAPTION (lower margin): *LION DE L'ATLAS.*

CAT. 67

Young Tiger Playing with Its Mother (Study of Two Tigers)
1830
Oil on canvas
51⁹⁄₁₆ x 76⁹⁄₁₆ in. (131 x 194.5 cm)
Signed and dated (lower left): *Eug. Delacroix. / 1830.*
Musée du Louvre, Paris, Département des Peintures, Bequest of Maurice Cottier, 1881 (with life interest), entered the collection in 1903 (RF 1943)
J 59
repr. p. 42

PROVENANCE: thought to have been purchased from the artist by Auguste Thuret (probably 1830–at least 1862); [Francis Petit, Paris, in 1865]; Maurice Cottier (until d. 1881; his bequest to the Louvre with life interest to his wife; entered Louvre in 1903)

SELECTED EXHIBITIONS: Paris 1830c, no. 55; Paris (Salon) 1831, no. 516; Paris 1861–62; Paris 1885, no. 51; Paris (Mémorial) 1963, no. 134; Karlsruhe 2003–4, no. 82; Madrid–Barcelona 2011–12, no. 73

CAT. 68

The Battle of Poitiers
1830
Oil on canvas
44⅞ x 57½ in. (114 x 146 cm)
Signed and dated (lower left): *E. Delacroix, 1830*
Musée du Louvre, Paris, Département des Peintures (RF 3153)
J 141
New York only
repr. p. 105

PROVENANCE: the artist (until 1831; commissioned in 1829 by the duchesse de Berry and apparently delivered to her; she fled to England during the July Revolution of 1830, leaving it unpaid for; her sale, Paris, December 8, 1830, no. 10, but apparently withdrawn, the artist having regained possession, possibly by obtaining an injunction to prevent its sale; in November 1831 he arranged for its sale by Monsieur Paillet, commissaire-expert des Musées Royaux); vicomte d'Osembray (possibly from 1831, certainly by 1855–at least 1864); Marmontel (until 1868; his sale, Hôtel Drouot, Paris, May 11–14, 1868, no. 6); Monsieur Edwards (until 1870; his sale, Hôtel Drouot, Paris, March 7, 1870, no. 4, to Aguado); Eugène Pereire (in 1885); [Barbazanges, in December 1921]; [Hodebert, in 1925]; [Matthiesen, Berlin, by 1926–31; sold to Louvre]

SELECTED EXHIBITIONS: Paris 1855, no. 2919; Paris 1864b, no. 6 (probably this work); Paris 1885, no. 214; Paris (Mémorial) 1963, no. 123; Tokyo–Nagoya 1989, no. 18; Rouen 1998, no. 149; Madrid–Barcelona 2011–12, no. 72

English forces led by Edward, Prince of Wales, known as the Black Prince (1330–1376), won this battle of 1356, part of the Hundred Years' War, against King Jean II of France (1319–1364).

CAT. 69

The Battle of Nancy and the Death of Charles the Bold, Duke of Burgundy, January 5, 1477
1831
Oil on canvas
93⁵⁄₁₆ in. x 11 ft. 8³⁄₁₆ in. (237 x 356 cm)
Signed and dated (lower right): *EUG. DELACROIX. / F. 1831.*
Musée des Beaux-Arts, Nancy (inv. MPR 1809)
J 143
repr. p. 58

PROVENANCE: commissioned by King Charles X on August 28, 1828, for the municipal museum of Nancy; delivered in 1833

SELECTED EXHIBITIONS: Paris (Salon) 1834, no. 494; Paris 1855, no. 2920; Paris 1864b, no. 2; Paris 1885, no. 157; Paris (Mémorial) 1963, no. 196; Zürich–Frankfurt 1987–88, no. 37; Tokyo–Nagoya 1989, no. 69; Rouen 1998, no. 151

Charles the Bold was vanquished by forces led by René II, duc de Lorraine.

CAT. 70

Boissy d'Anglas at the Convention, sketch
1831
Oil on canvas
31⅛ x 40¹⁵⁄₁₆ in. (79 x 104 cm)

Signed and dated (lower left): *Eug. Delacroix 1831*
Musée des Beaux-Arts, Bordeaux (inv. Bx E 820)
J 147
New York only
repr. p. 106

PROVENANCE: Bouruet-Aubertot (in 1860); Amédée Larrieu, Bordeaux (in May 1869); John Saulnier, Bordeaux (by 1885–86; his estate sale, Hôtel Drouot, Paris, June 5, 1886, no. 34, to the city of Bordeaux for the Musée des Beaux-Arts)

SELECTED EXHIBITIONS: Paris 1831; Paris 1855, no. 2925; Paris 1860, supplement no. 344; Paris 1885, no. 196; Paris (Mémorial) 1963, no. 142; Zürich–Frankfurt 1987–88, no. 39; Rouen 1998, no. 152; Karlsruhe 2003–4, no. 91; Leipzig 2015–16, no. 4

François Antoine de Boissy d'Anglas (1756–1826) retained his composure throughout an extended speech delivered before a riotous crowd at the National Convention on May 20, 1795. This sketch was submitted for a competition to decorate the wall behind the rostrum of the Chamber of Deputies in the Palais Bourbon, but was not selected.

CAT. 71

Interior of a Dominican Convent in Madrid (L'Amende Honorable)
1831
Oil on canvas
51¼ x 63¾ in. (130.2 x 161.9 cm)
Signed and dated (lower center): *EUG. DELACROIX 1831*
Philadelphia Museum of Art: Purchased with the W. P. Wilstach Fund, 1894 (W 1894-1-2)
J 148
New York only
repr. p. 62

PROVENANCE: Ferdinand Philippe, duc d'Orléans (by 1836–d. 1842); his widow (1842–53; her sale, Hôtel des Ventes, Paris, January 18, 1853, no. 18); van Isacker (until 1857; his sale, rue Drouot, 5, Paris, April 24, 1857, no. 14, to Bouruet-Aubertot); A. Bouruet-Aubertot (until at least 1864, possibly until d. 1869); [Brame, Paris]; Monsieur Edwards (until 1870; his sale, Hôtel Drouot, Paris, March 7, 1870, no. 3, apparently bought in or sold to a family member); [Durand-Ruel, Paris, in 1872]; James Duncan of Benmore (by 1885–89; his sale, Hôtel Drouot, Paris, April 15, 1889, no. 10, to Durand-Ruel); [Durand-Ruel, Paris, from 1889]; Philadelphia Museum of Art (from 1894)

SELECTED EXHIBITIONS: Paris (Salon) 1834, no. 495; Paris 1846b, no. 20; Paris 1860, supplement no. 343; Paris 1864b, no. 132; Paris 1885, no. 74; Paris (Mémorial) 1963, no. 199; Zürich–Frankfurt

1987–88, no. 38; Rouen 1998, no. 60; London–Minneapolis–New York 2003–4, no. 60; Madrid–Barcelona 2011–12, no. 75

The scene is drawn from Charles Robert Maturin's novel *Melmoth the Wanderer*, published in English in 1820 and in French the following year.

CAT. 72

Jewish Woman of Tangier
1832
Pencil on paper
11 x 8 in. (27.9 x 20.3 cm)
Dated (lower right): *28 jr*
Private collection
New York only
repr. p. 80

PROVENANCE: the artist's estate sale, Hôtel Drouot, Paris, February 17–29, 1864, probably one of two drawings under no. 556, one to Emile Gavet and the other to Francis Petit; Roger Marx, Paris; his son, Claude Roger-Marx, Paris; Henri Benezit; [Paris art market, until ca. 2005]; private collection

In a *Journal* entry that corresponds to the date inscribed on this sheet, January 28, 1832, Delacroix recorded a visit to the home of his interpreter, Abraham Ben-Chimol (Delacroix 2009, vol. 1, p. 201). This may be one of Ben-Chimol's daughters, one of whom appears in the slightly later watercolor exhibited here as cat. 76.

CAT. 73

Portrait of Schmareck, Tanner at Tangier
1832
Watercolor with red and black chalk on paper
10¼ x 7⅛ in. (26 x 18.1 cm)
Stamped (lower right): *ED*
Private collection
New York only
repr. p. 83

PROVENANCE: the artist's estate sale, Hôtel Drouot, Paris, February 17–29, 1864; Dr. Paul Brodin (in 1916); Etienne Moreau-Nélaton, Paris; by descent to private collection; [Galerie de Bayser, Paris; until 2009; sold to private collection]; private collection (from 2009)

In a *Journal* entry written at Tangier on January 28, 1832, Delacroix described "Schmareck in his shirt and leather apron"; the latter has been identified as a tanner employed by Abraham Ben-Chimol (Delacroix 2009, vol. 1, pp. 201, 203). For a summary sketch of the figure and a mention of "la tanerie," see fig. 30.

CAT. 74

Standing Moroccan

1832

Watercolor and pencil on paper

10⅝ x 7 1/16 in. (27 x 18 cm)

Dated and inscribed (lower left): *2 mars / promenade avec M. Hay / diné chez lui*; stamped (lower right): *ED*

Private collection

New York only

repr. p. 83

PROVENANCE: the artist's estate sale, Hôtel Drouot, Paris, February 17–29, 1864, one of lots 543–547, to Andrieu; Pierre Andrieu, Paris (from 1864); Edgar Degas, Paris (until d. 1917; his estate sale, Galerie Georges Petit, Paris, November 15–16, 1918, no. 152, to Guérin); Marcel Guérin, Paris (1918–at least 1936); Guérin family, by descent; [Brame, Paris]; private collection

SELECTED EXHIBITIONS: Frankfurt 1987–88, no. H 18; Zürich 1987–88, no. 34; Paris 1994–95, no. 3; New York 1997–98, no. 390

The same figure appears seated, without burnoose, in cat. 75. The Monsieur Hay named in the inscription was Edward William Auriol Drummond-Hay (1785–1845), British consul in Morocco.

CAT. 75

A Man of Tangier

1832

Watercolor and pencil on paper

10½ x 7 5/16 in. (26.7 x 18.6 cm)

Inscribed in pencil (upper left): *Bajador / Cedria*; stamped (lower right): *ED*

The Morgan Library & Museum, New York, Thaw Collection (2017.63)

New York only

repr. p. 82

PROVENANCE: the artist's estate sale, Hôtel Drouot, Paris, February 17–29, 1864, one of lots 543–47, to Robaut; Alfred Robaut, Paris (catalogues for his sales of December 2, 1907, and December 18, 1907, do not include this drawing); Paul-Arthur Chéramy, Paris (until d. 1912; his estate sale, Hôtel Drouot, Paris, April 14–16, 1913, part of no. 98, to Guérin); Marcel Guérin, Paris (1913–at least 1936); Guérin family, by descent; [Brame, Paris]; Eugene V. and Clare E. Thaw, New York (until 2017; gift to Morgan)

SELECTED EXHIBITIONS: Paris 1994–95, no. 4

CAT. 76

Saada, the Wife of Abraham Ben-Chimol, and Préciada, One of Their Daughters

1832

Watercolor over graphite on wove paper

8¾ x 6⅜ in. (22.2 x 16.2 cm)

Signed (lower left): *Eug Delacroix*

The Metropolitan Museum of Art, New York, Bequest of Walter C. Baker, 1971 (1972.118.210)

New York only

repr. p. 81

PROVENANCE: the artist, Paris (part of an album of eighteen watercolors of Moroccan subjects, now in various collections, given to Mornay in 1832 or soon after); comte Charles de Mornay, Paris (until 1877; his sale, Hôtel Drouot, Paris, March 29, 1877, no. 10, to Hecht); Albert Hecht, Paris (from 1877); Edouard Aynard (until d. 1913; his estate sale, Galerie Georges Petit, Paris, December 1–4, 1913, no. 2); Walter C. Baker, New York (until d. 1971)

SELECTED EXHIBITIONS: Paris (Mémorial) 1963, no. 162; New York 1991, no. 27

Delacroix is thought to have produced the watercolors for Mornay immediately upon returning from North Africa, while he was in quarantine in Toulon between July 5 and 20, 1832.

CAT. 77

Street in Meknes

1832

Oil on canvas

18¼ x 25¼ in. (46.4 x 64.1 cm)

Signed and dated (lower right): *Eug. Delacroix / 1832*

Collection Albright-Knox Art Gallery, Buffalo, New York, Elisabeth H. Gates and Charles W. Goodyear Funds, 1948 (1948:4)

J 352

repr. p. 86

PROVENANCE: Robert Pelleve de la Motte-Ango, marquis de Flers (until 1907; sold on May 17 to Bernheim); [Bernheim-Jeune, Paris, 1907–9; sold on April 23, 1909, to Ebenrod]; Friedrich, Ritter von Wolff-Ebenrod, Düsseldorf (1909–d. 1920); his son-in-law, Friedrich August Feldhoff, Langenberg (until at least 1929); [Fine Arts Associates, New York, until 1948; sold on October 6 to Albright Art Gallery]

SELECTED EXHIBITIONS: Paris (Salon) 1834, no. 496; Paris (Mémorial) 1963, no. 200; Paris 1994–95, no. 59; Rouen 1998, no. 119; Madrid–Barcelona 2011–12, no. 90

CAT. 78

Moroccan Military Exercises

1832

Oil on canvas

23⅝ x 28 13/16 in. (60 x 73.2 cm)

Signed (lower center): *Eug Delacroix / 1832.*

Musée Fabre, Montpellier Méditerranée Métropole (inv. 868.1.37)

J 351

repr. p. 84

PROVENANCE: presumably acquired from the artist by comte Charles de Mornay, Paris (until 1850; ?his anonymous sale, Hôtel des Ventes, Paris, January 18–19, 1850, no. 119; Alfred Bruyas, Montpellier (1850/51–68; his gift to the city of Montpellier)

SELECTED EXHIBITIONS: Montpellier 1860, no. 77; Paris (Mémorial) 1963, no. 187; Paris 1994–95, no. 58; Paris 2002–3, no. 209; Richmond–Williamstown–Dallas–San Francisco 2004–5, no. 41; Madrid–Barcelona 2011–12, no. 89 (Barcelona only)

CAT. 79

Arab Cavalry Practicing a Charge (Fantaisie Arabe)

1833

Oil on canvas

23 13/16 x 29 5/16 in. (60.5 x 74.5 cm)

Signed and dated (lower right): *Eug Delacroix / 1833.*

Städel Museum, Frankfurt am Main, Property of the Städelscher Museums-Verein e.V. (inv. 1466)

J 353

New York only

repr. p. 84

PROVENANCE: M. de Schomberg (until 1849; his sale, Paris, April 28, 1849, no. 40); Monsieur van Isacker (until 1852; his sale, Hôtel des Ventes, Paris, May 15, 1852, no. 12); M. B. (until 1855; his sale, Hôtel des Commissaires-Priseurs, Paris, March 30, 1855, no. 19, to Getting); Count Anatole Demidoff, prince of San Donato, Paris and Florence (1856–70; his sale, Boulevard des Italiens, no. 26, Paris, February 21–22, 1870, no. 28, to Petit); [Petit]; Louis Lefebvre, Roubaix (by 1873–96; his posthumous sale, Galerie Georges Petit, Paris, May 4, 1896, no. 12, to Knoedler); [Knoedler, New York, 1896; sold in July to Kauffman]; J. W. Kauffman, St. Louis (1896–1905; his posthumous sale, Mendelssohn Hall, New York, February 3, 1905, no. 70, to Lehman); M. H. Lehman; [Knoedler, New York, until 1909, sold May 7 to Arnold & Tripp]; [Arnold & Tripp, Paris, 1909–10; sold December 19, 1910, to Städelsches Kunstinstitut]

SELECTED EXHIBITIONS: London 1851, no. 67; Paris 1885, no. 126; Paris (Mémorial) 1963, no. 188; Zürich–Frankfurt 1987–88, no. 43; Karlsruhe 2003–4, no. 112

CAT. 80
A Blacksmith
1833
Aquatint on laid paper, with drypoint sketches in
the margins; second state of six
Sheet 8⅜ x 5⅜ in. (21.3 x 13.6 cm), trimmed within
the plate
The Metropolitan Museum of Art, New York,
Purchase, Rogers Fund and Jacob H. Schiff Bequest,
1922 (22.60.13)
D-S 19
New York only
repr. p. 63

PROVENANCE: Alfred Beurdeley, Paris (d. 1919);
[Maurice Gobin, Paris, until 1922; sold to MMA]

SELECTED EXHIBITIONS (this impression): Paris–
New York 2002–3, no. 121 (New York only)

The print repeats the composition of a painting
believed to have been painted about 1825 (location
unknown, J L115).

CAT. 81
Collision of Arab Horsemen
1833/34
Oil on canvas
31¹¹⁄₁₆ x 39⁹⁄₁₆ in. (80.5 x 100.5 cm)
Signed (lower left): *Eug. Delacroix*
Private collection
J 355
New York only
repr. p. 85

PROVENANCE: Salomon Hayum Goldschmidt, Paris
(until d. 1888; his estate sale, Galerie Georges Petit,
Paris, May 17, 1888, no. 29, to his heirs); by descent
to Madame Bicart-Sée; sale, Piasa, Paris, June 19,
1998, no. 28); private collection (from 1998)

SELECTED EXHIBITIONS: rejected by the jury of the
Paris Salon of 1834; Nantes 1839 (unidentified
exhibition)

CAT. 82
Figure Study for "The Women of Algiers"
1833/34
Graphite and watercolor on wove paper
12¹³⁄₁₆ x 8³⁄₁₆ in. (32.5 x 20.8 cm)
Stamped (lower left): *ED*
The Metropolitan Museum of Art, New York,
Bequest of Walter C. Baker, 1971 (1972.118.209)
New York only
repr. p. 79

PROVENANCE: the artist's estate sale, Hôtel Drouot,
Paris, February 17–29, 1864, no. unknown; [Georges
Bernier, Paris]; Walter C. Baker, New York (until
d. 1971)

For this study and at least one other (Louvre,
RF 9290), Delacroix employed a European model to
research the pose of the black maidservant in the
Women of Algiers (cat. 83).

CAT. 83
Women of Algiers in Their Apartment
1834
Oil on canvas
70⅞ x 90³⁄₁₆ in. (180 x 229 cm)
Signed and dated (bottom right): *EUG. DELACROIX.
/ F.1834.*
Musée du Louvre, Paris, Département des Peintures
(3824)
J 356
repr. p. 78

PROVENANCE: King Louis-Philippe, Paris (1834; bought
from the artist on June 26 and allocated to the Musée
du Luxembourg); Musée du Luxembourg, Paris
(1834–74; transferred in November 1874 to Louvre)

SELECTED EXHIBITIONS: Paris (Salon) 1834, no. 497;
Paris 1855, no. 2931; Paris 1864b, no. 297; Paris
(Mémorial) 1963, no. 394; Nantes–Paris–Piacenza
1995–96, no. 74; Madrid–Barcelona 2011–12, no. 99

CAT. 84
The Natchez
1823–24 and 1835
Oil on canvas
35½ x 46 in. (90.2 x 116.8 cm)
Signed (lower right): *EugDelacroix*
The Metropolitan Museum of Art, New York,
Purchase, Gifts of George N. and Helen M. Richard
and Mr. and Mrs. Charles S. McVeigh and Bequest
of Emma A. Sheafer, by exchange, 1989 (1989.328)
J 101
New York only
repr. p. 229

PROVENANCE: the artist, Paris (until 1837; possibly
sold to baron Charles Rivet; lottery, Lyon, 1837 or
1838, possibly won by Paturle); Monsieur Paturle
(until 1872; his sale, Hôtel Drouot, Paris, February
28, 1872, no. 7, to Febvre); [Alexis Joseph Febvre,
Paris, from 1872]; Charles Sedelmeyer, Paris (until
1877; his sale, Hôtel Drouot, Paris, April 30, 1877,
no. 25); Paul Demidoff, prince of San Donato,
Florence and St. Petersburg (in 1878); Monsieur
Perreau (until 1881; sold on October 24, to Goupil);
[Goupil & Cie, Paris, 1881–87; stock no. 15678; their

sale, Hôtel Drouot, Paris, May 25, 1887, no. 44, to
Escribe for Boussod, Valadon, but probably bought
in and sold to Guillot]; Edmond Guillot, Paris (until
1888; sold on December 31 to Boussod, Valadon);
[Boussod, Valadon & Cie, Paris, 1888; stock
no. 19615, sold on December 31, to Michel]; F.
Michel (from 1888); Philippe George, Aÿ (until 1891;
his sale, Galerie Georges Petit, Paris, June 2, 1891,
no. 17); his widow, Madame Philippe George
(until 1898; sold on May 16 to Durand-Ruel);
[Durand-Ruel, Paris, 1898–99; stock no. 4666; sold
on January 26, 1899, to Bernheim-Jeune]; [Galerie
Bernheim-Jeune, Paris, from 1899]; Monsieur
Bessonneau, Angers (by 1916); his son-in-law(?),
Monsieur Frappier (by 1923); Madame Frappier
(by 1923–at least 1930); sale, former collection
Bessonneau d'Angers, Galerie Charpentier, Paris,
June 15, 1954, no. 31, to Reid & Lefevre; [Reid &
Lefevre, London, 1954–at least 1956]; Lord and Lady
Walston, Thriplow, Cambridge (by 1959–89; on loan
to National Gallery, London, April 1988–May 1989;
sale, Christie's, New York, November 14, 1989,
no. 31, to MMA)

SELECTED EXHIBITIONS: Paris (Salon) 1835, no. 556;
Moulins 1836, suppl. no. 266; Lyon 1837, no. 72;
Zürich–Frankfurt 1987–88, no. 7; New York 1991,
no. 3; Rouen 1998, no. 52; Madrid–Barcelona
2011–12, no. 76

For the subject, see the essay by Asher Miller in the
present volume.

CAT. 85
Christ on the Cross
1835
Oil on canvas
71⅝ x 53⅛ in. (182 x 135 cm)
Signed and dated (lower left): *Eug. Delacroix. / 1835*
Musée des Beaux-Arts, Vannes (inv. 2017.001.001)
J 421
repr. p. 122

PROVENANCE: purchased from the artist by the French
state in 1835 and given to the municipality of Vannes
(first installed in the church of Saint-Patern; displayed in the office of the mayor, 1865; transferred in
1908 to museum; final transfer from the French state
to the city of Vannes concluded in 2017)

SELECTED EXHIBITIONS: Paris (Salon) 1835, no. 554;
Paris 1864b, no. 295; Paris 1885, no. 227; Paris
(Mémorial) 1963, no. 214; Tokyo–Nagoya 1989,
no. 26; Vannes 1993, no. 13; Rouen 1998, no. 153;
Madrid–Barcelona 2011–12, no. 103

CAT. 86

Hamlet and Horatio in the Graveyard

1835

Oil on canvas

39 x 31¹¹⁄₁₆ in. (99 x 80.5 cm)

Signed and dated (lower left): *Eug. Delacroix / 1835*

Städel Museum, Frankfurt am Main, Property of the Städelscher Museums-Verein e.V. (inv. 2155)

J 258

repr. p. 159

PROVENANCE: Achille Ricourt (bought in summer 1836); [Durand-Ruel, in 1845]; ?M. A. Dugléré (until 1853; his sale, Hôtel des Ventes Mobilières, Paris, February 1, 1853, no. 42); Bouruet (in 1864); Monsieur Edwards (until 1870; his sale, Hôtel Drouot, Paris, March 7, 1870, no. 8, to Heine); Michel Heine (1870–at least 1885); [Marlborough Fine Art, London]; Geoffrey Gorer, Sussex, England (by 1959–1982); sale, Sotheby's, London, June 15, 1982, no. 11, to Colnaghi; [Colnaghi, London, from 1982]; Städelsches Kunstinstitut, Frankfurt (purchased in 1987)

SELECTED EXHIBITIONS : rejected by the jury of the Paris Salon of 1836; Amiens 1836 (unidentified exhibition); Paris 1885, no. 239; Zürich–Frankfurt 1987–88, no. 45; Copenhagen 2000, no. 24; Karlsruhe 2003–4, no. 125; Winterthur 2008, no. 13; Marseilles–Rovereto–Toronto 2009–10, no. 92 (Marseilles and Rovereto only); Leipzig 2015–16, no. 61

This scene is based on Shakespeare's *Hamlet*, act 5, scene 1.

CAT. 87

Combat of the Giaour and Hassan

1835

Oil on canvas

29⅛ x 23⅝ in. (74 x 60 cm)

Signed and dated (lower right): *Eug. Delacroix. 1835.*

Petit Palais, Musée des Beaux-Arts de la Ville de Paris, Collection Dutuit (inv. PDUT1162)

J 257

repr. p. 35

PROVENANCE: presumably comte Charles de Mornay, Paris (until 1850; ?his anonymous sale, Hôtel des Ventes, Paris, January 18–19, 1850, no. 117, to Collot); Collot (1850–52; his sale, Hôtel des Ventes, Paris, May 29, 1852, no. 9, to Davin); Monsieur Davin (until 1863; his sale, Hôtel Drouot, Paris, March 14, 1863, no. 7, to Pereire); Emile Pereire (from 1863); Gavet (in 1873); Laurent Richard (until 1878; his sale, Hôtel Drouot, Paris, May 23–25, 1878, no. 13, bought in); baron Gérard (in August 1878); comte de Lastours (in 1930); François-Charles-Jean-Marie, duc d'Harcourt (until 1963, sold to Petit Palais)

SELECTED EXHIBITIONS: Paris 1848, no. 26; Paris 1855, no. 2927; Paris 1860, no. 168; Paris 1864b, no. 76; Paris 1885, no. 92; Paris (Mémorial) 1963, no. 220; Zürich–Frankfurt 1987–88, no. 44; Bordeaux–Paris–Athens 1996–97, no. 31; Paris 2002–3, no. 211; Karlsruhe 2003–4, no. 113; Madrid–Barcelona 2011–12, no. 102; Minneapolis–London 2015–16, no. 17

This painting reprises a subject treated in cat. 27.

CAT. 88

Léon Riesener (1808–1878)

1835

Oil on canvas

21¼ x 17⁵⁄₁₆ in. (54 x 44 cm)

Musée du Louvre, Paris, Département des Peintures (RF 1960-58)

J 225

New York only

repr. p. 6

PROVENANCE: presumably painted for the sitter (d. 1878) or his mother (d. 1847); the sitter's daughter, Madame Rosalie Pillaut (by 1885–d. 1913; her bequest to Louvre; entered museum in 1960)

SELECTED EXHIBITIONS: Paris 1885, no. 164; Karlsruhe 2003–4, no. 71; Madrid–Barcelona 2011–12, no. 101

The sitter, a painter, was Delacroix's first cousin; his mother is depicted in cat. 89.

CAT. 89

Madame Henri François Riesener (Félicité Longrois, 1786–1847)

1835

Oil on canvas

29¼ x 23¾ in. (74.3 x 60.3 cm)

The Metropolitan Museum of Art, New York, Gift of Mrs. Charles Wrightsman, 1994 (1994.430)

J 226

New York only

repr. p. 6

PROVENANCE: ?the sitter, the artist's maternal aunt, Frépillon, near Montmorency, and Paris (until d. 1847); her son, Léon Riesener, Paris (1847–d. 1878); his widow, Madame Léon Riesener (1878–at least 1885); their daughter, Louise Riesener, later Madame Claude Léouzon-le-Duc, ?Paris (by 1916–at least 1936); Léon Salavin, Paris (by 1952–at least 1969); [Galerie Schmit, Paris, until 1971, sold on January 11 to Rosenberg]; [Paul Rosenberg, New York, 1971; stock no. 6409; sold on February 22 to Wrightsman]; Mr. and Mrs. Charles Wrightsman, New York (1971–his d. 1986); Mrs. Charles Wrightsman (1986–94)

SELECTED EXHIBITIONS: Paris 1885, no. 167; Paris (Mémorial) 1963, no. 219

The sitter was Delacroix's aunt by marriage on his mother's side. Her husband, Henri François Riesener (1767–1828), was a painter who specialized in portraiture.

CAT. 90

Saint Sebastian Tended by the Holy Women

1836

Oil on canvas

84⅝ in. x 9 ft. 2¼ in. (215 x 280 cm)

Signed and dated (lower right): *Eug. Delacroix 1836*

Church of Saint-Michel, Nantua (Ain); Fonds National d'Art Contemporain (inv. FNAC PFH-5176); placed on deposit by the Centre National des Arts Plastiques at the Collégiale de Nantua since 1837

J 422

repr. p. 112

PROVENANCE: sold by the artist in 1837 to the French state; sent to Nantua at the request of Girot, deputy from Ain; sold by the parish council of Ain to the dealers Brame and Durand-Ruel, Paris, in 1869, but sale annulled by the court of Lyon in 1873; painting returned to Church of Saint-Michel

SELECTED EXHIBITIONS: Paris (Salon) 1836, no. 499; Paris 1864b, no. 296; Paris (Mémorial) 1963, no. 227; Zürich–Frankfurt 1987–88, no. 47; Tokyo–Nagoya 1989, no. 50; Madrid–Barcelona 2011–12, no. 104

The scene is drawn from the *Golden Legend*, also known as the *Lives of the Saints*, compiled in the late thirteenth century by Jacobus de Voragine, archbishop of Genoa.

CAT. 91

Medea About to Kill Her Children, sketch

ca. 1836

Oil on canvas

18⅛ x 14¹⁵⁄₁₆ in. (46 x 38 cm)

Palais des Beaux-Arts, Lille (inv. P. 933)

J 259

repr. p. 114

PROVENANCE: the artist's estate sale, Hôtel Drouot, Paris, February 17–29, 1864, possibly no. 139, to Reynart for Musée des Beaux-Arts, now Palais des Beaux-Arts, Lille

SELECTED EXHIBITIONS: Paris (Mémorial) 1963, no. 246; Zürich–Frankfurt 1987–88, no. 48; Karlsruhe 2003–4, no. 126; Paris 2001, no. 38; Madrid–Barcelona 2011–12, no. 105; Paris 2013–14, no. 16

CAT. 92

Moroccan Chieftain Receiving Tribute

1837

Oil on canvas

38⁹⁄₁₆ x 49⁵⁄₈ in. (98 x 126 cm)

Signed and dated (lower right): *Eug. Delacroix / 1837.*

Musée d'Arts de Nantes, Nantes Métropole
(inv. 892)

J 359

repr. p. 89

PROVENANCE: the artist, Paris (until 1839; sold in June to the Musée des Beaux-Arts, Nantes)

SELECTED EXHIBITIONS: Paris (Salon) 1838, no. 458; Nantes 1839 (unidentified exhibition); Paris 1864b, no. 3; Paris (Mémorial) 1963, no. 257; Zürich–Frankfurt 1987–88, no. 49; Paris 1994–95, no. 69; Rouen 1998, no. 120; Paris 2002–3, no. 212; Karlsruhe 2003–4, no. 141; Madrid–Barcelona 2011–12, no. 111 (Madrid only); Chantilly 2012–13, no. 58; Paris 2014–15, no. 41

CAT. 93

Self-Portrait in a Green Vest

ca. 1837

Oil on canvas

25⁹⁄₁₆ x 21⁷⁄₁₆ in. (65 x 54.5 cm)

Musée du Louvre, Paris, Département des Peintures, Gift of Madame Zélie Duriez de Verninac through Pierre Andrieu, 1872 (RF 25)

J 230

repr. p. 98

PROVENANCE: the artist, Paris (until d. 1863; bequeathed to Le Guillou with the verbal request that she give it to the Louvre if the Orléans family returned to power; see Robaut 1885, p. 82, under no. 295); his housekeeper, Jenny Le Guillou (1863–d. 1869; bequeathed to Verninac); the artist's cousin Madame Zélie Duriez de Verninac (until 1872; her gift to the Louvre, with Pierre Andrieu as intermediary)

SELECTED EXHIBITIONS: Paris (Mémorial) 1963, no. 243; Madrid–Barcelona 2011–12, no. 110; Minneapolis–London 2015–16, no. 1 (London only)

CAT. 94

Medea About to Kill Her Children (Medée furieuse)

1838

Oil on canvas

8 ft. 6³⁄₈ in. x 64¹⁵⁄₁₆ in. (260 x 165 cm)

Signed and dated (lower left): *EUG DELACROIX / 1838*

Palais des Beaux-Arts, Lille (inv. P. 542)

J 261

repr. p. 115

PROVENANCE: the artist (until July 31, 1838; sold to the French state for Musée des Beaux-Arts, now Palais des Beaux-Arts, Lille)

SELECTED EXHIBITIONS: Paris (Salon) 1838, no. 456; exhibited at the Musée du Luxembourg, Paris, for one year following its purchase by the state prior to being sent to Lille; Paris 1855, no. 2913; Paris 1885, no. 130; Paris (Mémorial) 1963, no. 245; Tokyo–Nagoya 1989, no. 41; Nantes–Paris–Piacenza 1995–96, no. 68; Paris 2001, no. 39; Madrid–Barcelona 2011–12, no. 114

According to the Greek mythological tale, Medea became enraged by Jason's infidelity (with Glauce, daughter of the king of Corinth), taking revenge by killing their children.

CAT. 95

Cleopatra and the Peasant

1838

Oil on canvas

38½ x 50 in. (97.8 x 127 cm)

Signed and dated (upper right): *Eug. Delacroix / 1838.*

Collection of the Ackland Art Museum, University of North Carolina at Chapel Hill, Ackland Fund
(59.15.1)

J 262

repr. p. 118

PROVENANCE: presumably comte Charles de Mornay, Paris (probably from 1847–50; ?his anonymous sale, Hôtel des Ventes, Paris, January 18–19, 1850, no. 116, possibly to Delacroix); ?Eugène Delacroix, Paris (from 1850); private collection, Toulouse (in 1865); Madame Carayon-Talpayrac (in 1874); her family (until at least 1893); Denys Cochin (by 1916–19; his sale, Galerie Georges Petit, Paris, March 26, 1919, no. 12); Dr. Emil Hahnloser, Zürich (in 1921); his family (until ca. 1957); [Schaeffer Galleries, New York, 1957/58–59; sold in October 1959 to Ackland]

SELECTED EXHIBITIONS: Paris (Salon) 1839, no. 524; Paris 1846b, no. 21; Paris (Mémorial) 1963, no. 280; Madrid–Barcelona 2011–12, no. 115; Minneapolis–London 2015–16, no. 50

The subject is drawn from Shakespeare's *Antony and Cleopatra*, act 5, scene 2.

CAT. 96

Hamlet and Horatio in the Graveyard

1839

Oil on canvas

32¹⁄₁₆ x 25¾ in. (81.5 x 65.4 cm)

Signed and dated (lower center): *Eug. Delacroix / 1839.*

Musée du Louvre, Paris, Département des Peintures, Bequest of Maurice Cottier, 1883 (with life interest), entered the collection in 1903 (RF 1942)

J 267

repr. p. 161

PROVENANCE: Ferdinand Philippe, duc d'Orléans (by 1836–d. 1842); his widow (1842–53; her sale, Hôtel des Ventes, Paris, January 18, 1853, no. 19, to Cottier); Maurice Cottier (1853–d. 1881; bequeathed to Louvre with life interest to his widow; entered museum in 1903)

SELECTED EXHIBITIONS: Paris (Salon) 1839, no. 525; Bordeaux 1852, no. 133; Paris 1855, no. 2936; Paris 1860, no. 171; Paris 1885, no. 49; Paris (Mémorial) 1963, no. 281; Nantes–Paris–Piacenza 1995–96, no. 69; Madrid–Barcelona 2011–12, no. 117

This painting reprises the subject of cat. 86.

CAT. 97

Startled Arabian Horse in a Landscape

ca. 1835–40

Watercolor and gouache with gum arabic on paper

6⁷⁄₈ x 9⁵⁄₈ in. (17.5 x 24.5 cm)

Signed (lower left): *Eug Delacroix*

Private collection

New York only

repr. p. 88

PROVENANCE: [?Adolphe Beugniet, Paris]; [Galerie Susse, Paris, until 1856; their anonymous sale, Hôtel des Commissaires-Priseurs, Paris, January 10, 1856, no. 35, to Moreau]; Adolphe Moreau père, Paris (from 1856); private collection, Lyon; [Paris art market, until ca. 1987; sold to private collection]

SELECTED EXHIBITIONS: Paris 2002–3, no. 208

CAT. 98

The Shipwreck of Don Juan

1840

Oil on canvas

53¹⁄₈ x 77³⁄₁₆ in. (135 x 196 cm)

Signed and dated (lower left): *Eug. Delacroix. / 1840.*

Musée du Louvre, Département des Peintures, Paris, Gift of Adolphe Moreau, 1883 (RF 359)

J 276

repr. p. 118

PROVENANCE: [Cheradane, ca. 1845]; Adolphe Moreau père, Paris (bought no later than January 1847); his widow and their son, Adolphe Moreau fils (until 1883; their gift to Louvre)

SELECTED EXHIBITIONS: Paris (Salon) 1841, no. 510; Paris 1855, no. 2937; Paris 1860, no. 169; Paris (Mémorial) 1963, no. 303; Paris 2004, no. 46; Madrid–Barcelona 2011–12, no. 120

The subject is drawn from Lord Byron's poem *Don Juan*, initially published in parts between 1819 and 1824.

CAT. 99

Christ on the Lake of Genesareth
ca. 1841
Oil on canvas
17¾ x 21⅝ in. (45.1 x 54.9 cm)
Signed (lower right, on boat): *Eug. Delacroix.*
Portland Art Museum, Oregon, Gift of Mrs. William Mead Ladd and her children: William Sargent Ladd, Charles Thornton Ladd, and Henry Andrews Ladd in memory of William Mead Ladd (31.4)
J 452
New York only
repr. p. 190

PROVENANCE: ?Mlle Micheline Dziekańska; Van Praet, Brussels (by 1873–d. 1888); his nephew, Paul Devaux (d. ca. 1892); Henri Garnier (1893–94; bought with Van Praet collection en bloc; his sale, Galerie Georges Petit, Paris, December 3–4, 1894, no. 43, to Durand-Ruel in shares with Boussod-Valadon); [Durand-Ruel, Paris, and Boussod, Valadon, Paris, 1894–95, until the former sold share to latter on May 30]; [Boussod-Valadon, 1895; sold on July 1 to Cottier]; [Cottier, New York, from 1895]; William Ladd, Portland, Oregon (by 1913–d. 1931; on loan to Portland Art Museum, 1913–30; in care of Dr. Louis Ladd, New York, 1930–31); his widow, Mrs. William Ladd (1931); her gift in February 1931 to Portland Art Museum)

SELECTED EXHIBITIONS: possibly exhibited in Paris in 1841; Paris (Mémorial) 1963, no. 448; Zürich–Frankfurt 1987–88, no. 93; Paris–Philadelphia 1998–99, no. 114

When awakened by his terrified disciples during a storm on the Lake of Genesareth, also known as the Sea of Galilee and by other names, Christ scolded them for their lack of trust in Providence. The story is recounted in three of the Gospels: Matthew 8:23–27, Luke 8:22–25, and Mark 4:36–41. There are two other treatments of the subject in the present catalogue (cats. 129 and 131).

CAT. 100

Pietà, first sketch
by 1843
Oil on paper, laid down on canvas, with strip of wood added at bottom edge

12½ x 17 in. (31.8 x 43.2 cm)
Signed (at bottom, right of center): *Eug. Delacroix.*
Private collection
J 562
repr. p. 124

PROVENANCE: Gustave-Joseph-Marie Lassalle Bordes, Paris (received from the artist by 1853); de La Rosière (by 1864); [Durand-Ruel, August 1872]; private collection, Brussels (until 2016); private collection (from 2016)

SELECTED EXHIBITIONS: Paris 1864b, no. 116; Madrid–Barcelona 2011–12, no. 109

Elements of this sketch for the wall painting in the church of Saint-Denys-du-Saint-Sacrement, Paris (1844), most notably the angels drawing back the curtains, were subsequently abandoned; see cat. 101.

CAT. 101

Pietà, second sketch
by 1843
Oil on canvas
11⅝ x 17⅛ in. (29.5 x 43.5 cm)
Musée du Louvre, Paris, Département des Peintures, Bequest of Armand Dorville, 1942 (RF 1943-6)
J 563
repr. p. 125

PROVENANCE: the artist's estate sale, Hôtel Drouot, Paris, February 17–29, 1864, no. 7, to Lambert; Lambert (from 1864); Georges Aubry (until 1933; his sale, Hôtel Drouot, Paris, March 11, 1933, no. 82, to Schoeller); Armand Dorville (until d. 1941; his bequest to Louvre, 1942; delivered to Louvre in June 1943)

SELECTED EXHIBITIONS: Madrid–Barcelona 2011–12, no. 108

The composition of this sketch was adopted, in reverse, for the painting in Saint-Denys-du-Saint-Sacrement.

CAT. 102

Christ on the Cross, sketch
1845
Oil on wood
14⁹⁄₁₆ x 9¹³⁄₁₆ in. (37 x 25 cm)
Museum Boijmans Van Beuningen, Rotterdam (inv. 2625 [OK])
J 432
repr. p. 126

PROVENANCE: Alexandre Dumas fils (in 1845); Paul Meurice (by 1885–d. 1905; his estate sale, Hôtel Drouot, Paris, May 25, 1906, no. 80, probably to a member of his family); Madame Albert

Clemenceau-Meurice (in 1927); [Vitale Bloch, ca. 1960–61; sold in 1961 to Boijmans]

SELECTED EXHIBITIONS: Paris 1845; Paris 1885, no. 146; Zürich–Frankfurt 1987–88, no. 60; Paris–Philadelphia 1998–99, no. 119; Copenhagen 2000, no. 18

CAT. 103

Christ on the Cross
1846
Oil on canvas
31½ x 25¼ in. (80 x 64.1 cm)
Signed and dated (lower right): *Eug. Delacroix 1846*
The Walters Art Museum, Baltimore, Maryland (37.62)
J 433
repr. p. 127

PROVENANCE: Paul Barroilhet (bought from the artist by April 1847); ?Van Cuyck; J. P. Bonnet (by 1853–at least 1855; his sale, Hôtel des Ventes Mobilières, Paris, February 19, 1853, no. 10, to de Breville, possibly bought in for Bonnet); Solar; Osiris; ?Gavet; Fanien (by 1873/74; sold to Petit); [Georges Petit, Paris]; Monsieur Defoer (by 1883–86; his sale, Galerie Georges Petit, Paris, May 22, 1886, no. 10, to Montaignac for Walters); William T. Walters, Baltimore (1886–d. 1894); his son, Henry Walters (1894–d. 1931; his bequest to Walters Art Museum)

SELECTED EXHIBITIONS: Paris (Salon) 1847, no. 459; Paris 1855, no. 2909; Paris 1885, no. 52; Paris (Mémorial) 1963, no. 360; Columbia–Rochester–Santa Barbara 1989–90, no. 169; New York 1991, no. 6; Paris–Philadelphia 1998–99, no. 120; Madrid–Barcelona 2011–12, no. 132

CAT. 104

The Death of Sardanapalus
1845–46
Oil on canvas
29 x 32⁷⁄₁₆ in. (73.7 x 82.4 cm)
Philadelphia Museum of Art: The Henry P. McIlhenny Collection in memory of Frances P. McIlhenny, 1986 (1986-26-17)
J 286
repr. p. 52

PROVENANCE: the artist, Paris (until d. 1863; bequeathed to his executor, Legrand); Eugène-François-Charles Legrand, Paris; Prosper Crabbe, Brussels (in 1873); A. Bellino (by 1885–92; his sale, Galerie Georges Petit, Paris, May 20, 1892, no. 11, bought in); [Wildenstein, New York, in 1930]; [Paul Rosenberg, Paris and New York, by April 1934–35; sold to McIlhenny]; Henry P. McIlhenny, Philadelphia (1935–d. 1986; his bequest to Philadelphia Museum of Art)

SELECTED EXHIBITIONS: Paris 1864b, no. 144; Paris 1885, no. 8; New York 1991, no. 4; London–Minneapolis–New York 2003–4, no. 78; Minneapolis–London 2015–16, no. 18

The artist produced this reduced version of the painting he had exhibited at the Salon of 1827–28 (fig. 20) at the time he sold the larger picture to the collector Daniel Wilson.

CAT. 105

The Abduction of Rebecca
1846
Oil on canvas
39½ x 32¼ in. (100.3 x 81.9 cm)
Signed and dated (lower right): *Eug. Delacroix / 1846*
The Metropolitan Museum of Art, New York, Catharine Lorillard Wolfe Collection, Wolfe Fund, 1903 (03.30)
J 284
repr. p. 174

PROVENANCE: Collot, Paris (by 1846–52; his sale, Hôtel des Ventes Mobilières, Paris, May 28, 1852, no. 11); M. T. . . , Brussels (until 1856; his sale, Hôtel des Commissaires-Priseurs, Paris, February 9, 1856, no. 12, to Bouruet-Aubertot); [Jean-Hector Bouruet-Aubertot, Paris, 1856–68; sold June 1868 to Durand-Ruel and Brame]; [Durand-Ruel and Hector Brame, Paris, 1868, in equal shares; Durand-Ruel archives, stock 1868–73, no. 10953; sold in June 1868, to Gavet]; Emile Gavet, Paris (from 1868); Edwards, Paris (until 1870; his sale, Hôtel Drouot, Paris, March 7, 1870, no. 7, to Sabatier); Raymond Sabatier, Paris (1870–83; sale, Hôtel Drouot, Paris, May 30, 1883, no. 12); Salomon Hayum Goldschmidt, Paris (1883–88; his estate sale, Galerie Georges Petit, Paris, May 17, 1888, no. 34, to Knoedler for Lyall); David C. Lyall, Brooklyn (1888–d. 1892; his estate sale, American Art Association, New York, February 10, 1903, no. 96, to Durand-Ruel); [Durand-Ruel, New York, 1903; sold half-share on February 26 to Knoedler]; [Durand-Ruel and Knoedler, New York, 1903; stock no. 10184 sold on March 2 to MMA]

SELECTED EXHIBITIONS: Paris (Salon) 1846, no. 502; Paris 1846a, suppl. no. 164; Paris 1864b, no. 129 (possibly this work); New York 1991, no. 5

The subject is drawn from Sir Walter Scott's historical novel *Ivanhoe*, published in English in 1820 and translated into French the following year.

CAT. 106

The Lamentation (Christ at the Tomb)
1847–48
Oil on canvas
64 x 52 in. (162.6 x 132.1 cm)
Signed and dated (lower left): *Eug. Delacroix. / 1848*
Museum of Fine Arts, Boston, Gift by contribution in memory of Martin Brimmer (96.21)
J 434
repr. p. 128

PROVENANCE: comte Théodore de Geloës, probably Paris, but possibly Château d'Osen, near Roermund, the Netherlands (1847–70; bought from the artist on April 28, 1847, while the painting was still incomplete; sold to Faure); Jean-Baptiste Faure, Paris (1870–73; his sale, Boulevard des Italiens, no. 26, Paris, June 7, 1873, no. 7, to Durand-Ruel); [Hector Brame, Paris, in 1878]; baron Etienne Martin de Beurnonville (until 1880; his sale, Hôtel Drouot, Paris, April 29, 1880, no. 11, possibly to Brame for Tavernier); Tavernier (1880–94; his sale, Galerie Georges Petit, Paris, June 11, 1894, no. 5, to Durand-Ruel); [Durand-Ruel, Paris and New York, 1894–96; sold Museum of Fine Arts, Boston]

SELECTED EXHIBITIONS: Paris (Salon) 1848, no. 1157; Paris 1855, no. 2910; Paris (Mémorial) 1963, no. 383; Paris–Philadelphia 1998–99, no. 125; Minneapolis–London 2015–16, no. 37

CAT. 107

Arab Players
1848
Oil on canvas
37¹³⁄₁₆ x 51³⁄₁₆ in. (96 x 130 cm)
Signed and dated (lower left): *Eug. Delacroix / 1848.*
Musée des Beaux-Arts de Tours (inv. 1848-1-1)
J 380
repr. p. 88

PROVENANCE: sold by the artist in 1848 to the French state and deposited at the Musée des Beaux-Arts, Tours; transferred by the state to the city of Tours in 2010

SELECTED EXHIBITIONS: Paris 1848, no. 1160; Paris 1864b, no. 14; Paris 1885, no. 220; Paris (Mémorial) 1963, no. 389; Zürich–Frankfurt 1987–88, no. 68; Nantes–Paris–Piacenza 1995–96, no. 72; Copenhagen 2000, no. 8; Karlsruhe 2003–4, no. 211; Madrid–Barcelona 2011–12, no. 136

CAT. 108

Arch of Morning Glories, study for "Basket of Flowers"
1848/49
Pastel on blue paper
12¹⁄₁₆ x 18 in. (30.6 x 45.7 cm)
The Metropolitan Museum of Art, New York, Bequest of Miss Adelaide Milton de Groot (1876–1967), 1967 (67.187.4)
Johnson 1995, no. 10
New York only
repr. p. 142

PROVENANCE: the artist's estate sale, Hôtel Drouot, Paris, February 17–29, 1864, no. 616, to Casavy; Casavy (from 1864); Charles Paravey (his sale, Hôtel Drouot, Paris, April 13, 1878, not listed in catalogue); Victor Chocquet, Paris (until d. 1891); his widow, Augustine Marie Caroline Chocquet, née Buisson, Paris (1891–d. 1899; her sale, Galerie Georges Petit, Paris, July 1, 3–4, 1899, no. 177; [Wildenstein, New York, in 1952]; Adelaide Milton de Groot, New York (until d. 1967)

SELECTED EXHIBITIONS: New York 1991, no. 17; Paris–Philadelphia 1998–99, no. 28 (Paris only); Paris 2012–13, unnumbered catalogue (fig. 85)

This pastel is a study for cat. 109.

CAT. 109

Basket of Flowers
1848–49
Oil on canvas
42¼ x 56 in. (107.3 x 142.2 cm)
The Metropolitan Museum of Art, New York, Bequest of Miss Adelaide Milton de Groot (1876–1967), 1967 (67.187.60)
J 502
repr. p. 142

PROVENANCE: the artist, Paris (until d. 1863; his estate sale, Hôtel Drouot, Paris, February 17–18, 1864, no. 88, to Sourigues); Monsieur Sourigues (1864–81; his sale, Hôtel Drouot, Paris, February 28, 1881, no. 14, to Durand-Ruel); [Durand-Ruel, Paris, 1881; stock no. 882; sold on March 5 to Feder]; Jules Feder, Paris (from 1881); Vice-Admiral Auguste Bosse, Paris (in 1885); Erwin Davis, New York (by 1888–at least 1911; on deposit with Durand-Ruel, New York, December 27, 1897–December 30, 1911; deposit no. 5645); Albert Gallatin, New York (by 1936–at least 1938); [Wildenstein, New York, by 1943–56; stock no. 16861; sold to de Groot]; Adelaide Milton de Groot, New York (1956–d. 1967)

SELECTED EXHIBITIONS: Paris (Salon) 1849, no. 504; Bordeaux 1854, probably no. 157; Paris 1855, part of no. 2941; Paris 1862; Paris 1864b, no. 308 (in supplement to 3rd ed. of catalogue); Paris–Philadelphia 1998–99, no. 29; Karlsruhe 2003–4, no. 154

CAT. 110

Basket of Flowers and Fruit
1849
Oil on canvas
42⅝ x 56⅜ in. (108.3 x 143.2 cm)
Philadelphia Museum of Art: John G. Johnson
Collection, 1917 (Cat. 974)
J 501
repr. p. 143

PROVENANCE: the artist, Paris (until d. 1863; his estate
sale, Hôtel Drouot, Paris, February 17–29, 1864,
no. 90, to Piron); Achille Piron (1864–d. 1865; his
estate sale, Hôtel Drouot, Paris, April 21, 1865, no. 2);
[Durand-Ruel, Paris, in 1873]; Fanien (by 1873–at
least 1878); [Georges Petit, Paris, in 1884]; John G.
Johnson, Philadelphia (possibly by 1888, certainly
by 1892–d. 1917; his bequest to Philadelphia Museum
of Art)

SELECTED EXHIBITIONS: Paris (Salon) 1849, no. 505;
Bordeaux 1854, no. 158; Paris 1855, no. 2942; Paris
1862; Paris 1885, no. 234; Paris–Philadelphia 1998–99,
no. 30; Copenhagen 2000, no. 42; Karlsruhe
2003–4, no. 153; Minneapolis–London 2015–16,
no. 64

CAT. 111

Basket of Flowers
ca. 1848–50
Oil on canvas
24⁷⁄₁₆ x 34¼ in. (62 x 87 cm)
Signed (lower right, on table): *Eug. Delacroix*
Palais des Beaux-Arts, Lille (inv. P. 533)
J 504
repr. p. 139

PROVENANCE: Monsieur Panis; Delaroche (in
December 1893); Musée des Beaux-Arts, now Palais
des Beaux-Arts, Lille (purchased in July 1895)

SELECTED EXHIBITIONS: Copenhagen 2000, no. 43;
Karlsruhe 2003–4, no. 152; Paris 2012–13, unnumbered catalogue (fig. 27)

CAT. 112

Christ at the Column
probably 1849
Oil on canvas
14 x 10¾ in. (35.6 x 27.3 cm)
Signed (lower right): *Eug. Delacroix.*
National Gallery of Canada, Ottawa, Purchased 2014
(inv. 46341)
J 439
repr. p. 134

PROVENANCE: the artist (probably until March 1849;
probably sold to Lefebvre); [Lefebvre]; Barre,
Chaussée d'Antin, Paris (until 1890; sold on February
6 to Boussod, Valadon); [Boussod, Valadon et Cie,
Paris, 1890–91; sold on July 4 to Chase); [J. E.
Chase, Boston, from 1891]; ?Mrs. Samuel D. Warren,
Boston (until d.; her estate sale, American Art
Association, New York, January 8–9, 1903, no. 30, to
Healy); A. A. Healy (from 1903); private collection,
Venice (until ca. 1962); private collection, Rio de
Janeiro (in 1977); sale, Sotheby's, London, June 23,
1981, no. 10, to Whitney; Wheelock Whitney, New
York (1981–2014); National Gallery of Canada,
Ottawa (from 2014)

SELECTED EXHIBITIONS: Zürich–Frankfurt 1987–88,
no. 69; Madrid–Barcelona 2011–12, no. 137

CAT. 113

Landscape at Champrosay
possibly 1849
Oil on paper on cardboard
15¹⁄₁₆ x 18³⁄₁₆ in. (38.3 x 46.2 cm)
Kunsthalle Bremen—Der Kunstverein in Bremen
(inv. 121-1927/8)
J 480
repr. p. 183

PROVENANCE: the artist's estate sale, Hôtel Drouot,
Paris, February 17–29, 1864, part of no. 219, to Belly;
Léon Belly (1864–d. 1877; his estate sale, Hôtel
Drouot, Paris, February 11–12, 1878, no. 209, to
Dollfus); Jean Dollfus (1878–d. 1911; his estate sale,
Galerie Georges Petit, Paris, March 2, 1912, no. 31, to
Hessel); Jos Hessel, Paris (from 1912); [Moderne
Galerie Thannhauser, Munich, in 1916]; Curt Glaser,
Berlin (in 1921); [Kunstsalon Paul Cassirer, Berlin,
until 1927; sold on October 6 to Kunsthalle Bremen]

SELECTED EXHIBITIONS: Paris 1885, no. 89; Paris
(Mémorial) 1963, no. 402; Winterthur 2008, no. 19

CAT. 114

Michelangelo in His Studio
1849–50
Oil on canvas
15¾ x 12⅝ in. (40 x 32 cm)
Signed (lower left): *Eug. Delacroix.*
Musée Fabre, Montpellier Méditerranée Métropole
(inv. 868.1.40)
J 305
New York only
repr. p. 119

PROVENANCE: [Thomas, from 1853; bought from the
artist in March]; Alfred Bruyas, Montpellier (by
1854–68; his gift to the city of Montpellier)

SELECTED EXHIBITIONS: Montpellier 1860, no. 75;
Paris 1864b, no. 299; Nantes–Paris–Piacenza 1995–
96, no. 75; Richmond–Williamstown–Dallas–San
Francisco 2004–5, no. 45; Winterthur 2008, no. 17;
Madrid–Barcelona 2011–12, no. 142

CAT. 115

View in the Forest of Sénart
ca. 1849–50
Oil on canvas
12¹¹⁄₁₆ x 18⅛ in. (32.2 x 46 cm)
Private collection, courtesy of Art Cuéllar-Nathan
J 482a
repr. p. 196

PROVENANCE: the artist's estate sale, Hôtel Drouot,
Paris, February 17–29, 1864, probably part of no. 219,
to Aubry; Monsieur Aubry, Paris (from 1864);
[Vuillier, Paris, until 1898; sold to Launay]; Louis
de Launay (from 1898); de Launay family, by descent
(until at least 1986); private collection (from at
least 1998)

SELECTED EXHIBITIONS: Paris–Philadelphia 1998–99,
no. 38

CAT. 116

Forest View with an Oak Tree
ca. 1849–50
Watercolor with yellow opaque watercolor over
black chalk on paper
12¼ x 8⅞ in. (31.1 x 22.5 cm)
Stamped (lower left): *ED*
The Morgan Library & Museum, New York,
Thaw Collection (2017.67)
New York only
repr. p. 182

PROVENANCE: the artist's estate sale, Hôtel Drouot,
Paris, February 17–29, 1864, unidentified no.; Alfred
Beurdeley (until d. 1919; his estate sale, Galerie
Georges Petit, Paris, December 1–2, 1920, no. 121);
Boutet Roulier; Eugene V. and Clare E. Thaw, New
York (until 2017; their gift to Morgan)

SELECTED EXHIBITIONS: New York 1991, no. 68;
Paris–Philadelphia 1998–99, no. 39 (Paris only)

Features of this oak were incorporated into cats. 119,
120, and subsequently, fig. 69.

CAT. 117

The Triumph of Genius over Envy
ca. 1849–51
Pen and brown ink over graphite on laid paper,
mounted on cardboard
10³⁄₈ x 13¹³⁄₁₆ in. (26.4 x 35.1 cm)
Inscribed in graphite (lower center): *Serpent*; (lower
right): *plus grand le monstre*; (upper left): [illegible];
stamped (lower right): *ED*
The Metropolitan Museum of Art, New York, Rogers
Fund, 1961 (61.160.1)
New York only
repr. p. 153

PROVENANCE: the artist's estate sale, Hôtel Drouot,
Paris, February 17–29, 1864, part of no. 378, possibly
to Sensier; Alfred Sensier, Paris (1864–d. 1877;
reportedly his estate sale, Hôtel Drouot, Paris,
December 12, 14–16, 1877, to Burty); Philippe Burty,
Paris (until d. 1890; his estate sale, Hôtel Drouot,
Paris, March 2–3, 1891, no. 71); [Otto Wertheimer,
Paris, until 1937; sold on December 18 to
Feilchenfeldt]; Walter and Marianne Feilchenfeldt,
Amsterdam and Zürich (1937–his d. 1953); Marianne
Feilchenfeldt, Zürich (1953–61; sold to MMA)

SELECTED EXHIBITIONS: Paris 1885, not in catalogue;
Paris (Mémorial) 1963, no. 294; New York 1991,
no. 45; Paris–Philadelphia 1998–99, no. 63
(Paris only)

CAT. 118

Jacob Struggling with the Angel
1850
Graphite over traces of red chalk on two sheets of
beige laid paper, joined horizontally at the center
22¼ x 15⅛ in. (56.5 x 38.4 cm)
Inscribed (lower left): *vert*; stamped (lower right):
ED
Harvard Art Museums/Fogg Museum, Cambridge,
Mass., gift of Philip Hofer (1934.3)
New York only
repr. p. 170

PROVENANCE: the artist's estate sale, Hôtel Drouot,
Paris, February 17–29, 1864, part of no. 297; Alfred
Robaut, Paris; Denys Darcy; Georges Aubry, Paris;
Maurice Gobin, Paris (sold to Hofer); Philip Hofer,
Cambridge, Mass. (until 1934)

SELECTED EXHIBITIONS: Paris (Mémorial) 1963,
no. 517; Frankfurt 1987–88, no. K 8; New York 1991,
no. 47; Karlsruhe 2003–4, no. 168

This drawing and cats. 119 and 120 are studies for
the painting in the church of Saint-Sulpice, Paris
(fig. 69). Their subject is drawn from Genesis
32:22–32.

CAT. 119

Jacob Wrestling with the Angel
1850
Black chalk on tracing paper
21⁷⁄₈ x 14⁹⁄₁₆ in. (55.6 x 37 cm)
Stamped (lower left): *ED*
The Morgan Library & Museum, New York, gift of
Mrs. Landon K. Thorne, 1964 (1964.2)
New York only
repr. p. 170

PROVENANCE: the artist's estate sale, Hôtel Drouot,
Paris, February 17–29, 1864, part of lot 297; Alfred
Robaut, Paris; Paul-Arthur Chéramy, Paris (until
1908; his sale, Galerie Georges Petit, Paris, May 5–7,
1908, no. 351); Alfred Beurdeley, Paris (until d. 1919;
his estate sale, Galerie Georges Petit, Paris,
November 30–December 2, 1920, no. 118); Edouard
Napoléon César Edmond Mortier, duc de Trévise,
Paris (until 1938; his sale, Galerie Charpentier, Paris,
May 19, 1938, no. 3); Mrs. Landon K. Thorne (until
1964; her gift to Morgan)

SELECTED EXHIBITIONS: Frankfurt 1987–88, no. K 9;
New York 1991, no. 46

CAT. 120

Jacob Wrestling with the Angel
1850
Oil over pen and ink on tracing paper; mounted on
canvas and backed with linen
22⅜ x 16 in. (56.8 x 40.6 cm)
The Metropolitan Museum of Art, New York, Gift
from the Karen B. Cohen Collection of Eugène
Delacroix, in honor of Philippe de Montebello, 2016
(2016.759)
J 595
New York only
repr. p. 171

PROVENANCE: the artist (possibly given to Andrieu);
Pierre Andrieu, Paris (until at least 1864); member of
the Orléans family, possibly Philippe, comte de Paris,
Château d'Eu, Normandy (by 1891–d. 1894); his
daughter princesse Hélène, duchess of Aosta
(1895–d. 1951); her daughter-in-law Irene, duchess of
Aosta, Florence (from 1951–at least 1959, when
consigned to Michael Harvard, London); [Claude
Aubry, Paris, by 1963]; [Eugene V. Thaw, New York,
by 1967]; [Salander-O'Reilly, New York, until 1985];
Karen B. Cohen, New York (1985–2016)

SELECTED EXHIBITIONS: Paris 1864b, no. 87; New
York 1991, no. 8; New York 2000–2001, no. 44; Paris
2009–10, no. 15; Paris 2018, no. 39

CAT. 121

Sunset
ca. 1850
Pastel on blue laid paper, mounted on paper board
Overall: 8¹⁄₁₆ x 10³⁄₁₆ in. (20.4 x 25.9 cm)
Stamped (verso): *ED*
The Metropolitan Museum of Art, New York, Gift
from the Karen B. Cohen Collection of Eugène
Delacroix, in honor of Philippe de Montebello, 2014
(2014.732.4)
Johnson 1995, no. 44
New York only
repr. p. 184

PROVENANCE: the artist's estate sale, Hôtel Drouot,
Paris, February 17–29, 1864, one of seventeen pastel
studies of skies included in nos. 608–13; Alfred
Robaut, Paris; baron Joseph Vitta, Paris (by 1930);
[Hazlitt, Gooden & Fox, London, until 1988];
Karen B. Cohen, New York (1988–2014)

SELECTED EXHIBITIONS: New York 1991, no. 16;
Paris–Philadelphia 1998–99, no. 62 (Philadelphia
only); New York 2000–2001, no. 45; Paris 2009–10,
no. 104; New York 2018, no. 101

CAT. 122

Apollo Slays the Python, sketch
ca. 1850
Oil on paper on canvas
26¹⁄₁₆ x 23¾ in. (66.2 x 60.3 cm)
Van Gogh Museum, Amsterdam (purchased with
support from the BankGiro Loterij)
(inv. s0526S2012)
J 575
New York only
repr. p. 144

PROVENANCE: the artist's estate sale, Hôtel Drouot,
Paris, February 17–29, 1864, no. 30, to Dauzats;
Adrien Dauzats (from 1864); count of Villagonzalo,
Paris (from ca. 1870); by descent to private collec-
tion, Madrid (until 2012; sale, Christie's, London,
June 12, 2012, no. 24); Van Gogh Museum,
Amsterdam (from 2012)

SELECTED EXHIBITIONS: Madrid–Barcelona 2011–12,
no. 147; Minneapolis–London 2015–16, no. 11

The subject of this sketch and cat. 123 is a Greek myth
recounted by the Roman poet Ovid in *Metamorphoses*
(1.438–72). Both works are related to the ceiling
painting in the Gallery of Apollo in the Louvre
(fig. 53).

CAT. 123

Apollo Victorious over the Serpent Python, sketch
ca. 1850
Oil on canvas
54⅛ x 40³⁄₁₆ in. (137.5 x 102 cm)
Musées Royaux des Beaux-Arts de Belgique, Brussels
(inv. 1727)
J 576
repr. p. 145

PROVENANCE: the artist's estate sale, Hôtel Drouot, Paris, February 17–29, 1864, no. 28, withdrawn by Delacroix's legatee, Piron; Achille Piron (1864–d. 1865; his estate sale, Hôtel Drouot, Paris, April 21, 1865, no. 1, to Stevens); [Arthur Stevens, Brussels, 1865; sold to Musées Royaux des Beaux-Arts de Belgique, Brussels]

SELECTED EXHIBITIONS: Paris 1861–62; Bordeaux 1862, no. 223; Paris (Mémorial) 1963, no. 419; Paris–Philadelphia 1998–99, no. 64 (in catalogue but not in exhibition)

CAT. 124

Pietà
ca. 1850
Oil on canvas
13¾ x 10⅝ in. (35 x 27 cm)
Signed (lower center): *Eug. Delacroix.*
The National Museum of Art, Architecture and Design, Oslo (inv. NG.M.01179)
J 443
repr. p. 135

PROVENANCE: Narcisse-Virgile Diaz de la Peña (in 1855); Paul Tesse (in 1864); Elisabeth, Queen consort of Romania (in 1889; d. 1916); National Gallery, Oslo (from 1918; acquired as gift from the Friends of the National Gallery)

SELECTED EXHIBITIONS: Paris 1864a; Zürich–Frankfurt 1987–88, no. 73; Copenhagen 2000, no. 19; Madrid–Barcelona 2011–12, no. 146

CAT. 125

The Agony in the Garden
1851
Oil on canvas
13⅜ x 16⁹⁄₁₆ in. (34 x 42 cm)
Signed and dated (lower left): *Eug. Delacroix / 1851*
Van Gogh Museum, Amsterdam. On loan from Rijksmuseum, Amsterdam (gift of M. C. Baroness Van Lynden-Van Pallandt, The Hague)
(inv. s0086B1991)
J 445
repr. p. 133

PROVENANCE: the artist (until 1851; sold in December, through the Société des Amis des Arts, Bordeaux, probably to Damblat); Monsieur F. E. Damblat (in 1864); Madame Ingres or Monsieurs T. and X. (until 1894; posthumous sale of Madame Ingres and modern pictures belonging to MM. T. and X., Hôtel Drouot, Paris, April 10, 1894, no. 28, to Arnold & Tripp]; [Arnold & Tripp, 1894; sold August 7 to Van Lynden]; Baron R. van Lynden, The Hague (1894–his d.); his widow (until 1900; her gift to Rijksmuseum)

SELECTED EXHIBITIONS: Bordeaux 1851, no. 144; Winterthur 2008, no. 24

CAT. 126

Study of the Sea
1851(?)
Watercolor on paper, with inscription in graphite
10 x 15¼ in. (25.4 x 38.7 cm)
Possibly inscribed or dated (lower right): *51*; stamped (lower right): *ED* [Lugt 838]
Roberta J. M. Olson and Alexander B. V. Johnson
New York only
repr. p. 185

PROVENANCE: presumably acquired from the artist by Pierre Andrieu (d. 1892), Paris, and sold by him or his widow to Vuillier; [Vuillier, Paris]; private collection, France; [David & Constance Yates, New York, until 1995; sold to Olson and Johnson]

CAT. 127

Marphise
1852
Oil on canvas
32⁵⁄₁₆ x 39¾ in. (82.1 x 101 cm)
Signed and dated (lower left): *Eug. Delacroix / 1852.*
The Walters Art Museum, Baltimore, Maryland (37.10)
J 303
repr. p. 200

PROVENANCE: the artist (sold to Bonnet); J. P. Bonnet (until 1853; his sale, Hôtel des Ventes Mobilières, Paris, February 19, 1853, no. 9, to Bulloz); Bulloz (from 1853); sale, Hôtel Drouot, Paris, May 20, 1881, no. 9, presumably to Haro, possibly for Balay; Balay (by 1885); [Arnold & Tripp, Paris, in half-shares with Knoedler, New York, 1901–4; sold to Walters]; Henry Walters, Baltimore (1904–d. 1931; his bequest to Walters Art Museum)

SELECTED EXHIBITIONS: Paris 1885, no. 107; Paris (Mémorial) 1963, no. 429; Zürich–Frankfurt 1987–88, no. 84; Paris–Philadelphia 1998–99, no. 87; Copenhagen 2000, no. 30

The scene is drawn from the epic poem *Orlando furioso* (1516), by Ludovico Ariosto (1474–1533).

CAT. 128

The Sea at Dieppe
1852
Oil on cardboard, laid down on wood
13¾ x 20¹⁄₁₆ in. (35 x 51 cm)
Musée du Louvre, Paris, Département des Peintures, Bequest of Marcel Beurdeley, 1979 (RF 1979-46)
J 489
repr. p. 186

PROVENANCE: the artist's estate sale, Hôtel Drouot, Paris, February 17–29, 1864, no. 98, to Duchâtel; comte Duchâtel (1864–at least 1885); Alfred Beurdeley (by 1912–d. 1919; his estate sale, Galerie Georges Petit, Paris, May 6–7, 1920, no. 35, to Beurdeley); his son, Marcel Beurdeley (1920–d. 1979; his bequest to Louvre)

SELECTED EXHIBITIONS: Paris 1864b, no. 149; Paris 1885, no. 70; Paris (Mémorial) 1963, no. 453; Paris–Philadelphia 1998–99, no. 53; Madrid–Barcelona 2011–12, no. 155

CAT. 129

Christ Asleep during the Tempest
ca. 1853
Oil on canvas
20 x 24 in. (50.8 x 61 cm)
Signed (lower left): *Eug. Delacroix*
The Metropolitan Museum of Art, New York, H. O. Havemeyer Collection, Bequest of Mrs. H. O. Havemeyer, 1929 (29.100.131)
J 454
repr. p. 191

PROVENANCE: ?[Francis Petit, Paris, from 1853]; ?Bouruet-Aubertot, Paris (by 1860); ?Monsieur R.-L. L. (until 1876; his sale, Paris, April 22, 1876, no. II); John Saulnier, Bordeaux (by 1873?–d. 1886; his estate sale, Hôtel Drouot, Paris, June 5, 1886, no. 35, bought in; his estate sale, Galerie Charles Sedelmeyer, Paris, March 25, 1892, no. 8, to Durand-Ruel); [Durand-Ruel, Paris, 1892; stock no. 2066; sold on December 13 to Durand-Ruel, New York]; [Durand-Ruel, New York, 1892–94; sold on January 16, 1894, to Havemeyer]; Mr. and Mrs. H. O. Havemeyer, New York (1894–his d. 1907); Mrs. H. O. (Louisine W.) Havemeyer, New York (1907–d. 1929)

SELECTED EXHIBITIONS: Paris 1860, no. 349; Paris 1864b, no. 125; Zürich–Frankfurt 1987–88, no. 95; New York 1991, no. 9; Paris–Philadelphia 1998–99, no. 115; Karlsruhe 2003–4, no. 172; Minneapolis–London 2015–16, no. 43

CAT. 130

Saint Stephen Borne Away by His Disciples
1853
Oil on canvas
58¼ x 45¼ in. (148 x 115 cm)
Signed and dated (lower left): *Eug. Delacroix 1853*
Musée des Beaux-Arts, Arras (inv. 859.1)
J 449
repr. p. 131

PROVENANCE: the artist, Paris (until 1859; sold to the municipality of Arras for the Musée des Beaux-Arts)

SELECTED EXHIBITIONS: Paris (Salon) 1853, no. 350; Paris 1885, no. 5; Paris (Mémorial) 1963, no. 437; Zürich–Frankfurt 1987–88, no. 88; Paris–Philadelphia 1998–99, no. 111; Karlsruhe 2003–4, no. 181; Madrid–Barcelona 2011–12, no. 160; Leipzig 2015–16, no. 81

The subject is drawn from the New Testament (Acts of the Apostles 6 and 7:55–60).

CAT. 131

Christ on the Sea of Galilee
1854
Oil on canvas
23⁹⁄₁₆ x 28⅞ in. (59.8 x 73.3 cm)
Signed and dated (lower right): *Eug. Delacroix / 1854*
The Walters Art Museum, Baltimore, Maryland (37.186)
J 456
repr. p. 191

PROVENANCE: [Adolphe Beugniet, Paris, 1854/55; presumably bought from the artist; sold to Troyon]; Constant Troyon, Paris (by 1855–d. 1865); his mother (1865; to Frémyn); Frémyn (from 1865); Tabourier (in 1878); Gustave Viot (by 1883–86; his sale, Galerie Georges Petit, Paris, May 25, 1886, no. 2, to Levesque); Levesque (from 1886); William T. Walters, Baltimore (until d. 1894); his son, Henry Walters (1894–d. 1931; his bequest to Walters Art Museum)

SELECTED EXHIBITIONS: Bordeaux 1855, no. 170; Paris (Mémorial) 1963, no. 450; Zürich–Frankfurt 1987–88, no. 96; New York 1991, no. 10; Paris–Philadelphia 1998–99, no. 118; Madrid–Barcelona 2011–12, no. 165

CAT. 132

The Sea at Dieppe
probably 1854
Watercolor on laid paper
10½ x 17⁹⁄₁₆ in. (26.7 x 44.6 cm)
Inscribed in graphite (at right): *presque toujours brume grisatre violete* [sic] */ à l'horizon entre le ton de la mer / et le bleu du ciel / par le beau temps / les montagnes /*

violatres / le ton de la mer / paraissant d'un vert / charmant mais / mêlé de vert d'arc en ciel / où le vert domine (almost always a grayish violet haze at the horizon, between the tone of the sea and the blue of the sky—in clear weather the violet peaks—the tone of the sea appears green, delightful but mixed with the green [these two last words struck out] of a rainbow, in which green predominates); stamped (lower right): *ED*
The Metropolitan Museum of Art, New York, Gift from the Karen B. Cohen Collection of Eugène Delacroix, in honor of Jill Newhouse, 2014 (2014.732.1)
New York only
repr. p. 187

PROVENANCE: the artist's estate sale, Hôtel Drouot, Paris, February 17–29, 1864, part of no. 600; private collection, Paris; [Jill Newhouse]; Karen B. Cohen, New York

SELECTED EXHIBITIONS: New York 1991, no. 69; Paris–Philadelphia 1998–99, no. 57 (Paris only); Paris 2009–10, no. 105

CAT. 133

A Lion and a Tiger, Fighting
ca. 1854
Graphite on wove paper
12⁵⁄₁₆ x 9½ in. (31.3 x 24.1 cm)
Stamped (lower right): *ED*
The Metropolitan Museum of Art, New York, Bequest of Gregoire Tarnopol, 1979, and Gift of Alexander Tarnopol, 1980 (1980.21.13)
New York only
repr. p. 146

PROVENANCE: the artist's estate sale, Hôtel Drouot, Paris, February 17–29, 1864, no. 470; Alfred Robaut, Fontenay-sous-Bois (d. 1909); Georges Aubry, Paris (by 1927); Maurice Gobin, Paris (by 1930–at least 1939); Grégoire Tarnopol (until d. 1979) and his brother Alexander Tarnopol, New York (until 1980)

SELECTED EXHIBITIONS: Frankfurt 1987–88, no. I 26; New York 1991, no. 53; Paris–Philadelphia 1998–99, no. 8 (Philadelphia only); Karlsruhe 2003–4, no. 183

CAT. 134

Lion Hunt, sketch
1854
Oil on canvas
35⁷⁄₁₆ x 45¹⁵⁄₁₆ in. (90 x 116.7 cm)
Musée d'Orsay, Paris (RF 1984-33)
J 197
repr. p. 147

PROVENANCE: the artist's estate sale, Hôtel Drouot, Paris, February 17–29, 1864, no. 148, to Riesener; Léon Riesener (1864–79; his estate sale, Hôtel Drouot, Paris, April 10–11, 1879, no. 222); his widow, Madame Léon Riesener (1879–at least 1885); their daughter, Madame Alexandre (Louise Thérèse) Lauwick (until d. 1932); by descent to Madame Georges (Gabrielle) Itasse (by 1933–?1984); [E. V. Thaw, New York, 1984]; purchased in 1984 by the Musées Nationaux for Musée d'Orsay

SELECTED EXHIBITIONS: Paris 1864b, no. 140; Paris 1885, no. 169; Paris (Mémorial) 1963, no. 467; Paris–Philadelphia 1998–99, no. 12; Copenhagen 2000, no. 12; Madrid–Barcelona 2011–12, no. 168; Paris 2013–14, no. 25

CAT. 135

Lion Hunt (fragment)
1855
Oil on canvas
68⅞ in. x 11 ft. 9⁵⁄₁₆ in. (175 x 359 cm)
Signed and dated (lower center): *Eug. Delacroix 1855.*
Musée des Beaux-Arts, Bordeaux (inv. Bx E 469)
J 198
repr. p. 147

PROVENANCE: commissioned from the artist by the state on March 20, 1854, with payment completed in November 1855; allocated in 1856 to the Musée de Bordeaux

SELECTED EXHIBITIONS: Paris 1855, no. 2939; Bordeaux 1857, no. 154; Paris (Mémorial) 1963, no. 466; Paris–Philadelphia 1998–99, no. 14

The original dimensions of this painting were 260 x 359 cm; the perimeter, notably the top portion, was lost to fire in 1870.

CAT. 136

Lion Hunt
1855–56
Oil on canvas
22⁷⁄₁₆ x 29⅛ in. (57 x 74 cm)
Signed and dated (lower right): *Eug. Delacroix. 1856.*
Nationalmuseum, Stockholm (inv. NM 6350)
J 199
repr. p. 150

PROVENANCE: [Détrimont; bought from the artist upon completion in April 1856; possibly sold to Goldsmith (or Goldschmidt)]; Adolf Liebermann von Wahlendorf (until 1876; his sale, Hôtel Drouot, Paris, May 8–9, 1876, no. 24, bought in); Fop Smit, Rotterdam (until 1893; sold on February 4 to Durand-Ruel); [Durand-Ruel, Paris, 1893–95; sold on

April 30 to Heugel]; Henri Heugel (1895–1905; his sale, Galerie Georges Petit, Paris, May 26, 1905, no. 5, to Bauml); Bauml (from 1905); A. F. Klaveness, Oslo (in 1929); Philip and Grace Sandblom, Lund (until 1970; their gift to Nationalmuseum)

SELECTED EXHIBITIONS: Paris–Philadelphia 1998–99, no. 13 (Paris only); Madrid–Barcelona 2011–12, no. 169

CAT. 137
Hilly Landscape
ca. 1855
Oil on paper, laid down on canvas
7½ x 11⅛ in. (19.1 x 28.3 cm)
Private collection, New York
J 484a
New York only
repr. p. 183

PROVENANCE: the artist's estate sale, Hôtel Drouot, Paris, February 17–29, 1864, probably part of no. 219; Sir Michael Sadler, Oxford (by 1932–d. 1943; exhibited, presumably as part of his estate, at Leicester Galleries, London, 1944, and sold by them to Russell); Mrs. Gilbert Russell, possibly Mottisfont, Hampshire, until 1972, and thereafter London (1944–d. 1982; her estate sale, Phillips, London, November 27, 1984, no. 110, to Emery); Dr. and Mrs. Eric Emery (1984–87; sold through Richard Nathanson, London, to O'Reilly); [William O'Reilly, New York, 1987–88; sold to private collection]; private collection (since 1988)

SELECTED EXHIBITIONS: New York 1991, no. 11; New York 2000–2001, no. 46; Paris 2009–10, no. 103

CAT. 138
The Sultan of Morocco and His Entourage
1856
Oil on canvas
25⁹⁄₁₆ x 21⅝ in. (64.9 x 54.9 cm)
Signed and dated (lower right): *Eug. Delacroix / 1856*
Private collection
J 401
New York only
repr. p. 109

PROVENANCE: Frédéric Hartmann, Paris (1856–d. 1880; commissioned from the artist; delivered October 1856; his estate sale, rue de Courcelles, no. 18, Paris, May 7, 1881, no. 1, to Pereire); Gustave Pereire, Paris (from 1881); his son-in-law, Eugène Mir (by 1928–d. 1930); [Brame, Paris, until 1972]; Norton Simon Foundation, Pasadena (1972–at least 1986; inv. F. 72.33.P); private collection

This is a reduced variant of the prime version, exhibited at the Salon of 1845, and now in the Musée des Augustins, Toulouse (fig. 37).

CAT. 139
The Bride of Abydos (Selim and Zuleika)
1857
Oil on canvas
18¾ x 15¾ in. (47.6 x 40 cm)
Signed and dated (lower left): *Eug. Delacroix / 1857.*
Kimbell Art Museum, Fort Worth, Texas
(AP 1986.04)
J 325
repr. p. 155

PROVENANCE: gift of the artist to his landlord, Jules Hurel, Paris (March 15, 1858–at least 1889); [E. Le Roy et Cie, Paris; sold to Knoedler]; [Knoedler, Paris, until 1913; sold in June to Soucaret]; Madame Soucaret (from 1913); Madame Emile Dhainaut (until 1924; her sale, Galerie Georges Petit, Paris, May 19, 1924, no. 6, to Diehl); Marchal Diehl (from 1924); private collection, Switzerland (from 1980); [Lentes Trading S.A., Zug, Switzerland]; Kimbell Art Museum, Fort Worth (purchased in 1986)

SELECTED EXHIBITIONS: Zürich–Frankfurt 1987–88, no. 105; New York 1991, no. 12; New Orleans–New York–Cincinnati 1996–97, no. 13; Paris–Philadelphia 1998–99, no. 85; Copenhagen 2000, no. 34; Minneapolis–London 2015–16 (Minneapolis only)

This is the last of four painted versions of this subject, drawn from Lord Byron's poem *The Bride of Abydos* (1813), published in French in 1821.

CAT. 140
Lamentation over the Body of Christ
1857
Oil on canvas
14¹⁵⁄₁₆ x 18¼ in. (38 x 46.3 cm)
Signed and dated (lower left): *Eug. Delacroix. 1857.*
Staatliche Kunsthalle Karlsruhe (inv. 2661)
J 466
repr. p. 136

PROVENANCE: probably bought from the artist by Bouruet-Aubertot (by 1864–his d.; his estate sale, Hôtel Drouot, Paris, February 22, 1869, no. 7, withdrawn and sold privately, probably to Gavet); Gavet (?from 1869; sold to Laurent-Richard); Laurent-Richard (until 1878; his sale, Hôtel Drouot, Paris, May 23–25, 1878, no. 15, bought in); Albert de Saint-Albin; John Balli, London (until 1913; his sale, Galerie Georges Petit, Paris, May 22, 1913, no. 11); Laroche Gand; Le Roy, Paris; Mrs. Walter Feilchenfeldt, Zürich (until 1978; sold to Staatliche Kunsthalle Karlsruhe)

SELECTED EXHIBITIONS: Paris 1864b, no. 103; Paris–Philadelphia 1998–99, no. 124 (Paris only); Copenhagen 2000, no. 20; Karlsruhe 2003–4, no. 179; Winterthur 2008, no. 22; Madrid–Barcelona 2011–12, no. 172; Leipzig 2015–16, no. 87

This is a reduced variant of the painting in Saint-Denys-du-Saint-Sacrement, Paris (fig. 48), with the composition reversed (as in cats. 100 and 101).

CAT. 141
Abduction of Rebecca
1858
Oil on canvas
41⁵⁄₁₆ x 32¹⁄₁₆ in. (105 x 81.5 cm)
Signed and dated (lower center, on stone block): *Eug. Delacroix 1858.*
Musée du Louvre, Paris, Département des Peintures, Bequest of George Thomy-Thiéry, 1902 (RF 1392)
J 326
repr. p. 175

PROVENANCE: the artist, Paris (sold in 1858 to Hartmann); Jacques Hartmann, Mulhouse (1858–76; his anonymous sale, Hôtel Drouot, Paris, May 11, 1876, no. 10; to Bague); [Bague, Paris, in 1876]; F. Kramer (in 1878); [Arnold & Tripp and Bague et Cie, 1882; bought from an unspecified source in half-shares with another purchaser on April 21, 1882; sold the same day to Secrétan]; Eugène Secrétan (from 1882); comte de Jaucourt; George Thomy-Thiéry (by January 1889–1902; his bequest to Louvre)

SELECTED EXHIBITIONS: Paris (Salon) 1859, no. 824; Paris (Mémorial) 1963, no. 501; Zürich–Frankfurt 1987–88, no. 111; Paris–Philadelphia 1998–99, no. 91; Copenhagen 2000, no. 35; Madrid–Barcelona 2011–12, no. 173

This is a different treatment of the subject depicted in cat. 105.

CAT. 142
Ovid among the Scythians
1859
Oil on canvas
34⅝ x 51³⁄₁₆ in. (88 x 130 cm)
Signed and dated (lower right): *Eug. Delacroix / 1859*
The National Gallery, London, Bought, 1956 (inv. NG6262)
J 334
repr. p. 219

PROVENANCE: Benoît Fould (commissioned from the artist in March 1856; Fould died in July 1858, before the painting was completed, but the commission was honored by his widow); his widow, Madame Fould; their niece, Madame de Sourdeval (in 1892); her daughter, Madame Charles Demachy; her daughter, baronne Ernest Seillière; her heirs (sold to de Hauke by 1956); [César de Hauke, until 1956; sold to National Gallery]

SELECTED EXHIBITIONS: Paris (Salon) 1859, no. 822, Paris 1861–62; Zürich–Frankfurt 1987–88, no. 114; Paris–Philadelphia 1998–99, no. 95; Karlsruhe 2003–4, no. 209; Madrid–Barcelona 2011–12, no. 176; Minneapolis–London 2015–16, no. 56

In A.D. 8, the Roman poet Ovid (43 B.C.–A.D. 17) was banished by Emperor Augustus to the banks of the Black Sea, where, according to the Greek historian Strabo, he was greeted with hospitality by the Scythians, who fed him mare's milk.

CAT. 143

Amadis de Gaule Delivers a Damsel from Galpan's Castle
1859–60
Oil on canvas
21½ x 25¾ in. (54.6 x 65.4 cm)
Signed and dated (lower left): *Eug. Delacroix 1860*
Virginia Museum of Fine Arts, Richmond, Adolph D. and Wilkins C. Williams Fund (57.1)
J 336
repr. p. 176

PROVENANCE: the artist, Paris (sold prior to completion in late 1859 to Cachardy); [Cachardy, in 1859; sold to Gerantet]; Claudius Gerantet, Saint-Etienne (by January 4, 1860; d. 1889); [Gustave Tempelaere, 1898; bought at Saint-Etienne in November; sold on November 11 to Arnold & Tripp]; [Arnold & Tripp, Paris, 1898–99; sold on July 19 to Knoedler]; [Knoedler, New York, 1899; sold in August to Henry]; H. S. Henry, Philadelphia (1899–1907; his sale, American Art Association, New York, January 25, 1907, no. 15, to Montaignac); I. Montaignac (from 1907); Charles Viguier, Paris (in 1910); Eugène(?) Blot; Dr. H. Graber, Zürich (in 1939); [Raeber Gallery, Basel, inv. 44435]; private collection, Basel (until 1954; sold on February 25 to Knoedler); [Knoedler, New York, 1954–57; sold to Virginia Museum of Fine Arts]

SELECTED EXHIBITIONS: Paris (Mémorial) 1963, no. 508; Zürich–Frankfurt 1987–88, no. 118; New Orleans–New York–Cincinnati 1996–97, no. 11; Paris–Philadelphia 1998–99, no. 96

The subject is drawn from the chivalric romance *Amadis de Gaule*, which originated in fourteenth-century Spain or Portugal. Delacroix likely knew the version by Louis-Elisabeth de la Vergne, comte de Tressan, published in Amsterdam in 1779.

CAT. 144

Arab Horses Fighting in a Stable
1860
Oil on canvas
25⅜ x 31⅞ in. (64.5 x 81 cm)
Signed and dated (lower left): *Eug. Delacroix / 1860*
Musée d'Orsay, Paris, on deposit from the Musée du Louvre, Bequest of comte Isaac de Camondo, 1911 (RF 1988)
J 413
repr. p. 212

PROVENANCE: [Estienne; thought to have been commissioned from the artist]; Allou or Erler (until 1872; their sale, Hôtel Drouot, Paris, February 12, 1872, no. 13, to Durand-Ruel); [Durand-Ruel, Paris, 1872–73]; John Saulnier, Bordeaux (in 1873); Charles Hayem, Bordeaux (in 1885); comte Isaac de Camondo (until d. 1911; his bequest to Louvre)

SELECTED EXHIBITIONS: Paris 1885, no. 96; Paris (Mémorial) 1963, no. 506; Paris 1994–95, no. 102; Paris–Philadelphia 1998–99, no. 108; Karlsruhe 2003–4, no. 220; Madrid–Barcelona 2011–12, no. 179; Paris 2014–15, no. 72

CAT. 145

Shipwreck on the Coast
1862
Oil on canvas
15¼ x 18 in. (38.7 x 45.7 cm)
Signed and dated (lower right): *Eug. Delacroix / 1862.*
Museum of Fine Arts, Houston, Museum purchase funded by the Agnes Cullen Arnold Endowment Fund, 2004 (2004.1693)
J 490
repr. p. 196

PROVENANCE: Victor Chocquet, Paris (by 1864–d. 1891); his widow, Marie Chocquet (1891–d. 1899; her estate sale, Galerie Georges Petit, Paris, July 1–4, 1899, no. 47, to Durand-Ruel); [Durand-Ruel, Paris, from 1899]; Denys Cochin (in 1916); Boner, Berlin (in 1930); A. M. Haussmann (or Hausamann), Zürich (in 1956); by descent to private collection (until 2002; sale, Christie's, London, June 20, 2002, no. 138); [Richard Feigen, New York, 2002–4; sold to Museum of Fine Arts, Houston]

SELECTED EXHIBITIONS: Paris (Mémorial) 1963, no. 527; Madrid–Barcelona 2011–12, no. 180; Minneapolis–London 2015–16, no. 74

Autograph Manuscripts by Delacroix
Lent by the Library of the Institut National d'Histoire de l'Art, Paris

School Notebook no. 8
1815
Folio 1
Collections Jacques Doucet (Ms 246–8)

Journal, 1822–24
First Notebook (September 3–October 27, 1822)
Folios 15v and 16r (October 8, 1822)
Collections Jacques Doucet (Ms 247–1)

Second Notebook (April 15, 1823–January 27, 1824)
Folio 22v (January 27, 1824)
Collections Jacques Doucet, gift of David David-Weill, 1924 (Ms 247–2)

Fourth Notebook (April 16–May 15, 1824)
Folios 15v and 16r (May 7, 1824)
Collections Jacques Doucet (Ms 247–4)

Fifth Notebook (May 18–October 5, 1824)
Folios 2v and 3r (June 1, 1824)
Collections Jacques Doucet, gift of David David-Weill, 1924 (Ms 247–5)

Journal, 1847
Folios 18v and 19r (March 12–15, 1847)
Collections Jacques Doucet (Ms 253–1)

Journal, 1850
Folios 72v and 73r (October 14–17, 1850)
Collections Jacques Doucet (Ms 253–2)
New York only

Journal, 1855
Folios 129v and 130r (October 3–4, 1855)
Collections Jacques Doucet (Ms 253–3)

Journal, 1857
Folios 118v and 119r (August 24–25, 1857)
Collections Jacques Doucet, bequest of Etienne Moreau-Nélaton, 1927 (Ms 253–5)

Lettres d'Eugène Delacroix (1815–1863) recueillies et publiées par M. Philippe Burty
Bound volume containing 33 letters and 3 prints
Open to Frédéric Villot, *Portrait of Eugène Delacroix (after a Self-Portrait)*, 1847, mezzotint and drypoint on chine collée (for another impression, see fig. 1)
Collections Jacques Doucet, gift of David David-Weil, 1926 (Ms 248)
New York only

Bibliography

Allard 2004
Allard, Sébastien. "Delacroix au Salon de 1822: La stratégie de la conquête." In Paris 2004, pp. 13–35.

Allard 2005
Allard, Sébastien, ed. *Paris 1820: L'affirmation de la génération romantique; actes de la journée d'étude organisée par le Centre André Chastel le 24 mai 2004.* Bern: Peter Lang, 2005.

Allard 2010
Allard, Sébastien. "Delacroix, Delaroche, and the Place of the Spectator." In Marseilles–Rovereto–Toronto 2009–10 (Italian ed.), pp. 130–39. (2009 French ed., pp. 122–31.)

Allard 2011
Allard, Sébastien. "Delacroix et l'idée du sujet en peinture." In Madrid–Barcelona 2011–12, pp. 24–60.

Allard and Chaudonneret 2006
Allard, Sébastien, and Marie-Claude Chaudonneret. *Ingres: La réforme des principes, 1806–1834.* Lyon: Fage, 2006.

Allard and Chaudonneret 2010
Allard, Sébastien, and Marie-Claude Chaudonneret. *Le Suicide de Gros: Les peintres de l'Empire et la génération romantique.* Paris: Gourcuff Gradenigo, 2010.

Alliez 2007
Alliez, Eric. *L'oeil-cerveau: Nouvelles histoires de la peinture moderne.* Paris: Vrin, 2007.

Angers 2011
Guillaume Bodinier (1795–1872): Un peintre angevin en Italie. Musée des Beaux-Arts, Angers, France, May 27–September 18, 2011. Exh. cat. by Patrick Le Nouëne. Angers: Musées d'Angers; Editions Expressions Contemporaines, 2011.

Angers 2012
La Dernière Nuit de Troie: Histoire et violence autour de "La Mort de Priam" de Pierre Guérin. Musée des Beaux-Arts, Angers, France, May 25–September 2, 2012. Exh. cat. by Mehdi Korchane. Paris: Somogy; Angers: Musées d'Angers, 2012.

Anon. 1824
Anonymous (*L'amateur sans prétention*). "Salon de 1824: Septième article." *Le Mercure du dix-neuvième siècle* 7 (1824), pp. 199–210.

Anon. 1836
Anonymous. "Salon de 1836 (IIe article). Peinture." *L'artiste* 11, no. 7 (1836), pp. 77–78.

Ariosto 1850
Ariosto, Ludovico. *Roland furieux.* French translation by the comte de Tressan. 2 vols. Paris: Ruel aîné, 1850.

Astruc 1859
Astruc, Zacharie. *Les 14 stations du Salon 1859, suivies d'un récit douloureux.* Paris: Poulet-Malassis et de Broise, 1859.

Bandiera 1980
Bandiera, John. "Byron's 'Lara' as a Source for an Early Work by Delacroix." *Marsyas: Studies in the History of Art* 20 (1979–80, pub. 1980), pp. 57–60, pls. 26, 27.

Baroni 2016
Baroni, Jean-Luc. *Paintings, Drawings, Sculptures.* London: Jean-Luc Baroni, 2016.

Baudelaire 1845 (1976 ed.)
Baudelaire, Charles. "Salon de 1845." In Baudelaire 1976, vol. 2, pp. 351–407.

Baudelaire 1846 (1976 ed.)
Baudelaire, Charles. "Salon de 1846." In Baudelaire 1976, vol. 2, pp. 415–96. Originally published Paris: Michel Lévy Frères, 1846.

Baudelaire 1855 (1976 ed.)
Baudelaire, Charles. "Exposition universelle, 1855." In Baudelaire 1976, vol. 2, pp. 575–97. Originally published in *Le pays* (May 26 and June 3, 1855) and *La portefeuille* (August 12, 1855).

Baudelaire 1856 (1976 ed.)
Baudelaire, Charles. "Edgar Poe, sa vie et ses oeuvres." In Baudelaire 1976, vol. 2, pp. 296–318. Originally published in *Histoires extraordinaires*, 1856.

Baudelaire 1859a (1976 ed.)
Baudelaire, Charles. "Philibert Rouvière." In Baudelaire 1976, vol. 2, pp. 60–65. Originally published in *L'artiste*, n.s., 8 (December 1, 1859), pp. 158–59.

Baudelaire 1859b (1976 ed.)
Baudelaire, Charles. "Salon de 1859." In Baudelaire 1976, vol. 2, pp. 608–82. Originally published in *Revue française* (June 10, June 20, July 1, and July 20, 1859).

Baudelaire 1863 (1976 ed.)
Baudelaire, Charles. "L'oeuvre et la vie d'Eugène Delacroix." In Baudelaire 1976, vol. 2, pp. 742–70. Originally published in *L'opinion nationale* (September 2–November 22, 1863).

Baudelaire 1976
Baudelaire, Charles. *Oeuvres complètes.* Edited by Claude Pichois. 2 vols. New ed. Bibliothèque de la Pléiade 7. Paris: Gallimard, 1976.

Baudelaire 1981
Baudelaire, Charles. *Art in Paris, 1845–1862: Salons and Other Exhibitions Reviewed by Charles Baudelaire.* Translated and edited by Jonathan Mayne. 2nd ed. Oxford: Phaidon Press, 1981. Originally published 1965.

Bazin 1987–97
Bazin, Germain. *Théodore Géricault: Etude critique, documents et catalogue raisonné.* 7 vols. Paris: La Bibliothèque des Arts, 1987–97.

Bernast 2001
Bernast, Virginie. "Les sources littéraires et musicales de *Médée furieuse*." In Paris 2001, pp. 32–44.

Blanc 1870
Blanc, Charles. *Grammaire des arts du dessin: Architecture, sculpture, peinture.* 2nd ed. Paris: Renouard, 1870.

Blanc 1876
Blanc, Charles. *Les artistes de mon temps.* Paris: Firmin-Didot, 1876.

Bordeaux 1851
Société des Amis des Arts de Bordeaux, première exposition. Opened November 15, 1851. Exh. cat., *Explication des ouvrages de peinture, sculpture, architecture, graveur et lithographie des artistes vivants exposés dans la Galerie de la Société des Amis des Arts de Bordeaux.* Bordeaux: Chez Gounouilhou, 1851.

Bordeaux 1852
Société des Amis des Arts de Bordeaux. 3rd exhibition.
Opened November 15, 1852. Exh. cat., *Explication
des ouvrages de peinture, sculpture, architecture, graveur
et lithographie des artistes.* Bordeaux: Chez
Gounouilhou, 1852.

Bordeaux 1854
Société des Amis des Arts de Bordeaux. 5th exhibition.
Opened November 12, 1854. Exh. cat., *Explication
des ouvrages de peinture, sculpture, architecture, graveur
et lithographie des artistes.* Bordeaux: Chez
Gounouilhou, 1854.

Bordeaux 1855
Société des Amis des Arts de Bordeaux. 6th exhibition.
Opened December 30, 1855. Exh. cat., *Explication
des ouvrages de peinture, sculpture, architecture, graveur
et lithographie des artistes.* Bordeaux: Chez
Gounouilhou, 1855.

Bordeaux 1857
Société des Amis des Arts de Bordeaux. 7th exhibition.
Opened March 8, 1857. Publication not located.

Bordeaux 1862
Société des Amis des Arts de Bordeaux. 11th exhibition.
Opened March 17, 1862. Publication not located.

Bordeaux–Paris–Athens 1996–97
*La Grèce en révolte: Delacroix et les peintres français,
1815–1848.* Musée des Beaux-Arts, Bordeaux,
June 14–September 8, 1996; Musée National
Eugène-Delacroix, Paris, October 8, 1996–January
13, 1997; Ethnikē Pinakothēkē, Mouseion Alexandrou
Soutsou, Athens, February 12–April 25, 1997. Exh. cat.
edited by Claire Constans, with contributions by
Dominique Cante et al. Paris: Réunion des Musées
Nationaux, 1996.

Bordes 2012
Bordes, Phillippe. "Après la Révolution: L'Antiquité
au-delà de la raison." In Angers 2012, pp. 31–41.

Bresc-Bautier 2004
Bresc-Bautier, Geneviève, ed. *The Apollo Gallery in
the Louvre.* Paris: Musée du Louvre; Gallimard, 2004.

Bruyas 1876
Bruyas, Alfred. *Musée de Montpellier: La Galerie
Bruyas.* Paris: Imprimerie de J. Claye, 1876.

Cantaloube 1864
Cantaloube, Amédée. *Eugène Delacroix:
L'homme et l'artiste, ses amis et ses critiques.* Paris:
E. Dentu, 1864.

Castagnary 1892
Castagnary, Jules. *Salons (1857–1870).* 2 vols. Paris:
Bibliothèque-Charpentier, 1892.

Cavé 1850
Cavé, Marie-Elisabeth. *Le dessin sans maître: Méthode
pour apprendre à dessiner de mémoire.* Paris: MM. Susse
Frères, 1850.

Chantilly 2012–13
*Delacroix et l'aube de l'orientalisme, de Decamps à
Fromentin, peintures et dessins.* Musée Condé,
Chantilly, September 30, 2012–January 7, 2013.
Exh. cat. by Nicole Garnier-Pelle. Paris: Somogy;
Chantilly, 2012.

**Charleroi–La Chaux-de-Fonds–Coutances
1999–2000**
*François-Joseph Navez (Charleroi 1787–Bruxelles
1869): La nostalgie de l'Italie.* Musée des Beaux-Arts,
Charleroi, November 20, 1999–February 20, 2000;
Musée de La Chaux-de-Fonds, March 19–May 21,
2000; Musée de Coutances, July 8–October 15,
2000. Exh. cat. by Denis Coekelberghs, Alain
Jacobs, and Pierre Loze. Ghent: Snoeck-Ducaju &
Zoon, 1999.

Chaudonneret 1999
Chaudonneret, Marie-Claude. *L'Etat et les artistes:
De la Restauration à la monarchie de juillet (1815–1833).*
Paris: Flammarion, 1999.

Chauvin 1825
Chauvin, Auguste. *Salon de mil huit cent vingt-quatre.*
Paris: Chez Pillet ainé, 1825.

Chenique 2015
Chenique, Bruno. *Géricault-Delacroix: "La Barque de
Dante," ou la naissance du romantisme révolutionnaire.*
Paris: L'Echoppe, 2015.

Chesneau 1859
Chesneau, Ernest. "Libre étude sur l'art contemporain: Salon de 1859." *Revue des races* 14 (May 1859),
pp. 164–66.

Clark 1982
Clark, T. J. *The Absolute Bourgeois: Artists and Politics
in France, 1848–1851.* Princeton: Princeton University
Press, 1982.

Clément de Ris 1851
Clément de Ris, Louis. "Le Salon." *L'artiste,* ser. 5, 6
(February 1, 1851), pp. 3–9.

Clément de Ris 1857
Clément de Ris, Louis. "Artistes contemporains:
Eugène Delacroix." 2 parts. *Revue française,* ann. 3, 8
(1857), pp. 354–63, 414–24.

Columbia–Rochester–Santa Barbara 1989–90
The Art of the July Monarchy: France, 1830 to 1848.
Museum of Art and Archaeology, University of
Missouri, Columbia, October 21–December 3,
1989; Memorial Art Gallery at the University of
Rochester, January 21–March 12, 1990; Santa Barbara
Museum of Art, March 31–May 20, 1990. Catalogue
by Robert J. Bezucha et al. Columbia: University of
Missouri Press, 1989.

Copenhagen 2000
Delacroix: The Music of Painting. Ordrupgaard
Museum, Copenhagen, September 13–December 30,
2000. Exh. cat. by Thomas Lederballe, with contri-
butions by Anne-Birgitte Fonsmark and Vincent
Pomarède. Copenhagen: Ordrupgaard and
Rhodos, 2000.

Corbin, Courtine, and Vigarello 2011
Corbin, Alain, Jean-Jacques Courtine, and
Georges Vigarello, eds. *Histoire du corps.* Vol. 2,
De la Révolution à la Grande Guerre. Paris: Editions
du Seuil, 2011.

Courbet 1992
Courbet, Gustave. *Letters of Gustave Courbet.*
Edited and translated by Petra ten-Doesschate Chu.
Chicago: University of Chicago Press, 1992.

Courbet 1996
Courbet, Gustave. *Correspondance de Courbet.*
Edited by Petra ten-Doesschate Chu. Paris:
Flammarion, 1996.

Damisch 2001
Damisch, Hubert. *La peinture en écharpe: Delacroix, la
photographie.* Brussels: Yves Gevaert Editeur, 2001.

Debord 1997
Debord, Jean-François. "À propos de quelques
dessins anatomiques de Géricault." In *Géricault:
Dessins et estampes des collections de l'École des Beaux-
Arts,* edited by Emmanuelle Brugerolles, pp. 43–66.
Exh. cat. Paris: École Nationale Supérieure des
Beaux-Arts, 1997.

Decamps 1834
Decamps, Alexandre. *Le Musée: Revue du Salon de
1834.* Paris: A. Ledoux, 1834.

Delacroix 1846
Delacroix, Eugène. "Peintres et sculpteurs modernes.
II, Prudhon." *Revue des deux mondes* 16 (November 16,
1846), pp. 432–51.

Delacroix 1848
Delacroix, Eugène. "Peintres et sculpteurs modernes.
III, Gros." *Revue des deux mondes* 23 (September 1,
1848), pp. 649–73.

Delacroix 1854
Delacroix, Eugène. "Questions sur le beau." *Revue des deux mondes*, ser. 2, 7 (July 15, 1854), pp. 306–15.

Delacroix 1857
Delacroix, Eugène. "Des variations du beau." *Revue des deux mondes*, ser. 2, 9 (June 15, 1857), pp. 908–19.

Delacroix 1878
Delacroix, Eugène. *Lettres de Eugène Delacroix (1815 à 1863)*. Edited by Philippe Burty. Paris: A. Quantin, 1878.

Delacroix 1935–38
Delacroix, Eugène. *Correspondance générale d'Eugène Delacroix*. Edited by André Joubin. 5 vols. Paris: Librairie Plon, 1935–38.

Delacroix 1954
Delacroix, Eugène. *Lettres intimes. Correspondance inédite*. Edited by Alfred Dupont. Paris: Gallimard, 1954.

Delacroix 1991
Delacroix, Eugène. *Eugène Delacroix: Further Correspondence, 1817–1863*. Edited by Lee Johnson. Oxford: Clarendon Press, 1991.

Delacroix 1995a
Delacroix, Eugène. *The Journal of Eugene Delacroix: A Selection*. Edited by Hubert Wellington; translated by Lucy Norton. 3rd ed. London: Phaidon Press, Arts and Letters, 1995. Originally published 1951.

Delacroix 1995b
Delacroix, Eugène. *Lettres intimes*. Edited by Alfred Dupont. Paris: Gallimard, 1995. Originally published 1954.

Delacroix 1999
Delacroix, Eugène. *Souvenirs d'un voyage dans le Maroc*. Edited by Laure Beaumont-Maillet, Barthélémy Jobert, and Sophie Join-Lambert. Paris: Gallimard, 1999.

Delacroix 2000
Delacroix, Eugène. *Nouvelles lettres*. Edited by Lee Johnson and Michèle Hannoosh. Bordeaux: William Blake, 2000.

Delacroix 2001
Delacroix, Eugène. *Selected Letters, 1813–1863*. Selected and translated by Jean Stewart. Boston: MFA Publications; artWorks, 2001. Originally published 1970.

Delacroix 2009
Delacroix, Eugène. *Journal*. Edited by Michèle Hannoosh. 2 vols. New ed. Domaine romantique series. Paris: José Corti, 2009.

Delacroix 2014
Delacroix, Eugène. *Eugène Delacroix: Ecrivain, témoin de son temps; écrits choisis*. Edited by Catherine Adam-Sigas, Arlette Sérullaz, Dominique de Font-Réaulx, and Marie-Christine Mégevand. Ecrire l'art series. Paris: Flammarion, 2014.

Delacroix sale 1865
Tableaux, aquarelles, dessins, croquis, études, planches gravées à l'eau forte par Eugène Delacroix. Preface by Fréderic Villot. Sale cat., Hôtel Drouot, Paris, February 11, 1865.

Delécluze 1828a
Delécluze, Etienne-Jean. "Beaux-Arts: Salon de 1827 (douzième article)." *Journal des débats politiques et littéraires*, March 21, 1828, pp. 1–3.

Delécluze 1828b
Delécluze, Etienne-Jean. *Précis d'un traité de peinture, contenant les principes du dessin, du modelé et du coloris, et leur application à l'imitation des objets et à la composition . . . .* Paris: Bureau de l'Encyclopédie Portative, 1828.

Delteil and Strauber 1997
Delteil, Loys. *Delacroix: The Graphic Work; A Catalogue Raisonné*. Rev. ed. Translated and edited by Susan Strauber. San Francisco: Alan Wofsy Fine Arts, 1997. Originally published 1908 as *Le peintre-graveur illustré (XIXᵉ et XXᵉ siècles)*, vol. 3, *Ingres et Delacroix*.

Douai 1827
Explication des ouvrages de peinture, dessin, sculpture, modelure, gravure et objets d'industrie exposés au Salon de la Ville de Douai. Douai, unknown venue, July 8–August 8, 1827. Exh. cat. Douai: De l'imp. de Villette-Jacquart, 1827.

Du Camp 1855
Du Camp, Maxime. *Les beaux-arts à l'Exposition universelle de 1855: Peinture—sculpture*. Paris: Librairie Nouvelle, 1855.

Du Camp 1859
Du Camp, Maxime. *Le Salon de 1859*. Paris: Librairie Nouvelle, 1859.

Du Camp 1882
Du Camp, Maxime. "Souvenirs littéraires. Douzième partie (1), XXIII—Ateliers de peintres." *Revue des deux mondes*, ser. 3, 52 (1882), pp. 241–74.

Du Camp 2002
Du Camp, Maxime. *Souvenirs littéraires: Flaubert, Fromentin, Gautier, Musset, Nerval, Sand*. Le regard littéraire 67. Brussels: Editions Complexe, 2002.

Du Pays 1859
Du Pays, A. J. "Salon de 1859." *L'illustration*, May 21, 1859, pp. 339–42.

Duprat 1997
Duprat, Annie. "Des femmes sur les barricades de juillet 1830: Histoire d'un imaginaire social." In *La barricade: Actes du colloque organisé les 17, 18 et 19 mai 1995*, edited by Alain Corbin and Jean-Marie Mayeur, pp. 197–208. Paris: Publications de la Sorbonne, 1997.

Durand-Ruel 1845
Galerie Durand-Ruel. *Spécimens les plus brillants de l'école moderne*. Part 1, *Peinture: Ecole moderne*. Paris: La Galerie, 1845.

Font-Réaulx 2017
Font-Réaulx, Dominique de. "Les manuscrits de Delacroix." *Grande Galerie: Le journal du Louvre*. Special issue: hors série, no. 1, *La recherche au Musée du Louvre 2016* (May 2017), pp. 72–79.

Frankfurt 1987–88
Eugène Delacroix: Themen und Variationen; Arbeiten auf Papier. Städtische Galerie im Städelschen Kunstinstitut, Frankfurt am Main, September 24, 1987–January 10, 1988. Exh. cat. by Margret Stuffmann, with contributions by Petra Bopp et al. Frankfurt am Main: Städtische Galerie im Städelschen Kunstinstitut, 1987.

Fraser 1998
Fraser, Elisabeth A. "Uncivil Alliances: Delacroix, the Private Collector, and the Public." *Oxford Art Journal* 21, no. 1 (January 1998), pp. 87–103.

Fromentin 1984
Fromentin, Eugène. *Oeuvres complètes*. Edited by Guy Sagnes. Paris: Gallimard, 1984.

Gasquet 1921
Gasquet, Joachim. *Cézanne*. Paris: Bernheim-Jeune, 1921.

Gautier 1836
Gautier, Théophile. "Beaux-arts. Peintures de la Chambre des Députés: Salle du Trône." *La presse*, August 26, 1836, pp. 1–2.

Gautier 1838
Gautier, Théophile. "Exposition du Louvre." *La presse*, March 22, 1838, pp. 3–4.

Gautier 1841
Gautier, Théophile. "Salon de 1841." *Revue de Paris,*
April 18, 1841, p. 160.

Gautier 1847a
Gautier, Théophile. "Feuilleton de *La presse*. La Croix
de Berny [bibliothèque de la Chambre des Pairs]."
La presse, January 31, 1847, pp. [1–2].

Gautier 1847b
Gautier, Théophile. "Salon of 1847." *La presse,*
April 1, 1847.

Gautier 1849
Théophile Gautier, "Salon de 1849, cinquième
article: Peinture." *La presse,* August 1, 1849, pp. [1–2].

Gautier 1855a
Gautier, Théophile. "Exposition universelle de 1855:
Peinture, sculpture. XVII. M. Eugène Delacroix."
Le moniteur universel, July 19, 1855.

Gautier 1855b
Gautier, Théophile. "Exposition universelle de 1855:
Peinture, sculpture. XVII. M. Eugène Delacroix."
Le moniteur universel, July 25, 1855.

Gautier 1856–57
Gautier, Théophile. *Les beaux-arts en Europe 1855.*
Première série. Paris: Michel Lévy Frères, 1856–57.

Gautier 1874
Gautier, Théophile. *Histoire du romantisme.* Paris:
Charpentier, 1874.

Grigsby 2002
Grigsby, Darcy Grimaldo. *Extremities: Painting Empire
in Post-Revolutionary France.* New Haven: Yale
University Press, 2002.

Haussard 1849
Haussard, Prosper. "Le Salon de 1849." *Le national,*
August 7, 1849.

Houyoux and Sulzberger 1964
Houyoux, Rose, and Suzanne J. Sulzberger. "Fernand
Khnopff et Eugène Delacroix." *Gazette des beaux-arts,*
ser. 6, 64 (September 1964), pp. 183–85.

Howell 1994
Howell, Joyce Bernstein. "Delacroix's Lithographs of
Antique Coins." *Gazette des beaux-arts,* ser. 6, 124
(1994), pp. 15–24.

Jal 1824
Jal, Augustin. *L'artiste et le philosophe: Entretiens
critiques sur le Salon de 1824.* Paris: Ponthieu, 1824.

Jal 1828
Jal, Auguste. *Esquisses, croquis, pochades et tout ce qu'on
voudra sur le Salon de 1827.* Paris: A. Dupont, 1828.

Jobert 1997
Jobert, Barthélemy. *Delacroix.* Paris: Gallimard, 1997.

Johnson 1981–2002
Johnson, Lee. *The Paintings of Eugène Delacroix:
A Critical Catalogue, 1816–1831.* 7 vols. Oxford:
Clarendon Press, 1981–89 (vols. 1–6); Oxford
University Press, 2002 (vol. 7: *Fourth Supplement and
Reprint of Third Supplement*).

Johnson 1995
Johnson, Lee. *Delacroix's Pastels.* New York: George
Braziller, 1995.

Karlsruhe 2003–4
Eugène Delacroix. Staatliche Kunsthalle Karlsruhe,
November 1, 2003–February 1, 2004. Exh. cat.
edited by Jessica Mack-Andrick, with contributions
by Astrid Reuter et al. Heidelberg: Kehrer, 2003.

Korchane 2003
Korchane, Mehdi. "L'Académie de France à Rome,
1815–1830: Un Romantisme impossible." In *Maestà di
Roma: Da Napoleone all'unità d'Italia; D'Ingres à Degas:
Les artistes français à Rome*, edited by Olivier Bonfait,
pp. 107–15. Exh. cat. Milan: Electa; Rome: Académie
de France, 2003.

Korchane 2005a
Korchane, Mehdi. "Guérin et ses élèves: Paternité et
filiation paradoxales." In Allard 2005, pp. 85–99.

Korchane 2005b
Korchane, Mehdi. "Pierre Narcisse Guérin (1774–
1833) et l'art français de la Révolution à la monarchie
de Juillet." 2 vols. PhD diss., Université Lumière
Lyon 2, 2005.

Korchane 2018
Korchane, Mehdi. *Pierre Guérin (1774–1833).* Paris:
Mare et Martin, 2018.

Landon 1824
Landon, Charles Paul. *Salon de 1824. Annales du Musée
et de l'Ecole Moderne des Beaux-Arts.* 2 vols. Paris:
Bureau des Annales du Musée, 1824.

Landon 1827
Landon, Charles Paul. *Annales de l'Ecole Française des
Beaux-Arts . . . Salons de 1808 à 1824.* Paris: Chez
Pillet, 1827.

Lapauze 1924
Lapauze, Henry. *Histoire de l'Académie de France à
Rome.* Paris: Plon-Nourrit, 1924.

Larue 1996
Larue, Anne. "Delacroix et ses élèves d'après un
manuscrit inédit." *Romantisme: Revue du dix-neuvième
siècle* 26, no. 93 (1996), pp. 7–20.

Lederballe 2000
Lederballe, Thomas. "Delacroix's Enthusiasm:
Abduction as a Genre in His Painting." In
Copenhagen 2000, pp. 103–21.

Le Men 2018
Le Men, Ségolène. "Delacroix et l'estampe." In
Paris–New York 2018–19, pp. 375–83.

Le Normand-Romain, Fossier, and Korchane 2005
Le Normand-Romain, Antoinette, François Fossier,
and Mehdi Korchane, eds. *Correspondance des
directeurs de l'Académie de France à Rome.* Vol. 4,
Pierre-Narcisse Guérin, 1823–1828. Société de l'histoire
de l'art français, n.s., XIX siècle. Troyes: Le Trait
d'Union; Rome: Académie de France à Rome; Paris:
Archives de l'Art Français, 2005.

Le Tourneur 1835
Le Tourneur, Pierre, trans. *Oeuvres dramatiques de
Shakspeare.* Edited by Henri-Horace Meyer. New ed.
2 vols. Paris: Imprimerie d'Amédée Saintin, 1835.

Leipzig 2015–16
*Eugène Delacroix & Paul Delaroche: Geschichte als
Sensation; mit einem Verzeichnis der Sammlung Adolph
Heinrich Schletter.* Museum der Bildenden Künste
Leipzig, October 11, 2015–January 17, 2016. Exh. cat.
edited by Hans-Werner Schmidt, Jan Nicolaisen, and
Martin Schieder, with contributions by Sébastien
Allard et al. Petersberg: Michael Imhof Verlag, 2015.

Lichtenstein 1979
Lichtenstein, Sara. *Delacroix and Raphaël.* New York:
Garland, 1979.

Loddé 2003
Loddé, Isabelle. "Charles-Philippe Larivière, grand
prix de Rome de 1824, ou les dangers d'un séjour en
Italie." *Studiolo: Revue d'histoire de l'art de l'Académie de
France à Rome* 2 (2003), pp. 76–106.

London 1828
*A Catalogue of the Works of British and French Artists
Composing Mr. Hobday's Gallery of Modern Art, no. 54,
Pall Mall.* Hobday's Gallery, London, opened by
June 7, 1828. Exh. cat. London: A. A. Paris, 1828.

London 1830
Royal Academy, London. 1830. Publication
not located.

London 1851
General Exhibition of Paintings by the Living Painters of the Schools of All Countries. Lichfield House, St. James's Square, London, June 1851. Publication not located.

London–Minneapolis–New York 2003–4
Crossing the Channel: British and French Painting in the Age of Romanticism. Tate Britain, London, February 5–May 11, 2003; The Minneapolis Institute of Arts, June 8–September 7, 2003; The Metropolitan Museum of Art, New York, October 7, 2003–January 4, 2004. Exh. cat. edited by Patrick Noon, with contributions by Stephen Bann et al. London: Tate Pub., 2003.

Loyrette 1995
Loyrette, Henri. "Delacroix's 'Ovid in Exile.'" *Burlington Magazine* 137, no. 1111 (October 1995), pp. 682–83.

Lyon 1837
Exposition de la Société des Amis des Arts de Lyon. Lyon, 1837. Publication not located.

Madrid–Barcelona 2011–12
Delacroix: De l'idée à l'expression (1798–1863). CaixaForum Madrid, October 19, 2011–January 15, 2012; CaixaForum Barcelona, February 15–May 20, 2012. Exh. cat. by Sébastien Allard. Madrid: Ediciones El Viso; Barcelona: Fundació "La Caixa," 2011.

Mantz 1847
Mantz, Paul. "Bibliothèque de la Chambre des Pairs: Coupole de M. Eugène Delacroix." *L'artiste,* ser. 4, 8 (February 7, 1847), pp. 218–21.

Mantz 1855
Mantz, Paul. "Salon de 1855, sections V, VI: France." *Revue française,* ann. 1, 2 (June 1855), pp. 170–77.

Mantz 1859
Mantz, Paul. "Salon de 1859." *Gazette des beaux-arts* 2 (May 1, 1859), pp. 129–41.

Marseilles–Rovereto–Toronto 2009–10
Drama and Desire: Art and Theatre from the French Revolution to the First World War. Musée Cantini, Marseilles, October 6, 2009–January 3, 2010; Museo di Arte Moderna e Contemporanea di Trento e Rovereto, February 6–May 23, 2010; Art Gallery of Ontario, Toronto, June 19–September 26, 2010. Exh. cat. edited by Guy Cogeval and Beatrice Avanzi. Milan: Skira, 2010. (French ed.: *De la scène au tableau: David, Füssli, Klimt, Moreau, Lautrec, Degas, Vuillard.* Paris: Skira Flammarion, 2009.)

Medwin 1824
Medwin, Thomas. *Conversations of Lord Byron, Noted during a Residence with His Lordship at Pisa in the Years 1821 and 1822.* London: Henry Colburn, 1824.

Minneapolis–London 2015–16
Delacroix and the Rise of Modern Art. Minneapolis Institute of Art, October 18, 2015–January 10, 2016; The National Gallery, London, February 17–May 22, 2016. Exh. cat. by Patrick Noon and Christopher Riopelle. London: National Gallery; Minneapolis: Minneapolis Institute of Art, 2015.

Montier 2017
Montier, Manon. "Aux origines de l'illustration shakespearienne en France: Des *Oeuvres de Jean-François Ducis* aux *Souvenirs du théâtre anglais à Paris* (1813–1827)." *Actes des congrès de la Société française Shakespeare* 35 (2017). http://journals.openedition.org/shakespeare/3955.

Montpellier 1860
Salon de Montpellier. Opened May 1, 1860. Publication not located.

Moreau 1873
Moreau, Adolphe. *E. Delacroix et son oeuvre; avec des gravures en fac-simile des planches originales les plus rares.* Paris: Librairie des Bibliophiles, 1873.

Motherwell 2007
Motherwell, Robert. "Introduction to *The Journal of Eugène Delacroix,* 1972." In *The Writings of Robert Motherwell,* edited by Dore Ashton and Joan Banach, pp. 286–87. Documents of Twentieth-Century Art. Berkeley and Los Angeles: University of California Press, 2007.

Moulins 1836
Exposition de 1836. Société Centrale des Amis des Arts en Province, Moulins, 1836. Moulins: Imprimerie P. A. Desrosiers, 1836.

Nantes–Paris–Piacenza 1995–96
Les années romantiques: La peinture française de 1815 à 1850. Musée des Beaux-Arts de Nantes, December 4, 1995–March 17, 1996; Galeries Nationales du Grand Palais, Paris, April 16–July 15, 1996; Palazzo Gotico, Piacenza, September 6–November 17, 1996. Exh. cat. by Isabelle Julia, Jean Lacambre, et al. Paris: Réunion des Musées Nationaux, 1995.

Néto 1995
Néto, Isabelle. *Granet et son entourage.* Archives de l'art français, n.s., 31. Nogent-le-Roi: Librarie des Arts et Métiers-Editions Jacques Laget, 1995.

New Orleans–New York–Cincinnati 1996–97
Romance and Chivalry: History and Literature Reflected in Early Nineteenth-Century French Painting. New Orleans Museum of Art, June 23–August 25, 1996; Stair Sainty Matthiesen Inc., New York, September 25–November 2, 1996; Taft Museum, Cincinnati, December 12, 1996–February 9, 1997. Exh. cat. by Nadia Tscherny, Guy Stair Sainty, et al. London and New York: Matthiesen Gallery and Stair Sainty Matthiesen, 1996.

New York 1991
Eugène Delacroix (1798–1863): Paintings, Drawings, and Prints from North American Collections. The Metropolitan Museum of Art, New York, April 10–June 16, 1991. Exh. cat. by Lee Johnson. New York: The Metropolitan Museum of Art, 1991.

New York 1997–98
"The Private Collection of Edgar Degas." The Metropolitan Museum of Art, New York, October 1, 1997–January 11, 1998. Exh. cat., *The Private Collection of Edgar Degas: A Summary Catalogue,* compiled by Colta Ives, Susan Alyson Stein, and Julie A. Steiner, with contributions by Ann Dumas, Rebecca A. Rabinow, and Gary Tinterow. New York: The Metropolitan Museum of Art, 1997.

New York 2000–2001
Romanticism and the School of Nature: Nineteenth-Century Drawings and Paintings from the Karen B. Cohen Collection. The Metropolitan Museum of Art, New York, October 17, 2000–January 21, 2001. Exh. cat. by Colta Ives, with contributions by Elizabeth E. Barker. New York: The Metropolitan Museum of Art, 2000.

New York 2018
"Devotion to Drawing: The Karen B. Cohen Collection of Eugène Delacroix." The Metropolitan Museum of Art, New York, July 17–November 12, 2018. Exh. cat., *Delacroix Drawings: The Karen B. Cohen Collection,* by Ashley E. Dunn, with contributions by Colta Ives and Marjorie Shelley. New York: The Metropolitan Museum of Art, 2018.

Orléans 1997–98
Le temps des passions: Collections romantiques des musées d'Orléans. Musée des Beaux-Arts d'Orléans, November 7, 1997–March 31, 1998. Exh. cat. by Eric Moinet, Isabelle Klinka, Mehdi Korchane, et al. Orléans: Musée des Beaux-Arts d'Orléans, 1997.

Paris 1826a
Explication des ouvrages de peinture exposés au profit des Grecs. Galerie Lebrun, rue du Gros-Chenet, nº 4, Paris, May 15–July 3, 1826. Exh. cat. Paris: Firmin Didot, 1826.

Paris 1826b
Explication des ouvrages de peinture exposes au profit des Grecs. Galerie Lebrun, rue du Gros-Chenet, n° 4, Paris, July 16–November 19, 1826.

Paris 1829a
Catalogue des tableaux et objets d'art exposés dans le Musée Colbert. Musée Colbert, Paris, November 1829. Exh. cat. Paris: Henri Gaugain et Cie; Imprimerie de J. Tastu, 1829.

Paris 1829b
Catalogue des tableaux et objets d'art exposés dans le Musée Colbert. 2nd exhibition. Musée Colbert, Paris, December 1829. Exh. cat. Paris: Henri Gaugain et Cie; Imprimerie de J. Tastu, 1829.

Paris 1830a
Catalogue des tableaux et objets d'art exposés dans le Musée Colbert. 3rd exhibition. Musée Colbert, Paris, February 1830. Exh. cat. Paris: Henri Gaugain et Cie; Imprimerie de J. Tastu, 1830.

Paris 1830b
Catalogue des tableaux et objets d'art exposés dans le Musée Colbert. 4th exhibition. Musée Colbert, Paris, May 1830. Publication not located.

Paris 1830c
Explication des ouvrages de peinture, sculpture, architecture, gravure, dessins et lithographies, exposés dans la galerie de la Chambre des Pairs, au profit des blessés des 27, 28 et 29 juillet 1830. Palais du Luxembourg, Paris, opened October 14, 1830. Exh. cat. Paris: Vinchon, 1830.

Paris 1831
École des Beaux-Arts, Paris, April 1831. Publication not located.

Paris 1832
Explication des ouvrages de peinture, sculpture, architecture et gravure, exposés à la galerie du Musée Colbert, le 6 mai 1832, par MM. les Artistes, au profit des indigens des douze arrondissemens de la ville de Paris, atteints de la maladie épidémique. Musée Colbert, Paris, opened May 6, 1832. Exh. cat. Paris: Imprimerie de Dezauche, 1832.

Paris 1845
Théâtre de l'Odéon, Paris, opened November 1845. No catalogue.

Paris 1846a
Explication des ouvrages de peinture exposés dans la Galerie des Beaux-Arts, boulevard Bonne-Nouvelle, 22. Au profit de la Caisse de Secours et pensions de la Société des Artistes . . . . Galerie des Beaux-Arts, Paris, opened January 11, 1846. (Delacroix's work appears in "suites du Supplément.")

Paris 1846b
Explication des ouvrages de peinture exposés dans la Galerie des Beaux-Arts, boulevard Bonne-Nouvelle, 22. Au profit de la Caisse de Secours et pensions de la Société des Artistes . . . "Deuxième année," but now at 75 rue Saint-Lazare. Galerie des Beaux-Arts, Paris, opened December 15, 1846.

Paris 1848
Explication des ouvrages de peinture, sculpture et architecture: exposées à la Galerie Bonne-Nouvelle, au profit de la Caisse des secours et pensions de l'Association. Galeries Bonne-Nouvelle, Paris, "Troisième année," January 1848.

Paris 1855
Exposition Universelle de 1855: Ouvrages de peinture, sculpture, gravure, lithographie et architecture des artistes vivants, étrangers et français. Palais des Beaux-Arts, Paris, May 1–October 31, 1855. Exh. cat. Paris: Vinchon, 1855.

Paris 1860
Catalogue de tableaux tirés de collections d'amateurs et exposés au profit de la Caisse de Secours des Artistes, Peintres, Sculpteurs, Architectes et Dessinateurs. [Galerie Louis Martinet], 26, Boulevard des Italiens, Paris, opened by early February 1860 and replenished in May. Exh. cat. Paris: Imprimerie de J. Claye, 1860.

Paris 1861–62
"Exposition de peinture" (until May or June 1862); "Société Nationale des Beaux-Arts: Première exposition des sociétaires fondateurs" (from June 1862). [Galerie Louis Martinet], 26, Boulevard des Italiens, Paris, Spring 1861–Spring 1862. Exhibition contents changed during this time. No catalogue.

Paris 1862
Exhibition title unknown. Galerie du Cercle des Beaux-Arts [Francis Petit], rue de Choiseul, Paris, May–June 1862. No catalogue.

Paris 1864a
"Exposition du Cercle de la Rue de Choiseul et de la Société Nationale des Beaux-Arts." Paris, unknown venue near the rue de Choiseul, February 1864. Organized by Francis Petit. No catalogue.

Paris 1864b
Oeuvres d'Eugène Delacroix. Société Nationale des Beaux-Arts, held at [Galerie Louis Martinet], 26, Boulevard des Italiens, Paris, opened August 13, 1864. Publication not located.

Paris 1885
Exposition Eugène Delacroix au profit de la souscription destinée à élever à Paris un monument à sa mémoire. Ecole Nationale des Beaux-Arts, Paris, March 6–April 15, 1885. Exh. cat. by Auguste Vacquerie and Paul Mantz. Paris: Imprimerie Pillet et Dumoulin, 1885.

Paris 1930
Exposition Eugène Delacroix: Peintures, aquarelles, pastels, dessins, gravures, documents. Musée du Louvre, Paris, June–July 1930. Exh. cat. preface by Paul Jamot. Paris: Musées Nationaux, Palais du Louvre, 1930.

Paris (Mémorial) 1963
"Eugène Delacroix, 1798–1863: Exposition du centenaire." Musée du Louvre, Paris, May–September 1963. Exh. cat., *Mémorial de l'exposition Eugène Delacroix . . . à l'occasion du centenaire de la mort de l'artiste,* by Maurice Sérullaz. Rev. and enl. ed. Paris: Editions des Musées Nationaux, 1963.

Paris 1982–83
La Liberté guidant le peuple. Musée du Louvre, Paris, November 1982–February 7, 1983. Exh. cat. by Hélène Toussaint. Paris: Editions de la Réunion des Musées Nationaux, 1982.

Paris 1994–95
Delacroix in Morocco. Institut du Monde Arabe, Paris, September 27, 1994–January 15, 1995. Exh. cat. by Brahim Alaoui, Maurice Sérullaz, Maurice Arama, Lee Johnson, and Arlette Sérullaz; translated by Tamara Blondel. Paris: Flammarion, 1994. (French ed., *Delacroix, le voyage au Maroc.* Paris: Institut du Monde Arabe, 1994.)

Paris 1995
Eugène Delacroix à l'Assemblée nationale: Peintures murales, esquisses, dessins. Palais Bourbon, Paris, February 16–April 1, 1995. Exh. cat. by Arlette Sérullaz and Nicole Moulonguet. Paris: L'Assemblée, 1995.

Paris 2001
Médée furieuse. Musée National Eugène-Delacroix, Paris, April 24–July 30, 2001. Exh. cat. by Arlette Sérullaz et al. Paris: Réunion des Musées Nationaux, 2001.

Paris 2002–3
Chevaux et cavaliers arabes dans les arts d'Orient et d'Occident. Institut du Monde Arabe, Paris, November 26, 2002–March 30, 2003. Exh. cat. edited by Jean-Pierre Digard. Paris: Institut du Monde Arabe; Gallimard, 2002.

Paris 2004
"Dante et Virgile aux Enfers" d'Eugène Delacroix. Musée du Louvre, Paris, April 9–July 5, 2004. Exh. cat. by Sébastien Allard. Les dossiers du Musée du Louvre 65. Paris: Réunion des Musées Nationaux, 2004.

Paris 2008–9
Delacroix et la photographie. Musée National Eugène-Delacroix, Paris, November 28, 2008–March 2, 2009. Exh. cat. by Christophe Leribault, with contributions by Sylvie Aubenas, Françoise Heilbrun, Fiona Le Boucher, and Sabine Slanina. Paris: Musée du Louvre Éditions; Le Passage, 2008.

Paris 2009–10
Une passion pour Delacroix: La collection Karen B. Cohen. Musée National Eugène-Delacroix, Paris, December 16, 2009–April 5, 2010. Exh. cat. by Christophe Leribault et al. Paris: Musée du Louvre Editions, 2009.

Paris 2011–12
Fantin-Latour, Manet, Baudelaire: L'hommage à Delacroix. Musée National Eugène-Delacroix, Paris, December 7, 2011–March 19, 2012. Exh. cat. by Christophe Leribault, Stéphane Guégan, Marie-Pierre Salé, and Amélie Simier. Paris: Musée du Louvre Editions; Le Passage, 2011.

Paris 2012–13
Delacroix, Othoniel, Creten: Des Fleurs en hiver. Musée National Eugène-Delacroix, Paris, December 12, 2012–March 18, 2013. Exh. cat. by Christophe Leribault, Stéphane Guégan, and Michèle Hannoosh. Paris: Musée du Louvre Editions; Le Passage, 2012.

Paris 2013–14
Esquisses peintes de l'époque romantique: Delacroix, Cogniet, Scheffer . . . . Musée de la Vie Romantique, Paris, September 17, 2013–February 2, 2014. Exh. cat. edited by Sophie Eloy, with contributions by Olivia Voisin et al. Paris: Paris-Musées, 2013.

Paris 2014–15
Delacroix: Objets dans la peinture; souvenir du Maroc. Musée National Eugène-Delacroix, Paris, November 5, 2014–February 2, 2015. Exh. cat. edited by Dominique de Font-Réaulx, with contributions by Catherine Adam-Sigas et al. Paris: Le Passage, 2014.

Paris 2017
Maurice Denis et Eugène Delacroix: De l'atelier au musée. Musée National Eugène-Delacroix, Paris, May 3–August 28, 2017. Exh. cat. by Isabelle Collet, Dominique de Font-Réaulx, Anne Robbins, Marie-Pierre Salé, Arlette Sérullaz, and Fabienne Stahl. Paris: Musée du Louvre Éditions; Le Passage, 2017.

Paris 2018
Une Lutte moderne: De Delacroix à nos jours. Musée National Eugène-Delacroix, Paris, April 11–July 23, 2018. Exh. cat. edited by Dominique de Font-Réaulx and Marie Monfort. Paris: Louvre Editions; Le Passage, 2018.

Paris–New York 1994–95
Origins of Impressionism. Galeries Nationales du Grand Palais, Paris, April 19–August 8, 1994; The Metropolitan Museum of Modern Art, New York, September 27, 1994–January 8, 1995. Exh. cat. by Gary Tinterow and Henri Loyrette. New York: The Metropolitan Museum of Art, 1994.

Paris–New York 2002–3
Manet/Velázquez: The French Taste for Spanish Painting. Musée d'Orsay, Paris, September 16, 2002–January 12, 2003; The Metropolitan Museum of Art, New York, March 4–June 8, 2003. Exh. cat. by Gary Tinterow and Geneviève Lacambre with contributions by Deborah L. Roldan, Juliet Wilson-Bareau, et al. New York: The Metropolitan Museum of Art, 2003. (French ed., *Manet, Velázquez: La manière espagnole au XIXᵉ siècle.* Paris: Réunion des Musées Nationaux, 2002.)

Paris–New York 2018–19
Delacroix. Musée du Louvre, Paris, March 29–July 23, 2018; The Metropolitan Museum of Art, New York, September 13, 2018–January 6, 2019. Exh. cat. by Sébastien Allard, Côme Fabre, Catherine Adam-Sigas, Dominique de Font-Réaulx, Michèle Hannoosh, Mehdi Korchane, Ségolène Le Men, Catherine Meneux, Asher Miller, and Marie-Pierre Salé. French ed. Paris: Hazan, 2018.

Paris–New York–Montpellier 2007–8
Gustave Courbet. Galeries Nationales du Grand Palais, Paris, October 13, 2007–January 28, 2008; The Metropolitan Museum of Art, New York, February 27–May 18, 2008; Musée Fabre, Montpellier, June 14–September 28, 2008. Exh. cat. by Dominique de Font-Réaulx, Laurence des Cars, Michel Hilaire, Bruno Mottin, and Bertrand Tillier. New York: The Metropolitan Museum of Art; Ostfildern: Hatje Cantz, 2008. (French ed., Paris: Réunion des Musées Nationaux, 2007.)

Paris–Philadelphia 1998–99
Delacroix: The Late Work. Galeries Nationales du Grand Palais, Paris, April 7–July 20, 1998; Philadelphia Museum of Art, September 15, 1998–January 3, 1999. Exh. cat. by Arlette Sérullaz et al. Philadelphia: Philadelphia Museum of Art, 1998. (French ed., *Delacroix: Les dernières années.* Paris: Réunion des Musées Nationaux, 1998.)

Perrier 1855
Perrier, Charles. "L'Exposition universelle des Beaux-Arts IV, La peinture française: M. Eugène Delacroix." *L'artiste,* ser. 5, 15 (June 10, 1855), pp. 71–75.

Perrier 1859
Perrier, Charles. "Le Salon de 1859." *La revue contemporaine,* ser. 2, 9 (May–June 1859), pp. 287–324.

Petroz 1855
Petroz, Pierre. "Exposition universelle des Beaux-Arts, III: M. Eugène Delacroix." *La presse,* June 5, 1855, pp. [1–2].

Phelps Bailey 1964
Phelps Bailey, Helen. *Hamlet in France from Voltaire to Laforgue.* Geneva: Librairie Droz, 1964.

Planche 1834
Planche, Gustave. "Histoire et philosophie de l'art, IV: De l'Ecole française au Salon de 1834." *Revue des deux mondes* 2 (April 1, 1834), pp. 47–84.

Planche 1836 (1855 ed.)
Planche, Gustave. "Salon de 1836." Part 9. *Chronique de Paris,* April 24, 1836. Reprinted in Planche 1855, vol. 2, pp. 21–31.

Planche 1838
Planche, Gustave. "Salon de 1838." Part 1. *Revue du XIXᵉ siècle,* 1838. Reprinted in Planche 1855, vol. 2, pp. 107–21.

Planche 1846
Planche, Gustave. "Peintures monumentales de MM. Eugène Delacroix et Hippolyte Flandrin à la Chambre des députés et à Saint-Germain-des-Prés." *Revue des deux mondes,* July 1, 1846.

Planche 1855
Planche, Gustave. *Etudes sur l'école française (1831–1852): Peinture et sculpture.* 2 vols. Paris: Michel Lévy Frères, 1855.

Ratliff 1992
Ratliff, Floyd. *Paul Signac and Color in Neo-Impressionism; Including the First English Edition of "From Eugène Delacroix to Neo-Impressionism" by Paul Signac.* Translated from the 1921 French ed. by Willa Silverman. New York: Rockefeller University Press, 1992.

Richmond–Williamstown–Dallas–San Francisco 2004–5
"Bonjour, Monsieur Courbet!": The Bruyas Collection from the Musée Fabre, Montpellier. Virginia Museum of Fine Arts, Richmond, March 26–June 13, 2004; Sterling and Francine Clark Art Institute, Williamstown, Mass., June 27–September 6, 2004; Dallas Museum of Art, October 17, 2004–January 2, 2005; Fine Arts Museums of San Francisco, January 22–April 3, 2005. Exh. cat. edited by Sarah Lees, with contributions by Michel Hilaire et al. Paris: Réunion des Musées Nationaux; Williamstown, Mass.: Sterling and Francine Clark Art Institute, 2004.

Robaut 1885
Robaut, Alfred. *L'oeuvre complet de Eugène Delacroix: Peintures, dessins, gravures, lithographies.* Comments by Ernest Chesneau. Paris: Charavay Frères Editeurs, 1885.

Roque 1997
Roque, Georges. *Art et science de la couleur: Chevreul et les peintres de Delacroix à l'abstraction.* Nîmes: Jacqueline Chambon, 1997.

Rouen 1998
Delacroix: La naissance d'un nouveau romantisme. Musée des Beaux-Arts, Rouen, April 4–July 15, 1998. Exh. cat. by Claude Pétry, Lee Johnson, Barthélémy Jobert, et al. Paris: Réunion des Musées Nationaux, 1998.

Rousseau 1859
Jean Rousseau. "Salon de 1859, III: Ce qui reste de Delacroix." *Figaro,* May 10, 1859, pp. 3–4.

Saint-Victor 1859
Saint-Victor, Paul de. "Salon de 1859." *La presse,* April 23, 1859, pp. 1–2.

Sérullaz 1963
Sérullaz, Maurice. *Les peintures murales de Delacroix.* Paris: Editions du Temps, 1963.

Sérullaz 1989
Sérullaz, Maurice. *Delacroix.* Paris: Fayard, 1989.

Sérullaz et al. 1984
Sérullaz, Maurice, ed. *Dessins d'Eugène Delacroix, 1798–1863.* With contributions by Arlette Sérullaz, Louis-Antoine Prat, and Claudine Ganeval. 2 vols. Musée du Louvre, Cabinet des Dessins, Inventaire générale des dessins école française. Paris: Réunion des Musées Nationaux, 1984.

Signac 1911
Signac, Paul. *D'Eugène Delacroix au Néo-Impressionnisme.* New ed. Paris: H. Floury, 1911.

Silvestre 1856
Silvestre, Théophile. "Eugène Delacroix." In *Histoire des artistes vivants, français et étrangers: Etudes d'après nature,* pp. 41–75. Paris: E. Blanchard, 1856.

Silvestre 1859
Silvestre, Théophile. *L'art, les artistes et l'industrie en Angleterre: Discours prononcé devant la Société des Arts de Londres.* London: W. Trounce, 1859.

Souvenirs du théâtre anglais à Paris 1827
Souvenirs du théâtre anglais à Paris dessinés par MM. Devéria et Boulanger avec un texte par M. Moreau. Paris: Henri Gaugain, Lambert et Compagnie, 1827.

Stendhal 2002
Stendhal [Marie-Henri Beyle]. *Salons.* Edited by Stéphane Guégan and Martine Reid. Paris: Gallimard, 2002.

Taine 1905
Taine, Hippolyte. *Nouveaux essais de critique et d'histoire.* 8th ed. Paris: Librairie Hachette, 1905.

Tardieu 1837
T[ardieu], A[mbroise]. "Salon de 1837." Part 4. *Le courrier français,* March 16, 1837.

Tasso 1825
Tasso, Torquato. *Tasso's Jerusalem Delivered: An Heroic Poem.* Translated by John H. Hunt. 2 vols. Philadelphia: John Laval and Samuel F. Bradford, 1825.

Thénot 1839
Thénot, Jean-Pierre. *Les règles de la perspective pratique mise à la portée de toutes les intelligences.* Paris: Chez l'auteur, 1839.

Thiers 1822
Thiers, Adolphe. "Le Salon de 1822." Part 5. *Le constitutionnel,* May 11, 1822, pp. 3–4.

Thiers 1824
[Thiers, Adolphe.] "Beaux-Arts: Exposition de 1824 (IIIe article): M. Delacroix." *Le globe,* September 28, 1824, pp. 27–28.

Thoré 1837
Thoré, Théophile. "Artistes contemporains: Eugène Delacroix." 2 parts. *Le siècle,* February 24, 1837, pp. [1–2]; February 25, 1837, pp. [1–3].

Tokyo–Nagoya 1989
Delacroix et le romantisme français. National Museum of Western Art, Tokyo, August 5–October 1, 1989; Municipal Museum of Fine Arts, Nagoya, October 10–November 23, 1989. Exh. cat. by Jacques Thuillier, Shuji Takashina, Francis Haskell, et al. Tokyo: Kokuritsu Seiyo Bijutsukan, 1989.

Tours 1998
Delacroix en Touraine. Musée des Beaux-Arts de Tours, May 16–July 31, 1998. Exh. cat. by Philippe Le Leyzour, Sophie Join-Lambert, et al. Tours: Musée des Beaux-Arts de Tours, 1998.

Vannes 1993
Autour de Delacroix: La peinture religieuse en Bretagne au XIXe siècle. Musée des Beaux-Arts, Vannes, 1993. Exh. cat. edited by Brigitte Nicolas et al. Vannes: Sagemor, 1993.

Vauday 2006
Vauday, Patrick. *La décolonisation du tableau. Art et politique au XIXe siècle: Delacroix, Gauguin, Monet.* Paris: Seuil, 2006.

Véron 1853–55
Véron, Louis-Désiré. *Mémoires d'un bourgeois de Paris.* 5 vols. Paris: Gabriel de Gonet, 1853–55.

Vieillard 1825
Vieillard, Pierre Ange. *Salon de mil huit cent vingt-quatre: Revue des ouvrages de peinture, sculpture, etc., des artistes vivans.* Paris: Pillet ainé, 1825. Extract from *Journal des Maires.*

Vitet 1826
Vitet, Ludovic. "Exposition de tableaux en bénéfice des Grecs; IIe article: M. Delacroix." *Le globe,* June 3, 1826, pp. 372–74.

Vitet 1828
Vitet, Ludovic. "Beaux-Arts. [Salon de 1827] (IVe article): M. Gérard, MM. Delacroix, Scheffer, Steuben, Gudin, Robert, Delaroche." *Le globe,* March 8, 1828, pp. 252–55.

Voutier 1823
Voutier, Olivier. *Mémoires du Colonel Voutier sur la guerre actuelle des Grecs.* Paris: Bossange Frères, 1823.

Wildenstein and Wildenstein 1973
Wildenstein, Daniel, and Guy Wildenstein. *Documents complémentaires au catalogue de l'oeuvre de Louis David.* Paris: Fondation Wildenstein, 1973.

Winterthur 2008
Eugène Delacroix, Reflections: Tasso in the Madhouse. Oskar Reinhart Collection "Am Römerholz," Winterthur, September 6–December 14, 2008. Exh. cat. by Margret Stuffmann, Norbert Miller, and Karlheinz Stierle. Munich: Hirmer, 2008.

Zürich 1987–88
Eugène Delacroix: Arbeiten auf Papier. Kunsthaus Zürich, June 5–August 23, 1987. Exh. cat. by Harald Szeemann. Zürich: Kunsthaus Zürich, 1987.

Zürich–Frankfurt 1987–88
Eugène Delacroix. Kunsthaus Zürich, June 5–August 23, 1987; Städtische Galerie im Städelschen Kunstinstitut, Frankfurt am Main, September 24, 1987–January 10, 1988. Exh. cat. by Harald Szeemann et al. Cologne: DuMont Buchverlag, 1987.

Index

Note: Italic page numbers refer to illustrations. Paintings are identified by their catalogue raisonné number in Johnson 1981–2002, abbreviated as "J" followed by the number. Prints are identified by the number in Delteil and Strauber 1997, abbreviated as "D-S" followed by the number.

Photography Credits

Courtesy of the Ackland Art Museum: cat. 95

Courtesy of Albertina, Vienna: fig. 77

Albright-Knox Art Gallery / Art Resource, NY: cat. 77

Allen Phillips\Wadsworth Atheneum: fig. 85

Courtesy of Art Cuéllar-Nathan: cats. 32, 115

© Artcurial – Paris: fig. 113

The Art Institute of Chicago / Art Resource, NY: cats. 27, 61, fig. 58

© Assemblée Nationale-2018: figs. 38–39, 97

Courtesy Bibliothèque de l'Institut National d'Histoire de l'Art: figs. 103–4, 106

Courtesy of Bibliothèque Nationale de France, Paris: figs. 1, 87, 117–18

bpk Bildagentur / Alte Pinakothek, Bayerische Staatsgemälde-sammlungen, Munich / Art Resource, NY: fig. 101

bpk Bildagentnr / Bayerische Staatsgemäldesammlungen, Alte Pinakothek / Art Resource, NY: fig. 59

bpk Bildagentur / Berlin / Elke Estel / Hans-Peter Klut / Art Resource, NY: fig. 79

bpk Bildagentur / Hans-Peter Klut / Art Resource, NY: fig. 43

bpk Bildagentur / Nationalgalerie, Staatliche Museen, Berlin, Germany / Jörg P. Anders / Art Resource, NY: cat. 2

bpk Bildagentur / Staatliche Kunsthalle Karlsruhe / Annette Fischer/Heike Kohler / Art Resource, NY: cat. 140

bpk Bildagentur / Staatsgalerie Stuttgart / Art Resource, NY: fig. 60

© Gérard Blot /Réunion des Musées Métropolitains Rouen Normandie: figs. 35, 49

Dominic Büttner, Zürich: fig. 15

© Patrick Cadet / Centre des monuments nationaux: fig. 76

© COARC / Roger-Viollet: fig. 70

Courtesy of Collection particulière / photo Thomas Agnews & Son: fig. 114

Courtesy of Conseil départemental de l'Ain / J. Alves: cat. 90

© Christophe Fouin/COARC/Roger-Viollet: fig. 48

Courtesy of galerie Jean-Luc Baroni: fig. 109

Courtesy of Patrick Goetelen: cat. 3

Houghton Library, Harvard University: cats. 37, 44, 46

Image © Metropolitan Museum of Art: cats. 1, 6, 9, 19–21, 29, 57–60, 62–63, 65–66, 76, 80, 82, 84, 108, 117, 120–21, 132–33, 137, figs. 16, 64–65, 100, 102, 123

Image © Metropolitan Museum of Art, photo by Erica Allen: cats. 35, 72, 74

Image © Metropolitan Museum of Art, photo by Hyla Skopitz: cats. 15, 126

Image © Metropolitan Museum of Art, photo by Juan Trujillo: cats. 84, 89, 100, 105, 109, 129, 138

Imaging Department © President and Fellows of Harvard College: cats. 11, 118

Courtesy of Kimbell Art Museum, Fort Worth, Texas: cat. 139

© Kunsthalle Bremen – Lars Lohrisch – ARTOTHEK: cat. 113, fig. 51

Kunstmuseum Basel, Martin P. Bühler: cats. 5, 22

Photograph by Jean-François Le Sénéchal: fig. 110

© Lyon MBA – Photo Alain Basset: cat. 33

The Mesdag Collection, The Hague: fig. 13

© Emmanuel Michot / COARC / Roger-Viollet: fig. 69

Courtesy of Minneapolis Institute of Arts/Bridgeman Images: figs. 34, 90

Courtesy of Morgan Library & Museum: cats. 75, 116, 119

© Jean-Marc Moser / COARC / Roger-Viollet: cat. 17

© Musées d'Angers: fig. 111

© Musées d'Angers, P. David: fig. 115

Courtesy of Musée des Beaux-Arts d'Arras and the Louvre: cat. 130

© Musée des Beaux-Arts de Dijon/Michel Bourquin: fig. 27

Courtesy of Musée des Beaux-Arts de Tours, photo: Dominique Couineau: cat. 107

Courtesy Musée des Beaux-arts, Orléans: cat. 7

Image courtesy of Musée des Beaux-Arts Vannes: cat. 85

© Musée des Beaux-Arts, ville de Bordeaux: cats. 26, 70, 135

Musée des Beaux-Arts de la Ville de Reims © Photo: C. Devleeschauwer: fig. 62

© Musée du Louvre, Dist. RMN-Grand Palais / Philippe Fuzeau / Art Resource, NY: fig. 26

© Musée Fabre de Montpellier Méditerranée Métropole - photograph by Frédéric Jaulmes: cats. 10, 78, 114, figs. 32, 86

Musées municipaux de Rochefort / © Studio Sebert: fig. 12

© Museo Thyssen-Bornemisza, Madrid: cat. 24

Museum Boijmans Van Beuningen, Rotterdam / Creditline photographer: Studio Tromp, Rotterdam: cat. 102

© 2018 Museum of Fine Arts, Boston: cat. 106

Courtesy of Museum of Fine Arts, Houston/Bridgeman Images: cat. 145

© Museum Folkwang Essen – ARTOTHEK: fig. 99

Courtesy Nancy, musée des beaux-arts © P. Mignot: cat. 69

© Nasjonalmuseet: cat. 124

Courtesy Nathan Fine Art (Zürich / Potsdam): cat. 8

© The National Gallery, London: cats. 30, 142, fig. 52

© National Gallery in Prague 2018: cat. 25

Courtesy of National Galleries of Scotland, Edinburgh: fig. 54

Courtesy National Gallery of Art, Washington.: fig. 92

© Nationalmuseet: cat. 136, fig. 68

NGC: cat. 112, fig. 116

NMWA / DNPartcom: fig. 89

Courtesy Ny Carlsberg Glyptotek, Copenhagen, photo: Ole Haupt: fig. 24

© Paris, Les Arts Décoratifs / Jean Tholance: cat. 28

Courtesy of Pérez Simón Collection, Mexico © Arturo Piera: cat. 23

© Petit Palais / Roger-Viollet: cats. 38–43, 45, 47, 48–56, 87, fig. 67

Courtesy Philadelphia Museum of Art: cats. 71, 104, 110

Courtesy of The Phillips Collection, Washington, D.C.: fig. 91

Polistena, 2008, p. 171. Image © Metropolitan Museum of Art, photo by Heather Johnson: fig. 40

Courtesy of the Portland Art Museum, Oregon: cat. 99

Private Collection Photo © Christie's Images/Bridgeman Images: fig. 95

Courtesy of Rijksmuseum, Amsterdam: cat. 125

© RMN-Grand Palais / Art Resource, NY: fig. 2

© RMN-Grand Palais / Art Resource, NY. Photo: Daniel Arnaudet: fig. 23

© RMN-Grand Palais / Art Resource, NY. Photo: Martine Beck-Coppola: cat. 68

© RMN-Grand Palais / Art Resource, NY. Photo: Michèle Bellot: fig. 57

© RMN-Grand Palais / Art Resource, NY. Photo: Jean-Gilles Berizzi: cats. 12, 141, fig. 88

© RMN-Grand Palais / Art Resource, NY. Photo: Gerard Blot: cats. 92, 98, figs. 14, 55, 71, 96

© RMN-Grand Palais / Art Resource, NY. Photo: Angèle Dequier: cat. 96, figs. 20, 33, 98

© RMN-Grand Paiais / Art Resource, NY Photo: Adrien Didierjean; cat. 31

© RMN-Grand Palais / Art Resource, NY. Photo: Philippe Fuzeau: cats. 88, 101, 128, figs. 22, 66, 75, 83

© RMN-Grand Palais / Art Resource, NY. Photo: Thierry Le Mage: figs. 3, 28

© RMN-Grand Palais / Art Resource, NY. Photo: Hervé Lewandowski: figs. 4, 8

© RMN-Grand Palais / Art Resource, NY. Photo: Stéphane Maréchalle: cats. 91, 94, figs. 17, 31

© RMN-Grand Palais / Art Resource, NY. Photo: Stéphane Marechalle / Adrien Didierjean: fig. 5

© RMN-Grand Palais / Art Resource, NY. Photo: Rene-Gabriel Ojeda: cats. 4, 14, figs. 50, 72, 78

© RMN-Grand Palais / Art Resource, NY. Photo: Olivier Ouadah: fig. 53

© RMN-Grand Palais / Art Resource, NY. Photo: Jacques Quecq d'Henripret: fig. 41

© RMN-Grand Palais / Art Resource, NY. Photo: Tony Querrec: cats. 34, 64, fig. 42

© RMN-Grand Palais / Art Resource, NY. Photo: Mathieu Rabeau: fig. 9, cat. 13

© RMN-Grand Palais / Art Resource, NY. Photo: Franck Raux: cats. 67, 83, 134, 144, figs. 19, 61, 80, 105

© RMN-Grand Palais / Art Resource, NY. Photo: Franck Raux / Rene-Gabriel Ojeda: cat. 111, figs. 11, 36

© RMN-Grand Palais / Art Resource, NY. Photo: Benoit Touchard: fig. 112

© RMN-Grand Palais / Art Resource, NY. Photo: Michel Urtado: cat. 93, figs. 6, 7, 21, 29, 30, 44–47, 63, 73–74, 82, 107–8, 122

© Royal Museums of Fine Arts of Belgium (RMFAB), Brussels: cat. 123

Scala / Art Resource, NY: fig. 56

Städel Museum – ARTOTHEK: cat. 86

Städel Museum – U. Edelmann – ARTOTHEK: cat. 79

Studio Tromp, Rotterdam: fig. 81

Courtesy of Szépművészeti Museum, Budapest: figs. 18, 93

© Tate, London 2017: fig. 120

Courtesy of Toledo Museum of Art: fig. 121

Toulouse, Musée des Augustins. Photo Daniel Martin: fig. 37

Courtesy of Van Gogh Museum, Amsterdam: cat. 122

© Viking Company: cat. 18

Von der Heydt-Museum Wuppertal / Photo: AntjeZeis-Loi, Medienzentrum Wuppertal: fig. 94

© The Wallace Collection: fig. 25

Courtesy of The Walters Art Museum, Baltimore: cats. 103, 127, 131

Katherine Wetzel © Virginia Museum of Fine Arts: cat. 143